READING POPULAR CULTURE

An Anthology for Writers

Michael Keller

South Dakota State University

with Contributions by

Kelly Bradbury

Dakota State University

and

Carey Denman

University of Sioux Falls

KENDALL/HUNT PUBLISHING COMPANY
4050 Westmark Drive   Dubuque, Iowa 52002

Contents

PART 2   FASHION AND THE BODY

PART 3   DOMESTICITY, CONSUMPTION, AND THE
          CREATION OF TRADITION

CHAPTER IV   DUMB AND DUMBER: ANTI-INTELLECTUALISM
              IN AMERICAN LIFE

CHAPTER V   THAT'S ENTERTAINMENT: POLITICS AND THE NEWS

CHAPTER VI   IS NOTHING WHAT IT SEEMS?: MEDIATION AND
         ITS PROBLEMS

CASE STUDY: REPRESENTING THE WEST

Thematic Contents

Chapter III   Gender Matters

Part 1   Representations of Men and Women on Television, in Film, and in Literature

Part 2   Fashion and the Body

PART 3   DOMESTICITY, CONSUMPTION, AND THE
CREATION OF TRADITION

CHAPTER IV   DUMB AND DUMBER: ANTI-INTELLECTUALISM
IN AMERICAN LIFE

CHAPTER V   THAT'S ENTERTAINMENT: POLITICS AND THE NEWS

CHAPTER VI IS NOTHING WHAT IT SEEMS?: MEDIATION AND ITS PROBLEMS

CASE STUDY: REPRESENTING THE WEST

CHAPTER 1

It's a Material World: Tales of Consumption

■━━━━━━━━━━━━━━━━━━━━━━━━━━━━━━━━■

Beyond Veblen: Rethinking Consumer Culture in America

Jackson Lears

A portrait of Thorstein Veblen in the faculty lounge at Yale University shows him lean-ing back in his chair, one leg tossed easily over the other, smoking a cigarette. He is surveying the passing scene of academic pomp with just the hint of a twinkle in his eye. Despite his mythic marginality, Veblen looks more bemused than embittered. And were he alive today, Veblen might be pardoned some bemusement. The ideas of the celebrated icon-oclast have become part of the conventional wisdom about American society and conspicu-ous consumption. Many serious analysts of American culture have clasped Veblen to their bosoms, and more than a few would agree with Max Lerner's assertion that Veblen pos-sessed "the most creative mind American social thought has produced."[1]

In many ways the reputation is deserved. Veblen broke new ground, much of which is still neglected. He was one of the first theorists to move away from the producer orientation of nineteenth-century economics and focus on consumption as an important category of social and economic behavior. He rejected the utilitarian psychology of orthodox economic thought, demolished through caricature the "Economic Man," and effectively focused on the irrationality and absurdity inherent in many acts of consumption. Having immersed himself in anthropological literature, Veblen could add a cultural dimension to Karl Marx's famous distinction between use-value and exchange-value. Much of what passed for exchange-value, he noted, was also a form of symbolic value. The orgies of display at Newport and the parading of ornamental wives on Fifth Avenue corresponded to similar ceremonies among "primitive" tribes: the captain of industry, like the Kwakiutl chieftain, was eager to demonstrate his prowess by showing off his trophies. But unlike many anthro-pologists of his own time or ours, Veblen preserved a keen sense of hierarchical social struc-ture and of how that structure was reinforced by patterns of consumption. By remaining sensitive to the interaction between culture and power relations, Veblen plunged forward where orthodox Marxism pulled up short. He was able to see how subordinate groups could develop allegiances to a dominant culture that may not have reflected their own best interests. He anticipated some of Antonio Gramsci's insights into the ways dominant groups exercise cultural hegemony under organized capitalism.[2]

Despite Veblen's achievements, his persistent influence has been a mixed blessing. His republican moral commitments prevented him from realizing the near universality of conspicuous consumption and conspicuous display. He himself habitually resorted to conspicuous display in the guise of antidisplay. Veblen's unkempt appearance and bizarre attire, his thick woolen stockings supported by pins clipped to his trouser legs, were aspects of costume that contributed crucially to his legendary status as a bohemian intellectual. Despite his anthropological perspective, he could not see accumulation and display as patterns interwoven by different social groups throughout the whole fabric of a culture. He insisted on attributing the dominant patterns of consumption to the pernicious influence of a parasitic "leisure class." His assumption that cultural influences flow only from the top downward is not borne out by the historical record. Lois Banner's recent and comprehensive study of American fashion, for example, demonstrates that the pacesetters in the beauty sweepstakes were courtesans and chorus girls who were often aped by their social betters.[3]

Veblen's top-down model of cultural domination melded with his desire to stress the irrationality of consumption. As a result, his psychology remained narrow. His thinking was, to be sure, a step beyond the simple-minded utilitarianism of orthodox economics, but he still reduced complex social rituals to one-dimensional examples of "pecuniary emulation." Nothing—from a funeral to a wedding to any form of "devout observance"—was allowed its true, multivalent significance. Veblen realized that all consumption enacted cultural meaning, but he was willing to assign it only one meaning: status-striving. Moreover, since nearly all cultural artifacts and practices contain elements of display, Veblen's furious assault on display amounted to an "attack on culture" itself, as Theodor Adorno recognized more than forty years ago.[4] Veblen's polemical intent led him to a sweeping dismissal of art, religion, and nearly all sensuous or material cultural forms in the name of a utopian alternative: a rational state where sturdy producer-citizens would be ruled by the discipline of the machine rather than the irrationalities of consumption.

What is amazing is how often this bleak vision has continued to inspire critics of consumer culture, particularly on the Left, and how often they have perpetrated Veblen's misconceptions.[5] Why has Veblen's influence been so durable? In part, I would suggest, because his critique resonates with a long tradition in Anglo-American Protestant culture: the Puritan's plain-speak assault on theatrical artifice and effete display. The ensuing essay furthers this argument by situating Veblen historically by tracing the tensions between authenticity and artifice in nineteenth-century American market culture and by suggesting how those tensions were reorchestrated during the period from 1880 to 1920, the period when Veblen consolidated his data base.

The origins of the plain-speech tradition lay in a fundamental project of the Protestant Reformation: the effort to create an alternative to the method of constructing meaning through the assemblage and display of objects, the method that anthropologists claim is virtually universal and timeless. The pietist tradition in Protestantism insisted that salvation lay in faith rather than works, in inner being rather than outward form. They believed that the objective surface of things concealed rather than revealed meaning. Appearances, for the early Protestant, were always deceptive.[6]

The problem of appearances was exacerbated by the emergence of a modern, placeless market, as Jean-Christophe Agnew has persuasively argued. Theatrical modes of artifice were detached from their customary ritual moorings; they became modes of self-aggrandizement in the fluid, boundless world of market relations.[7] Puritan and later evangelical Protestants aimed to create a new and tighter set of boundaries around the simple, striving self and to control the flood of meanings unleashed in market society by insisting on unadorned communication in language as well as material goods. Plain speech complemented plain living: both served the vision of social transparency; that is, a society where people said what they meant and meant what they said. That vision, of course, remained provokingly just out of reach, as market society multiplied goods and the meanings attached to them.

The tension between authenticity and artifice transferred slowly to American shores. American public culture was born in opposition to European-style luxury and display, nurtured in dreams of Spartan simplicity. But by the early and mid nineteenth century, representatives of the national and international market began to fan out from the cities into a countryside that was still dominated in many areas by household production. We are just beginning to glimpse the ways that this expanding world of goods was represented in popular culture, but preliminary evidence suggests that it may be a mistake to argue a shift from the plodding nineteenth century to the carnivalesque twentieth: the carnival may have been in town all the time.[8]

Certainly the nineteenth-century market signified entertainment and exoticism, offering new sensations as well as new goods. Exotica were the stock-in-trade of museum promoters from P. T. Barnum to his backwoods emulators; Barnum's first and most famous estate—itself a gigantic advertisement for his work—was Iranistan, a fabulous oriental villa built in 1846. From the 1830s on, many consumer goods (such as clothing, cosmetics, jewelry, patent medicines) were surrounded by an aura of sensuous mystery, even magical self-transformation. The mysterious East had long been associated with marketable goods, and mid Victorian writers kept that link before the reading public. "India is the Ophir of commerce," a *Godey's Lady's Book* contributor announced in 1853. Fashion magazines printed engravings of bare-breasted brown ladies, such as "The Circassian Beauty" in *Peterson's* for 1851, providing a kind of sanctioned Victorian pornography. By the 1850s, fashionable clothes were often surrounded with exotic attributes: the Turkish shawl, the Castilian cloak, the Echarpe Orientale. New York department store magnate A. T. Stewart chose oriental motifs for the interior of the store he built at Broadway and Tenth Street in 1863, complete with "luxurious hassocks . . . soft Persian mats . . . [and] fairy-like frostings of lace draperies." The tie between the market and exotic oriental goods was firmly implanted in the bourgeois imagination.[9] Representatives of the market reinforced those connections. Many, to be sure, were complaisant shopkeepers; but many others were more aggressive and intrusive peddlers whose wares were sometimes just as enticing as those found in the fashionable shops.

For many Americans, particularly those outside the urban upper classes, the market was personified in the itinerant peddler. The primal scene of the emerging market culture in the mid nineteenth century was the peddler entering the isolated village or rural community, laden with glittering goods that were ornamental as well as useful: scissors, knives, tools, tinware, clocks, patent medicines, jewelry, perfumes, and fabrics. The peddler embodied a multitude of cultural associations. Certainly he was a trickster figure, a confidence man who achieved his goal through guile rather than strength, particularly through a skillful theatricality. What was perhaps most striking about the peddler was his liminality. He was constantly on the move, scurrying along the fringes of established society. He occupied the threshold not only between the village and the cosmopolitan world beyond but also between the natural and the supernatural. He was an emissary of the marvelous, promising his audience magical transformations not through religious conversion, but through the purchase of a bit of silk, a pair of earrings, or a mysterious elixir. Like the traditional conjurer multiplying rabbits, doves, or scarves, the peddler opened his pack and presented a startling vision of abundance. (In Clement Moore's famous poem "A Visit from St. Nicholas" [1822], Santa Claus himself "looked like a peddler opening his pack.") Despite his secular concerns, the peddler, particularly if he was the impresario of a patent medicine show, had much in common with the evangelical ministry: itinerancy, a special appeal to women, and a rhetorical style that combined exhortation with the invocation of testimonials from the saved. From Johnson Jones Hooper's Simon Suggs to Mark Twain's Beriah Sellers, humorists presented the confidence man as preacher, and vice versa.[10]

The peddler's persona resonated with magic and religion. Those resonances varied depending on regional or ethnic circumstances. Folklore tended to label all peddlers (at least up to the Civil War) as either Yankees or Jews. Both groups were proverbially alleged to be rootless and conniving avatars of the market, aggressively penetrating the countryside, and both provoked a mingling of fear, hostility, and fascination. After the 1830s, as German Jews became a more palpable presence in peddling and its lore, popular assumptions tended increasingly to conflate the peddler's mobility and marginality with his Jewishness. "The Jews are proverbially a restless, roving class," announced Luke Shortfield, the hero of John Beauchamp Jones's *Western Merchant* (1849). "The Shylocks prefer to be on navigable streams, where it is convenient for them to take passage for 'parts unknown,' should their necessities or indications render it expedient for them to do so." Mid Victorian imagery presented the Jew as a liminal figure who was even more exotic than the Yankee. "These wonderful people bear the imprint of their Oriental origin even to this day," wrote novelist Joseph Holt Ingraham in 1860. In physical appearance and social behavior, the Jewish peddler epitomized the commercial arts of the mysterious East. Beginning with *The Monk,* written by

Monk Lewis in 1796, the literary Wandering Jew was gradually transformed from an exemplar of Christian doctrine to "a black magician whose sorcery was interesting on secular grounds." The peddler was a Wandering Jew with a pack on his back, promising a brief deliverance through the magical powers of purchase.[11] Whatever his ethnic persuasion, the peddler became a lighting rod for the anxieties and aspirations of a developing market society. The encounter between the peddler and his prospective customer was exciting but also disturbing. It prefigured later, more structured rituals of purchase in department stores and other urban settings.

The common link between earlier and later cultural forms was the tendency to see selling as seduction. The peddler was not only a potential poacher on what the husband conceived to be his private sexual realm but also a participant in the mysterious power of "influence"— the Victorian belief in the capacity of one individual to form or deform another's malleable character forever. The peddler—like that other liminal confidence man, the mesmerist— seemed particularly adept at influencing women. If he sold patent medicine, he also resembled the mesmerist in his access to hidden lore: the word *nostrum* derives from *our secret.* If he sold clothes, perfume, and jewelry, he dealt in "fascination" and "glamour"; both words originally referred to magic spells.[12]

The peddler's brand of influence had powerful connotations; at its worst, it could even promote a kind of addiction. This was suggested by Ann Porter's "Banishment of the Peddlers," a *Godey's* poem published in 1848, deep enough into the era of German Jewish peddling to contain a harsh note of anti-Semitism. The poem tells the story of a small town where the ladies decide to boycott the shopkeepers until they refuse to sell any more liquor. All but one yield.

> "Ladies," said he, "you know full well,
>   That peddlers haunt this place
> And for their knick-knacks take your cash,
>   A low and vulgar race.
> But if you will refuse to trade,
>   With this same Jewish clan,
> I'll quit the sale of spirits now,
>   Nor sell a dram again."

Although "the ladies had some feeling for these men of heavy packs," they bow to the will of the "brave man": peddlers and liquor alike are banished from the village. This poem dramatizes a developing social conflict between established Protestant retailers and itinerant Jewish peddlers: it is not consumption per se that is equated with addiction to alcohol, but consumption from a particularly "influential" source. In suggesting that equation, "The Banishment of the Peddlers" identified the act of purchase as an arena of gender conflict; it also evoked the fear that, without proper boundaries, the market could undermine self-control.[13]

That fear lay at the heart of Victorian moralism. Participation in the market, given its associations with avarice and exotic sensuality, posed fundamental temptations. The moralists' nightmarish vision was that the self's moral and intellectual gyroscope would spin out of control as it entered the magnetic field of market relations, resulting in the pursuit of worldly goods that would lead to madness and death. Novelist Catherine Sedgwick, recalling the speculative fever of the 1830s, charged, "the atmosphere was poisoned, and the silly and the wise alike went mad." Popular fiction confirmed the threat, as the mad speculator became a stock figure. An 1858 *Godey's* story introduced a Mr. Brandon, who, "in the reckless spirit of the age, had entered speculation after speculation until success had made him mad; and when failure had met him he still madly persisted until inevitable ruin stared him in the face." Nor were women immune. A *Peterson's* editorial of 1866 presented an imaginary conversation between a doctor and another male observer at a fashionable ball; their decorous exchange is frequently interrupted by the screeching "mad laugh" of a lovely and elegant young matron, the most fashionably dressed and wittiest woman in the room. The doctor believes that he detects insanity in her laugh, and, sure enough, after her husband's death in a warehouse accident six months later, the woman has to be admitted to an asylum. The quest for social brilliance could be as perilous as the speculative plunge, sapping one's resources and leaving one vulnerable to psychic as well as financial collapse.[14]

The fears of self-ruination, rooted in a persistent Puritan-republican ethos, pervaded bourgeois culture throughout much of the nineteenth century. So it should come as no surprise that the proliferation of marketable goods and sensations generated protest as well as fascination. Among artisans and farmers, heirs of the plain-speech tradition mounted a powerful critique of individual accumulation at the expense of the social whole, a critique energized by the principles of labor republicanism. Among intellectuals, dreams of social transparency led to discomfort amid a new world of manufactured appearances, expressed as longings to strike through the pasteboard mask of artifice (as Melville's Ahab said), and experience unmediated life directly.[15] Longings could be expressed in the idiom of romantic transcendentalism or, later, as austere positivist scientism. Veblen participated in this latter trend; nearly all his work is pervaded by the desire to unmask the duplicities of polite society or conventional wisdom.

During the mid nineteenth century (1840–80), the arbiters of taste in fashion magazines and other popular periodicals groped for a middle ground between authenticity and artifice. Sensing that market relations could be integrated into bourgeois society only if their centrifugal impact were controlled, these makers of mainstream culture sought an idiom that would meld aristocratic fashion and republican simplicity. They wanted to penetrate behind the veil of appearances, but not too far. They implicitly anticipated an idea articulated by Joseph Conrad, Henrik Ibsen, and Sigmund Freud at the end of the century: the notion that civilization was in some sense dependent on a delicate tissue of necessary lies.

Longings for sincerity persisted, however, and led to a bit of a muddle. Fashion was justifiable only insofar as it expressed the true self within; appearances meant everything and nothing.[16] Aesthetic moralists wanted to maintain a tightly controlled equipoise between respectability and extravagance, authenticity and artifice. As expressed by Charles J. Peterson, editor of *Peterson's* magazine, in 1873, "Wise men or women make their dress so thoroughly in accordance with their person or character, that no one notices it any more than the frame of a picture; but to be clothed shabbily in the hopes that our inner perfections will overshadow our dress, is but the extreme of vanity." Yet in the same magazine, one finds extraordinarily elaborate directions for assembling the appropriate ensemble at the appropriate time, as in these comments on the chemisette from an 1851 issue: "The undersleeves should correspond as nearly as possible, in style and pattern, with the collar and chemisette with which they are intended to be worn. This rule should be observed whether the undersleeves are open or closed at the end. We may mention that undersleeves should be reserved exclusively for evening dress, or at least confined to indoor wear." One can find similar descriptions in almost any issue of *Peterson's, Godey's,* or other fashion magazines during the middle decades of the nineteenth century, coexisting with obsessive references to simplicity and suitability. The editors recognized the need to express one's true self, but also to fit in, not to appear eccentric.[17] A sense of unified character began to erode gradually beneath the layers of appearances. What emerged was an antifashionable ideology of fashion, in which the authentic self became a constructed objet d'art, carefully framed by its material surroundings.

Fashion ideologues constantly emphasized the control and care with which clothes and other goods should be presented to the world. The meanings associated with goods, especially fashionable or luxury goods, were always shifting, unstable, and perhaps even dangerous; they embodied the decadence of the aristoi, the sybaritic delights of the demimonde, and the exotic sensuality of the "uncivilized" periphery. Madness, the literature implied, bubbled just beneath the surface of select society. So there was a constant need to organize the meanings attached to consumption—to domesticate and moralize them. This was the role played by fashion magazine editors and authors of advice literature.

The tendency to link the glittering theatricality of consumer culture with a frightening loss of control was more than puritanism; it was rooted in the insecurities of everyday life in an expanding market society. Popular fiction and the files of Dun and Bradstreet were pervaded by tales of rapid rise and overnight ruin. In searching for explanations for wild fluctuations of fortune, moralists predictably conflated the impersonal operations of the market with personal moral choice, in particular the choice of extravagance or overconsumption. They flayed men for indulging in wine, cigars, and stag outings and criticized women for improvident expenditures on clothes and household furnishings.[18]

The idiom of control was sentimental moralism, and its material embodiment was the domestic household. Home became the necessary counterweight to the centrifugal forces unleashed by the market. Few scenes were more distressing to moralists than the forced auction of household goods—the invasion of the home by the corrosive powers of cash. Used repeatedly as a symbol of doom in popular fiction, the unwise purchase of a Brussels carpet meant that the household gods would soon be toppled from their pedestals and the auctioneer's red flag would soon be hoisted over the family home. In "The New Carpets" (1881), Fannie Swift decides that she must have new carpets even though things are difficult financially for her husband, Charlie. Charlie's banker sees the carpets being delivered, considers the purchase to be a wild extravagance, given Charlie's current financial condition, and decides that Charlie is a poor credit risk. Three weeks after the banker turns down Charlie for a crucial loan, the auctioneer's flag signals the dissolution of the Swift home. It is a bitter lesson, but Fannie learns it. Through industry and economy, she and Charlie fight their way back from ruin. In this story, as in many others, not only extravagance but also the appearance of extravagance is the key to a disastrous fall. Appearances, so often dismissed as nothing, again turn out to be everything.[19]

Overall, during the period from 1840 to 1880, fashion ideologues were engaged in a continuing search for some means of organizing and controlling the chaotic potential of the proliferating meanings attached to commodities. The search was pervaded by tension between simplicity and extravagance, as well as authenticity and artifice, and by the implicit realization that obsessive preoccupation with either authenticity or artifice could lead to catastrophe. The result was the well-known Victorian compromise, respectability, rooted in tense ambivalence.

From 1880 to 1920, the period when Veblen began to survey the dominant culture, the tensions between authenticity and artifice increased for a wide variety of reasons. The most obvious reasons involved the increase of wealth, the elaboration of ornament, and the strutting social performance among elites—the tendencies that Veblen anatomized and anathematized in *The Theory of the Leisure Class* (1899). Another reason was the rise of European aestheticism, which exalted fluid theatricality and the manipulation of surfaces. The career of Oscar Wilde personified these tendencies. His delight in language as artifice, as well as his flamboyant self-fashionings, rejection of conventional gender roles, and dramaturgical conception of life, all dramatized the blurring of boundaries that Victorians attempted to control. Americans' ambivalent fascination with Wilde deserves closer scrutiny. It is worth noting that a character in an 1882 story names her rooster after him and that trade cards for goods from fertilizer to perfume satirized Wildean poseurs through the 1890s. An additional reason for increasing anxiety over issues of authenticity and artifice was the arrival of immigrants from non-Protestant traditions of ritual and carnivalesque display. Finally, within what might be called the vernacular entrepreneurial tradition, there was a continuing elaboration of exotic, sensuous display in trade card iconography and, as William Leach and John Kasson have shown, the rise of two new institutions for popularizing exoticism and commercial theatricality: department stores and amusement parks. It is not surprising that Veblen and other, more conventional plain speakers felt ill at ease in this developing cultural environment.[20]

At the same time, the fin de siècle also saw a new and more rigorous search for dark truth behind the veil of appearances. For J. G. Frazer, Freud, and others, the surface of civilization was nothing, a mere veneer covering primal irrationality. In both high and popular cultures, one can see an emergent fascination with instinctual experience unmediated by surface conventionality, a quest for what D. H. Lawrence called "blood knowledge." As Lionel Trilling suggested, the Victorian ideal of simplicity was becoming the modernist ideal of authenticity: more rigorous, demanding, and dangerous.[21]

Both the spread of exotic theatricality and the recovery of primal irrationality involved the resurfacing of instinctual energy that was submerged, although never absent, in the Victorian imagination. Both pointed toward the upsetting of equipoise, the loss of control, and the renewed need to balance tension between authenticity and artifice. Fortunately for the survival of civilization as we know it, cultural elites did develop new means of orchestrating familiar tensions—new ways of mediating the meanings attached to goods, domesticating fashion, and sanitizing exoticism. The idiom of mediation shifted from moralism to professionalism as new structures of control arose, including professional associations, national corporations, and bureaucratic organizations of all kinds. Licensing laws stopped the mobile peddler in his tracks and put him behind the counter of a department store, transforming him from a liminal figure into a complaisant shopkeeper. Advertising sought to shed its Barnumesque inheritance and achieve professional respectability. Corporations acquired unprecedented control over the visual and verbal images attached to goods. These changes helped to reorganize cultural meanings in many different arenas of consumption, of which two are particularly representative: the domestic interior and the body. There was a similar pattern in both cases: a moralized nature had become increasingly surfeited with lush and decadent imagery. Professional designers on the one hand and professional advertisers on the other sought to sanitize that imagery and to purge it of unhealthy exoticism.

The nineteenth-century interior was the woman's sphere. Women not only provided moral uplift but also gave constant attention to the messy details of biological existence often ignored or denied by the male world outside. It is therefore no surprise that the Victorian interior embodied the iconography of female experience; it domesticated and moralized natural fecundity and sexual energy with floral wallpaper, globular lamps, cavorting cupids in the bedroom, and Ceres in the dining room. The vogue of potted plants epitomized the pattern of a domesticated nature straining at the seams of its civilized constraints.[22] For men—and for some more privileged women—the interior was associated with retreat to a world of private revery and leisured aesthetic contemplation. Late Victorian architects aimed to individualize and compartmentalize interior space as much as possible. Alongside natural imagery, exoticism and theatrical display intensified during the last two decades of the nineteenth century. Curio cabinets filled with bric-a-brac from many lands, the Turkish corner, the Egyptian booth, the vogue of chinoiserie, and the riot of eclectic architectural motifs, all betokened the rise of the interior as a stage set for private fantasy. As fiction and advice literature makes clear, some parts of that domestic stage could also be set for fashionable social performance.[23]

But by the turn of the century, there was a growing sense of oppressiveness, nearly suffocation, amid the clutter of theatrical props. Male fantasies of entombment, which pervaded the work of Edgar Allan Poe, Joris-Karl Huysmans, and Gustav Klimt, became more widespread and less gender-specific. In Charlotte Perkins Gilman's "Yellow Wallpaper" (1891), for example, the narrator not only recoils from the "sprawling, flamboyant patterns" in the wallpaper but also associates its "florid arabesque" with a nightmarish vision of fecundity—a fungus: "if you could imagine a toadstool in joints, an interminable string of toadstools, budding and sprouting in endless convolutions—why, that is something like it." Here and elsewhere, domestic artifice can hardly contain the monstrous energies of nature.[24]

The more drastic aesthetic response to this oppressive anxiety was enacted by the European modernists, who preached a gospel of secular puritanism, rationality, and efficiency in the guise of liberation from the airless, closed box of the nineteenth-century interior. In a sense, European modernism was a return to plain speech in architectural style. Severe functionalists like Ludwig Mies van der Rohe and Gerrit Rietveld were animated by a blend of Dutch Calvinism and German pietism; the bedrooms designed by Marcel Breuer began to look like gymnasiums.[25] Anglo-Americans never warmed to this sterilized vision, although there was a brief flurry of scientific management in the home. Ellen Richards introduced "euthenics"—the "science of the controlled environment"—to middle-class audiences who were initially enthusiastic, but the appeal of euthenics never went beyond a few ideologues. It is also true that *House Beautiful* magazine and the arts and crafts movement attacked "the tyranny of things" and "the poor taste of the rich," warring against clutter in the name of taste, health, and sanity. They argued in the new professional/scientific language of expertise to do away with heavy drapes that sheltered microbes and "nervous, discordant" colors that bred neurasthenia. The overall result of American design reform, however, was a compromise between puritanical plain speech and riotous ornament.[26]

Frank Lloyd Wright's prairie houses expressed that compromise perfectly. He opened up and deindividualized the floor plan, providing fewer opportunities for morbid introspection and private fantasy. He brought the outdoors indoors, using the large, flat sheets of plate glass that were industrially available for the first time in the 1880s. These were moves in the direction of Bauhaus-style functionality. Wright used wood and stone rather than steel in keeping with the "organic" preoccupations of the arts and crafts movement. And he never fully rationalized the domestic ideal; he aimed to impart a sacramental aura to traditional family gathering places like the hearth and the dining room. In the pages of *House Beautiful* and other decorating magazines, the compromise was even more apparent. A good deal of ornament survived the assault on clutter, and by the 1910s a Morrisite commitment to "sincerity" in design—always an ambiguous goal at best—had given way to a tasteful eclecticism.[27]

The sanitizing of late Victorian imagery was even more apparent in the commercial iconography of the body. There was a dramatic movement away from exoticism and display, toward rationality and control. The vernacular entrepreneurial tradition of trade cards and patent medicine almanacs yielded to national corporate advertising planned by bureaucratic organizations—called advertising agencies—in New York City. These organizations were staffed overwhelmingly by educated, upper-class, WASP men with the same social and cultural background as the Protestant arbiters of nineteenth-century taste.[28]

Through the late nineteenth century, patent medicine advertising had preserved an exotic aura. Advertisements were steeped in herbalist lore and claims of primitive tribal origin. They fell into a common imperialist pattern: the white man penetrates the dark interior of a tropical land, extracts mysterious remedies, and puts them to the service of "civilization." A Warner's

Safe Remedy pamphlet from 1882 captures the imperialist pattern; it shows a white man's head on a muscular brown body, paddling a canoe toward the heart of primitive darkness.[29]

Advertising for cosmetics also wallowed in exotic settings redolent of luxuriant sensuality during the late nineteenth century. Often advertisements toyed with overt eroticism in displaying the languorous ease of voluptuous women from the subculture of sensuality. Corsets were associated with images of explosive fecundity and even peep show-style prurience. These advertisements suggest a more complex picture of late Victorian culture than the prim and bloodless one presented by its early twentieth-century critics.[30]

After 1900 exoticism survived within the entrepreneurial tradition, inscribed on the walls of restaurants and movie theaters; however, in corporate iconography, it declined or was channeled into more productive outlets. Advertisers who promoted the tanning vogue of the early twentieth century, for example, detached dark skin from overtones of tropical sensuality and linked it with bracing outdoor vigor. The imperialist pattern was transformed from extraction of dark secrets to imposition of white values. In an Ivory soap series from 1900, for instance, an assembly of Plains Indians recalled that their blankets had been smeared with "grease and stains / from buffalo meat and settlers' veins" until "Ivory soap came like a ray / of light across our darkened way." Cleanliness had been a key emblem of refinement for at least half a century; what emerged after the turn of the century was a certain kind of cleanliness, purged of decadent hedonistic associations, oriented toward productive activism and a broader agenda of control. In corporate advertising, there was a growing emphasis on standardized, sanitized images of youthful physical perfection: the voluptuous woman and the bearded man yielded to smoother, cleaner, more activist and athletic models of beauty. The sanitation of body imagery was paralleled by an increased sensitivity to odors, culminating in the drive for "an absolute cleanliness of person, a real surgical cleanliness" announced by Zonite antiseptic in 1932. Euthenics triumphed in advertising, if not in actuality; a Lysol campaign from the early 1930s showed a cellophane-wrapped guest at a suburban front door, claiming, "If callers also arrived in sanitary packages, we wouldn't need Lysol."[31]

There are a number of explanations for this intensified emphasis on control of the biological universe. One involves the consolidation of scientific authority because of therapeutic breakthroughs and the growing preoccupation with the germ theory of disease. Another encompasses the broad process that Max Weber identified as the "disenchantment of the world": the reduction of nature, including one's own body, to a commodity, a manipulable thing. But there are more specific historical reasons as well, involving the ethnic, class, and intellectual background of the ad men themselves. They were members of a WASP elite group surrounded by swarming immigrants and troubling Darwinian theories. If one had apes for ancestors and Hottentots for cousins, the old cultural boundaries between civilization and barbarism, body and soul, no longer seemed so clear. Anglo-Saxon elites felt a strong need to distinguish themselves from primitives, exotics, and the "lower races"—the whole lot of brute creation. As Mary Douglas has suggested, a concern with bodily purification can reflect broader anxieties; pollution taboos reassert the reality of established social boundaries. The American preoccupation with sanitized, hairless bodies and sterile house-holds was a means of redrawing familiar boundaries in a period of critical social stress. The standardized model of physical perfection offered a distinct alternative to the simian stereotypes of immigrant ethnic groups, the sort of people that Attorney Gen. A. Mitchell Palmer characterized in 1919 as "alien filth with sly and crafty eyes, lopsided faces, sloping brows, and misshapen features." Correct appearance became a mark of political normality and of civilization itself. More dramatically than in the domestic interior, in the iconography of the body one sees a farewell to exoticism, a triumph of control, and a steering away from both primitivism and decadence in favor of a moderate norm.[32]

One can only imagine what Veblen would think of this analysis. Maybe he would see the rationalizing tendencies I have described as a partial vindication of his own critique, a process by which the American ruling class refused to become a leisure class, instead creating new sanctions for self-control and disciplined achievement. And perhaps he would recognize that the reorganization of cultural meaning between 1880 and 1920 was too complex to be captured in any linear scheme of progress or decline. What is particularly suspect is the idea, derived partly from Veblen, that the emergence of new ways of assigning meaning to goods meant the rise of self-indulgent materialism and hedonism. We have always had materialism with us, in the sense that people have always used material goods to make cultural meaning; the history of hedonism has yet to be written.

Meanwhile, the tension between authenticity and artifice is still very much alive. Indeed it has acquired a global significance, as multinational corporations cry their commodities in every corner of the "developing" world. The cacophony helps to conceal older, quieter relationships of imperial coercion, at least from postmodern theorists in the West who have taken to celebrating the agreeably meaningless signifiers of mass cultural fashion. But the discourse of authenticity survives outside Anglo-Saxon traditions of plain speech, among anti-imperialist leaders in the third world who invoke national or tribal loyalties in their attempts to exorcise the demons of Western artifice. Whether their project will be any more successful than Veblen's remains to be seen.

ENDNOTES

[1] Max Lerner, ed., *The Portable Veblen* (New York: Viking Press, 1948), back cover.

[2] Thorstein Veblen, *The Theory of the Leisure Class: An Economic Study in the Evolution of Institutions* (New York: Macmillan Co., 1899); John Patrick Diggins, *The Bard of Savagery* (New York: Seabury Press, 1978); T. J. Jackson Lears, "The Concept of Cultural Hegemony: Problems and Possibilities," *American Historical Review* 90, no. 3 (June 1985): 567–93.

[3] Lois Banner, *American Beauty* (New York: Alfred A. Knopf, 1983). For an influential discussion of consumption as a way that various groups throughout a society can create cultural meaning, see Mary Douglas and Baron Isherwood, *The World of Goods: Towards an Anthropology of Consumption* (New York: W. W. Norton, 1979). For a somewhat more sophisticated version of this argument, see Mihaly Csikszentmihalyi and Eugene Rochberg-Halton, *The Meaning of Things: Domestic Symbols and the Self* (New York: Cambridge University Press, 1981).

[4] Theodor Adorno, "Veblen's Attack on Culture" (1941), reprinted in Theodor Adorno, *Prisms,* trans. Samuel and Sherry Weber (Cambridge, Mass.: MIT Press, 1981), pp. 73–94.

[5] See, for example, Stuart Chase, *The Tragedy of Waste* (New York: Macmillan, 1925); John Kenneth Galbraith, *The Affluent Society* (New York: New American Library, 1958); and John Kenneth Galbraith, *The New Industrial State* (Boston: Houghton Mifflin Co., 1967).

[6] This issue is discussed in Edmund Morgan, *Visible Saints: The History of a Puritan Idea* (New York: New York University Press, 1963); and the issue is deftly brought into the nineteenth century in Karen Halttunen, *Confidence Men and Painted Women: A Study of Middle-Class Culture in America, 1830–1870* (New Haven: Yale University Press, 1982), esp. p. 45.

[7] Jean-Christophe Agnew, *Worlds Apart: The Market and the Theater in Anglo-American Thought, 1550–1750* (New York: Cambridge University Press, 1986).

[8] Here I do not mean to abandon my own and other historians' stress on the late nineteenth century as a period of crucial transformation. But I now believe that an understanding of that transformation requires a subtler conceptual framework than simply the notion of a shift from a Protestant "producer culture" to a secular "consumer culture." For statements of that earlier view, see T. J. Jackson Lears, "From Salvation to Self-Realization: Advertising and the Therapeutic Roots of the Consumer Culture, 1880-1930," in *The Culture of Consumption: Critical Essays in American History, 1880–1980,* ed. Richard Wightman Fox and T. J. Jackson Lears (New York: Pantheon Books, 1983) pp. 3–38; and Warren I. Susman, *Culture as History: The Transformation of American Society in the Twentieth Century* (New York: Pantheon Books, 1984), esp. Introduction.

[9] P. T. Barnum, *Struggles and Triumphs; or, Forty Years' Recollections of P. T. Barnum* (Buffalo: Warren, Johnson, 1872), p. 263; Henry P. Haynes, "The East," *Godey's Lady's Book* 47 (July 1853): 33; engraving, "The Circassian Beauty," in *Peterson's* 29, no. 3 (September 1851), frontispiece; "Work Department: The Ottoman," *Godey's Lady's Book* 56 (June 1858): 555; advertisement for "The Castiglione" in *Godey's Lady's Book* 58 (January 1858): 9; Emily May, "The Echarpe Orientale," *Peterson's* 27, no. 1 (January 1855): 89–90; "Chitchat upon Prevailing Fashions," *Godey's Lady's Book* 48 (May 1854): 479–80; Alice B. Haven, "A Morning at Stewart's," *Godey's Lady's Book* 66 (May 1863): 429–33.

[10] The standard works on peddlers are Richardson Wright, *Hawkers and Walkers in Early America: Strolling Peddlers, Preachers, Lawyers, Doctors, Players, and Others, from the Beginning to the Civil War* (Philadelphia: J. B. Lippincott Co., 1927); and J. R. Dolan, *The Yankee Peddlers of Early America* (New York: Clarkson N. Potter, 1964). Also helpful are Frazar Kirkland, *Cyclopedia of Commercial and Business Anecdotes,* 2 vols. (New York: D. Appleton, 1864); and B. A. Botkin, *A Treasury of New England Folklore* (rev. ed.; New York: Crown Publishers, 1965). The concept of liminality is associated with the work of Victor Turner, who is threatening to displace Clifford Geertz as the anthropologist most cited by historians. The most relevant writings on liminality include Victor Turner, *The Ritual Process: Structure and Anti-Structure* (Chicago: University of Chicago Press, 1969), esp. chap. 3; and Victor Turner, *Dramas, Fields, and Metaphors* (Ithaca: Cornell University Press, 1974), esp. chaps. 1, 6, 7. On the link between ancient conjuring lore and dreams of fantastic abundance, see Paul Bouissac, *Circus and Culture: A Semiotic Approach* (Bloomington: Indiana University Press, 1975), p. 78. See also Clement Moore, "A Visit from St. Nicholas" (1822), reprinted as *The Night before Christmas* (Philadelphia: J. B. Lippincott Co., 1954); Johnson Jones Hooper, *Adventures of Capt. Simon Suggs* (Philadelphia: T. B. Peterson Co., 1846); Samuel L. Clemens and Charles Dudley Warner, *The Gilded Age: A Tale of To-Day* (1872; reprint, Indianapolis: Bobbs-Merrill, 1972).

[11] John Beauchamp Jones, *The Western Merchant* (Philadelphia: Grigg, Elliot, 1849), p. 289; Joseph Holt Ingraham, *The Sunny South; or, The Southerner at Home, Embracing Five Years' Experience of a Northern Governess in the Land of Sugar and the Cotton* (1860; reprint, New York: Negro Universities Press, 1968); Edgar Rosenberg, *From Shylock to Svengali: Jewish Stereotypes in English Fiction* (Stanford: Stanford University Press, 1960), p. 206. See also Louis Harap, *The Image of the Jew in American Literature, from the Early Republic to Mass Immigration* (Philadelphia: Jewish Publication Society, 1974); Rudolf Glanz, *The Jew in the Old American Folklore* (New York: Privately printed, 1961), esp. pp. 2–8, 187 n. 21; and Mac E. Barrick, "The Image of the Jew in South-Central Pennsylvania," *Pennsylvania Folklife* 34, no. 3 (Spring 1985): 133–38.

[12] On influence, see Halttunen, *Confidence Men,* pp. 4–5. The explicitly sexual connotations of mesmerism are discussed in John Haller, *American Medicine in Transition, 1840–1910* (Urbana: University of Illinois Press, 1974), p. 105. For the etymologies mentioned in this paragraph, see the relevant entries in *Oxford English Dictionary,* s. v. "fascination," "glamour." On fascination in particular, see Herbert Leventhal, *The Shadow of the Enlightenment* (New York: New York University Press, 1974), pp. 138–39.

[13] Ann E. Porter, "The Banishment of the Peddlers," *Godey's Lady's Book* 37 (October 1848): 227.

[14] Mrs. C. M. Sedgwick, "Wilton Harvey," *Godey's Lady's Book* 24 (March 1842): 122; "Blanche Brandon," *Godey's Lady's Book* 56 (April 1858): 306; "Editor's Table," *Peterson's* 50, no. 3 (September 1866): 210.

[15] Herman Melville, *Moby Dick; or, The White Whale* (1851; reprint, New York: New American Library, 1961), p. 167.

[16] "All is not gold that glitters" was an obsessive theme in women's magazines throughout the 1840–80 period; for example, see Harriet Beecher Stowe, "Art and Nature," *Godey's Lady's Book* 19 (September 1839); Ellen Ashton, "Keeping Up Appearances," *Peterson's* 24, no. 6 (December 1853): 283–84; and L. MacDonnell, "Grace Eversleigh's Golden Hair," *Peterson's* 62, no. 1 (July 1872): 23–24.

[17] "Editor's Table," *Peterson's* 63, no. 6 (June 1873): 442; "Fashions for September, " *Peterson's* 20, no. 3 (September 1851): 134. See also "Editor's Table," *Peterson's* 28, no. 6 (December 1855): 410; "Descriptions of Fashions," *Godey's Lady's Book* 18 (January 1839); "The Art of Dress," *Godey's Lady's Book* 57 (October 1848); and "New Furniture," *Godey's Lady's Book* 40 (February 1850): 152–53.

[18] Mrs. Lambert, "Margaret Compton," *Lady's National* 4, no. 4 (October 1843): 109–18; Alice B. Neal, "Furnishing; or, Two Ways of Commencing Life," *Godey's Lady's Book* 41 (November 1850): 299–305; Mrs. Child, "Our Treasury: Hints about Furniture," *Godey's Lady's Book* 46 (June 1853): 467–68; Charles J. Peterson, "Waifs by the Wayside," *Peterson's* 32, no. 3 (September 1857): 247; Mrs. J. E. M'Conaughey, "Saving Matches," *Peterson's* 69, no. 2 (February 1876): 109–10.

[19] Mrs. J. E. M'Conaughey, "The New Carpets," *Peterson's* 80, no. 2 (August 1881): 148–49. See also Edgar Wayne, "Eleanor Hartley," *Lady's National* 11, no. 6 (June 1847): 201; and Helen B. Thornton, "The Red Flag," *Peterson's* 58, no. 2 (August 1870): 101–2.

[20] Veblen, *Theory,* pp. 33–131; Mary Hayes, "An Esthete's Heart," *Peterson's* 81, no. 5 (November 1882): 371–77; John F. Kasson, *Amusing the Millions: Coney Island at the Turn of the Century* (New York: Hill and Wang, 1978); William Leach, "Transformations in a Culture of Consumption: Women and Department Stores, 1890–1925," *Journal of American History* 71, no. 2 (September 1984): 319–42.

[21] James G. Frazer, *The Golden Bough: A Study in Comparative Religion,* 2 vols. (London and New York: Macmillan Co., 1890); Sigmund Freud, *The Interpretation of Dreams,* trans. A. A. Brill (New York: Macmillan Co., 1913); D. H. Lawrence, *Studies in Classic American Literature* (1924; reprint, London: William Heinemann, 1937), p. 86; Lionel Trilling, *Sincerity and Authenticity* (Cambridge, Mass.: Harvard University Press, 1972).

[22] Bonnie G. Smith, *Ladies of the Leisure Class: The Bourgeoises of Northern France in the Nineteenth Century* (Princeton: Princeton University Press, 1981), pp. 82–85, 87; Mario Praz, *An Illustrated History of Furnishing from the Renaissance to the Twentieth Century,* trans. William Weaver (New York: George Braziller, 1964), p. 327; Carroll Smith-Rosenberg, "The Female World of Love and Ritual," *Signs* 1, no. 1 (Autumn 1975): 1–29; Catharine E. Beecher and Harriet Beecher Stowe, *The American Woman's Home, or, Principles of Domestic Science; Being a Guide to the Formation and Maintenance of Economical, Healthful, Beautiful, and Christian Homes* (1869; reprint, Hartford, Conn.: Stowe-Day Foundation, 1975).

[23] Walter Benjamin, "Paris, Capital of the Nineteenth Century," in Walter Benjamin, *Reflections,* trans. Edmund Jephcott (New York: Harper and Row, 1978), esp. pp. 154–56; Gwendolyn Wright, *Moralism and the Model Home: Domestic Architecture and Cultural Conflict in Chicago, 1873–1913* (Chicago: University of Chicago Press, 1980), pp. 28–40.

[24] Charlotte Perkins Gilman, "The Yellow Wallpaper" (1891) in *A Charlotte Perkins Gilman Reader,* ed. Anne Lane (New York: Pantheon Books, 1980), pp. 3–20. For other examples of these developing claustrophobic sentiments, see Joris-Karl Huysmans, *Against the Grain,* trans. John Howard (New York: Modern Library, 1930); and Carl Schorske, *Fin de Siècle Vienna: Politics and Culture* (New York: Alfred A. Knopf, 1980), esp. chap. 5.

[25] Herbert Bayer, Walter Gropius, and Ise Gropius, *Bauhaus, 1919–1928* (2nd ed.; Boston: Houghton Mifflin Co., 1952), esp. p. 126; Charles Edouard Jeanneret-Gris [Le Corbusier, pseud.], *The New World of Space* (New York: Reynal and Hitchcock, 1948), p. 48; Hans Ludwig C. Jaffee, *De Stijl 1917–1931: The Dutch Contribution to Modern Art* (Amsterdam: J. M. Meulenhoff, 1956), pp. 5, 42, 59.

[26] See, for example, Helen Campbell, "Household Art and the Microbe," *House Beautiful* 6, no. 5 (October 1899): 218–20; Esther Morton, "The Tyranny of Things," *House Beautiful* 36, no. 4 (September 1914): 113; Katherine W. Hand, "Nerves and Decoration," *House Beautiful* 37, no. 6 (May 1915): 184–85; and Wright, *Moralism,* pp. 234, 291. On feminist efforts to create alternative household arrangements, see Dolores Hayden, *The Grand Domestic Revolution* (Cambridge, Mass.: MIT Press, 1981).

[27] Here I follow the stimulating suggestions of Robert Twombly, "Saving the Family: Middle Class Attraction to Wright's Prairie House, 1901–1909," *American Quarterly* 27, no. 1 (March 1975): 57–72. See, for example, Claude Bragdon, "The Architecture of the Home: Some Fundamental Principles," *House Beautiful* 16, no. 1 (June 1904): 10; and Richard Bowland Kimball, "Keeping the House Alive," *House Beautiful* 47, no. 5 (May 1920): 404.

[28] On the social background of advertising agency people, see Roland Marchand, *Advertising the American Dream: Making Way for Modernity, 1920–1940* (Berkeley: University of California Press, 1985), pp. 130–38; and Wallace Boren, "Bad Taste in Advertising," *JWT Forum,* January 7, 1936 (J. Walter Thompson Company Archives, New York).

[29] *Wright's Indian Vegetable Pills* (Philadelphia, 1844), box 33, Lyon Manufacturing Co., *Morning, Noon, and Night* (1872), box 20, *Peruvian Catarrh Cure* (New York, 1890), box 25, *Warner's "Safe"*

Remedies (Rochester, N.Y., 1883), box 34, in Patent Medicines, Warshaw Collection of Business Americana, National Museum of American History, Smithsonian Institution.

[30] In addition to those illustrated, see trade cards for F. J. Taney and Co. Angostura Bitters, 1876, box 31a, Patent Medicines, and Love's Incense, 1880, and Taylor's Premium Cologne, ca. 1890, box 108, Cosmetics, Warshaw Collection. For other examples of nineteenth-century exoticism, see Banner, *American Beauty,* esp. pp. 111–17

[31] Advertisement for Mennen's Borated Talcum Powder, in *Town and Country,* June 19, 1909, in box 109, Cosmetics, Warshaw Collection; Ivory Soap Co., *What a Cake of Soap Will Do* (ca. 1900), in box "Proctor and Gamble," Soap, Warshaw Collection; advertisement for Zonite Antiseptic, *Good Housekeeping* 92, no. 4 (April 1931): 126; advertisement for Lysol Antiseptic, *Good Housekeeping* 90, no. 4 (April 1930): 143. The upper-class counterattack on the belle ideal of voluptuous womanhood is discussed in Banner, *American Beauty,* pp. 130–31.

[32] On the consolidation of authority by the mainstream medical profession, see Paul Starr, *The Social Transformation of American Medicine* (New York Basic Books, 1982), esp. chap. 3. The best concise explication of disenchantment is Peter Berger, *The Sacred Canopy: Elements of a Sociological Theory of Religion* (Garden City, N.Y.: Doubleday, 1967). For an insightful discussion of late Victorian anxieties about the blurred boundaries between humanity and animality, see James Turner, *Reckoning with the Beast: Animals, Pain, and Humanity in the Victorian Mind* (Baltimore: Johns Hopkins University Press, 1980), esp. pp. 63–69. The classic analysis of the relationship between pollution taboos and social boundaries is Mary Douglas, *Purity and Danger: An Analysis of Concepts of Pollution and Taboo* (London: Routledge and Kegan Paul, 1966). Palmer is quoted in Michael Paul Rogin, *Ronald Reagan, the Movie, and Other Episodes in Political Demonology* (Berkeley: University of California Press, 1987), pp. 238–39.

Name: _____ Date: _____

UNDERSTANDING THE TEXT

1. Though he commends Veblen for his many insights into the nature of consumpton, Lears finds some of Veblen's thinking on the topic limited. Discuss one such instance.

2. According to Lears, peddlers in the nineteenth century exerted an especially powerful, seductive influence upon which group of consumers?

3. According to Lears, how did "the tension between authenticity and artifice" shape consumer culture in late-nineteenth/early-twentieth-centuty America?

Transformations in a Culture of Consumption: Women and Department Stores, 1890–1925

William R. Leach

"We dream, we work, we wake!" declared Artemas Ward, one of America's first great advertising geniuses, in 1892. "The world seems real only when it answers to our individual touch. Yet, beyond our touch, beyond our waking, beyond our working, and almost in the land of dreams, lie things beyond our present thought, greater, wider, stronger, than those we now lay hold on. To each a world opens; to everyone possibilities are present."[1] Ward captured here what I wish to develop at much greater length in this essay on the culture of consumption and women. America at the close of the nineteenth century and at the beginning of the next was, indeed, a land of "possibilities" and "dreams" that flowered within the heart of a new culture and that had the power to change older patterns that had hitherto distinguished the behavior of many women.

As recent historical study of women has so consistently shown, nineteenth-century middle-class Americans viewed women as dependent, emotional, deeply religious, and sexually pure beings who were supposed to tend the domestic fires and to bear and rear children. Men, on the other hand, were thought of as stalwart citizen-producers, family providers, rational people who found personal fulfillment in public life and in the individual ownership of property. The public life was male, and individualism a male legacy that only a few women dared claim as their own. By 1915 that older paradigm had been deeply weakened by the transformation of work. Men now received wages and salaries in factories or in ever-expanding corporate and bureaucratic structures, while many women had entered the work force, some finding jobs in the new consumer, service-oriented industries.[2]

Alongside those changes in work emerged a vast culture of consumption. Forged by merchants in the company of enthusiastic politicians, reformers, educators, and artists, this capitalist culture was so powerful as nearly to dwarf all alternative cultures. Advertising gave it shape; a new abundance of commodities established its foundation. The culture of consumption was an urban and secular one of color and spectacle, of sensuous pleasure and dreams. It subverted, but never overturned, the older mentality of repression, practical utilitarianism, scarcity, and self-denial. It slowly encompassed service and comfort as desirable goals, intermingling competition and cooperation, blurring the lines between work and leisure.[3]

The culture of consumption had a transformative effect on women. Many of them imaginatively reconceived themselves as women within that dense and volatile situation. Such an imaginative reconception, the principal subject of this essay, developed out of a capitalist culture that had both strong manipulating and strong utopian currents, and it was freely chosen by individual women who interpreted that culture in their own ways. The focus here is on the emancipating impact of consumer culture on two kinds of women—working women who had power within consumer institutions and mostly middle-class women who shopped and spent much time in such institutions. This is not to deny that much could be said about the more grim components of consumer experience: gross material indulgence; the dominance of men in the manufacture of fantasy and in managerial hierarchies; unfair wage scales for women and the exploitation of women in consumer industries; the reification of women as objects of desire in advertising; and the misery many poor women must have felt as they passed the windows of city retail stores, which revealed to them an unobtainable world of luxury. These aspects of consumer life, among others, must be considered if we are to have a fully dialectical, historical assessment of consumption.

However, at the risk of losing such a dialectical perspective, this essay deals largely with those patterns of consumer life that implied a new freedom from self-denial and from repression, a liberation that promised to expand the province of rewarding work and of individual expression for women. Too often leftist historians of consumer society have interpreted the modern quest for individual autonomy as manipulated, based on the consumer desire for commodities and determined by the needs of managerial elites. Although those critics are partly correct, they have tended to exaggerate the extent to which the mass of women (and men) are manipulatable and passive. As a result, they cannot account for the way early consumer capitalism—even though that capitalism often miserably failed to live up to its promises—secured the loyalties of otherwise intelligent, resourceful, and thoughtful women. The explanation lies in the opportunities and in the imaginative culture that arose from early consumer capitalism. It can be seriously argued that over time that culture, as well as the work provided by consumer institutions that have proletarianized much female labor and that have established even clearer class distinctions among women, has ceased to generate the same enthusiasm it once did.[4] It would be mistaken, however, to conclude, on the basis of that shift, that such enthusiasm never existed and that the justification for it was not compelling. To make such a judgment would be to forfeit the chance to understand how consumer capitalism appealed so well to the longings and desires of many individual women.

The essay is divided into two equal parts. The first part lays out in detail the distinguishing elements of the culture of consumption and uses the department store as the main institutional focus. The second part describes how the behavior of women was affected and transformed by the culture of consumption in general and by the department store in particular.

By the 1890s such consumer businesses as restaurants, hotels, theaters, and dry goods houses had been converted into festival environments severed from their former identities. Like the architects of any great cultural venture, many merchants placed much stock in the powers of the imagination to invent a new institutional world. "Imagination urges on," wrote H. Gordon Selfridge, the American founder of the London department store Selfridge's in 1909, in his lyrical book *The Romance of Commerce.* "It is the yeast of progress. It pictures the desirable." Consumer culture, as it took shape and ever widened like an enchanted circle until it touched every nook and cranny of city life, was above all an imaginative, improvisational, even surreal culture, freely mixing often contradictory elements into fascinating and original patterns that took somewhat different forms in cities from New York to San Francisco. Such improvisational richness acted as a check against the standardizing and homogenizing thrust of modern capitalist industry so long as the major cities and the regions surrounding them retained control over their own productive resources.[5]

Department stores pictured the desirable as did no other contemporary institution. Launched as early as the 1870s by the demands of the market, made possible by mass concentrations of capital and people and by the expansion of the transportation system, department stores had appeared in thousands of cities by the 1890s and had grown into the palatial giants of urban retail. They had little in common with the drab try goods houses of the earlier period, which had been operated by pious Protestant merchants. In the language of W. F. Hotchkin, an advertising manager at John Wanamaker's, store decorators "transfigured" and "transposed" the stores as well as the goods into "pictures" to impress the customers. Behaving like revolutionary actors, the stores occupied urban space in both physical and psychological ways. They sought to weaken resistance on the part of people unaccustomed to this form of buying; they attempted to control markets formerly dominated by smaller retail establishments; and they competed successfully with popular street culture, which struggled to consume much of the same urban space. Bolstered by their own passions, store merchants labored to justify their right to exist and to command large markets; and they did it, partly, through festive, celebratory methods.[6]

The stores conducted street fairs and carnivals in the spring and the fall, reritualizing the passage of time. Long before R. H. Macy sponsored its famous Thanksgiving Day affair, first organized in 1924 by its immigrant employees, department stores had had similar floral and float parades. The stores knit the days between Thanksgiving and Easter more closely together. They resurrected older holidays and dreamed up new ones, such as Ladies' Day and the Fete d'Automne. "Everyday must be a special day." By 1900 seasonal, festive, and exotic themes—"central," or "single," "ideas" around which the details of store life were orchestrated—had become part of the everyday presentation of commodities. Stores were decorated to look like French salons, rose and apple-blossom festivals, "the streets of Paris,"

Egyptian temples, semitropical refuges in the middle of winter, Japanese gardens, the "October woods." *The Thousand and One Nights* served as a nearly inexhaustible source for fanciful display ideas. In May 1913 the huge rotunda of Wanamaker's New York store was voluptuously decked out like a vision from that collection of tales. Although interest in that Oriental text, and in ones similar to it, ran deep in the stream of nineteenth-century urban cultural life, it did not take such widespread institutional expression until this time. Fascination with it was a mark of new desires pervasively taking shape within the culture of consumption, which many Americans projected into faraway lands.[7]

Department stores were among the first modern institutions to disseminate the new technologies of color, glass, and light. The adoption of those technologies for display further enhanced the festive atmosphere of the stores, decisively setting off the world of consumption from that of production. Throughout the 1890s and beyond, merchants helped make a new glass environment, using curved or straight glass doors and shelves, glass counters and containers, and, by 1905, forty-one different kinds of glass showcases. In a major departure, the social implications of which have yet to be examined, glass mediated between people and goods in a new way; it permitted everything to be seen and at the same time rendered it inaccessible. Mirrors of all kinds appeared to create the "illusion" of space and abundance, to "conceal" defects in store architecture, and to make each article "show to advantage."[8] Some mirrors multiplied images, whether of customers or of commodities, to infinity.

From the 1870s observers of the American commercial scene recognized the radical cultural significance of the use of color in display, that its adoption would act as a "handmaiden to luxury," as "an aid to comfort." "The effects of color," wrote journalist Gail Hamilton in 1873, "bring an exquisite enjoyment which scarcely anything else equals." Display managers learned the new color theory and exploited color, often in the most adroit ways. They decorated with puffed archways of colored silk; they hung garlands of flowers, draperies of colored plush, cages of colored birds. The biggest stores designed rooms, individual displays, the entire store around a single color scheme. Green in all its tints and shades prevailed from basement to roof at William Filene's Sons in Boston in 1901. In 1907 green was everywhere in Greenhut's, one of the last great stores to serve downtown Manhattan trade: carpets, side walls, stool seats, and desk blotters wore different shades of green; window backgrounds were green velvet, and the store attendants dressed in green; there were green stationery, green stock boxes and wrapping paper, green string, even green ink and green ribbon for the green store typewriters. Perhaps most important of all, customers saw in the department store, as in no other institution, the spectrum of new colors manufactured from chemical dyes. They viewed "fast colors," colors in all combinations, colors that melted into one another, inspired by Loie Fuller, the American dancer who performed in flowing draperies under colored lights. Fuller ushered into existence new prismatic blends of tints in gauzes, artificial flowers, plumes, and ribbons. After 1893 people could observe in the stores colors that no one had ever seen before.[9]

Artificial and natural lighting transfigured the stores into "refined Coney Islands." Retailers moved swiftly from gas and blinding arc light to prismatic light, which efficiently focused daylight into the stores, and to electric light from tungsten filaments in globed containers. After 1905 specially constructed, concealed lamps erased shadows and evenly diffused a soft radiance throughout interiors. Combined with the technologies of color and glass, the effect of light could be stunning. Some stores had fountains illuminated by colored light and had electrical towers that projected "varying hues." In 1902 Marshall Field in Chicago erected its magnificent opalescent glass dome, designed by the Louis C. Tiffany Studios and illuminated by four "golden globes of light" suspended beneath, the largest single piece of iridescent glass mosaic in the world. By the early 1920s decorators adopted spotlighting and colored screens to transform interiors into beautiful spaces.[10]

Exterior display was no less ingenious or spectacular in its mingling of color, glass, and light. The stores floodlighted their exteriors or outlined them in light. They relied on poster art, electrical signs, and illuminated and painted billboards—all new kinds of advertising blanketing the cityscape by 1915 and producing such sights as the "Blazing Trail" or the "Great White Way." In 1913 Gimbel Brothers of Milwaukee put up the biggest electrical sign in the world. Hoisted to the top of a fourteen-story building in the heart of Milwaukee and spelled out by 2,500 lamps, the word "GIMBELS" could be read thirty miles away. Those clearly focused signs, commercial guides through the spectacle of American abundance, brought great color and light to the city streets. Outdoor advertisers loved the idea that they had the whole sky as a background (and who else in that era had such rights to the sky?). Such advertising, as retailers themselves liked to claim, was created to communicate only "agreeable sensations," to make people smile and to forget their worries (and, of course, to buy); like other forms of advertising, it was supposed to "command involuntary attention." It invited projection into a new world of fantasy and personal transformation. As one observer said of the poster art of Jules Cheret, the Frenchman who had a decisive impact on American dry goods poster design: "We sigh for things that never have been, never can be and never would have been suggested except for the [poster artist]."[11]

That desire to show things off, to publicize or to advertise whatever American capitalism yielded, marked a critical moment in the formation of a new culture of consumption. The concept of show invaded the domain of culture, whether in the shape of a theatrical show, a baby show, a show girl, a showplace, or a showroom. Perhaps inadvertently, the desire to show things off helped to loosen the resistance to personal sexual display and performance in public that had hitherto distinguished American social behavior. As Elbert Hubbard, one of the great pioneers in retail advertising, declared, "life is too short for you to hide yourself away mantled in your own modesty."[12]

The department store show window, emerging as a major instrument of advertising, added to this development. Through its windows the department store exercised its most magical and immediate external appeal to women, as well as to the men who stopped to peer into them. Plate-glass windows, along with the windows of other consumer and business institutions, dramatically altered the appearance of city streets. Technological invention and advertising needs made store windows, only erratically and unsystematically developed for display in the nineteenth century, central to the success of department store business in the early twentieth century. With the advent of the cheap manufacture of plate glass in this country in the mid-1890s, show windows became much stronger, larger, and perfectly clear. By 1915 great banks of store windows extended not only along the streets but beneath them as well, at subway stops in many major cities.[13]

After 1915 many of the largest stores were transforming their windows into little stage sets, wherein single commodities might be presented in the best possible light. "You must offer an easily realized view of something in my Lady's Mind," one retailer advised his peers, "and she injected with that invigorant, is going to buy it, wants it, will have it." By looking into and actively interpreting those windows, women might have been stirred, not by an "invigorant" to buy, but by some other stimulus, by some longing, perhaps, for something far beyond what any commodity in the window might satisfy. Many stores went out of their way to make their windows into "people's picture galleries," displaying the best in art. Before World War I people could see classical and Renaissance art, art nouveau, cubism, and futurism; and by the late 1920s, art deco. The windows as a whole were often more important than the goods within them: they communicated festivity, vitality, beauty, and fantasy, revealing the signature of individual stores and the inner possibilities of store life.[14]

Department stores seemed as if they were not stores at all but theatrical havens, imaginative mediums that depended on the existence of commodities and that transcended them at the same time. As one store decorator, Jerome Koerber, declared, the point was to "eliminate the store." Store merchants destroyed the older reality associated with retail selling and created a new reality that voraciously incorporated every myth and fantasy, every custom and tradition to entice people to shop and to keep them in the stores. The department store borrowed from other mass consumer and public institutions, as they did from it. By 1920 the department store was a zoo (Bloomingdale's and Wanamaker's in New York had enormous pet stores), a botanical garden (floral shops, miniature conservatories, roof gardens), a restaurant (some of the major stores had lavish restaurants bigger than any other in their cities), a barber shop, a butcher shop, a museum (gift and art shops, art exhibits), a world's fair, a library, a post office, a beauty parlor.[15]

As early as the 1890s, when merchants started to build their own auditoriums, department stores literally became theaters, putting on plays, musicals, concerts, and, in some instances, spectacular extravaganzas. In 1904 Richard Strauss conducted the world premier performance of his *Symphonia Domestica* in the big rotunda of Wanamaker's New York store. Display managers used theatrical strategies inside and outside the stores. Windows not only were conceived as stage sets but also often depicted scenes from the latest theatrical productions. By 1900 customers did not see the bleaker areas in the stores, the counting and bookkeeping rooms, the manufacturing floors if there were any. "The selling departments," said one observer in 1902, "is the stage upon which the play is enacted."[16] Signs of hard work were placed out of sight. The low wages and mixed feelings of salesclerks were hidden behind courteous smiles and fashionable clothes or uniforms.

Had they been alive to witness it, the merchants of the 1840s would have blinked at such a transformation. What, they would have asked, is an auditorium doing in a retail store? a restaurant? a roof garden? a beauty parlor? What is a beauty parlor in the first place?

Immersed in those theatrical, surreal settings, commodities themselves acquired new life, new meanings. By 1900 the American economy was based on commodity exchange markets, cut off from traditional forms of barter and gift exchange. This economy produced a plethora of goods that in turn created what the poet and essayist Lewis Hyde describes as an "excitement of possibility." Unlike traditional gifts (modern gifts begin as commodities), which cannot be sold on the market, which circulate only in tightly knit communities, and which bind individuals to and within the group, commodities circulate freely and have no binding power. That liberating character of commodities, according to Hyde, generates an excitement that gifts do not contain. "The excitement of commodities," he writes, "is the excitement of possibility, of floating away from the particular to taste the range of available life." In a way unsurpassed by any other institution of the time, the department store housed a vast range of exciting commodities. What women formerly made at home and in private—foods, clothing, soap, cosmetics, and so on—was now arrayed before them in public, made available by revolutions in transportation and communications to anyone who could afford to buy it. From the early 1890s the stores showed an unprecedented quantity of goods, from coffee and exotic fruits to linen and woven rugs from far-off places. The stores marketed out-of-season flowers and in their own pet shops sold anything from rare birds to marmoset monkeys.[17] For the first time, women of nearly any economic bracket could choose from a spectrum of mass-produced, increasingly streamlined everyday wear and sportswear. By purchasing imitation jewels, artificial silk and furs, cheap perfume—all new on the market—women could partake of both the luxury and the theatrical behavior of the rich.

Department stores, however, did not simply "sell" commodities: they intervened with advertising skills to amplify the excitement of possibility inherent in the commodity form. They attempted to endow the goods with transformative messages and associations that the goods did not objectively possess. As Marshall Field's advertising put it in 1912, "through the development of ideas this store becomes a vast repository of possibilities to the individual customer."[18] To buy a shawl in a "Japanese garden," therefore, was to appropriate not only the shawl but the exoticism injected into it by its setting.

Fashion intensified the excitement of commodities. "Fashion," observed a retailer in 1908, "imparts to merchandise a value over and above its intrinsic worth" and "imbues with special desirability goods which otherwise would excite only languid interest." The compelling power of that value rests on what René Girard has described in another context as the "model" of "desire." This model has attributes that people seek to emulate and that they hope will set them apart from other people, heightening their desirability. Fashion intervenes between the commodity and the consumer to erect a structure of "triangular desire" and is especially potent in a fluent society where class lines are unclear. Relentlessly shifting, fashion causes anxiety in those who obey its laws; thus because the model of desire is always embraced by many people at the same time, it at once loses its appeal, to be cast away for a newer model, and then a newer one.[19] Fashion has another dimension: it is playful and secular. Like the merchants who constantly change store interiors and exteriors, fashion designers exult in the imaginative reconstruction of reality, the mixing of discordant elements, the exploitation of all styles from traditional to modern. Fashion dwells on custom only as it enhances the value of the goods.

The American department store did more than any other institution to bring fashion to multitudes of people. From the 1870s it tied the glamour of Paris, of aristocracy and nobility, and later the aura of the theater and the movie screen to the goods on display. In the early 1900s American merchants took a revolutionary step by installing the exclusive and intimate Paris fashion show in the department store, a mass consumer institution. Ehrich Brothers of New York gets the credit for conducting the first show in 1903, soon after eclipsed by Wanamaker's impressive shows and the *"promenade des toilettes"* at Gimbels. Exhibiting clothes designed by Europeans and later by Americans, and accompanied by the requisite ramps and stages and by the first live female models, adult and juvenile, fashion shows were immediately popular in stores everywhere in the country. After 1915 there were style shows and children's fashion shows; united fashion and style shows organized by several stores at once; fashion movies; and, finally, the great fashion pageants of the late 1910s and early 1920s, spectacular, multimedia affairs with orchestras, models, special effects, and theatrical performances and with thousands of people in attendance. The first pageant, held in St. Louis in the summer of 1917, closed with "Revels of Dionysius," a fully choreographed dance number. Two years later a pageant entitled "The Garden of Enchantment" was mounted around "Aladdin and the Wonderful Lamp."[20]

Limited in the nineteenth century to a small section of the population living in relatively large cities, fashion swelled to huge proportions by the 1920s. The engine of fashion existed now in thousands of cities at the heart of everyday life, churning up desire for commodities that carried with them the promise of personal transformation.[21]

A related feature of consumer life was its sensually suggestive and remissive side. Department stores did little to prevent or to control the loosening of sensual boundaries; indeed, they promoted it, even in the face of much opposition from purity and reform groups. "Certain organizations of women," declared the editors of the *Dry Goods Economist*, the main trade voice for the stores, "are claiming [that] the stores . . . are ruining the youth of the land by display of corsets and garments" and "that the 'scandalous hussies [wax figures]' should not be permitted to display their waxen charms so publicly. What sort of minds do these venerable women possess? Do they suppose that the youth of our land are equally advanced in prurience with themselves?" By the turn of the century, store windows showed everything from bedroom sets to teacups, from lingerie to evening gowns that clearly outlined the body with "slits up one side to leave still less to the imagination." With the opening of their liquor and wine departments in the late 1890s, the big stores opposed all efforts by temperance groups to restrict sales. Store advertising, moreover, sought to trigger buying on impulse, by feeling and not by rational thought, and to open people further to sensual suggestion. By creating artificial, festive environments and by saturating goods and stores with meaning, merchants conjured up what can only be called a potentially uncontrollable circumstance of longing and desire. The outcome must have been to widen the terrain in which many forms of desire were given expression.[22]

Department stores contributed to the formation of an image-producing culture that further weakened sensual controls. By their very nature, colorful images, whether in the form of windows, illustrations, posters, or billboards, appealed directly to the visual sense and had the power to stir the imagination in a less mediated way than did white and black copy or illustration. Retail advertisers were quick to grasp that fact and by 1910 were regularly replacing what Robert Ogden, Wanamaker's pioneering advertising manager, called "cold print" with "hot pictures." Endowed with color, those images possessed carnivalesque properties, sensual concreteness, plasticity, and zest.[23]

Service was another remarkable feature of the stores and of other consumer institutions. From the moment that the dry goods houses began rapidly developing in the 1870s in a climate of intense rivalry, service was grafted to store practice. Consumption and service evolved together. Ladies' parlors, restaurants and lunch counters, the practice of giving free gifts and souvenirs such as flowers and ice cream, free checking services—all had reached the commonplace by the 1890s. As early as 1895 many stores were offering free child-care facilities—small nurseries and, later, elaborate playgrounds staffed by trained personnel—that gave customers the chance to wander about and to shop alone. Orchestras and small bands that played for the customers became so popular that people "expected to do their shopping to the accompaniment of music." Siegel-Cooper even stationed an all-women orchestra in its grocery department. By 1910 people could attend free art exhibitions, lectures, plays, and "extravaganzas" organized for them in store theaters and recital halls. In 1903 Siegel-Cooper, famous for its "spectacular extravaganzas," produced in its fifth-floor auditorium a six-week-long "Carnival of Nations," climaxing in August with "Oriental Week" and highlighted by an exotic show called "Phantasma, The Enchanted Bower." That show, embellished by "thrilling" light-and-color effects, delivered a "glimpse of the Orient— a turkish harem, a parade of turkish dancing girls, a 'genie' of the lamp" and "Cleopatra of the Nile." A year later the store staged its "Amazma" show, which consisted of "incandescent illusions," "weird transformations," and "startling and beautiful electrical displays."[24]

The big stores had branch public libraries and tiny hospitals to care for ailing shoppers. Store "hostesses" guided and entertained the "guests" who might otherwise have been befuddled or lost. From the late 1890s merchants began to extend charge privileges to more and more women. By 1902 charge accounts had achieved full and widespread legitimacy; in that year every store in New York but one had fallen in line with the credit ranks.[25]

Over time many Americans had come to consider the department store as an "eleemosynary institution maintained for the purpose of serving the public without regard for profit." Visitors to the United States were astonished by the extent of the service. As an English advertising manager from Harrods in London declared in 1919, "I do not know whether stores have created and fostered the demand for service, or whether it has developed because there was a desire for service which department stores recognized and met; but it certainly causes a tremendous amount of overhead expense, and it is a question if it has not been carried too far."[26]

Service fit, yet did not fit, the American scene. On the one hand, merchants, by dispensing services or gifts and by proclaiming that all customers would be cared for in the stores and that no comfort would not be forthcoming, challenged both the atomism of the commodity market and the older republican-individualist contention that people must be self-reliant and independent. On the other hand, service appeared to fulfill the utopian American promise that the happiness and well-being of everyone could be provided for. The emphasis was on individual happiness, although it was to be satisfied within institutional settings. Service could be described as a peculiar American variant of neosocialism (I do not think "corporate paternalism" quite captures the meaning here), existing in tension with the imperatives of commodity selling. Many merchants viewed the stores as public, not private, institutions and were so enthusiastic about service that their commitment to it threatened to overturn the system of profit that gave birth to it in the first place. Of the established merchants, John Wanamaker approached a utopian perspective. In 1897 he seriously proposed that his store was not a "capitalist" or "Wanamaker store" serving mercenary motives: it was a "people's store." Most merchants, however, tried to resolve the tension between service and profit in behalf of profit. At the risk of losing customers, they passed on service expenses to consumers in the form of higher prices; they cut back on services or introduced self-service; they levied charges for such things as alterations and deliveries. Nevertheless, the troubling fact remained that customers could enjoy many of the services without ever making a purchase.[27]

The combined elements of consumer life—fantasy exteriors and interiors, commodity excitements, fashion, service—created a dynamic chemistry capable of influencing, even changing, individual identities and gender behavior. White middle-class women were the first to experience that world at the closest range, the first to feel its transformative power. The impact was complex.

On the one hand, such consumer businesses as department stores deepened and reinforced gender distinctions; store decorators, by consciously crafting interior spaces and schemes, forcefully institutionalized stereotypes and images that may have been incompletely realized only in the minds of most men and women. Thus the color in the stores, the fashion and the theater, the indulgence and the impulse became ever more associated in the minds of both sexes with femininity. Those conditions would go unchanged even as department stores opened their doors to men in a big way in the early 1920s. Over time men had separate street and elevator entrances and separate departments, or "stores," dressed in dark and "rugged" colors. Everything was done to create distinct gender spaces for men and women, even as (or especially because) the exigencies of the capitalist market pulled them more closely together than ever before in the public domain. The motive was not to prevent sexual interaction in public (which might have been the case in another culture) but to give men psychological peace of mind.[28]

On the other hand, at the same time that consumer life reinforced sexual differences, it also challenged them. The most obvious change for women came in the area of work, although to a limited degree. In that new context, the older sexual division of labor, which connected women with the production of household commodities, functioned in behalf of female independence outside the home. In the period after 1890, many women across the country worked as editors and copywriters for fashion and advertising periodicals, as poster and billboard advertisers in advertising agencies, as dress designers and illustrators, and as directors or owners of cosmetic firms. Although men indisputably filled the highest managerial ranks, women worked at nearly every other level of the department store hierarchy. By 1912 Mary H. Tolman, an analyst of the stores, could say that "here more than anywhere else, equal pay and equal opportunities have been offered to those who show results—whether they are men or women." Here, moreover, as Achsah Gardner, style coordinator at Marshall Field in the 1920s, proclaimed, "a great many girls who aren't married, and a lot of those choosing not to be married, are having lives of their own that are more exciting and stimulating than anything they dreamed could ever happen to them."[29]

Middle-class women found jobs as store doctors, as assistant merchandising managers, as professional shoppers, and as traveling models. In many stores they predominated as advertising managers and as educational social-welfare directors. A number of women traveled the world as sales representatives, a job so unusual, so new, that it inspired Edna Ferber to fictionalize the experience of such a woman, the first depiction in American literature, according to Ferber, of the life of an "American business woman." Above all, women worked as buyers, often gaining such status after years of hard toil in the stores. Female buyers, commonly labeled the "prima donnas" or "queens" of retailing, commanded their own budgets, acted as individual merchants in their own departments, received excellent salaries, and went everywhere in the country and abroad to discover markets and styles. By 1916 almost one-third of department store buyers were women; by 1924, over one-third, a surprising figure given the central importance of the department store to the American economy.[30]

At one significant level, then, consumer life provided a minority of women with independence where once they had been constrained by dependence. The possibility for gender transformation, however, existed on a multitude of planes, touching both women who worked and those middle-class women who shopped and spent much of their time in the stores.

As early as the 1840s and 1850s, especially in the urban centers, shopping had become a woman's job, reflecting the gender differentiation of roles that resulted from the separation of workplace and home and that was supported by the rise of wage and salaried male labor. An index of the control many middle-class women had over the family budget, shopping gave them a measure of economic power they lacked by not working. After the Civil War the number of shopping women increased. In the late 1860s Alexander Turney Stewart, the first great department store prince, pioneered in institutionalizing shopping as a female activity. It was one of his dreams to see "two acres of ladies all shopping at one time." By the 1880s the *New York Times* could report "the awful prevalence of the vice of shopping among women," an addiction, it warned, "every bit as bad as male drinking or smoking." As retail institutions and districts expanded, shopping became possible for more and more women. By 1915 women were doing between 80 and 85 percent of the consumer purchasing in the United States.[31]

In the early period shopping was only a minor incident in the round of domestic chores performed by most middle-class women. Moreover, as many diaries of such women indicate, it never superseded such public activities as churchgoing and charity or moral reform work. For example, the diary of Mary Lester Harris, wife of a New York City dry goods merchant, never mentions shopping; rather, Harris is concerned with her family and, particularly, with religion. "This is the last day of the year," she writes typically in 1848, "and what have I done for Christ?" By 1880 Christian reform work increasingly competed with shopping for the attention of city women. Sophie C. Hall, wife of an Episcopalian minister, begins her diary with religious reflections and describes in subsequent pages her prayer meetings and missionary work. But Hall also shops, often much longer than she wishes. "Got to Macy's Emporium," she writes in January 1879. "I saw so many beautiful things that we found it a trying matter to get out."[32]

By the turn of the century, shopping had developed into an almost full-time secular and public business. It was also an adventure bursting with new meanings. In that new context shopping posed many dangers for middle-class women who were dependent on male incomes. Through a multitude of display devices, merchants "encouraged" women to "indulge their own desires," to buy without much thought or reflection.[33] Such encouragement might have released unsettling impulses, leading some women to shoplifting. Still other women, who enjoyed the benefits of the new liberal credit policies, might have bought compulsively; they might have confused the possession of goods with the fulfillment of their longing for happiness. The outcome in both instances might have been great psychological disorientation and intense marital and family conflict.

Throughout that period an increasing number of court cases pitted wives, who bought well beyond their means, against husbands, who refused to pay their wives' debts. Some judges ruled in favor of the husbands; they argued that the common-law concept of "necessaries," which required husbands to pay for their wives' bed, board, clothing, and so forth, did not cover the cost of fur coats and jewelry or of any other superfluous commodity. Other judges, who expanded the meaning of necessaries and thus elicited the thanks of merchants, backed the wives. Those cases as a whole illustrate the strain placed on marriage by the spread of credit and fashion and by the new abundance of commodities. Such new realities threatened the relatively stable equilibrium between the sexes that marked nineteenth-century social life.[34]

All women were potentially vulnerable to the perils of shopping, but most, it is probably safe to say, suffered very little from them. As the diaries of many metropolitan women of the upper-middle class indicate, many of those women were not so much disoriented by consumer life as fascinated with it and with the new opportunities for escape and pleasure. Marjorie Reynolds, a young New York woman, writes on February 18, 1908: "Gorgeous day, 5th Ave. a dream. To Wanamaker's alone for errand." And on April 2, 1909: "To Papa's office. Lunched with him at the Down Town Club with glee. . . . Thence uptown again. I love the whirl of these streets! Marianne down from Litchfield—met her at Altman's and had some confab." Mrs. George Richards, an affluent woman from upstate New Jersey, went shopping every second or third day. A few of her diary entries are as follows:

> January 12, 1903. Mother and I to town on 10.57. Altman's, Arnold's. Lunched with Kate Mitchell at the Woman's Club, 9 E 46. Called then on Mrs. Hornblower, Wanamaker's, home on 5.15.

> January 17, 1903. Went to town on the Erie, at 9.46. Stern's, Mirrian's, Aitken's, Vautin's, Johnson and Faulkner, Macy's. Lunch 168. M. and I to Marquand Pictures. Home on 4.55.

> February 26, 1903. To town at 12:30. O'Neill's, Altman's. Lunch at tea rooms on 20th st. . . . Stern's, McCreery's. . . . home 4.55.

> March 2, 1903. To town on 9:30. . . . to Lax, Macy, Altman's, O'Neill's, Simpson and Arnold's, looking for a grey suit. Arnold's $25. Shoes at Alexander's. Home on 5:15 with George.

The Richards diary is remarkable for several reasons. It reflects the character of time in an upper-middle-class woman's life: flexible, fluent, unlike male work rhythms, although determined at its outer limits by male time. The diary is utterly unintrospective; it has virtually nothing in it but shopping dates and excursions, records of departures to and from Manhattan or Newark, ritual data of great importance to this woman. The diary shows how much Richards did not like being cooped up at home. She spent much of her time in public— shopping.[35]

Even more interesting are the personal writings of Mary Antin and Marguerite Delavarre DuBois. Antin, a Jewish immigrant who came to the "Promised Land" in 1898, lived most of her youth in the Chelsea district of Boston. Every Saturday night she and her girlfriends would "march up Broadway, and [take] possession of all we saw . . . or desired," staying out "till all hours." They pressed their "noses and fingers on plate glass windows ablaze with electric lights and alluring with display." They inspected "tons of cheap candy, to find a few pennies' worth of the most enduring kind." Such experiences, Antin said, planted "treasures [in] my brain," which she later drew on as an adult. What were those treasures but the content of a new identity, a new kind of person who would regard the future as one of "shining," unfolding possibility. Blocking out the inequities and miseries that burdened the immigrant community from which she came, Antin compared her life to a "fairy story," observing how she moved from one "transformation" to another. "I have reached," she declared as an adult, "what was the second transformation of my life, as truly as my coming to America was the first great transformation." Part of that first transformation took place in a "dazzlingly beautiful palace called a 'department store,'" when she and her sister "exchanged our hateful homemade European costumes . . . for real American machine-made garments, and issued forth glorified in each other's eyes."[36]

A Manhattan teenager, DuBois lived with her working mother in a reasonably comfortable midtown apartment. On clear, bright days in 1907 when she was not learning French, sewing, or attending art classes, DuBois loved to go walking on Broadway, bounded on every turn by consumer institutions. For her, nearly every day in New York was "swell elegant," "peachy," "scrumptuous," and "glorious," especially those days that freed her to go into the streets. "I may as well take up residence on Broadway," she said in her diary, so often did she go abroad. Characteristically, she wrote: "Up early and went down to Myra's. We went downtown and shopped and walked up Broadway to Macy's—had more fun than a 'barrel of monkeys.'" DuBois's diary reports phone calls, outings with the camera, subway journeys to the new theaters and soda fountains, visits to the Knickerbocker and Waldorf-Astoria hotels, and, above all, shopping jaunts to such stores as Macy's, B. Altman, and James McCreery. She met her friends at the stores and ate with them in the store restaurants. She traveled the elevators and escalators to see the abundance of goods, and she witnessed the entertainment supplied by the stores to women who had the leisure to enjoy them.[37]

These diaries and autobiographical accounts show how far the secularization of thought and behavior had proceeded in the lives of many women, whose daily activity seems to have been barely touched by religious reflection or works of charity. Such accounts and diaries also display how much middle-class women had come to occupy and to move comfortably within the public domain. Their new freedom was made possible by the emergence of a quintessentially feminine world constructed around the commodity form that had come to dominate the urban scene by 1915. F. Laurent Godinez, one of the first important authorities on city street lighting, clearly hinted at that relationship when he wrote in 1914, "The American city is in a state of evolution, due largely to woman's influence, and there is a rapidly spreading sentiment to the effect that our cities . . . must be something more than bare shelters for enormous aggregations of humanity. . . . They must be places to live in . . . and must afford facilities for recreation and the attainment of an artistic ideal." Once considered only private beings with identities circumscribed by the limits of the domestic frontier, women had now entered a public space no longer principally masculine in character. Moreover, by 1920 many women, working in fashion and consumer industries, had acquired the power to shape in some degree the public culture of consumption. An utterly different social context had appeared, far removed from the early capitalist one John Mack Farragher describes in *Women and Men on the Overland Trail,* where men controlled the public life and where women's culture was tethered to the hearth.[38] A public life in cultural tension in which the lives of women and men interfused and competed for influence had emerged.

The culture and institutions of consumption did much more, however, than make the lives of women more secular and public. As the women's personal statements also reveal, they drew women deeply into a new individualism founded on commodity consumption, not on the production of goods or on the individual ownership of property. Fostering the idea that women ought to be treated as individuals with special interests and with desires for comfort and pleasure, consumer service must have induced many women to believe that they ought to be served, not to serve others. In the minds of at least some women, that conviction had considerable implications for the sexual relation, suggesting that men ought to entertain and to serve women, not the other way around. The idea was to take its most extreme expression in an article by journalist Helen Lawrenson, written for *Esquire Magazine* in the 1930s. Lawrenson argued that the "new modern man" ought to imitate the "gigolo," because gigolos understand the "feminine yearning to get away from home" and "offer" women "the whole world as a playground." "Service for ladies is his watchword"; and his motto, "The customer is always right."[39]

The inventive, surreal, multicolored, and image-saturated texture of consumer life, the excitement of possibility inherent in the commodity form, the aura of fashion, the appeals of desire and fulfillment—all stimulated women to imagine a more varied range of individual expression and experience. An upsurge of longing, a diffuse desire for something better or, perhaps, a quest focused on a concrete change, was a hallmark of the consumer culture. In Florence Peck, a young librarian from Boston who knew consumer life very well, the longing assumed its diffuse form. "Have you ever had the desire," she mused in her 1903 diary, "the awful longing for something, some one that you could not have—away down in your heart—that dreadful longing for something, some one." DuBois, on the other hand, had a better grip on her dreams. After visiting the White Line Pier in New York, to watch the departure of the magnificent luxury liner *Oceanic,* she exclaimed, "Oh! Gee how I longed to stay on board—Just think what oodles and oodles of fun we'd have—With a heavy heart I left that ship. Oh! to be in *Rome! London!* and the *Ocean* just seems to call me!"[40]

The thought and behavior of American feminists before World War I also displayed the imprint of the culture of consumption. Feminist ideology, once partly based on the individualist demand that women be given independence through productive work, now began to absorb the newer individualist demand for greater sensual gratification and experience. That process is discernible as early as the late 1880s, when such leaders of the women's rights movement as Lucy Stone, Mary Livermore, Julia Ward Howe, and Charlotte Perkins Gilman joined the ranks of Nationalism, an indigenous socialist movement founded by Edward Bellamy, which put the department store at the core of its vision. Although most of the women of that movement did not discard older commitments to productive labor or to the belief in rational, well-balanced behavior, some of them did begin to reject inherited notions of thrift, temperance, and self-denial. Nationalist Jane Croly, a noted fashion columnist and a women's rights leader, declared that all men and women ought to have "warmth, luxury, and the softness of blended colors, the freedom from the rude influences of life environed by material beauty and comfort" and "the right to participate in whatever life has to bestow."[41]

Many women who headed the woman movement in the late nineteenth and the early twentieth centuries felt unease and unrest in the face of the new culture. They struggled over its moral and social implications, the way it turned away from established traditions and settled forms and threatened to uproot women from traditional familial settings, making them vulnerable to exploitation in a new and anonymous communal forum. In the midst of the department store revolution in retailing, many women, from different perspectives within the woman movement, were fighting to erase prostitution, to eliminate the peddling of false images of women in the media, to protect women and children from the dangers of city life, and to legislate against intemperance.[42] At the same time, suffragists and social reformers, as well as the "new feminists" of the early twentieth century, could hardly escape the impact of the culture of consumption, not a surprising fact given the magnitude of the changes then taking place. Often competing with the older faith in balance, symmetry, rational control, and loyalty to productive work, this culture was felt by different women in different ways. Nevertheless, we can see the power of the new experience breaking in on the political practice and social behavior of many feminist and suffragist women.

The mainstream suffrage publications, such as the *Woman Voter,* invited department stores to advertise in their pages. The *Woman's Journal* employed advertising agents. Ebulliently, suffragists emulated advertising strategies and purveyed the "art of publicity." They devised suffrage billboards and posters, calendars and movies and conducted great parades and pageants, which echoed those arranged by department stores and which "transformed" even the streets of Boston into "carnivals of color, sound, and animation." A purple, violet, and gold color scheme unified the Washington parade of 1913. "Yellow rallies" were held in New York with marchers wearing yellow capes and carrying "yellow balls of light in the shape of lanterns." In May 1914 twelve little girls dressed as butterflies, symbolizing the suffrage states, led decorated floats and bedecked automobiles in a handsome parade down the main thoroughfare of Louisville, Kentucky. Behind the girls trotted a little boy, consigned to the garb of a "gray moth, representing Kentucky just ready to emerge from its cocoon."[43]

Like liberal and leftist political activists in other countries, American feminists relied on an aesthetic politics of mass spectacle that imitated the practices forged by the urban merchant class. Suffragists used advertising space in the streetcars, where they tacked up "vivid yellow, black, and white placards." With the willing consent of department stores, they decorated store windows in the "colors of the Suffrage Party." Stores everywhere volunteered their windows and their interiors for suffrage advertising. In June 1916 Chicago's Carson Pirie Scott installed a wax figure of a suffragist in one of its windows, a herald of the coming convention of the Woman's Party in that city. At about the same time, Wanamaker's set a precedent by permitting all female employees to march in suffrage parades during working hours. In 1912 suffragists chose Macy's in New York as the headquarters for suffragette supplies, including marching gowns, bonnets, and hatpins.[44]

Women's rights leaders published magazines that reflected the clear merger of feminism, marked by a secular, internationalist perspective, with the cosmopolitan, heterogeneous culture of consumption. The magazine *Madame,* printed in Indianapolis as the official organ of the National Council of Women, appeared in 1903. Nearly a cousin of *Harper's Bazaar, Madame* mixed articles on jewelry, cosmetics, food, theater, and department stores with descriptions of woman's advancement in public life. Also in 1903 the short-lived *American Business Woman's Magazine,* the first of its kind in America, was published in Denver, Colorado. It was followed in 1915 by a hardier version, *Business Woman's Magazine,* a Manhattan periodical that was kindred to the official bulletin of the National Federation of Business and Professional Women's Clubs, the *Independent Woman,* in print four years later. Ardent defenders of women's right to have families and professional careers at the same time, both *Business Woman's Magazine* and the *Independent Woman* generously made space for articles on department stores, and both would have agreed with the Department Store, a fleeting and expensive retail journal of the time, that the department store constituted "the first true expression of the cresting wave of feminism," where women "ruled" and were recognized as "salesgirls, department heads, and buyers." The two magazines promoted a liberal, individualistic feminism, and both described the business woman as the "new feminist," who sought to release herself from all fetters and to enjoy life to the fullest. "The business woman it is who extracts from life its best flower and romance. The modern girl wants to come into contact with the *live forces* of the busy old world which is moving every day."[45]

Many of the newer feminists, who also worked for suffrage, had some connection with the commercial world, and still others were attracted to the urban centers, so revitalized by the "palaces of consumption." The novelist and feminist Edna Ferber, whose father owned a retail store, adored the consumer life, although she could be extremely critical of it as well. In 1916 Elsa Maxwell and Alva Belmont, the president of the Congressional Union for Woman Suffrage, wrote a fund-raising suffrage operetta, "Melinda and Her Sisters," an innovation perhaps never repeated. Maxwell, a feminist all her life, acquired fame as a columnist and party giver. The socialist-feminist Crystal Eastman worked for a while as director of the sales department of the Maxwell Automobile Company, which engaged fifty women on the same terms as its male employees to sell its cars. And, as the *Woman's Journal* contended, all female department store advertisers were suffragists.[46]

Of that younger generation of women, Rheta Childe Dorr and Inez Haynes Irwin exemplified most vividly in their behavior and beliefs the shaping power of the culture of consumption. Dorr was a militant feminist leader in the 1910s, editor of the *Suffragist,* the official organ of the Congressional Union for Woman Suffrage, precursor of the National Woman's Party. A socialist for a short while, she later denounced Bolshevism, in 1917, and campaigned for Warren G. Harding, in 1920. Dorr claimed her right to independence, her freedom to leave her family and home at any time for places unknown. As a child she had said, "When I grow up if I don't like my family I won't live with 'em. If I don't like the town I live in I'll move away. I'm never going to *have* anything I don't want, and I'm never going to *do* anything I don't like, not so long as I live." In 1890, against her family's opposition, she went to New York City to become an artist. Her exposure to the consumer life of the city must have completed her "transformation" into one of the new feminists, who increasingly tried to integrate an older interest in woman's public advancement with a new, passionate concern for personal enrichment and sensual expression. Dorr was an important consumer activist who joined other reformers in demanding better treatment of saleswomen in department stores; at the same time she was pleased to report that women, having "risen" in the stores, "keep on rising. One-fourth of the department store buyers and managers in the sixteen biggest stores on [Chicago's] State [Street] are women." Moreover, she could describe State Street, the major retail thoroughfare in Chicago, as a "pavilion where people ought to dance in the open air."[47]

Born in 1873, Irwin came from a genteel, New England middle-class family, which, significantly, made its living managing hotels in Boston, perhaps Irwin's first contact with modern consumer life. In the early 1900s she moved to Greenwich Village, wrote articles for the radical periodical the *Masses,* and joined the National Advisory Council of the National Woman's Party. Irwin's fame rests largely on her important history, *The Story of the Woman's Party,* but she also wrote many journalistic pieces and novels that showed her nearly uncritical approach to the culture of consumption. Like many of her contemporaries, Irwin seemed to lose touch with its grimmer side, its class character, the way it depended on discipline and exploitation, and, above all, the way it seemed to threaten fragmentation and disorientation. She was so fascinated by the tendency toward play and leisure in this culture that she confused work with play. For example, after spending a year in California, she wrote in 1916 that Californians "make every task a game and a play and a lark—a joy and delight."[48]

Irwin was convinced that women could achieve true humanity and modernity only by living in the cosmopolitan city with its wealth of consumer institutions. Her novel *The Lady of Kingdoms* depicts the emerging liberation of her female characters as they abandon what she describes as the provincial and sexually "starved" life of a small country town for the "seething" pleasures of "metropolitan experience." Her main heroine, Southward Drake, epitomizes the new feminist of the day. She has money and a driving need for independence. Restless and athletic, slender and beautiful, she yearns for unknown and vital experience. As the novel begins Southward is living in her grandparents' mansion in rural Connecticut, where she has fashioned for herself a fantastic "garret" high up in the house, well beyond the reach of her family. Southward consumes the novels of Jules Verne and the early fairy tales of H. G. Wells in this secluded place, which has all the trappings of a cosmopolitan dream. The decor mixes Occidental with Oriental motifs; the walls are covered with colorful crepe, turning the room into a rajah's quarters. "It makes me think of the *Arabian Nights,*" observes one of her few visitors. Here Southward dons Chinese clothes taken from the family trunk: a "tomato-coloured prince's coat" and "a high Chinese head-dress" with feathers and flowers, "many coloured silk pompons," and "streamers of silk trimmed with mirrors."[49]

Toward the middle of the novel, Southward has found her emancipation in New York, surfeited with skyscrapers, theaters, restaurants, dinner parties, and department stores, all of which are described in the book. She has encountered intellectual and sexual freedom. She has discovered and realized her true self. But, then, all Irwin's major female characters in the novel experience their true selves in the city, are transformed by the "seething quality of its social life," its "gorgeous restaurant night life." Even the most dour, Dickensian woman in the novel, Mrs. Crowell, mother of Southward's best friend, Hester, undergoes a dramatic conversion. Trapped in a "little dead country village," Mrs. Crowell seems buried under the weight of puritan repression and fear and of outmoded family conventions; but, in San Francisco, where she has gone with her emancipated daughter at the end of the novel, she lives through a great change. Together, the Crowells "[wander] about the streets of the shopping districts, gazing into the windows that offer the stranger unlimited entertainment." At night, before going home, they pass "through the department-store area, staring into the big lighted windows where groups of wax figures [display] the latest fashion caprice from Paris."

They enter the glories of Chinatown, startled by the "vegetable shops, meat shops, fish shops, crowded with familiar wares in strange shapes; the side streets papered for intervals with scarlet posters . . . the constant procession of men in all possible variations of Oriental and Occidental wear."[50]

After feeling the accumulated power of a series of such experiences, Mrs. Crowell says to her daughter, "I feel . . . as though I'd died and come to life in another world." As Irwin writes: "It was as though, having cast all the associations of her past life overboard, she were trying to fill out the shape of her soul with a new cargo, a cargo which should make up in degree of its colour and strangeness for all the lost greynesses and familiarities." Mrs. Crowell comes to accept the liberation of her daughter and begins to chart her own. She has forfeited "greyness" for color, taking part in a major ritual of transformation in a culture of consumption.[51]

Irwin depicted journeys of transformation in her fiction that other American women took in real life. In those early, nearly euphoric days of consumer capitalism, textured so much by the department store, many women thought they had discovered a more exciting, more appealing life; freedom remade within a consumer matrix. Their participation in consumer experience challenged and subverted that complex of qualities traditionally known as feminine—dependence, passivity, religious piety, domestic inwardness, sexual purity, and maternal nurture. Mass consumer culture presented to women a new definition of gender that carved out a space for individual expression similar to men's and that stood in tension with the older definition passed on to them by their mothers and grandmothers. This tension, clearly established in that transformative moment in history, would take many forms but would remain a fixed and fundamental part of female experience for decades to come.

ENDNOTES

[1] Artemas Ward, "Stray Shots," *Fame,* 1 (Dec. 1892), 323.

[2] Alice Kessler-Harris, *Out to Work: A History of Wage-Earning Women in the United States* (New York, 1982), 75–217; Nick Salvatore, *Eugene V. Debs: Citizen and Socialist* (Urbana, 1982), 23–177.

[3] David M. Potter, *People of Plenty: Economic Abundance and the American Character* (Chicago, 1954), 78–195; Joyce Appleby, "The Social Origins of American Revolutionary Ideology," *Journal of American History,* 64 (March 1978), 935–58; Daniel J. Boorstin, *The Americans: The Democratic Experience* (New York, 1973), 97–225; Ann Douglas, *The Feminization of American Culture* (New York, 1977), 3–13, 200–256; Karen Halttunen, *Confidence Men and Painted Women: A Study of Middle-Class Culture in America, 1830–1870* (New Haven, 1982), 1–91, 191–210; Altina L. Waller, *Reverend Beecher and Mrs. Tilton: Sex and Class in Victorian America* (Amherst, Mass., 1982), 1–53, 64–81; John Higham, "The Reorientation of American Culture in the 1890s," in John Higham, *Writing American History: Essays on Modern Scholarship* (Bloomington, Ind., 1970), 73–102; John F. Kasson, *Amusing the Million: Coney Island at the Turn of the Century* (New York, 1978); T. J. Jackson Lears, *No Place of Grace: Antimodernism and the Transformation of American Culture,*

1880–1920 (New York, 1981), 4–47; Warren I. Susman, "'Personality' and the Making of Twentieth-Century Culture," in *New Directions in American Intellectual History,* ed. John Higham and Paul Conkin (Baltimore, 1979), 212–26.

[4] Stuart Ewen and Elizabeth Ewen, *Channels of Desire: Mass Images and the Shaping of American Culture* (New York, 1982), 1–77; Barry Bluestone, Patricia Hanna, Sarah Kuhn, and Laura Moore, *The Retail Revolution: Market Transformation, Investment, and Labor in the Modern Department Store* (Boston, 1981), 98–151.

[5] Hugh Dalziel Duncan, *Culture and Democracy: The Struggle for Form in Society and Architecture in Chicago and the Midwest during the Life and Times of Louis H. Sullivan* (Totowa, N.J., 1965), 113–52; Lewis A. Erenberg, *Steppin' Out: New York Nightlife and the Transformation of American Culture, 1890–1930* (Westport, Conn., 1981), 113–230; Elizabeth Kendall, *Where She Danced* (New York, 1979), 4–68; H. Gordon Selfridge, *The Romance of Commerce* (London, 1918), 16; Jane Jacobs, *Cities and the Wealth of Nations: Principles of Economic Life* (New York, 1984), 54–113, 227–30; Warren Susman, "The Culture of Abundance," typescript, Sept. 15, 1983, pp. 1–35 (in Leach's possession); William R. Taylor, "Toward the Launching of a Commercial Culture: New York City, 1860–1939," typescript, March 16, 1984, pp. 19–22 (in Leach's possession).

[6] *Dry Goods Economist,* Jan. 5, 1901, p 7. No book that discusses these strategies as a whole exists, although the following are useful: William Leach, *True Love and Perfect Union: The Feminist Reform of Sex and Society* (New York, 1980), 213–60; Harry E. Ressequie, "Alexander Turney Stewart's Marble Palace: The Cradle of the Department Store," *New-York Historical Society Quarterly,* 48 (April 1964), 131–62; and Susan Benson Porter, "Palace of Consumption and Machine for Selling: The American Department Store, 1880–1940," *Radical History Review,* 21 (Fall 1979), 199–221.

[7] L. Frank Baum, *The Art of Decorating Dry Goods Windows* (Chicago, 1900), 165–66; *Dry Goods Economist,* March 20, 1897, p. 97; *ibid.,* Oct. 6, 1900, p. 20; *ibid.,* May 24, 1902, p. 73; *ibid.,* July 8, 1905, p. 79; W. H. Barley, "Power of Store Decoration," *Store Life,* 1 (Oct. 1904), 7–8; Dolf Sternberger, *Panorama of the Nineteenth Century,* trans. Joachim Neugroshel (New York, 1977), 38–52.

[8] *Dry Goods Economist,* Sept. 24, 1898, p. 9; *ibid.,* April 14, 1900, p. 14; *ibid.,* Jan. 21, 1905, p. 55; Warren C. Scoville, *Revolution in Glassmaking: Entrepreneurship and Technological Change in the American Industry, 1880–1920* (Cambridge, Mass., 1948), 78–83, 103–04, 253–59; Freda Diamond, *The Story of Glass* (New York, 1953), 79–128.

[9] Gail Hamilton, "A New Art," *Harper's Bazaar,* Oct. 18, 1873, p. 658; *Dry Goods Economist,* March 25, 1893, p. 16; *ibid.,* June 29, 1893, p. 21; *ibid.,* March 24, 1894, p. 83; *ibid.,* Jan. 4, 1896, p. 7; *ibid.,* March 27, 1897, pp. 39–41; *ibid.,* April 6, 1901, p. 51; *ibid.,* Feb. 2, 1904, p. 58; *ibid.,* Sept. 21, 1907, p. 36; *ibid.,* April 3, 1920, pp. 103–07; K. Venkataramen, *The Chemistry of Synthetic Dyes* (2 vols., New York, 1952), I, 1–4; David Paterson, *The Science of Colour Mixing: A Manual Intended for the Use of Dyers, Calico Printers, and Colour Chemists* (London, 1900), 85–111; Faber Birren, *Color and Human Response: Aspects of Light and Color Bearing on the Reaction of Living Things and the Welfare of Human Beings* (New York, 1978), 60–107.

[10] *Philadelphia Retail Ledger,* Jan. 17, 1923, p. 3; M. Luckiesh, *Light and Color in Advertising and Merchandising* (New York, 1923), 146–70, 207–17; *Dry Goods Economist,* Dec. 23, 1893, p. 38;

ibid., Oct. 26, 1912, p. 16; *ibid.,* Aug. 30, 1919, p. 99; "Through English Eyes," *Store Life,* 1 (Oct. 1904), 8.

[11] "Poster Art in France," *Poster,* 1 (1896), 55; "Posters in America," *Poster and Art Collector,* 1 (July 1898), 64–65; "Gimbel's Will Have the Biggest Electric Sign in the World," *Signs of the Times: The Journal of Advertising Devoted to the Interest of the Advertiser, the Agency and the Purveyor of Publicity,* 20 (Jan. 1913), 28; *Dry Goods Economist,* Aug. 17, 1907, p. 263; *ibid.,* April 27, 1912, p. 95; "Schack's New Wonder Spot and Floodlights," *Merchants' Record and Show Window,* 59 (Sept. 1926), 58; "Advertising Art," *Advertising World: The Retail Merchants' Magazine of Advertising,* 3 (May 15, 1898), 1–2; Herbert Cecil Duce, *Poster Advertising* (Chicago, 1912), 126.

[12] Milton Fuessle, "Elbert Hubbard, Master of Advertising and Retailing," *Advertising World,* 20 (Aug.–Sept. 1915), 142.

[13] Leonard S. Marcus, *The American Store Window* (New York, 1978), 13–20; Barry James Wood, *Show Windows: 75 Years of the Art of Display* (New York, 1982), 1–18; Pittsburgh Plate Glass, *Glass: History, Manufacture, and Its Universal Application* (Pittsburgh, 1923), 33–40.

[14] Marcus, *American Store Window,* 23, 54, 56–57; Robert Grier Cooke, "Show Window Displays: The People's Picture Galleries," *American Magazine of Fine Arts,* 2 (April 1921), 115–17; *Dry Goods Economist,* Nov. 12, 1898, p. 31.

[15] Neil Harris, "Museums, Merchandising, and Popular Taste: The Struggle for Influence," in *Material Culture and the Study of American Life,* ed. Ian M. G. Quimby (New York, 1978), 140–74; "Store Decoration," *Merchants' Record and Show Window,* 2 (April 1912), 54; "The Unique Gift Shop," *Pet Dealer,* 2 (Sept. 1927), 20; "The Wanamaker Pet Shop," *Pet Shop,* 1 (July 1926), 3.

[16] *Dry Goods Economist,* Aug. 23, 1902, p. 21; Grover Whalen, *Mr. New York: The Autobiography of Grover Whalen* (New York, 1955), 20.

[17] Lewis Hyde, *The Gift: Imagination and the Erotic Life of Property* (New York, 1983), 67–68; "Wanamaker Pet Shop," 3–5.

[18] *Advertising World,* 16 (March 1912), 11.

[19] *Dry Goods Economist,* Aug. 15, 1908, p. 3; René Girard, *Deceit, Desire, and the Novel: Self and Other in Literary Structure,* trans. Yvonne Freccero (Baltimore, 1965), 1–52. René Girard does not deal with fashion; I have applied his arguments to the subject.

[20] "Showing Gowns on Living Models," *Merchants' Record and Show Window,* 25 (Nov. 1909), 39; "Living Models," *ibid.,* 22 (May 1908), 45; *Dry Goods Economist,* Oct. 10, 1903, p. 14; *ibid.,* Aug. 19, 1911, p. 49; *ibid.,* April 12, 1913, p. 55; *ibid.,* Oct. 3, 1914, pp. 45–46; *ibid.,* Oct. 10, 1914, p. 34; *ibid.,* April 1, 1916, pp. 73–75; *ibid.,* March 3, 1917, p. 15; *ibid.,* Aug. 25, 1917, pp. 77, 95; *ibid.,* July 12, 1919, p. 24; *ibid.,* Aug. 27, 1921, pp. 16–17; "Cooperative Show Window Advertising," *Signs of the Times,* 16 (June 1912), 28; Lillian Drain, "Many Artists in Fashion Show Poster Contest," *Poster,* 3 (Oct. 1912), 23–24; Albert Morenson, "Fashion Show Posters in Los Angeles," *ibid.* (April 1913), 43–44; "How New Styles Are Shown by Means of Moving Pictures," *Department Store,* 1 (April 1914), 14.

[21] Lois W. Banner, *American Beauty* (New York, 1983), 17–85, 175–225.

[22] *Dry Goods Economist,* Nov. 17, 1900, p. 14; *ibid.,* Nov. 30, 1901, p. 71; *ibid.,* May 2, 1903, p. 68; *ibid.,* July 4, 1908, p. 4; "Mobs View Directoire," *Dry Goods Reporter,* 1 (Aug. 15, 1908), 12;

"Costume and Morality," *ibid.,* 2 (July 17, 1909), 12. Practically any issue of the *Dry Goods Economist* after 1895 shows photographs of underwear or lingerie windows, but see the photograph of a boudoir window with two women dressed in underwear in *Dry Goods Economist,* Oct. 19, 1901, p. 55.

[23] "Advertising Art," *Advertising World,* 3 (May 15, 1898), 1–2; Jean-Christophe Agnew, "The Consuming Vision of Henry James," in *The Culture of Consumption: Critical Essays in American History, 1880–1980,* ed. Richard Wightman Fox and T. J. Jackson Lears (New York, 1983), 65–100; Neil Harris, "Iconography and Intellectual History: The Half-Tone Effect," in *New Directions in American Intellectual History,* ed. Higham and Conkin, 196–211; Estelle Jussim, *Visual Communication and the Graphic Arts: Photographic Technologies in the Nineteenth Century* (New York, 1974), 69–144; Peter C. Marzio, *The Democratic Art: Pictures for a 19th-Century America: Chromolithography, 1840–1900* (Boston, 1979), 1–27.

[24] Siegel-Cooper advertisement, in Bella Landauer, comp., retail advertisement scrapbook, n.p., Bella Landauer Collection of Advertising Art (New-York Historical Society, New York City); *Dry Goods Economist,* March 16, 1895, p. 32; *ibid.,* June 13, 1896, p. 10; *ibid.,* Aug. 22, 1896, p. 16; *ibid.,* March 27, 1897, pp. 39–41; *ibid.,* July 16, 1898, p. 79; *ibid.,* Nov. 17, 1900, p. 15; *ibid.,* April 21, 1906, p. 87; *ibid.,* Sept. 28, 1907, p. 95; *Siegel-Cooper Company of New York: A Bird's Eye View of New York* (New York, 1898), 134–35; "New York's New Store," *Store Life,* 1 (May 1904), 25–27; "Through English Eyes," 8; Leach, *True Love and Perfect Union,* 234–35.

[25] *Dry Goods Economist,* April 26, 1902, p. 18; *ibid.,* Feb. 28, 1903, p. 68; *ibid.,* Jan. 16, 1904, p. 21; *ibid.,* Aug. 22, 1908, p. 9; "A Branch of the New York Public Library to Be Opened Shortly in the Big Store," *Thought and Work,* 1 (Jan. 15, 1905), 6. The term *guests* was commonly used by merchants to describe their customers. Barley, "Power of Store Decoration," 7–8.

[26] *Dry Goods Economist,* Oct. 28, 1916, p. 55; *ibid.,* Aug. 30, 1919, p. 49.

[27] *Ibid.,* Aug. 7, 1897, p. 67; *ibid.,* Jan. 20, 1917, pp. 7–13, 29; *ibid.,* May 19, 1917, pp. 7, 13, 17; *ibid.,* March 16, 1918, pp. 7–11, 33.

[28] *Ibid.,* April 3, 1920, pp. 235–37.

[29] Emily Kimbrough, *Through Charley's Door* (New York, 1952), 178; Mary H. Tolman, *Positions of Responsibility in Department Stores and Other Retail Selling Organizations: A Study of Opportunities for Women* (New York, 1921), 37; "Business Notes," *Poster,* 3 (Nov. 1912), 9; Edmund Arrowsmith, "Women in the Poster Advertising Field," *ibid.* (Dec. 1912), 19–21; "She Puts the 'Flash' in Flashers," *Signs of the Times,* 20 (Oct. 1, 1913), 38; "'We Are Seven,' Say the Olivie Sisters, Hair Specialists," *Independent Woman,* 7 (Sept. 1927), 18–19, 47; Rose Gotthold, "One Woman's Success," *Business Woman's Magazine,* 1 (Nov. 1914), 38–39; "Business Helps, Money-Making Plans for the Ambitious Girl," *ibid.,* 63–65; Catharine Oglesby, *Fashion Careers American Style* (New York, 1930), 35–266.

[30] Louise Robinson Blaisdell, "From Cash Girl to Buyer," *Business Woman's Magazine,* 2 (April 1915), 50–52; Mae De Mon Sutton, *I Reminisce—* (Fort Lauderdale, 1942), 29–39, 59–67; Estelle Hamburger, *It's a Woman's Business* (New York, 1939), 106–08, 114–15, 174–75, 192–93, 228–29; *Woman's Journal,* Aug. 5, 1916, p. 251; "Places in the Sun," *Independent Woman,* 1 (Oct. 1920), 7; Elizabeth Hale Lally, "The Big Department Store: The Advertising Manager's Job," in *Advertising Careers for Women,* ed. Blanche Clair and Dorothy Dignam (New York, 1939), 35; Merle Higley, *Women in Advertising in New York Agencies* (New York, 1924), 1–18; Beulah Elfreth Kennard, *The Educational Director in the Retail Store* (New York, 1918), 1–12; Edna Ferber, *Emma McChesney and Co.* (New York, 1915); Edna Ferber, *A Peculiar Treasure* (New York, 1939), 172–73. The figures

on buyers are from *Sheldon's Retail Trade in the United States* (New York, 1916, 1924). This directory furnished the retail business with a list of all buyers in the country and is still published today. The 1916 percentage is based on a sample of 3,592 buyers in major cities in New York, Illinois, Pennsylvania, California, Massachusetts, Connecticut, and the Deep South, 1,315 of whom were women; the 1924 figure of 7,922, which covers more cities in the country, includes 3,040 women. *Ibid.,* 1–289. The figures do not reflect the total number of buyers in both years.

[31] "Women Control the Family Purse," *Advertising World,* 33 (July 1928), 44–45; D. J. K., "Shopping at Stewart's," *Hearth and Home,* 1 (Jan. 9, 1869), 43; Joel Benton, "The Woman Buyer," *Fame,* 7 (Oct. 1898), 403; *New York Times,* June 13, 1881, p. 13.

[32] Mary Lester Harris Diary, Dec. 30, 1848, Harris Collection (Manuscripts Division, New-York Historical Society, New York City); Sophie C. Hall Diary, Monday morning, Jan. 1879 (Manuscripts Division, New York Public Library).

[33] *Dry Goods Economist,* Sept. 15, 1894, p. 25.

[34] *Ibid.,* July 12, 1902, p. 62; *ibid.,* Oct. 24, 1903, p. 49; *ibid.,* July 5, 1905, p. 61.

[35] Marjorie Reynolds Diary, Feb. 18, 1903, April 2, 1909, Reynolds Family Papers (Manuscripts Division, New-York Historical Society); Mrs. George Richards Diary, Jan. 12, Jan. 17, Feb. 26, March 2, 1903, Richards Family Papers, *ibid.*

[36] Mary Antin, *The Promised Land* (Boston, 1912), 187, 261–62, 321.

[37] Marguerite Delavarre DuBois Diary, Feb. 2, Feb. 8, March 1, March 8, March 27, April 28, May 10, May 29, Nov. 13, Dec. 11, Dec. 28, 1907 (Manuscripts Division, New York Public Library) .

[38] F. Laurent Godinez, *Display Window Lighting and the City Beautiful: Facts, and New Ideas for Progressive Merchants* (New York, 1914), 19; John Mack Farragher, *Women and Men on the Overland Trail* (New Haven, 1979), 110–43.

[39] Helen Lawrenson, "Wanted: A New Modern Man," *Esquire Magazine,* 40 (Jan. 1939), 35, 127–29.

[40] Florence Peck Diary, April 12, 1903 (Manuscripts Division, New York Public Library); DuBois Diary, July 3, 1907.

[41] Mari Jo Buhle, *Women and American Socialism, 1870–1920* (Urbana, 1981), 75–90, 246–85; Jennie June [Jane Croly], "The New Point of View," *Nationalist,* 1 (Oct. 1889), 195–97; William Leach, "Looking Forward Together: Feminists and Edward Bellamy," *democracy,* 1 (Jan. 1982), 120–34.

[42] Linda Gordon, *Woman's Body, Woman's Right: A Social History of Birth Control in America* (New York, 1976), 236–40; David Nasaw, "Children of the Street," typescript, Sept. 26, 1982, pp. 1–24 (in Leach's possession).

[43] *Woman's Journal,* May 16, 1914, p. 154; *ibid,* May 2, 1914, p. 139; *ibid.,* May 30, 1914, p. 174; *ibid.,* Oct. 10, 1914, p. 273; *ibid.,* May 15, 1915, p. 10; *ibid.,* May 29, 1915, p. 12; *Woman Voter,* 4 (Jan. 1913), 2; "The Washington Parade and Pageant," *ibid.* (March 1913), 10–11; Adaline W. Sterling, "Yellow Rallies," *ibid.,* 6 (Sept. 1915), 22; "Why We March: A Symposium," *ibid.,* 3 (May 1912), 3–5.

[44] F. F. Purdy, "Notes for New York," *Merchants' Record and Show Window,* 31 (Dec. 1912), 40; *Suffragist,* June 3, 1916, p. 11; *Woman's Journal,* Jan. 10, 1914, p. 10; *ibid.,* April 24, 1915, p. 128; Frank Trommler, "Working-Class Culture and Modern Mass Culture before World War I," *New German Critique,* 29 (Spring–Summer 1983), 57–70.

[45] "The Feminist and All Feminism," *Business Woman's Magazine,* 1 (Oct. 1914), 31–34; "An Appreciation of the Department Store," *Department Store,* 1 (April 1914), 67; Edmund Russell,

"Realism and Jewels," *Madame,* 2 (Sept. 1904), 173–74; Stella Stuart, "The Quest for Beauty," *ibid.,* 4 (June 1904), 277; Elizabeth Buckham, "Chicago's Noted Social Settlement," *ibid.* (July 1905), 289; "Madame's Fashion Department," *ibid.,* 3 (Oct. 1904), 20–22.

[46] *Woman's Journal,* Aug. 5, 1916, p. 251; *Suffragist,* Feb. 26, 1916, p. 6; Ferber, *Peculiar Treasure,* 6, 27, 187–88, 217; Edna Ferber, "One of the Old Girls," *American Magazine,* 72 (Sept. 1911), 552–58; Edna Ferber, "May Meys from Cuba," *ibid.,* 705–11.

[47] Rheta Childe Dorr, *A Woman of Fifty* (New York, 1924), 6–7, 9–14, 39; Edward T. James and Janet Wilson James, eds., *Notable American Women, 1607–1950: A Biographical Dictionary* (3 vols., Cambridge, Mass., 1971), I, 503–04; William Hard and Rheta Dorr, "The Woman's Invasion," *Everybody's Magazine,* 20 (Jan. 1909), 81–85; "Christmas from behind the Counter," *Independent,* Dec. 5, 1907, pp. 1340–47.

[48] Barbara Sicherman and Carol Hurd Green, eds., *Notable American Women: The Modern Period: A Biographical Dictionary* (Cambridge, Mass., 1980), 368–70; Inez Haynes Irwin, *The Story of the Woman's Party* (New York, 1921); Inez Haynes Irwin, *The Californiacs* (New York, 1916), 54–55, 60.

[49] Inez Haynes Irwin, *The Lady of Kingdoms* (New York, 1917), 24, 99–103, 472, 475.

[50] *Ibid.,* 213–45, 468–72, 475.

[51] *Ibid.,* 471–72.

Name: _____   Date: _____

UNDERSTANDING THE TEXT

1. Based on your reading of Leach's essay, briefly characterize the large urban department store of the late nineteenth century. According to Leach, what forces made such stores possible? (Identify two.)

2. According to Lewis Hyde, what is the difference between a gift and a commodity?

3. Leach claims that "[w]hite middle-class women were the first to experience . . . the transformative power" of the new style of consumption afforded by department stores. How did it transform them? (Identify and discuss two examples.)

Two Cheers for Materialism

James Twitchell

Of all the strange beasts that have come slouching into the 20th century, none has been more misunderstood, more criticized, and more important than materialism. Who but fools, toadies, hacks, and occasional loopy libertarians have ever risen to its defense? Yet the fact remains that while materialism may be the most shallow of the 20th century's various -isms, it has been the one that has ultimately triumphed. The world of commodities appears so antithetical to the world of ideas that it seems almost heresy to point out the obvious: most of the world most of the time spends most of its energy producing and consuming more and more stuff. The really interesting question may be not why we are so materialistic, but why we are so unwilling to acknowledge and explore what seems the central characteristic of modern life.

When the French wished to disparage the English in the 19th century, they called them a nation of shopkeepers. When the rest of the world now wishes to disparage Americans, they call us a nation of consumers. And they are right. We are developing and rapidly exporting a new material culture, a mallcondo culture. To the rest of the world we do indeed seem not just born to shop, but alive to shop. Americans spend more time tooling around the mallcondo—three to four times as many hours as our European counterparts—and we have more stuff to show for it. According to some estimates, we have about four times as many things as Middle Europeans, and who knows how much more than people in the less developed parts of the world. The quantity and disparity are increasing daily, even though, as we see in Russia and China, the "emerging nations" are playing a frantic game of catch-up.

This burst of mallcondo commercialism has happened recently—in my lifetime—and it is spreading around the world at the speed of television. The average American consumes twice as many goods and services as in 1950; in fact, the poorest fifth of the current population buys more than the average fifth did in 1955. Little wonder that the average new home of today is twice as large as the average house built in the early years after World War II. We have to put that stuff somewhere—quick!—before it turns to junk.

Sooner or later we are going to have to acknowledge the uncomfortable fact that this amoral consumerama has proved potent because human beings love things. In fact, to a considerable degree we live for things. In all cultures we buy things, steal things, exchange things, and horde things. From time to time, some of us collect vast amounts of things, from tulip bulbs to paint drippings on canvasses to matchbook covers. Often these objects have no observable use.

We live through things. We create ourselves through things. And we change ourselves by changing our things. In the West, we have even developed the elaborate algebra of commercial law to decide how things are exchanged, divested, and recaptured. Remember, we call these things "goods," as in "goods and services." We don't—unless we are academic critics—call them "bads." This sounds simplistic, but it is crucial to understanding the powerful allure of materialism.

Our commercial culture has been blamed for the rise of eating disorders, the spread of "affluenza," the epidemic of depression, the despoliation of cultural icons, the corruption of politics, the carnivalization of holy times like Christmas, and the gnat-life attention span of our youth. All of this is true. Commercialism contributes. But it is by no means the whole truth. Commercialism is more a mirror than a lamp. In demonizing it, in seeing ourselves as helpless and innocent victims of its overpowering force, in making it the scapegoat du jour, we reveal far more about our own eagerness to be passive in the face of complexity than about the thing itself.

Anthropologists tell us that consumption habits are gender-specific. Men seem to want stuff in the latent and post-midlife years. That's when the male collecting impulse seems to be felt. Boys amass playing marbles first, Elgin marbles later. Women seem to gain potency as consumers after childbirth, almost as if getting and spending is part of a nesting impulse.

Historians, however, tell us to be careful about such stereotyping. Although women are the primary consumers of commercial objects today, they have enjoyed this status only since the Industrial Revolution. Certainly in the pre-industrial world men were the chief hunter-gatherers. If we can trust works of art to accurately portray how booty was split (and cultural historians such as John Berger and Simon Schama think we can), then males were the prime consumers of fine clothes, heavily decorated furniture, gold and silver articles, and of course, paintings in which they could be shown displaying their stuff.

Once a surplus was created, in the 19th century, women joined the fray in earnest. They were not duped. The hegemonic phallocentric patriarchy did not brainwash them into thinking goods mattered. The Industrial Revolution produced more and more things not simply because it had the machines to do so, and not because nasty producers twisted their handlebar mustaches and whispered, "We can talk women into buying anything," but because both sexes are powerfully attracted to the world of things.

Karl Marx understood the magnetism of things better than anyone else. In The Communist Manifesto (1848), he wrote:

> The bourgeoisie, by the rapid improvement of all instruments of production, by the immensely facilitated means of communication, draws all, even the most barbarian nations into civilization.

The cheap prices of its commodities are the heavy artillery with which it batters down all Chinese walls. . . . It compels all nations, on pain of extinction, to adopt the bourgeois mode of production; it compels them to introduce what it calls civilization into their midst, i.e. to become bourgeois themselves. In one word, it creates a world after its own image.

Marx used this insight to motivate the heroic struggle against capitalism. But the struggle should not be to deter capitalism and its mad consumptive ways, but to appreciate how it works so its furious energy may be understood and exploited.

Don't turn to today's middle-aged academic critic for any help on that score. Driving about in his totemic Volvo (unattractive and built to stay that way), he can certainly criticize the bourgeois afflictions of others, but he is unable to provide much actual insight into their consumption practices, much less his own. Ask him to explain the difference between "Hilfiger" inscribed on an oversize shirt hanging nearly to the knees and his rear-window university decal (My child goes to Yale, sorry about yours), and you will be met with a blank stare. If you were then to suggest that what that decal and automotive nameplate represent is as overpriced as Calvin Klein's initials on a plain white T-shirt, he would pout that you can't compare apples and whatever. If you were to say next that aspiration and affiliation are at the heart of both displays, he would say that you just don't get it, just don't get it at all.

If you want to understand the potency of American consumer culture, ask any group of teenagers what democracy means to them. You will hear an extraordinary response. Democracy is the right to buy anything you want. Freedom's just another word for lots of things to buy. Appalling perhaps, but there is something to their answer. Being able to buy what you want when and where you want it was, after all, the right that made 1989 a watershed year in Eastern Europe. Recall as well that freedom to shop was another way to describe the right to be served in a restaurant that provided one focus for the early civil rights movement. Go back further. It was the right to consume freely which sparked the fires of separation of this country from England. The freedom to buy what you want (even if you can't pay for it) is what most foreigners immediately spot as what they like about our culture, even though in the next breath they will understandably criticize it.

The pressure to commercialize—to turn things into commodities and then market them as charms—has always been particularly Western. As Max Weber first argued in *The Protestant Ethic and the Spirit of Capitalism* (1905), much of the Protestant Reformation was geared toward denying the holiness of many things that the Catholic church had endowed with meanings. From the inviolable priesthood to the sacrificial holy water, this deconstructive movement systematically unloaded meaning. Soon the marketplace would capture this off-loaded meaning and apply it to secular things. Buy this, you'll be saved. You deserve a break today. You, you're the one. We are the company that cares about you. You're worth it. You are in good hands. We care. Trust in us. We are here for you.

Materialism, it's important to note, does not crowd out spiritualism; spiritualism is more likely a substitute when objects are scarce. When we have few things we make the next world holy. When we have plenty we enchant the objects around us. The hereafter becomes the here and now.

We have not grown weaker but stronger by accepting the self-evidently ridiculous myths that sacramentalize mass-produced objects; we have not wasted away but have proved inordinately powerful; have not devolved and been rebarbarized, but seem to have marginally improved. Dreaded affluenza notwithstanding, commercialism has lessened pain. Most of us have more pleasure and less discomfort in our lives than most of the people most of the time in all of history.

As Stanley Lebergott, an economist at Wesleyan University, argues in *Pursuing Happiness* (1993), most Americans have "spent their way to happiness." Lest this sound overly Panglossian, what Lebergott means is that while consumption by the rich has remained relatively steady, the rest of us—the intractable poor (about four percent of the population) are the exception—have now had a go of it. If the rich really are different, as F. Scott Fitzgerald said, and the difference is that they have longer shopping lists and are happier for it, then we have, in the last two generations, substantially caught up.

The most interesting part of the book is the second half. Here Lebergott unloads reams of government statistics and calculations to chart the path that American consumption has taken in a wide range of products and services: food, tobacco, clothing, fuel, domestic service, and medicine—to name only a few. Two themes emerge strongly from these data. The first, not surprisingly, is that Americans were far better off by 1990 than they were in 1900. And the second is that academic critics—from Robert Heilbroner, Tibor Scitovsky, Robert and Helen Lynd, and Christopher Lasch to Juliet Schor, Robert Frank, and legions of others—who've censured the waste and tastelessness of much of American consumerism have simply missed the point. Okay, okay, money can't buy happiness, but you stand a better chance than with penury.

The cultural pessimists counter that it may be true that materialism offers a temporary palliative against the anxiety of emptiness, but we still must burst joy's grape. Consumption will turn sour because so much of it is based on the chimera of debt. Easy credit = overbuying = disappointment = increased anxiety.

This is not just patronizing, it is wrongheaded. As another economist, Lendol Calder, has argued in *Financing the American Dream* (1999), debt has been an important part of families' financial planning since the time of Washington and Jefferson. And although consumer debt has consistently risen in recent times, the default rate has remained remarkably stable. More than 95.5 percent of consumer debt gets paid, usually on time. In fact, the increased availability of credit to a growing share of the population, particularly to lower-income individuals and families, has allowed many more "have nots" to enter the economic mainstream.

There is, in fact, a special crippling quality to poverty in the modern Western world. For the penalty of intractable, transgenerational destitution is not just the absence of things; it is also the absence of meaning, the exclusion from participating in the essential socializing events of modern life. When you hear that some ghetto kid has killed one of his peers for a pair of branded sneakers or a monogrammed athletic jacket you realize that chronically unemployed poor youths are indeed living the absurdist life proclaimed by existentialists. The poor are truly the self-less ones in commercial culture.

Clearly what the poor are after is what we all want: association, affiliation, inclusion, magical purpose. While they are bombarded, as we all are, by the commercial imprecations of being cool, of experimenting with various presentations of disposable self, they lack the wherewithal to even enter the loop.

The grandfather of today's academic scolds is Thorstein Veblen (1857–1929), the eccentric Minnesotan who coined the phrase "conspicuous consumption" and has become almost a cult figure among critics of consumption. All of his books (save for his translation of the *Lexdaela Saga*) are still in print. His most famous, *The Theory of the Leisure Class,* has never been out of print since it was first published in 1899. Veblen claimed that the leisure class set the standards for conspicuous consumption. Without sumptuary laws to protect their markers of distinction, the rest of us could soon make their styles into our own—the Industrial Revolution saw to that. But since objects lose their status distinctions when consumed by the hoi polloi, the leisure class must eternally be finding newer and more wasteful markers. Waste is not just inevitable, it is always increasing as the foolish hounds chase the wily fox.

Veblen lumped conspicuous consumption with sports and games, "devout observances," and aesthetic display. They were all reducible, he insisted, to "pecuniary emulation," his characteristically inflated term for getting in with the in-crowd. Veblen fancied himself a socialist looking forward to the day when "the discipline of the machine" would be turned around to promote stringent rationality among the entire population instead of wasted dispersion. If only we had fewer choices we would be happier, there would be less waste, and we would accept each other as equals.

The key to Veblen's argumentative power is that like Hercules cleaning the Augean stables, he felt no responsibility to explain what happens next. True, if we all purchased the same toothpaste things would be more efficient and less wasteful. Logically we should all read *Consumer Reports,* find out the best brand, and then all be happy using the same product. But we aren't. Procter & Gamble markets 36 sizes and shapes of Crest. There are 41 versions of Tylenol. Is this because we are dolts afflicted with "pecuniary emulation," obsessed with making invidious distinctions, or is the answer more complex? Veblen never considered that consumers might have other reasons for exercising choice in the marketplace. He never considered, for example, that along with "keeping up with the Joneses" runs "keeping away from the Joneses."

Remember in *King Lear* when the two nasty daughters want to strip Lear of his last remaining trappings of majesty? He has moved in with them, and they don't think he needs so many expensive guards. They whittle away at his retinue until only one is left. "What needs one?" they say. Rather like governments attempting to redistribute wealth or like academics criticizing consumption, they conclude that Lear's needs are excessive. They are false needs. Lear, however, knows otherwise. Terrified and suddenly bereft of purpose, he bellows from his innermost soul, "Reason not the need."

Lear knows that possessions are definitions—superficial meanings, perhaps, but meanings nonetheless. And unlike Veblen, he knows those meanings are worth having. Without soldiers he is no king. Without a BMW there can be no yuppie, without tattoos no adolescent rebel, without big hair no Southwestern glamourpuss, without Volvos no academic intellectual, and, well, you know the rest. Meaning is what we are after, what we need, especially when we are young.

What kind of meaning? In the standard academic view, growing out of the work of the Frankfurt school theorists of the 1950s and '60s (such as Antonio Gramsci, Theodor Adorno, and Max Horkheimer) and later those of the Center for Contemporary Cultural Studies at the University of Birmingham, it is meaning supplied by capitalist manipulators. What we see in popular culture, in this view, is the result of the manipulation of the many for the profit of the few.

For an analogy, take watching television. In academic circles, we assume that youngsters are being reified (to borrow a bit of the vast lexicon of jargon that accompanies this view) by passively consuming pixels in the dark. Meaning supposedly resides in the shows and is transferred to the sponge-like viewers. So boys, for example, see flickering scenes of violence, internalize these scenes, and willy-nilly are soon out jimmying open your car. This is the famous Twinkie interpretation of human behavior—consuming too much sugar leads to violent actions. Would listening to Barry Manilow five hours a day make adolescents into loving, caring people?

Watch kids watching television and you see something quite different from what is seen by the critics. Most consumption, whether it be of entertainment or in the grocery store, is active. We are engaged. Here is how I watch television. I almost never turn the set on to see a particular show. I am near the machine and think I'll see what's happening. I know all the channels; any eight-year-old does. I am not a passive viewer. I use the remote control to pass through various programs, not searching for a final destination but making up a shopping basket, as it were, of entertainment.

But the academic critic doesn't see this. He sees a passive observer who sits quietly in front of the set letting the phosphorescent glow of mindless infotainment pour over his consciousness. In the hypodermic analogy beloved by critics, the potent dope of desire is pumped into the bleary dupe. This paradigm of passive observer and active supplier, a receptive moron and smart manipulator, is easily transported to the marketplace. One can see why such a system would appeal to the critic. After all, since the critic is not being duped, he should be empowered to protect the young, the female, the foreign, the uneducated, and the helpless from the onslaught of dreck.

In the last decade or so, however, a number of scholars in the humanities and social sciences have been challenging many of the academy's assumptions.[1] What distinguishes the newer thinking is that scholars have left the office to actually observe and question their subjects. Just one example: Mihaly Csikszentmihalyi, a psychology professor at the University of Chicago, interviewed 315 Chicagoans from 82 families, asking them what objects in the home they cherished most. The adult members of the five happiest families picked things that reminded them of other people and good times they'd had together. They mentioned a memento (such as an old toy) from their childhood 30 percent of the time. Adults in the five most dissatisfied families cited such objects only six percent of the time.

In explaining why they liked something, happy family members often described, for example, the times their family had spent on a favorite couch, rather than its style or color. Their gloomier counterparts tended to focus on the merely physical qualities of things. What was clear was that both happy and unhappy families derived great meaning from the consumption and interchange of manufactured things. The thesis, reflected in the title of his co-authored 1981 book, *The Meaning of Things: Domestic Symbols and the Self,* is that most of the "work" of consumption occurs after the act of purchase. Things do not come complete; they are forever being assembled.

Twentieth-century French sociologists have taken the argument even further. Two of the most important are Pierre Bourdieu, author of *Distinction: A Social Critique of the Judgement of Taste* (1984), and Jean Baudrillard, whose books include *The Mirror of Production* (1983) and *Simulacra and Simulation* (1994). In the spirit of reader-response theory in literary criticism, they see meaning not as a single thing that producers affix to consumer goods, but as something created by the user, who jumbles various interpretations simultaneously. Essentially, beneath the jargon, this means that the Budweiser you drink is not the same as the one I drink. The meaning tastes different. The fashion you consider stylish, I think is ugly. If we buy the package not the contents, it is because the package means more.

The process of consumption is creative and even emancipating. In an open market, we consume the real and the imaginary meanings, fusing objects, symbols, and images together to end up with "a little world made cunningly." Rather than lives, individuals since midcentury have had lifestyles. For better or worse, lifestyles are secular religions, coherent patterns of valued things. Your lifestyle is not related to what you do for a living but to what you buy. One of the chief aims of the way we live now is the enjoyment of affiliating with those who share the same clusters of objects as we do.

Mallcondo culture is so powerful in part because it frees us from the strictures of social class. The outcome of material life is no longer preordained by coat of arms, pew seat, or trust fund. Instead, it evolves from a never-ending shifting of individual choice. No one wants to be middle class, for instance. You want to be cool, hip, with it, with the "in" crowd, instead.

One of the reasons terms like Yuppie, Baby Boomer, and GenX have elbowed aside such older designations as "upper middle class" is that we no longer understand social class as well as we do lifestyle, or what marketing firms call "consumption communities." Observing stuff is the way we understand each other. Even if no one knows exactly how much money it takes to be a yuppie, or how young you have to be, or how upwardly aspiring, everybody knows where yuppies gather, how they dress, what they play, what they drive, what they eat, and why they hate to be called yuppies.

For better or worse, American culture is well on its way to becoming world culture. The Soviets have fallen. Only quixotic French intellectuals and anxious Islamic fundamentalists are trying to stand up to it. By no means am I sanguine about such a material culture. It has many problems that I have glossed over. Consumerism is wasteful, it is devoid of other-worldly concerns, it lives for today and celebrates the body, and it overindulges and spoils the young with impossible promises.

"Getting and spending" has eclipsed family, ethnicity, even religion as a defining matrix. That doesn't mean that those other defining systems have disappeared, but that an increasing number of young people around the world will give more of their loyalty to Nike than to creeds of blood, race, or belief. This is not entirely a bad thing, since a lust for upscale branding isn't likely to drive many people to war, but it is, to say the least, far from inspiring.

It would be nice to think that materialism could be heroic, self-abnegating, and redemptive. It would be nice to think that greater material comforts will release us from racism, sexism, and ethnocentrism, and that the apocalypse will come as it did at the end of romanticism in Shelley's *Prometheus Unbound,* leaving us "Scepterless, free, uncircumscribed . . . Equal, unclassed, tribeless, and nationless."

But it is more likely that the globalization of capitalism will result in the banalities of an ever-increasing worldwide consumerist culture. The French don't stand a chance. The untranscendent, repetitive, sensational, democratic, immediate, tribalizing and unifying force of what Irving Kristol calls the American Imperium need not necessarily result in a Bronze Age of culture. But it certainly will not produce what Shelley had in mind.

We have not been led into this world of material closeness against our better judgment. For many of us, especially when young, consumerism is our better judgment. We have not just asked to go this way, we have demanded. Now most of the world is lining up, pushing and shoving, eager to elbow into the mall. Getting and spending has become the most passionate, and often the most imaginative, endeavor of modern life. While this is dreary and depressing to some, as doubtless it should be, it is liberating and democratic to many more.

ENDNOTE

[1] This reconsideration of consumption is an especially strong current in anthropology, where the central text is *The World of Goods: Towards an Anthropology of Consumption* (1979), by Mary Douglas and Baron Isherwood. It can also be seen in the work of scholars such as William Leiss in communication studies; Dick Hebdige in sociology; Jackson Lears in history; David Morley in cultural studies; Michael Schudson in the study of advertising; Sidney Levy in consumer research; Tyler Cowan in economics; Grant McCracken in fashion; and Simon Schama in art history. There are many other signs of change. One of the more interesting recent shows at the Museum of Modern Art, "Objects of Desire: The Modern Still Life," actually focused on the salutary influence of consumer culture on high culture.

Name: _____ Date: _____

UNDERSTANDING THE TEXT

1. In Twitchell's opinion, what does he readily acknowledge that most academics don't?

2. According to Twitchell, what is the nature of the relation between materialism and spiritualism?

3. Why, ultimately, does Twitchell think that we collect possessions—that, in most cases, we seek to have more rather than fewer of them?

Why Johnny Can't Dissent

Thomas Frank

The public be damned! I work for my stockholders.
—William H. Vanderbilt, 1879

Break the rules. Stand apart. Keep your head. Go with your heart.
—TV commercial for Vanderbilt perfume, 1994

Capitalism is changing, obviously and drastically. From the moneyed pages of the *Wall Street Journal* to TV commercials for airlines and photocopiers we hear every day about the new order's globe-spanning, cyber-accumulating ways. But our notion about what's wrong with American life and how the figures responsible are to be confronted haven't changed much in thirty years. Call it, for convenience, the "countercultural idea." It holds that the paramount ailment of our society is conformity, a malady that has variously been described as over-organization, bureaucracy, homogeneity, hierarchy, logocentrism, technocracy, the Combine, the Apollonian. We all know what it is and what it does. It transforms humanity into "organization man," into "the man in the gray flannel suit." It is "Moloch whose mind is pure machinery," the "incomprehensible prison" that consumes "brains and imagination." It is artifice, starched shirts, tailfins, carefully mowed lawns, and always, always, the consciousness of impending nuclear destruction. It is a stiff, militaristic order that seeks to suppress instinct, to forbid sex and pleasure, to deny basic human impulses and individuality, to enforce through a rigid uniformity a meaningless plastic consumerism.

As this half of the countercultural idea originated during the 1950s, it is appropriate that the evils of conformity are most conveniently summarized with images of 1950s suburban correctness. You know, that land of sedate music, sexual repression, deference to authority, Red Scares, and smiling white people standing politely in line to go to church. Constantly appearing as a symbol of arch-backwardness in advertising and movies, it is an image we find easy to evoke.

The ways in which this system are to be resisted are equally well understood and agreed-upon. The Establishment demands homogeneity; we revolt by embracing diverse, individual lifestyles. It demands self-denial and rigid adherence to convention; we revolt through immediate gratification, instinct uninhibited, and liberation of the libido and the appetites. Few have put it more bluntly than Jerry Rubin did in 1970: "Amerika says: Don't! The yippies say: Do It!" The countercultural idea is hostile to any law and every establishment. "Whenever we see a rule, we must break it," Rubin continued. "Only by breaking rules do we discover who we are." Above all rebellion consists of a sort of Nietzschean antinomianism, an automatic questioning of rules, a rejection of whatever social prescriptions we've happened to inherit. Just Do It is the whole of the law.

The patron saints of the countercultural idea are, of course, the Beats, whose frenzied style and merry alienation still maintain a powerful grip on the American imagination. Even forty years after the publication of *On the Road,* the works of Kerouac, Ginsberg, and Burroughs remain the *sine qua non* of dissidence, the model for aspiring poets, rock stars, or indeed anyone who feels vaguely artistic or alienated. That frenzied sensibility of pure experience, life on the edge, immediate gratification, and total freedom from moral restraint, which the Beats first propounded back in those heady days when suddenly everyone could have their own TV and powerful V-8, has stuck with us through all the intervening years and become something of a permanent American style. Go to any poetry reading and you can see a string of junior Kerouacs go through the routine, upsetting cultural hierarchies by pushing themselves to the limit, straining for that gorgeous moment of original vice when Allen Ginsberg first read "Howl" in 1955 and the patriarchs of our fantasies recoiled in shock. The Gap may have since claimed Ginsberg and *USA Today* may run feature stories about the brilliance of the beloved Kerouac, but the rebel race continues today regardless, with ever-heightening shit-references calculated to scare Jesse Helms, talk about sex and smack that is supposed to bring the electricity of real life, and ever-more determined defiance of the repressive rules and mores of the American 1950s—rules and mores that by now we know only from movies.

But one hardly has to go to a poetry reading to see the countercultural idea acted out. Its frenzied ecstasies have long since become an official aesthetic of consumer society, a monotheme of mass as well as adversarial culture. Turn on the TV and there it is instantly: the unending drama of consumer unbound and in search of an ever-heightened good time, the inescapable rock 'n' roll soundtrack, dreadlocks and ponytails bounding into Taco Bells, a drunken, swinging-camera epiphany of tennis shoes, outlaw soda pops, and mind-bending dandruff shampoos. Corporate America, it turns out, no longer speaks in the voice of oppressive order that it did when Ginsberg moaned in 1956 that *Time* magazine was

> always telling me about responsibility. Business-
> men are serious. Movie producers are serious.
> Everybody's serious but me.

Nobody wants you to think they're serious today, least of all Time Warner. On the contrary: the Culture Trust is now our leader in the Ginsbergian search for kicks upon kicks. Corporate America is not an oppressor but a sponsor of fun, provider of lifestyle accouterments, facilitator of carnival, our slang-speaking partner in the quest for that ever-more apocalyptic orgasm. The countercultural idea has become capitalist orthodoxy, its hunger for transgression upon transgression now perfectly suited to an economic-cultural regime that runs on ever-faster cyclings of the new; its taste for self-fulfillment and its intolerance for the confines of tradition now permitting vast latitude in consuming practices and lifestyle experimentations.

Consumerism is no longer about "conformity" but about "difference." Advertising teaches us not in the ways of puritanical self-denial (a bizarre notion on the face of it), but in orgiastic, never-ending self-fulfillment. It counsels not rigid adherence to the tastes of the herd but vigilant and constantly updated individualism. We consume not to fit in, but to prove, on the surface at least, that we are rock 'n' roll rebels, each one of us as rule-breaking and hierarchy-defying as our heroes of the 60s, who now pitch cars, shoes, and beer. This imperative of endless difference is today the genius at the heart of American capitalism, an eternal fleeing from "sameness" that satiates our thirst for the New with such achievements of civilization as the infinite brands of identical cola, the myriad colors and irrepressible variety of the cigarette rack at 7-Eleven.

As existential rebellion has become a more or less official style of Information Age capitalism, so has the countercultural notion of a static, repressive Establishment grown hopelessly obsolete. However the basic impulses of the countercultural idea may have disturbed a nation lost in Cold War darkness, they are today in fundamental agreement with the basic tenets of Information Age business theory. So close are they, in fact, that it has become difficult to understand the countercultural idea as anything more than the self-justifying ideology of the new bourgeoisie that has arisen since the 1960s, the cultural means by which this group has proven itself ever so much better skilled than its slow-moving, security-minded forebears at adapting to the accelerated, always-changing consumerism of today. The anointed cultural opponents of capitalism are now capitalism's ideologues.

The two come together in perfect synchronization in a figure like Camille Paglia, whose ravings are grounded in the absolutely noncontroversial ideas of the golden sixties. According to Paglia, American business is still exactly what it was believed to have been in that beloved decade, that is, "puritanical and desensualized." Its great opponents are, of course, liberated figures like "the beatniks," Bob Dylan, and the Beatles. Culture is, quite simply, a binary battle between the repressive Apollonian order of capitalism and the Dionysian impulses of the counterculture. Rebellion makes no sense without repression; we must remain forever convinced of capitalism's fundamental hostility to pleasure in order to consume capitalism's rebel products as avidly as we do. It comes as little surprise when, after criticizing the "Apollonian capitalist machine" (in her book, *Vamps & Tramps*), Paglia applauds American mass culture (in *Utne Reader*), the preeminent product of that "capitalist machine," as a "third great eruption" of a Dionysian "paganism." For her, as for most other designated dissidents, there is no contradiction between replaying the standard critique of capitalist conformity and repressiveness and then endorsing its rebel products—for Paglia the car culture and Madonna—as the obvious solution: the Culture Trust offers both Establishment and Resistance in one convenient package. The only question that remains is why Paglia has not yet landed an endorsement contract from a soda pop or automobile manufacturer.

Other legendary exponents of the countercultural idea have been more fortunate—William S. Burroughs, for example, who appears in a television spot for the Nike corporation. But so openly does the commercial flaunt the confluence of capital and counterculture that it has brought considerable criticism down on the head of the aging beat. Writing in the *Village Voice,* Leslie Savan marvels at the contradiction between Burroughs' writings and the faceless corporate entity for which he is now pushing product. "Now the realization that *nothing* threatens the system has freed advertising to exploit even the most marginal elements of society," Savan observes. "In fact, being hip is no longer quite enough—better the pitchman be 'underground.'" Meanwhile Burroughs' manager insists, as all future Cultural Studies treatments of the ad will no doubt also insist, that Burroughs' presence actually makes the commercial "deeply subversive"—"I hate to repeat the usual mantra, but you know, homosexual drug addict, manslaughter, accidental homicide." But Savan wonders whether, in fact, it is Burroughs who has been assimilated by corporate America. "The problem comes," she writes, "in how easily any idea, deed, or image can become part of the sponsored world."

The most startling revelation to emerge from the Burroughs/Nike partnership is not that corporate America has overwhelmed its cultural foes or that Burroughs can somehow remain "subversive" through it all, but the complete lack of dissonance between the two sides. Of course Burroughs is not "subversive," but neither has he "sold out": His ravings are no longer appreciably different from the official folklore of American capitalism. What's changed is not Burroughs, but business itself. As expertly as Burroughs once bayoneted American proprieties, as stridently as he once proclaimed himself beyond the laws of man and God, he is today a respected ideologue of the Information Age, occupying roughly the position in the pantheon of corporate-cultural thought once reserved strictly for Notre Dame football coaches and positive-thinking Methodist ministers. His inspirational writings are boardroom favorites, his dark nihilistic burpings the happy homilies of the new corporate faith.

For with the assumption of power by Drucker's and Reich's new class has come an entirely new ideology of business, a way of justifying and exercising power that has little to do with the "conformity" and the "establishment" so vilified by the countercultural idea. The management theorists and "leadership" charlatans of the Information Age don't waste their time prattling about hierarchy and regulation, but about disorder, chaos, and the meaninglessness of convention. With its reorganization around information, capitalism has developed a new mythology, a sort of corporate antinomianism according to which the breaking of rules and the elimination of rigid corporate structure have become the central article of faith for millions of aspiring executives.

Dropping *Naked Lunch* and picking up *Thriving on Chaos,* the groundbreaking 1987 management text by Tom Peters, the most popular business writer of the past decade, one finds more philosophical similarities than one would expect from two manifestos of, respectively, dissident culture and business culture. If anything, Peters' celebration of disorder is, by virtue of its hard statistics, bleaker and more nightmarish than Burroughs'. For this popular lecturer on such once-blithe topics as competitiveness and pop psychology there is nothing, absolutely nothing, that is certain. His world is one in which the corporate wisdom of the past is meaningless, established customs are ridiculous, and "rules" are some sort of curse, a remnant of the foolish fifties that exist to be defied, not obeyed. We live in what Peters calls "A World Turned Upside Down," in which whirl is king and, in order to survive, businesses must eventually embrace Peters' universal solution: "Revolution!" "To meet the demands of the fast-changing competitive scene," he counsels, "we must simply learn to love change as much as we have hated it in the past." He advises businessmen to become Robespierres of routine, to demand of their underlings, "'What have you changed lately?' 'How fast are you changing?' and 'Are you pursuing bold enough change goals?'" "Revolution," of course, means for Peters the same thing it did to Burroughs and Ginsberg, Presley and the Stones in their heyday: breaking rules, pissing off the suits, shocking the bean-counters: "Actively and publicly hail defiance of the rules, many of which you doubtless labored mightily to construct in the first place." Peters even suggests that his readers implement this hostility to logocentrism in a carnivalesque celebration, drinking beer out in "the woods" and destroying "all the forms and rules and discontinued reports" and, "if you've got real nerve," a photocopier as well.

Today corporate antinomianism is the emphatic message of nearly every new business text, continually escalating the corporate insurrection begun by Peters. Capitalism, at least as it is envisioned by the best-selling management handbooks, is no longer about enforcing Order, but destroying it. "Revolution," once the totemic catchphrase of the counterculture, has become the totemic catchphrase of boomer-as-capitalist. The Information Age businessman holds inherited ideas and traditional practices not in reverence, but in high suspicion. Even reason itself is now found to be an enemy of true competitiveness, an out-of-date faculty to be scrupulously avoided by conscientious managers. A 1990 book by Charles Handy entitled *The Age of Unreason* agrees with Peters that we inhabit a time in which "there can be no certainty" and suggests that readers engage in full-fledged epistemological revolution: "Thinking Upside Down," using new ways of "learning which can . . . be seen as disrespectful if not downright rebellious," methods of approaching problems that have "never been popular with the upholders of continuity and of the status quo." Three years later the authors of *Reengineering the Corporation* ("A Manifesto for Business Revolution," as its subtitle declares) are ready to push this doctrine even farther. Not only should we be suspicious of traditional practices, but we should cast out virtually everything learned over the past two centuries!

Business reengineering means putting aside much of the received wisdom of two hundred years of industrial management. It means forgetting how work was done in the age of the mass market and deciding how it can best be done now. In business reengineering, old job titles and old organizational arrangements—departments, divisions, groups, and so on—cease to matter. They are artifacts of another age.

As countercultural rebellion becomes corporate ideology, even the beloved Buddhism of the Beats wins a place on the executive bookshelf. In *The Leader as Martial Artist* (1993), Arnold Mindell advises men of commerce in the ways of the Tao, mastery of which he likens, of course, to surfing. For Mindell's Zen businessman, as for the followers of Tom Peters, the world is a wildly chaotic place of opportunity, navigable only to an enlightened "leader" who can discern the "timespirits" at work behind the scenes. In terms Peters himself might use were he a more meditative sort of inspiration professional, Mindell explains that "the wise facilitator" doesn't seek to prevent the inevitable and random clashes between "conflicting field spirits," but to anticipate such bouts of disorder and profit thereby.

Contemporary corporate fantasy imagines a world of ceaseless, turbulent change, of centers that ecstatically fail to hold, of joyous extinction for the craven gray-flannel creature of the past. Businessmen today decorate the walls of their offices not with portraits of President Eisenhower and emblems of suburban order, but with images of extreme athletic daring, with sayings about "diversity" and "empowerment" and "thinking outside the box." They theorize their world not in the bar car of the commuter train, but in weepy corporate retreats at which they beat their tom-toms and envision themselves as part of the great avant-garde tradition of edge-livers, risk-takers, and ass-kickers. Their world is a place not of sublimation and conformity, but of "leadership" and bold talk about defying the herd. And there is nothing this new enlightened species of businessman despises more than "rules" and "reason." The prominent culture-warriors of the right may believe that the counterculture was capitalism's undoing, but the antinomian businessmen know better. "One of the t-shirt slogans of the sixties read, 'Question authority,'" the authors of *Reengineering the Corporation* write. "Process owners might buy their reengineering team members the nineties version: 'Question assumptions.'"

The new businessman quite naturally gravitates to the slogans and sensibility of the rebel sixties to express his understanding of the new Information World. He is led in what one magazine calls "the business revolution" by the office-park subversives it hails as "business activists," "change agents," and "corporate radicals." He speaks to his comrades through commercials like the one for "Warp," a type of IBM computer operating system, in which an electric guitar soundtrack and psychedelic video effects surround hip executives with earrings and hairdos who are visibly stunned by the product's gnarly 'tude (It's a "totally cool way to run your computer," read the product's print ads). He understands the world through *Fast Company,* a successful new magazine whose editors take their inspiration from Hunter S. Thompson and whose stories describe such things as a "dis-organization" that inhabits an "anti-office" where "all vestiges of hierarchy have disappeared" or a computer scientist who is also "a rabble rouser, an agent provocateur, a product of the 1960s who never lost his activist fire or democratic values." He is what sociologists Paul Leinberger and Bruce Tucker have called "The New Individualist," the new and improved manager whose arty worldview and creative hip derive directly from his formative sixties days. The one thing this new executive is definitely *not* is Organization Man, the hyper-rational counter of beans, attender of church, and wearer of stiff hats.

In television commercials, through which the new American businessman presents his visions and self-understanding to the public, perpetual revolution and the gospel of rule-breaking are the orthodoxy of the day. You only need to watch for a few minutes before you see one of these slogans and understand the grip of antinomianism over the corporate mind:

Sometimes You Gotta Break the Rules	*—Burger King*
If You Don't Like the Rules, Change Them	*—WXRT-FM*
The Rules Have Changed	*—Dodge*
The Art of Changing	*—Swatch*
There's no one way to do it.	*—Levi's*
This is different. Different is good.	*—Arby's*
Just Different From the Rest	*—Special Export beer*
The Line Has Been Crossed: The Revolutionary New Supra	*—Toyota*
Resist the Usual	*—the slogan of both Clash Clear Malt and Young & Rubicam*
Innovate Don't Imitate	*—Hugo Boss*
Chart Your Own Course	*—Navigator Cologne*
It separates you from the crowd	*—Vision Cologne*

In most, the commercial message is driven home with the vanguard iconography of the rebel: screaming guitars, whirling cameras, and startled old timers who, we predict, will become an increasingly indispensable prop as consumers require ever-greater assurances that, Yes! You *are* a rebel! Just look at how offended they are!

Our businessmen imagine themselves rebels, and our rebels sound more and more like ideologists of business. Henry Rollins, for example, the maker of loutish, overbearing music and composer of high-school-grade poetry, straddles both worlds unproblematically. Rollins' writing and lyrics strike all the standard alienated literary poses: He rails against overcivilization and yearns to "disconnect." He veers back and forth between vague threats toward "weak" people who "bring me down" and blustery declarations of his weightlifting ability and physical prowess. As a result he ruled for several years as the preeminent darling of *Details* magazine, a periodical handbook for the young executive on the rise, where rebellion has achieved a perfect synthesis with corporate ideology. In 1992 *Details* named Rollins a "rock 'n' roll samurai," an "emblem . . . of a new masculinity" whose "enlightened honesty" is "a way of being that seems to flesh out many of the ideas expressed in contemporary culture and fashion." In 1994 the magazine consummated its relationship with Rollins by naming him "Man of the Year," printing a fawning story about his muscular worldview and decorating its cover with a photo in which Rollins displays his tattoos and rubs his chin in a thoughtful manner.

Details found Rollins to be such an appropriate role model for the struggling young businessman not only because of his music-product, but because of his excellent "self-styled identity," which the magazine describes in terms normally reserved for the breast-beating and soul-searching variety of motivational seminars. Although he derives it from the quality-maximizing wisdom of the East rather than the unfashionable doctrines of Calvin, Rollins' rebel posture is identical to that fabled ethic of the small capitalist whose regimen of positive thinking and hard work will one day pay off. *Details* describes one of Rollins' songs, quite seriously, as "a self-motivational superforce, an anthem of empowerment," teaching lessons that any aspiring middle-manager must internalize. Elsewhere, Iggy Pop, that great chronicler of the ambitionless life, praises Rollins as a "high achiever" who "wants to go somewhere." Rollins himself even seems to invite such an interpretation. His recent spoken-word account of touring with Black Flag, delivered in an unrelenting two-hour drill-instructor staccato, begins with the timeless bourgeois story of opportunity taken, of young Henry leaving the security of a "straight job," enlisting with a group of visionaries who were "the hardest working people I have ever seen," and learning "what hard work is all about." In the liner notes he speaks proudly of his Deming-esque dedication to quality, of how his bandmates "Delivered under pressure at incredible odds." When describing his relationship with his parents for the readers of *Details,* Rollins quickly cuts to the critical matter, the results that such dedication has brought: "Mom, Dad, I outgross both of you put together," a happy observation he repeats in his interview with the *New York Times Magazine.*

Despite the extreme hostility of punk rockers with which Rollins had to contend all through the 1980s, it is he who has been chosen by the commercial media as the godfather of rock 'n' roll revolt. It is not difficult to see why. For Rollins the punk rock decade was but a lengthy seminar on leadership skills, thriving on chaos, and total quality management. Rollins' much-celebrated anger is indistinguishable from the anger of the frustrated junior executive who finds obstacles on the way to the top. His discipline and determination are the automatic catechism of any small entrepreneur who's just finished brainwashing himself with the latest leadership and positive-thinking tracts; his poetry is the inspired verse of *21 Days to Unlimited Power* or *Let's Get Results, Not Excuses.* Henry Rollins is no more a threat to established power in America than was Dale Carnegie. And yet Rollins as king of the rebels—peerless and ultimate—is the message hammered home wherever photos of his growling visage appear. If you're unhappy with your lot, the Culture Trust tells us with each new tale of Rollins, if you feel you must rebel, take your cue from the most disgruntled guy of all: Lift weights! Work hard! Meditate in your back yard! Root out the weaknesses deep down inside yourself! But whatever you do, *don't* think about who controls power or how it is wielded.

The structure and thinking of American business have changed enormously in the years since our popular conceptions of its problems and abuses were formulated. In the meantime the mad frothings and jolly apolitical revolt of Beat, despite their vast popularity and insurgent air, have become powerless against a new regime that, one suspects, few of Beat's present-day admirers and practitioners feel any need to study or understand. Today that beautiful countercultural idea, endorsed now by everyone from the surviving Beats to shampoo manufacturers, is more the official doctrine of corporate America than it is a program of resistance. What we understand as "dissent" does not subvert, does not challenge, does not even question the cultural faiths of Western business. What David Rieff wrote of the revolutionary pretentions of multiculturalism is equally true of the countercultural idea: "The more one reads in academic multiculturalist journals and in business publications, and the more one contrasts the speeches of CEOs and the speeches of noted multiculturalist academics, the more one is struck by the similarities in the way they view the world." What's happened is not co-optation or appropriation, but a simple and direct confluence of interest.

The problem with cultural dissent in America isn't that it's been co-opted, absorbed, or ripped-off. Of course it's been all of these things. But it has proven so hopelessly susceptible to such assaults for the same reason it has become so harmless in the first place, so toothless even before Mr. Geffen's boys discover it angsting away in some bar in Lawrence, Kansas: It is no longer any different from the official culture it's supposed to be subverting. The basic impulses of the countercultural idea, as descended from the holy Beats, are about as threatening to the new breed of antinomian businessmen as Anthony Robbins, selling success & how to achieve it on a late-night infomercial.

The people who staff the Combine aren't like Nurse Ratched. They aren't Frank Burns, they aren't the Church Lady, they aren't Dean Wormer from *Animal House,* they aren't those repressed old folks in the commercials who want to ban Tropicana Fruit Twisters. They're hipper than you can ever hope to be because *hip is their official ideology,* and they're always going to be there at the poetry reading to encourage your "rebellion" with a hearty "right on, man!" before you even know they're in the auditorium. You can't outrun them, or even stay ahead of them for very long: it's their racetrack, and that's them waiting at the finish line to congratulate you on how *outrageous* your new style is, on how you *shocked* those stuffy prudes out in the heartland.

Name: _____ Date: _____

UNDERSTANDING THE TEXT

1. According to Frank, how did the counterculture of the 1950s and 1960s view corporate America?

2. How does Frank suggest we view corporate America today?

3. What is Frank's assessment of Henry Rollins?

ADDITIONAL READINGS

Bronner, Simon J., ed. *Consuming Visions: Accumulation and Display of Goods in America, 1880–1920.* New York: Norton, 1989.

Ewen, Stuart. *Captains of Consciousness: Advertising and the Social Roots of the Consumer Culture.* 1976. New York: Basic Books, 2001.

Frank, Thomas. *The Conquest of Cool: Business Culture, Counterculture, and the Rise of Hip Consumerism,* U of Chicago P, 1997.

———. *One Market Under God: Extreme Capitalism, Market Populism, and the End of Economic Democracy.* New York: Doubleday, 2000.

Frank, Thomas and Matt Weiland, eds. *Commodify Your Dissent: Salvos from the* Baffler. New York: Norton, 1997.

Lears, Jackson. *Fables of Abundance: A Cultural History of Advertising in America.* New York: Basic Books, 1994.

Ohmann, Richard. *Selling Culture: Magazines, Markets, and Class at the Turn of the Century.* The Haymarket Series. London: Verso, 1996.

Rosenblatt, Roger, ed. *Consuming Desires: Consumption, Culture, and the Pursuit of Happiness.* Washington: Shearwater Books-Island Press, 1999.

Twitchell, James B. *Lead Us Into Temptation: The Triumph of American Materialism.* New York: Columbia UP, 1999.

Veblen, Thorstein. *The Theory of the Leisure Class.* 1899. New York: Viking, 1967.

CHAPTER II

After These Messages:
Advertising and Its Effects

"In Your Face . . . All over the Place": Advertising Is Our Environment

Jean Kilbourne

Advertisers like to tell parents that they can always turn off the TV to protect their kids from any of the negative impact of advertising. This is like telling us that we can protect our children from air pollution by making sure they never breathe. Advertising is our *environment*. We swim in it as fish swim in water. We cannot escape it. Unless, of course, we keep our children home from school and blindfold them whenever they are outside of the house. And never let them play with other children. Even then, advertising's messages are inside our intimate relationships, our homes, our hearts, our heads.

Advertising not only appears on radio and television, in our magazines and newspapers, but also surrounds us on billboards, on the sides of buildings, plastered on our public transportation. Buses now in many cities are transformed into facsimiles of products, so that one boards a bus masquerading as a box of Dunkin' Donuts (followed, no doubt, by a Slimfast bus). The creators of this atrocity proudly tell us in their ad in *Advertising Age,* "In your face . . . all over the place!" Indeed.

Trucks carry advertising along with products as part of a marketing strategy. "I want every truck we have on the road making folks thirsty for Bud Light," says an ad in *Advertising Age,* which refers to a truck as a "valuable moving billboard." Given that almost half of all automobile crashes are alcohol-related, it's frightening to think of people becoming thirsty for Bud Light while driving their cars. A Spanish company has paid the drivers of seventy-five cars in Madrid to turn their cars into Pall Mall cigarette packages, and hopes to expand its operation throughout Spain. Imagine cars disguised as bottles of beer zipping along our highways. If we seek to escape all this by taking a plane, we become a captive audience for in-flight promotional videos.

Ads are on the videos we rent, the shopping carts we push through stores, the apples and hot dogs we buy, the online services we use, and the navigational screens of the luxury cars we drive. A new device allows advertisers to print their messages directly onto the sand of a beach. "This is my best idea ever—5,000 imprints of Skippy Peanut Butter jars covering the beach," crowed the inventor. Added the promotion director, "I'm here looking at thousands of families with kids. If they're on the beach thinking of Skippy, that's just what we want." Their next big idea is snow imprinting at ski resorts. In England the legendary white cliffs of Dover now serve as the backdrop for a laser-projected Adidas ad. American consumers have recently joined Europeans in being offered free phone calls if they will also listen to commercials. Conversations are interrupted by brief ads, tailored to match the age and social profiles of the conversants. And beer companies have experimented with messages posted over urinals, such as "Time for more Coors" or "Put used Bud here."

The average American is exposed to at least three thousand ads every day and will spend three years of his or her life watching television commercials. Advertising makes up about 70 percent of our newspapers and 40 percent of our mail. Of course, we don't pay direct attention to very many of these ads, but we are powerfully influenced, mostly on an unconscious level, by the experience of being immersed in an advertising culture, a market-driven culture, in which all our institutions, from political to religious to educational, are increasingly for sale to the highest bidder. According to Rance Crain, editor-in-chief of *Advertising Age,* the major publication of the advertising industry, "Only eight percent of an ad's message is received by the conscious mind; the rest is worked and reworked deep within the recesses of the brain, where a product's positioning and repositioning takes shape." It is in this sense that advertising is subliminal: not in the sense of hidden messages embedded in ice cubes, but in the sense that we aren't consciously aware of what advertising is doing.

Children who used to roam their neighborhoods now often play at McDonald's. Families go to Disneyland or other theme parks instead of state and national parks—or to megamalls such as the Mall of America in Minneapolis or Grapevine Mills in Texas, which provide "shoppertainment." One of the major tourist destinations in historic Boston is the bar used in the 1980s hit television series *Cheers*. The Olympics today are at least as much about advertising as athletics. We are not far off from the world David Foster Wallace imagined in his epic novel *Infinite Jest,* in which years are sponsored by companies and named after them, giving us the Year of the Whopper and the Year of the Tucks Medicated Pad.

Commercialism has no borders. There is barely any line left between advertising and the rest of the culture. The prestigious Museum of Fine Arts in Boston puts on a huge exhibit of Herb Ritts, fashion photographer, and draws one of the largest crowds in its history. In 1998 the museum's Monet show was the most popular exhibit in the world. Museum officials were especially pleased by results of a survey showing 74 percent of visitors recognized that the show's sponsor was Fleet Financial Group, which shelled out $1.2 million to underwrite the show.

Bob Dole plays on his defeat in the presidential election in ads for Air France and Viagra, while Ed Koch, former mayor of New York City, peddles Dunkin' Donuts' bagels. Dr. Jane Goodall, doyenne of primatology, appears with her chimpanzees in an ad for Home Box Office, and Sarah Ferguson, the former duchess of York, gets a million dollars for being the official spokeswoman for Weight Watchers (with a bonus if she keeps her weight down).

Dead celebrities, such as Marilyn Monroe and Humphrey Bogart and John Wayne, are brought to life through computer magic and given digitized immortality in ads (how awful it is to see classy Fred Astaire dancing with electric brooms and hand vacs). Even worse, advertising often exploits cultural icons of rebellion and anticommercialism. Jimi Hendrix was raised from the dead by Aiwa to sell stereos, and John Lennon's haunting song "Imagine" is used by American Express. The Beatles' "Revolution," Bob Dylan's classic anthem "The Times They Are A-Changin'," and Janis Joplin's "Oh Lord, won't you buy me a Mercedes-Benz?" have all been used as advertising jingles, appealing to baby-boomers' nostalgia while completely corrupting the meaning of the songs. And the Rolling Stones, those aging rebels, have allowed Sprint to put a straight-pin through the band's tongue logo. However, when Neil Young recorded a video for his song "This Note's for You," which states that he won't sing for Pepsi or Coke and includes the lines "I don't sing for nobody/Makes me look like a joke," MTV refused to run it.

Live celebrities line up to appear in ads and people who simply appear in ads become celebrities. Today little girls constantly rate the supermodels high on their list of heroes, and most of us know them by their first names alone . . . Cindy, Elle, Naomi, Iman. Imagine—these women are *heroes* to little girls, not because of their courage or character or good deeds, but because of their perfect features and poreless skin. Models become more famous than film and television stars and rock stars, and the stars themselves often become pitchmen (and women) for a variety of products ranging from candy to cigarettes to alcohol.

Stars such as Harrison Ford, Woody Allen, Paul Newman, Whoopi Goldberg, and Bruce Willis, who don't want to tarnish their image in the United States, gladly appear in foreign television ads and commercials. Antonio Banderas and Kevin Costner have pushed cars, Brad Pitt watches, Dennis Hopper bath salts, Michael J. Fox fishing tackle, and Jennifer Aniston shampoo. In a commercial for Nippon Ham, Sylvester Stallone munched sausages at a garden party. After the success of *Titanic,* Leonardo DiCaprio was paid $4 million to play a noodle-eating detective in a Japanese commercial for credit cards. And in a commercial for Austrian Railways, Arnold Schwarzenegger rebuffs a steward who offers him a drink with the reply, "Hasta la vista, baby." Not surprisingly, he agreed to make the commercial only on the condition that the international media not be told about it. Madonna has a similar deal with Max Factor, which is paying her $6.5 million to sell cosmetics on TV, billboards, and in magazines throughout Britain, Europe, and Asia, but is prohibited from circulating photos from the ad campaign in the United States.

We are also influenced by advertising that we do not recognize as such, like the use of brand names during televised sporting events (during one ninety-minute car race, the word "Marlboro" appeared 5,933 times). In 1983 Sylvester Stallone wrote a letter to the Brown &

Williamson tobacco company in which he promised to use their tobacco products in five feature films in exchange for half a million dollars. Compare this with the old days of "Brand X," the days when Julia Child covered the brand name "Pyrex" on her measuring cup!

Increasingly, films and television shows carry these hidden commercials. Often characters use certain products, the brands are prominently displayed, but the audience remains unaware that money has changed hands. New technology allows advertisers to have products digitally added to a scene, such as a Coca-Cola can on a desk or commercial billboards in the background of baseball games. At the very least, these "commercials" should be directly acknowledged in the credits. Writer and cartoonist Mark O'Donnell suggests that someday there will be tie-ins in literature as well, such as "All's Well That Ends With Pepsi," "The Old Man, Coppertone and the Sea," and "Nausea, and Periodic Discomfort Relief."

Sometimes the tie-ins are overt. Diet Coke obtained the rights to the cast of the hit series *Friends* and built a promotion around a special episode of the show that aired after the Super Bowl. In 1997 ABC and American Airlines announced a program that grants bonus miles and vacation credits to enrolled members who can correctly answer questions about shows that recently aired on the network. In the spring of 1998 product peddling on television was brought to new heights (or a new low) when a character in the hit show *Baywatch* created a line of shoes in her fashion-design class that viewers can actually buy. Stay tuned for *Shoe-watch*.

Far more important than the tie-ins, however, is the increasing influence of advertising on the form and content of films, television shows, and music videos (which aren't so much *like* ads as they *are* ads). Among other things, advertisers prefer that their products be associated with upbeat shows and films with happy endings, shows that leave people in the mood to buy. "People have become less capable of tolerating any kind of darkness or sadness," says media scholar Mark Crispin Miller. "I think it ultimately has to do with advertising, with a vision of life as a shopping trip." Steven Stark, another media critic, holds advertising responsible for a shift in television programs from glamorizing private detectives to glamorizing the police. According to Stark, "A detective show often leaves the audience with the impression that the system, police included, is corrupt and incompetent. An audience left with that message is in less mood to buy than an audience reassured, night after night, that the system works because the police are doing their job."

The cast of *Seinfeld* were the most successful hucksters in TV history, so successful that in 1994 *Advertising Age* gave their Star Presenter of the Year award to the entire cast. As Jerry Seinfeld, star of the show, said, "It is a good combination. When you're on TV in a sitcom, there's a loose reality that lends itself to doing commercials, which are also on TV. As long as you're on TV pretending to be something you're not anyway, why not do it for a commercial?" Opening an advertising agency, one of the paths Seinfeld is reportedly now considering, wouldn't be much of a leap (not that there's anything wrong with that). No wonder Seinfeld was one of the celebrities featured in a 1999 ad placed by *Forbes* magazine in *Advertising Age* that said, "These days, kids don't want to grow up to be athletes, comedians or movie stars. They want to be highly leveraged brands." The ad continues, "The real power in America no longer belongs to the most talented celebrities. But the most marketable ones."

The 1997 James Bond film *Tomorrow Never Dies* broke new ground for global integrated film tie-ins. In an ongoing effort to raise its profile, beer marketer Heineken USA featured James Bond, portrayed by Pierce Brosnan, in point-of-purchase displays worldwide and also offered a James Bond holiday catalog of electronic devices. During one scene in the film Bond crashes a car into a Heineken truck. Other marketers with major tie-ins to the film include Heublein's Smirnoff vodka brand, Omega watches, Avis, L'Oreal, and Visa International. More recently, the 1998 hit movie *You've Got Mail* basically costarred America Online, which in turn spent millions on television and online advertising for the movie. "Warner Brothers came to us and we agreed to be as helpful as we possibly could," said an AOL spokeswoman.

And independent films are becoming as tight with Madison Avenue as are the big flicks. Although I have no evidence that it was intentional, *The Brothers McMullen* prominently featured Heineken and Budweiser beer, which was ironic given its underlying theme of the havoc wreaked by family alcoholism. According to Ted Hope, the film's producer, "We struggle with product placement all the time, and I know other producers and directors struggle with it. I actively discourage it in movies but there are times when I contradict myself."

According to Paul Speaker, director of marketing for the independent production company responsible for *Sling Blade,* the key "is not only to find opportunities to seamlessly place products, but more importantly to associate brand to the entire film relevance." In order to appear hip and cool, major clothing manufacturers, such as Dockers, Tommy Hilfiger, and Polo Ralph Lauren, are associating their products with the low-budget independent films that are usually seen as "counterculture." Hilfiger provided the wardrobe for the independent film *The Faculty* and, in exchange, the teenage actors in the film appeared in commercials for Hilfiger. Andy Hilfiger, the company's vice-president of marketing, said, "The cast is great, and they went so well with our clothing."

The music world is in the game too, as rappers launch clothing lines and designers start record labels. Maurice Malone, who designs sportswear and has a record company, says, "You can use your music videos and your artists on your label to show your clothes," and, "You can talk about your clothes in the songs and hype the name." In 1999 designer Tommy Hilfiger sponsored concert tours for the Rolling Stones, Lilith Fair, and Britney Spears. All the musicians wore Hilfiger items onstage, while ads in fashion magazines depicted staged scenes from the concerts.

Not everyone is enthusiastic about this trend. Chris Gore, publisher of the Webzine *Film Threat,* thinks that sponsorship will inevitably guide what kinds of films get made, discouraging those with less consumer-friendly content. "Think of classic movies, like *The Wizard of Oz* or *Gone With the Wind,* and the products that could have been branded with them," he said. "Not only would that date them, it would be pathetic. We're not creating classics here—this is about commerce."

In spite of the fact that we are surrounded by more advertising than ever before, most of us still ridicule the idea that we might be personally influenced by it. The ridicule is often extremely simplistic. The argument essentially is, "I'm no robot marching down to the store to do advertising's bidding and therefore advertising doesn't affect me at all." This argument was made by Jacob Sullum, a senior editor at *Reason* magazine, in an editorial in *The New York Times*. Writing about "heroin chic," the advertising fad in the mid-1990s of using models who looked like heroin addicts, Sullum says, "Like you, I've seen . . . ads featuring sallow, sullen, scrawny youths. Not once have I had an overwhelming urge to rush out and buy some heroin." He concludes from this in-depth research that all critics of advertising are portraying "people not as independent moral agents but as mindless automatons," as if there were no middle ground between rushing out to buy heroin and being completely uninfluenced by the media images that surround us—or no possibility that disaffected teens are more vulnerable than middle-aged executives. After all, Sullum is *not* the target audience for heroin chic ads.

Of course, most of us feel far superior to the kind of person who would be affected by advertising. *We* are not influenced, after all. We are skeptical, even cynical . . . but ignorant (certainly not stupid, just uninformed). Advertising is familiar, but not known. The fact that we are surrounded by it, that we can sing the jingles and identify the models and recognize the logos, doesn't mean that we are educated about it, that we understand it. As Sut Jhally says, "To not be influenced by advertising would be to live outside of culture. No human being lives outside of culture."

Advertisers want us to believe that we are not influenced by ads. As Joseph Goebbels said, "This is the secret of propaganda: Those who are to be persuaded by it should be completely immersed in the ideas of the propaganda, without ever noticing that they are being immersed in it." So the advertisers sometimes play upon our cynicism. In fact, they co-opt our cynicism and our irony just as they have co-opted our rock music, our revolutions and movements for liberation, and our concern for the environment. In a current trend that I call "anti-advertising," the advertisers flatter us by insinuating that we are far too smart to be taken in by advertising. Many of these ads spoof the whole notion of image advertising. A scotch ad tells the reader "This is a glass of Cutty Sark. If you need to see a picture of a guy in an Armani suit sitting between two fashion models drinking it before you know it's right for you, it probably isn't."

And an ad for shoes says, "If you feel the need to be smarter and more articulate, read the complete works of Shakespeare. If you like who you are, here are your shoes." Another shoe ad, this one for sneakers, says, "Shoe buying rule number one: The image wears off after the first six miles." What a concept. By buying heavily advertised products, we can demonstrate that we are not influenced by advertising. Of course, this is not entirely new. Volkswagens were introduced in the 1960s with an anti-advertising campaign, such as the ad that pictured the car and the headline "Lemon." But such ads go a lot further these days, especially the foreign ones. A British ad for Easy jeans says, "We don't use sex to sell our jeans. We don't even screw you when you buy them." And French Connection UK gets away with a double-page spread that says "fcuk advertising."

A Sprite campaign plays on this cynicism. One commercial features teenagers partying on a beach while drinking a soft drink called Jooky. As the camera pulls back, we see that this is a fictional television commercial being watched by two teens, who open their own cans of Jooky and experience absolutely nothing. "Image is nothing. Thirst is everything," says the slogan. However, there is nothing in the ad about thirst—or taste, for that matter—or anything intrinsic to Sprite. The campaign is about nothing but image. Of course, what other way is there to sell sweetened, flavored carbonated water? If thirst is really everything, our best bet is water, and not high-priced bottled water either, such as Evian, which costs more than some champagne (no wonder that Evian backward spells "naive").

When Nike wanted to reach skateboarders, it had to overcome the fact that skateboarders are "about the most cynical bunch of consumers around" and often downright hostile to the idea of Nike entering the market. By putting a humorous spin on a powerful insight about how skateboarders want to be treated, Nike created the "What if we treated all athletes the way we treat skateboarders?" campaign, which has "won over skateboarders around the country and made them believe that Nike knows them and has the guts to defend them and their sport." Who cares if this is true—what is important is that skateboarders believe that it is true.

Some advertisers use what they chillingly call "viral communications" as a way to reach teenagers alienated from traditional forms of advertising. They use posters on construction sites and lampposts, sidewalk markings, and e-mail to infiltrate youth culture and cultivate the perception that their product is hot. One marketing consultant suggests picturing the mind as a combination lock and says, "One has to know what the particular stimuli are that are the 'clicks' heard by the inner mind of the target market and then allow the target market to open the lock so it is their own 'Aha!'—their own discovery, and so their own commitment."

Some ads make fun of high-pressure tactics. "Perhaps you'd consider buying one," says an ad for Saturn, and then in brackets below, "Sorry, we didn't mean to pressure you like that." Another car ad declares, "We're not trying to sell you this car. We're just letting you know it exists." An ad for sneakers tells us that "marketing is just hype." This is a bit like a man unbuttoning a woman's blouse, all the while telling her that she is far too smart to be seduced by the likes of him.

Cynicism is one of the worst effects of advertising. Cynicism learned from years of being exposed to marketing hype and products that never deliver the promised goods often carries over to other aspects of life. This starts early: A study of children done by researchers at Columbia University in 1975 found that heavy viewing of advertising led to cynicism, not only about advertising, but about life in general. The researchers found that "in most cultures, adolescents have had to deal with social hypocrisy and even with institutionalized lying. But today, TV advertising is stimulating *preadolescent* children to think about socially accepted hypocrisy. They may be too young to cope with such thoughts without permanently distorting their views of morality, society, and business." They concluded that "7- to 10-year-olds are strained by the very existence of advertising directed to them." These jaded children become the young people whose mantra is "whatever," who admire people like David Letterman (who has made a career out of taking nothing seriously), whose response to almost every experience is "been there, done that," "duh," and "do ya think?" Cynicism is not criticism. It is a lot easier than criticism. In fact, easy cynicism is a kind of naiveté. We need to be more critical as a culture and less cynical.

Cynicism deeply affects how we define our problems and envision their solutions. Many people exposed to massive doses of advertising both distrust every possible solution *and* expect a quick fix. There are no quick fixes to the problems our society faces today, but there are solutions to many of them. The first step, as always, is breaking through denial and facing the problems squarely. I believe it was James Baldwin who said, "Not everything that is faced can be changed, but nothing can be changed until it is faced." One of the things we need to face is that we and our children are indeed influenced by advertising.

Although some people, especially advertisers, continue to argue that advertising simply reflects the society, advertising does a great deal more than simply reflect cultural attitudes and values. Even some advertisers admit to this: Rance Crain of *Advertising Age* said great advertising "plays the tune rather than just dancing to the tune." Far from being a passive mirror of society, advertising is an effective and pervasive medium of influence and persuasion, and its influence is cumulative often subtle, and primarily unconscious. Advertising performs much the same function in industrial society as myth performed in ancient and primitive societies. It is both a creator and perpetuator of the dominant attitudes, values, and ideology of the culture, the social norms and myths by which most people govern their behavior. At the very least, advertising helps to create a climate in which certain attitudes and values flourish and others are not reflected at all.

Advertising is not only our physical environment, it is increasingly our spiritual environment as well. By definition, however, it is only interested in materialistic values. When spiritual values or religious images show up in ads, it is only to appropriate them in order to sell us something. Sometimes this is very obvious. Eternity is a perfume by Calvin Klein. Infiniti is an automobile and Hydra Zen a moisturizer. Jesus is a brand of jeans. "See the light," says an ad for wool, while a face powder ad promises "an enlightening experience" and "absolute heaven." One car is "born again" and another promises to "energize your soul." In a full-page ad in *Advertising Age,* the online service Yahoo! proclaims, "We've got 60 million followers. That's more than some religions," but goes on to assure readers, "Don't worry. We're *not* a religion." When Pope John Paul II visited Mexico City in the winter of 1999, he could have seen a smiling image of himself on bags of Sabritas, a popular brand of potato chips, or a giant street sign showing him bowing piously next to a Pepsi logo with a phrase in Spanish that reads, "Mexico Always Faithful." In the United States, he could have treated himself to pope-on-a-rope soap.

An ad for kosher hot dogs pictures the Bible beside a hot dog with the caption, "If you liked the book, you'll love the hot dog." The campaign slogan is, "We answer to a higher authority." "God bless America," says a full-page newspaper ad featuring a little boy with his hand over his heart. The copy continues, "Where else can you find one company that offers phone, cable and internet service?" And an ad for garage doors says, "The legendary architect Mies van der Rohe said, 'God is in the details.' If that's so, could these be the pearly gates?"

Sometimes the allusion to the spiritual realm is more subtle, as in the countless alcohol ads featuring the bottle surrounded by a halo of light. Indeed products are often displayed, such as jewelry shining in a store window, as if they were sacred objects. Buy this and your life will be better. Advertising co-opts our sacred symbols and sacred language in order to evoke an immediate emotional response. Neil Postman refers to this as "cultural rape" that leaves us deprived of our most meaningful images.

But advertising's co-optation of spirituality goes much deeper than this. It is commonplace these days to observe that consumerism has become the religion of our time (with advertising its holy text), but the criticism usually stops short of what is most important, what is at the heart of the comparison. Advertising and religion share a belief in transformation and transcendence, but most religions believe that this requires work and sacrifice. In the world of advertising, enlightenment is achieved instantly by purchasing material goods. As James Twitchell, author of *Adcult USA*, says, "The Jolly Green Giant, the Michelin Man, the Man from Glad, Mother Nature, Aunt Jemima, Speedy Alka-Seltzer, the White Knight, and all their otherworldly kin are descendants of the earlier gods. What separates them is that they now reside in manufactured products and that, although earlier gods were invoked by fasting, prayer, rituals, and penance, the promise of purchase calls forth their modern ilk."

Advertising constantly promotes the core belief of American culture: that we *can* re-create ourselves, transform ourselves, transcend our circumstances—but with a twist. For generations Americans believed this could be achieved if we worked hard enough, like Horatio Alger. Today the promise is that we can change our lives instantly, effortlessly—by winning the lottery, selecting the right mutual fund, having a fashion makeover, losing weight, having tighter abs, buying the right car or soft drink. It is this belief that such transformation is possible that drives us to keep dieting, to buy more stuff, to read fashion magazines that give us the same information over and over again. Cindy Crawford's makeup is carefully described as if it could transform us into her. On one level, we know it won't—after all, most of us have tried this approach many times before. But on another level, we continue to try, continue to believe that this time it will be different. This American belief that we can transform ourselves makes advertising images much more powerful than they otherwise would be.

The focus of the transformation has shifted from the soul to the body. Of course, this trivializes and cheapens authentic spirituality and transcendence. But, more important, this junk food for the soul leaves us hungry, empty, malnourished. The emphasis on instant salvation is parodied in an ad from *Adbusters* for a product called Mammon, in which a man says, "I need a belief system that serves my needs right away" The copy continues, "Dean Sachs has a mortgage, a family and an extremely demanding job. What he doesn't need is a religion that complicates his life with unreasonable ethical demands." The ad ends with the words, "Mammon: Because you deserve to enjoy life—guilt free."

As advertising becomes more and more absurd, however, it becomes increasingly difficult to parody ads. There's not much of a difference between the ad for Mammon and the real ad for cruises that says "It can take several lifetimes to reach a state of inner peace and tranquillity. Or, it can take a couple of weeks." Of course, we know that a couple of weeks on a cruise won't solve our problems, won't bring us to a state of peace and enlightenment, but it is so tempting to believe that there is some easy way to get there, some ticket we can buy.

To be one of the "elect" in today's society is to have enough money to buy luxury goods. Of course, when salvation comes via the sale, it becomes important to display these goods. Owning a Rolex would not impress anyone who didn't know how expensive it is. A Rolex ad itself says the watch was voted "most likely to be coveted." Indeed, one of advertising's purposes is to create an aura for a product, so that other people will be impressed. As one marketer said recently in *Advertising Age,* "It's no fun to spend $100 on athletic shoes to wear to high school if your friends don't know how cool your shoes are."

Thus the influence of advertising goes way beyond the target audience and includes those who could never afford the product, who will simply be envious and impressed—perhaps to the point of killing someone for his sneakers or jacket, as has sometimes happened in our poverty-stricken neighborhoods. In the early 1990s the city health commissioner in Philadelphia issued a public health warning cautioning youths against wearing expensive leather jackets and jewelry, while in Milwaukee billboards depicted a chalk outline of a body and the warning, "Dress Smart and Stay Alive." Poor children in many countries knot the laces of their Nikes around their ankles to avoid having them stolen while they sleep.

Many teens fantasize that objects will somehow transform their lives, give them social standing and respect. When they wear a certain brand of sneaker or jacket, they feel, "This is important, therefore I am important." The brand gives instant status. No wonder they are willing, even eager, to spend money for clothes that advertise the brands. A *USA Today*-CNN-Gallup Poll found that 61 percent of boys and 44 percent of girls considered brand names on clothes "very important" or "somewhat important." As ten-year-old Darion Sawyer from Baltimore said, "People will tease you and talk about you, say you got on no-name shoes or say you shop at Kmart." Leydiana Reyes, an eighth-grader in Brooklyn, said, "My father always tells me I could buy two pairs of jeans for what you pay for Calvin Klein. I know that. But I still want Calvin Klein." And Danny Shirley, a fourteen-year-old in Santa Fe decked out in Tommy Hilfiger regalia, said, "Kids who wear Levi's don't really care about what they wear, I guess."

In the beginning, these labels were somewhat discreet. Today we see sweatshirts with fifteen-inch "Polo" logos stamped across the chest, jeans with four-inch "Calvin Klein" labels stitched on them, and a jacket with "Tommy Hilfiger" in five-inch letters across the back. Some of these outfits are so close to sandwich boards that I'm surprised people aren't paid to wear them. Before too long, the logo-free product probably will be the expensive rarity.

What people who wear these clothes are really buying isn't a garment, of course, but an *image*. And increasingly, an image is all that advertising has to sell. Advertising began centuries ago with signs in medieval villages. In the nineteenth century, it became more common but was still essentially designed to give people information about manufactured goods and services. Since the 1920s, advertising has provided less information about the product and focused more on the lives, especially the emotional lives, of the prospective consumers. This shift coincided, of course, with the increasing knowledge and acceptability of psychology, as well as the success of propaganda used to convince the population to support World War I.

Industrialization gave rise to the burgeoning ability of businesses to mass produce goods. Since it was no longer certain there would be a market for the goods, it became necessary not just to mass-produce the goods but to mass-produce markets hungry for the goods. The problem became not too little candy produced but not enough candy consumed, so it became the job of the advertisers to *produce consumers*. This led to an increased use of psychological research and emotional ploys to sell products. Consumer behavior became recognized as a science in the late 1940s.

As luxury goods, prepared foods, and nonessential items have proliferated, it has become crucial to create artificial needs in order to sell unnecessary products. Was there such a thing as static cling before there were fabric softeners and sprays? An ad for a "lip renewal cream" says, "I never thought of my lips as a problem area until Andrea came up with the solution."

Most brands in a given category are essentially the same. Most shampoos are made by two or three manufacturers. Blindfolded smokers or beer-drinkers can rarely identify what brand they are smoking or drinking, including their own. Whether we know it or not, we select products primarily because of the image reflected in their advertising. Very few ads give us any real information at all. Sometimes it is impossible to tell what is being advertised. "This is an ad for the hair dryer," says one ad, featuring a woman lounging on a sofa. If we weren't told, we would never know. A joke made the rounds a while ago about a little boy who wanted a box of tampons so that he could effortlessly ride bicycles and horses, ski, and swim.

Almost all tobacco and alcohol ads are entirely image-based. Of course, when you're selling a product that kills people, it's difficult to give honest information about it. Think of all the cigarette ads that never show cigarettes or even a wisp of smoke. One of the most striking examples of image advertising is the very successful and long-running campaign for Absolut vodka. This campaign focuses on the shape of the bottle and the word "Absolut," as in "Absolut Perfection," which features the bottle with a halo. This campaign has been so successful that a coffee-table book collection of the ads published just in time for Christmas, the perfect gift for the alcoholic in your family, sold over 150,000 copies. Collecting Absolut ads is now a common pastime for elementary-school children, who swap them like baseball cards.

Adbusters magazine often parodies the Absolut ads. One such parody, headlined "Absolut Nonsense," pictures a bottle with the following copy on the label: "This superb marketing scheme has been carefully distilled for smoothness. . . . Although no one pays attention to advertising, after one year of this campaign, sales soared from 54,000 cases to 2.4 million cases." Since all vodka is essentially the same, all the campaign can sell us is image.

Even the advertisers admit to this. Carol Nathanson-Moog, an advertising psychologist, said, "More and more it seems the liquor industry has awakened to the truth. It isn't selling bottles or glasses or even liquor. It's selling fantasies." An article in *Advertising Age* went further, stating that "product image is probably the most important element in selling liquor. The trick for marketers is to project the right message in their advertisements to motivate those often motionless consumers to march down to the liquor store or bar and exchange their money for a sip of image."

"A sip of image." Just as simple films relying on crude jokes and violence are perfect for the global marketplace, since they require little translation, so is advertising that relies entirely on image. Bare breasts and phallic symbols are understood everywhere. As are the nude female buttocks featured in the Italian and German ads for similar worthless products to remedy the imaginary problem of cellulite. Unfortunately, such powerful imagery often pollutes the cultural environment. Certainly this is so with the Olivetti ad that ran in a Russian publication. In case the image is too subtle for some, the copy says "Fax me." Sexism in advertising, although increasingly recognized as a problem, remains an ongoing global issue.

How does all this affect us? It is very difficult to do objective research about advertising's influence because there are no comparison groups, almost no people who have not been exposed to massive doses of advertising. In addition, research that measures only one point in time does not adequately capture advertising's real effects. We need longitudinal studies, such as George Gerbner's twenty-five-year study of violence on television.

The advertising industry itself can't prove that advertising works. While claiming to its clients that it does, it simultaneously denies it to the Federal Trade Commission whenever the subject of alcohol and tobacco advertising comes up. As an editorial in *Advertising Age* once said, "A strange world it is, in which people spending millions on advertising must do their best to prove that advertising doesn't do very much!" According to Bob Wehling, senior vice-president of marketing at Procter & Gamble, "We don't have a lot of scientific studies to support our belief that advertising works. But we have seen that the power of advertising makes a significant difference."

What research can most easily prove is usually what is least important, such as advertising's influence on our choice of brands. This is the most obvious, but least significant, way that advertising affects us. There are countless examples of successful advertising campaigns, such as the Absolut campaign, that have sent sales soaring. A commercial for I Can't Believe It's Not Butter featuring a sculptress whose work comes alive in the form of romance-novel hunk Fabio boosted sales about 17 percent. Tamagotchis—virtual pets in an egg—were introduced in the United States with a massive advertising campaign and earned $150 million in seven months. And Gardenburger, a veggie patty, ran a thirty-second spot during the final episode of *Seinfeld* and, within a week, sold over $2 million worth, a market share jump of 50 percent and more than the entire category sold in the same week the previous year. But advertising is more of an art than a science, and campaigns often fail. In 1998 a Miller beer campaign bombed, costing the company millions of dollars and offending a large segment of their customers. The 1989 Nissan Infiniti campaign, known as the "Rocks and Trees" campaign, was the first ever to introduce a car without showing it and immediately became a target for Jay Leno's monologues. And, of course, the Edsel, a car introduced by Ford with great fanfare in 1957, remains a universal symbol of failure.

The unintended effects of advertising are far more important and far more difficult to measure than those effects that are intended. The important question is not "Does this ad sell the product?" but rather "What else does this ad sell?" An ad for Gap khakis featuring a group of acrobatic swing dancers probably sold a lot of pants, which, of course, was the intention of the advertisers. But it also contributed to a rage for swing dancing. This is an innocuous example of advertising's powerful unintended effects. Swing dancing is not binge drinking, after all.

Advertising often sells a great deal more than products. It sells values, images, and concepts of love and sexuality, romance, success, and, perhaps most important, normalcy. To a great extent, it tells us who we are and who we should be. We are increasingly using brand names to create our identities. James Twitchell argues that the label of our shirt, the make of our car, and our favorite laundry detergent are filling the vacuum once occupied by religion, education, and our family name.

Even more important, advertising corrupts our language and thus influences our ability to think clearly. Critic and novelist George Steiner once talked with an interviewer about what he called "anti-language, that which is transcendentally annihilating of truth and meaning." Novelist Jonathan Dee, applying this concept to advertising, writes that "the harm lies not in the ad itself; the harm is in the exchange, in the collision of ad language, ad imagery, with other sorts of language that contend with it in the public realm. When Apple reprints an old photo of Gandhi, or Heineken ends its ads with the words 'Seek the Truth,' or Winston suggests that we buy cigarettes by proposing (just under the surgeon general's warning) that 'You have to appreciate authenticity in all its forms,' or Kellogg's identifies itself with the message 'Simple is Good,' these occasions color our contact with those words and images in their other, possibly less promotional applications." The real violence of advertising, Dee concludes, is that "words can be made to mean anything, which is hard to distinguish from the idea that words mean nothing." We see the consequences of this in much of our culture, from "art" to politics, that has no content, no connection between language and conviction. Just as it is often difficult to tell what product an ad is selling, so is it difficult to determine what a politician's beliefs are (the "vision thing," as George Bush so aptly called it, albeit unintentionally) or what the subject is of a film or song or work of art. As Dee says, "The men and women who make ads are not hucksters; they are artists with nothing to say, and they have found their form." Unfortunately, their form deeply influences all the other forms of the culture. We end up expecting nothing more.

This has terrible consequences for our culture. As Richard Pollay says, "Without a reliance on words and a faith in truth, we lack the mortar for social cohesion. Without trustworthy communication, there is no communion, no community, only an aggregation of increasingly isolated individuals, alone in the mass."

Advertising creates a worldview that is based upon cynicism, dissatisfaction, and craving. The advertisers aren't evil. They are just doing their job, which is to sell a product, but the consequences, usually unintended, are often destructive to individuals, to cultures, and to the planet. In the history of the world, there has never been a propaganda effort to match that of advertising in the twentieth century. More thought, more effort, and more money go into advertising than has gone into any other campaign to change social consciousness. The story that advertising tells is that the way to be happy, to find satisfaction—and the path to political freedom, as well—is through the consumption of material objects. And the major motivating force for social change throughout the world today is this belief that happiness comes from the market.

So, advertising has a greater impact on all of us than we generally realize. The primary purpose of the mass media is to deliver us to advertisers. Much of the information that we need from the media in order to make informed choices in our lives is distorted or deleted on behalf of corporate sponsors. Advertising is an increasingly ubiquitous presence in our lives, and it sells much more than products. We delude ourselves when we say we are not influenced by advertising. And we trivialize and ignore its growing significance at our peril.

BIBLIOGRAPHY

Ads not infinitum (1998, December 14). *People,* 10–11.

Angier, N. (1996, November 24). Who needs this ad most? *New York Times,* 4E.

Arndofer, J. B. (1997, July 28). 007's sponsor blitz. *Advertising Age,* 24.

Bauder, D. (1999, March 31). Ads creep into TV content. *Boston Globe,* E6.

Bernstein, S. (1978, August 7). Do ads promote spirited imbibing? *Advertising Age,* 14.

Bever, T. G., Smith, M. L., Bengen, B., and Johnson, T. G. (1975). Young viewers' troubling response to TV ads. *Harvard Business Review,* 53, 109–20.

Bidlake, S. (1997, September). Commercials support free phone calls. *Advertising Age International,* I47, I49.

Chacon, R. and Ribadeneira, D. (1999, January 22), *Boston Globe,* A1, A10.

Cheers and Jeers (1997, June 21). *TV Guide,* 10.

Cortissoz, A. (1998, July 25). For young people, swing's the thing. *Boston Globe,* A1, A10.

Crain, R. (1997, June 9). Who knows what ads lurk in the hearts of consumers? The inner mind knows. *Advertising Age,* 25.

Crain, R. (1998, November 30). Miller's horrendous mistake example of how little we know. *Advertising Age,* 24.

Crain, R. (1999, January 18). When ads don't produce sales, watch the (phony) excuses fly. *Advertising Age,* 23.

Curtis, J. (1998, May/June). Wait a minute, Mr. Postman. *Applied Arts Magazine,* 49–54.

Dee, J. (1999, January). But is it advertising? *Harper's,* 61–72.

Enrico, D. (1997, September 15). Absolut vodka's ad spots withstand the test of time. *USA Today,* 4B.

Espen, H. (1999, March 21). Levi's blues. *New York Times Magazine,* 54–59.

Gardenburger hits the spot (1998, September 14). *Advertising Age,* 17.

Gleason, M. (1997, March 17). Events & promotions. *Advertising Age,* S1.

Goldner, B. (1998, June 29). Tamagotchi. *Advertising Age,* S43.

Grunwald, M. (1997, December 9). Megamall sells stimulation. *Boston Globe,* A1, A26.

Haran, L. (1996, March 18). Madison Avenue visits dream land. *Advertising Age,* 12.

Horton, C. (1996, January 8). Admen lament: If only we could take it back. *Advertising Age,* S28, S30, S48.

Hudes, K. (1998, November 15). Independent film, but with a catch: a corporate logo. *New York Times,* 43.

Jacobson, M. F. and Mazur, L. A. (1995). *Marketing Madness: A survival guide for a consumer society.* Boulder, CO: Westview Press.

Jhally, S. (1998). Advertising and the end of the world (a video). Northampton, MA: Media Education Foundation.

Kakutani, M. (1997, November 9). Bananas for rent. *New York Times Magazine,* 32.

Lee, L. (1998, May 31). Pass the popcorn (and the khakis). *New York Times,* 2 ST.

Leonhardt, D. (1997, June 30). Hey kid, buy this! *Business Week,* 61–67.

Levin, M. (1994, May 19). Tobacco firm paid $950,000 to place cigarettes in films. *Los Angeles Times,* 1.

Lewis, M. (1997, February 9). Royal scam. *New York Times Magazine,* 22.

Liu, E. (1999, March 25). Remember when public space didn't carry brand names? *USA Today,* 15A.

Logan, M. (1998, April 18). A big step for *Baywatch. TV Guide,* 8.

Maddox, K. and Jensen, J. (1998, October 5). Online marketers race for tie-ins with *You've Got Mail. Advertising Age,* 48.

Mandese, J. (1995, September 25). Star presenter of the year. *Advertising Age,* 1, 6.

McCarthy, C. (1990, November 11). In thingdom, laying waste our powers. *Washington Post,* F3.

Mohl, B. (1999, January 13). Lend them your ear, and your call is free. *Boston Globe,* A1, A10.

Monet show sets world record (1999, February 2). *Boston Globe,* E2.

Nathanson-Moog, C. (1984, July 26). Brand personalities undergo psychoanalysis. *Advertising Age,* 18.

Nike (1997). *30 years of Effie.* New York: American Marketing Association.

O'Donnell, M. (1995, January 22). From the notebooks of a genius. *New York Times Magazine,* 64.

Orlando, S. (1999, May 19). A material world: Defining ourselves by consumer goods. *http://www.sciencedaily.com/releases/1999/05/990518114815.htm.*

Pareles, J. (1998, February 8). Edging off rock's high road. *New York Times,* D1, D30.

Peppers, D. and Rogers, M. (1997, June 2). Marketer-customer dialogue comes to fore. *Advertising Age,* 32.

Pollay, R. W. (1986, April). The distorted mirror: reflections on the unintended consequences of advertising. *Journal of Marketing,* vol. 50, 18–36.

Rosenberg, A. S. (1999, February 1). Ad ideas etched in sand. *Boston Globe,* A3.

Ryan, S. (1996, December 18). They're not afraid to be labeled. *Boston Globe,* D1, D5.

Ryan, S. C. (1999, May 26). Fusion is the fashion. *Boston Globe,* F1, F6.

Sharkey, J. (1998, July 5). Beach-blanket babel: Another reason to stay at the pool. *New York Times,* 2.

Stark, S. (1990, July 23). Cops are tops—cowboys out. *Boston Globe,* 15.

Sullum, J. (1997, May 23). Victims of everything. *New York Times,* A31.

Tagliabue, J. (1997, September 28). Europe offering free calls, but first a word from . . . *New York Times,* 1, 8.

Twitchell, J. B. (1996). *Adcult USA: The triumph of advertising in American culture.* New York: Columbia University Press.

Tye, L. (1997, January 5). For some, it's an Absolut mania. *Boston Globe,* 1, 13.

Wallace, D. F. (1996). *Infinite jest.* Boston: Little Brown.

Wentz, L. (1998, May 11). Global village. *Advertising Age International,* 12.

What do they have in common? (1994, Summer). *Tobacco-Free Youth Reporter,* 3–4.

Woods, G. B. (1995). *Advertising and marketing to the new majority.* Belmont, CA: Wadsworth.

Worthington, R. (1992, January 19). 'Cultural psychosis' defense in teen fashion killing. *Chicago Tribune,* 15.

ENDNOTES

[73] *"advertising's messages are inside":* Jhally, 1998.

[73] *"almost half of all automobile crashes":* According to the U.S. Department of Transportation, over 40 percent of all fatal traffic accidents in 1996 were alcohol-related. National Highway Traffic Safety Administration, 1999.

[74] *"'This is my best idea ever'":* Sharkey, 1998, 2.

[74] *"Their next big idea":* Rosenberg, 1999, A3.

[74] *"In England the legendary white cliffs of Dover":* Liu. 1999, 15A.

[74] *"American consumers have recently joined Europeans":* Mohl, 1999, Al. Also Tagliabue, 1997, 1.

[74] *"Conversations are interrupted":* Bidlake, 1997, I49.

[74] *"beer companies have experimented":* Twitchell, 1996, 62.

[74] *"The average American is exposed":* Jacobson and Mazur, 1995, 13.

[74] *"Advertising makes up about 70 percent of our newspapers":* Twitchell, 1996, 71.

[74] *"40 percent of our mail":* McCarthy, 1990, F3.

[74] *"According to Rance Crain":* Crain, 1997, 25.

[74] *"advertising is subliminal":* Twitchell, 1996, 116.

[74] *"Grapevine Mills in Texas":* Grunwald, 1997, Al.

[74] *"the world David Foster Wallace imagined":* Wallace, 1996.

[74] *"In 1998 the museum's Monet show":* Monet show sets world record, 1999, E2.

[75] *"Bob Dole plays on his defeat":* Angier, 1996, 4E.

[75] *"Sarah Ferguson":* Lewis, 1997, 22.

[75] *"And the Rolling Stones, those aging rebels":* Pareles, 1998, D1.

[75] *"when Neil Young recorded a video":* Twitchell, 1996, 21–22.

[75] *"Stars such as Harrison Ford":* Angier, 1996, 4E.

[75] *"Antonio Banderas and Kevin Costner have pushed cars":* Ads not infinitum, 1998, 10.

[75] *"Leonardo DiCaprio was paid $4 million":* Wentz, 1998, 12.

[75] *"In 1983 Sylvester Stallone wrote":* What do they have in common? 1994, 4. Also Levin, 1994, 1.

[76] *"New technology allows":* Bauder, 1999, E6.

[76] *"Writer and cartoonist Mark O'Donnell":* O'Donnell, 1995, 64.

[76] *"Diet Coke obtained the rights":* Gleason, 1997, S1.

[76] *"In 1997 ABC and American Airlines":* Cheers & Jeers, 1997, 10.

[76] *"a character in the hit show* Baywatch": Logan, 1998, 8.

[76] *"'People have become less capable'"*: Kakutani, 1997, 32.

[76] *"Steven Stark, another media critic"*: Stark, 1990, 15.

[76] *"As Jerry Seinfeld, star of the show, said"*: Mandese, 1995, 1.

[77] *"The 1997 James Bond film"*: Arndofer, 1997, 24

[77] *"the 1998 hit movie* You've Got Mail": Maddox and Jensen, 1998, 48.

[77] *"And independent films are becoming as tight"*: Hudes, 1998, 43.

[77] *"Hilfiger provided the wardrobe"*: Lee, 1998, 2 ST.

[77] *"Maurice Malone"*: Ryan, 1999, F1.

[77] *"Chris Gore, publisher of the Webzine* Film Threat": Lee, 1998, 2 ST.

[78] *"This argument was made by Jacob Sullum"*: Sullum, 1997, A31.

[78] *"As Sut Jhally says"*: Jhally, 1998.

[78] *"As Joseph Goebbels"*: Goebbels, 1933, March 28. Quoted in Jacobson and Mazur, 1995, 15.

[79] *"no wonder that Evian backwards"*: My thanks to Bob McCannon for this observation.

[79] *"When Nike wanted to reach skateboarders"*: Nike, 1997, 54.

[79] *"Some advertisers use what they chillingly call"*: Espen, 1999, 54–59.

[79] *"One marketing consultant suggests"*: Crain, 1997, 25.

[79] *"A study of children done by researchers at Columbia University"*: Bever, Smith, Bengen, and Johnson, 1975, 119.

[80] *"'7- to 10-year-olds are strained'"*: Bever, Smith, Bengen, and Johnson, 1975, 120.

[80] *"Rance Crain of Advertising Age"*: Crain, 1999, 23.

[80] *"When Pope John Paul II"*: Chacon and Ribadeneira, 1999, A8.

[81] *"Neil Postman refers"*: Curtis, 1998, 49.

[81] *"'The Jolly Green Giant'"*: Twitchell, 1996, 30.

[82] *"'It's no fun to spend $100 on athletic shoes'"*: Peppers and Rogers, 1997, 32.

[82] *"the city health commissioner in Philadelphia"*: Worthington, 1992, 15.

[82] *"A USA Today-CNN-Gallup Poll"*: Jacobson and Mazur, 1995, 26.

[82] *"Leydiana Reyes"*: Leonhardt, 1997, 65.

[82] *"Danny Shirley"*: Espen, 1999, 59.

[82] *"sweatshirts with fifteen-inch 'Polo' logos"*: Ryan, 1996, D1.

[83] *"Consumer behavior"*: Woods, 1995.

[83] *"Most shampoos"*: Twitchell, 1996, 252.

[83] *"Blindfolded smokers"*: Twitchell, 1996, 125.

[83] *"This campaign has been so successful"*: Enrico, 1997, 4B.

[83] *"Collecting Absolut ads"*: Tye, 1997, 1, 13.

[84] *"Carol Nathanson-Moog, an advertising psychologist"*: Nathanson-Moog, 1984, 18.

[84] *"product image is probably the most important element"*: Nathanson-Moog, 1984, 18.

[84] *"'A strange world it is'"*: Bernstein, 1978, August 7.

[84] *"According to Bob Wehling"*: Crain, 1998, 24.

[84] *"A commercial for I Can't Believe It's Not Butter"*: Haran, 1996, 12.

[84] *"Tamagotchis"*: Goldner, 1998, S43.

[84] *"And Gardenburger"*: Gardenburger hits the spot, 1998, 17.

[85] *"In 1998 a Miller beer campaign"*: Crain, 1998, 24.

[85] *"The 1989 Nissan Infiniti"*: Horton, 1996, S28.

[85] *"the Edsel":* Horton, 1996, S30.

[85] *"An ad for Gap khakis":* Cortissoz, 1998, A10.

[85] *"James Twitchell argues":* University of Florida news release, quoted by Orlando, 1999, http://www.sciencedaily.com/releases/1999/05/990518114815.htm.

[85] *"Critic and novelist George Steiner":* Dee., 1999, 65–66.

[85] *"As Richard Pollay":* Pollay, 1986.

[86] *"there has never been a propaganda effort":* Jhally, 1998.

Name: _____ Date: _____

Understanding the Text

1. Ironically, says Kilbourne, "[a]dvertisers want us to believe that we are not influenced by ads." How does she think advertisers benefit from this strategy?

2. According to Kilbourne, what do advertising and religion have in common? Why does she find this commonality troubling?

3. Kilbourne claims that "[t]he unintended effects of advertising are far more important . . . than those effects that are intended." Why does she think so?

Reading Bodies

Susan Bordo

For sometime during the last seven years, we seem to have entered an unabashed Reign of the Ram. Fashion ads today routinely feature men in underwear who are amazingly endowed ("He looks like he has *two* penises in there!" a student of mine said of one), their poses directing the viewer's attention to their crotches. Some ads show men cupping their genitals; in others, the penis seems to be fully erect. *Playgirl,* clearly doing double duty for both gay and straight readers, has become a cornucopia of humongous male organs of every race, class, and age. Rap musicians (and, aping them, Madonna) have made crotch grabbing a common cultural code for sexual power and virility. Surgical phalloplasty is big business today—and, by the way, has provided John Bobbitt with a new, happier ending to his saga. Bobbit has not only been re-membered but enhanced ("It's like a beer can," he boasted after the operation). So will someone send a thank-you card to Lorena already?

This is not the first time in history that penises have been culturally visible. Modernity has been especially squeamish, it seems, about the male body. Until the creation of trousers at the beginning of the eighteenth century, men's pants were more like what we call "tights," through which the shape of the genitals could often be clearly discerned. However, as Anne Hollander points out in *Sex and Suits,* the simulation or suggestion of male nakedness had a very different significance then than it does today. In 1998, we look at the frontal bulges of fashion models clad in clinging jersey briefs and think: "Sex." From the early Renaissance to the eighteenth century, it was just the opposite. Revealing the basic outline of male legs and genitals while covering those parts of a woman's body with voluminous materials, drapes, hoops, and the like meant the male body was a more utilitarian, "authentic," no-nonsense, *truthful* body, while the woman's body was an object of artifice, fantasy, and illusion, her clothing designed to stimulate the sexual imagination rather than represent her anatomy accurately.

The example shows that exploring attitudes toward clothing, nakedness, and masculinity means recognizing their historical and cultural variability. It also suggests that we need to think about the body not only as a physical entity—which it assuredly is—but also as a cultural form that carries *meaning* with it. The notion that bodies are just material things, collections of instincts, mechanical processes put in place by God the watchmaker, ticking away in pretty much the same way from culture to culture, era to era, goes back to the philosopher Descartes. Darwinian science profoundly altered the Cartesian picture by showing that the body's mechanisms aren't timeless and unchanging, but have evolved dramatically over time. What's still missing from this picture, though—and what was ultimately supplied in the twentieth century—is the recognition that when we look at bodies (including our own in the mirror), we don't just see biological nature at work, but values and ideals, differences and similarities that *culture* has "written," so to speak, on those bodies.

What this means is that the body doesn't carry only DNA, it also carries human history with it. Biologically, a penis is a penis (more or less). But as Hollander's research shows, a seventeenth-century spectator would have seen something very different than we do when confronted with the sight of a man in genital-revealing tights. Another example of how history and culture affect the way we see bodies is provided by the Jockey ad on the next page. The two parts to the ad are parallel—five good-looking men (doctors, surgeons, and physical therapists) and five good-looking women (riders, ranchers, and cowgirls) with their pants around their ankles, revealing their Jockeys underneath. Some features of these ads are pretty obvious. The open expressions on the women's faces versus the mostly serious, semi-challenging male stares; the men's "feet planted firm" posture versus the women's flirtatiously bent knees—these are standard stuff in the depiction of men and women's bodies. As for what's "new"—Jockey clearly means to tweak the cultural stereotypes of doctors and cowboys with its unexpectedly muscular, macho docs and curvy, feminine ranchers. And to convey a message of equality too, by having the women and men in equal states of undress.

The thing is, they're *not* in equal states of undress—because pants-around-the-ankles convey something different on the bodies of the men than they do on the bodies of the women. The men's genitals in the Jockey ad are much more visible than the women's. Actually, the women, by contemporary standards, are hardly undressed at all. Yet somehow, they *seem* more exposed than the men. It's those pants around the ankles. Mentally remove them—or just cover them up with your hands—and you get a very different feeling from the ad. With the men, on the other hand, the "dropped trou"—the expression seems appropriate for them, but not for the girls—barely signify at all. Cover them up or leave them in, the guys' bodies project much the same confident, slightly challenging machismo either way. Their bodies are very sexy. But they do not seem stripped or exposed.

Partly, this is because we read the bodies in the Jockey ad against the backdrop of depictions of male and female bodies that we are used to, and until recently, the conventions governing the two sexes have been very different. In countless movies, we've grown used to seeing women take off their clothes for sex, or to display themselves erotically, or to be unsuspectingly spied on. The act of getting undressed is an act of uncovering, exposing; a secret sexual self is revealed. In contrast, men, until very recently, would only be shown undressing with some "utilitarian" fiction written into the scene—changing from business

suits into sweats, putting on athletic uniforms, and so on. Anne Hollander would probably argue that all of this has to do with the lingering of those old ideas about the utilitarian form of the male body. And when you examine the accessories that have been included in the Jockey ads, it seems that there's something to that. The docs seem ready to get to work. They've got their stethoscopes around their necks, their surgical masks ready to tie on; all they need to do is pull up those pants, whip out that knife, and start bossing the nurses around. The cowgirls, in contrast, are ill equipped to round up anything beyond male winks. (Those hats are cute, though.)

There's a more unnerving piece to this too. With women, pants-around-the-ankles subtly recalls movie scenes of rape (think Jodie Foster on that pinball machine in *The Accused*) and the discovered bodies of female murder victims. Such images are not part of a feminist's paranoid delusion, but belong to a common lexicon of cultural motifs that we are almost all familiar with and are very difficult (if not impossible) to erase from the unconscious. The fact that the models in the Jockey ad are *not* coming on like sexual temptresses but have bright, sunny smiles only enhances the lascivious juxtaposition between their own definition of themselves (as active, happy girls) and the perspective of the viewer, in whose eyes they seem vulnerable, unknowingly exposed. You feel, in some subliminal corner of the brain, that while the men have "dropped trou" themselves someone has pulled those girls' pants down (or asked them to pull them down, or is peeping around the corner). Yes, I know the *actual* models don't feel that way at all . . . and would probably have a good hoot if they read this too. I'm not talking about how the models *feel* but about elements suggested in the representation they posed for.

You may not see the same things in this ad that I do. Representations of the body have a history, but so too do viewers, and they bring that history—both personal and cultural—to their perception and interpretation. Different viewers may see different things. In pointing to certain elements in ads, or movies, or fashion, I'm not ignoring the differences in how people may see things, but deliberately trying to direct your attention to what I see as significant. I'm making an argument, and you may or may not find it convincing. You might think—as my students sometimes do—that I'm "making too much" of certain elements. Or your own background, values, "ways of seeing" may enable you to discern things that I do not. Or it may be that even as I offer my ideas, the cultural context has already begun to shift in ways that answer my interpretation or make it obsolete. Cultural interpretation is an ongoing, always incomplete process, and no one gets the final word.

Hollander's insights, for example, while useful in interpreting some aspects of the Jockey ad, ultimately come up against the fact that we *do* live in the second half of the twentieth century, and despite the utilitarian accessorizing, the doctors' discernible genitals, no less than the girls' body parts, *are* the stuff of sex. With all the naked bodies around nowadays, this sensibility may ultimately reach its historical limit too, as we get jaded and bored with all the (mostly plastic) flesh around. But for now, as a general rule, the more a piece of clothing outlines and reveals what's underneath, the "sexier" it is to our cultural eyes.

The kind of sex the docs project is different, though, than the sex the cowgirls project. Nowadays, men—the Chippendales, for example, and men in ads as well—*do* strip for erotic display. But when they do so, they tend to present their bodies aggressively and so rarely seem truly exposed. Being undressed does not necessarily mean being naked. Most men in underwear ads today . . . Well, you wouldn't want to meet one coming round a dark corner. When, in the 1996 French film *Ridicule,* an aristocrat took his penis out of his pants and pissed in the lap of another man, he seemed more to be whipping out a weapon than a body part. And what can a viewer's eyes do but admire the bulging bundles and gleaming muscles of the Chippendales and their ilk? Their bodies are a kind of natural armor. Being "stripped," it seems—much more than merely being undressed—has been anathema to masculinity.

BIBLIOGRAPHY

Hollander, Anne. (1994). *Sex and Suits: The Evolution of Modern Dress.* New York: Kodansha International.

Name: _____ Date: _____

Understanding the Text

1. In the west, from the Renaissance to the eighteenth century, what did men wear instead of trousers?

2. According to Anne Hollander, what did this article of clothing signify?

3. Though both the men and women in the Jockey ad Bordo describes are in "equal states of undress," this condition, she argues, signifies something different for each sex. What does it signify for each?

Getting Dirty

Mark Crispin Miller

We are outside a house, looking in the window, and this is what we see: a young man, apparently nude and half-crazed with anxiety, lunging toward the glass. "Gail!" he screams, as he throws the window open and leans outside, over a flowerbox full of geraniums: "The most important shower of my life, and you switch deodorant soap!" He is, we now see, only half-naked, wearing a towel around his waist; and he shakes a packaged bar of soap—"Shield"—in one accusing hand. Gail, wearing a blue man-tailored shirt, stands outside, below the window, clipping a hedge. She handles this reproach with an ease that suggests years of contempt. "Shield is better," she explains patiently, in a voice somewhat deeper than her husband's. "It's extra strength." (Close-up of the package in the husband's hand, Gail's efficient finger gliding along beneath the legend, THE EXTRA STRENGTH DEODORANT SOAP.) "Yeah," whimpers Mr. Gail, "but my first call on J. J. Siss [sic], the company's *toughest customer,* and now *this*!" Gail nods with broad mock-sympathy, and stands firm: "Shield fights odor better, so you'll feel *cleaner,*" she assures her husband, who darts away with a jerk of panic, as Gail rolls her eyes heavenward and gently shakes her head, as if to say, "What a half-wit!"

Cut to our hero, as he takes his important shower. No longer frantic, he now grins down at himself, apparently delighted to be caked with Shield, which, in its detergent state, has the consistency of wet cement. He then goes out of focus, as if glimpsed through a shower door. "Clinical tests prove," proclaims an eager baritone, "Shield fights odor better than the *leading* deodorant soap!" A bar of Shield (green) and a bar of that other soap (yellow) zip up the screen with a festive toot, forming a sort of graph which demonstrates that Shield does, indeed, "fight odor better, so you'll feel *cleaner!*"

This particular contest having been settled, we return to the major one, which has yet to be resolved. Our hero reappears, almost transformed: calmed down, dressed up, his voice at least an octave lower. "I *do* feel cleaner!" he announces cheerily, leaning into the doorway of a room where Gail is arranging flowers. She pretends to be ecstatic at this news, and he comes toward her, setting himself up for a profound humiliation by putting on a playful air of suave command. Adjusting his tie like a real man of the world, he saunters over to his wife and her flower bowl, where he plucks a dainty purple flower and lifts it to his lapel: "And," he boasts throughout all this, trying to make his voice sound even deeper, "with old J. J.'s business and my brains—" "—you'll . . . *clean up again?*" Gail asks with suggestive irony, subverting his authoritative pose by leaning against him, draping one hand over his shoulder to dangle a big yellow daisy down his chest. Taken aback, he shoots her a distrustful look, and she titters at him.

Finally, the word SHIELD appears in extreme close-up and the camera pulls back, showing two bars of the soap, one packaged and one not, on display amidst an array of steely bubbles. "Shield fights odor better, so you'll feel *cleaner!*" the baritone reminds us, and then our hero's face appears once more, in a little square over the unpackaged bar of soap: "I feel *cleaner* than *ever before!*" he insists, sounding faintly unconvinced.

Is all this as stupid as it seems at first? Or is there, just beneath the surface of this moronic narrative, some noteworthy design, intended to appeal to (and to worsen) some of the anxieties of modern life? A serious look at this particular trifle might lead us to some strange discoveries.

We are struck, first of all, by the commercial's pseudofeminism, an advertising ploy with a long history, and one ubiquitous on television nowadays. Although the whole subject deserves more extended treatment, this commercial offers us an especially rich example of the strategy. Typically, it woos its female viewers—i.e., those who choose the soap in most households—with a fantasy of dominance; and it does so by inverting the actualities of woman's lot through a number of imperceptible details. For instance, in this marriage it is the wife, and not the husband, who gets to keep her name; and Gail's name, moreover, is a potent one, because of its brevity and its homonymic connotation. (If this housewife were more delicately named, called "Lillian" or "Cecilia," it would lessen her illusory strength.) She is also equipped in more noticeable ways: she's the one who wears the button-down shirt in this family, she's the one who's competent both outdoors and in the house, and it is she, and only she, who wields the tool.

These visual details imply that Gail is quite a powerful housewife, whereas her nameless mate is a figure of embarrassing impotence. This "man," in fact, is actually Gail's *wife*: he is utterly feminized, striking a posture and displaying attributes which men have long deplored in women. In other words, this commercial, which apparently takes the woman's side, is really the expression (and reflection) of misogyny. Gail's husband is dependent and hysterical, entirely without that self-possession which we expect from solid, manly types, like Gail. This is partly the result of his demeanor: in the opening scene, his voice sometimes cracks ludicrously, and he otherwise betrays the shrill desperation of a man who can't remember where he left his scrotum. The comic effect of this frenzy, moreover, is subtly enhanced by the mise-en-scène, which puts the man in a conventionally feminine position—in dishabille, looking down from a window. Thus we infer that he is sheltered and housebound, a modern Juliet calling for his/her Romeo; or—more appropriately—the image suggests a scene in some suburban red-light district, presenting this husband as an item on display, like the flowers just below his stomach, available for anyone's enjoyment, at a certain price. Although in one way contradictory, these implications are actually quite congruous, for they both serve to emasculate the husband, so that the wife might take his place, or play his part.

Such details, some might argue, need not have been the conscious work of this commercial's makers. The authors, that is, might have worked by instinct rather than design, and so would have been no more aware of their work's psychosocial import than we ourselves: they just wanted to make the guy look like a wimp, merely for the purposes of domestic comedy. While such an argument certainly does apply to many ads, in this case it is unlikely. Advertising agencies do plenty of research, by which we can assume that they don't select their tactics arbitrarily. They take pains to analyze the culture which they help to sicken, and then, with much wit and cynicism, use their insights in devising their small dramas. This commercial is a subtle and meticulous endorsement of castration, meant to play on certain widespread guilts and insecurities; and all we need to do to demonstrate this fact is to subject the two main scenes to the kind of visual analysis which commercials, so brief and broad, tend to resist (understandably). The ad's visual implications are too carefully achieved to have been merely accidental or unconscious.

The crucial object in the opening shot is that flower box with its bright geraniums, which is placed directly in front of the husband's groin. This clever stroke of composition has the immediate effect of equating our hero's manhood with a bunch of flowers. This is an exquisitely perverse suggestion, rather like using a cigar to represent the Eternal Feminine: flowers are frail, sweet, and largely ornamental, hardly an appropriate phallic symbol, but (of course) a venerable symbol of *maidenhood.* The geraniums stand, then, not for the husband's virility, but for its absence.

More than a clever instance of inversion, furthermore, these phallic blossoms tell us something odd about this marital relationship. As Gail, clippers in hand, turns from the hedge to calm her agitated man, she appears entirely capable of calming him quite drastically, if she hasn't done so already (which might explain his hairless chest and high-pitched voice). She has the power, that is, to take away whatever slender potency he may possess, and uses the power repeatedly, trimming her husband (we infer) as diligently as she prunes her foliage. And, as she can snip his manhood, so too can she restore it, which is what the second scene implies. Now the flower bowl has replaced the flower box as the visual crux, dominating the bottom center of the frame with a crowd of blooms. As the husband, cleaned and dressed, comes to stand beside his wife, straining to affect a new authority, the flower bowl too appears directly at his lower center; so that Gail, briskly adding flowers to the bouquet, appears to be replenishing his vacant groin with extra stalks. He has a lot to thank her for, it seems: she is his helpmate, confidante, adviser, she keeps his house and grounds in order, and she is clearly the custodian of the family jewels.

Of course, her restoration of his potency cannot be complete, or he might shatter her mastery by growing a bit too masterful himself. He could start choosing his own soap, or take her shears away, or—worst of all—walk out for good. Therefore, she punctures his momentary confidence by taunting him with that big limp daisy, countering his lordly gesture with the boutonniere by flaunting that symbol of his floral status. He can put on whatever airs he likes, but she still has his fragile vigor firmly in her hand.

Now what, precisely, motivates this sexless battle of the sexes? That is, what really underlies this tense and hateful marriage, making the man so weak, the woman so contemptuously helpful? The script, seemingly nothing more than a series of inanities, contains the answer to these questions, conveying, as it does, a concern with cleanliness that amounts to an obsession: "Shield fights odor better, so you'll feel cleaner!" "I *do* feel cleaner!" "Shield fights odor better, so you'll feel *cleaner!*" "I feel *cleaner* than *ever before!*" Indeed, the commercial emphasizes the feeling of cleanliness even more pointedly than the name of the product, implying, by its very insistence, a feeling of dirtiness, an apprehension of deep filth.

And yet there is not a trace of dirt in the vivid world of this commercial. Unlike many ads for other soaps, this one shows no sloppy children, no sweatsoaked workingmen with blackened hands, not even a bleary housewife in need of her morning shower. We never even glimpse the ground in Gail's world, nor is her husband even faintly smudged. In fact, the filth which Shield supposedly "fights" is not physical but psychological besmirchment: Gail's husband feels soiled because of what he has to do for a living, in order to keep Gail in that nice big house, happily supplied with shirts and shears.

"My first call on J. J. Siss, the company's *toughest customer,* and now *this!*" The man's anxiety is yet another feminizing trait, for it is generally women, and not men, who are consumed by doubts about the sweetness of their bodies, which must never be offensive to the guys who run the world. (This real anxiety is itself aggravated by commercials.) Gail's husband must play the female to the mighty J. J. Siss, a name whose oxymoronic character implies perversion: "J. J." is a stereotypic nickname for the potent boss, while "Sis" is a term of endearment, short for "sister" (and perhaps implying "sissy," too, in this case). Gail's husband must do his boyish best to please the voracious J. J. Siss, just as a prostitute must satisfy a demanding trick, or "tough customer." It is therefore perfectly fitting that this employee refer to the encounter, not as a "meeting" or "appointment," but as a "call"; and his demeaning posture in the window—half dressed and bent over—conveys, we now see, a definitive implication.

Gail's job as the "understanding wife" is not to rescue her husband from these sordid obligations, but to help him meet them successfully. She may seem coolly self-sufficient, but she actually depends on her husband's attractiveness, just as a pimp relies on the charm of his whore. And, also like a pimp, she has to keep her girl in line with occasional reminders of who's boss. When her husband starts getting uppity *après la douche,* she jars him from the very self-assurance which she had helped him to discover, piercing that "shield" which was her gift.

"And, with old J. J.'s business and my brains—" "— you'll . . . *clean up again?*" He means, of course, that he'll work fiscal wonders with old J. J.'s account, but his fragmentary boast contains a deeper significance, upon which Gail plays with sadistic cleverness. "Old J. J.'s business and my brains" implies a feminine self-description, since it suggests a variation on the old commonplace of "brains vs. brawn": J. J.'s money, in the world of this commercial (as in ours), amounts to brute strength, which the flexible husband intends to complement with his mother wit. Gail's retort broadens this unconscious hint of homosexuality: "—you'll . . . *clean up again?*" Given the monetary nature of her husband's truncated remark, the retort must mean primarily, "You'll make a lot of money." If this were all it meant, however, it would not be a joke, nor would the husband find it so upsetting. Moreover, we have no evidence that Gail's husband ever "cleaned up"—i.e., made a sudden fortune—in the past. Rather, the ad's milieu and *dramatis personae* suggest upward mobility, gradual savings and a yearly raise, rather than one prior killing. What Gail is referring to, in fact, with that "again," is her husband's shower: she implies that what he'll have to do, after his "call" on J. J. Siss, is, quite literally, wash himself off. Like any other tidy hooker, this man will have to clean up after taking on a tough customer, so that he might be ready to take on someone else.

These suggestions of pederasty are intended, not as a literal characterization of the husband's job, but as a metaphor for what it takes to get ahead: Gail's husband, like most white-collar workers, must debase himself to make a good impression, toadying to his superiors, offering himself, body and soul, to the corporation. Maybe, therefore, it isn't really Gail who has neutered him; it may be his way of life that has wrought the ugly change. How, then, are women represented here? The commercial does deliberately appeal to women, offering them a sad fantasy of control; but it also, perhaps inadvertently, illuminates the unhappiness which makes that fantasy attractive.

The husband's status, it would seem, should make Gail happy, since it makes her physically comfortable, and yet Gail can't help loathing her husband for the degradations which she helps him undergo. For her part of the bargain is, ultimately, no less painful than his. She has to do more than put up with him; she has to prepare him for his world of affairs, and then must help him to conceal the shame. Of course, it's all quite hopeless. She clearly despises the man whom she would bolster; and the thing which she provides to help him "feel cleaner than ever before" is precisely what has helped him do the job that's always made him feel so dirty. "A little water cleans us of this deed" is her promise, which is false, for she is just as soiled as her doomed husband, however fresh and well-ironed she may look.

Of course, the ad not only illuminates this mess, but helps perpetuate it, by obliquely gratifying the guilts, terrors, and resentments that underlie it and arise from it. The strategy is not meant to be noticed, but works through the apparent comedy, which must therefore be studied carefully, not passively received. Thus, thirty seconds of ingenious advertising, which we can barely stand to watch, tell us something more than we might want to know about the souls of men and women under corporate capitalism.

Name: _____ Date: _____

UNDERSTANDING THE TEXT

1. Miller claims that the ad for Shield soap is "pseudofeminist." What does this mean and what evidence does he cite to support his claim? (Identify and discuss two examples.)

2. Miller suggests that a careful reading of this ad might reveal that it seeks "to appeal to (and to worsen) some of the anxieties of modern life[.]" How might such a tactic encourage consumers to buy soap?

3. According to Miller, why does the husband feel "soiled"?

Naughty but Nice: Food Pornography

Rosalind Coward

There's a full-page spread in a woman's magazine. It's captioned Breakfast Special, and shows a picture of every delicious breakfast imaginable. The hungry eye can delight in croissants with butter, exquisitely prepared bacon and eggs, toasted waffles with maple syrup. But over the top of the pictures there's a sinister message: 430 calories for the croissants; 300 for the waffles. The English breakfast takes the biscuit with a top score of 665 calories. It must be a galling sight for the readers of this particular magazine. Because it's *Slimmer* magazine. And one presumes the reader looks on these pleasures in the full knowledge that they had better not be indulged.

This pleasure in looking at the supposedly forbidden is reminiscent of another form of guilty-but-indulgent looking, that of sexual pornography. Sexual pornography as a separate realm of imagery exists because our society defines some explicit pictures of sexual activity or sexual parts as 'naughty', 'illicit'. These images are then made widely available through a massive and massively profitable industry.

The glossy pictures in slimming magazines show in glorious Technicolor all the illicit desires which make us fat. Many of the articles show almost life-size pictures of the real baddies of the dieting world—bags of crisps, peanuts, bars of chocolate, cream puddings. Diet foods are advertised as sensuously as possible. The food is made as appetizing as possible, often with explicit sexual references: 'Tip Top. For Girls who used to say No'; 'Grapefruits. The Least Forbidden Fruit'.

Pictures in slimming magazines and those circulated around the slimming culture are only the hard core of food pictures which are in general circulation in women's magazines. Most women's magazines carry articles about food, recipes or advertising. All are accompanied by larger-than-life, elaborate pictures of food, cross-sections through a cream and strawberry sponge, or close-ups of succulent Orange and Walnut Roast Beef. Recipe books often dwell on the visual impact of food. In the street, billboards confront us with gargantuan cream cakes.

But it is only the unfortunate readers of the slimming magazines who are supposed to use the pictures as a substitute for the real thing. While other forms of food photography are meant to stimulate the desire to prepare and eat the food, for the slimmers it is a matter of feasting the eyes only.

Like sexual pornography, pictures of food provide a photographic genre geared towards one sex. And like sexual pornography, it is a regime of 'pleasure' which is incomprehensible to the opposite sex. This is because these pornographies are creating and indulging 'pleasures' which confirm or trap men and women in their respective positions of power and subordination.

Sexual pornography is an industry dealing in images geared towards men. Sexual pornography is dominated by pictures of women. It shows bits of women's bodies, women engaged in sex acts, women masturbating, women supposedly having orgasms. When the women look at the camera, it is with an expression of sexual arousal, interest and availability. The way in which women are posed for these images presupposes a male viewer, behind the camera, as it were, about to move in on the act.

Pornography is only the extreme end of how images of women are circulated in general in this society. Pornography is defined as being illicit, naughty, unacceptable for public display (though definitions of what is acceptable vary from one epoch to the next). It shows things which generally available images don't—penetration, masturbation, women's genitals. The porn industry then thrives on marketing and circulating these 'illicit' images. But if pornography is meant to be illicit, and hidden, the kinds of images it shows differ little from the more routinely available images of women. Page three nudes in daily papers, advertisements showing women, the representation of sex in non-pornographic films, all draw on the conventions by which women are represented in pornography. Women are made to look into the camera in the same way, their bodies are arranged in the same way, the same glossy photographic techniques are used, there is the same fragmentation of women's bodies, and a concomitant fetishistic concentration on bits of the body.

Many women now think that the way male arousal is catered for in these images is a problem. These images feed a belief that men have depersonalized sexual needs, like sleeping or going to the lavatory. Pornography as it is currently practiced suggests that women's bodies are available to meet those needs. Men often say that porn is just fantasy, a harmless way of having pleasure as a substitute for the real thing. But women have begun to question this use of the term 'pleasure'. After all, the pleasure seems conditional on feeling power to use women's bodies. And maybe there's only a thin line between the fantasy and the lived experience of sexuality where men do sometimes force their sexual attentions on women.

If sexual pornography is a display of images which confirm men's sense of themselves as having power over women, food pornography is a regime of pleasurable images which has the opposite effect on its viewers—women. It indulges a pleasure which is linked to servitude and therefore confirms the subordinate position of women. Unlike sexual pornography, however, food porn cannot even be used without guilt. Because of pressures to diet, women have been made to feel guilty about enjoying food.

The use of food pornography is surprisingly widespread. All the women I have talked to about food have confessed to enjoying it. Few activities it seems rival relaxing in bed with a good recipe book. Some indulged in full colour pictures of gleaming bodies of Cold Mackerel Basquaise lying invitingly on a bed of peppers, or perfectly formed chocolate mousse topped with mounds of cream. The intellectuals expressed a preference for erotica, Elizabeth David's historical and literary titillation. All of us used the recipe books as aids to oral gratification, stimulants to imagine new combinations of food, ideas for producing a lovely meal.

Cooking food and presenting it beautifully is an act of servitude. It is a way of expressing affection through a gift. In fact, the preparation of a meal involves intensive domestic labour, the most devalued labour in this society. That we should aspire to produce perfectly finished and presented food is a symbol of a willing and enjoyable participation in servicing other people.

Food pornography exactly sustains these meanings relating to the preparation of food. The kinds of pictures used always repress the process of production of a meal. They are always beautifully lit, often touched up. The settings are invariably exquisite—a conservatory in the background, fresh flowers on the table. The dishes are expensive and look barely used.

There's a whole professional ideology connected with food photography. The *Focal Encyclopaedia of Photography* tells us that in a 'good food picture', 'the food must be both perfectly cooked and perfectly displayed' if it is to appeal to the magazine reader. The photographer 'must decide in advance on the correct style and arrangement of table linen, silver, china, flowers. Close attention to such details is vital because the final pictures must survive the critical inspection of housewives and cooks.' Food photographers are supposed to be at the service of the expert chef, but sometimes 'the photographer learns by experience that certain foodstuffs do not photograph well'. And in such circumstances, 'he must be able to suggest reasonable substitutes'. Glycerine-covered green paper is a well-known substitute for lettuce, which wilts under the bright lights of a studio. And fast-melting foods like ice-cream pose interesting technical problems for the food photographer. Occasionally, they do get caught out—I recently saw a picture of a sausage dinner where a nail was clearly visible, holding the sausage to its surroundings! Virtually all meals shown in these photos are actually inedible. If not actually made of plaster, most are sprayed or treated for photographing. How ironic to think of the perfect meal destined for the dustbin.

Food photographs are the culinary equivalent of the removal of unsightly hairs. Not only do hours of work go into the preparation of the settings and the dishes, but the finished photos are touched up and imperfections removed to make the food look succulent and glistening. The aim of these photos is the display of the perfect meal in isolation from the kitchen context and the process of its production. There are no traces of the hours of shopping, cleaning, cutting up, preparing, tidying up, arranging the table and the room which in fact go into the production of a meal. Just as we know that glamorous models in the adverts don't really look as they appear, so we know perfectly well about the hours of untidy chaos involved in the preparation of a meal. We know that photos of glamour models are touched up, skin blemishes removed, excess fat literally cut out of the picture. And—subconsciously at least—we probably realize the same process has been at work on the Black Forest Gâteau. But the ideal images still linger in our minds as a lure. A meal should really look like the pictures. And that's how the images produce complicity in our subordination. We aim at giving others pleasure by obliterating the traces of our labour.

But it is not as if, even if we could produce this perfect meal, we could wholeheartedly enjoy it. Because at the same time as food is presented as the one legitimate sensual pleasure for women we are simultaneously told that women shouldn't eat too much. Food is Naughty but Nice, as the current Real Dairy Cream advertisement announces.

This guilt connected with eating has become severe over the last few decades. It's a result of the growing pressure over these years towards the ideal shape of women. This shape is more like an adolescent than a woman, a silhouette rather than a soft body. There's a current dictum in slimming circles: 'If you can pinch an inch, you may need to lose weight.' This seems a particularly vicious control of female contours in a society obsessed with eating and uninterested in physical exertion. Dieting is the forcible imposition of an ideal shape on a woman's body.

The presentation of food sets up a particular trap for women. The glossy, sensual photography legitimates oral desires and pleasures for women in a way that sexual interest for women is never legitimated. At the same time, however, much of the food photography constructs a direct equation between food and fat, an equation which can only generate guilt about oral pleasures. Look at the way advertising presents food, drawing a direct equation between what women eat and what shape they will be. Tab is the low-calorie drink from Coca-Cola. Its advertising campaign shows a glass of the stuff which is in the shape of a woman's body! Beside the glass are the statistics 35″ 22″ 35″. A Sweetex advertisement shows two slender women and exhorts 'Take the lumps out of your life. Take Sweetex'! Heinz promotes its 'Slimway Mayonnaise' with a picture of a very lurid lobster and the caption 'Mayonnaise without guilt'. Tea even 'adds a little weight to the slimming argument'. Another soft-drink company exhorts: 'Spoil yourself, not your figure', which is a common promise for slimming foods. Nor is this phenomenon confined to slimming foods. Women's magazines have articles about whether 'your taste buds are ruining your figure', and creamy foods are offered as wicked but worth it.

An equation is set up in this kind of writing and these pictures between what goes into the mouth and the shape your body will be. It is as if we swallow a mouthful and it goes immediately, without digestion, to join the 'cellulite'. If we give this a moment's thought, we realize it is nonsense. There's no direct correlation between food into the mouth and fat; that's about the *only* thing on which all the diet experts agree. People have different metabolisms, use food differently. Different things in different people's lives affect what they eat and what effect that eating has on overall health. But the simplistic ideologies behind food and dieting cultures reinforce the guilt associated with food for women. Oral pleasures are only really permissible when tied to the servicing of others in the production of a meal. Women are controlled and punished if they indulge themselves.

The way images of food are made and circulated is not just an innocent catering for pleasures. They also meddle in people's sense of themselves and their self-worth. In a sexually divided and hierarchical society, these pleasures are tied to positions of power and subordination.

Name: _____ Date: _____

UNDERSTANDING THE TEXT

1. According to Coward, what makes images of food in women's magazines pornographic?

2. Coward argues that food pornography "indulges a pleasure which is linked to servitude and therefore confirms the subordinate position of women." To what specific form of "servitude" does she refer?

3. Ultimately, Coward suggests, food ads are a form of social control. How so? And who is controlling whom?

Weasel Words

William Lutz

One problem advertisers have when they try to convince you that the product they are pushing is really different from other, similar products is that their claims are subject to some laws. Not a lot of laws, but there are some designed to prevent fraudulent or untruthful claims in advertising. Even during the happy years of nonregulation under President Ronald Reagan, the FTC did crack down on the more blatant abuses in advertising claims. Generally speaking, advertisers have to be careful in what they say in their ads, in the claims they make for the products they advertise. Parity claims are safe because they are legal and supported by a number of court decisions. But beyond parity claims there are weasel words.

Advertisers use weasel words to appear to be making a claim for a product when in fact they are making no claim at all. Weasel words get their name from the way weasels eat the eggs they find in the nests of other animals. A weasel will make a small hole in the egg, suck out the insides, then place the egg back in the nest. Only when the egg is examined closely is it found to be hollow. That's the way it is with weasel words in advertising: Examine weasel words closely and you'll find that they're as hollow as any egg sucked by a weasel. Weasel words appear to say one thing when in fact they say the opposite, or nothing at all.

"Help"—The Number One Weasel Word

The biggest weasel word used in advertising doublespeak is "help." Now "help" only means to aid or assist, nothing more. It does not mean to conquer, stop, eliminate, end, solve, heal, cure, or anything else. But once the ad says "help," it can say just about anything after that because "help" qualifies everything coming after it. The trick is that the claim that comes after the weasel word is usually so strong and so dramatic that you forget the word "help" and concentrate only on the dramatic claim. You read into the ad a message that the ad does not contain. More importantly, the advertiser is not responsible for the claim that you read into the ad, even though the advertiser wrote the ad so you would read that claim into it.

The next time you see an ad for a cold medicine that promises that it "helps relieve cold symptoms fast," don't rush out to buy it. Ask yourself what this claim is really saying. Remember, "helps" means only that the medicine will aid or assist. What will it aid or assist in doing? Why, "relieve" your cold "symptoms." "Relieve" only means to ease, alleviate, or mitigate, not to stop, end, or cure. Nor does the claim say how much relieving this medicine will do. Nowhere does this ad claim it will cure anything. In fact, the ad doesn't even claim it will *do* anything at all. The ad only claims that it will aid in relieving (not curing) your cold symptoms, which are probably a runny nose, watery eyes, and a headache. In other words, this medicine probably contains a standard decongestant and some aspirin. By the way, what does "fast" mean? Ten minutes, one hour, one day? What is fast to one person can be very slow to another. Fast is another weasel word.

Ad claims using "help" are among the most popular ads. One says, "Helps keep you young looking," but then a lot of things will help keep you young looking, including exercise, rest, good nutrition, and a facelift. More importantly, this ad doesn't say the product will keep you young, only "young *looking*." Someone may look young to one person and old to another.

A toothpaste ad says, "Helps prevent cavities," but it doesn't say it will actually prevent cavities. Brushing your teeth regularly, avoiding sugars in food, and flossing daily will also help prevent cavities. A liquid cleaner ad says, "Helps keep your home germ free," but it doesn't say it actually kills germs, nor does it even specify which germs it might kill.

"Help" is such a useful weasel word that it is often combined with other action-verb weasel words such as "fight" and "control." Consider the claim, "Helps control dandruff symptoms with regular use." What does it really say? It will assist in controlling (not eliminating, stopping, ending, or curing) the *symptoms* of dandruff, not the cause of dandruff nor the dandruff itself. What are the symptoms of dandruff? The ad deliberately leaves that undefined, but assume that the symptoms referred to in the ad are the flaking and itching commonly associated with dandruff. But just shampooing with *any* shampoo will temporarily eliminate these symptoms, so this shampoo isn't any different from any other. Finally, in order to benefit from this product, you must use it regularly. What is "regular use"—daily, weekly, hourly? Using another shampoo "regularly" will have the same effect. Nowhere does this advertising claim say this particular shampoo stops, eliminates, or cures dandruff. In fact, this claim says nothing at all, thanks to all the weasel words.

Look at ads in magazines and newspapers, listen to ads on radio and television, and you'll find the word "help" in ads for all kinds of products. How often do you read or hear such phrases as "helps stop . . . ," "helps overcome . . . ," "helps eliminate . . . ," "helps you feel . . . ," or "helps you look . . ."? If you start looking for this weasel word in advertising, you'll be amazed at how often it occurs. Analyze the claims in the ads using "help," and you will discover that these ads are really saying nothing.

There are plenty of other weasel words used in advertising. In fact, there are so many that to list them all would fill the rest of this book. But, in order to identify the doublespeak of advertising and understand the real meaning of an ad, you have to be aware of the most popular weasel words in advertising today.

Virtually Spotless

One of the most powerful weasel words is "virtually," a word so innocent that most people don't pay any attention to it when it is used in an advertising claim. But watch out. "Virtually" is used in advertising claims that appear to make specific, definite promises when there is no promise. After all, what does "virtually" mean? It means "in essence or effect, although not in fact." Look at that definition again. "Virtually" means *not in fact*. It does *not* mean "almost" or "just about the same as," or anything else. And before you dismiss all this concern over such a small word, remember that small words can have big consequences.

In 1971 a federal court rendered its decision on a case brought by a woman who became pregnant while taking birth control pills. She sued the manufacturer, Eli Lilly and Company, for breach of warranty. The woman lost her case. Basing its ruling on a statement in the pamphlet accompanying the pills, which stated that, "When taken as directed, the tablets offer virtually 100% protection," the court ruled that there was no warranty, expressed or implied, that the pills were absolutely effective. In its ruling, the court pointed out that, according to *Webster's Third New International Dictionary,* "virtually" means "almost entirely" and clearly does not mean "absolute" (*Whittington* v. *Eli Lilly and Company,* 333 F. Supp. 98). In other words, the Eli Lilly company was really saying that its birth control pill, even when taken as directed, *did not in fact* provide 100 percent protection against pregnancy. But Eli Lilly didn't want to put it that way because then many women might not have bought Lilly's birth control pills.

The next time you see the ad that says that this dishwasher detergent "leaves dishes virtually spotless," just remember how advertisers twist the meaning of the weasel word "virtually." You can have lots of spots on your dishes after using this detergent and the ad claim will still be true, because what this claim really means is that this detergent does not *in fact* leave your dishes spotless. Whenever you see or hear an ad claim that uses the word "virtually," just translate that claim into its real meaning.

So the television set that is "virtually trouble free" becomes the television set that is not in fact trouble free, the "virtually foolproof operation" of any appliance becomes an operation that is in fact not foolproof, and the product that "virtually never needs service" becomes the product that is not in fact service free.

New and Improved

If "new" is the most frequently used word on a product package, "improved" is the second most frequent. In fact, the two words are almost always used together. It seems just about everything sold these days is "new and improved." The next time you're in the supermarket, try counting the number of times you see these words on products. But you'd better do it while you're walking down just one aisle, otherwise you'll need a calculator to keep track of your counting.

Just what do these words mean? The use of the word "new" is restricted by regulations, so an advertiser can't just use the word on a product or in an ad without meeting certain requirements. For example, a product is considered new for about six months during a national advertising campaign. If the product is being advertised only in a limited test market area, the word can be used longer, and in some instances has been used for as long as two years.

What makes a product "new"? Some products have been around for a long time, yet every once in a while you discover that they are being advertised as "new." Well, an advertiser can call a product new if there has been "a material functional change" in the product. What is "a material functional change," you ask? Good question. In fact it's such a good question it's being asked all the time. It's up to the manufacturer to prove that the product has undergone such a change. And if the manufacturer isn't challenged on the claim, then there's no one to stop it. Moreover, the change does not have to be an improvement in the product. One manufacturer added an artificial lemon scent to a cleaning product and called it "new and improved," even though the product did not clean any better than without the lemon scent. The manufacturer defended the use of the word "new" on the grounds that the artificial scent changed the chemical formula of the product and therefore constituted "a material functional change."

Which brings up the word "improved." When used in advertising, "improved" does not mean "made better." It only means "changed" or "different from before." So, if the detergent maker puts a plastic pour spout on the box of detergent, the product has been "improved," and away we go with a whole new advertising campaign. Or, if the cereal maker adds more fruit or a different kind of fruit to the cereal, there's an improved product. Now you know why manufacturers are constantly making little changes in their products. Whole new advertising campaigns, designed to convince you that the product has been changed for the better, are based on small changes in superficial aspects of a product. The next time you see an ad for an "improved" product, ask yourself what was wrong with the old one. Ask yourself just how "improved" the product is. Finally, you might check to see whether the "improved" version costs more than the unimproved one. After all, someone has to pay for the millions of dollars spent advertising the improved product.

Of course, advertisers really like to run ads that claim a product is "new and improved." While what constitutes a "new" product may be subject to some regulation, "improved" is a subjective judgment. A manufacturer changes the shape of its stick deodorant, but the shape doesn't improve the function of the deodorant. That is, changing the shape doesn't affect the deodorizing ability of the deodorant, so the manufacturer calls it "improved." Another manufacturer adds ammonia to its liquid cleaner and calls it "new and improved." Since adding ammonia does affect the cleaning ability of the product, there has been a "material functional change" in the product, and the manufacturer can now call its cleaner "new," and "improved" as well. Now the weasel words "new and improved" are plastered all over the package and are the basis for a multimillion-dollar ad campaign. But after six months the word "new" will have to go, until someone can dream up another change in the product. Perhaps it will be adding color to the liquid, or changing the shape of the package, or maybe adding a new dripless pour spout, or perhaps a _____. The "improvements" are endless, and so are the new advertising claims and campaigns.

"New" is just too useful and powerful a word in advertising for advertisers to pass it up easily. So they use weasel words that say "new" without really saying it. One of their favorites is "introducing," as in, "Introducing improved Tide," or "Introducing the stain remover." The first is simply saying, here's our improved soap; the second, here's our new advertising campaign for our detergent. Another favorite is "now," as in, "Now there's Sinex," which simply means that Sinex is available. Then there are phrases like "Today's Chevrolet," "Presenting Dristan," and "A fresh way to start the day." The list is really endless because advertisers are always finding new ways to say "new" without really saying it. If there is a second edition of this book, I'll just call it the "new and improved" edition. Wouldn't you really rather have a "new and improved" edition of this book rather than a "second" edition?

Acts Fast

"Acts" and "works" are two popular weasel words in advertising because they bring action to the product and to the advertising claim. When you see the ad for the cough syrup that "Acts on the cough control center," ask yourself what this cough syrup is claiming to do. Well, it's just claiming to "act," to do something, to perform an action. What is it that the cough syrup does? The ad doesn't say. It only claims to perform an action or do something on your "cough control center." By the way, what and where is your "cough control center"? I don't remember learning about that part of the body in human biology class.

Ads that use such phrases as "acts fast," "acts against," "acts to prevent," and the like are saying essentially nothing, because "act" is a word empty of any specific meaning. The ads are always careful not to specify exactly what "act" the product performs. Just because a brand of aspirin claims to "act fast" for headache relief doesn't mean this aspirin is any better than any other aspirin. What is the "act" that this aspirin performs? You're never told. Maybe it just dissolves quickly. Since aspirin is a parity product, all aspirin is the same and therefore functions the same.

Works Like Anything Else

If you don't find the word "acts" in an ad, you will probably find the weasel word "works." In fact, the two words are almost interchangeable in advertising. Watch out for ads that say a product "works against," "works like," "works for," or "works longer." As with "acts," "works" is the same meaningless verb used to make you think that this product really does something, and maybe even something special or unique. But "works," like "acts," is basically a word empty of any specific meaning.

Like Magic

Whenever advertisers want you to stop thinking about the product and to start thinking about something bigger, better, or more attractive than the product, they use that very popular weasel word, "like." The word "like" is the advertiser's equivalent of a magician's use of misdirection. "Like" gets you to ignore the product and concentrate on the claim the advertiser is making about it. "For skin like peaches and cream" claims the ad for a skin cream. What is this ad really claiming? It doesn't say this cream will give you peaches-and-cream skin. There is no verb in this claim, so it doesn't even mention using the product. How is skin ever like "peaches and cream"? Remember, ads must be read literally and exactly, according to the dictionary definition of words. (Remember "virtually" in the Eli Lilly case.) The ad is making absolutely no promise or claim whatsoever for this skin cream. If you think this cream will give you soft, smooth, youthful-looking skin, you are the one who has read that meaning into the ad.

The wine that claims "It's like taking a trip to France" wants you to think about a romantic evening in Paris as you walk along the boulevard after a wonderful meal in an intimate little bistro. Of course, you don't really believe that a wine can take you to France, but the goal of the ad is to get you to think pleasant, romantic thoughts about France and not about how the wine tastes or how expensive it may be. That little word "like" has taken you away from crushed grapes into a world of your own imaginative making. Who knows, maybe the next time you buy wine, you'll think those pleasant thoughts when you see this brand of wine, and you'll buy it. Or, maybe you weren't even thinking about buying wine at all, but now you just might pick up a bottle the next time you're shopping. Ah, the power of "like" in advertising.

How about the most famous "like" claim of all, "Winston tastes good like a cigarette should"? Ignoring the grammatical error here, you might want to know what this claim is saying. Whether a cigarette tastes good or bad is a subjective judgment because what tastes good to one person may well taste horrible to another. Not everyone likes fried snails, even if they are called escargot. (*De gustibus non est disputandum,* which was probably the Roman rule for advertising as well as for defending the games in the Colosseum.) There are many people who say all cigarettes taste terrible, other people who say only some cigarettes taste all right, and still others who say all cigarettes taste good. Who's right? Everyone, because taste is a matter of personal judgment.

Moreover, note the use of the conditional, "should." The complete claim is, "Winston tastes good like a cigarette should taste." But should cigarettes taste good? Again, this is a matter of personal judgment and probably depends most on one's experiences with smoking. So, the Winston ad is simply saying that Winston cigarettes are just like any other cigarette:

Some people like them and some people don't. On that statement R. J. Reynolds conducted a very successful multimillion-dollar advertising campaign that helped keep Winston the number-two-selling cigarette in the United States, close behind number one, Marlboro.

CAN IT BE UP TO THE CLAIM?

Analyzing ads for doublespeak requires that you pay attention to every word in the ad and determine what each word really means. Advertisers try to wrap their claims in language that sounds concrete, specific, and objective, when in fact the language of advertising is anything but. Your job is to read carefully and listen critically so that when the announcer says that "Crest can be of significant value . . ." you know immediately that this claim says absolutely nothing. Where is the doublespeak in this ad? Start with the second word.

Once again, you have to look at what words really mean, not what you think they mean or what the advertiser wants you to think they mean. The ad for Crest only says that using Crest "can be" of "significant value." What really throws you off in this ad is the brilliant use of "significant." It draws your attention to the word "value" and makes you forget that the ad only claims that Crest "can be." The ad doesn't say that Crest *is* of value, only that it is "able" or "possible" to be of value, because that's all that "can" means.

It's so easy to miss the importance of those little words, "can be." Almost as easy as missing the importance of the words "up to" in an ad. These words are very popular in sale ads. You know, the ones that say, "Up to 50% Off!" Now, what does that claim mean? Not much, because the store or manufacturer has to reduce the price of only a few items by 50 percent. Everything else can be reduced a lot less, or not even reduced. Moreover, don't you want to know 50 percent off of what? Is it 50 percent off the "manufacturer's suggested list price," which is the highest possible price? Was the price artificially inflated and then reduced? In other ads, "up to" expresses an ideal situation. The medicine that works "up to ten times faster," the battery that lasts "up to twice as long," and the soap that gets you "up to twice as clean" all are based on ideal situations for using those products, situations in which you can be sure you will never find yourself.

UNFINISHED WORDS

Unfinished words are a kind of "up to" claim in advertising. The claim that a battery lasts "up to twice as long" usually doesn't finish the comparison—twice as long as what? A birthday candle? A tank of gas? A cheap battery made in a country not noted for its technological achievements? The implication is that the battery lasts twice as long as batteries made by other battery makers, or twice as long as earlier model batteries made by the advertiser, but the ad doesn't really make these claims. You read these claims into the ad, aided by the visual images the advertiser so carefully provides.

Unfinished words depend on you to finish them, to provide the words the advertisers so thoughtfully left out of the ad. Pall Mall cigarettes were once advertised as "A longer finer and milder smoke." The question is, longer, finer, and milder than what? The aspirin that claims it contains "Twice as much of the pain reliever doctors recommend most" doesn't tell you what pain reliever it contains twice as much of. (By the way, it's aspirin. That's right; it just contains twice the amount of aspirin. And how much is twice the amount? Twice of what amount?) Panadol boasts that "nobody reduces fever faster," but, since Panadol is a parity product, this claim simply means that Panadol isn't any better than any other product in its parity class. "You can be sure if it's Westinghouse," you're told, but just exactly what it is you can be sure of is never mentioned. "Magnavox gives you more" doesn't tell you what you get more of. More value? More television? More than they gave you before? It sounds nice, but it means nothing, until you fill in the claim with your own words, the words the advertiser didn't use. Since each of us fills in the claim differently, the ad and the product can become all things to all people, and not promise a single thing.

Unfinished words abound in advertising because they appear to promise so much. More importantly, they can be joined with powerful visual images on television to appear to be making significant promises about a product's effectiveness without really making any promises. In a television ad, the aspirin product that claims fast relief can show a person with a headache taking the product and then, in what appears to be a matter of minutes, claiming complete relief. This visual image is far more powerful than any claim made in unfinished words. Indeed, the visual image completes the unfinished words for you, filling in with pictures what the words leave out. And you thought that ads didn't affect you. What brand of aspirin do you use?

Some years ago, Ford's advertisements proclaimed "Ford LTD—700% quieter." Now, what do you think Ford was claiming with these unfinished words? What was the Ford LTD quieter than? A Cadillac? A Mercedes Benz? A BMW? Well, when the FTC asked Ford to substantiate this unfinished claim, Ford replied that it meant that the inside of the LTD was 700% quieter than the outside. How did you finish those unfinished words when you first read them? Did you even come close to Ford's meaning?

Combining Weasel Words

A lot of ads don't fall neatly into one category or another because they use a variety of different devices and words. Different weasel words are often combined to make an ad claim. The claim, "Coffee-Mate gives coffee more body, more flavor," uses Unfinished Words ("more" than what?) and also uses words that have no specific meaning ("body" and "flavor"). Along with "taste" (remember the Winston ad and its claim to taste good), "body" and "flavor" mean nothing because their meaning is entirely subjective. To you, "body" in coffee might mean thick, black, almost bitter coffee, while I might take it to mean a light brown, delicate coffee. Now, if you think you understood that last sentence, read it again, because it said nothing of objective value; it was filled with weasel words of no specific meaning: "thick," "black," "bitter," "light brown," and "delicate." Each of those words has no specific, objective meaning, because each of us can interpret them differently.

Try this slogan: "Looks, smells, tastes like ground-roast coffee." So, are you now going to buy Taster's Choice instant coffee because of this ad? "Looks," "smells," and "tastes" are all words with no specific meaning and depend on your interpretation of them for any meaning. Then there's that great weasel word "like," which simply suggests a comparison but does not make the actual connection between the product and the quality. Besides, do you know what "ground-roast" coffee is? I don't, but it sure sounds good. So, out of seven words in this ad, four are definite weasel words, two are quite meaningless, and only one has any clear meaning.

Remember the Anacin ad—"Twice as much of the pain reliever doctors recommend most"? There's a whole lot of weaseling going on in this ad. First, what's the pain reliever they're talking about in this ad? Aspirin, of course. In fact, any time you see or hear an ad using those words "pain reliever," you can automatically substitute the word "aspirin" for them. (Makers of acetaminophen and ibuprofen pain relievers are careful in their advertising to identify their products as nonaspirin products.) So, now we know that Anacin has aspirin in it. Moreover, we know that Anacin has twice as much aspirin in it, but we don't know twice as much as what. Does it have twice as much aspirin as an ordinary aspirin tablet? If so, what is an ordinary aspirin tablet, and how much aspirin does it contain? Twice as much as Excedrin or Bufferin? Twice as much as a chocolate chip cookie? Remember those Unfinished Words and how they lead you on without saying anything.

Finally, what about those doctors who are doing all that recommending? Who are they? How many of them are there? What kind of doctors are they? What are their qualifications? Who asked them about recommending pain relievers? What other pain relievers did they recommend? And there are a whole lot more questions about this "poll" of doctors to which I'd like to know the answers, but you get the point. Sometimes, when I call my doctor, she tells me to take two aspirin and call her office in the morning. Is that where Anacin got this ad?

Name: _____ Date: _____

UNDERSTANDING THE TEXT

1. According to Lutz, what are "weasel words," and why are advertisers so eager to use them?

2. According to Lutz, what is the particular effect of the word "like"?

3. What is an example of an "unfinished word," and why might advertisers find it useful?

ADDITIONAL READINGS

Kilbourne, Jean. *Deadly Persuasion: Why Women and Girls Must Fight the Addictive Power of Advertising.* New York: Free Press, 1999.

Marchand, Roland. *Advertising the American Dream: Making Way for Modernity, 1920–1940.* Berkeley: U of California P, 1985.

Savan, Leslie. *The Sponsored Life: Ads, TV, and American Culture.* Philadelphia: Temple UP, 1994.

Schudson, Michael. *Advertising: The Uneasy Persuasion: Its Dubious Impact on American Society.* New York: Basic Books, 1984.

Twitchell, James B. *ADCULT USA: The Triumph of Advertising in American Culture.* New York: Columbia UP, 1996.

CHAPTER III

Gender Matters

PART ONE

Representations of Men and Women on Television, in Film, and in Literature

Genies and Witches

Susan Douglas

While my friends and I were upstairs blasting Beatles records and planning how many times we would go see *A Hard Day's Night,* our mothers were downstairs in the kitchen or the laundry room fuming, and fantasizing about a jailbreak of their own. They soon discovered they weren't alone. Political rumblings about women's second-class status, and their desire for more opportunities and choices, now registered on America's media seismographs. Some of our mothers, it turned out, wanted to break down some barricades themselves. The prevailing line in the print media of the early 1960s was that American women, as the *Ladies' Home Journal* put it, "never had it so good": they controlled the family's purse strings and the nation's wealth, had an array of household technologies that made housework effortless, had plenty of free time to play bridge or do volunteer work, and enjoyed unprecedented equality. The *Journal* continued, "They have rights and opportunities today the likes of which the Western world has never seen. . . . Indeed, women today are in many respects much better off than men." In its special supplement of October 1962 entitled "The American Female," *Harper's* maintained that American women were "repelled by the slogans of old-fashioned feminism."[1]

But *Harper's* also thought it saw a trend in 1962 and named it "crypto-feminism." Women were reexamining their roles as "wives, mothers, and members of the human race" because motherhood was short-lived as a full-time job, more women wanted or needed to work outside the home, yet many women found that "the institutions that are supposed to serve women are not very helpful." Women, in fact, faced a "void." Articles kept appearing in the early and mid-1960s with titles like "Our Greatest Waste of Talent Is Women," "Women—Neglected Assets," and "Women—Emancipation Is Still to Come," articles at odds with the "women have it made" line. Clearly, a new turbulence was emerging.

Professional women, in particular, were fed up with their second-class salaries and their image as freaks of nature, and they lobbied the Kennedy administration to do something. In one of the more famous scenes from John Kennedy's press conferences, the indefatigable journalist May Craig stood up and asked the president what he was doing for women. Kennedy quipped that he was sure that, whatever it was, it wasn't enough, implying that women were *never* satisfied, and shared a big laugh with the predominantly male press corps. Nonetheless, in 1961, Kennedy established a Presidential Commission on the Status of Women, with Eleanor Roosevelt as its head, to ascertain how to eradicate the "prejudices and outmoded customs [that] act as barriers to the full realization of women's basic rights." The Kennedy administration also outlawed discrimination in the federal civil service and in 1963 pushed through Congress the Equal Pay Act, which prohibited paying men and women different salaries for the same jobs. The Kennedy Commission's report, *American Women,* published just six weeks before the president's death, recommended the establishment of child-care services, advocated equal opportunities for women in employment and education, urged women to seek public office, and argued that the government's mission should be to secure "equality of rights for women." The front-page story in *The New York Times* headlined the report with "U.S. Panel Urges Women to Sue for Equal Rights."[2]

The real tip-off that many of our mothers hated their assigned positions, weren't sure whether to hate themselves or the men around them, and were tired of straddling the untenable contradictions in their lives was the eagerness with which thousands of them ran out to buy Betty Friedan's *The Feminine Mystique,* which they put on the best-seller list from April through July 1963. In 1964, while teenagers were discovering the Beatles, older women made *The Feminine Mystique* the number one best-selling paperback in the country.[3] Trashing "biology as destiny," Freud, and penis envy, castigating the phony happy housewife heroine of the women's magazines, and enumerating the emptiness, resentments, and self-doubt of many housewives' lives, Friedan reminded women of the unfinished work of the women's movement and urged her sisters to stop being doormats and to fight for equality.

Portions of Friedan's book were condensed in women's magazines, and the book inspired other investigations into the status of women. In "Whatever Happened to Women's Rights?" published in the *Atlantic Monthly* in March 1964, Paul Foley stacked up a tower of statistics to emphasize women's second-class status. Only two U.S. senators and 11 of the 435 members of the House of Representatives were women. Only 3 of the 422 federal judges were female. Women were confined to low-paying, dead-end jobs, they married too young, and they were not encouraged to pursue advanced degrees. Foley's article was condensed and reprinted in *Reader's Digest.*[4] *U.S. News and World Report* in 1966 also itemized the various ways in which women were discriminated against and underrepresented in American business and political institutions, and it noted that sociologists "warn that the U.S. may be building up a new generation of 'unhappy women.'" The article also focused on a significant trend: women were "going to work in droves," often combining a job, marriage, and motherhood. But the article concluded that "'full equality' for women appears far off."[5] Foley, however, claimed that "for public scrutiny on the American woman, 1963 was a banner year," and he was right: this was to be a turning point.

It was within this context of prefeminist agitation, combined with the unsettling phenomenon of wild packs of girls chasing the four mop-tops across America, that there appeared on TV, and with a vengeance, a new female mutant, a hybrid of old and new, of negative and positive stereotypes. We saw the ghoulish Morticia in *The Addams Family* as a femme fatale; a genie who was not a rotund, balding man but a shapely and beautiful young woman; a witch who was not a murderous old hag but an attractive young housewife; a cute, perky nun who could fly.

All of a sudden, female characters in TV sitcoms were capable of magic. They had fantastic supernatural powers. Yet this was more than just the ultimate in kitsch or the triumph of special effects. If we put these TV shows and the impulses behind them on the shrink's couch for a minute, we see that a significant proportion of the pop culture moguls were trying to acknowledge the impending release of female sexual and political energy, while keeping it all safely in a straitjacket. Sure, it would be great if women, especially young women, were more sexually liberated. But prefeminist rumblings about economic and political liberation were another matter. You could almost see these guys holding their nuts for dear life. Sensing they were playing with fire, they tried to contain it technologically, through images of levitation, twitching noses, and poofs of fake smoke.

In these shows, the potentially monstrous and grotesque was beautified and tamed; what we saw, in other words, was the containment of the threat posed by unleashed female sexuality, especially in the wake of Beatlemania and Helen Gurley Brown. Since viewers had been socialized to regard female sexuality as monstrous, TV producers addressed the anxieties about letting it loose by domesticating the monster, by making her pretty and sometimes slavish, by shrinking her and keeping her locked up in a bottle, and by playing the situation for laughs.[6]

In shows like *Bewitched, I Dream of Jeannie,* and *The Flying Nun,* a new version of Pandora's box was acted out. Seemingly normal-looking female characters possessed magical powers, which men begged them not to use; if women did use them, their powers had to be confined to the private sphere. Whenever women used these powers outside the home, in the public sphere, the male world was turned completely upside down. Business simply could not be conducted as usual, and logic and rationality were often overthrown and rendered useless. Men were made impotent by these powers, and the husbands (or husband figures) of such women were stripped of their male authority and made to look foolish and incompetent in front of their male superiors. After all, how can you explain men turned into dogs, or co-workers sent to Antarctica? Although the men insisted (usually unsuccessfully) that their women not use these powers, there were three exceptions that the shows' narrative systems permitted: to complete domestic chores, to compete over men, and to help the men out of embarrassing situations, which usually had been created by the woman's unauthorized use of her magic powers in the first place.

The two most successful examples of this genre were *Bewitched* and *I Dream of Jeannie. Bewitched* was extremely popular; it was the biggest hit series produced by ABC up to that time, running from 1964 to 1972. For its first five seasons it was among the top twenty highest rated shows; the year of its debut, it soared to number two, topped only by *Bonanza*.[7] It is easy to dismiss *Bewitched* as one of the dumbest and kitchiest shows ever produced, but it would be a mistake to do so. *Bewitched* was such a success in part because of its novelty and its skillful use of special effects, which played to some fairly basic fantasies about magic and control. But it was also successful because it was one of the few shows with an appealing female lead character who offered female viewers a respite from, as well as a critique of, male domination. In *Bewitched* we have a woman's dream and a man's nightmare. Darrin was surrounded by an endearing yet constantly troublesome matriarchy, a domestic situation in which his wife, mother-in-law, daughter, and other relatives were all witches, endowed with magical powers, which constantly threatened his professional status and his authority as head of the household.

A show like *Bewitched* was an updated, blander, yet trickier version of *I Love Lucy*. Lucy didn't have magical powers, and she certainly didn't need them to get into trouble. Always struggling to break out of the confines of the domestic sphere and enter Ricky's glamorous world in the public limelight, Lucy was set up by the physical slapstick of the show as a clown, as a woman constantly using her face and body to fight the strictures of femininity. Samantha, however, was not a clown: she always remained a lady. This was one of the show's many concessions to traditional femininity and conventional gender roles. Elizabeth Montgomery didn't have to use her face or body the way Lucy did: she had technically mastered special effects to be disruptive for her. Aside from twitching her nose, nodding her head, or raising her hands, she did not become physically grotesque when disrupting Darrin's world. Young, slim, blond, and beautiful, with practical, intelligent ideas about what needed to be done in her community, yet a witch, Samantha stood at the intersection between middle-class definitions of the ideal young wife and rebelliousness against those definitions.

Samantha embodied important contradictions, for she was a happy, respectable suburban housewife who exerted power beyond the kitchen or the living room. She was at once traditional and modern. The show often suggested that women, especially younger women, were smarter, more creative, and more versatile than men. Samantha had magical powers, but she also excelled at the more mundane female duties of ensuring that social interactions ran smoothly. Often it was up to her to come up with an explanation to Darrin's boss or other outsiders for the bizarre goings-on. Invariably, her explanation placated the irate or confused father figure, and often she succeeded in using the explanation to make Darrin or some other hapless man look good in the eyes of the older male authority figure. Samantha engineered the outcome so that Darrin got the credit for coming up with a great idea or doing a great job, but the audience knew who was the real power behind the throne. And it was key to the show that Darrin have all the sex appeal of egg albumen. Had he really been handsome, sexy, or magnetic, her magic and power would have been too threatening, both to the man and to the viewer.

The question of whether Samantha could use her powers, and under what circumstances, defined the entire series. In the first show, on their wedding night, just before they are supposed to go to bed, Samantha reveals to Darrin that she is a witch. Dressed in her peignoir, Samantha shows a skeptical Darrin just what she can do by making a broken cigarette lighter he's trying to use suddenly ejaculate a flame and by moving an ashtray around the coffee table so he can't successfully flick his ash. (And you thought all that subliminal stuff only went on in liquor ads.) When he nearly faints realizing she really is a witch, Samantha kisses him seductively and he says they'll discuss the problem tomorrow. We know what happens next. The mere suggestion that these two are going to have sex was revolutionary for television at that time. The next day, Darrin makes Samantha promise never to use her powers again. Samantha assures him, "Darling, I'll be the best wife a man ever had." He gets specific. "You're going to have to learn how to be a suburban housewife. . . . And you'll have to learn to cook and clean and keep house and go to my mother's house every Friday night." Samantha says it sounds wonderful. We don't believe her for a minute. There wasn't a woman in the audience who would have given up that kind of power.

We know she won't be able to keep her promise, and her restraint is tested right away. A former girlfriend of Darrin's, dark-haired, rich, seductive, and patronizingly sophisticated—in other words, a bitch—invites Darrin and Samantha over for dinner. During the course of the evening, she openly flirts with Darrin while making insufferably catty remarks to Samantha about her hair and clothes; she's clearly the real demon here. Under an assault like this, when another woman is challenging her for her man, Samantha can't possibly keep her promise to Darrin. Using her magical powers, she makes the rival's hair fall into her eyes, places a large hunk of spinach on one of her front teeth, has her dinner slide into her lap, her dress nearly fall off, and her wig blow off her head. The rival is humiliated and Samantha's use of witchcraft completely justified. At the end of the show, in what became a classic scene in *Bewitched,* Darrin is urging Samantha to come up to bed, and we know exactly what he's got on his mind. But the kitchen is a mess. Samantha says she'll be right up, then raises her arms and zaps the kitchen clean. She says with a self-satisfied smile, "Maybe I'll taper off," a joke rife with ambiguity. Taper off, my ass.

It is also important to note that Samantha's mother—indeed, all her relatives—is strongly opposed to Samantha not using her powers just because of Darrin. Endora constantly casts him as a mere mortal to whom Samantha is superior, and as someone who is constraining Samantha, trying to make her life too confined, boring, and predictable. For Endora, Samantha has another, more exciting destiny, a destiny that spans history and geography. And while Samantha insists that marriage to Darrin is what she wants, she gets to have it both ways, to have the reassurances of being a suburban wife and the adventures of being a more unconventional woman.

What is especially interesting about the show, premiering as it did in 1964, not long after Betty Friedan's *The Feminine Mystique* was a best-seller, is the way it offered, yet sought to diminish, a criticism of female confinement in the home. It is hard to imagine a woman watching who did not identify with the fantasy of cleaning the kitchen or preparing dinner just by twitching her nose. But there were other telling fantasies, repeated week in and week out, about having some real influence in the outside world, and how the world might be better if men just listened to women once in a while. In an episode from the first season, Samantha and Endora eat at Mario's Pizza and decide the food is so good that Mario deserves some publicity. Samantha, by twitching her nose, stops the presses at the local paper and inserts a full-page ad that reads "Eat at Mario's." When the ad comes out, Mario's competitor, the head of Perfect Pizza, is outraged and drops Darrin's ad agency for letting Mario's get the upper hand. When Samantha learns that her husband's account is in jeopardy, she works to repair the damage. She and Endora, using their magic, fill the town's billboards with ads, cover the sky with skywriting, and place "Eat Perfect Pizza" placards on all the pedestrians in town. The delight they take in orchestrating this ad campaign is clear as each tackles a new medium, giggling and saying, "It's your turn," and "Now yours." At the end of the show, with the account saved, Darrin complains, "I'd appreciate your letting me handle my accounts by myself," to which Endora responds sarcastically, "Do you think you can?" Samantha insists with a smile, "Of course he can—except under special circumstances."

In other episodes, Samantha uses her magic to get the mayor to fix the town's traffic lights, to persuade a French fashion designer to design clothes that look good on "the average American woman" and not just on fashion models, and to expose political corruption and help get a reform candidate elected to the city council. In this last episode, Darrin wrongly accuses a corrupt councilman of fraudulent dealings in a city construction contract. Samantha and Endora transport themselves to the councilman's office and use their witchcraft to open his locked file cabinet and study his records. It takes Samantha just a few seconds to confirm that all his dealings, with the sole exception of the one that pea-brained Darrin had tried to expose, had been crooked, another Darrin blunder that causes Endora great mirth. Yet Endora casts various spells to vindicate Darrin and indict the councilman. At the end of the show, we see Darrin, completely befuddled, mumbling to himself as he walks upstairs, while Samantha and Endora stand shoulder to shoulder, leaning slightly into each other with their arms crossed over their chests, smiling knowingly and patronizingly at poor, dumbo Darrin.

The repeated combination of magic, diplomacy (her forte), and good common sense made Samantha's solutions to problems the ones that were clearly the most viable and sensible. Here was a housewife with logical and creative ideas about how to make the world better, and with an ability to act on those ideas and get them a fair hearing, even if she had to do so through her bumbling surrogate, Darrin. (The character was such a zero that Dick York, Darrin number one, was easily replaced in 1969 by another Dick, last name Sargent, as Darrin number two.) Samantha's interventions in advertising, politics, and marketing were a mixed blessing, but often they expedited the solution to a particular problem. And despite his anger and frustration over the personal humiliations, Darrin always loved and admired Samantha. This was one of the first post-1950s sitcoms to show a husband and wife sharing a double bed, and we often saw Darrin looking at Sam with desire.

Samantha stood in contrast to the older women in the show, who were grotesque by comparison and conformed more closely to the age-old archetype of the witch as a wrinkled and disorderly crone.[8] Grotesque women—the battle-axes, villainesses, shrews, and over-the-hill whores of popular culture—with their aging faces and sagging, protruding bodies, were ostracized, pitied, and often destroyed in movies and TV shows because they had moved outside the norms of femininity. But such women also rebelled against and often disrupted the rigid gender codes of society, and the female grotesque par excellence of *Bewitched*— Endora—was no exception. With her overly bouffant, bright red hairdos, two-inch-long false eyelashes, and thick eyeliner that shot up at a forty-five-degree angle to her eyes, Endora made gestures to femininity that were exaggerated, like a Mardi Gras mask. But it was this defiance that gave her power, and made her such a liberatory character. Darrin hated her interventions, and often Samantha did too. She was blunt, honest, catty, and self-indulgent, and she did not waste her time trying to soothe others' feelings or placate men the way Samantha did. She was a caricature of the meddling, hard-edged mother-in-law girls were supposed to cast themselves against. But as played by Agnes Moorehead, Endora also had an arch sophistication and a biting tongue that enabled her to get away with—and enjoy—her assaults on arbitrary male authority, especially when it was imposed on her daughter. Female viewers agreed with her dismissive assessment of Darrin as an impotent doofus and took great delight in her outrageous transgressions, and in her unmovable loyalty to Samantha. Endora got to say what many women wished they could say, and her complete indifference to the approval of men was a joy and relief to watch, even as we knew we did not want to be like her.

The other grotesque female, the baggy-faced, chinless, relentlessly nosy neighbor Mrs. Kravitz, was given none of Endora's protective coloration. There was no masquerade of femininity here. Mrs. Kravitz was a warning, the darker side of female aging. She kept spying on the Stevens house, looking where she wasn't supposed to. Thus, even though she saw "the truth," her reports made her appear crazy. Ugly, unadorned, shrill, she never succeeded in getting anyone else to see what she saw. She was the parody of the old housewife with too much time on her hands and nothing to do except live through others. Old women who become voyeurs, who neglect their appearance and their husbands, are pathetic. This, girls, is who you could become if you pay too much attention to the outside world and not enough to your face, body, and home. Mrs. Kravitz embodied the costs of not adhering to traditional femininity: her husband held her in contempt, and everyone else laughed at and pitied her. Unlike Samantha, who knew how to juggle her domestic duties and her forays into the outside world, Mrs. Kravitz had lost her balance. She spent too much time looking out her window and not enough looking in her mirror, too much surveillance in the wrong direction.

The character we identified with, Samantha—most frequently referred to by her masculine nickname, Sam—was passive and active, flouted her husband's authority yet complied with the role of suburban housewife, was both conforming and rebellious: she gave expression to traditional norms and prefeminist aspirations. The show hailed young female viewers by providing, and seeking to reconcile, images of female equality—and, often, even images of female superiority—with images of female subordination. Samantha's talent and success as a wife lay in knowing when to intervene and when to hold back. She often made mistakes, but because she had the traditional female traits of empathy, tact, flattery, and the ability to craft a compromise, all coupled with her magic, she was able repeatedly to rescue her husband, herself, and her marriage.

The show acknowledged that young women wanted more than confinement in the home, that housework was drudgery, and that husbands were often inept clods. Samantha skillfully managed the contradictions of being a superior being (a witch with power) and a subordinate being (a wife with a husband). She made these contradictions work for her, and she also smoothed them over, demonstrating the juggling act young girls were meant to do when they got married. While the show reaffirmed the primacy of traditional female roles and behaviors, it also provided powerful visual representations of what many young women would like to do if they just had a little power: zap that housework and a few men as well.

I Dream of Jeannie ran from 1965 to 1970 and also featured a woman with magical powers, but this show was predicated on a more flagrant sexual display of Jeannie's body and her desires, even if the network censors made sure Barbara Eden's belly button was discreetly hidden. The premise rested on a male fantasy of a regular guy discovering a beautiful, naive, unworldly woman who will do anything for him and calls him "master," or, more formally, by his military title. (That the "regular guy" was an astronaut played into another male fantasy for good measure.) But the implied power and availability of Jeannie's sexuality were always a threat to her master, Captain (later, Major) Tony Nelson, and sometimes he was most relieved and happiest when she was "in her bottle." Jeannie was always more amorous and sexualized than her master, and this, of course, is what got them into so much trouble. Captain Nelson tried in vain to contain Jeannie both physically and sexually, and in those episodes where Jeannie's bottle was lost, there was considerable tension until it was found and Jeannie could get back inside it again.

I Dream of Jeannie differed from *Bewitched* in crucial ways that already suggested a backlash against the earlier show's discourse of empowerment. Jeannie did not intervene in community affairs the way Samantha did; in fact, she cared little for the public sphere. She was not the ideal 1960s wife who happened to have magical powers. In her pink chiffon harem pants, red bra, pom-pom-trimmed bolero jacket, and chiffon-draped headpiece, Jeannie was from another place and time, an anachronism in 1960s suburban America. She was the dumb, shapely, ditzy blonde with too much power, which she often used impetuously. Hyperfeminized, Jeannie was unreasonably jealous and possessive, giggled a lot, and was overly enthusiastic about whatever her master did: in fact, she often behaved and was treated like a child. Although she got her master into embarrassing situations, unlike Samantha she left him to explain his own way out. She was not seen as shrewder or more creative than Captain Nelson; after all, he was an astronaut, embedded in a world of science, technology, and the military-industrial complex women allegedly *couldn't* master. Jeannie's main goal was to serve Captain Nelson obsequiously, get him to pay more attention to her, and, she hoped, get him to marry her. Although Captain Nelson kept insisting he was the master of the house, Jeannie's magic constantly undermined that assertion. Yet the balance of power always tilted toward him, because Jeannie was more devoted to him and more emotionally dependent on him than he was on her.

The fact that Jeannie didn't know how to behave like a "normal" woman was the basis for a number of the plots in the show. In one telling episode, we see how this show, despite its reliance on many of the same visual gags and tricks as *Bewitched,* differed ideologically from its predecessor. In a 1965 episode, "The Americanization of Jeannie," Jeannie comes to feel that Captain Nelson devotes too much time and attention to his work and not enough to her. She reads a women's magazine and finds an article titled "The Emancipation of Modern Women." She asks, "What does emancipation mean?" and he answers, "You don't have to worry about anything like that." "Oh, yes I do," she insists. "I want to understand your way of life so I can please you." She continues reading the article. "Are you a loser in the battle between the sexes? Is the man in your life aloof, indifferent, difficult to please? Does he fail to appreciate what you have to offer as a female? Answer: Challenge his masculine arrogance. Be independent, self-reliant, unpredictable. You must learn to cope with him on his own grounds. In short, you must become a modern, American woman."

The next day, Nelson comes home to find the house a mess and no dinner on the table. Jeannie walks into the living room in a bathrobe and curlers and says, "Hiya, old boy," instead of her usual, more fawning greeting. Nelson accuses her of not doing any housework, but Jeannie responds by citing part of her magazine article, "How Not to Be a Drudge." "'Share the work with him,'" reads Jeannie as she reaches for a box of chocolates. "I'm an astronaut, not a housekeeper," explodes Nelson. "You must broaden your horizons," retorts Jeannie as she hands him a broom.

Needless to say, Nelson tells Jeannie that a real woman doesn't behave this way, and his reactions, as well as the narrative, repudiate the role reversal she proposes. At the end of the episode, their original relationship is restored, and Nelson advises her, "You need an outlet for your affection. You need a pet." Advice from a magazine about female emancipation turns out to be very bad advice because it undermines the woman's femininity, makes her appear ridiculous, and alienates the man's affections. The advice, of course, is a parody of feminism, for it urges women to be deliberately unattractive and completely self-indulgent, and to make men do the housework while the women do nothing at all.

Bewitched never took such a head-on approach to role reversal, thus it didn't draw such stark boundaries between male and female spheres. *Bewitched* blurred gender roles; *I Dream of Jeannie* accentuated them. Yet both shows anticipated feminism and hailed the prefeminist viewer. Samantha was clearly a role model, while Jeannie was an extreme version of femininity that girls ought not to model themselves after. When women like that got power, look out. Thus, *I Dream of Jeannie* was more of a warning. In *Bewitched,* Darrin's work in an advertising agency was repeatedly compromised by the inappropriate exercise of female power. In *I Dream of Jeannie,* the ante was upped: now, magic inspired by female desire, jealousy, and possessiveness threatened to disrupt one of the crowning achievements of 1960s male technocracy, the U.S. space program. Even NASA was no match for female power and sexuality run amok. In *Bewitched,* female power could be accommodated; in *Jeannie,* it could not. Because of these differences, the central mixed message remains: female power, when let loose in the public sphere, is often disruptive to male authority, but sometimes it also bolsters that authority. These colliding messages made *Bewitched* and *I Dream of Jeannie* simultaneously cautionary and liberatory. The schizophrenic female persona such shows helped constitute saw female obsequiousness amply rewarded. But she also had empowering images of physically zapping things—and men—into their proper place.

In 1964 and 1965, images of female possession were everywhere. In two sitcoms, *The Munsters* and *The Addams Family,* the mothers were black-clad female vampires with often macabre idiosyncrasies. The antithesis of Donna Reed, these moms did not bake chocolate chip cookies or take the PTA seriously. They were more likely making frog-eyeball stew or teaching the kids how to tie hangman's knots and build toy guillotines. Again, it was only through such quasimonsters—totally unrealistic yet unthreatening women from the realms of the supernatural—that females' rebellion against their traditional roles got expressed on TV. And as with *Bewitched* and *I Dream of Jeannie,* the sexual tension between regular guys and newly empowered women was a prominent subtext. A running joke on *The Addams Family* had Gomez unable to restrain himself from planting passionate kisses all along Morticia's irresistible arm. Here we saw the clearest connection between female sexuality and ghoulishness: her monstrous power turned him into a helpless, slavering fool.

Then, in the 1967–68 season, we had a fusion of *Bewitched* and *Gidget,* in the form of the poor, benighted Sally Field as Sister Bertrille. In *The Flying Nun,* perkiness took to the air. It took Sally Field ten years and the ability to portray dozens of personalities in *Sybil* to live down this role. Now we had a female character who could fly, but lest anyone do a Freudian reading, she was, by vocational choice, chaste and asexual. Her flying wasn't always in her control, but when you walk around with headgear shaped like a paper airplane on steroids, the updrafts sometimes just take you away. She often ended up in places where females, especially those from nunneries, weren't supposed to be; she was once nearly shot down as an enemy plane and, on another occasion, pursued by a lovestruck pelican.[9] Here we see the progression from Samantha to Sister Bertrille, from the woman having control of her magical powers and using them, at times, in ways that embarrassed men to the woman's magical powers having control of and embarrassing her. This was, of course, wishful thinking on the part of TV producers, for out in the viewing audience young women were feeling more, not less, empowered.

It is no surprise that, at the moment girls took to the streets in an outpouring of female resistance against the status quo, and in pursuit of new, supposedly false gods, while their mothers flocked to buy a book demanding equal rights for women, the witch and other women with supernatural powers would reappear on the cultural landscape of America. Television shows tried to suggest that if girls and women were feeling a bit restless, a tad mischievous, a mite defiant, these unruly impulses could be managed. But in an effort to co-opt this rebellion, and to translate it into Nielsen ratings, this media strategy backfired. For as we watched Darrin Stevens turned into a Yorkshire terrier, or Major Tony Nelson transported to seventh-century Persia, we saw that male authority wasn't so impregnable or impressive at all.

In real life, teenage girls blithely ignored or pushed through police barricades, with few negative consequences. What many of us experienced and saw, although we barely knew it at the time, was the beginning of a war. It was a battle between sexual rebellion and sexual containment, between the old masculinity and the new androgyny, a fight over how much more masquerading had to go on between men and women. After trying on the personas of the rebel, the sexual sophisticate, the knowing girl who was bonded to other girls in a group, the pursuer, and the witch, some girls decided they didn't want to imagine, fantasize, or pretend anymore. Girls were stepping over old boundaries, and there was no going back. We were on the verge of revolt.

ENDNOTES

[1] "The American Female," *Harper's,* October 1962, p. 117.

[2] Marjorie Hunter, "U.S. Panel Urges Women to Sue for Equal Rights," *New York Times,* October 12, 1963, p. 1.

[3] *Publisher's Weekly,* January 18, 1965, pp. 68, 72.

[4] Paul Foley, "Whatever Happened to Women's Rights," *Atlantic Monthly,* March 1964, pp. 63–65; Foley, "Women's Rights—and What They Don't Do about Them," *Reader's Digest,* May 1964, pp. 22–23.

[5] "How Women's Role in U.S. Is Changing," *U.S. News & World Report,* May 30, 1966, pp. 58–60.

[6] For a discussion of the monstrosity of female sexuality see Linda Williams, "When the Woman Looks," in Mary Ann Doane et al., eds., *Re-Vision: Essays in Feminist Film Criticism* (Frederick, MD: University Publications of America, 1984).

[7] Tim Brooks and Earle Marsh, *The Complete Directory to Prime Time Network TV Shows* (New York: Ballantine, 1979), pp. 62, 806–808.

[8] The term and concept of the female grotesque comes from Mary Russo, "Female Grotesques: Carnival and Theory," in Teresa de Lauretis, ed., *Feminist Studies/Critical Studies* (Bloomington: University of Indiana Press, 1986).

[9] Brooks and Marsh, *Complete Directory,* p. 205.

Name: _____ Date: _____

UNDERSTANDING THE TEXT

1. According to Douglas, what social and political factors in the early 1960s gave rise to *Bewitched* and *I Dream of Jeannie?* (Identify and discuss two.)

2. According to Douglas, what message did *Bewitched's* Mrs. Kravitz send to viewers?

3. Douglas argues that *Bewitched* and *I Dream of Jeannie* "differed ideologically." What was the difference?

Ally McBeal's Younger Sisters

Jane Rosenzweig

In the premiere of *Wasteland,* ABC's new prime-time soap by the creator of the WB Network's *Dawson's Creek* and the film *Scream,* 26-year-old Dawnie theorizes that her generation is experiencing a "second coming of age" in which twenty- and thirty-somethings face uncertainties of growing up that used to be the exclusive province of adolescents.

"Look at me," she says. "I've spent my entire life in school, my parents still support me, human relationships baffle me, and I am acutely self-aware—to the point where I am clueless and slightly suicidal." (She is also, in an interesting twist on television's conventional mores, a virgin.) Whether or not Dawnie's hypothesis is applicable to real people—and with any luck for ABC, this will be a subject of fervent water-cooler debate around the country—it certainly applies to the young women of prime time, who are trapped in the most protracted adolescence in television history.

It is perhaps no accident that at a time when youth sells (advertising slots for shows about teenagers, like *Dawson's Creek,* can command more money than those for the consistently top-10 rated *Touched by an Angel*), American pop culture has become preoccupied with our collective inability to grow up. People are staying single longer, and the beauty industry is constantly coaxing us to make ourselves look younger if we want to stay in romantic business.

But the proliferation of teen shows is one thing; the packaging of female adulthood as an extended adolescence is something else altogether. Indeed, what's most interesting about this infantilization of twenty- and thirty-something women—a trend started by David Kelley's *Ally McBeal* and perpetuated by the women of *Wasteland, Providence,* and to varying degrees a number of new fall programs—is that it coincides with a flood of shows about teenage girl characters who are more assertive, more independent, and more interesting than their adult counterparts. I'd say Ally McBeal ought to grow up—except the real problem seems to be that she already has and is still less mature than the average television teenager.

Reprinted with permission from *The American Prospect,* Volume 11, Number 1: November 23, 1999. The American Prospect, 5 Broad Street, Boston, MA 02109. All rights reserved.

Q: What makes your problems bigger than everyone else's?

A: They're mine.

—Ally McBeal

Most of the people here have been saved by you or helped by you at one time or another.

—A classmate speaking to Buffy Summers,
Buffy the Vampire Slayer

The preoccupations of young women are not new to television; women have always been the key audience for advertisers. A teenage girl in 1963 could flip on the TV to look for fac-similes of herself on *The Patty Duke Show* and *Gidget.* Young adult women, of course, have a long history of television "role models": think of June Cleaver, Donna Reed, and Laura Petrie—or, more recently, Mary Tyler Moore. And the history of television is rife with ambiguous portrayals of women: Are they empowered or trapped in traditional roles (think of *I Dream of Jeannie* and *Charlie's Angels*)? Can brains and femininity be reconciled in a single character, or must they always be dichotomized into either *Cagney and Lacey* or *Baywatch?* Or if they can be reconciled, must the result be *Xena: Warrior Princess?* But for all this history of mixed messages, there has never been a time when the girls were more like women and the women more like girls than right now.

True, the conventional wisdom these days is that the line between adolescence and adult-hood is blurring: the young are getting older, the old younger. Though if that's the case, shouldn't our television counterparts be meeting in the middle? Why, instead, do television teenagers have more mature relationships with men than the thirty-somethings do? Why are Buffy the vampire slayer, Felicity, and the girls of *Party of Five* and *Dawson's Creek* so much more emotionally intelligent than the grown-ups on other shows? Harvard psycholo-gist Carol Gilligan and others have observed that the confidence and self-esteem of young girls diminish when they reach adolescence, at which point girls start downplaying their intellects and compromising their personalities in order to adapt to society's expectations—and to be attractive to boys. If current television is any indication, the cultural manifestation of this trend now occurs twice (*Wasteland's* Dawnie may be onto something bigger than she knows): if girls go ditzy when they reach adolescence, they seem to be going ditzier still as they pass into young adulthood.

This phenomenon, I think, can be explained at least in part by our cultural preoccupation with women's biological clocks, a preoccupation that has clearly constrained the imagina-tions of today's television writers. Can't they conceive of any other kinds of lives for women? If we succumb to the creative failure represented by the latest crop of television shows, the danger is that we, as viewers, will find ourselves accepting these same constraints in our own lives.

I want to save the world. I just want to get married first.

—Ally McBeal

It has become fashionable to loathe Ally McBeal. Her contribution to the putative death of feminism, her diminutive cuteness, her short skirts, and her perky pouts all combine to make her an insult to any actual Harvard law graduate—or any graduate of any school in any field, for that matter. While the show is still at times clever and even resonant in its focus on the lonely search for a soul mate, Ally is a hard character to sympathize with. It may be kind of funny when she says, "I'm tempted to become a street person cut off from society, but then I wouldn't get to wear my outfits," but it's also pathetic. By the end of last season, when she schemed to win back her boyfriend by hiring a gigolo to make him jealous and then propositioned the gigolo, she'd lost all credibility as an adult character. Mary Tyler Moore wouldn't be caught dead messing up her life like this.

While originally hailed as whimsical and imaginative, and even as it continues to garner accolades (most recently, in September, an Emmy for Best Comedy Series), *Ally McBeal* is well on its way to being the biggest failure of the imagination in prime time. But because of its early critical and ongoing ratings success, Ally has basically created a new category of women on television: pretty young things who, in the guise of successful career women, are actually completely defined by an inability to find a husband and have children. Ally is stalked by a holographic dancing baby meant to remind her (and us) that her biological clock is ticking. While there are women in her age group on television who do care about their careers in some workplace-centered shows—most notably Carol Hathaway on *ER*—most of the dramas and comedy-dramas that focus on personal lives feature immature women who share more with Ally McBeal than with the people we know in real life. Lindsay Dole on Kelley's *The Practice* throws tantrums in court; her unhappy housemate, played by Lara Flynn Boyle, appears more anorexic than Calista Flockhart's Ally and seems even more ill-equipped to handle her personal life. It's as though you're supposed to look at Boyle and think, If only she had a nice husband to take care of her, maybe she would eat.

Perhaps the worst example of TV's confused conception of the single woman is Dr. Sydney Hansen of NBC's *Providence,* which debuted last season. After coming home to find her boyfriend in the shower with another man, she left her lucrative job as an L.A. plastic surgeon and moved home to practice medicine at a free clinic in Providence. Sleeping once again in the room she grew up in, she regularly wakes, sweating, from dreams in which her dead mother is chastising her about her inability to find a man. Syd consistently makes dating decisions more worthy of a teenager than a smart, adult woman, which is what she is theoretically supposed to be. And her skirts are as short as Ally McBeal's; most real doctors and lawyers, it's safe to say, don't dress like that.

Unfortunately, the new fall season offers more of the same. In addition to Dawnie on *Wasteland,* there are the women of NBC's *Cold Feet,* one of whom strikes a blow to sexism by marching into her husband's business meeting to demand, for once and for all, a nanny. (And never mind that the husband appears to have no interest in either wife or child.) Another of the main characters in *Cold Feet* runs off to sulk at her mother's house when she argues with her husband. These characters are like early adolescents who relate to one another by screaming, pouting, and stamping their feet.

Funny thing is, turn the channel to the WB Network, which has made the strongest effort to stake out the youth market, and you find that the characters who actually are adolescent girls do not stamp their feet. They are calm and collected, surprisingly analytical. Television's message: only when they're not worrying about their biological clocks can women have fully developed characters. Is it really the case that only women who are still in high school have the luxury of thinking about things other than themselves without constantly being interrupted by thoughts of their own reproductive limits?

> I need to find out if I'm capable of being a whole person without you.
> > —15-year-old Joey Potter to her boyfriend Dawson
> > on the WB's *Dawson's Creek*

Don't get me wrong: teenage girls on television are not ideal role models. They all have clear skin and shiny hair and don't seem afflicted by any of the maladies of girlhood described by experts. It's not hard to see how some critics would assert that these characters are the primary contributors to body image problems of ordinary girls. (The actress who plays Buffy, Sarah Michelle Gellar, is a spokesmodel for Maybelline cosmetics, whose ads run throughout the show.) And some characters are perhaps more sexually active earlier than we would like the role models for our children to be. But I would rather have my girls watch *Dawson's Creek* or *Buffy* than *Ally McBeal*.

Say what you will about the fanciful premise of *Buffy,* in which Buffy Summers fights the evil denizens of hell in order to save her town. But Buffy is neither man obsessed nor self-absorbed, and she refuses to see her problems, like Ally McBeal does, as bigger than everyone else's. In fact, she balances her personal life quite elegantly with her responsibility to protect her community from evil vampires (okay, so that sounds ridiculous on its face; nevertheless, the lesson it conveys is a worthy one). The problems are of a different scale. She misses out on her own prom in order to make school safe for her friends; she gives up something but earns loyalty and respect in return. Also, her best friend Willow is intelligent, sensitive, principled, and the least stereotypical Jewish woman on television.

Similarly, peel away the music-video veneer from *Dawson's Creek* or *Party of Five* and you'll find some young women who clearly have their feet planted firmly on the ground, even in the context of formulaic television plots. Joey Potter, for example, in spite of having a dead mother and a jailed father, has enough self-awareness to realize that there is an asymmetry between her boyfriend Dawson's passion for filmmaking and her own passion for Dawson. After some initial sadness, she pulls herself together enough to think about what she really wants out of life—and to realize the folly of a self-definition that requires always having a man. Ally McBeal never shows this kind of independence. The tragedy is that, assuming television convention holds, if Joey graduates from college without having landed a husband, she'll be reduced to jabbering preadolescence. (The self-reliant title character of the WB Network's *Felicity* suggests that college women still have their own identities and therefore that it is sometime after college that life begins to be about having babies.)

Sometimes the divide between adolescent maturity and post-adolescent immaturity is starkly evident even within a single show. *Party of Five,* for instance, depicts both teenage girls and twenty-something women. The differences are striking. (Originally about a family of orphans trying to raise themselves, the show has turned into a fairly formulaic soap about adolescents and young adults coexisting in an adult-free San Francisco universe.) Sarah—whose character, now 19, is spinning off this season to a new show called *Time of Your Life*—was one of the first TV characters I saw with the self-awareness to realize that her coquettish attempts to win her boyfriend's heart (in a batch of episodes a few years ago) were not only a waste of her time but also a challenge to her self-esteem, and that she shouldn't have to compromise her intelligence to win love. In an episode at the end of last season, Sarah, now older, attempted to teach this lesson to 16-year-old Claudia while at the same time struggling to maintain her own interests as her life was increasingly overtaken by her boyfriend's responsibilities.

In contrast, twenty-something Kirsten, the girlfriend of the show's oldest sibling, is a uni-dimensional character painted almost entirely in terms of her inability to have children. The chain of events that followed her learning this fact was over the top: she plagiarized her Ph.D. thesis, had a nervous breakdown, married a man she didn't love, and spent several seasons obsessing about how she would hold onto a man if she couldn't bear children. Meanwhile, the only other twenty-something women on this show have been a stripper who doesn't love her child, an alcoholic who depends on a 19-year-old man to take care of her, and a hard-edged and independent—but, alas, unlovable and unappealing—social worker.

What is it in the logic of television that demands that self-possessed girls full of possibility must evolve into women who are defined entirely by their marriage status and act like spoiled children? To the extent that television reflects or defines many of our central preoccupations as a society, this is a question to take seriously. Mightn't television capture some more complex way of thinking about the role of women in society? Or must television continue to make women into one-issue vessels when they reach childbearing age? The women I know lead richly textured lives, and the ones who do feel the loneliness of being single do not deal with it by throwing tantrums in court or moving home to live with their parents; surely it's the same for the women you know, too. But that's not the impression your daughters would get—or your sons, for that matter—from watching TV.

Sadly, shows featuring teen girls are becoming more and more formulaic, their lead characters more and more flat and conventional. Television producers are like sheep; thus a few dramas about teenagers from the last two seasons have generated a trend that will feature as many as 10 such shows this season, not counting the returning sitcoms *Moesha* and *Sabrina the Teenage Witch,* or the *Moesha* spinoff *The Parkers.* As the new season starts, it will be worth watching to see which of these teen girls can sustain their level of maturity as they age and which will become ditzy stereotypes. We can only hope the girls don't lose character definition as these shows become the norm. One thing is certain: if Buffy Summers grows up to be Ally McBeal, there will be hell to pay. Literally.

Can *Buffy's* Brilliance Last?

Garrett Epps

When future critics ask whether turn-of-the-century American TV produced any works of genius, the verdict on the entire medium—all 128 channels of it—is likely to depend on their assessment of a cult teen hit currently airing on UPN, with syndicated reruns on FX.

At first glance, *Buffy the Vampire Slayer* seems indistinguishable from the WB's rancid *Dawson's Creek* or the *American Pie* movies: An all-white cast of impossibly nubile women and muscular men (they call themselves "the Scooby gang") pretend to be teenagers while modeling the latest in Southern California teen slang and sportswear. But there's a difference: The other shows paste a veneer of realism over a fantasy of adolescence; *Buffy* adopts a facade of fantasy to cover a portrayal of the teen years as they really are. The show is a worthy successor to school stories like *Nicholas Nickleby, Stalky & Co.*, and *The Catcher in the Rye.*

When I was 12, I stumbled across George Orwell's "Such, Such Were the Joys," a scathing memoir of his days at a minor British prep school. I was transfixed: As a student at a segregated southern boys' day school that self-consciously modeled itself on the English public schools (except, as Buffy might say, for the whole "education" part), I was amazed that an adult really *understood.* Such a small place—with its snobbery of wealth and station, its sadistic teachers and bullying classmates, its cult of team sports, and its unremitting anti-intellectualism—becomes, for children immured in it, an entire cosmos of danger and significance, to be survived, if at all, only by guile, silence, and inner escape. Like Orwell's essay, the best of the school-story genre exert a horrid fascination that even much great adult narrative cannot match.

No matter what kind of school they attend, teenagers live in a world resembling that of ancient Greek mythology: Uncaring and capricious adults, like the Olympian gods, hold arbitrary power over their lives, ritual mistakes may bring irrevocable ruin, and each day offers a chance to answer the riddle of the Sphinx and learn, for good or ill, who they really are. In that world, "small" things—first loves and best friends, small successes and seemingly monstrous failures—matter as much as or more than the larger crises that lie ahead in adulthood. The overwhelming fact that teens know and adults seek to ignore is that what happens in those years does matter almost as much as it seems to at the time. The identities we take on then—class brain, prom queen, rebel, popular jock, geeky misfit—play out insistently under the surface of our later lives.

Most pop-culture re-creations of adolescence focus on the electric sexuality that teens swim in—the obsession with dating and looks, music and dancing, making out and scoring. But Joss Whedon, creator of the *Buffy the Vampire Slayer* TV series and its precursor, the 1992 theatrical film, focuses instead on his characters' all-encompassing fear. For Whedon, high school literally is the mouth of hell, and the ill-equipped teens must rely on their own resources to survive such perils as a seductive substitute teacher (she's actually a huge praying mantis), a bullying potential stepfather (he's a homicidal robot), or a demon who persuades the local chapter of "Mothers Opposed to the Occult" to move from locker searches and a school-library purge at Sunnydale High to full-fledged witch burnings at city hall.

Whedon's dramatic triumph is Buffy's tortured romance with Angel, played by the gifted comic actor David Boreanaz. Angel was my own high-school nightmare, the "older guy" who bewitched the girls with mystery, muscles, and menace—and just a hint of a heart of gold. Whedon's older guy is a 245-year-old vampire cursed by Gypsies with a soul. He fights evil and then wanders off in search of babes to lure to his graveyard bachelor's lair. On Buffy's 16th birthday, matters proceed to their inevitable consummation, and the curse truly kicks in: The loving, gentle Angel reverts to vile vampirehood, spreading terror among the Scoobys and—even worse—vicious gossip among the boys of Sunnydale. As a depiction of male sexual ambivalence and fecklessness, the story surpasses anything ever shown on HBO's *Sex and the City*.

The dimwitted adults in Sunnydale carry on as if the fate of the entire cosmos were not at stake in each weekly episode. Only Giles, the kindly librarian (Anthony Stewart Head), treats the Scoobys with respect, helping them find their way through each tiny apocalypse with a mixture of kindness, erudition, and wry mockery.

Though it has links to Dickens and Kipling, *Buffy* is, of course, different in one important regard: It is a story of *female* self-discovery. Buffy, the heroine, discovers that underneath her silly first name and petite cheerleader looks she is really what every teenager longs to be: a unique and important being with gifts that matter to the world. In her postfeminist case, the talents are superstrength and killer reflexes, and her life's mission is to save the universe while looking fabulous. For most of us, the discoveries are more mundane. But what matters to surviving adolescence is that the moment of self-recognition does come.

This brings us to the other brute teenage fact: sex. I first began watching *Buffy* because its star, Sarah Michelle Gellar—known to the faithful as "SMG"—is hypnotically beautiful. But soon I began corralling my children ("Watch *Buffy* or I won't let you do your homework") because the program treats teen sexuality with a moral seriousness missing in the rest of the teen-exploitation genre.

It goes without saying that our infatuation with vampires derives from the unholy power of sex to unbalance the human soul. The original Dracula was the quintessential Victorian-era seducer. With his continental accent and bedroom eyes, he stood for the return of the repressed—big time. What is interesting is that the myth survived the repression that spawned it. By the dawn of the 1970s, Count Yorga, played by Robert Quarry, appeared as the consummate swinger, soullessly pursuing pleasure across a landscape of emotional entropy. (I discovered vampires at this low point. As an undergraduate, I kept inviting young women to vampire flicks, hoping that terror would drive them into my manly arms. Wise girls, they invariably fled back to their dorm rooms, knowing that what I really wanted was to bite their necks.)

Sex is omnipresent in *Buffy,* but it has been transformed for the era of teen pregnancy and sexually transmitted diseases. In Sunnydale the vampire's kiss offers no pleasure, only loneliness and death. The bodily-fluids metaphor is patent; but the lesson goes deeper. Advocates of "abstinence" clothe their message to the young in religious, economic, or public-policy terms that are, to most teens, utterly irrelevant. In a society where Viagra poster child Bob Dole barks after Britney Spears in commercials, by far the most consistent adult pressure on teens is not to abstain from anything but to score early and often.

For cultural reasons I cannot pretend to fathom, our society has eroticized the adolescent body more thoroughly than any previous one of which I am aware. In advertising, in popular entertainment, and even in the lubricious piety of media prophets like William Bennett, American adults betray an unbecoming obsession about what children may be up to underneath the sheets.

Though their glands are unquestionably supercharged, many teens are reluctant, frightened, or even repulsed by sex. But too often they are coerced by conformism and pop culture into experimenting before they are ready. (The only other convincing portrayal of this painful rite of passage I've seen came during the too-short run of the magnificent TV series *My So-Called Life.*) *Buffy* dramatizes the case for waiting in the only terms the adolescent mind can grasp: If it doesn't feel good, don't do it. Sunnydale is packed with largely male bloodsuckers who will do almost anything to get into a girl's veins; a moment's weakness or inattention will leave her dead—a physical death that is a powerful metaphor for the inner necrosis of unfeeling promiscuity. (Female bloodsuckers also lurk in Sunnydale's shadows, though we see less of the havoc they wreak.)

But *Buffy's* triumph during its early seasons is its problem today. "Where do we go from here?" sang the cast at the end of a special musical episode this fall. Adolescents grow up: Those awkward bundles of promise slowly congeal into more defined, and sometimes duller, adults. That's happening to the Scoobys now. Two years ago, they graduated from Sunnydale High after a moving ceremony at which Mayor Wilkins ate Principal Snyder. Now the gang are young adults. Willow Rosenberg, valedictorian and computer geek (played by the unlikely sex star Allyson "Band Camp" Hannigan) has become a powerful witch; her troubled romance with the vulnerable Tara (Amber Benson) is the most complex lesbian relationship a TV series has ever attempted. Class clown Xander Harris (Nicholas Brendon) is uneasily facing marriage to the terrifyingly monogamous former revenge demon Anya (Emma Caulfield). Their concerns are now less *I Was a Teenage Werewolf* than *I Dream of Jeannie.* The danger is that the show—like Fox's once electrifying *X-Files*—will drift into ignominious self-parody.

But where there's undeath, there's hope. Last season, a league of monks from another dimension created a "sister" for Buffy. (Has any older sibling ever not suspected that a younger one is a supernatural interloper?) The new character, Dawn—played by the winsome Michelle Trachtenberg—is now a freshman at Sunnydale High, dealing hesitantly with peer pressure, shoplifting, gym class, and really cute vampires. If Joss Whedon can surround this new potential slayer with a suitable crowd of Scoobinis, there's hope for the series.

For each of us, adolescence mercifully ends; the drama itself rolls on, with new tearstained, pimply faces in the archetypal roles. Growing up entails loss as well as gain; it will be sad if the passing years rob us of *Buffy's* brilliant satire.

Name: _____ Date: _____

UNDERSTANDING THE TEXT

1. Epps favorably compares *Buffy* to the works of Dickens, Kipling, Orwell, and Salinger. Yet, he says, it is "different in one important regard." What is it?

2. According to Epps, why do we find vampires so fascinating?

3. Ultimately, why does Epps praise *Buffy* so highly?

Gentleman or Beast? The Double Bind of Masculinity

Susan Bordo

THE DOUBLE BIND OF MASCULINITY

In 1956, psychologist Gregory Bateson formulated the concept of the "double bind." A double bind is any situation in which a person is subject to mutually incompatible instructions, in which they are directed to fulfill two contradictory requirements at the same time. Bateson's emphasis was on the double messages that parents send to children—for example, demanding that they stand on their own but at the same time encouraging dependency. But the concept is socially applicable too. In a previous book, *Unbearable Weight,* I used the concept of the double bind to explore some of the contradictions that face young women today, living at a time when girls are encouraged to compete alongside men, to "be all that they can be," to "just do it," and so on—at the same time as they take care to not lose their femininity in the process. So we get superbly skilled, fearless young female athletes who speak in baby voices and bat their eyes like Ally McBeal.

Clearly, this culture places young boys in a double bind too. We fabulously reward those boys who succeed in our ritual arenas of primitive potency, and humiliate the boy whose sexual aggression quota doesn't match up to those standards. But at the same time, we want male aggression to bow to civilization when a girl says "no" and to be transformed into tender passion when she says "yes." The fact that these contradictory directives put a *real* person in a difficult (if not impossible) double bind gets masked by the fact that we've created numerous *fictional* heroes who successfully embody both requirements, who have the sexual charisma of an untamed beast and are unbeatable in battle, but are intelligent, erudite, and gentle with women.

Edgar Rice Burroughs's Tarzan is an exemplar. The genetic offspring of British aristocrats, but raised by apes, he combines (as historian Gail Bederman puts it) "the ultimate in Anglo-Saxon manliness with the most primal masculinity . . . violent yet chivalrous; moral yet passionate . . . [and] with a superb body." These qualities make their appearance in every version of the Tarzan story that I've seen, including the recent *George of the Jungle* (Brendan Fraser had the most superb body yet). In a similar vein, Mel Gibson's Braveheart is a fluent linguist, educated in Latin, well-traveled, and a tender, sweet lover. None of that gets in the way, however, when he's called upon to lead an animal-house army of howling Scotsmen against their cruel (and effete) British oppressors. The heroes of *Pulp Fiction* are able to discourse at one moment on abstract intellectual conundrums of philosophy and religion (not to mention cultural variants of the "Big Mac") and in the next, without raising their pulses, blast away at a roomful of human beings.

The mixed messages about manliness get directed at girls as well as boys—and catch them at a very young age. In Disney's most recent version of *Beauty and the Beast,* the beast-hero not only looks and acts quite a bit like a man, but is the keeper of the flame of civilization. True, he must learn to control his anger and to have good table manners. But he owns a high-ceilinged library full of books, and is continually contrasted in the film with the provincial, arrogant, ferociously anti-intellectual hunter Gaston, whom Belle describes at one point as "primeval." (Gaston's room is decorated with antlers; even his furniture is made of antlers.) Gaston, who is a "normal" man, is represented as the truly uncivilized male of the story, because he has no appreciation for beauty (double meaning intended), while the beast, although full of animal rage to begin with, becomes fully tamed under the spell of his love for Belle.

But at the same time as the (tamed) Disney beast represents the virtues of masculine civility, he is also far more romanticized and sexualized *as* beast than in earlier versions of the tale. He growls impressively, rears up on his hind legs in phallic splendor, and has a wild passionate nature that seems almost the cartoon equivalent of Mel Gibson's William Wallace. His aggression is pure of heart, but, like Wallace's, it's pretty potent when it gets going. And this isn't lost on Beauty. In earlier versions of the story—the original tale and various movies based on it, as well as the popular television show—the main idea of the story is that love requires learning to see beyond externals, as the heroine learns to see past the grotesque exterior of the beast to discover the "real" person within (symbolized by the handsome prince who emerges at the end of the story). But in the Disney version, Beauty doesn't really need to see past the beast's externals, for he's pretty magnificent as he is. In fact, as Elaine Showalter writes, "it's a distinct letdown when the Beast turns into a blue-eyed prince"; I agree, the prince is rather lame compared to the commanding figure of the beast. (For Showalter, even the beast was "a bit too gentle for her tastes"; now there's a lover of the wild man!)

The Disney people recognized the erotic charge of their beast; they delayed making the film for a decade, worried about the sexual overtones of the story, until they finally hit on the solution of having constant chaperones around in the castle, in the form of all those talking teapots and dinnerware. But it was the makers of the film, of course, who endowed the beast with all that sex appeal to begin with. As such, the "learning to see past externals" theme becomes merged with, even supplanted by, a version of the "sleeping beauty" motif, whose main point is not the heroine's spiritual education but her sexual awakening. (That's the way contemporary Freudian commentators like Bruno Bettelheim have interpreted the beauty and beast tale too—as about the young girl's initiation into the power of male sexuality.) It's frightening for her at first ("strange, and a bit alarming," as the Disney heroine sings), but it ultimately allows her to unleash the beast within herself. Women, being ovens by nature, need the spark of the male blowtorch to set their instinctual fires going.

The notion that men's more forceful, hotter sexuality is required to turn on a woman's slow-heating oven—an idea which has a certain amount of charm, no doubt about it—is unfortunately also part of the mythology that teaches men not to take "no" for an answer. For in this version of sexual "complementarity," the woman *requires* for her own awakening that the man see past the veneer of civilization motivating her "no" to the *real,* albeit latent, desires within. Of course it's going to take a while . . . she's a slow cooker, remember. But don't give up; she'll come around. That's the way it happens in the movies, isn't it? There, you'll never see the woman who won't let go depicted as anything other than deranged (as in *Fatal Attraction*) or power-mad (as in *Disclosure*). But numerous romantic comedies reward the persistent male suitor for his efforts—with the girl's affections. Popular culture *admires* the man who won't take no for an answer.

When date rape workshops focus on women's learning to say "no" in a way that will be clear and unequivocal, they don't alter this mythology much either. For these (well-meaning) workshops are clearly still imagining women as the gatekeepers of male desire, tamers of the beast, domesticators, while continuing to view men as primitive animals who, if left to their own devices, would naturally plunder everything in sight. The script still has the male in hot pursuit, the woman with the "stop" and "go" signs. Here, women are getting some mixed messages too. John Gray says we should flirt, to stoke the fires of male desire. But popular college training manuals for the prevention of acquaintance rape seem to recommend otherwise. They caution that "flirting," which suggests a certain indecisiveness, a "wait and see what he does for me" attitude, is exactly what should be avoided: "An important part of assertiveness," one of these manuals reads, "includes clearly indicating what is intended with both words and actions. If a woman says 'no' with her mouth, and 'yes' with her body, she is giving a mixed and inconsistent message. She must know what she wants clearly before she can ask for it."

To slightly adapt the refrain that Maurice Chevalier sings in *Gigi:* "Oh, I'm so gla-ad that I-I'm not young . . . nowadays."

"THE MALE ANIMAL" AS IDEOLOGY

Destructive double messages aside, it might seem that science ought to have the last word here about what differences in male and female sexuality are "real" and which are the creations of culture. The findings of evolutionary science should be taken very seriously. I think it's also important to take note that scientific ideas about these matters have changed over time, and in not entirely disinterested or objective ways.

It might come as a surprise to contemporary men and women, but throughout the ancient and medieval periods of Western history, it was women, not men, whom science regarded as the hot-blooded, sexually insatiable sex. Women were believed to have a greater sexual appetite than men and to be less capable of controlling their urges. But these qualities carried meanings different from dominant contemporary notions that equate hair-trigger sexuality with virility. Both Greek and early Christian cultures valued sexual self-control highly (although for different reasons) and viewed domination by one's passions as a sign of weakness, *not* manliness. The truly virile man (or, within Christian tradition, the chaste and godly man) was the master of his own body. Being more at the mercy of our sexual urges was thus among the traits that, ancient science argued, were a sign of women's inferiority to men.

Women's lesser control over our sexual impulses was connected to what was believed to be our greater "passivity"—another feature of our natural inferiority. We've already seen, in an earlier chapter, how approval of male "activity" and revulsion with the man who puts himself in a passive, "feminine" position, affected Greek ideas about sex between men (and still inform some homosexual cultures). The same set of values (male = active = admirable; female = passive = inferior) also were embedded in ideas about reproduction, and demonstrate how profoundly gender ideology is capable of shaping even how "hard" scientists interpret their observations. According to Aristotle, the conception of a living being involves the vitalization of the purely material contribution of the female by the "effective, active" element— the male sperm:

> . . . [T]here must be that which generates and that from which it generates, even if these be one, still they must be distinct in form and their essence must be different . . . If, then, the male stands for the effective and active, and the female, considered as female, for the passive, it follows that what the female would contribute would not be semen but material for the semen to work upon. This is just what we find to be the case, for the catamenia (menstrual material) have in their nature an affinity to the primitive matter.

In other words, what the female contributes to conception is mere glop. The forces that will shape that glop into a distinctive human being are all contributed by the male. This view of things was so powerful that when Leeuwenhoek in 1677 first examined sperm under the newly invented microscope, he saw tiny "animalcules" in it—the "form" of the future being, to be stamped onto the shapeless dough of the menstrual matter. We no longer believe in this cookie-cutter version of reproduction, in which female stuff just lies there, waiting to be penetrated and molded by male form. But if you think we've gone beyond mistaken notions about males as "active" and females as "receptive" in the act of conception, consider this account from Alan Guttmacher's drugstore guide *Pregnancy, Birth and Family Planning*:

> Some of the sperm swim straight up the one-inch, mucus-filled canal with almost purposeful success, while others bog down on the way, getting hopelessly stranded in tissue bays and

coves. A small proportion of the total number ejaculated eventually reach the cavity of the uterus and begin their upward two-inch excursion through its length . . . The undaunted ones, those not stranded in this veritable everglade, reach the openings of the two fallopian tubes . . . The one sperm that achieves its destiny has won against gigantic odds, several hundred million to one . . . No one knows just what selective forces are responsible for the victory. Perhaps the winner had the strongest constitution; perhaps it was the swiftest swimmer of all the contestants entered in the race . . . If ovulation occurred within several minutes to twenty-four hours before the sperm's journey ends, the ovum will be in the tube, awaiting fertilization; if ovulation took place more than twenty-four hours before insemination, the egg cell will already have begun to deteriorate and fragment, rendering it incapable of being fertilized by the time the spermatozoon reaches it. On the other hand, if ovulation has not yet occurred, but takes place within two or three days after intercourse, living spermatozoa will be cruising at the tubal site . . .

Guttmacher's drama of driven, supercharged sperm racing to be the first to penetrate a waiting egg is duplicated in the opening credits of *Look Who's Talking,* which depict the perilous journey of "the undaunted ones" to the tune of "I Get Around," and have the successful sperm (the one "who achieves his destiny") provide a running commentary on his progress. And there, at the end of his journey is the giant beach ball of an egg, languorously bobbing, killing time, awaiting the victor's arrival. But this picture is totally inaccurate as a depiction of a typical act of conception. On most occasions, when fertilization occurs it is actually the *egg* that travels to rendezvous with sperm that have been lolling around, for as much as three days, waiting for *her* to show up. What Guttmacher and *Look Who's Talking* present as their model is an act of intercourse at ovulation—by no means representative of the majority of fertilizations. Yet it has somehow become our paradigm. Could it be that it goes against the grain to imagine males (or their sperm surrogates) passively hanging around, waiting for Ms. Egg to "call"? (To be fair, Guttmacher does allow that sometimes the sperm will be waiting for the egg. But, significantly, he doesn't describe them as "waiting"; rather, they are "cruising," like guys driving their cars down the street, looking for chicks.)

During the Renaissance and Enlightenment, ideas about sexuality were focused less on men and women and more on race, as the group of people who now came to be seen by Western science as having a naturally hotter, more "primitive" sexuality were the "uncivilized" people of non-European descent: African, West Indian, and Native American Indian (both male and female). As Bryan Edward, a Jamaican planter and English politician, wrote in 1793:

The Negroes in the West Indies, both men and women, would consider it to be the great exertion of tyranny, and the most cruel of all hardships, to be compelled to confine themselves to a single connection with the other sex. Their passion is mere animal desire, implanted by the great Author of all things for the preservation of the species. This the Negroes, without a doubt, possess in common with the rest of the animal creation, and they indulge it, as inclination prompts, in an almost promiscuous intercourse with the other sex.

The notion that the passion of the Negroes is "mere animal desire" was confirmed by pre-evolutionary (and, later, evolutionary) science, which plotted degrees of similarity and difference between the apes and various racial groups; drawings of Africans, the appropriate features exaggerated, were placed closest to those of apes, while sketches of fine-featured Europeans with noble expressions on their faces occupied the other end of the spectrum. Artists depicted "historical" matings between Africans and orangutans. These ideas that the African man (and woman) is closer to purely instinctual, animal nature still survive today, not only in overt racial stereotypes but also in more subtle ways. Actor Laurence Fishburne was recently depicted in *Vanity Fair* in a series of photographs posing him in menacing, lionlike postures, with captions like: "Laurence has natural grace, but he's not afraid to be savage" and "He's like a dangerous, magnificent beast."

How did we get from the identification of animal sexuality with non-Europeans of both sexes to the current notion that *men*—of all races—are hotter-blooded and more promiscuous in nature than women? It wasn't discoveries in evolutionary science that led the way, but changes in perceptions of what constituted the ideal man in an industrial, increasingly competitive society. By the end of the nineteenth century, Europeans began rethinking their attitudes toward the primitive "savage," not out of any sense of morality or political correctness, but because the primitive savage was beginning to be seen as having something the European gentleman lacked and needed. As we've seen in an earlier chapter, it was a time when the prestige of older notions of manliness was eroding, since those notions revolved around qualities no longer very useful to success in a market-driven economy. Being a "civilized gentleman" didn't get you very far in the competitive jungle of the marketplace. At the same time, "civilization" itself was increasingly being viewed as a source of human "discontent" (as Freud put it) responsible for numerous new nervous disorders seen as being caused by the stresses and strain of modern industrial life.

One of the most interesting expressions of this new mistrust of the suppression of instinct by civilization is found in the French nineteenth-century literature on rabies, which imagined the disease as an eruption of the beast through the suffocating veneer of civilization, turning the human sufferer into an animal, wild, uncontrollable, and dangerous, prone to biting and tearing apart everything in sight. Remarkably but consistently, rabies in dogs too was viewed as the result of hypercivilization and sexual repression! It was believed that dogs in the wild rarely developed rabies, that it was produced by the "unwholesome conditions of domesticity" where dogs are forced into "unnatural chastity by their mistresses."

In this context of growing concern and anxiety about the repressive effects of civilization and its "softening" of men (and dogs), fantasies of recovering an unspoiled, primitive masculinity began to emerge, and with them, a "flood of animal metaphors" poured forth to animate a new conception of masculinity. White men drew on the images and ideology of the savage Other to help them articulate this emerging construction of "passionate manhood" (as historian Anthony Rotundo calls it). The depiction of historical scenes of European rape and pillage—a motif that was formerly most prominent only in racist representations of the black male rapist or marauding Indian—became especially fashionable. Africans and other "primitive" peoples were also playacted in clubs and lodges. Bourgeois, white, American men began to speak of themselves in terms of "animal instincts" and "animal energy." They began to believe that "this nature was their male birthright and that it demanded expression."

In this way, arguably, the notion that men are passionate beasts by nature, who cannot and should not be expected to control themselves, gained cultural cachet—a cachet that has created a special sort of double bind for black men. Within racist mythology, being more instinctual means being a mere animal, a brute. But to the extent that being an untamed animal has become part of the definition of being a potent man, then being associated with sexual instinct and animal magnetism gives one the gender edge. It's no wonder, then, that black artists and athletes have sometimes exploited the stereotypes that endow them with greater potency and "animal" sexuality. Particularly when one has been historically deprived of most of the social privileges of masculinity, it would be hard to relinquish the one advantage one has. Unfortunately, the advantage comes at a high price, for that old racial mythology is still there, ready to be activated. When a white boy acts like a thug, he proves he's not a sissy to the other white guys in his group; when a black boy engages in the same behavior, the same white boys may view it as proof that he's a jungle brute after all.

Today, with many men feeling that women—particularly feminists—have been pushing them around for a couple of decades, the idea of a return to manhood "in the raw" has a refreshed, contemporary appeal. The "Return of the Alpha Male" literature and a good deal of the mythopoetic men's movement seem clearly to be "backlash" reclamations of manhood, which, like some of their Victorian counterparts, view women as responsible for having tamed the beast in man. Other Victorian conceptions, as we've seen, put the chief blame on civilization—and plenty of contemporary ads exploit that notion too, urging escape into the wild (in a luxury four-wheel-drive car). In neither case, however, is the ideal *really* for men to revert to the jungle (except perhaps on a weekend jaunt). For at the same time as we romanticize the wild man and scorn the wimp, we also—like the Greeks—still place great stock in masculine self-control. It's just that we expect it to have a potent, aggressive edge.

Such notions, and the ambivalence about "civilization" and "nature" that underlies them, are vividly illustrated in Mike Nichols's recent contemporary reworking of the werewolf story, in the movie *Wolf.* This film plays with the same idea which was so prominent in the Victorian era—that hypercivilization has made man soft, ineffective, and deadened and that his revitalization requires reconnection with his "animal" nature. Jack Nicholson's character, Will Randall, is a book editor at—oh, dear—"McLeash" House, where he performs his job with "taste, individuality and civility" and is given, at parties, to bemoaning the death of art and the triumph of TV talk shows. He's also a wonderfully "nice" person, as his boss Raymond Alden tells him, explaining why he's replacing him with his unscrupulous, ambitious assistant (who is also having an affair with Randall's wife). "What are you, the last civilized man?" the boss's daughter (Michelle Pfeiffer, wearing a buckskin jacket, by the way) cracks when he apologizes for finishing her drink, spelling it out for those of us who haven't gotten it yet. Randall is civilized, all right. But Nichols can't decide whether or not that's a good thing.

On the one hand, his niceness and love of art and gentleness are favorably contrasted with the ruthless crudeness of his boss and assistant, and the heroine explains that she loves him because he's a "good man" and that's "very exotic" to her. On the other hand, we are encouraged to see him as wimpy. He accepts being fired passively and uncomplainingly; his feminist wife (Kate Nelligan) nags and scolds him. At the beginning of the movie, the night he gets bitten by the wolf, he has just returned from closing a deal with an author; when asked by his wife how he got the author to sign the contract, he says he did it "the old-fashioned way; I begged." But being bitten changes all that for him. He gets in touch with his sexuality and aggression, makes love "like an animal" (as his wife tells him), begins to crave raw meat, and starts stalking game at night. And he gets even in primitive but effective ways with those who cross him. (For example, in a Bernhard Goetz white-man retribution moment, he bites off the fingers of a black gang member who tries to rob him in the park. In another scene, which must have delighted Camille Paglia, he pisses on the shoes of his assistant: "Just marking my territory and you got in the way," he says.)

All these, arguably, are in keeping with traditional werewolf stuff, albeit modernized. But becoming a wolf also makes Will more effective in the world of business—he sees and hears acutely, and uses this to his advantage—and most strikingly, his new wolfness makes him adept at the very kinds of ruthless machinations that the movie had portrayed so negatively earlier and juxtaposed against Will's civilized "niceness." He engineers a brilliant yet deceptive scheme to get his job back, and earns the respect of all around him. "You're my god," says his faithful editorial assistant (David Hyde Pierce) when he discovers that Will's scheme to get his job back is a bluff, based on a lie. And when the scheme succeeds, his boss tells him that if he'd known Will was "this ruthless, I'd never have fired you in the first place."

Here, the idea that real manliness (and sexual vitality and zest for life) is to be found outside man-made culture is merged with the idea of the workplace as the man-made jungle where a man might realize himself, if he's the right sort of animal. Will's transformation gives him the right stuff, and in the process he becomes something of an incoherency. He begins to speak like a character from a whole other movie. "The worm has turned and is packing an Uzi," he declares to his secretary. The bite of the wolf has turned Jack Nicholson into Arnold Schwarzenegger! Wolf man as terminator? Somehow I think the metaphors are getting mixed. In the end, the movie does suggest a final exit, with Michelle Pfeiffer, into the real jungle, where they will live fully as animals. But until then, the wolf man is allowed to have it all—spontaneous and playful animal sex with Michelle Pfeiffer, carnivorous romps in the woods, aggressive vengeance against his enemies— and more business smarts than Malcolm Forbes.

BIBLIOGRAPHY

Aristotle. (1941). "On the Generation of Animals." Trans. Arthur Platt, 729a 25–30, p. 676. In Richard McKeon (ed). *The Basic Works of Aristotle.* New York: Random House.

Bederman, Gail. (1995). *Manliness and Civilization.* Chicago: University of Chicago Press.

Bettelheim, Bruno. (1977). *The Uses of Enchantment: The Meaning and Importance of Fairy Tales.* New York: Vintage Books.

Gray, John. (1997). *Mars and Venus on a Date.* New York: HarperCollins.

Gray, John. (1992). *Men Are from Mars, Women Are from Venus.* New York: HarperCollins.

Guttmacher, Alan. (1987). *Pregnancy, Birth and Family Planning.* New York: Signet Books.

Showalter, Elaine. (1997). "Beauty and the Beast: Disney Meets a Liberated Love Story for the 90's," *Premiere,* October, p. 66.

Singer, A. L. (1991). *Disney's Beauty and the Beast.* New York: Disney Press.

Name: _____ Date: _____

UNDERSTANDING THE TEXT

1. According to Bordo, what is "the double bind of masculinity"?

2. According to Bordo, how did science before the Renaissance view women's sexuality?

3. According to Bordo, why did the status of the "civilized gentleman" in Europe decline as the nineteenth century drew to a close?

Consumer Republic

Debra Goldman

Is *Fight Club* an assault on consumer culture or a treatise on the sorry state of manhood? It was near the end of *Fight Club,* when Brad Pitt hurls the epithet "Ikea Boy" at Ed Norton, that I had a paranoid thought: Is this a product placement?

Think about it: Have you read a single review of *Fight Club,* director David Fincher's fantasy of male rebellion against the Empire of Brands, that failed to mention Ikea? When we meet Norton's character, Jack, he's flipping through an Ikea catalog, the camera peering over his shoulder as he ponders which dining room set "defines me as a person." Of course, he's being ironic—like, duh. Yet I haven't seen so much screen time devoted to a product since Q introduced James Bond to the latest BMW.

Then there's the visual motif of crumpled Krispy Kreme bags and the totemic shot of a Starbucks cup. If nothing else, the presence of these brands is a tribute to their mighty meme power, further proof that one logo-ed grande latte is worth a thousand words. When Jack grumbles, "We used to read pornography. Now it is the Horchow Home Collection," I understand: I'm on the Horchow Home Collection mailing list, too.

Yet Jack has another problem with consumer culture: His manhood is at risk, held hostage to his cushy condo lifestyle. "How do guys like us know what a duvet is?" complains Pitt's Tyler Durden. Before meeting Tyler, poor wussy, alienated Jack seeks comfort in 12-step programs, where the afflicted hug and weep like girls. Then Tyler teaches him—and, ultimately, every bus boy, barkeep and beat cop in the nation—to take spiritual nourishment from a knuckle sandwich.

The movie's antidote to a consumer culture that promises 24/7 pleasure is pain, inflicted mano-a-mano—a thesis that provides the excuse for lots of nasty, mesmerizing fight scenes during which a succession of faces are pummeled into purplish goo.

Fight Club has attracted controversy not just for its seductively stylish brutality, which has been damned as irresponsible in post-Columbine America. It also touches a sociocultural nerve in the era of erectile dysfunction ads: consumer culture as the emasculator of men.

In the heyday of feminism, consumer culture was the agent of patriarchy, reducing women to sex objects in service to the marketplace. Today, it's the long arm of feminization, offering men empty narcissism in place of masculine achievement.

Wipe the fake blood off the movie's characters and they'd make perfect subjects for a chapter in Susan Faludi's *Stiff: The Betrayal of American Men.* Like Faludi's lost boys, Jack and Tyler are literally and/or spiritually fatherless. In place of meaningful work or the heroic demands of war, they have credit cards. They traverse, as Faludi herself wrote in *Newsweek,* "a barren landscape familiar to many men who must contend with a world stripped of socially useful male roles and saturated with commercial images of masculinity."

What is to be done? Faludi's vision of manhood redeemed looks a lot like a WPA mural, resplendent with the lunch-pail solidarity of men who labor with their hands and their brawn to put food on the table. Fincher's is more like an apocalyptic music video, in which the guys find redemption through the fascist bonds of blood and obedience.

In truth, it's difficult to decide which of these scenarios is more unlikely: the resurrection of worker solidarity or the conversion of today's iconoclastic consumers into brainwashed, black-shirted terrorists. Both are pretty farfetched, though the fascism gambit makes a more commercial movie.

In my more generous moments, I think of *Fight Club* not as a celebration of fascism as the cure for consumer culture but as a satire of it. Jack and Tyler's all-powerful-leader fantasy is the kind of photogenic evil you'd dream up if you were someone who spent a lot of time watching movies like *Fight Club,* complete with buckets of special-effects blood and an artfully engineered soundtrack of fists thudding and skulls cracking.

We must be meant to laugh at the final scene, in which Ikea Boy and his nihilistic soul mate Maria clasp hands while they watch the destruction of capitalism's infrastructure as if it were a movie. Surely it's all a big goof on virtual violence, the opiate of the male masses in a post-masculine consumer age.

If *Fight Club* is not a satire, however, then it's one of the most cynical movies I've ever seen. It pretends to criticize the deadening effects of consumer culture so it can push the hot buttons of its young male target audience. In that case, I would like to propose a sequel.

In *Fight Club II,* Jack and Tyler return with their homemade bombs and their ambition to bring down the advertising-industrial complex. But instead of blowing up credit-card companies, they'll plant them in movie theaters—the ones showing *Fight Club.*

Name: _____ Date: _____

UNDERSTANDING THE TEXT

1. *Fight Club* appears to be highly critical of consumer culture. According to Goldman, how has this culture typically affected women, and how, as represented in the film, has it begun to affect men?

2. What does the film propose men do to counter this effect?

3. In her conclusion, Goldman offers a story line for a sequel. What is it, and why does she think it might be appropriate?

Rip Van Winkle

Washington Irving

The following Tale was found among the papers of the late Diedrich Knickerbocker, an old gentleman of New York, who was very curious in the Dutch history of the province, and the manners of the descendants from its primitive settlers. His historical researches, however, did not lie so much among books, as among men; for the former are lamentably scanty on his favourite topics; whereas he found the old burghers, and still more, their wives, rich in that legendary lore so invaluable to true history. Whenever, therefore, he happened upon a genuine Dutch family, snugly shut up in its low roofed farm house, under a spreading sycamore, he looked upon it as a little clasped volume of black letter, and studied it with the zeal of a bookworm.

The result of all these researches was a history of the province during the reign of the Dutch governors, which he published some years since. There have been various opinions as to the literary character of his work and, to tell the truth, it is not a whit better than it should be. Its chief merit is its scrupulous accuracy, which indeed was a little questioned on its first appearance, but has since been completely established; and it is now admitted into all historical collections as a book of unquestionable authority.

The old gentleman died shortly after the publication of his work, and now that he is dead and gone, it cannot do much harm to his memory to say that his time might have been much better employed in weightier labours. He, however, was apt to ride his hobby his own way; and though it did now and then kick up the dust a little in the eyes of his neighbours, and grieve the spirit of some friends for whom he felt the truest deference and affection; yet his errors and follies are remembered "more in sorrow than in anger," and it begins to be suspected that he never intended to injure or offend. But however his memory may be appreciated by criticks, it is still held dear by many folk whose good opinion is well worth having; particularly by certain biscuit bakers, who have gone so far as to imprint his likeness on their new year cakes, and have thus given him a chance for immortality, almost equal to being stamped on a Waterloo medal, or a Queen Anne's farthing.

Rip Van Winkle

A Posthumous Writing of Diedrich Knickerbocker

> By Woden, God of Saxons,
> From whence comes Wensday, that is Wodensday,
> Truth is a thing that ever I will keep
> Unto thylke day in which I creep into
> My sepulchre—
>
> *Cartwright*

Whoever has made a voyage up the Hudson must remember the Kaatskill mountains. They are a dismembered branch of the great Appalachian family, and are seen away to the west of the river swelling up to noble height and lording it over the surrounding country. Every change of season, every change of weather, indeed every hour of the day, produces some change in the magical hues and shapes of these mountains, and they are regarded by all the good wives far and near as perfect barometers. When the weather is fair and settled they are clothed in blue and purple, and print their bold outlines on the clear evening sky; but sometimes, when the rest of the landscape is cloudless, they will gather a hood of grey vapours about their summits, which, in the last rays of the setting sun, will glow and light up like a crown of glory.

At the foot of these fairy mountains the voyager may have descried the light smoke curling up from a village, whose shingle roofs gleam among the trees, just where the blue tints of the upland melt away into the fresh green of the nearer landscape. It is a little village of great antiquity, having been founded by some of the Dutch colonists in the early times of the province, just about the beginning of the government of the good Peter Stuyvesant, (may he rest in peace!) and there were some of the houses of the original settlers standing within a few years; built of small yellow bricks brought from Holland, having latticed windows and gable fronts, surmounted with weathercocks.

In that same village, and in one of these very houses (which to tell the precise truth was sadly time worn and weather beaten) there lived many years since, while the country was yet a province of Great Britain, a simple good natured fellow of the name of Rip Van Winkle. He was a descendant of the Van Winkles who figured so gallantly in the chivalrous days of Peter Stuyvesant, and accompanied him to the siege of Fort Christina. He inherited, however, but little of the martial character of his ancestors. I have observed that he was a simple good natured man; he was moreover a kind neighbour, and an obedient, henpecked husband. Indeed to the latter circumstance might be owing that meekness of spirit which gained him such universal popularity; for those men are most apt to be obsequious and conciliating abroad, who are under the discipline of shrews at home. Their tempers doubtless are rendered pliant and malleable in the fiery furnace of domestic tribulation, and a curtain lecture is worth all the sermons in the world for teaching the virtues of patience and long suffering.

A termagant wife may therefore in some respects be considered a tolerable blessing—and if so, Rip Van Winkle was thrice blessed.

Certain it is that he was a great favourite among all the good wives of the village, who as usual with the amiable sex, took his part in all family squabbles, and never failed, whenever they talked those matters over in their evening gossippings, to lay all the blame on Dame Van Winkle. The children of the village too would shout with joy whenever he approached. He assisted at their sports, made their play things, taught them to fly kites and shoot marbles, and told them long stories of ghosts, witches and Indians. Whenever he went dodging about the village he was surrounded by a troop of them hanging on his skirts, clambering on his back and playing a thousand tricks on him with impunity; and not a dog would bark at him throughout the neighbourhood.

The great error in Rip's composition was an insuperable aversion to all kinds of profitable labour. It could not be from the want of assiduity or perseverance; for he would sit on a wet rock, with a rod as long and heavy as a Tartar's lance, and fish all day without a murmur, even though he should not be encouraged by a single nibble. He would carry a fowling piece on his shoulder for hours together, trudging through woods, and swamps and up hill and down dale, to shoot a few squirrels or wild pigeons; he would never refuse to assist a neighbour even in the roughest toil, and was a foremost man at all country frolicks for husking Indian corn, or building stone fences; the women of the village too used to employ him to run their errands and to do such little odd jobs as their less obliging husbands would not do for them—in a word Rip was ready to attend to any body's business but his own; but as to doing family duty, and keeping his farm in order, he found it impossible.

In fact he declared it was of no use to work on his farm; it was the most pestilent little piece of ground in the whole country; every thing about it went wrong and would go wrong in spite of him. His fences were continually falling to pieces; his cow would either go astray or get among the cabbages, weeds were sure to grow quicker in his fields than any where else; the rain always made a point of setting in just as he had some outdoor work to do. So that though his patrimonial estate had dwindled away under his management, acre by acre until there was little more left than a mere patch of Indian corn and potatoes, yet it was the worst conditioned farm in the neighbourhood.

His children too were as ragged and wild as if they belonged to nobody. His son Rip, an urchin begotten in his own likeness, promised to inherit the habits with the old clothes of his father. He was generally seen trooping like a colt at his mother's heels, equipped in a pair of his father's cast off galligaskins, which he had much ado to hold up with one hand, as a fine lady does her train in bad weather.

Rip Van Winkle, however, was one of those happy mortals of foolish, well oiled dispositions, who take the world easy, eat white bread or brown, whichever can be got with least thought or trouble, and would rather starve on a penny than work for a pound. If left to himself, he would have whistled life away in perfect contentment, but his wife kept continually dinning in his ears about his idleness, his carelessness and the ruin he was bringing on his family. Morning noon and night her tongue was incessantly going, and every thing he said or did was sure to produce a torrent of household eloquence. Rip had but one way of replying to all lectures of the kind, and that by frequent use had grown into a habit. He shrugged his shoulders, shook his head, cast up his eyes, but said nothing. This, however, always provoked a fresh volley from his wife, so that he was fain to draw off his forces and take to the outside of the house—the only side which in truth belongs to a henpecked husband.

Rip's sole domestic adherent was his dog Wolf who was as much henpecked as his master, for Dame Van Winkle regarded them as companions in idleness, and even looked upon Wolf with an evil eye as the cause of his master's going so often astray. True it is, in all points of spirit befitting an honourable dog, he was as courageous an animal as ever scoured the woods—but what courage can withstand the ever during and all besetting terrors of a woman's tongue? The moment Wolf entered the house his crest fell, his tail drooped to the ground or curled between his legs, he sneaked about with a gallows air, casting many a sidelong glance at Dame Van Winkle, and at the least flourish of a broomstick or ladle he would fly to the door with yelping precipitation.

Times grew worse and worse with Rip Van Winkle as years of matrimony rolled on; a tart temper never mellows with age, and a sharp tongue is the only edged tool that grows keener with constant use. For a long while he used to console himself when driven from home, by frequenting a kind of perpetual club of the sages, philosophers and other idle personages of the village which held its sessions on a bench before a small inn, designated by a rubicund portrait of his majesty George the Third. Here they used to sit in the shade, through a long lazy summer's day, talking listlessly over village gossip, or telling endless sleepy stories about nothing. But it would have been worth any statesman's money to have heard the profound discussions that sometimes took place, when by chance an old newspaper fell into their hands from some passing traveller. How solemnly they would listen to the contents as drawled out by Derrick Van Bummel the schoolmaster, a dapper, learned little man, who was not to be daunted by the most gigantic word in the dictionary; and how sagely they would deliberate upon public events some months after they had taken place.

The opinions of this junto were completely controlled by Nicholaus Vedder, a patriarch of the village, and landlord of the inn, at the door of which he took his seat from morning till night, just moving sufficiently to avoid the sun and keep in the shade of a large tree; so that the neighbours could tell the hour by his movements as accurately as by a sun dial. It is true he was rarely heard to speak, but smoked his pipe incessantly. His adherents, however (for every great man has his adherents), perfectly understood him and knew how to gather his opinions. When any thing that was read or related displeased him, he was observed to smoke his pipe vehemently and to send forth short, frequent and angry puffs; but when pleased he would inhale the smoke slowly and tranquilly and emit it in light and placid clouds, and sometimes taking the pipe from his mouth and letting the fragrant vapour curl about his nose, would gravely nod his head in token of perfect approbation.

From even this strong hold the unlucky Rip was at length routed by his termagant wife who would suddenly break in upon the tranquility of the assemblage and call the members all to naught; nor was that august personage Nicholaus Vedder himself sacred from the daring tongue of this terrible virago, who charged him outright with encouraging her husband in habits of idleness.

Poor Rip was at last reduced almost to despair; and his only alternative to escape from the labour of the farm and the clamour of his wife, was to take gun in hand and stroll away into the woods. Here he would sometimes seat himself at the foot of a tree and share the contents of his wallet with Wolf, with whom he sympathised as a fellow sufferer in persecution. "Poor Wolf," he would say, "thy mistress leads thee a dog's life of it, but never mind my lad, whilst I live thou shalt never want a friend to stand by thee!" Wolf would wag his tail, look wistfully in his master's face, and if dogs can feel pity I verily believe he reciprocated the sentiment with all his heart.

In a long ramble of the kind on a fine autumnal day, Rip had unconsciously scrambled to one of the highest parts of the Kaatskill mountains. He was after his favourite sport of squirrel shooting and the still solitudes had echoed and re-echoed with the reports of his gun. Panting and fatigued he threw himself, late in the afternoon, on a green knoll, covered with mountain herbage, that crowned the brow of a precipice. From an opening between the trees he could overlook all the lower country for many a mile of rich woodland. He saw at a distance the lordly Hudson, far, far below him, moving on its silent but majestic course, with the reflection of a purple cloud, or the sail of a lagging bark here and there sleeping on its glassy bosom, and at last losing itself in the blue highlands.

On the other side he looked down into a deep mountain glen, wild, lonely and shagged, the bottom filled with fragments from the impending cliffs and scarcely lighted by the reflected rays of the setting sun. For some time Rip lay musing on this scene, evening was gradually advancing, the mountains began to throw their long blue shadows over the valleys, he saw that it would be dark, long before he could reach the village, and he heaved a heavy sigh when he thought of encountering the terrors of Dame Van Winkle.

As he was about to descend he heard a voice from a distance hallooing "Rip Van Winkle! Rip Van Winkle!" He looked around, but could see nothing but a crow winging its solitary flight across the mountain. He thought his fancy must have deceived him and turned again to descend, when he heard the same cry ring through the still evening air: "Rip Van Winkle! Rip Van Winkle!"—at the same time Wolf bristled up his back and giving a low growl, skulked to his master's side, looking fearfully down into the glen. Rip now felt a vague apprehension stealing over him; he looked anxiously in the same direction and perceived a strange figure slowly toiling up the rocks and bending under the weight of something he carried on his back. He was surprised to see any human being in this lonely and unfrequented place, but supposing it to be some one of the neighbourhood in need of his assistance he hastened down to yield it.

On nearer approach he was still more surprised at the singularity of the stranger's appearance. He was a short, square built old fellow, with thick bushy hair and a grizzled beard. His dress was of the antique Dutch fashion, a cloth jerkin strapped round the waist, several pair of breeches, the outer one of ample volume decorated with rows of buttons down the sides and bunches at the knees. He bore on his shoulder a stout keg that seemed full of liquor, and made signs for Rip to approach and assist him with the load. Though rather shy and distrustful of this new acquaintance Rip complied with his usual alacrity, and mutually relieving each other they clambered up a narrow gully apparently the dry bed of a mountain torrent. As they ascended Rip every now and then heard long rolling peals like distant thunder, that seemed to issue out of a deep ravine or rather cleft between lofty rocks, toward which their rugged path conducted. He paused for an instant, but supposing it to be the muttering of one of those transient thunder showers which often take place in mountain heights, he proceeded. Passing through the ravine they came to a hollow like a small amphitheatre, surrounded by perpendicular precipices, over the brinks of which impending trees shot their branches, so that you only caught glimpses of the azure sky and the bright evening cloud. During the whole time Rip and his companion had laboured on in silence, for though the former marvelled greatly what could be the object of carrying a keg of liquor up this wild mountain, yet there was something strange and incomprehensible about the unknown, that inspired awe and checked familiarity.

On entering the amphitheatre new objects of wonder presented themselves. On a level spot in the centre was a company of odd looking personages playing at ninepins. They were dressed in a quaint outlandish fashion—some wore short doublets, others jerkins with long knives in their belts and most of them had enormous breeches of similar style with that of the guide's. Their visages too were peculiar. One had a large head, broad face and small piggish eyes. The face of another seemed to consist entirely of nose, and was surmounted by a white sugarloaf hat, set off with a little red cock's tail. They all had beards of various shapes and colours. There was one who seemed to be the Commander. He was a stout old gentleman, with a weatherbeaten countenance. He wore a laced doublet, broad belt and hanger, high crowned hat and feather, red stockings and high heel'd shoes with roses in them. The whole group reminded Rip of the figures in an old Flemish painting, in the parlour of Dominie Van Schaick the village parson, and which had been brought over from Holland at the time of the settlement.

What seemed particularly odd to Rip was, that though these folks were evidently amusing themselves, yet they maintained the gravest faces, the most mysterious silence, and were, withal, the most melancholy party of pleasure he had ever witnessed. Nothing interrupted the stillness of the scene, but the noise of the balls, which, whenever they were rolled, echoed along the mountains like rumbling peals of thunder.

As Rip and his companion approached them they suddenly desisted from their play and stared at him with such fixed statue like gaze, and such strange uncouth, lack lustre countenances, that his heart turned within him, and his knees smote together. His companion now emptied the contents of the keg into large flagons and made signs to him to wait upon the company. He obeyed with fear and trembling; they quaffed the liquor in profound silence and then returned to their game.

By degrees Rip's awe and apprehension subsided. He even ventured, when no eye was fixed upon him, to taste the beverage, which he found had much of the flavour of excellent hollands. He was naturally a thirsty soul and was soon tempted to repeat the draught. One taste provoked another, and he reiterated his visits to the flagon so often that at length his senses were overpowered, his eyes swam in his head—his head gradually declined and he fell into a deep sleep.

On awaking he found himself on the green knoll from whence he had first seen the old man of the glen. He rubbed his eyes—it was a bright, sunny morning. The birds were hopping and twittering among the bushes, and the eagle was wheeling aloft and breasting the pure mountain breeze. "Surly," thought Rip, "I have not slept here all night." He recalled the occurrences before he fell asleep. The strange man with a keg of liquor—the mountain ravine—the wild retreat among the rocks—the woe begone party at ninepins—the flagon—"ah! that flagon! that wicked flagon!" thought Rip—"what excuse shall I make to Dame Van Winkle?"

He looked round for his gun, but in place of the clean well oiled fowling piece he found an old firelock lying by him, the barrel encrusted with rust; the lock falling off and the stock worm eaten. He now suspected that the grave roysters of the mountain had put a trick upon him, and having dosed him with liquor, had robbed him of his gun. Wolf too had disappeared, but he might have strayed away after a squirrel or partridge. He whistled after him and shouted his name—but all in vain; the echoes repeated his whistle and shout, but no dog was to be seen.

He determined to revisit the scene of the last evening's gambol, and if he met with any of the party, to demand his dog and gun. As he arose to walk he found himself stiff in the joints and wanting in his usual activity. "These mountain beds do not agree with me," thought Rip, "and if this frolick should lay me up with a fit of the rheumatism, I shall have a blessed time with Dame Van Winkle." With some difficulty he got down into the glen; he found the gully up which he and his companion had ascended the preceding evening, but to his astonishment a mountain stream was now foaming down it; leaping from rock to rock, and filling the glen with babbling murmurs. He, however, made shift to scramble up its sides working his toilsome way through thickets of birch, sassafras and witch hazel, and sometimes tripped up or entangled by the wild grape vines that twisted their coils and tendrils from tree to tree, and spread a kind of net work in his path.

At length he reached to where the ravine had opened through the cliffs, to the amphitheatre—but no traces of such opening remained. The rocks presented a high impenetrable wall over which the torrent came tumbling in a sheet of feathery foam, and fell into a broad deep basin black from the shadows of the surrounding forest. Here then poor Rip was brought to a stand. He again called and whistled after his dog—he was only answered by the cawing of a flock of idle crows, sporting high in air about a dry tree that overhung a sunny precipice; and who, secure in their elevation seemed to look down and scoff at the poor man's perplexities.

What was to be done? The morning was passing away and Rip felt famished for want of his breakfast. He grieved to give up his dog and gun; he dreaded to meet his wife; but it would not do to starve among the mountains. He shook his head, shouldered the rusty fire lock and with a heart full of trouble and anxiety, turned his steps homeward.

As he approached the village he met a number of people, but none whom he knew, which somewhat surprised him for he had thought himself acquainted with every one in the country round. Their dress too was of a different fashion from that to which he was accustomed. They all stared at him with equal marks of surprise, and whenever they cast their eyes upon him, invariably stroked their chins. The constant recurrence of this gesture induced Rip involuntarily to do the same, when to his astonishment he found his beard had grown a foot long!

He had now entered the skirts of the village. A troop of strange children ran at his heels, hooting after him and pointing at his grey beard. The dogs too, not one of which he recognized for an old acquaintance, barked at him as he passed. The very village was altered—it was larger and more populous. There were rows of houses which he had never seen before, and those which had been his familiar haunts had disappeared. Strange names were over the doors—strange faces at the windows—every thing was strange. His mind now misgave him; he began to doubt whether both he and the world around him were not bewitched. Surely this was his native village which he had left but the day before. There stood the Kaatskill mountains—there ran the silver Hudson at a distance—there was every hill and dale precisely as it had always been—Rip was sorely perplexed—"That flagon last night," thought he, "has addled my poor head sadly!"

It was with some difficulty that he found the way to his own house, which he approached with silent awe, expecting every moment to hear the shrill voice of Dame Van Winkle. He found the house gone to decay—the roof fallen in, the windows shattered and the doors off the hinges. A half starved dog that looked like Wolf was skulking about it. Rip called him by name but the cur snarled, shewed his teeth and passed on. This was an unkind cut indeed— "My very dog," sighed poor Rip, "has forgotten me!"

He entered the house, which, to tell the truth, Dame Van Winkle had always kept in neat order. It was empty, forlorn and apparently abandoned. This desolateness overcame all his connubial fears—he called loudly for his wife and children— the lonely chambers rung for a moment with his voice, and then all again was silence.

He now hurried forth and hastened to his old resort, the village inn—but it too was gone. A large, ricketty wooden building stood in its place, with great gaping windows, some of them broken, and mended with old hats and petticoats, and over the door was printed "The Union Hotel, by Jonathan Doolittle." Instead of the great tree, that used to shelter the quiet little Dutch inn of yore, there now was reared a tall naked pole with something on top that looked like a red night cap, and from it was fluttering a flag on which was a singular assemblage of stars and stripes—all this was strange and incomprehensible. He recognized on the sign, however, the ruby face of King George under which he had smoked so many a peaceful pipe, but even this was singularly metamorphosed. The red coat was changed for one of blue and buff; a sword was held in the hand instead of a sceptre; the head was decorated with a cocked hat, and underneath was printed in large characters GENERAL WASHINGTON.

There was as usual a crowd of folk about the door; but none that Rip recollected. The very character of the people seemed changed. There was a busy, bustling disputatious tone about it, instead of the accustomed phlegm and drowsy tranquility. He looked in vain for the sage Nicholaus Vedder with his broad face, double chin and fair long pipe, uttering clouds of tobacco smoke instead of idle speeches. Or Van Bummel the schoolmaster doling forth the contents of an ancient newspaper. In place of these a lean bilious looking fellow with his pockets full of hand bills, was haranguing vehemently about rights of citizens—elections—members of Congress—liberty—Bunker's hill—heroes of seventy six—and other words which were a perfect babylonish jargon to the bewildered Van Winkle.

The appearance of Rip with his long grizzled beard, his rusty fowling piece his uncouth dress and an army of women and children at his heels soon attracted the attention of the tavern politicians. They crowded around him eying him from head to foot, with great curiosity. The orator bustled up to him, and drawing him partly aside, enquired "on which side he voted?"—Rip stared in vacant stupidity. Another short but busy little fellow, pulled him by the arm and rising on tiptoe, enquired in his ear " whether he was Federal or Democrat?"—Rip was equally at a loss to comprehend the question—when a knowing, self important old gentleman, in a sharp cocked hat, made his way through the crowd, putting them to the right and left with his elbows as he passed, and planting himself before Van Winkle, with one arm akimbo, the other resting on his cane, his keen eyes and sharp hat penetrating as it were into his very soul, demanded in an austere tone—"what brought him to the election with a gun on his shoulder and a mob at his heels, and whether he meant to breed a riot in the village?"—"Alas gentlemen," cried Rip, somewhat dismayed, "I am a poor quiet man, a native of the place, and a loyal subject of the King—God bless him!"

Here a general shout burst from the byestanders—"A tory! a tory! a spy! a Refugee! hustle him! away with him!"—It was with great difficulty that the self important man in the cocked hat restored order; and having assumed a ten fold austerity of brow demanded again of the unknown culprit, what he came there for and whom he was seeking. The poor man humbly assured him that he meant no harm; but merely came there in search of some of his neighbours, who used to keep about the tavern.

"—Well—who are they?—name them."

Rip bethought himself a moment and enquired, "Where's Nicholaus Vedder?"

There was a silence for a little while, when an old man replied, in a thin, piping voice, "Nicholaus Vedder? why he is dead and gone these eighteen years! There was a wooden tombstone in the church yard that used to tell all about him, but that's rotted and gone too."

"Where's Brom Dutcher?"

"Oh he went off to the army in the beginning of the war; some say he was killed at the storming of Stoney Point—others say he was drowned in a squall at the foot of Antony's Nose—I don't know—he never came back again."

"Where's Van Bummel the schoolmaster?"

"He went off to the wars too—was a great militia general, and is now in Congress."

Rip's heart died away at hearing of these sad changes in his home and friends, and finding himself thus alone in the world—every answer puzzled him too by treating of such enormous lapses of time and of matters which he could not understand—war—Congress, Stoney Point—he had no courage to ask after any more friends, but cried out in despair, "Does nobody here know Rip Van Winkle?"

"Oh. Rip Van Winkle?" exclaimed two or three—"oh to be sure!—that's Rip Van Winkle— yonder—leaning against the tree."

Rip looked and beheld a precise counterpart of himself, as he went up the mountain: apparently as lazy and certainly as ragged! The poor fellow was now completely confounded. He doubted his own identity, and whether he was himself or another man. In the midst of his bewilderment the man in the cocked hat demanded who he was,—what was his name?

"God knows," exclaimed he, at his wit's end, "I'm not myself.—I'm somebody else— that's me yonder—no—that's somebody else got into my shoes—I was myself last night; but I fell asleep on the mountain—and they've changed my gun—and every thing's changed—and I'm changed—and I can't tell what's my name, or who I am!"

The byestanders began now to look at each other, nod, wink significantly and tap their fingers against their foreheads. There was a whisper also about securing the gun, and keeping the old fellow from doing mischief—at the very suggestion of which, the self important man in the cocked hat retired with some precipitation. At this critical moment a fresh likely looking woman pressed through the throng to get a peep at the greybearded man. She had a chubby child in her arms, which frightened at his looks began to cry. "Hush Rip," cried she, "hush you little fool, the old man won't hurt you." The name of the child, the air of the mother, the tone of her voice all awakened a train of recollections in his mind. "What is your name my good woman?" asked he.

"Judith Gardenier."

"And your father's name?"

"Ah, poor man, Rip Van Winkle was his name, but it's twenty years since he went away from home with his gun and never has been heard of since—his dog came home without him—but whether he shot himself, or was carried away by the Indians no body can tell. I was then but a little girl."

Rip had but one question more to ask, but he put it with a faltering voice—

"Where's your mother?"—

Oh she too had died but a short time since—she broke a blood vessel in a fit of passion at a New England pedlar.—

There was a drop of comfort at least in this intelligence. The honest man could contain himself no longer—he caught his daughter and her child in his arms.—"I am your father!" cried he—"Young Rip Van Winkle once—old Rip Van Winkle now!—does nobody know poor Rip Van Winkle!"

All stood amazed, until an old woman tottering out from among the crowd put her hand to her brow and peering under it in his face for a moment exclaimed—"Sure enough!— it is Rip Van Winkle—it is himself—welcome home again old neighbour—why, where have you been these twenty long years?"

Rip's story was soon told, for the whole twenty years had been to him but as one night. The neighbours stared when they heard it; some were seen to wink at each other and put their tongues in their cheeks, and the self important man in the cocked hat, who when the alarm was over had returned to the field, screwed down the corners of his mouth and shook his head—upon which there was a general shaking of the head throughout the assemblage.

It was determined, however, to take the opinion of old Peter Vanderdonk, who was seen slowly advancing up the road. He was a descendant of the historian of that name, who wrote one of the earliest accounts of the province. Peter was the most ancient inhabitant of the village and well versed in all the wonderful events and traditions of the neighbourhood. He recollected Rip at once, and corroborated his story in the most satisfactory manner. He assured the company that it was a fact handed down from his ancestor the historian, that the Kaatskill mountains had always been haunted by strange beings. That it was affirmed that the great Hendrick Hudson, the first discoverer of the river and country, kept a kind of vigil there every twenty years, with his crew of the Half Moon—being permitted in this way to revisit the scenes of his enterprize and keep a guardian eye upon the river and the great city called by his name. That his father had once seen them in their old Dutch dresses playing at nine pins in a hollow of the mountain; and that he himself had heard one summer afternoon the sound of their balls, like distant peals of thunder.

To make a long story short—the company broke up, and returned to the more important concerns of the election. Rip's daughter took him home to live with her; she had a snug well furnished house, and a stout cheery farmer for a husband whom Rip recollected for one of the urchins that used to climb upon his back. As to Rip's son and heir, who was the ditto of himself seen leaning against the tree; he was employed to work on the farm; but evinced an hereditary disposition to attend to any thing else but his business.

Rip now resumed his old walks and habits; he soon found many of his former cronies, though all rather the worse for the wear and tear of time; and preferred making friends among the rising generation, with whom he soon grew into great favour. Having nothing to do at home, and being arrived at that happy age when a man can be idle, with impunity, he took his place once more on the bench at the inn door and was reverenced as one of the patriarchs of the village and a chronicle of the old times "before the war." It was some time before he could get into the regular track of gossip, or could be made to comprehend the strange events that had taken place during his torpor. How that there had been a revolutionary war—that the country had thrown off the yoke of Old England and that instead of being a subject of his majesty George the Third, he was now a free citizen of the United States. Rip in fact was no politician; the changes of states and empires made but little impression on him; but there was one species of despotism under which he had long groaned and that was petticoat government. Happily that was at an end—he had got his neck out of the yoke of matrimony, and could go in and out whenever he pleased without dreading the tyranny of Dame Van Winkle. Whenever her name was mentioned, however, he shook his head, shrugged his shoulders and cast up his eyes; which might pass either for an expression of resignation to his fate or joy at his deliverance.

He used to tell his story to every stranger that arrived at Mr. Doolittle's Hotel. He was observed at first to vary on some points, every time he told it, which was doubtless owing to his having so recently awaked. It at last settled down precisely to the tale I have related and not a man woman or child in the neighbourhood but knew it by heart. Some always pretended to doubt the reality of it, and insisted that Rip had been out of his head, and that this was one point on which he always remained flighty. The old Dutch inhabitants, however, almost universally gave it full credit—Even to this day they never hear a thunder storm of a summer afternoon about the Kaatskill, but they say Hendrick Hudson and his crew are at their game of nine pins; and it is a common wish of all henpecked husbands in the neighbourhood, when life hangs heavy on their hands, that they might have a quieting draught out of Rip Van Winkle's flagon.

NOTE

The foregoing tale one would suspect had been suggested to Mr. Knickerbocker by a little German superstition about the emperor Frederick *der Rothbart* and the Kypphauser Mountain; the subjoined note, however, which he had appended to the tale, shews that it is an absolute fact, narrated with his usual fidelity.—

"The story of Rip Van Winkle may seem incredible to many, but nevertheless I give it my full belief, for I know the vicinity of our old Dutch settlements to have been very subject to marvellous events and appearances. Indeed I have heard many stranger stories than this, in the villages along the Hudson; all of which were too well authenticated to admit of a doubt. I have even talked with Rip Van Winkle myself, who when last I saw him was a very venerable old man and so perfectly rational and consistent on every other point, that I think no conscientious person could refuse to take this into the bargain—nay I have seen a certificate on the subject taken before a country justice and signed with a cross in the justice's own hand writing. The story therefore is beyond the possibility of doubt.

D.K."

POSTSCRIPT

The following are travelling notes from a memorandum book of Mr. Knickerbocker.

The Kaatsberg or Catskill mountains have always been a region full of fable. The Indians considered them the abode of spirits who influenced the weather, spreading sunshine or clouds over the landscape and sending good or bad hunting seasons. They were ruled by an old squaw spirit, said to be their mother. She dwelt on the highest peak of the Catskills and had charge of the doors of day and night to open and shut them at the proper hour. She hung up the new moons in the skies and cut up the old ones into stars. In times of drought, if properly propitiated, she would spin light summer clouds out of cobwebs and morning dew, and send them off, from the crest of the mountain, flake after flake, like flakes of carded cotton to float in the air: until, dissolved by the heat of the sun, they would fall in gentle showers, causing the grass to spring, the fruits to ripen and the corn to grow an inch an hour. If displeased, however, she would brew up clouds black as ink, sitting in the midst of them like a bottle bellied spider in the midst of its web; and when these clouds broke— woe betide the valleys!

In old times say the Indian traditions, there was a kind of Manitou or Spirit, who kept about the wildest recesses of the Catskill mountains, and took a mischievous pleasure in wreaking all kinds of evils and vexations upon the red men. Sometimes he would assume the form of a bear a panther or a deer, lead the bewildered hunter a weary chace through tangled forests and among rugged rocks; and then spring off with a loud ho! ho! leaving him aghast on the brink of a beetling precipice or raging torrent.

The favorite abode of this Manitou is still shewn. It is a great rock or cliff in the loneliest part of the mountains, and, from the flowering vines which clamber about it, and the wild flowers which abound in its neighborhood, is known by the name of the Garden Rock. Near the foot of it is a small lake the haunt of the solitary bittern, with water snakes basking in the sun on the leaves of the pond lillies which lie on the surface. This place was held in great awe by the Indians, insomuch that the boldest hunter would not pursue his game within its precincts. Once upon a time, however, a hunter who had lost his way, penetrated to the garden rock where he beheld a number of gourds placed in the crotches of trees. One of these he seized and made off with it, but in the hurry of his retreat he let it fall among the rocks, when a great stream gushed forth which washed him away and swept him down precipices where he was dashed to pieces, and the stream made its way to the Hudson and continues to flow to the present day; being the identical stream known by the name of the Kaaters-kill.

Name: _____ Date: _____

UNDERSTANDING THE TEXT

1. Characterize Rip Van Winkle and his wife in detail. What is Rip's attitude toward work? What is his wife's response to this attitude?

> Rip was a nice caring guy who would help anyone out in the village! When it came to his farm, nothing ever was really taken care of Rip did not work hard on his farm. He didn't care to work
>
> Rips wife is good looking, but she is very bossy and mean. She is loud and is always getting on him when he comes home

2. Why does Rip go to the mountains, and what happens to him there? What happens to his wife back in the village?

> Rip goes to the mountains to escape his wife and shoot squirrels. While he was in the mountains, he fell asleep. He woke up in the morning 20 years later! He went back to the village to find that it has changed. He went to his house to find his wife and children gone. His wife passed away.

3. When he returns home, what does Rip discover has happened in the country and in his village? How many other Rips does he encounter? Who are they?

Rip has noticed the village has grown, and there are a lot of unfamiliar faces. His country had gone to war and most of his friends passed away. His dog didn't recognize him.

Rip comes across three Rips. His daughter, son, and grandson.

PART TWO

Fashion and the Body

Dress for Effect: Paris Creations, Power Suits and Punk Put-Ons, Your Style Affects Both You and Your Public

Michael R. Solomon

"Clothes make the man." "Dress for success." "Feeling down? Go out and buy new clothes." Popular culture is replete with references to the potency of clothing as symbol in everyday life. But although many people will attest to the power of clothing to influence self-esteem, mood and the impressions we make on others, the evidence for these claims has been largely anecdotal. Gradually, however, empirical evidence has been mounting to confirm the long-held belief that the meanings transmitted by clothing profoundly affect the perception and thinking not only of the viewer but of the wearer as well.

People are social animals, and clothing is very much a social invention. It is laden with symbolism that provides information about social and occupational standing, sex-role identification, political orientation, ethnicity and esthetic priorities. Clothing is a potent—and highly visible—medium of communication that carries a flood of information about who a person is, who a person is not and who a person would like to be. It is an important mediator of social life.

Popular wisdom tells us, for example, never to underestimate the power of a first impression. Within the first few seconds after encountering strangers, people very quickly and confidently form judgments about their religious, political and ethnic background and make snap decisions regarding their social, professional or sexual desirability. Although first impressions are often wrong, psychologists have shown that they have a tendency to persist, even in the face of later evidence to the contrary.

Clothing is an important source of information during this process. Unlike the contents of a wallet or one's personal values, clothing is highly visible and is brimming with clues about the wearer's background. Many clothing items, such as a priest's collar, are worn because they have symbolic significance. We are expected to draw conclusions about a person's identity from such symbols and to act accordingly.

Observers often use clothing to infer social status, for example. People become more "legitimate" if they are dressed appropriately. This effect has been documented experimentally as long ago as the 1950s, when psychologists Monroe Lefkowitz, Robert R. Blake and Jane Srygley Mouton examined the willingness of pedestrians to violate the social norm against jaywalking. When strangers saw a well-dressed person of high status (actually a confederate in the experiment) jaywalk, they were more likely to follow his example than if the same accomplice was dressed in soiled and patched clothing.

These findings extend to the political arena as well. For example, research by psychologist Peter Suedfeld and others has documented the impact of apparel on the likelihood of petition signing. He has shown that people who dress like their potential supporters will be more successful in gathering signatures. When campaigning for a liberal cause, the person dressed more casually (who corresponds with our expectations of what such a person should look like) is more likely to collect names.

The exact nature of these expectations is constantly evolving. While faded jeans, army fatigues and hiking boots were associated with political activism in the 1960s, such fashions have been coopted by mass culture and have lost much of their original meaning. Clothing researcher Charlene Lind at Brigham Young University and sociologist Mary Ellen Roach-Higgins at the University of Wisconsin-Madison have demonstrated that as the unconventional dress of '60s activists became the fashionable norm, it lost its power as a social and political statement.

Aside from generalizations about large groups, clues about individuals can be gleaned from apparel. These clues can be subtle. A man wearing a silk rep tie may be classified differently than one wearing a plaid bow tie. To the practiced observer, even subtle variations in the colors or stripe widths of a rep tie can speak volumes about the wearer.

Marketing researchers Shelley Harp and Shirley Stretch and telecommunications professor Dennis Harp investigated the effect of apparel on the credibility of television newscasters while at Texas Tech University. They simulated excerpts of 60-second newsbreaks using a man and a woman (both were actually professional broadcasters) to deliver a news report. The videotaped excerpts showed the female member of the news team reading a breaking story. While the clothing of the broadcasters was either conservative, casual or trendy, the color of the clothing and content of the news story were always the same.

Each viewer rated the personality of the female broadcaster on believability, competence and honesty, which the researchers combined to form an index of "perceived credibility." Viewers were also asked to indicate their own preferred style of dress.

The newscasters' clothing style exerted a strong effect on whether the viewers found them believable. When both actors were dressed conservatively, ratings were more positive than in any other case. It is likely that this type of dress was consistent with what the viewers expected newscasters to wear.

In general, researchers find that people agree on what certain types of clothes mean. In a study of adolescent girls in Great Britain, psychologist Keith Gibbins found that the girls could easily agree on the life-styles of girls who wore various outfits, including the number of boyfriends they probably had as well as whether they smoked or drank.

If there is widespread agreement about the meaning of clothing symbolism, then it stands to reason that we must all learn, to some degree, the same language of fashion—although we speak it with differing degrees of fluency. But when does the learning process begin? A recent study by sociologist Robert Mayer and consumer psychologist Russell Belk at the University of Utah underscores the idea that such associations take root at an early age.

For four products (jeans, shoes, video games and bicycles), Mayer and Belk showed slides of different types and brands to 384 fourth- and sixth-grade children. The children rated the owners of these products on personality characteristics such as popularity, attractiveness and friendliness. They also reported which products and brands they owned themselves.

The children were shown three types of children's jeans—a designer brand (Calvin Klein), a medium-priced traditional brand (Levi Strauss) and an inexpensive store brand (Sears Toughskins)—and the children did in fact attribute different personalities to owners of the different jeans. Levis wearers were perceived more favorably than wearers of Calvin Kleins, although the latter are more expensive, while Toughskin wearers were rated the most negatively.

Observers use clothing cues to categorize people, but what is the effect of clothing on the wearer? Within the limits of the fashion market, people can and do exercise control over what they wear, spending a great deal of time, effort and money on clothing. The hours spent agonizing over clothing choices in the store, deliberating over what to wear or preening in front of the mirror testify to the psychic importance of these decisions.

Concern with such decisions extends well beyond the minority who are slavishly committed to wearing the latest fashions. While many people profess not to be concerned with wearing fashionable clothing, most are concerned with owning clothing that is appropriate to the social, sexual, athletic or professional roles they perform in life. Since people are now aware that apparel cues are instrumental in communicating social information, the reason for being interested in clothing has changed from concern about esthetics to strategy.

Psychologist John Schopler and I have found that this connection is more likely to be made by people who see themselves as actors on life's stage. We tested the degree to which students at the University of North Carolina at Chapel Hill were aware of themselves as social entities and we also asked them to complete a questionnaire on their interest in clothing and fashion. We found that students who view themselves as taking an active role in their interpersonal relationships also tend to be concerned about costumes they must wear to successfully play those roles.

If these people rely upon appropriate clothing to convince their "audience" of the veracity of their social "roles," at what point will they come to believe in their own parts? Many people can relate instances in which the clothing they wore changed the way they felt about themselves, or the way they behaved. Clothing can be used to alter mood; indeed, some therapists I have interviewed recommend the purchase of new clothing to certain depressed clients.

Clothing may also be used to gain confidence when one must engage in stressful situations, ranging from first dates and courtroom appearances to job interviews. Of course, different people feel confident wearing different things. I recently explored the nature of people's attachment to blue jeans for Levi Strauss & Co. and found that about a quarter of the people felt more confident in social situations when they wore Levis.

Often we estimate how we are perceived by others and incorporate this image into our own self-perception. In another study at the University of North Carolina, I established a fake corporate office and conducted mock job interviews with male undergraduate business students. I predicted that these students would incorporate information about how they thought they looked into their overall self-image and that the quality of this image itself would have an impact on them.

The students were not told how to dress, but by carefully scheduling the appointments, I made sure that some would have to come directly from class while others would have an opportunity to change into more formal interview clothing. After the interview, students were asked how they thought the interviewer had perceived them. Those who were dressed in the proper "uniform" for the part—jacket and tie—felt that the interviewer had a higher opinion of their abilities than did those who were dressed in less appropriate ways. Moreover, when asked to name a figure that they would consider to be an appropriate starting salary for themselves, the more formally dressed students asked for $4,000 more than the others, on average.

The power of clothing to affect self-definition in a given social role may depend upon one's actual experience at playing that role. In a series of studies with marketing researcher Susan Douglas at New York University concerning female executives, I have found that the strategic value of a professional appearance is emphasized most by those who are relative newcomers to their positions or who are less confident in their ability to play those roles. People, it turns out, are most reliant upon the symbolism of clothing during the process of transition from a familiar role to an unfamiliar one. Many people believe that the business suit, for example, can function as a magic amulet that protects the wearer during the rite of passage to a new role as an "executive."

Such a proposition is consistent with work done by psychologists Robert Wicklund and Peter Gollwitzer while at the University of Texas at Austin. In their study, Wicklund and Gollwitzer found that business students with less likelihood of career success (measured by grade-point average and number of job offers, for example) were also more likely to wear expensive watches, accessories and shoes normally associated with the role of the executive.

In fact, the issue of appropriate clothing has probably received more attention in the business world than anywhere else. Intense competition for jobs, coupled with our society's emphasis on professional success and upward mobility, has prompted many to focus on possible competitive advantages that were previously ignored or underplayed. The "dress for success" movement has spawned an entire industry devoted to providing the work force with appropriate sartorial symbols and a heightened awareness of the power of clothing to influence outcomes in all types of settings.

Paradoxically, recent concerns about dressing correctly are antithetical to the traditional concerns of fashion. Whereas fashion has always meant personal expression, esthetics and, above all, constant change, the new emphasis upon strategic business clothing emphasizes conformity, rigidity and continuity. A survey of American men that I conducted for the Celanese Corporation illustrates the need to dress appropriately. When I asked these men what they wanted their clothing to say about them, most chose "confident" as opposed to rich, sophisticated, sexy or stylish.

The issue of clothing and self-definition in the workplace is even more pressing for women, who do not yet have the well-defined precedents and role models that men do but who nevertheless view their image as crucial to success. Many women in business are unsure about the appropriate mixture of masculine and feminine attributes desirable in female professional dress. And the array of choices for women is much wider than it is for men: Women must choose among alternatives ranging from severely cut business suits to dresses or skirts.

Anxiety over this issue appears to be well-founded. Psychologist Thomas Cash at Old Dominion University has conducted several studies on the effect of grooming styles on the personnel evaluations of women in corporate management. In one study, executives were asked to evaluate personnel folders in which they saw photographs of various female job "applicants." Cash found that women who displayed a "managerial" (or less feminine) grooming style—characterized by shorter hairstyles, only moderate use of cosmetics and plainly tailored clothing—were preferred over those displaying more traditional, feminine grooming styles.

In addition, although the latter style tends to be more esthetically appealing to members of the opposite sex, men are more consistently biased against feminine grooming when evaluating executives. As one male executive recruiter confided to me, "A sexy-looking woman is definitely going to get a longer interview, but she won't get a job."

Women in general, and executive women in particular, seem to understand this. Two years ago, Douglas and I surveyed the readers of a magazine for female executives. On the basis of more than 8,000 responses, we found that although many of the women were in an ideal position to be fashion trend-setters (that is, between the ages of 25 and 35, well-educated and with good incomes), they reported little interest in fashion. In contrast, these women were extremely involved with the tactical properties of clothing and strongly agreed that "dressing well is important for advancement in one's career."

We are starting to understand, in an empirical way, how clothing affects those who wear it and those who see it. But psychologists and other social scientists concerned with issues such as self-image and interpersonal relationships are like fish who are constantly surrounded by water yet only dimly aware of its importance. Social psychologists, for example, who have documented the effects of physical attractiveness on self-esteem, tend to focus mainly on the effects of facial features. Such studies have, for the most part, ignored the importance of fashion, which is potentially as important as any other factors.

We are just beginning to understand the pervasive impact that clothing and other symbolically-laden products can exert on self-definition and behavior in interpersonal relationships. As more systematic research is performed, we will better appreciate the role played by clothing in the fabric of social life.

Name: _____   Date: _____

UNDERSTANDING THE TEXT

1. According to researchers, what happened to the message sent by the nonconformist clothing styles of the 1960s once they "became the fashionable norm"?

2. What style of clothing did researchers report lends the greatest "credibility" to newscasters?

3. In their research, what did the author and his associate discover about clothing choices "made by people who see themselves as actors on life's stage"?

Haute Porn, Hard-Core Couture

John Leo

Naomi Wolf's book, *The Beauty Myth,* which is getting a good ride in the press now, argues that men are imposing a cruel "cult of female beauty" as a political weapon to impede women's progress. Though the book has the feel of an overwrought feminist tract circa 1980, the core thesis is not foolish at all, and Wolf is sharp on a number of side issues. Here she is on the connection between fashion and pornography:

> Midway through the 1970s, the punk-rock scene began to glorify S and M: High-school girls put safety pins through their ears, painted their lips bruise-blue, and ripped their clothing to suggest sexual battle. By the end of the decade, S and M had ascended from street fashion to high fashion in the form of studded black leather, wrist cuffs, and spikes. Fashion models adopted from violent pornography the furious pouting glare of the violated woman.

I first noticed the porn-fashion connection in 1975, when *Vogue* magazine ran a seven-photo fashion spread featuring a man in a bathrobe battering a screaming model in a lovely peach jumpsuit ($140 from Saks Fifth Avenue, pictures by Avedon). Though I was shocked, the model didn't seem to be, since on the next page, apparently refreshed by being slapped around in a fashionable manner, she and the perpetrator were nuzzling happily next to the headline "Together Again!" Though peace had broken out, he did seem to be choking her with both hands in a tiny photo on the bottom of the page, possibly because he just hated her plaided silk crepe de Chine separates (about $1,050, from Geoffrey Beene).

As Wolf notes, the conventions of hard-core porn, including the violent ones, began to take hold in the fashion world in the 70s. Some photographers rode to glory on pictures debasing women, including the late Chris von Wangenheim, with his dogs-and-women shots, and Helmut Newton, who injected the leather-and-bondage themes of male porn directly into the high-fashion world. Images of sexual violence and murder sprouted in fashion magazines and window displays of Fifth Avenue stores.

Bondage chic. Many people in the fashion industry downplay the porn-fashion connection, calling it a brief foray into titillation that has ended. In a way, it has. The battered-women fashion spreads and gun-toting mannequins are gone. But the images and conventions of porn came to stay. The Guess? jeans ads, for instance, rework familiar male porn, from the image of the docile young woman on her knees, gazing submissively up at a dominant older male, to the ad of a man seizing a woman from behind on a motorcycle, which looks like a rape.

In her book *Female Perversions,* psychoanalyst Louise J. Kaplan argues that pornographers once groped for style among fashion magazines and Bloomingdale's catalogs, but now the fashion world and the porn world use one another quite openly as resources. Kaplan writes: "Nobody knew quite how it happened, but there came a day when nobody could tell who was emulating whom."

The bodysuits and bathing suits cut high up on the thigh, for example, come from the world of porn and were introduced into the fashion world via the bunny costumes designed by Hugh Hefner. Many women like them because they make the legs look longer and sleeker. Some men, at least, seem to like them because of the fetishistic look of a high-riding, hip-baring style that makes the suit look like an arrow aimed at the female genitals.

Against all predictions, the garter belt—very likely the most fetishized garment in the imagination of the American male—has made an amazing comeback. Madonna has helped popularize many porn styles—pointy bras, tight bustiers and, in general, the underwear-as-outer-wear look that plays to female defiance and male voyeurism. In the 50s, Maidenform ads played with the fantasy of a woman confidently walking around town in a bra. Now the fantasy has more or less come true.

The current fetishization of fashion extends to body parts, too. Plastic surgeons report that women showing up for breast enlargement operations commonly bring along pictures torn out of *Penthouse* and *Playboy* to indicate the size they want. Following the big-breast obsession of American men, the size is often much larger than that sought in similar operations in Europe. In fact, it has been reported that many American women are enlarging their breasts to the exact point where French women come in and ask for breast reduction.

Well, now that bullet bras, garter belts, spiked chokers, slave bracelets and outdoor underwear are in fashion, what else can porn contribute to high style? Would you believe the piercing of the body in strange places? Yes, newspapers report a trend to wearing rings in the nipples and genitals. This is the clear imagery of sexual slavery, springing from the hardest-core, most hostile porn, but it is presented as a natural and harmless extension of earrings and nose jewelry. One California business reports over 600 body piercings in April, including the nipples of a bank president and the genitals of many Orange County housewives. "It became cool; it became fashion," a Manhattan piercer told the *New York Times.* Yet another quiet fashion triumph of the pornographic imagination.

Name: _____ Date: _____

UNDERSTANDING THE TEXT

1. When did Leo first notice that high fashion was drawing its images and motifs from pornography? What did the ads he encountered on this occasion depict?

2. What look in women's fashion does Leo trace back to Hugh Hefner's influence?

3. According to Leo, what kinds of images have encouraged the "piercing of the body in strange places"?

Dress Reform and the Bloomer

Jennifer Ladd Nelson

In the mid-nineteenth century, the ideology of separate "spheres" for men and women dictated the nature of their activities and was both symbolized and reinforced by their clothing. If the saying "clothes make the man" is true, it was doubly so for the Victorian woman. A writer of the time noted, "Fashion says that the chief use of woman is to exhibit dry goods fantastically arranged on her person" (Russell 500). The accuracy of this statement was evident in the extensive wardrobes of middle- and upper-class women of the period. Composed of ornamental, cumbersome, impractical garments, the wearer was rendered largely incapable of participating in public life and relegated to the domestic sphere assigned to women.

Several groups within society recognized the absurdity of women's fashions and shared a commitment to reforming dress in spite of emphasizing different concerns. Orthodox or allopathic physicians were interested in dress reform due to the health effects of the corset and petticoat and their impact on childbearing, a central responsibility within a woman's sphere. Practitioners of alternative medicine, including hydropathy or the water-cure, emphasized good health as a right of all individuals, including women, and believed that without dress reform, women's health would continue to be compromised along with their achievements. Feminists, too, acknowledged the health effects of the day's fashions but also called attention to dress as an impediment to women's full participation in society and their freedom to choose their own course in life. While each of these interested parties contributed to dress reform at various stages, it was the mainstream feminists, under the leadership of Amelia Bloomer and Elizabeth Cady Stanton, who brought dress reform to the attention of society with the introduction of the Bloomer costume. Ironically, it was also these same feminists, including Bloomer and Stanton who, in their promotion of women's rights, were among the first to abandon wearing the new costume.

In *Beyond Her Sphere,* Barbara Harris identifies four ideas that formed the "cult of true womanhood" in the nineteenth century. These included, "a sharp dichotomy between the home and the economic world outside that paralleled a sharp contrast between female and male natures, the designation of the home as the female's only proper sphere, the moral superiority of woman, and the idealization of her function as mother" (33). Together, these interconnected ideas outline the dominant nineteenth-century view of women and provide the foundation upon which their assigned role was built.

As the United States moved from a rural, agrarian society to a nation of industrial, urban centers, Americans felt the anxiety of such a significant change and the weakening of traditional class distinctions (Berg 61). The nature of work altered as the location of employment shifted from the home to places of industry, and wealth, as a source of security in a changing world, was sought to provide identity and to obtain an elevated position in a new hierarchy. Increasingly, the home, identified as women's sphere, was segregated from what was seen as the capitalistic, base world of the workplace, recognized as the domain of men. Having lost the tranquility of the rural countryside, men sought comfort in their homes, viewing them as havens in which the financial rewards of labor were enjoyed and displayed. Women oversaw as well as participated in this display of affluence. Just as the homes of the wealthy were decorated with "satin and velvet draperies, rich Axminster carpets, marble and inlaid tables, and large looking-glasses, the style in general being Parisian," so were women adorned in the latest, most extravagant fashions from Paris (Berg 61–62). Both a man's home and wife served to proclaim his financial success and to elevate his position in society. This relationship between men and women, in which men participated in the public realm for economic gains while women remained in the home, became entrenched within society, reinforced by men's characterization of women.

The popular view of women held that they were delicate, submissive, of inferior intellect, and prone to nervousness and hysteria. In short, women were believed to require protection and a provider as they were inherently incapable of competing in a man's world. They were, therefore, most naturally suited to the mentally and physically less taxing duties of the home. This image of women was repeatedly portrayed in magazines and novels including *The True Woman* in which the author wrote that man "may appear upon the stage of public and professional life. . . . But woman, timid, shrinking, retiring woman was formed for kindlier labor, where delicate sentiment . . . can soften the asperities of life" (Berg 70). Additionally, women were viewed as religious by nature and therefore responsible for the morality of both their families and society. As the keepers of religion and morality, women were charged to maintain their virtue, although it was understood that men, having a more sensual nature than women, would inevitably try to assault it (Welter 155). Women were to uphold moral standards, absolving men of any failings while using their influence to guide them in living a purer life. Likewise, children were believed to inherit traits from their mother, leaving women responsible for their children's morality and the advancement of a noble society. This notion of women's moral superiority further reinforced the idea that women were not suited to engage in what was deemed to be the amoral world of business, but instead were to be preserved from its effronteries. In *About Woman, Love and Marriage,* Frederick Saunders told women:

To you is committed the nobler task of moulding the infant mind, giving character to succeed-
ing ages,—to control the stormy passions of man, inspiring him with those sentiments which
elevate his nature,—to open to him the truest and purest sources of happiness and prompt him
to the love of virtue and religion. A wife, a mother! How sacred and venerable are these names!
(226–27)

It was difficult for women to challenge this ideology. To do so was to defy God and nature
and to reject what was presented as a sphere of equal importance to that of men's. In the
end, by assigning women characteristics and roles that precluded their participation in men's
activities, society ensured that women would not pose any challenge to men's position or
authority. Further ensuring this were women's fashions.

The clothing of mid-nineteenth-century America functioned as an "identity kit," reinforcing society's distinctions between men and women by symbolizing their natures, roles, and
responsibilities (Roberts 555). Thus, men, being serious, active, strong and aggressive, wore
clothing that was dark, allowed movement, emphasized broad chests and shoulders and presented sharp, definite lines. Conversely, women, regarded as frivolous, inactive, delicate and
submissive, dressed in decorative, light pastel colored clothing which inhibited movement,
accentuated tiny waists and sloping shoulders and presented an indefinite silhouette (555).
Women who challenged these dress codes were considered to be unnatural, and a perversion
of the "true" woman. Yet, simultaneously, women were belittled for succumbing to the dictates of fashion. Their slavish devotion to clothing that compromised their health, mobility,
and comfort left men to conclude that this was evidence of women's inferiority. Addressing
the constricting nature of women's clothing, one observer noted, "She struts or wriggles and
minces along in the most ridiculous fashion" (Haller 164). In fact, women's willingness to
wear the prescribed clothing was evidence of their upbringing which trained them to submit
to the wishes of men in order to secure their future well-being through marriage. Men desired
their wives to be fashionable and women acquiesced. One male correspondent wrote of his
appreciation for corsets in a popular women's magazine. "As a gentleman I admire exceed-
ingly, not only a small, but a well-laced-in waist in a lady, and I believe nine out of ten of us
do the same" (Roberts 565). Women responded to such admiration by willingly wearing the
garments that both psychologically and physically rendered them subordinate to men.

Corsets, stays, petticoats, bustles, high heels, and crinolines dominated the wardrobes of
fashionable women. Such clothing announced to the world that the wearer was a woman of
leisure, requiring servants to assist her. Chief among these was the corset. Frequently compared to the binding of Chinese women's feet, "tight-lacing" was used to achieve a waist
size of as little as seventeen or eighteen inches (Roberts 558). At an early age, young girls,
even infants, were introduced to corsets (Haller 152). Mothers would have been considered
negligent had they not provided such garments, as they were responsible for preparing their
daughters to enter fashionable society. It was believed to be better to begin shaping the figure early than to allow the waist to become "clumsy" and more difficult to control later.
Moreover, the corset came to be associated with morality and was therefore an indication of

a woman's character. According to one fashion magazine, "The corset is an ever-present monitor indirectly bidding its wearer to exercise self-restraint: it is evidence of a well-disciplined mind and well-regulated feelings" (Roberts 565). Numerous companies produced a wide variety of corsets, each proclaiming their product's merits. Madame Caplin, a prolific designer, created approximately twenty-three corsets to meet women's needs throughout their lives. Among these were the Juvenile Hygienic Corset "for young ladies growing too rapidly," the Self-Regulating Gestation Corset "calculated to answer all the phases of pregnancy," and the Corporiform for "corpulent ladies" (Haller 152). The corset significantly restricted a woman's movement, reinforcing her ornamental presence in the home. Likewise, the petticoat, worn five or six at a time, impeded a woman by adding to her frame an additional weight of as much as fifteen pounds (Coale 105). In public, women's clothing was a nuisance if not a hazard. Wide skirts supported by crinolines produced a circumference sometimes exceeding five yards, making it difficult to navigate stairs and public transportation. Inclement weather resulted in soaked skirts, stockings, and shoes while women routinely "cleaned" the floors of public buildings as well as streets with the hems of their dresses. Chided for the frivolous and impractical nature of their clothing, women were dressed for the role they had been assigned, and they continued to endure the resulting diminishment of their lives and health.

The state of women's health in the mid-nineteenth century was widely recognized as deplorable. Reformer Catherine Beecher claimed that she could not recall among her "immense circle of friends and acquaintances all over the Union, so many as ten married ladies born in this century and country, who are perfectly sound, healthy, and vigorous" (Berg 114). This state of affairs was largely attributed to the corset and petticoat. The constriction produced by the corset prevented the development and proper functioning of a woman's organs and was blamed for a myriad of illnesses, including consumption. Both the tight-lacing of the corset and the constant pull of heavy petticoats on a woman's lower back and stomach were held responsible for the many cases of prolapsed uteri or the falling of the womb. This painful condition was of great concern because of its impact on women's ability to produce healthy babies. As a result, many physicians were critical of women's fashions, urging them to modify their dress. Yet, for the majority of society, illness was understood to be part of a fashionable woman's life. It both proclaimed her frail and delicate nature while it maintained her dependent status.

The combination of the sphere assigned to women, the clothing designed for this sphere and the resulting physical incapacitation and illness, defined the existence of most middle- and upper-class women in mid-nineteenth-century America. It was an elaborate and complex system of beliefs and values adhered to by both men and women in order to maintain the constructs of Victorian society. However, as numerous overlapping reform movements gained momentum, including abolitionism, women began to explore the restraints of their sphere and to ask why they could not use their talents and abilities to participate in a broader spectrum of life. Among those asking such questions were feminists, and at least one answer to the question of what prevented women's participation was their dress.

In the February 1851 issue of *The Lily,* a publication "devoted to the interests of women," editor Amelia Bloomer entered the debate surrounding women's dress with an article entitled "Female Attire" (13). In her writing, she noted the control men exerted over women's dress and the tendency for women to acquiesce to the tastes of men. Concurrently, Bloomer was visited by Elizabeth Smith Miller who wore a short skirt and full Turkish trousers which she had adopted out of frustration with the "shackle" of fashionable dress. Two months later, Bloomer announced to her readers that she had donned a short skirt and trousers. *The New York Tribune* noticed her article and subsequently made her announcement known to its thousands of readers (Bloomer, "Survey" 326). In no time, Amelia Bloomer was notoriously identified with the new costume dubbed by the media the "Bloomer costume," and the dress reform movement was launched. Through the Bloomer, Victorian society was forced to engage in consideration of women's rights, including their right to choose their own style of dress, even one that facilitated their movement into the public realm. These were radical notions for the time, threatening the established roles of men and women.

The nature of the threat was summed up in the nineteenth-century belief that, "Men will lose their manliness when women lose their womanliness" (Saunders 246–47). Since articles of clothing had been designated as masculine or feminine, to disregard these distinctions was to disregard the relationship between the sexes as it was ordained by God. Dress reformers challenged this belief arguing for a new dress that expressed the "sameness of humanity" (Leach 246). Elizabeth Cady Stanton believed men and women had a "common nature" which should guide the wearing of a common dress. In 1856, she wrote to fellow reformer Gerrit Smith: "Believing as you do in the identity of the sexes, that all the difference we see in tastes, in character, is entirely the result of education—that 'man is woman and woman is man'—why keep up these distinctions of dress. Surely, whatever dress is convenient for one sex must be for the other also" (Leach 246–47). For Stanton and other women who adopted the Bloomer, the new costume served to lessen the distinctions of dress. While Amelia Bloomer emphasized individual taste and style in the design of the costume, in general the outfit consisted of a "skirt reaching down to a little below the knee, and not made quite so full as is the present fashion. Underneath this skirt, trousers made moderately full" (Gattey 58). A variety of materials and decorative trim were used to make the Bloomer, depending upon the season, occasion, and wearer's means. The result was a garment that emphasized both beauty and comfort.

For women who wore the costume, the response was unbridled enthusiasm. Women noted the ease of movement the Bloomer afforded them, their ability to go out in inclement weather and to stay warm in the winter, as well as their newly found independence. As one wearer expressed, "I only wished to tell you how free I feel, how light and comfortable—I am like the uncaged bird, I feel as though I could almost fly" (Selby 131). For others, particularly men, the sight of women in pants provoked intense anger and hostility. Wearers of the Bloomer were subjected to taunts and jeers in public and were repeatedly ridiculed in songs, cartoons, and editorials. They were accused of immodesty, "aping men," and of usurping what was rightfully man's. As the editor of the *New York Times* wrote:

We regret to see how obstinately our American women are bent on appropriating more than their fair share of Constitutional privileges. Not that the efforts ever amount to anything more than the reaffirmation of certain arrant heresies . . . the propriety of endowing their delicate forms with the apparel, appurtenances, and insignia of "manhood." But there is an obvious tendency to encroach upon masculine manners manifested ever in trifles, which cannot be too severely rebuked or too speedily repressed. (Lauer 582)

The Bloomer then came to symbolize the movement for women's rights, and the feminists were the most visible wearers of the new dress.

The furor surrounding the Bloomer initially assisted the feminists' efforts. Both the media and the public turned out in large numbers to attend conferences and to hear prominent movement leaders including Amelia Bloomer, Elizabeth Cady Stanton, Lucy Stone, and Susan B. Anthony speak on the advancement of women's status. Ultimately, the incessant attention and ridicule attached to the Bloomer caused feminists to return to wearing long dresses. Amelia Bloomer wrote, "We all felt that the dress was drawing attention from what we thought to be of far greater importance—the question of woman's right to better education, to a wider field of employment, to better remuneration for her labor, and to the ballot for the protection of her rights" (Gattey 113). While some prominent women continued to wear the Bloomer until their death, the dress was never fully accepted within middle- and upper-class society. In spite of women's knowledge of the health effects and their personal experience with its inconvenience, the majority of women continued to wear the prescribed fashions. However, among the working class, the Bloomer helped to promote change, enabling those performing manual labor to wear garments that facilitated safety and movement.

Although feminists sidelined dress reform, the movement continued throughout the nineteenth century, advocated largely by practitioners of hydropathy and various reform organizations including the National Dress Reform Association and American Free Dress League. In the February 1852 issue of *The Water-Cure Journal,* a writer examined the impact of dress reform on women's advancement. "Whether any radical reform will follow immediately upon the agitation of this subject is doubtful; but emancipation must come—it may be slowly—but it must and will come" (43).

In fact, the appearance of the Bloomer and dress reform movement did not result in radical reform. However, they undoubtedly paved the way for significant change. In 1891, at the meeting of the National Council of Women of the United States, a committee was established to consider women's dress and the need for clothing suitable for business and public activities (Sewall 488–89). While the subject under discussion was reminiscent of that surrounding the Bloomer, the discourse had reached a higher level. Recognizing the advancements made in women's opportunities for education and work over the prior thirty years, it was now understood that a style of dress was needed to accommodate their new lifestyle. "We are ready for a short dress for business women and others, whose out-of-door duties require all the freedom possible. Public sentiment is very generally ready to concede this" (Miller 496).

No longer new or shocking, dress reform and its message of women's equality had clearly moved beyond society's earlier view of them as radical concepts. After decades of pushing against the confines of their limited sphere, women were beginning to see society's enormous resistance yield to their call for equal rights. The struggle for women's emancipation would continue into the twentieth century, but the early feminists' advocacy of the Bloomer and dress reform courageously set the stage for its achievement.

WORKS CITED

Berg, Barbara J. *The Remembered Gate: Origins of American Feminism.* New York: Oxford UP, 1978.

Bloomer, Amelia. "A Brief Survey of the American Dress Reform Movements of the Past, with Views of Representative Women." *The Arena* Aug. 1892: 325–39.

————. "Female Attire." *The Lily* Feb. 1851.

Coale, W. E. "A Cause of Uterine Displacements." *The Water-Cure Journal* Nov. 1851.

Gattey, Charles Neilson. *The Bloomer Girls.* New York: Coward-McCann, 1967.

Haller, John S., and Robin M. Hailer. *The Physician and Sexuality in Victorian America.* Chicago: U of Illinois P, 1974.

Harris, Barbara J. *Beyond Her Sphere: Women and the Professions in American History.* Westport: Greenwood, 1978.

Lauer, Jeanette C., and Robert H. Lauer. "The Battle of the Sexes: Fashion in 19th Century America." *Journal of Popular Culture* 13 (Spring 1980): 581–89.

Leach, William. *True Love and Perfect Union.* New York: Basic Books, 1980.

Miller, Jenness. "Symposium on Women's Dress." *The Arena* Sept. 1892: 488–507.

"The Prevailing Winter Fashions Illustrated and Contrasted." *The Water-Cure Journal* Feb. 1852.

Roberts, Helene E. "The Exquisite Slave: The Role of Clothes in the Making of the Victorian Woman." *Signs* (Spring 1977): 554–69.

Russell, Frances E. "Symposium on Women's Dress." *The Arena* Sept. 1892: 488–507.

Saunders, Frederick. *About Woman, Love and Marriage.* New York: G. W. Carleton and Company, 1868.

Selby, Sarah E. "A Bloomer to Her Sisters." *The Water-Cure Journal* June 1853.

Sewall, May Wright. "Symposium on Women's Dress." *The Arena* Sept. 1892: 488–502.

Welter, Barbara. "The Cult of True Womanhood: 1820–1860." *American Quarterly* 18 (1966): 151–74.

Name: _____ Date: _____

UNDERSTANDING THE TEXT

1. According to Nelson, what were some of the common beliefs about the nature of women? (Identify four.)

2. According to Nelson, why did many women wear garments they found to be uncomfortable, cumbersome, and potentially harmful to their health?

3. In Nelson's view, why did many nineteenth-century feminists who championed and wore the Bloomer give up doing so?

Hard Bodies

Stuart Ewen

Writing in 1934, the sociologists George A. Lundberg, Mirra Komarovsky, and Mary Alice McInerny addressed the question of "leisure" in the context of an emerging consumer society. Understanding the symbiotic relationship between mass-production industries and a consumerized definition of leisure, they wrote of the need for society to achieve a compatibility between the worlds of work and daily life. "The ideal to be sought," they proposed, "is undoubtedly the gradual obliteration of the psychological barrier which today distinguishes work from leisure."[1]

That ideal has been realized in the daily routine of Raymond H——, a thirty-four-year-old middle-management employee of a large New York City investment firm. He is a living cog in what Felix Rohatyn has termed the new "money culture," one in which "making things" no longer counts; "making money," as an end in itself, is the driving force.[2] His days are spent at a computer terminal, monitoring an endless flow of numerical data.

When his workday is done, he heads toward a local health club for the relaxation of a "workout." Three times a week this means a visit to the Nautilus room, with its high, mirrored walls, and its imposing assembly line of large, specialized "machines." The workout consists of exercises for his lower body and for his upper body, twelve "stations" in all. As he moves from Nautilus machine to Nautilus machine, he works on his hips, buttocks, thighs, calves, back, shoulders, chest, upper arms, forearms, abdomen, and neck, body part by body part.

At the first station, Raymond lies on the "hip and back machine," making sure to align his hip joints with the large, polished, kidney shaped cams which offer resistance as he extends each leg downward over the padded roller under each knee. Twelve repetitions of this, and he moves on to the "hip abduction machine," where he spreads his legs outward against the padded restraints that hold them closed. Then leg extensions on the "compound leg machine" are followed by leg curls on the "leg curl machine." From here, Raymond H—— proceeds to the "pullover/torso arm machine," where he begins to address each piece of his upper body.

After a precise series of repetitions on the "double chest machine," he completes his workout on the "four-way neck machine."

While he alternates between different sequential workouts, and different machines, each session is pursued with deliberate precision, following exact instructions.

Raymond H—— has been working on his body for the past three years, ever since he got his last promotion. He is hoping to achieve the body he always wanted. Perhaps it is fitting that this quintessential, single, young, urban professional—whose life has become a circle of work, money culture, and the cultivation of an image—has turned himself, literally, into a piece of work. If the body ideal he seeks is *lean,* devoid of fatty tissue, it is also *hard.* "Soft flesh," once a standard phrase in the American erotic lexicon, is now—within the competitive, upscale world he inhabits—a sign of failure and sloth. The hard shell is now a sign of achievement, visible proof of success in the "rat race." The goal he seeks is more about *looking* than *touching.*

To achieve his goal, he approaches his body piece by piece; with each machine he performs a discrete task. Along the way he also assumes the job of inspector, surveying the results of each task in the mirrors that surround him. The division of labor, the fragmentation of the work process, and the regulating function of continual measurement and observation—all fundamental to the principles of "scientific management"—are intrinsic to this form of recreation. Like any assembly line worker, H—— needs no overall knowledge of the process he is engaged in, only the specific tasks that comprise that process. "You don't have to understand *why* Nautilus equipment works," writes bodybuilder Mike Mentzer in the forward to one of the most widely read Nautilus manuals. "With a tape measure in hand," he promises, "you will see what happens."[3]

The body ideal Raymond H—— covets is, itself, an aestheticized tribute to the broken-down work processes of the assembly line. "I'm trying to get better definition," H—— says. "I'm into Nautilus because it lets me do the necessary touch-up work. Free weights [barbells] are good for building up mass, but Nautilus is great for definition."[4] By "definition," H—— is employing the lingo of the gym, a reference to a body surface upon which each muscle, each muscle group, appears segmented and distinct. The perfect body is one that ratifies the fragmentary process of its construction, one that mimics—in flesh—the illustrative qualities of a schematic drawing, or an anatomy chart.

Surveying his work in the mirror, H—— admires the job he has done on his broad, high pectorals, but is quick to note that his quadriceps "could use some work." This ambivalence, this mix of emotions, pursues him each time he comes for a workout, and the times in between. He is never quite satisfied with the results. The excesses of the weekend-past invariably leave their blemish. An incorrectly struck pose reveals an overmeasure of loose skin, a sign of weakness in the shell. Despite all efforts, photogenic majesty is elusive.

The power of the photographic idiom, in his mind's eye, is reinforced, again and again, by the advertisements and other media of style visible everywhere. The ideal of the perfectly posed machine—the cold, hard body in response—is paraded, perpetually, before his eyes and ours. We see him, or her, at every glance.

An advertisement for home gym equipment promises a "Body By Soloflex." Above is the silent, chiaroscuro portrait of a muscular youth, his torso bare, his elbows reaching high, pulling a thin-ribbed undershirt up over his head, which is faceless, covered by shadow. His identity is situated below the neck, an instrumentally achieved study in brawn. The powerful expanse of his chest and back is illuminated from the right side. A carefully cast shadow accentuates the paired muscle formations of his abdominal wall. The airbrush has done its work as well, effecting a smooth, standardized, molded quality, what John Berger has termed "the skin without a biography." A silent, brooding hulk of a man, he is the unified product of pure engineering. His image is a product of expensive photographic technology, and expensive technical expertise. His body—so we are informed—is also a technical achievement. He has reached this captured moment of perpetual perfection on a "machine that fits in the corner" of his home. The machine, itself, resembles a stamping machine, one used to shape standardized, industrial products. Upon this machine, he has routinely followed instructions for "twenty-four traditional iron pumping exercises, each correct in form and balance." The privileged guidance of industrial engineering, and the mindless obedience of work discipline, have become legible upon his body; yet as it is displayed, it is nothing less than a thing of beauty, a transcendent aspiration.

This machine-man is one of a generation of desolate, finely tuned loners who have cropped up as icons of American style. Their bodies, often lightly oiled to accentuate definition, reveal their inner mechanisms like costly, open-faced watches, where one can see the wheels and gears moving inside, revealing—as it were—the magic of time itself. If this is eroticism, it is one tuned more to the mysteries of technology than to those of the flesh.

In another magazine advertisement, for Evian spring water from France, six similarly anatomized figures stand across a black and white two-page spread. From the look of things, each figure (three men and three women) has just completed a grueling workout, and four of them are partaking of Evian water as part of their recovery. The six are displayed in a lineup, each one displaying a particularly well-developed anatomical region. These are the new icons of beauty, precisely defined, powerful machines. Below, on the left, is the simple caption: "Revival of the Fittest." Though part of a group, each figure is conspicuously alone.

Once again, the modern contours of power, and the structures of work discipline, are imprinted upon the body. In a world of rampant careerism, self-absorption is a rule of thumb. If the division of labor sets each worker in competition with every other, here that fragmentation is aestheticized into the narcissism of mind and body.

Within this depiction, sexual equality is presented as the meeting point between the anorectic and the "nautilized." True to gender distinctions between evanescent value and industrial work discipline, the three women are defined primarily by contour, by the thin lines that their willowy bodies etch upon the page. Although their muscles are toned, they strike poses that suggest pure, disembodied form. Each of the men, situated alternately between the women, gives testimony on behalf of a particular fraction of segmented flesh:

abdomen, shoulders and upper arms, upper back. In keeping with the assembly line approach to muscle building, each man's body symbolizes a particular station within the labor process.

Another ad, for a health and fitness magazine, contains an alarmingly discordant statement: "Today's women workers are back in the sweat shop." There is a basis to this claim. In today's world, powerful, transnational corporations search the globe looking for the cheapest labor they can find. Within this global economy, more and more women—from Chinatown to Taiwan—are employed at tedious, low-paying jobs, producing everything from designer jeans to computer parts.

Yet this is not the kind of sweatshop the ad has in mind. The photographic illustration makes this clear. Above the text, across the two-page color spread, is the glistening, heavily muscled back of a woman hoisting a chrome barbell. Her sweat is self-induced, part of a "new woman" life-style being promoted in *Sport* magazine, "the magazine of the new vitality." Although this woman bears the feminine trademark of blonde, braided hair, her body is decidedly masculine, a new body aesthetic in the making. Her muscles are not the cramped, biographically induced muscles of menial labor. Hers is the brawn of the purely symbolic, the guise of the middle-class "working woman."

While the text of the advertisement seems to allude to the real conditions of female labor, the image transforms that truth into beauty, rendering it meaningless. Real conditions are copywritten into catchy and humorous phrases. The harsh physical demands of women's work are reinterpreted as regimented, leisure-time workouts at a "health club." Real sweat is reborn as photogenic body oil.

The migration of women into the social structures of industrial discipline is similarly aestheticized in an ad for Jack LaLanne Fitness Centers. A black and white close-up of a young woman wrestling with a fitness "machine" is complemented by the eroticized grimace on her face. Once again, the chiaroscuro technique accentuates the straining muscles of her arms. The high-contrast, black and white motif may also suggest the "night and day" metamorphosis that will occur when one commits to this particular brand of physical discipline.

In large white letters, superimposed across the shadowy bottom of the photograph, are the words: "Be taut by experts." With a clever play on words the goal of education moves from the mind to the body. Muscle power is offered as an equivalent substitute for brain power. No problem. In the search for the perfectly regulated self, it is implicit that others will do the thinking. This woman, like the Soloflex man, is the product of pure engineering, of technical expertise:

> We were building bodies back when you were building blocks. . . . We know how to perfectly balance your workout between swimming, jogging, aerobics and weight training on hundreds of the most advanced machines available. . . . Sure it may hurt a little. But remember. *You only hurt the one you love* [emphasis added].

These advertisements, like Raymond H——'s regular visits to the Nautilus room, are part of the middle-class bodily rhetoric of the 1980s. Together they mark a culture in which self-absorbed careerism, conspicuous consumption, and a conception of *self* as an object of competitive display have fused to become the preponderant symbols of achievement. The regulated body is the nexus where a cynical ethos of social Darwinism, and the eroticism of raw power, meet. Yet despite the currency of this body ideal, the roots of the regulated body have been deeply implanted in the terrain of Western culture since the Enlightenment.

Within the dialectic of Enlightenment thinking, two different but interwoven conceptions of human perfectionism emerged. The first stood at the emancipatory heart of democratic movements and ideals. It held that with Reason, and through scientific, secular education ("improvement"), people could dismantle the repressive, unenlightened hierarchies of the past and become the masters of their own lives. Such thinking spurred ideas of cooperative commonwealth and individual liberty.

Yet the rise of commercial power in the Age of Reason also fueled more instrumental notions of human transformation. While likewise making reference to the touchstones of Reason and Science, these ideas suggested that the rational perfection of an individual could be engineered by another, armed with a knowledge of scientific law, and employing modern techniques of social management. Whereas the bodies within the egalitarian tradition of perfection were those of free individuals, this latter tradition gave rise to the notion of malleable bodies, trainable or teachable for whatever purpose. If the first tradition sparked ideas of liberation among the underclasses, the dark side of Enlightenment was possessed by ideas of controlling and shaping them.

From the mid-eighteenth century on, the rise of this managerial sensibility began to be imprinted on more and more bourgeois social institutions. Particularly where the social organization of power was essential, Michel Foucault has argued, "a policy of coercions that act upon the body, a calculated manipulation of its elements, its gestures, its behaviour," began to be employed.[5]

An example of this, discussed by Foucault, may be found in the military, in the body of the soldier. In the early seventeenth century, he relates, the "ideal figure of the soldier" was still conceived in reference to a great chain of being. His military bearing was understood to be inborn, inseparable from his identity as a person within the social order:

> To begin with, the soldier was someone who could be recognized from afar; he bore certain signs: the natural signs of his strength and his courage, the marks, too, of his pride; his body was the blazon of his strength and valour; and although it is true that he had to learn the profession of arms little by little—generally in actual fighting—movements like marching and attitudes like the bearing of the head belonged for the most part to a bodily rhetoric of honour; "The signs for recognizing those most suited to this profession are a lively, alert manner, an erect head, a taut stomach, broad shoulders, long arms, strong fingers, a small belly, thick thighs, slender legs and dry feet, because a man of such a figure could not fail to be agile and strong.[6]

The body of this soldier bore the marks of muscular strength, but it was also implicit that this strength was intrinsic to the man. He was motivated, from within, by natural courage and pride, not by the techniques of externally imposed discipline. His "strength and valour" were signs of his elite status among men.

By the end of the eighteenth century this had changed. With the consolidation of national sovereignty, the development of a world market, and the spread of colonialism, the military requirements of Europe escalated. The recruitment of armies from among the "masses" necessitated a technique for producing soldiers. Under the rubric of this priority, Foucault argues, the human body entered "a machinery of power that explores it, breaks it down and rearranges it." The notion of the born soldier gave way to that of *basic training:*

> By the late eighteenth century, the soldier has become something that can be made; out of a formless clay, an inapt body, the machine required can be constructed; posture is gradually corrected; a calculated constraint runs slowly through each part of the body, mastering it, making it pliable, ready at all times, turning silently into the automatism of habit; in short, one has "got rid of the peasant' and given him "the air of a soldier" (ordinance of 20 March 1764). Recruits become accustomed to "holding their heads high and erect; to standing upright, without bending the back, to sticking out the belly, throwing out the chest and throwing back the shoulders; and, to help them acquire the habit, they are given this position while standing against a wall in such a way that the heels, the thighs, the waist and the shoulders touch it, as also do the backs of the hands, as one turns the arms outwards, without moving them away from the body. . . . Likewise, they will be taught never to fix their eyes on the ground, but to look straight at those they pass . . . to remain motionless until the order is given, without moving the head, the hands or the feet . . . lastly to march with a bold step, with knee and ham taut, on the points of the feet, which should face outwards" (ordinance of 20 March 1764).[7]

Foucault's discussion, here, focuses on the changing conception of the soldier, but the implications of this discussion shed light on changes within an ever-widening sphere of social activities from the eighteenth century onward. In the routinization of labor, in the rote teaching of schoolchildren, in the measured strides of fashion models, even in the detailed positional instructions of exercise tapes or sex manuals, Foucault's "well-trained regiments" can be heard marching in the distance.

Against this historical panorama, the monitored, regulated and segmented body ideal goes against its own claims for itself. On the aesthetic plane of the commercial culture this bodily motif suggests self-motivated, individual power. But its historic roots and its method of construction ("bodybuilding") reveal a person who is, to quote Foucault, the "object and target of power."[8] In their aestheticization, the modern structures of power are turned on their heads, posed as symbols of a *free individual.* In the world of style, where images seem to float, disconnected from the world that produces them, mastery can be confused with obedience.

ENDNOTES

[1] George A. Lundberg et al., *Leisure: A Suburban Study* (1934), p. 3.

[2] *New York Times,* 3 June 1987, p. A27.

[3] Ellington Darden, *The Nautilus Bodybuilding Book* (1986), pp. viii–ix.

[4] Style Project, interview I-13.

[5] Michel Foucault, *Discipline and Punish* (1977), p. 138.

[6] *Ibid.,* p. 135.

[7] *Ibid.,* pp. 135–36, 138.

[8] *Ibid.,* p. 136.

Name: _____   Date: _____

UNDERSTANDING THE TEXT

1. According to Ewen, in what ways does Raymond H——'s "workout" replicate "the processes of the assembly line"?

2. One ad that Ewen examines, for Jack LaLanne Fitness Centers, urges readers to "Be taut by experts." How does Ewen interpret the pun on "taut"?

3. On the surface, bodybuilding represents "self-motivated, individual power," Ewen suggests. But in light of its "historic roots," what else does he think it represents?

Superstars, Superheroes and the Male Body Image: The Visual Implications of Football Uniforms

Charlotte A. Jirousek

INTRODUCTION

Anne Hollander has argued most successfully that there is a relationship between the cut of clothes and concepts of the ideal body, and that the body ideal changes as fashions change (84–87). Although football uniforms are not daily dress, they have been the costume of heroes idolized by young boys and grown men alike as the embodiment of American manhood in the middle of the twentieth century. It can be argued that the evolution of the high tech protective armor worn under the uniform created an exaggerated image of male musculature, particularly in the years from World War II through the 1980s. This silhouette has exerted a relentless pressure on the ideal form of the unadorned male body. This pressure can also be discerned in recent fashion trends.

To be sure, not all men are sports fans. Martin and Koda make a persuasive case for a set of options from which men can choose to define their personal style (7–9). The preeminent choice they offer is between the look of the "Jock" and the "Nerd." They present the recent rehabilitation of the fashion image of the Nerd as a backlash against the ultra-macho Jock notion of manhood. Even with this alternative, the relentless images of muscular bodies presented by the media must be difficult for any man to ignore completely.

Football has been described as the ultimate expression of manly skill and aggressiveness, a metaphor for male roles and social relationships. In the introduction to a history of the National Football League, football is described as a "symbolic war":

Professional football is basically a physical assault by one team upon another in a desperate fight for land. Most people see themselves as the sum of their possessions—I am what I own. The most basic possession, land, is the issue in football and the most basic weapon, the body, is the means of acquiring it. It is a game of physical dominance; the weak are punished unmercifully and the unskilled are run off the field. So much of a man's personality is at stake that the game becomes a fanatical crusade." (*The First Fifty Years*)

There are several possible reasons why football rose in importance by the midpoint of this century. Social scientists have made a case for territoriality as a basic human trait. As our population has grown, becoming more urban and crowded, the appeal of this turf-oriented sport increased. This has also been a period of unparalleled technical development, social upheaval, alienation and anger. Football reflects an increasingly high tech, fast-moving culture, generating metaphors of violence, high tech strategy, corporate style teamwork, and high tech-augmented physical power. These images resonate with the temper of society in a way that the slow-paced, graceful virtuosity of that other great American pastime, baseball, can no longer do as effectively. As football gained in popularity, it was discovered that television and football were remarkably well suited to each other. The continuous action and visual impact of football came across dramatically on television. The enormous success of televised football has firmly planted the football hero in the pantheon of male icons.

The Evolution of the Football Uniform

Football began as a college sport, and although in recent years professional football has gained preeminence, college football has retained a passionate following. Since its beginnings, football has been followed fervently at the University of Alabama, and with great success. This was particularly true during the tenure of coach Paul "Bear" Bryant from 1958 to 1982. The opening of the Paul W. Bryant Museum in 1988 celebrated this history. The museum houses an extensive archive of visual and written material on football. In addition, there is a collection of football uniforms, equipment, and related materials that document the history of football from its beginnings in the 19th century to the present. As seen in these collections, the Alabama experience of football encapsulates the national experience. This material can be used to illustrate some interesting parallels between the evolution of the football uniform and the evolution of ideals for male body image.

The first intercollegiate football game in the United States took place in 1869 between Princeton and Rutgers. Within the next two years, Yale, Columbia, and Harvard established teams, and the "Ivy League" was born. Alabama came to the sport as a relative latecomer in 1892, and the Southern Intercollegiate Athletic Conference was formed in 1894 (Edson 23).

Early football players had no protective gear to exaggerate the body silhouette. The body image of the Victorian and Edwardian football hero was that of the natural athletic body. In the nineteenth and early twentieth century, the ideal for the fit male body was slender, with smooth muscular definition, corresponding to Classical sculpture (Mrozek 21–22). On the first Alabama team, the average weight of the players was 148 pounds (Bolton 62). The uniform of Alabama's early teams consisted of ordinary knickers and a wool sweater.

At this early period in its development, the game of football was virtually without rules, a violent free-for-all that was little more than a planned brawl. Gradually, because of the serious injuries that occurred, protective features were added to football wear, although many players resisted these innovations. Initially these precautions were rather minimal. In 1894, Alabama players were photographed wearing thicker (probably canvas) pants. A sleeveless canvas vest and a jersey were also worn under or instead of the sweater. These specialized garments may have saved wear and tear on the player's personal wardrobe, but they provided little protection for his body. In 1896, some padding was added to the elbows, and by the turn of the century jerseys had replaced sweaters (Shores). Not until 1900 did the first helmet (a rather inadequate leather article) appear at Alabama. However, helmets would remain optional until the late 1920s. Also introduced at the University of Alabama in 1900 was a type of canvas pants with attached vest. This garment included quilted patches filled with cotton, which also might be stiffened with lead inserts. In addition, patches were sewn to the pants and/or vest, into which rows of small reeds were inserted.

By 1901, separate leather shoulder pads began to come into use. A photograph of the 1901 University of Michigan team includes a player with his sweater off and pads visible over his jersey. In 1903, the first shoulder pads appeared at Alabama. During the next 25 years, the size of shoulder pads would gradually increase, as would the bulk and padding of the canvas knee pants. However, protective shoulder padding continued to be relatively unobtrusive before World War I. Such gear was a personal choice, often added only to protect an injury that would otherwise prevent the player from playing. Routine use of excessive protective gear was generally considered unmanly, and the wide-shouldered look of pads was de-emphasized as a result.

After World War I, as a generation of American young men set off to college, America was in a youthful, freewheeling mood. The college boy and his sport of football surged in popularity. In 1919, professional football made its appearance with the founding of the National Football League. The NFL introduced football to non-college audiences in towns throughout the midwest, and eventually, the whole country. The 1920s has been described as "the decade in which sport assumed its modern position as a cornerstone of American culture" (McChesney 55). This was also the first era in which radio and especially film could bring sports and its stars to the broader public (Treat).

By the 1920s, the shoulder padding was sufficient to be noticeable, but still seemed not to exaggerate the shoulder musculature in the way later uniforms would do. The bulky pants in use by this time often made the legs and hips appear wider than the upper body. This was also a characteristic of men's suits in the late twenties. The suit jacket became somewhat wider in the shoulders, but although the waist was indicated, the jacket was essentially straight and loosely fitted, giving width to the whole body. Pants were also cut wide. In the extreme form, the youthful fad for a style of wide-legged pants known as "Oxford bags" decidedly counterbalanced any appearance of width in the shoulders.

By the 1930s, some players, particularly linemen, began to wear shoulder pads that did add substantial width to the shoulders as compared to the lower body. At the same time, the uniform pants became more closely fitted, following the narrower contour of leg and hips, but augmented by the protective thigh padding. The more noticeable pads began to take on the look of exaggerated muscle development in the shoulders and thighs. Men's suits also began to take the form of an inverted triangle; wide at the shoulders, tapering to a clearly demarcated waist, and descending to narrower hips and pants.

Over the years the game became somewhat more regulated and less overtly dangerous. From the 1940s to the 1970s the protective padding developed into a form of virtual armor that increasingly exaggerated the athletic male form, and therefore exaggerated the super-hero image of the football player. Thus, football became a less directly brutal spectacle, with the illusion of protection for its players, who at the same time evoked an image of superhuman size and strength. As the violence became more sublimated, the image of strength became more fantastic.

There is some evidence that the power of the football image is beginning to wane, however. Particularly among younger people, basketball has been on the rise as the sport of choice,[1] and basketball stars have gained prominence in television sports and advertising imagery (Weismann 810). This may signal a paradigm shift in the image offered by the sports hero. The basketball hero still offers a larger than life body image, but the uniform exposes the real body, significantly different in proportions from the artificially exaggerated football silhouette. Yet football continues to be the leading American sport in terms of attendance and earnings, and clearly continues to be a pervasive media presence.[2]

THE MEDIA AND THE DEVELOPMENT OF THE SUPERHERO BODY IMAGE

Football was first seen on television as a demonstration at the RCA pavilion during the New York World's Fair of 1939. Even in that first fuzzy broadcast football was seen as the perfect television sport:

> Science has scored a touchdown at the kickoff of football by television. So sharp are the pictures, that the televiewer sits in his parlor wondering why he should leave the comforts of home to watch a gridiron battle in a sea of mud on a chilly autumnal afternoon. . . . When the players gallop directly in front of the camera, the televiewer feels that he is plunging right through the line or sliding out of bounds with the ball runner. . . . There is plenty of action on the gridiron and that is why football is classed as a "natural" for the camera (Patton 15).

Commercial television had to wait until after World War II to become a reality. Football games were broadcast from time to time throughout the 1950s. However, it was not until after the spectacular sudden death National Championship game televised in 1958 that the networks took up football in earnest. In 1962, the first contract with the NFL was signed by CBS.

As televised football grew in popularity, the images of football increased in importance. Television created many individual stars, whose image and lifestyle had substantial influence. As a result, this period saw an increasing use of football and other sports stars for advertising, which further augmented their image power. Johnny Unitas, Frank Gifford, and Alex Karras were among the first beneficiaries of this attention (Patton 38–42). Joe Namath, whose career began at the University of Alabama, became one of the great celebrities of the sixties when he led the New York Jets to their first Superbowl victory. He was as well known for his playboy lifestyle and pantyhose ads as he was for his prowess on the field (Jenkins 42).

Although changes in male body image and fashions are certainly caused by a number of factors, the parallels between the functional evolution of the football player's protective gear and the aesthetic evolution of the male silhouette are striking. The steady rise in the popularity of football was concurrent with the increasing augmentation of the player's body. The protective gear under his uniform ultimately created an irresistible image of male power which has in turn affected standards of male strength and beauty. The power of this image has contributed to a national obsession with physical fitness and sport in general, in the pursuit of the ideal body (Ames 91–94). This trend has been particularly discernible in the last thirty years, the era in which football became the preeminent sport, its image and mythology promoted by the ubiquitous force of television.

It is interesting to compare the evolution of the football uniform with other media images of male strength and attractiveness in comparable periods. In the late 1930s and 1940s, comic books were a popular form of literature for children, particularly for boys. Superman first appeared in 1938, followed quickly by Batman in 1939 (*Superman at Fifty;* Vaz 31–32). These superheroes were idolized for their incredible bravery, moral superiority, and (for the time) fantastic physical strength and proportions. Since Superman and Batman were supposed to be more powerful than ordinary men, they were drawn with physiques that exceeded the currently accepted standards of strength and fitness. In every comic book there was also an ad for Charles Atlas's body building program, holding out the promise that even a "97-pound weakling" could hope to look like Superman. Of course, the image of Charles Atlas in the ads looked suspiciously like that of the superhero shown in the adventure stories. Clearly this advertiser thought that the muscular appearance of the comic heroes was fascinating to the young reader.

For the most part, real muscle men of the day could not match this super image. The accepted ideals of strength and fitness for men idealized the classical Greek prototype, with smooth sleek lines and limited muscle definition (Ames 91). In actual fact, few if any men then encountered in real life could be compared to Superman's original physique, with the possible exception of a few obscure body builders—and a uniformed football player. Apart from the cape, the uniform of Superman or Batman actually looked rather like the football uniform of the day, but with super shoulders instead of pads.

As football uniforms and padding grew more exaggerated in the years that followed World War II, these fictional superheroes seemed to grow more powerful in appearance as well. In their comic book versions, the physiques of Superman and Batman have decidedly improved with age. Between the late thirties and the post sixties era, the bulk and articulation of muscles increased markedly.

Even more dramatic is the contrast between Adam West's 1960s portrayal of Batman and Michael Keaton's 1989 movie version. Adam West was filming his campy television series at the beginning of the televised football era, before the subsequent fitness craze set in (Eisner 14). West's body looks quite unremarkable to our eyes today. On the other hand, Keaton's body had to be augmented with supermuscular armor to accomplish a satisfactory superhero effect. Clearly the standards for super bodies had been revised in the interim.

The most dramatic changes in the ideal body silhouette occurred after the introduction of regularly televised football in the 1960s. By the end of 1961, there were numerous assertions by the elder statesmen of both football and baseball that football had replaced baseball as the national pastime (Marshall 10; "National Game" 15). Although this was an opinion subject to debate, there was no question that football was now center stage.

Television enormously increased the impact of the football body image. It can be no coincidence that the rise of televised football also corresponded to an explosion of interest in physical fitness in general and the amateur sport of body building in particular. As football became more popular, football players were getting bigger, both in fact as well as in silhouette ("Hefty Pros" 43). Certainly factors such as improved nutrition had contributed to larger, stronger athletes, particularly in the first half of the century. Yet improved nutrition alone cannot account for the growing fascination with well developed muscles.

Although body building had a long history as a minor sport, it had not previously captured mainstream attention. As the new physical fitness craze began in the late 1950s, California led the way with the success of Vic Tanny's sanitized gyms that offered fitness regimes and weight training for the amateur, male or female (Bunzel 45). Throughout the 1960s, interest in body building grew. By the early 1970s, *Sports Illustrated,* for the first time, began to cover major body building events, such as the Mr. Olympia competition, on a regular basis (Kram 128–48; McDermott 92). This interest in body building began to produce real life superheroes whose bodies looked as though football pads had been installed underneath their skin. These images of exaggerated muscles, looked upon as freakish in earlier periods, were now admired. The standard for jock manliness-of-form had escalated right out of normal reality.

It might be a temptation to dismiss the extreme results of body building as an aberration, followed by a rather obsessive subculture, and not relevant to mainstream tastes. Yet even if one does not choose to participate in the pursuit of this physical ideal, the pressure of this superheroic image can modify tastes and attitudes. Definitions of physical attractiveness are to a large extent cultural. Therefore, self concept, and our response to the appearance of others, is colored by such norms. There is no denying that standards of male attractiveness, as represented by public taste in popular entertainment stars, have shifted toward the more muscular. It should be pointed out that these images are sometimes intended to appeal to a female public rather than a male one, and, therefore, may not always inspire male emulation. At least in some cases, the media hero's silhouette may be more of a reflection of changing standards of male attractiveness than a source of these standards. However, this does not change the fact that both female and male audiences gradually accepted a more exaggerated aesthetic for the ideal male body.

The earliest male heart-throbs were, if anything, on the skinny side, and exaggerated muscularity was absent even among the square-shouldered and square-jawed. In fact, the nude upper body was rarely seen except in rather exotic settings until the 1930s and after. Douglas Fairbanks was a rather small and slender hero of 1920s swashbuckler epics. He could be best described as wiry rather than muscular, although he was generally held to be a model of fitness and athleticism for his time (Mrozek 26). Like football stars, movie stars seemed to become more broad shouldered as time passed. In the thirties, Olympic swimming stars such as Johnny Weismuller and Buster Crabbe played superheroes Tarzan and Flash Gordon, while Clark Gable and Cary Grant were playing more conventional romantic leads. These stars offered an increasingly broad shouldered and solid silhouette, but not one with pronounced muscles. This was also the first period in which football uniforms presented a noticeably broad shouldered silhouette. In the forties and fifties, Kirk Douglas and Burt Lancaster played many romantic and adventure roles. They offered somewhat more muscular shoulders, but not a look that could qualify as superheroic by today's standards. Charlton Heston seemed to be the actor of choice for superheroic roles in the 1960s, and in this first decade of televised football, he provided an image which was both large of frame and decidedly muscular. However, as televised football grew, and the subsequent sports and fitness boom developed, the standard for the heroic body became Sylvester Stallone or Arnold Schwarzenegger. By the time Schwarzenegger appeared in *Conan the Barbarian* in 1982, movie stars had become truly larger than life (Kroll 100). The overdeveloped muscles of these stars would have seemed unnatural—even repugnant, to many—a few years earlier. Is it not possible that this silhouette had become acceptable, and in fact, necessary as a bodily image of superpower after years of continuous televised exposure to the supermen of the gridiron?

Certainly athletics has enormously influenced the marketing of clothing for both men and women in this century. Athletic wear such as turtle neck sweaters, T shirts, sweat shirts and jogging suits have all entered the wardrobes of even the most determined couch potato. Athletic images have also become stock-in-trade for marketing clothing and anything else that can be vaguely associated with sexual attractiveness. It can be said that the mark of fashion in the 1980s was the shoulder pad, which did with clothing what Arnold Schwarzenegger has done with the body. Although shoulder pads are certainly not a new idea, there has been no period in which they were more exaggerated.

Also, as in the movies, the individuals chosen to wear the clothing and underwear in magazine ads have decidedly more athletic-looking bodies than was the case in earlier decades. In fact, a perusal of male fashion layouts could create the impression that if a man wants a career in modeling today, he will need to include weight training in his plans.

In recent years, however, the more extreme body builder images have begun to decline somewhat in fashion spreads. Though it is still manifestly clear that male models weight train to maintain their athletic looks, the more exaggerated muscle men are being replaced by men with more balanced proportions. This may be a result of the sports trends which are leading away from the predominance of the football hero toward the more proportional athleticism of the basketball star, as described above. Yet, we still have super male models such as Fabio, and the muscle man has by no means disappeared from the media, any more than football has disappeared as a national sport (Linden 73). However, Fabio's image as a romance novel cover boy and fashion model is clearly aimed at women more than men. His image cannot be seen primarily as an icon of male aspirations. In any case, the media continue to offer professionally developed athletic bodies as the standard of attractiveness.

IMPLICATIONS

For men, athletics and fitness have been the source of standards of body image and appearance more than fashion images (Ames 91–92). The pursuit of beauty is therefore translated into the pursuit of a healthy athletic body. Indeed, until relatively recently, articles offering men advice on their appearance were invariably offered under the guise of health and fitness. The rare discussion of male concerns with appearance seemed to be confined to women's fashion magazines.[3] Even in these articles, male concerns are presented primarily as health issues. However, health is not the only concern. In a study by Larry Tucker conducted at Auburn University, self concepts of male students were examined (McCarthy 12). Tucker compared students in a health class with members of a weight training course. Although both groups displayed similar profiles on a pretest, there was a significant difference between the groups at the end of the course. The weight training students experienced an improvement in self-confidence and general satisfaction levels with their bodies which corresponded to the visible changes in their physique. In another study by Adam Drenowski and Doris Yee, it was determined that although men and women are equally likely to be unhappy with their weight, women want to lose weight, while men want to gain (626–634). Therefore, women diet, and men exercise.

Much has been said about the unrealistic standards of beauty that have been foisted upon women by movies and fashion marketing. Since the 1960s, fashion magazines have portrayed a feminine ideal body which is wholly unattainable for most. The medical community has decried the resulting epidemic of bulimia and anorexia as desperate young women tried to achieve the impossible.

It seems that the athletic heroes sold through the media as a standard for manhood have placed an unrealistic pressure on young men not unlike that presented by the fashion model to young women. Images of sports surround a boy from earliest childhood. Many adolescents and young men have been motivated to actively pursue the kind of superbody silhouette embodied in the uniformed football player. The result has been a boom in weight training. Certainly the desire to compete and succeed in a variety of athletic endeavors is an important stimulus for this trend; yet it is undeniable that muscle building is done for the sake of image and attractiveness. For some, the desire to achieve supermuscles has become so great that they turn to artificial aids. In the 1980s, use of anabolic steroids to achieve this goal became an epidemic among high school-aged as well as older athletes (Fackelmann 391).

Fitness is a laudable goal, and to the extent that health is improved, disciplines mastered, and excellence achieved, society is well served. However, the exaggerations of body form encouraged by media images are perhaps not so healthy. It would seem that the super body as envisioned in the image of the uniformed football hero has provided an unrealistic standard of male strength and beauty. In turn, this image became the measure for other male icons of physical beauty, such as movie stars and fashion models.

In an era of overwhelming change, constant crisis, and deep disillusionment with old values, the metaphor of football in particular and sports in general has fulfilled the immensely important role of a cultural myth. It is clear that the images of men reflected in the game and its players speak powerfully to many people, both men and women. Our institutions may help to select and shape these myths, but once they are in place, they shape us all.

ENDNOTES

[1] J. Fierman, "Advertisers Show Signs of Football Fatigue," *Fortune* 110 (15 Oct. 1984), 141. Fierman reports that for the first time ratings for ABC's Monday night football have dropped 12%, and other football broadcasts show similar declines. Meanwhile, basketball revenues and viewership were rising (B. Welling, "Basketball: Business is Booming," *Business Week* [28 Oct. 1985], 72–5; and M. Landler, "It's Not Just the Fans on the Edge of Their Seats: Advertisers on CBS are Reaping a Bonanza from NCAA Basketball Fever," *Business Week* [13 Apr. 1992], 40).

[2] J. Lieber, "Fat and Unhealthy," *Sports Illustrated* 76 (27 Apr. 1992), 32–4. Lieber reports that although football revenues appeared to have peaked in 1990–93, and basketball earnings have been rising steadily for a decade, projections for 1994 show that football revenues will still be almost triple those of basketball for the same period.

[3] Men In Vogue: Charlton Heston Stays in Shape and Tells How," *Vogue* 151 (1 Jan. 1968), 67; "Men and Their Looks," *Vogue* 146 (15 Nov. 1965), 181; and "Male Body Beautiful," *Harper's Bazaar* 105 (June 1972), 106.

WORKS CITED

Ames, W. "Does He or Doesn't He? Use of Anabolic Steroids." *Sports Illustrated* 5 Dec. 1977: 91–92.

Bolton, Carl. *The Crimson Tide: A Story of Alabama Football.* Birmingham: The Strode Publishers, 1972.

Bunzel, Peter. "Health Kick's High Priest." *Life* 29 Sept. 1958: 71–80.

Drenowski, Adam and Doris Yee. "Men and Body Image: Are Males Satisfied With Their Body Weight?" *Psychosomatic Medicine* 49 (1987): 626–34.

Edson, James S. *Alabama's Crimson Tide.* Montgomery: Paragon P, 1946.

Eisner, Joel. *The Official Batman Batbook.* Chicago: Contemporary Books, 1986.

Fackelmann, K. A. "Male Teenagers and Steroid Abuse." *Science News* 17 Dec. 1988: 391.

Fierman, J. "Advertisers Show Signs of Football Fatigue." *Fortune* 16 Oct. 1984: 141.

The First Fifty Years: A Celebration of the National Football League in its Fiftieth Season. Ed. B. Oates. New York: Simon & Schuster, 1970.

"Hefty Pros Get Even Heftier." *Life* 18 Nov. 1957: 68–70.

Hollander, Anne. *Seeing through Clothes.* New York: Penguin Books, 1988.

Jenkins, Dan. "Sweet Life of Swinging Joe." *Sports Illustrated* 17 Oct. 1966: 42–44.

Kram, Mark. "Looking for a Lift." *Sports Illustrated* 12 Sept. 1966: 128–48.

Kroll, J. "Conan the Barbarian." *Newsweek* 17 May 1982: 100.

Landler, M. "It's Not Just the Fans on the Edge of their Seats." *Business Week* 13 Apr. 1992: 40.

Lieber, J. "Fat and Unhealthy." *Sports Illustrated* 27 April 1992: 32–4.

Linden, D. W. and M. Rees. "Pinup Boy." *Forbes* 6 July 1992: 73.

"Male Body Beautiful." *Harpers Bazaar* 105 (1972): 106.

Marshall, George P. "Speaking Out: Baseball Isn't Our National Sport." *Saturday Evening Post* 9 Dec. 1961: 10–14.

Martin, Richard and Harold Koda. *Jocks and Nerds: Men's Style in the Twentieth Century.* New York: Rizzoli, 1989.

McCarthy, Paul. "Body Beautiful." *Psychology Today* July/Aug. 1988: 12.

McChesney, Robert W. "Media Made Sport: A History of Sports Coverage in the United States." *Media, Sports and Society.* Ed. L. A. Wenner. Newberry Park, CA: SAGE Publications, 1989.

McDermott, Barry. "Trying to Muscle In." *Sports Illustrated* 21 Oct. 1974: 92.

"Men and Their Looks." *Vogue* 15 Nov. 1965: 181–221.

"Men in Vogue: Charlton Heston Stays in Great Shape and Tells How." *Vogue* 1 Jan. 1968: 67.

Mrozek, Donald J. "Sport in American Life: From National Health to Personal Fulfillment, 1890–1940." *Fitness in American Culture.* Ed. K. Grover. Amherst, MA: U of Massachusetts P, 1989.

"National Game." *Sports Illustrated* 18 Dec. 1961: 7.

Patton, Phil. *Razzle Dazzle: The Curious Marriage of Television and Football.* New York: Doubleday and Co., 1984.

Shores, Gary. History of Football Uniforms at Alabama. Unpublished summary. Archives, Paul W. Bryant Museum, Tuscaloosa, AL: University of Alabama.

Superman at Fifty: The Persistence of a Legend. Eds. Dennis Dooley and Gary Engle. Cleveland: Octavia Press, 1987.

Treat, Roger. *The Encyclopedia of Football.* New York: A.S. Barnes & Co., 1979.

Vaz, Mark. *Tales of the Dark Knight: Batman's First Fifty Years, 1939–1989.* New York: Ballantine Books, 1989.

Weisman, J. "Acolytes in the Temple of Nike." *The Nation* 17 June 1991: 810.

Welling, B. "Basketball: Business is Booming." *Business Week* 28 Oct. 1985: 72–5.

Name: _____ Date: _____

UNDERSTANDING THE TEXT

1. According to Jirousek, why had football increased in popularity by the middle of the twentieth century?

2. In the early days of football, what, according to Jirousek, was the ideal body type for men? How did this change later, and why?

3. Jirousek claims that "the power of the football image is beginning to wane." What does she think is taking its place?

PART THREE

Domesticity, Consumption, and the Creation of Tradition

Les Très Riches Heures de Martha Stewart

Margaret Talbot

Every age gets the household goddess it deserves. The '60s had Julia Child, the sophisticated French chef who proved as permissive as Dr. Spock. She may have proselytized for a refined foreign cuisine from her perch at a Boston PBS station, but she was always an anti-snob, vowing to "take a lot of the la dee dah out of French cooking." With her madras shirts and her penumbra of curls, her 6′2″ frame and her whinny of a voice, she exuded an air of Cambridge eccentricity—faintly bohemian and a little tatty, like a yellowing travel poster. She was messy and forgiving. When Julia dropped an egg or collapsed a soufflé, she shrugged and laughed. "You are alone in the kitchen, nobody can see you, and cooking is meant to be fun," she reminded her viewers. She wielded lethal-looking kitchen knives with campy abandon, dipped her fingers into crème anglaise and wiped her chocolate-smeared hands on an apron tied carelessly at her waist. For Child was also something of a sensualist, a celebrant of appetite as much as a pedant of cooking.

In the '90s, and probably well into the next century, we have Martha Stewart, corporate overachiever turned domestic superachiever, Mildred Pierce in earth-toned Armani. Martha is the anti-Julia. Consider the extent of their respective powers. At the height of her success, Child could boast a clutch of bestselling cookbooks and a *gemütlich* TV show shot on a single set. At what may or may not be the height of her success, here's what Stewart can claim: a 5-year-old magazine, *Martha Stewart Living,* with a circulation that has leapt to 1.5 million; a popular cable TV show, also called *Martha Stewart Living* and filmed at her luscious Connecticut and East Hampton estates; a dozen wildly successful gardening, cooking and lifestyle books; a mail-order business, Martha-by-Mail; a nationally syndicated newspaper column, "Ask Martha"; a regular Wednesday slot on the *Today* show; a line of $110-a-gallon paints in colors inspired by the eggs her Araucana hens lay; plans to invade cyberspace—in short, an empire.

Julia limited herself to cooking lessons, with the quiet implication that cooking was a kind of synecdoche for the rest of bourgeois existence; but Martha's parish is vaster, her field is all of life. Her expertise, as she recently explained to *Mediaweek* magazine, covers, quite simply, "Beautiful soups and how to make them, beautiful houses and how to build them, beautiful children and how to raise them." (From soups to little nuts.) She presides, in fact, over a phenomenon that, in other realms, is quite familiar in American society and culture: a cult, devoted to her name and image.

In the distance between these two cynosures of domestic life lies a question: What does the cult of Martha mean? Or, to put it another way, what have we done, exactly, to deserve her?

If you have read the paper or turned on the television in the last year or so, you have probably caught a glimpse of the WASPY good looks, the affectless demeanor, the nacreous perfection of her world. You may even know the outlines of her story. Middle-class girl from a Polish-American family in Nutley, New Jersey, works her way through Barnard in the early '60s, modeling on the side. She becomes a stockbroker, a self-described workaholic and insomniac who by the '70s is making six figures on Wall Street, and who then boldly trades it all in . . . for life as a workaholic, insomniac evangelist for domesticity whose business now generates some $200 million in profits a year. (She herself, according to the *Wall Street Journal,* makes a salary of $400,000 a year from Time Inc., which generously supplements this figure with a $40,000 a year clothing allowance and other candies.) You may even have admired her magazine, with its art-book production values and spare design, every kitchen utensil photographed like an Imogen Cunningham nude, every plum or pepper rendered with the loving detail of an eighteenth-century botanical drawing, every page a gentle exhalation of High Class.

What you may not quite realize, if you have not delved deeper into Stewart's oeuvre, is the ambition of her design for living—the absurd, self-parodic dream of it. To read Martha Stewart is to know that there is no corner of your domestic life that cannot be beautified or improved under careful tutelage, none that should not be colonized by the rhetoric and the discipline of quality control. Work full time though you may, care for your family though you must, convenience should never be your watchword in what Stewart likes to call, in her own twee coinage, "homekeeping." Convenience is the enemy of excellence. "We do not pretend that these are 'convenience' foods," she writes loftily of the bread and preserves recipes in a 1991 issue of the magazine. "Some take days to make. But they are recipes that will produce the very best results, and we know that is what you want." Martha is a kitchen-sink idealist. She scorns utility in the name of beauty. But her idealism, of course, extends no further than surface appearances, which makes it a very particular form of idealism indeed.

To spend any length of time in Martha-land is to realize that it is not enough to serve your guests homemade pumpkin soup as a first course. You must present it in hollowed-out, hand-gilded pumpkins as well. It will not do to serve an Easter ham unless you have baked it in a roasting pan lined with, of all things, "tender, young, organically-grown grass that has not yet been cut." And, when serving a "casual" lobster and corn dinner al fresco, you really ought to fashion dozens of cunning little bamboo brushes tied with raffia and adorned with a chive so that each of your guests may butter their corn with something pretty.

To be a Martha fan (or more precisely, a Martha adept) is to understand that a terracotta pot is just a terracotta pot until you have "aged" it, painstakingly rubbing yogurt into its dampened sides, then smearing it with plant food or "something you found in the woods" and patiently standing by while the mold sprouts. It is to think that maybe you could do this *kind* of thing, anyway—start a garden, say, in your scruffy backyard—and then to be brought up short by Martha's enumeration, in *Martha Stewart's Gardening,* of forty-nine "essential" gardening tools. These range from a "polesaw" to a "corn fiber broom" to three different kinds of pruning shears, one of which—the "loppers"—Martha says she has in three different sizes. You have, perhaps, a trowel. But then Martha's garden is a daunting thing to contemplate, what with its topiary mazes and state-of-the-art chicken coop; its "antique" flowers and geometric herb garden. It's half USDA station, half Sissinghurst. And you cannot imagine making anything remotely like it at your own house, not without legions of artisans and laborers and graduate students in landscape design, and a pot of money that perhaps you'll unearth when you dig up the yard.

In *The Culture of Narcissism,* Christopher Lasch describes the ways in which pleasure, in our age, has taken on "the qualities of work," allowing our leisure-time activities to be measured by the same standards of accomplishment that rule the workplace. It is a phenomenon that he memorably characterizes as "the invasion of play by the rhetoric of achievement." For Lasch, writing in the early '70s, the proliferation of sex-advice manuals offered a particularly poignant example. Today, though, you might just as easily point to the hundreds of products and texts, from unctuous home-furnishings catalogs to upscale "shelter" magazines to self-help books like *Meditations for Women Who Do Too Much,* that tell us exactly how to "nest" and "cocoon" and "nurture," how to "center" and "retreat," and how to measure our success at these eminently private pursuits. Just as late-nineteenth-century marketers and experts promised to bring Americans back in touch with the nature from which modern industrial life had alienated them, so today's "shelter" experts—the word is revealingly primal— promise to reconnect us with a similarly mystified home. The bourgeois home as lost paradise, retrievable through careful instruction.

Martha Stewart is the apotheosis of this particular cult of expertise, and its most resourceful entrepreneur. She imagines projects of which we would never have thought—gathering dewy grass for our Easter ham, say—and makes us feel the pressing need for training in them. And she exploits, brilliantly, a certain estrangement from home that many working women feel these days. For women who are working longer and longer hours at more and more demanding jobs, it's easy to think of home as the place where chaos reigns and their own competence is called into doubt: easy to regard the office, by comparison, as the bulwark of order. It is a reversal, of course, of the hoary concept of home as a refuge from the tempests of the marketplace. But these days, as the female executives in a recent study attested, the priority they most often let slide is housekeeping: they'll abide disorder at home that they wouldn't or couldn't abide at the office. No working couple's home is the oasis of tranquility and Italian marble countertops that Marthaism seems to promise. But could it be? Should it be? Stewart plucks expertly at that chord of doubt.

In an era when it is not at all uncommon to be cut off from the traditional sources of motherwit and household lore—when many of us live far from the families into which we were born and have started our own families too late to benefit from the guidance of living parents or grandparents— domestic pedants like Martha Stewart rightly sense a big vacuum to fill. Stewart's books are saturated with nostalgia for lost tradition and old moldings, for her childhood in Nutley and for her mother's homemade preserves. In the magazine, her "Remembering" column pines moralistically for a simpler era, when beach vacations meant no television or video games, just digging for clams and napping in hammocks. Yet Stewart's message is that such simplicity can only be achieved now through strenuous effort and a flood of advice. We might be able to put on a picnic or a dinner party without her help, she seems to tell us, but we wouldn't do it properly, beautifully, in the spirit of excellence that we expect of ourselves at work.

It may be that Stewart's special appeal is to women who wouldn't want to take their mother's word anyway, to baby-boomer daughters who figure that their sensibilities are just too different from their stay-at-home moms', who can't throw themselves into housekeeping without thinking of their kitchen as a catering business and their backyards as a garden show. In fact, relatively few of Martha's fans are housewives—72 percent of the subscribers to *Martha Stewart Living* are employed outside the home as managers or professionals— and many of them profess to admire her precisely because she isn't one, either. As one such Martha acolyte, an account executive at a Christian radio station, effused on the Internet: "[Stewart] is my favorite independent woman and what an entrepreneur! She's got her own television show, magazine, books and even her own brand of latex paint. . . . Martha is a feisty woman who settles for nothing less than perfection."

For women such as these, the didactic faux-maternalism of Martha Stewart seems the perfect answer. She may dispense the kind of homekeeping advice that a mother would, but she does so in tones too chill and exacting to sound "maternal," singling out, for example, those "who will always be too lazy" to do her projects. She makes housekeeping safe for the professional woman by professionalizing housekeeping. And you never forget that Stewart is herself a mogul, even when she's baking rhubarb crisp and telling you, in her Shakeresque mantra, that "It's a Good Thing."

It is tempting to see the Martha cult purely as a symptom of anti-feminist backlash. Though she may not directly admonish women to abandon careers for hearth and home, Stewart certainly exalts a way of life that puts hearth and home at its center, one that would be virtually impossible to achieve without *somebody's* full-time devotion. (Camille Paglia has praised her as "someone who has done a tremendous service for ordinary women—women who identify with the roles of wife, mother, and homemaker.") Besides, in those alarming moments when Stewart slips into the social critic's mode, she can sound a wee bit like Phyllis Schlafly—less punitive and more patrician, maybe, but just as smug about the moral uplift of a well-ordered home. Her philosophy of cultivating your own walled garden while the world outside is condemned to squalor bears the hallmarks of Reagan's America—it would not be overreading to call it a variety conservatism. "Amid the horrors of genocidal war in Bosnia and Rwanda, the AIDS epidemic and increasing crime in many cities," Stewart writes in a recent column, "there are those of us who desire positive reinforcement of some very basic tenets of good living." And those would be? "Good food, gardening, crafts, entertaining and home improvement." (Hollow out the pumpkins, they're starving in Rwanda.)

Yet it would, in the end, be too simplistic to regard her as a tool of the feminine mystique, or as some sort of spokesmodel for full-time mommies. For one thing, there is nothing especially June Cleaverish, or even motherly, about Stewart. She has taken a drubbing, in fact, for looking more convincing as a businesswoman than a dispenser of milk and cookies. (Remember the apocryphal tale that had Martha flattening a crate of baby chicks while backing out of a driveway in her Mercedes?) Her habitual prickliness and Scotchguard perfectionism are more like the badges of the striving good girl, still cut to the quick by her classmates' razzing when she asked for extra homework.

Despite the ritual obeisance that Martha pays to Family, moreover, she is not remotely interested in the messy contingencies of family life. In the enchanted world of Turkey Hill, there are no husbands (Stewart was divorced from hers in 1990), only loyal craftsmen, who clip hedges and force dogwood with self-effacing dedication. Children she makes use of as accessories, much like Parisian women deploy little dogs. The books and especially the magazine are often graced with photographic spreads of parties and teas where children pale as waxen angels somberly disport themselves, their fair hair shaped into tasteful blunt cuts, their slight figures clad in storybook velvet or lace. "If I had to choose one essential element for the success of an Easter brunch," she writes rather menacingly in her 1994 *Menus for Entertaining,* "it would be children." The homemade Halloween costumes modeled by wee lads and lasses in an October 1991 issue of *Martha Stewart Living* do look gorgeous—the Caravaggio colors, the themes drawn from nature. But it's kind of hard to imagine a 5-year-old boy happily agreeing to go as an acorn this year, instead of say, Batman. And why should he? In Marthaland, his boyhood would almost certainly be overridden in the name of taste.

If Stewart is a throwback, it's not so much to the 1950s as to the 1850s, when the doctrine of separate spheres did allow married or widowed women of the upper classes a kind of power—unchallenged dominion over the day-to-day functioning of the home and its servants, in exchange for ceding the public realm to men. At Turkey Hill, Stewart is the undisputed chatelaine, micromanaging her estate in splendid isolation. (This hermetic pastoral is slightly marred, of course, by the presence of cameras.) Here the domestic arts have become ends in themselves, unmoored from family values and indeed from family.

Stewart's peculiar brand of didacticism has another nineteenth-century precedent—in the domestic science or home economics movement. The domestic scientists' favorite recipes—"wholesome" concoctions of condensed milk and canned fruit, rivers of white sauce—would never have passed Martha's muster; but their commitment to painstakingly elegant presentation, their concern with the look of food even more than its taste, sound a lot like Stewart's. And, more importantly, so does their underlying philosophy. They emerged out of a tradition: the American preference for food writing of the prescriptive, not the descriptive, kind, for food books that told you, in M. F. K. Fisher's formulation, not about eating but about what to eat. But they took this spirit much further. Like Stewart, these brisk professional women of the 1880s and '90s believed that true culinary literacy could not be handed down or casually absorbed; it had to be carefully taught. (One of the movement's accomplishments, if it can be called that, was the home ec curriculum.)

Like Stewart, the domestic scientists were not bent on liberating intelligent women from housework. Their objective was to raise housework to a level worthy of intelligent women. They wished to apply rational method to the chaos and the drudgery of housework and, in so doing, to earn it the respect accorded men's stuff like science and business. Neither instinct, nor intuition, nor mother's rough-hewn words of advice would have a place in the scientifically managed home of the future. As Laura Shapiro observes in *Perfection Salad,* her lively and perceptive history of domestic science, the ideal new housewife was supposed to project, above all, "self-sufficiency, self-control, and a perfectly bland façade." Sound familiar?

It is in their understanding of gender roles, however, that the doyennes of home ec most closely prefigure Marthaism. Like Stewart, they cannot be classified either as feminists or traditionalists. Their model housewife was a pseudo-professional with little time for sublimating her ego to her husband's or tenderly ministering to his needs. She was more like a factory supervisor than either the Victorian angel of the home or what Shapiro calls the courtesan type, the postwar housewife who was supposed to zip through her chores so she could gussy herself up for her husband. In Martha's world, too, the managerial and aesthetic challenges of "homekeeping" always take priority, and their intricacy and ambition command a respect that mere wifely duties never could. Her husbandless hauteur is rich with the self-satisfaction of financial and emotional independence.

In the end, Stewart's fantasies have as much to do with class as with gender. The professional women who read her books might find themselves longing for a breadwinner, but a lifestyle this beautiful is easier to come by if you've never needed a breadwinner in the first place. Stewart's books are a dreamy advertisement for independent wealth—or, more accurately, for its facsimile. You may not have a posh pedigree, but with a little effort (okay, a lot) you can adopt its trappings. After all, Martha wasn't born to wealth either, but now she attends the weddings of people with names like Charles Booth-Clibborn (she went to his in London, the magazine tells us) and caters them for couples named Sissy and Kelsey (see her *Wedding Planner,* in which their yacht is decorated with a "Just Married" sign).

She is not an American aristocrat, but she plays one on TV. And you can play one, too, at least in your own home. Insist on cultivating only those particular yellow plums you tasted in the Dordogne, buy your copper cleaner only at Delherin in Paris, host lawn parties where guests come "attired in the garden dress of the Victorian era," and you begin to simulate the luster of lineage. Some of Stewart's status-augmenting suggestions must strike even her most faithful fans as ridiculous. For showers held after the baby is born, Martha "likes presenting the infant with engraved calling cards that the child can then slip into thank you notes and such for years to come." What a great idea. Maybe your baby can gum them for a while first, thoughtfully imprinting them with his signature drool.

The book that best exemplifies her class-consciousness is *Martha Stewart's New Old House,* a step-by-step account of refurbishing a Federal-style farmhouse in Westport, Connecticut. Like all her books, it contains many, many pictures of Martha; here she's frequently shown supervising the work of plasterers, carpenters and other "seemingly taciturn men." *New Old House* establishes Stewart's ideal audience: a demographic niche occupied by the kind of people who, like her, can afford to do their kitchen countertops in "mottled, gray-green, hand-honed slate from New York state, especially cut" for them. The cost of all this (and believe me, countertops are only the beginning) goes unmentioned. If you have to ask, maybe you're not a Martha kind of person after all.

In fact, Stewart never seems all that concerned with reassuring her readers of their ability to afford such luxuries or their right to enjoy them. She's more concerned with establishing her own claims. Her reasoning seems to go something like this: the houses that she buys and renovates belong to wealthy families who passed them down through generations. But these families did not properly care for their patrimony. The widowed Bulkeley sisters, erstwhile owners of Turkey Hill, had let the estate fall "into great disrepair. All the farms and out-buildings were gone. . . . The fields around had been sold off by the sisters in 2-acre building lots; suburbia encroached." The owner of the eponymous New Old House was a retired librarian named Miss Adams who "had little interest in the house other than as a roof over her head. Clearly a frugal spirit, she had no plans to restore the house, and she lived there until she could no longer cope with the maintenance and upkeep of the place. The house was in dire need of attention, and since no other family member wanted to assume responsibility, Miss Adams reluctantly decided to sell her family home. I wanted very much to save the Adams house, to put it to rights, to return its history to it, to make it livable once again."

It's a saga with overtones of Jamesian comedy: a family with bloodlines but no money is simultaneously rescued and eclipsed by an energetic upstart with money but no bloodlines. The important difference—besides the fact that Martha is marrying the house, not the son— is that she also has taste. And it's taste, far more than money, she implies, that gives her the right to these splendid, neglected piles of brick. Unlike the "frugal" Misses Bulkeley, she will keep suburbia at bay; unlike the careless Miss Adams, she would never resort to "hideous rugs" in (yuck) shades of brown. They don't understand their own houses; she does, and so she *deserves* to own their houses. But leave it to Martha to get all snippy about these people's aesthetic oversights while quietly celebrating their reversion to type. They're useful to her, and not only because their indifference to decor bolsters her claim to their property. Like the pumpkin pine floors and original fixtures, these quaintly cheeseparing New Englanders denote the property's authenticity.

The fantasy of vaulting into the upper crust that Martha Stewart fulfilled, and now piques in her readers, is about more than just money, of course. Among other things, it's about time, and the luxurious plenitude of it. Living the Martha way would mean enjoying a surfeit of that scarce commodity, cooking and crafting at the artisanal pace her projects require. Trouble is, none of us overworked Americans has time to spare these days—and least of all the upscale professional women whom Stewart targets. Martha herself seemed to acknowledge this when she told *Inside Media* that she attracts at least two classes of true believers: the "Be-Marthas," who have enough money and manic devotion to follow many of her lifestyle techniques, and the "Do-Marthas, " who "are a little bit envious" and "don't have as much money as the Be-Marthas."

To those fulsome categories, you could surely add the "watch Marthas" or the "read Marthas," people who might consider, say, making their own rabbit-shaped wire topiary forms, but only consider it, who mostly just indulge in the fantasy of doing so, if only they had the time. There is something undeniably soothing about watching Martha at her absurdly time-consuming labors. A female "media executive" explained the appeal to Barbara Lippert in *New York* magazine: "I never liked Martha Stewart until I started watching her on Sunday mornings. I turn on the TV, and I'm in my pajamas, still in this place between sleep and reality. And she's showing you how to roll your tablecloths in parchment paper. She's like a character when she does her crafts. It reminds me of watching Mr. Green Jeans on Captain Kangaroo. I remember he had a shoebox he took out that was filled with craft things. There would be a close-up on his hands with his buffed nails. And then he would show you how to cut an oaktag with a scissor, or when he folded paper, he'd say: 'There you go, boys and girls,' and it was very quiet. It's like she brings out this great meditative focus and calm."

The show does seem strikingly unfrenetic. Unlike just about everything else on TV, including the *Our Home* show, which follows it on Lifetime, it eschews Kathy Lee-type banter, perky music, swooping studio shots and jittery handheld cameras. Instead there's just Martha, alone in her garden or kitchen, her teacherly tones blending with birdsong, her recipes cued to the seasons. Whimsical recorder music pipes along over the credits. Martha's crisply ironed denim shirts, pearl earrings, and honey-toned highlights bespeak the fabulousness of Connecticut. Her hands move slowly, deliberately over her yellow roses or her Depression glasses. Martha is a Puritan who prepares "sinful" foods—few of her recipes are low-fat or especially health-conscious—that are redeemed by the prodigious labors, the molasses afternoons, involved in serving them. (She preys upon our guilt about overindulgence, then hints at how to assuage it.) Here at Turkey Hill, time is as logy as a honey-sated bumblebee. Here on Lifetime, the cable channel aimed at baby-boom women, Martha's stately show floats along in a sea of stalker movies, Thighmaster commercials and "Weddings of a Lifetime" segments, and by comparison, I have to say, she looks rather dignified. Would that we all had these *très riches heures.*

But if we had the hours, if we had the circumstances, wouldn't we want to fill them with something of our own, with a domestic grace of our own devising? Well, maybe not anymore. For taste is no longer an expression of individuality. It is, more often, an instrument of conformism, a way to assure ourselves that we're living by the right codes, dictated or sanctioned by experts. Martha Stewart's "expertise" is really nothing but another name for the perplexity of her cowed consumers. A lifestyle cult as all-encompassing as hers could thrive only at a time when large numbers of Americans have lost confidence in their own judgment about the most ordinary things. For this reason, *Martha Stewart Living* isn't really living at all.

Name: _____ Date: _____

UNDERSTANDING THE TEXT

1. Based on your reading of Talbot's essay, describe the phenomenon of Martha Stewart.

2. "Every age gets the household goddess it deserves," Talbot proclaims in the first sentence of her essay. Why, in her view, do we deserve Martha Stewart? (Identify and discuss two reasons.)

3. According to Talbot, what was the main "objective" of the domestic science movement?

Selling to Ms. Consumer

Carol Ascher

Consumerism and its handmaiden, advertising, developed in the late 1800s and the first decades of the twentieth century. Like many historical trends, these two grew largely outside of any direct decisions by those who were most affected by them—in this case, women. The period around the turn of the century was a time when, in fact, fewer women held professional roles than they had only two or three decades earlier. Moreover, active women of the period threw their energies into either the suffrage movement or various social welfare fights. Even Florence Kelly, executive secretary to the Consumer Union in the early 1900s, saw it as her role to generate pressure to improve the working conditions in which products were made rather than to create a movement to fight the growth of advertising or buying.

Without women's participation at higher levels in business and industry or an active women's movement concerned with these issues, the home was increasingly shaped by forces whose interests were not its own. As one woman argued in 1908, "Perhaps the real danger to the home lies in the fact that women . . . are not free to control the industrial changes which affect it, and that these changes are being determined too largely by commercial interests."[1]

Nonetheless, there was much about the condition of women that made them receptive to the changes taking place. It is this receptivity that I want to explore. For history is never completely beyond people's control, even when they are not at the helm where decisions are made.

Between 1890 and 1920, when America became transformed into a consumer society, women's lives continued on the almost runaway course of change begun much earlier in the nineteenth century. For those women who moved outside the home, new supports and new possibilities for selfhood became potentially available, though none were easily won or even easy to live with once attained. But for women in the home, the period had a shattering quality, much as the late sixties and early seventies have had for housewives today. And the loss of old norms and ties made these women vulnerable to solutions posed by the world of commodities.

In the early 1900s central heating, gas appliances, and running hot and cold water lightened housework for a growing number of women, particularly in the middle class. Water no longer had to be boiled for washing, nor irons heated on a stove, and coal didn't have to be brought in from a cellar and stoked throughout the day. The introduction of the fireless cooker (gas stove) was a milestone for women of this period; it meant that temperature could be controlled, and cooking done more efficiently and with greater certainty than ever before.

In the next decade, many women were able to purchase washing machines, ice boxes, and vacuum cleaners. These household appliances lightened work inside the home, but they also necessitated a reordering of women's sense of housekeeping. An example can be given with the vacuum cleaner. Here much of the early advertising consisted of retraining women to see cleaning as the rather undramatic suction process, rather than as the visually reassuring display of stirred-up dust they were used to.[2] Christine Frederick, one of the few women working with industry, expressed the disequilibrium the housewife was experiencing in the late 1920s when she said that manufacturers had to help women transform their work from the "hand-craft age" into the era of the "machine operative."[3]

The spread of the kindergarten and compulsory schooling in the first decades of the twentieth century also took some of the old childrearing responsibilities away from women. More important, these new institutions, as well as their intellectual underpinnings, began to shift the notion of who knew best how to care for children. Emerging fields of child development and education offered new methods of mothering and critiqued the old. Early standardized tests, such as the Binet, measured "objectively" how smart the child was, rendering inadequate a mother's sense of her daughter or son. Although mothers still spent years caring for their children, they increasingly did so with the specter of professional judgment hanging over them.

Women in the home were also affected by the changing order of the work world. The early home economists—domestic scientists, as they were then called—had hoped to strengthen the family and improve the woman's place in it by also insisting on the authority of the husband-father. But the new organization of industry made it difficult for men to hold on to their old controls, either at work or at home. The geographic separation of the home and work worlds made it impossible for the father to maintain the authority he had once held when he worked inside the home alongside his family. At the same time, work for most men lost its craft, and an increasing proportion of men worked for wages in large, anonymous situations where they retained little control over their work. This breakdown in the material base for male authority gave a spurt to feminism. But it also made daily life more uncertain for those women who tried to adjust old patterns to new realities.

As men's work on the outside lost its dignity, their role inside the family turned from that of patriarch to that of provider. Not only did the home have to offer solace from the workday world, but women had to bolster the wounded egos it was causing in their menfolk. It was as if by making the home a castle, women could transform their husbands back into kings.

Given the hierarchical patterns women were used to, the decreased dominion of the husband-father opened the way for women to accept a new locus of authority. This authority was being developed by science and industry. Both would have new rationales for right and wrong, and both would turn all the family, including the father, into children, to be taught, teased, and coerced. One of the most self-conscious statements of this shift in authority came toward its end, in 1931, when Edward Filene, head of the great Boston department store, wrote,

> since the head of the family is no longer in control of the economic process through which the family must get its living, he must be relieved of many ancient responsibilities and therefore of many of his prerogatives. . . . Women . . . and children are likely to discover that their economic well-being comes not from the organization of the family but from the organization of industry, and they may look more and more for individual guidance, not to their fathers, but to the *truth* which science is discovering.[4]

Birth control also undermined old authority patterns as well as transformed women's work in and outside the home. The shrinking of family size had started in the early nineteenth century, but it became a public "problem" in the later decades of the century when a number of social movements advocated some form of birth control and when it became a common fear that the middle class would simply cease to reproduce itself. Margaret Sanger's first clinic, which opened in 1916, was the culmination of decades of struggle for public access to birth control.[5] By the 1920s 70 to 80 percent of all middle- and upper-class women were assumed to be using some form of contraception.[6] For the first time, sex became separated from reproduction. The 1920s was a time of tremendous sexual experimentation—a time in many ways as free as today. But along with increases in sexual freedom, divorce grew rapidly. Whereas in 1890 there had been only three divorces per thousand, by 1920 the number had risen to nearly eight per thousand.[7]

Even the older feminists were caught off base by the new sexuality. Jane Addams, for example, who had grown up in the period when womanhood meant motherhood—or its more liberated variant, social housekeeping—spoke publicly of her discontent with the emphasis on sexual gratification. And Charlotte Perkins Gilman condemned the risqué clothing of the flappers. Although she felt bound to endorse sexual liberation, she believed women were displaying a "backlash of primitive femininity" that stood in the way of real sexual equality.[8]

Birth control generated the potential for women's economic independence, but it also caused a great deal of uncertainty and retrenchment. By 1920 every third worker was a woman, and 20 percent of all married women worked.[9] The proportion of single women (including those widowed and divorced) had also increased significantly in the preceding thirty years.[10] Moreover, single women were holding jobs and living outside families, rather than doing chores in return for room and board with relatives, as had been the case several decades earlier. However, Charlotte Perkins Gilman was not wrong to fear the backlash of "primitive femininity." In the first decades of the twentieth century the proportion of professional women declined. Between 1910 and 1930, for example, women doctors declined by 7 percent and women musicians and composers by 6 percent.[11] By the time the Nineteenth Amendment was passed, women posed no threat as a voting block, and few women in the 1920s ran for political office. Although many women worked, they did not aspire to the heights they once had.

Changes in work and the family had made women at home insecure; but this insecurity was exacerbated by women's increasing isolation. An important source of this isolation stemmed, in turn, from changes in the organization of the home and its relationship to the outside world.

By the turn of the century, although apartments were being built in every city, the single-family home was becoming a reality as well as an ideal for more people. Public transportation had enabled housing to spread out from city centers. Suburbanization made it possible for workers' families to live with their own separate roofs over their heads. And industrialists, home economists, and social reformers alike argued the importance of providing such dwellings for workers and their families. The *Ladies' Home Journal,* the most influential of the women's magazines, featured a model house plan for a single-family home in each of its issues.[12] Many of the industrial towns built in the late 1800s contained single-family homes in order to develop in their workers a sense of the right way to live. Some went so far as to offer courses in home economics for the wives; these courses reinforced the importance of the single-family home and the role of women in it.[13]

After World War I, the automobile furthered the sprawl of residential areas outside the cities. Thousands of men were already traveling to work over an hour each way, and neighborhoods were becoming devoid of men during working hours. While most urban women emigrees to the suburbs complained of loneliness, the idea that suburban living was important to family life, and particularly to raising children, kept the flow of families outward from the cities.

With a revolution going on in Russia and the potential for social upheaval obvious in this country, single-family dwellings became fused with a vision of preventing revolution and communism. The women's magazines supported this vision. A 1920 issue of the *Ladies' Home Journal,* for instance, "intimated that the Bolsheviks wanted most of all to destroy the single-family house and replace it with 'nationalized woman' in mass housing." The magazine also connected feminism and communism as foes of the home and motherhood, asserting that women who selfishly chose not to have children or not to raise them by themselves at home were "aiding the red cause."[14]

Along with the ideal of the single-family home came new housing styles, which lessened the housework but opened the way for commodities to enter the home. The parlor, the repository of tradition, had been the first to go, aided by a virulent campaign against it in the 1890s by the editor of the *Ladies' Home Journal,* Ed Bok. The parlor symbolized holding on to old family heirlooms and relating to guests in old, formal ways. The living room, by contrast, was to be "lived in." It could embrace new styles in commodities and human relationships.

Along with the number of rooms, room size also shrank steadily. This trend was most obvious in the kitchen, a room that had once been the center of household production. Following the industrial ideal of specialization, architects now stripped all but food preparation from the room. The ideal size for a kitchen in the early 1900s had already shrunk from its nineteenth-century expansiveness to ten by twelve feet.[15] By the end of World War I, kitchenettes began to appear.[16] The elimination of laundry space in the kitchen went along with the growth of the commercial laundry, one of the few ultimately unsuccessful campaigns to commercialize what had been women's work.[17] Small kitchens and kitchenettes also eliminated the possibility of eating inside them, and by the early 1930s one author was noting that small kitchens had forced "a good deal of eating outside the house."[18]

Small kitchens were a sign of prestige, as they both followed the ideal of efficiency and specialization and were a visual display of the fact that the husband's salary enabled the family to buy, rather than produce, most of what it used. The inverse relationship between kitchen size and workers' incomes was drawn out with exquisite detail by a Harvard social scientist. In his view, among families whose income was ten dollars a week or less, the wife spent her time "cooking, washing, caring for the children, and doing outside washing or going herself to work." The kitchen in these homes was "perforce the family living room and should be made proportionately ample." In families whose weekly income approached eighteen dollars, while the family still ate in the kitchen, it would probably want "a 'best room' in which to receive callers, actual or hoped for." Among "families of a higher income class," however, a small kitchen was most appropriate. Here, in this analyst's view, "the housewife is quite willing to carry food and dishes into the dining-room in order to escape eating the food in the place where it was cooked; also a separate dining-room is deemed more comfortable by the rest of the family."[19] Thus the middle-class housewife paid for the greater gentility of her family by preparing food alone, in a small kitchen, and carrying it to and from the dining area.

By 1920, the isolation caused by single-family homes and the specialization of rooms within them had apparently caused enough widespread distress among women at home that a book could be written entitled *The Nervous Housewife*. The book combined popular psychoanalytic notions of human needs, an ideological commitment to the single-family home with its specialized quarters, and—despite the contradiction—a detailed study of the damage it was wreaking on women. In a poignant chapter called "The Housework and the Home as Factors in the Neuroses," the author, Abraham Myerson, listed as sources of women's contemporary neuroses not only their raised expectations but also, and more important, the isolation and monotony of their work:

> All work at home has the difficulty of the segregation, the isolation of the home. Man, the social animal who needs at least some one to quarrel with, has deliberately isolated his household—on a property basis. There has grown up a definite, aesthetic need of privacy; all of modesty and the essential feeling demand it.

This is good for the man, and perhaps for the children, but not for the woman. Her work is done all alone, and at the time her husband comes home and wants to stay there, she would like to get out. Work that is in the main lonely, and work that on the whole leaves the mind free, leads almost inevitably to daydreaming and introspection. These are essentials in the housework—monotony, daydreaming, and introspection.[20]

Because Myerson assumed that the need for privacy and segregation were worth nurturing in their current form, his solution to "the nervous housewife" was tentative and piecemeal. Like Charlotte Perkins Gilman, Myerson suggested that some housework would probably have to be made cooperative; but he was cautious to insist that this be done within the confines of the nuclear family and the single-family home.

Isolation inside the home began to impel women into shops and stores. Yet shopping itself provided less and less succor for isolation. For it too was becoming bereft of personal contact.

In the 1880s and 1890s department stores sprang up in all major cities. Since several hundred clerks could not be trusted to bargain in the manner of a shopkeeper, department stores began to institute the "fixed price." With the fixed price, the clerk was relegated to showing items and making change. In the same period, F. W. Woolworth began his five-and-dime stores. These further limited the contact between salesperson and customer by instituting open counters and displays. Woolworth's salespeople now only made change for purchases already chosen.

In food retailing, packaged foods around the turn of the century left the grocery store clerk without measuring functions, and shifted the focus from the actual product and the relationship between clerk and shopper to the product's appearance in its package. Brand names became the source by which the customer chose—and increasingly received her "human" contact. With packaging of food items, "self-service" came into existence. Now, instead of the storekeeper serving a woman as she filled her order, the woman was left to roam through the store while clerks stocked shelves and took inventory. Contact with the customer became limited to the checkout.

In the small shops, women had been allowed to charge and pay as their money came in. As the chain stores became the major self-service operators, the self-service stores demanded cash. The motto was "pay as you go," and nobody's personal relationship with the proprietor was good enough to warrant informal debts and charges. Instead, the larger stores began to offer installment plans, which—after some investigation of her or his personal finances—allowed the consumer to pay on time, at interest. Like self-service, installment buying aimed at stimulating purchases. But it did so without either the personal trust of the old charge account or the economic risks to the storekeepers.

Advertising developed its modern appeals during this period of upheaval and estrangement. The very technological improvements that furthered women's uncertainty and isolation also created the possibility for more effective selling. As old roles and relationships weakened, consumerism and advertising took upon themselves the burden of offering contact and promising love, trust, and security. Some of the changes in selling and advertising techniques—such as certain forms of packaging or the use of color photography—necessitated technological advances. But the dramatic alterations in the style and meaning of the messages had less to do with technology than with an increased understanding of human psychology, as it developed through psychoanalysis and its derivative movements, and with a conscious decision by businessmen to play an active role in helping to form what women and men wanted.

Before 1880, advertising messages had consisted largely of detailed instructions, diagrams and descriptions of the product by the manufacturer, or lengthy testimonials by its users. Images only indirectly connected to the product generally did not come into play. Around the 1890s, advertisers began to loosen up and experiment with new forms. Jingles and human interest trademarks appeared. Jingles told a story, often absurd, but focused on a phrase or an image that embedded the product in the customer's mind. While the emotional appeal of jingles was often their silliness, it was clear to sellers that catchy, emotionally appealing ideas, rather than long descriptions, were good selling devices. Human interest trademarks also followed the device of the simple message but began the trend of more "subjective" advertising. Human interest trademarks, such as the Wool Soap Kids or the H-O cereal baby, were characters who became known and loved for themselves.

Advertisers used images of children self-consciously in the 1890s, directing them specifically at women. *Printer's Ink,* the advertising trade journal, announced in 1896 that "the picture of a healthy, pretty child rivets the attention of most people, especially women. This fact is now generally recognized by advertisers, and the use of a multitude of child-faces as eye attractors is the result."[21] The effectiveness of children as an advertising device was heightened because motherhood had become a choice for many women. At the same time, the images served to draw women back in toward their mothering role.

From the outset, advertising theory, like much of psychoanalysis, was developed largely through experience with women. The psychology of advertising as a discipline has been dated as early as 1903, and certainly numerous insights about what motivated women were being developed around the turn of the century. However, it was with the end of World War I that an accelerated need to increase consumption and the spread of psychoanalysis in this country joined to create a new, scientific study of women as consumers. Notions about the nature of women quickly became embedded in analyses of how the consumer functioned.

Many advertising theorists took Freud's notion of the sexual drive or instinct and used it for their own purposes. Whereas Freud postulated only sexuality as an instinct that transcended history (and even this had a quite broad meaning, almost at the level of a life force), advertising theorists began to produce long lists of "instincts" that were clearly products of a specific culture and whose aim was to further embed people in that culture. For example, Christine Frederick, in her book *Selling to Mrs. Consumer,* listed eighteen "female instincts," among which were sex-love, mother-love, love of homemaking, vanity, love of mutation or change (that is, fashion), love of prestige, and love of reputation.[22] She even elevated the love of trading to an instinct in her attempt to rationalize and justify women's new consumer role. Designating all these traits as instincts removed them to a place where the society no longer had to take responsibility for their existence. Instead, those traits that would be developed, accentuated, and reinforced by advertising could be blamed on the instinctual structure.

Whatever the specific "instinct," emotionality and irrationality became the mainstay of advertising's notion of human or female nature. This was the vulgarized version of the psychoanalytic notion that the individual was driven by unconscious drives. And as emotionality and irrationality became embedded in the common sense of advertising practice, advertising language and imagery drew more and more on prestige, sexuality, isolation, and the alternative, love and contact. Carl Naether, in his classic *Advertising to Women,* argued that advertising should always "strike a personal note," because women were always involved in "the personal"; he suggested using "fanciful expressions" and "chatty tones" with women.[23] His suggestions implied an understanding that the messages of advertising would have to convey the personal contact lost to most people's lives. Like Naether, Christine Frederick also emphasized woman's emotionality. In Frederick's view, woman had a "natural" intelligence, which was "instinctive" and "practical"; but living emotionally, she often revived her spirits with "foolish purchases." Both Frederick and Naether were aware, however, of the changes women were experiencing. Whereas Naether warned industry that they must appeal to the "growing class of business women," Frederick told advertisers that "the present generation of women are not bound much by religious controls, nor by the feeling of being below men in political rights, mental ability or sex inhibition."[24]

Even in their most freedom-loving images, however, the advertisements of the 1920s never incorporated the full implications of the working woman or the possibilities of women living outside of families. Freedom was connected to leisure and romance; stability, to the family and the home. Women might hold jobs, but their main fantasies were still directed toward the family configuration. Whereas women had earlier produced the objects of their daily lives, now they were to buy them—from the objects that made them lovable (marriageable), to those that created a healthy family or a secure home life.

An analysis of the most common themes in advertising in the late 1920s is worth quoting in full, because of the clarity with which it outlines the new images of advertising. Based on a study of the *Woman's Home Companion,* the author, Otis Pease, reported two themes as paramount: "the American family at home" and "the importance of romantic love":

1. *The American family at home.* Home is never an apartment but a house, usually owned. It sanctifies leisure and recreation. It is invariably a "white collar" home. No one works or sweats; families only play at home. A housewife plays with her kitchen and her laundry, the husband plays with his boys or his radio. Homes usually have two cars and a dog. Mothers-in-law, uncles, and grandfathers live elsewhere. Single men and women do not exist. A successful man is a husband who is unfailingly cheerful, "sincere," and upwardly mobile. He may often acquire these virtues by correspondence courses and by other expenditures of money, but his failure to possess them would be a sign not of poverty, but of defective character. The worries, insecurities, and fears of modern men and women stem from failure to be liked, to adjust to one

another, to find adequate sexual satisfactions, but especially from failure to live amid the accoutrements of leisure. These criteria of security are surpassingly important to all families. To possess them is to be free from tension and misery. Harmony and happiness in fact depend on the rate of consumption of gadgets. Friends are always dropping in to view the Frigidaire or dance to the Philco. No more than a good meal and a quiet deodorant are needed to keep the affection of one's husband and children. The preparation and serving of food, to be sure, is a complex function; but the housewife may trust the food industry for advice and guidance. Other large institutions perpetually bolster the family: banks, insurance companies, and utilities stand ready to protect its security and preserve its happiness. Money spent in these institutions is never an expense but an investment.

2. *The importance of romantic love.* The satisfactions of sex and the criteria of romantic love are inextricably intertwined; but whereas romantic love is indispensable to sexual satisfaction, the reverse is not the case: romantic love is desirable in and of itself and is bound up with other ends, such as prestige, social success, power and wealth. The criteria of romantic love can be acquired cheaply by purchase: youth, smoothness of skin, a prominent bust, a deodorized body, a daily ritual of body care, handsome or alluring clothes, outward manners, and a ready affirmative response to these criteria in the other person. (Some women age so young and fade out—constipated. The wife of the Pretender to the throne of France is irresistible; she possesses the power to love; she commands attention; she uses Pond's. Look like a schoolgirl all your life; use Palmolive for your skin—it is made from natural African beauty oils.) Romantic love is available only to those who retain the appearance of youth. Men and women over forty are Mothers, Fathers, Grandmothers, Grandfathers, Business Executives, Professional People; they are no longer capable of romantic love or, therefore, of sexual interests. They seek, instead, prestige and social success; they are content merely to conform to their assigned roles as Mother, Father, etc. Romantic love is also a function of wealth and the ability to consume it. Romantic love depends on leisure time, shopping, parties, sports, vacations, cruises, night clubs, and usually on the premise that the pair are not yet married. Real satisfaction is attainable from sex only upon acquiring the criteria of romantic love.[25]

As women shopped, these images drew them in. They promised solutions to unfulfilled needs and escapes from anxieties. For isolation, there was the promise of contact and communication; for uncertainty, a world where values and ideals were clear. Adventure and freedom could be gained through romantic love; security, protection, and nourishment, through family life. The concrete solution to these desires, however, was to be mere things—commodities that had taken on the emotional overtones conveyed by the ads.

And if the anxieties and insecurities aroused naturally by contemporary life were not enough to sell products, then these feelings were provoked and drawn out by the advertisements themselves. Commodities from mouthwash to life insurance used the possibilities of marital disaster to sell their products. Women's beauty products, which became a major industry during the twenties, helped to inject into physical beauty much of the uncertainty about being a woman and maintaining a marriage. Advertisements were increasingly aimed at heightening women's insecurity so that their product might then be sold as a solution. As Stuart Ewen, who studied advertising in the 1920s, put it,

> Keen and critical glances constantly threatened her. As her home-making skills had become reconstituted into a process of accumulating possessions, her sexuo-economic capacities were reinforced on a commercial plane. An ad for Woodbury soap (1922) offered women "the possession of a beautiful skin" which might arm them to meet a hostile world "proudly—confidently—without fear." Another Woodbury ad warned women that "a man expects to find daintiness, charm, refinement in the woman he knows," and that in order to maintain his pleasure, a woman must constantly spend on her appearance.[26]

Without an alternative vision, women were easily caught in the solutions that advertising offered. If femininity was valued in a period of great instability between women and men, then the loveliness that cosmetics offered was hard to resist. If marriage seemed the only alternative in a time when so many forces made it less secure, then anything from life insurance to mouthwash might be grasped at. Commodities appeared to fill the cracks of a shattered world, and promised to make that world secure in an exciting new way.

The individual that psychoanalysis and psychology were discovering was rapidly channeled into a narrow range of possible wishes and desires. The liberating potential inherent in the loosening of family ties was transformed into a romance of sexuality and family life. Life choices would increasingly be seen in terms of choices about commodities, whose images would symbolize to the isolated, insecure consumer the satisfaction of her well-chiseled desires.

Endnotes

[1] Caroline Hunt, *Home Problems from a New Standpoint* (Boston: Whitcomb & Barrows, 1908), pp. 143–144.

[2] Frank G. Hoover, *Fabulous Dustpan* (Cleveland: The World, 1955).

[3] Christine Frederick, *Selling to Mrs. Consumer* (New York: The Business Course, 1929), p. 181.

[4] Edward Filene, *Successful Living in the Machine Age* (1931), p. 96; quoted in Stuart Ewen, "Advertising as a Way of Life," *Liberation,* January 1975, p. 17.

[5] Linda Gordon, *Woman's Body, Woman's Right: A Social History of Birth Control in America* (New York: Viking Press, 1976).

[6] Norman Himes, *Medical History of Contraception* (1963), p. 340; quoted in Mary P. Ryan, *Womanhood in America from Colonial Times to the Present* (New York: Franklin Watts, 1975), p. 268.

[7] Paul H. Jacobson, *American Marriage and Divorce* (New York: Holt, Rinehart, 1959), pp. 1–19.

[8] Ryan, *Womanhood in America,* p. 262.

[9] Margaret Mead and Frances Bagley Kaplan, eds., *American Woman: The Report of the President's Commission on the Status of Women, and other Publications of the Commission* (New York: Scribner, 1965), pp. 46–47.

[10] Mary Ross, "The New Status of Women in America," in *Women's Coming of Age: A Symposium,* ed. Samuel D. Schmalhausen and V. F. Calhoun (New York: Horace Liveright, 1931), p. 537.

[11] Sophonisba Breckinridge, "The Activities of Women Outside the Home" (1933), p. 723; quoted in William O'Neil, *Everyone Was Brave: A History of Feminism in America* (Chicago: Quadrangle, 1961), p. 305.

[12] An analysis of these homes, as well as other reforms proposed by the *Ladies' Home Journal* editor, Ed Bok, can be found in Helen Woodward, *The Lady Persuaders* (New York: Ivan Obolensky, 1960).

[13] G. W. W. Hanger, *Housing of the Working People in the United States,* Bulletin of the Bureau of Labor no. 54 (Washington, D.C.: GPO, 1904); quoted in Gwendolyn Wright, "A Woman's Place Is in the Home: Changes in Domestic Architecture and in American Family Life, 1880–1915" (UCLA, 1976, typescript).

[14] Quoted in Wright, "A Woman's Place."

[15] Isabel Bevier, *The House, Its Plan, Decoration and Care* (Chicago: American School of Home Economics, 1907), pp. 86–87.

[16] Stuart Ewen, *Captains of Consciousness: Advertising and the Social Roots of the Consumer Culture* (New York: McGraw-Hill, 1976), p. 28.

[17] Heidi Hartman, *Capitalism and Women's Work in the Home, 1900–1930* (Ph.D. diss., Yale University, 1974).

[18] Albert Farwell Bemes, *The Evolving House,* vol. 2: *The Economics of Shelter* (Cambridge, Mass.: MIT Press, 1934), p. 69.

[19] Winthrop Hamlin, "Low Cost Construction in America" (Cambridge, Mass.: Department of Social Ethics, Harvard University, 1917); quoted in Wright, "A Woman's Place."

[20] Abraham Myerson, *The Nervous Housewife* (Boston: Little, Brown, 1920), pp. 77–78.

[21] Frank Presbrey, *The History and Development of Advertising* (1928; New York: Greenwood, 1968), p. 387.

[22] Frederick, *Selling to Mrs. Consumer,* p. 45.

[23] Carl Naether, *Advertising to Women* (New York: Prentice-Hall, 1928).

[24] Frederick, *Selling to Mrs. Consumer,* p. 23.

[25] Otis Pease, *Responsibilities of American Advertising* (New Haven: Yale University Press, 1958), pp. 38–40.

[26] Stuart Ewen, *Captains of Consciousness,* p. 178.

Name: _____   Date: _____

UNDERSTANDING THE TEXT

1. According to Ascher, why were women around the turn of the last century especially "vulnerable to solutions posed by the world of commodities"? (Identify and discuss two reasons.)

2. During the same era, according to Ascher, what changes at home and at work were men experiencing?

3. According to Ascher, what became of the kitchen during this era? For what reasons?

The Making of the Domestic Occasion: The History of Thanksgiving in the United States

Elizabeth Pleck

Four historians, Leigh Eric Schmidt, John Gillis, Penne Restad, and Stephen Nissenbaum, have recently published books about the history of Christmas and several other major holidays in nineteenth-century Europe and the United States Their interpretations provide an organizing framework for understanding the evolution of another holiday, Thanksgiving, between the mid-nineteenth and early twentieth century. My aim is to account for the rise of Thanksgiving as a "domestic occasion" among the antebellum middle class, the extent that poor and working-class families adopted the holiday by the early twentieth century, and the addition of new elements to the celebration by the 1930s.

Schmidt, Gillis, Restad, and Nissenbaum traced the change in patterns of festivity between colonial days and the mid-nineteenth century. Communal celebration, often raucous, usually outdoors, which involved lower-class males demanding treats from the wealthy gave way gradually to private celebrations of the middle class, sedate but joyful. This historic change in the pattern of celebration I call the rise of the "domestic occasion."[1] By a domestic occasion, I mean a family gathering held in the home which paid homage to the ideal of the "affectionate family." Such a family was a privatized nuclear one, with a nurturant mother creating a proper home atmosphere, and providing children with a protected and supervised upbringing. Although the ideal of the affectionate family was a nuclear one, the domestic occasion was often a gathering of extended kin, a family homecoming. Sometimes families invited neighbors or strangers so that these non-family members would not feel lonely on a

From *Journal of Social History*, Summer 1999, Vol. 32, No. 4 by Elizabeth Pleck. Copyright © 1999 by Journal of Social History. Reprinted by permission.

day of family gathering. The domestic occasion was a culturally dominant form, practiced at first mainly by the upper classes and middle classes, which spread throughout the society in the twentieth century.

The four historians mentioned above regard the domestic occasion both as an expression of the middle-class ideology of the affectionate family and the result of it. This ideology divided the public and private into two separate spheres. The private sphere, that of the home, became "the empire of the woman," a quasi-sacred space over which the mother as homemaker presided.[2] Middle-class women, with or without the help of servants, organized and arranged the domestic occasion and found it an affirmation of their role in the home, despite occasional complaints about the burden of shopping and worries about indulging children.[3]

John Gillis, Leigh Eric Schmidt, and Stephen Nissenbaum offer additional explanations for the rise of the domestic occasion. Gillis sees it as a "moment in time" or "special time" for the family. The industrial revolution, he argues, gave birth to clock time, industrial discipline, and the schedule. Domestic occasions were scheduled events of family gathering during an epoch when some relatives had moved away from home and the family breadwinner was spending fewer hours with his family during the week. In addition, both Leigh Eric Schmidt and Stephen Nissenbaum explore the commercial origins of the domestic occasion. Nissenbaum shows that the luxury gift was central to the rise of the domestic Christmas. He notes that merchants were advertising gift books, published once a year, as one of the first Christmas and New Year's presents by the 1820s.[4]

Nissenbaum further argues that the urban upper class felt threatened by gang violence and unlicensed drunkenness during the Christmas season. They favored the homey, seemingly old-fashioned Christmas as a sober alternative to "hideous" cries from the street. Clement Moore's poem, "A Visit from St. Nicholas," popularly known as "The Night Before Christmas," written in 1822, described and helped further the ideal of a domesticated Christmas. Soon after Moore's poem was reprinted in newspapers, New York City replaced its relatively ineffective private watch with a professional police force. Thereafter the police arrested unruly masqueraders on Christmas, and the public came to regard drunken license on Christmas Eve as disreputable.[5] Nissenbaum admits that the rowdy way of celebrating Christmas never disappeared, but instead he believes it became stigmatized as crime, rather than as harmless festivity.

The four authors share a social constructionist approach toward the history of the domestic occasion. They place it in the category of an "invented tradition," a phrase devised by Eric Hobsbawm and Terence Ranger. Hobsbawm and Ranger considered an invented tradition a ritual implying continuity with the past, even though that continuity is largely fictitious.[6] Hobsbawm and Ranger traced the history of public rituals, not private ones, although their concept is elastic enough to apply to both. They argued that the invented tradition met the needs of people in the present for a sense of connection with the past, and a desire of people in a modern world "to structure at least some parts of social life within it [their modern world] as unchanging and invariant."[7] Bastille Day, kilt-wearing, and the pledge of allegiance, they noted, were all rituals invented between the end of the eighteenth century and the last third of the nineteenth century—kilt wearing in the late eighteenth century, the other two rituals in the late nineteenth century. These were entirely new ceremonies, they argued, intended to create the fiction of shared national identity and national unity. Unlike Hobsbawm and Ranger, the four historians I have mentioned located the origin of the domestic occasion in the early rather than the late nineteenth century.

Historians of the domestic occasion also tend to emphasize the equivalent of a "big bang theory," a single large cultural and economic change, occurring in the early nineteenth century which generated a fixed form and meaning for family ritual. Gillis traces our cultural difficulties in the present to the legacy of living with the myths the Victorians created. Nissenbaum ended his study of Christmas around 1900 because he believed that the holiday had acquired a fixed form by then.[8] A case study of a holiday other than Christmas allows examination of the relative significance of the factors already adduced as significant in the rise of domestic occasions. The second most popular domestic occasion in the modern United States, Thanksgiving, is surprisingly absent from the holidays recently studied. The history of Thanksgiving recounted here will show how the holiday was invented—and reinvented—over four major periods of time between the early nineteenth century and about 1930, how the domestic occasion initially coexisted and then eventually triumphed over more raucous forms of celebration, and how Thanksgiving spread from its initial enthusiasts in New England to become a holiday celebrated by people of many classes and regions.

The history of Thanksgiving is hallowed ground for antiquarians, popular writers, and even an occasional anthropologist.[9] The story begins with the Pilgrims who held a feast for themselves and their Wampanoag neighbors in October of 1621. Prior to Lincoln, three presidents, George Washington, John Adams, and James Madison, issued *ad hoc* proclamations of a *national day* of thanksgiving. Nonetheless, Thanksgiving in the early nineteenth century was mainly popular in New England and to a lesser extent the mid-Atlantic states. As of the 1850s, Thanksgiving was a legal holiday only in these states and in Texas.

Prior to Abraham Lincoln's proclamation in 1863 of an annual national holiday in November, Thanksgiving was a regional day, both secular and religious. In early nineteenth century New England Thanksgiving day might begin with a morning church service, followed by the large meal in the afternoon. Before or after attending church, men, musket in hand, might take aim at a wild turkey in the fields, or at paper targets. The winner usually won a turkey as his prize for good marksmanship. The food at the feast was bountiful but the setting was relatively modest. Most families did not own a long wooden dining table. They might have had a smaller one, which was set up in a sitting room, parlor, or the bedroom—any room that could be kept warm in winter. There were probably only two courses to the meal, the food for the main meal spread on the table, and the desserts served later.[10] Because the roads were poor, muddy or snow-covered, many relatives, eager to return home for the holidays, were unable to do so.

HALE, LINCOLN AND THE TOLERANCE OF MISRULE

Through the efforts of Sarah Josepha Hale, and later Abraham Lincoln, Thanksgiving became a holiday of the Union, with limited acceptance in the Southern states.[11] The editor of *Godey*'s magazine, Sarah Josepha Hale, issued yearly editorials beginning in 1846 encouraging the "Great American Festival" of Thanksgiving. Hale wrote letters to governors of states and territories, overseas missionaries, and navy commanders urging them to celebrate Thanksgiving and, in the case of the governors, to make Thanksgiving a legal holiday. Hale hoped that a unifying holiday would help avert the prospect of a civil war. Instead, the victory at Gettysburg as well as Hale's entreaties encouraged Abraham Lincoln in 1863 to declare a national day of thanksgiving in November.

As a holiday of "family homecoming," Thanksgiving eased the social dislocations of the industrial and commerical revolutions. The ritual of returning home at Thanksgiving, "when the fledged birds once more flew back to the mother nest," made it possible to reconcile individualism and obligation to family.[12] A man could be self-made and an obedient son, so long as he reunited with his family for Thanksgiving. The family homecoming also affirmed the importance of the extended family at a time when large-scale migration from New England had weakened kin ties. The ideal of Thanksgiving as a holiday of family reunion emerged at the height of the ideology of domesticity that made the home into a secular shrine. Sarah Josepha Hale thought the holiday established the importance of "the gratified hospitality, the obliging civility and unaffected happiness" of the American family.[13]

Why was it so important that domestic occasions appear to be "old fashioned?" The growth of commerce, industry, and urban life created a radical break between past and present, a gap that could be bridged by threshold reunions at the family manse. Nostalgia at Thanksgiving was a yearning for a simpler, more virtuous, more public-spirited and wholesome past, located in the countryside, not the city. In gaining wealth, the family and nation, it was believed, had lost its sense of spiritual mission. Perhaps celebrating one special day might help restore the religious morality of an earlier generation. In reprinting recipes for the feast, and publishing stories of prodigals returning home, Hale showed how Thanksgiving should be celebrated and explained its meaning. She assumed that the family would attend church the morning of the feast, although many Thanksgiving articles in *Godey*'s did not emphasize church-going.

By having Lincoln as its midwife, Thanksgiving also celebrated the blessings of American nationhood as well as its domestic ideals. Thanksgiving was—and is—a holiday of American civil religion, that is, religious belief in the national purpose and destiny. The nation, it was believed, was blessed by God and given a special purpose in the world.[14] (The distinction between Thanksgiving and Christmas in this regard is a matter of degree rather than of kind, since some Victorian Christmas trees in America might be decorated with the American flag and those in Britain were draped with the Union Jack.) To Lincoln, Thanksgiving was the time for a grateful nation to praise God for blessings bestowed, for the many years of "peace and prosperity," for the growth in national wealth, power, and population, "as no other nation has ever grown." Lincoln, or William H. Seward, who wrote the proclamation, saw Thanksgiving as a holiday when the "whole American people" invoked God but he also raised the troublesome idea that the country was at war because God was punishing it for a national sin.[15]

An earlier way of celebrating coexisted with the domestic occasion Hale and Lincoln reinvented. As William Dean Howells put it, "The poor recognize [Thanksgiving] as a sort of carnival," a masculine escape from the family, a day of rule breaking, and spontaneous mirth.[16] Thanksgiving had its own set of rowdies, akin to those at Christmas. Drunken men and boys, often masked, paraded from house to house and demanded to be treated. Boys misbehaved and men committed physical assaults on Thanksgiving as well as on Christmas.[17]

Groups of men, crossdressing, who called themselves the Fantastics or Fantasticals, masqueraded on Thanksgiving beginning in the 1780s. The name Fantastic was English and the practice seems to have been derived from English door to door masquerading for treats. Subsequently the Fantastics copied these and other elements of English mumming, such as drunkenness and ridiculing authority. At the end of the Revolutionary war veterans were dressing up in the rags of the Continental soldiers. The Fantastics paraded in rural and urban areas of eastern and central Pennsylvania, and New York City on Thanksgiving, New Year's Eve and Day, Battalion Day, Washington's Birthday, and the Fourth of July.[18]

The upper- and middle-class public, which so disliked noisy and threatening bands of youths on Christmas and New Year's Eve, was more accepting of Fantastical parades. An editorial in a Pennsylvania newspaper in 1870 defended the Fantastics, on the grounds that "it is better to be merry than sad, and if, as some genial writer asserts, a good hearty laugh takes a nail out of your coffin, a parade of the fantasticals can not fail to lessen the bills of mortality."[19] *The New York Times* in 1885 regarded the Fantastics as "hilarious" and "quaint."[20] In New York City the police and an occasional politician joined the parade. Most New York City Fantastics were Irish and working class; many were fish sellers at the Fulton Fish market, along with some politicians and prison guards. As a boy, growing up in the 1880s, the Democratic governor of New York state and later presidential candidate, Al Smith, worked at the market himself, and enjoyed watching the Fantastical parade.[21]

ATTACKS ON MISRULE AND IMMIGRANT CELEBRATION OF THANKSGIVING

Lower-class men had been making merry and poking fun at their betters for centuries, on Thanksgiving and other holidays. In the late 1880s the upper class developed its own form of misrule in their exuberance after Thanksgiving Day football games. An organization run by college students, the Intercollegiate Football Association, scheduled its first championship game on Thanksgiving Day in 1876. Two decades later the *Chicago Tribune* estimated that about 10,000 high school and college teams, and those of athletic clubs were playing football on Thanksgiving Day.[22]

The Thanksgiving Day game was controversial from the beginning. Walter Camp, the "father" of modern football, argued that the fact that fans willingly gave up—or in some cases, postponed—their Thanksgiving dinner to cheer for their team showed the popularity of the game.[23] To ministers and Ethelbret Warfield, president of Lafayette College, football on Thanksgiving desecrated "a great national feast-day." Warfield regarded Thanksgiving as a day to give thanks to God for the blessings of "the Christian home" and "citizenship." He believed that whooping college boys, storming theaters, starting fights at "saloons, dance halls, and worse" were taking the first steps in a life of "temptation and vice."[24] The collegians were also getting themselves arrested, disrupting Broadway performances, and throwing beer mugs and glasses at high-stepping showgirls.[25] In 1894 Ivy League college presidents, embarrassed by all this, shifted the day of the season-ending game to the Saturday before Thanksgiving, moved the location from Manhattan to college grounds, and insisted that students return to campus after the game had finished.[26]

A broader attack on the Fantastics began in these years as well. The *New York Times* in 1895 called the Fantastics "intolerable" and a "public nuisance"—although the newspaper conceded that children might think them funny.[27] We find decreasing tolerance for misrule on Thanksgiving not in the early nineteenth century, as had been the case with Christmas, but around 1890. Perhaps the immediate reasons for the change in opinion were double-digit rates of unemployment and civil unrest. Fearful of social disorder, the populace linked the Fantastics or drunken Princetonians with strikers at Pullman or marchers in Coxey's army. There is no evidence that misrule was more disruptive than before. The difference was that the public felt more threatened by even minor disturbances of the peace.

The Fantastics disappeared by the 1910s, although the masquerade and carnival cropped up in different incarnations. The ball, which had been held at the end of the day of masquerading, was now celebrated in the 1910s and 1920s by gay men in Greenwich Village, many of whom came in drag.[28] It is unclear whether male homosexuals had always been among the crossdressers in the Fantastics parade, or whether an entirely separate group of men had appropriated the ritual they might have witnessed in their neighborhood. Misrule at Thanksgiving also appeared in October. Halloween, rather than Thanksgiving, became the holiday for wearing costumes. Children, sometimes dressed in rags or wearing masks, had always followed the Fantastics on Thanksgiving Day, blowing horns and begging. Calling their ritual the Ragamuffin parade, children continued to beg on Thanksgiving. Although some of the child beggars were poor, more privileged ragamuffins in costume demanded coins or treats in New York City or upstate New York as late as the 1940s.[29]

Progressive era reformers regarded child begging on Thanksgiving as immoral and thought children who engaged in it should be arrested. Why were parents not able to control their offspring? the *New York Times* in 1903 wanted to know.[30] The newspaper castigated parents who allowed children to demand treats or money as indecent.[31] The police tried to enforce a ban against begging. In response to complaints from the public, the clergy, school superintendents, and classroom teachers issued warnings. The *New York Times* in November of 1930 worried that demanding coins could teach children to become professional beggars and blackmailers and that children were annoying the public.[32] Begging, decided the paper, was a "malicious influence on the morals of children of the city."[33] Boys' clubs and other child welfare agencies organized parades and costume contests as alternative activities. As a result of these efforts, child begging on Thanksgiving finally disappeared by the 1940s.[34]

Even before that, the festival of the home had become the dominant way of celebrating Thanksgiving. In the Progressive era Thanksgiving acquired a new meaning, as a domestic occasion that incorporated newcomers into American customs. Surveys of elementary school principals in the 1920s show that Thanksgiving was the most frequently celebrated holiday in the schools, even slightly edging out Christmas.[35] Public school teachers and settlement house workers hoped to assimilate immigrant children to America and use children as Americanizers of their parents. They wanted the children to become patriotic citizens who demonstrated their love of country through celebration of cherished American holidays. Hale helped to invent a domestic occasion, which emphasized family homecoming; Lincoln saw in the holiday an opportunity for a nation to give thanks for its blessings. Both of them used the language of civil religion, even though in the mid-nineteenth century the public still understood the holiday as a Protestant one. In the Progressive era teachers did not emphasize the Protestant origins or meaning of thanksgiving, and instead portrayed the holiday in secular, nationalist terms, as a day when all Americans could feel they belonged to the nation. (Families were expected to say grace before the feast, but churchgoing was no longer a required element of the ritual.)

This Progressive era invention of Thanksgiving made the Pilgrims into the first newcomers who shared the migration experience with subsequent immigrants. Even in Hale's day, the story of the Pilgrims was the first chapter in the American story. Reverend Samuel Francis Smith in 1831, in writing his hymn, "America," made clear that he thought that the "sweet land of liberty" originated as the "land of the Pilgrims' pride."[36] However, antebellum stories and popular paintings emphasized the landing at Plymouth Rock and the Pilgrims' first encounters with Indians. In the 1890s the public became as interested in the feast as in other Pilgrim activities. Americans of that era commonly confused the Puritans, the rather intolerant founders of the large Massachusetts Bay Colony, with the Pilgrims, religious separatists who left Holland to establish their own colony in Plymouth in 1620. Those who knew the difference recognized that the Pilgrims were relatively egalitarian, nonideological, and had initially friendly relations with Indians. They worked hard, too, and had been persecuted in Europe, which could not be said for the settlers in Jamestown, Virginia. By the late nineteenth century, the educated elite sought examples of "intense faith, imagination, and courage," respectable ancestors, founders of their country who "could not be accused of religious intolerance or intellectual arrogance."[37]

Beginning in the 1890s genealogical fever, snobbery, and the desire to differentiate themselves from the great wave of immigrants standing on the national doorstep led to the founding of the Daughters and Sons of the American Revolution, the Colonial Dames of America, the Society of Mayflower Descendants, and dozens of other patriotic societies. William DeLoss Love, a Congregationalist minister and member of the Sons of the American

Revolution, wrote the first history of Thanksgiving. He published *The Fast and Thanksgiving Days of New England* in 1895. Love argued that Plymouth was the birthplace of the nation and that the New England family of the past was "one of the grandest conceptions of family life known in history."[38]

Schoolteachers throughout the nation began to teach the story of the Pilgrims to their pupils.[39] Textbooks claimed that the Pilgrims believed in the democratic ideal, since they had drawn up the Mayflower Compact, the first democratic constitution in the New World. Many schools had been putting up Christmas trees and decorating them ever since about the 1870s, but had not made teaching about holidays part of the curriculum. Progressive era educators devised student art projects and contests as part of a social studies education which emphasized teaching about calendric holidays. The selection of the national secular and religious calendar as the form of instruction was an exercise in cultural power, providing children with a dominant set of symbols (the flag, turkeys, Pilgrims, Santas, Easter Bunnies).

Portraying Thanksgiving as a day to be thankful for the blessings of "home and community," teachers staged elaborate tableaux with girls dressed in white caps and cuffs made out of paper and boys in round collars and cuffs. They decorated their classrooms with pumpkins, ears of corn, and pictures of Pilgrims and turkeys. One Jewish immigrant recalled that schools emphasized "American holidays and our Puritan roots . . ." indicating the common confusion of the Pilgrims and Puritans. He added, "We had a textbook about Puritans, pictures of Puritans with the big hats and Thanksgiving and so on, and then about the Revolutionary War and the Fourth of July and Betsy Ross and George Washington, and those things we *learned*."[40]

Teachers told their students that all Americans were immigrants or their descendants, although some had arrived earlier than others. One Italian immigrant student grasped that "the Pilgrim fathers had come in pursuit of religious freedom; we had come in pursuit of more and better bread."[41] The schools recognized that they had to develop an emotional bond between the immigrant and the nation, a love of country. Immigrant children could be taught American history and learn about the holidays, but the home was where the deepest feelings of patriotism were conveyed.[42] Thus, the home celebration of holidays needed to be encouraged to reinforce the patriotism learned in the school. By holding a feast around a common table, an immigrant family could demonstrate its acceptance of American customs and knowledge of American history.

How were the teachers' efforts received? Gary Gerstle has asserted that because Thanksgiving was a cultural affirmation of "family," Catholic and Jewish households eagerly accepted it.[43] It is true that most states had passed legislation making Thanksgiving a legal holiday by the end of the nineteenth century. Even then, it seems likely that Thanksgiving celebration was most common among the middle and upper classes, in New England and the mid-Atlantic states, and among Protestants. The Catholic church opposed the holiday as a Protestant rite as late as the 1880s. Many in the South still thought of Thanksgiving as a Yankee day.[44] In the West the day was largely one for hunting, and the feast could be a brief and unassuming one. A Colorado pioneer, recalling his family's home celebration at the turn of the century, claimed that Thanksgiving was "like Sunday in the middle of the week."[45]

One reason that Thanksgiving was not frequently celebrated among the rural or urban poor was because they could not afford a turkey. Wardheelers brought free turkeys to poor families in immigrant neighborhoods, but not to every home. Some but certainly not the majority of employers handed out free turkeys.[46] Another reason is that Thanksgiving was still understood as a religious day. Around 1900, for example, blacks often went to church services on Thanksgiving but rarely had feasts at home.[47] Although it is impossible to establish the frequency of the celebration of Thanksgiving among the poor and working class, it is clear that schoolchildren were cultural conduits, bringing home ideas about celebration, national history, and cultural symbols learned at school. One boy even cut out paper pumpkins and turkeys and pasted them on the windowpanes of his apartment.[48] Children implored their mothers to buy a turkey and roast it. The immigrant child helped promote cultural change, making a request of his or her mother, who might veto it.

The reasons why Pearl Kazin's mother said no were overtly religious, and covertly cultural. Kazin, who lived in Brooklyn in the 1920s, asked her mother, "But Mama, *why* can't we have turkey for Thanksgiving like everybody else?"[49] Her mother replied, "Who's everybody?" Mother would say, without taking her eyes from the sewing machine, 'The Feins eat turkey Thanksgiving? . . . We don't have enough *our* holidays for you.'" The distinction between Jewish and school holidays revealed the distance between Mrs. Kazin's concept of a festival and the middle-class (Christian) one taught in the schools. A Chinese mother in California, also not a Christian, saw Thanksgiving as a means of extending Chinese hospitality to the host society. But her reasons were more complicated, as she explained, "We share the holiday of our American neighbors . . . because we wish to live in peace and harmony with them and because I do not wish you children to grow wicked with envy of others."[50]

Most immigrants sought a culinary fusion, which asserted a bit of group identity while embracing many elements of the dominant culture, even though there were a few families who adopted the entire American menu, including the chestnut stuffing and sweet potatoes.[51] The turkey became the symbol of the dominant culture, and the stuffing, the side dishes, and desserts the immigrant's contribution. Mothers added spices to the stuffing distinctive to the homeland. Greek families sprinkled pine nuts in the stuffing and the American-born wife of an Armenian husband added pomegranate and Oriental spices to hers. A Chinese-American mother steamed the turkey first, then stuffed it with the glutinous rice mixture she usually used with chicken.[52] Most groups were unconsciously making the statement that they were trying to assimilate by combining a few, selected elements of their culture with fealty to the national holiday and its cuisine. Only a few cooks discarded the traditional American meal entirely.[53]

COMMERCIALIZATION AND RADIO BROADCAST OF FOOTBALL

The Macy's Thanksgiving Day parade, begun in 1924, symbolized the commercialization of a holiday the general public regards as non-commercial. In truth, Thanksgiving was a minor gift-giving occasion in the early nineteenth century. A man might give his brother a Bible for a Thanksgiving present.[54] At first merchants, as Nissenbaum notes, were advertising gift books as suitable presents for Christmas and New Year's. By the 1850s publishers were also selling gift books for Thanksgiving.[55] Since we often assume that commerce expands exponentially, without interruption, it is puzzling to explain why these initial efforts at gift giving on Thanksgiving seem to have disappeared. Perhaps giving a Bible on Thanksgiving was no longer thought of as the holiday became more secular. And as Christmas gift lists grew longer, it might have seemed wasteful, even superfluous to buy a Thanksgiving present.

While gift giving seems to have disappeared, other forms of commercial goods, originally developed for Valentine's Day or Christmas, were sold for the Thanksgiving holiday. Greeting cards, paper goods (paper napkins and plates imprinted with pictures of Pilgrims and turkeys), candies, and flowers have been and are now marketed for Thanksgiving. Since the early twentieth century newspapers and magazines began to carry Thanksgiving ads. A Crisco ad from 1916 showed a grey-haired granny with wire-rimmed glasses holding her mince pie made with their product. Commercial foods, such as canned pumpkin, appeared about a decade later. In the Thanksgiving issue of the *Saturday Evening Post* for 1931, an advertisement for Camels touted the cigarettes as "something to be thankful for."[56]

There were at least two nineteenth-century antecedents to a parade on Thanksgiving, the Fantastics and football fans, riding atop horse-drawn carriages on their way to the Polo Grounds where the game was to be played.[57] What made Macy's parade different was that the department store wanted to stage a parade as a prelude to the Christmas shopping season. Appearing at the end of the parade, Santa symbolized the bounty of Christmas and the desire to shower children with presents. So clear was the connection between the two holidays that Macy's at first called its November spectacle a "Christmas parade."[58]

Macy's parade, even in the 1920s, existed not in the shadow of the family feast or the church service, but in competition with the afternoon football game. Football was clearly the more significant of the two forms of out-of-home entertainment, as changes in the timing of Macy's parade in the 1920s indicate. Initially Macy's parade offended patriotic groups, who decried a spectacle on "a national and essentially religious holiday."[59] Macy's hired a public relations man, who decided that the critics could be placated if the parade in the morning was postponed until at least after church services had ended. The parade, pushed back to the afternoon, began at the same time as the kickoff for most football games. Customers and football fans complained. By the late 1920s, Macy's had returned to an early morning parade, presumably so as not to compete with afternoon football games.

In the 1920s football finally moved into the home, rather than being merely a form of outdoor amusement which threatened to overwhelm the domestic celebration. The family might dine and then listen to a football game on the radio as a form of after-dinner entertainment. By 1956 football games were televised. Popular entertainment has enhanced home celebration in the twentieth century whether it was the Christmas program on radio or television or the broadcast of a football game. There is always the question of whether listening to the football game in the living room represented a distinct stage of reinvention of the holiday, or simply a new custom attached to the nineteenth-century notion of feast and homecoming. Men, listening avidly to the game at home, probably thought it was a significant reinvention. They quickly came to regard listening to the game as traditional, part of what made the ritual authentic and meaningful.

Families scheduled their dinner so that they would be finished eating by the time the football game began. Like all forms of mass culture, football has multiple meanings. Journalists, educators, ministers, coaches, and sports writers have interpreted the game as a metaphor for various American social ideals. To be sure, occasional opponents of the game thought the game too aggressive, violent, and dangerous. To the game's proponents football could be a training ground for war (a common World War I theme) or an antidote to it (a postwar theme). It could be a symbol of imperialism and social Darwinism (proof of the "dominance of the white race" and the success of the fittest). It might combine Christianity with male athleticism, or serve as an excellent preparation for bureaucracy, team work, and management (in the writings of the Yale "football coach," Walter Camp). Many late nineteenth century writers argued that football demonstrated the success of Victorian virtues, such as regularity, self-restraint, and fair play. Some writers also noticed that the Thanksgiving Day game generated loyalty among college students and alumni and that attendance at the Thanksgiving Day game provided an opportunity for a fur-coated elite to display status by arriving at the game in decorated carriages.[60]

What was lost on these devotees of the game was the irony in a family event, punctuated by (mostly) men listening to a game noted for its aggressive body contact, warlike language, male bonding, and the ability of contestants to withstand pain. There had always been gender segregation at the Thanksgiving meal, with men talking to other men, and women conversing with women before and after the meal. As women in the kitchen washed the dishes, and men listened to the game, one could recognize that women (willingly) gave up their leisure, and that men and children benefitted from female sacrifice. Men and women also occupied separate spaces in the home on Thanksgiving, although it was easier for a woman to enter the living room where men were listening to the game than for a man to don an apron and help in the kitchen.[61]

Encamping in the living room, men seemed to find solace in an all-male group, after having participated in an event so female in ambience. One function of football, even enjoyed vicariously, was to reaffirm men's bonds with other men and their masculinity, to inject some manliness into the sentimentality. Sons, listening to the game with their fathers, were learning the rules of male sociability—and being weaned away from their mothers. Listening to football was an additional masculine element that followed the ritual of carving the turkey, man the gladiator side by side with man the hunter. As such, the football game on Thanksgiving Day provided an added symbolic statement about the difference between the genders.[62]

What makes for a domestic occasion? Certainly the ideology of domesticity, the cultural and economic anxieties and dislocations of the industrial and commercial revolutions played a significant role. Middle-class women found the idea of the domestic occasion an affirmation of their nurturing role in the family, and an opportunity for kin to reunite. The compliments called out to them for their mince or pumpkin pie usually compensated for the burdens of cleaning and cooking. The nineteenth-century Thanksgiving was not entirely devoid of commercialism. Yet in the case of Thanksgiving, nationalism was a more significant feature than commerce. In that sense, Hobsbawm and Ranger were correct to draw attention to nationalism as a force in creating new traditions and reinvigorating others. Celebrating the national mission was an important impetus for the invention of Thanksgiving in the early nineteenth century and remains a central element in the holiday to this day.

Christmas, the most significant calendric holiday of the year, the most culturally rich one, and the most commercialized, does not provide the model for other holidays. Consumer culture has shaped *every* American domestic occasion, but not to the same degree. Exactly how commerce and sentiment were married varied for each occasion. Responding to petitions from merchants, Franklin D. Roosevelt in 1939 changed the date of Thanksgiving to the third Thursday in November to lengthen the Christmas shopping season. Two years later he admitted his mistake, and proclaimed again the fourth Thursday in November as the day for national Thanksgiving because the public did not want Christmas to intrude on Thanksgiving. Roosevelt had tampered with a fixed date, the public objected to. Nonetheless, a certain level of intrusion was accepted, since the crowds enjoyed Thanksgiving day parades even though such parades commercialized Thanksgiving on behalf of Christmas.

Nissenbaum argued that the domestic Christmas emerged as an upper-class and middle-class alternative to rowdy youth gangs rioting and disturbing the peace. At Thanksgiving, the domestic occasion coexisted with rowdiness, and significant efforts to eliminate misrule occurred decades after the domestic occasion had become the dominant form. The public seems to have tolerated misrule at Thanksgiving from the Federalist era to the Gilded Age. Attitudes began to change in the 1890s, perhaps because an economic depression and civil unrest made misrule appear more threatening. The antebellum New York City police took swift action to arrest the unruly on Christmas Eve; attempts to ban the Fantastics were sporadic, and took a long time to effect. The child begging on a sacred day went on, year after year, because the police and mothers tolerated it.

American nationalism has shaped the celebration of Thanksgiving since the days of Lincoln. Thanksgiving did not unify a war-torn nation, but the holiday probably did help unify the Northern side during the Civil War. In the Progressive era schoolteachers wanted to incorporate immigrants into the nation. They tried to broaden the appeal of the holiday, and draw in their immigrant students. Teachers followed the maxim, persuade the child, and the parents will follow; they seem to have succeeded in convincing their students of the importance of the holiday, and in getting them to plead with their parents to celebrate it. Nonetheless, many parents failed to grasp the significance of Thanksgiving. Quite a few mothers did not roast a turkey on Thanksgiving not simply because they could not afford one but because they considered Thanksgiving an alien holiday.

Thus, it took a long time before Thanksgiving became beloved in all classes and regions, or among most homemakers. The introduction of football made the holiday more appealing to many men. By adding listening to an athletic contest to a feast, families recognized that popular entertainment on the radio enhanced the celebration. Listening to the game was not simply a new custom added to the family feast; it became a central attraction of the holiday for men. While the domestic occasion of the early nineteenth century represented the feminization of the middle-class home, radio broadcast of the game at Thanksgiving helped masculinize the domestic festival.

The reinventions of Thanksgiving show the significance of American nationalism, the desire of (many) immigrants to adopt the national culture, but in a hyphenated form, the significance of children as agents of change, and the role of popular entertainment in enhancing modern festivity and in adding a masculine element to a highly feminine occasion. As this study of Thanksgiving demonstrates, Thanksgiving has been reinvented several times, with changes in both form and meaning. Tad Tuleja nicely summarized this evolution when he wrote that Thanksgiving has become "Puritans plus Sarah Josepha Hale and the Butterball trademark and football and (in some Italian families) lasagna as a traditional side dish."[63] Tuleja's list included only the elements grafted on to Thanksgiving. Through the efforts of teachers, the police, college presidents, and social agencies, we have also gradually subtracted a significant element, misrule, from the celebration of Thanksgiving.

ENDNOTES

Jacqueline Jones and John Gillis read earlier drafts of this essay. The author also acknowledges the comments and suggestions of Joseph Pleck and Frederic Cople Jaher.

[1] John R. Gillis, *A World of Their Own Making: Myth, Ritual, and the Quest for Family Values* (New York, 1997); Leigh Eric Schmidt, *Consumer Rites: The Buying and Selling of American Holidays* (Princeton, 1997); Penne Restad, *Christmas in America: A History* (New York, 1995); Stephen Nissenbaum, *The Battle for Christmas* (New York, 1996); John R. Gillis, "Ritualization of Middle-Class Family Life in Nineteenth Century Britain," *International Journal of Politics, Culture and Society* v. 3, No. 2 (Winter, 1989) 4–21.

[2] On the ideology of domesticity, see Nancy F. Cott, *The Bonds of Womanhood: "Woman's Sphere" in New England, 1780–1835* (New Haven, 1977); Ann Douglas, *The Feminization of American Culture* (New York, 1977); Mary P. Ryan, *Cradle of the Middle Class: The Family in Oneida County, New York, 1790–1865* (Cambridge, 1983); Kathryn Kish Sklar, *Catharine Beecher: A Study in American Domesticity* (New Haven, 1973); Lenore Davidoff and Catherine Hall, *Family Fortunes: Men and Women of the English Middle Class, 1780–1850* (Chicago, 1987); Jeanne Boydston, *Home and Work: Housework, Wages, and the Ideology of Labor in the Early Republic* (New York, 1990).

[3] Leigh Eric Schmidt in *Consumer Rites* emphasized the domestic occasion as an affirmation of middle-class women's role in the home.

[4] Stephen Nissenbaum, *The Battle for Christmas,* 140–155.

[5] Stephen Nissenbaum, *The Battle for Christmas,* ch. 3

[6] Eric Hobsbawm, "Introduction: Inventing Traditions," in Eric Hobsbawm and Terence Ranger, eds., *The Invention of Tradition* (Cambridge, 1983), 1–14.

[7] Eric Hobsbawm, "Introduction," 2.

[8] Stephen Nissenbaum, *The Battle for Christmas* (New York, 1996), XII.

[9] Janet Siskind, "The Invention of Thanksgiving: A Ritual of American Nationality," *Critique of Anthropology* v. 12, No. 2 (1992): 167–191; Diana Karter Appelbaum, *Thanksgiving: An American Holiday, An American History* (New York, 1984); William DeLoss Love, Jr., *The Fast and Thanksgiving Days of New England* (Cambridge, MA, 1985); Edwin T. Grenniger, "Thanksgiving: An American Holiday," *Social Science* v. 54, No. 4 (Winter, 1979): 3–15; Ralph and Adele Linton, *We Gather Together: The Story of Thanksgiving* (New York, 1949).

[10] For descriptions of Thanksgiving feasts in antebellum New England, see Jane C. Nylander, *Our Own Snug Fireside: Images of the New England Home 1760–1860* (New York, 1993), 261–282.

[11] Lincoln's proclamation also standardized the date of the celebration, since up to that time states had celebrated Thanksgiving on various days in November or even December. Jane C. Nylander, *Our Own Snug Fireside,* 263.

[12] Caroline Howard King, *When I Lived in Salem, 1822–1866* (Brattleboro, Vt, 1937), 108.

[13] Sarah Josepha Hale, *Northwood; or Life North and South* (New York, 1852), 91.

[14] Robert Bellah, "Civil Religion in America," in Robert Bellah, ed., *Beyond Belief: Essays on Religion in a Post-Traditional World* (New York, 1970), 168–192.

[15] "Proclamation of Thanksgiving," October 3, 1863, in Roy P. Basler, ed., *The Collected Works of Abraham Lincoln* (New Brunswick, 1953), 496–497; J. G. Randall, "Lincoln and Thanksgiving," *Lincoln Herald* v. 49, No. 3 (October, 1947), 10–13.

[16] W. D. Howells, *Through the Eye of the Needle* (New York, 1907), 49.

[17] Jack Santino, *All Around the Year: Holidays and Celebrations in American Life* (Urbana, 1994), 164–167; Robert J. Meyers, *Celebrations: The Complete Book of American Holidays* (Garden City, NY, 1972), 114–115.

[18] The Fantastics represented a "symbolic inversion" of the values of the family homecoming. Barbara Babcock defines symbolic inversion as "any act of expressive behavior which inverts, contradicts, abrogates, or in some fashion presents an alternative to commonly held cultural codes, values and norms be they linguistic, literary or artistic, religious, social and political." Barbara Babcock, *The Reversible World: Symbolic Inversion in Art and Society* (Ithaca, 1978), 14.

[19] Alfred L. Shoemaker, "Fantasticals," *Pennsylvania Dutchman* v. 4, No. 13 (1953), 31.

[20] "Fun of a Lively Sort," *New York Times* (November 27, 1885), 18.

[21] Alfred L. Shoemaker, "Fantasticals," *Pennsylvania Dutchman* v. 4, No. 13 (1953), 16. Al Smith indicates that in his childhood a fancy dress ball was held several days after the parade. Alfred E. Smith, *Up to Now: An Autobiography* (New York, 1929), 30; W. D. Howells, *Through the Eye of the Needle* (New York, 1907), 49.

[22] Michael Oriard, *Reading Football: How the Popular Press Created an American Spectacle* (Chapel Hill, 1995), 127.

[23] Walter Camp, "Intercollegiate Foot-Ball in America," *St. Nicholas* v. XVII, No. 3 (January, 1890), 241.

[24] Ethelbert D. Warfield, "Are Foot-Ball Games Educative or Brutalizing?" *Forum* v. 16 (January, 1894), 642, 652, as quoted in Michael Oriard, *Reading Football,* 181.

[25] "All the Town Wore Yellow," *New York Herald* (November 29, 1889), 4; "Dungeon Cells for College Boys," *New York Herald* (December 1, 1893), 5; "Not Red, But Blue, Did They 'Paint the

Town,'" *New York Herald* (November 25, 1892), 4; "Jubilators in Blue," *New York Herald* (November 24, 1895), 7.

[26] Michael Oriard argues that football games in New York City persisted after 1893, but they were contests between non-Ivy League teams which were sparsely attended. Michael Oriard, *Reading Football,* 92.

[27] "Fantastics," *New York Times* (November 29, 1902), 8; "Thanksgiving," *New York Times* (November 29, 1895), 4.

[28] George Chauncey, *Gay New York: Gender, Urban Culture, and the Making of the Gay Male World, 1890–1940* (New York, 1994), 294; Alfred L. Shoemaker, "Fantasticals," *Pennsylvania Folklife* v. 9 No. 1 (Winter, 1957–1958), 28–31.

[29] Mike Beno, *When Families Made Memories Together* (Greendale, WI, 1994), 157.

[30] "A Thanksgiving Day Abuse," *New York Times* (November 27, 1903), 8.

[31] *New York Times* (November 30, 1911), 12.

[32] *New York Times* (November 22, 1930), 17.

[33] *New York Times* (November 30, 1920), 10.

[34] W. D. Howells, *Through the Eye of the Needle,* 49.

[35] Clarice Whittenburg, "Holiday Observance in the Primary Schools," *Elementary School Journal* v. XXXV, No. 1 (September, 1934), 193–195.

[36] For varying political uses of this song, see Robert James Branham, "'Of Thee I Sing': Contesting 'America,'" *American Quarterly* v. 48, No. 4 (December, 1996), 623–652.

[37] Michael Kammen, *Mystic Chords of Memory: The Transformation of Tradition in American Culture* (New York, 1991), 206–211.

[38] William DeLoss Love, Jr., *The Fast and Thanksgiving Days of New England,* 429.

[39] On Thanksgiving in the schools see Marion S. Blaisdell, "Thanksgiving in the Past and Present," in Robert Haven Schauffler, ed., *Thanksgiving: Its Origin, Celebration and Significance as Related in Prose and Verse* (New York, 1927), 221–265 and Dorothy Canfield Fisher, "A New Pioneer," in Wilhelmina Harper, ed., *Stories of Thanksgiving Yesterday and Today* (New York, 1938), 186.

The pledge of allegiance to the flag, first devised in the 1890s, was another Americanizing ritual. Stuart McConnell argued that the pledge arose from the desire of native-born whites to express a more abstract ideal of national unity, larger in scope than the family, the village, or even a single region. Stuart McConnell, "Reading the Flag: A Reconsideration of the Patriotic Cults of the 1890s," in John Bodnar, ed., *Bonds of Affection: Americans Define Their Patriotism* (Princeton, 1996), 102–119.

[40] Stephen F. Brumberg, *Going to America, Going to School: The Jewish Immigrant Public School Encounter in Turn-of-the-Century New York City* (New York, 1986), 126.

[41] Angelo Pelligrini, *American Dream: An Immigrant's Quest* (San Francisco, 1986), 21.

[42] Stephen F. Brumberg, *Going to America,* 126. For Thanksgiving programs in segregated black schools in the South, see Chris Mayfield, *Growing Up Southern: Southern Exposure Looks at Childhood, Then and Now* (New York, 1972), 24.

[43] Gary Gerstle, *Working Class Americanism* (Cambridge, 1989), 191.

[44] Steven Pope argues that college football games on Thanksgiving helped to overcome Southern resistance to Thanksgiving. S. W. Pope, *Patriotic Games* (New York, 1997), 92.

[45] Hal Borland, *High, Wide and Lonesome* (Philadelphia and New York, 1956), 90, 176–177; Emmet Kelley, *Clown* (New York, 1954), 19; Eleanor Arnold, ed., *Voices of American Homemakers* (Bloomington, Indiana, 1985), 35.

[46] Holly Garrison, *The Thanksgiving Cookbook* (New York, 1991), 207; Harpo Marx with Rowland Barber, *Harpo Speaks* (New York, 1961), 27–28. Brooklyn Democratic politicians in the 1930s handed out turkeys. See Shirley Chisholm, *Unbought and Unbossed* (Boston, 1970), 63. Immigrants who were not politicians also left turkeys on the doorsteps of needy families. See Theresa F. Bucchieri, *Feasting with Nonna Serafina* (New York, 1966), 125.

[47] W. E. B. DuBois, *The Philadelphia Negro* (New York, 1899; New York, 1967), 196; Elizabeth Fox-Genovese, *Within the Plantation Household: Black and White Women of the Old South* (Chapel Hill, 1988), 364; Jon Gjerde, *The Minds of the West: Ethnocultural Evolution in the Rural Middle West, 1830–1917* (Chapel Hill, 1997), 230.

[48] Jeff Kisseloff, *You Must Remember This: An Oral History of Manhattan from the 1890s to World War II* (New York, 1989), 499.

[49] Pearl Kazin, "We Gather Together," *New Yorker* v. XXXI, No. 41 (November 26, 1955), 52–56.

[50] Pardee Lowe, *Father and Glorious Descendant* (Boston, 1943), 66.

[51] Gloria Braggiotti, *Born in a Crowd* (New York, 1957), 237.

[52] Ken Hom, *Easy Family Recipes from a Chinese-American Childhood* (New York, 1997), 146.

[53] Swedes were the exception in that they did not serve Swedish side dishes at the Thanksgiving meal. See Phebe Fjellstrom, *Swedish American Colonization in the San Joaquin Valley in California: a Study of the Acculturation and Assimilation of an Immigrant Group* (Upssala, 1970), 125. For examples of cultural and culinary melting pots, see Sylvia Torres Saillant, ed., *Hispanic Immigrant Writers and the Family* (Jackson Heights N.Y., 1989), 39; Arlene and Howard Eisenberg, "Thanksgiving with a Lebanese Flavor," *Good Housekeeping* v. 178 (November, 1971), 84, 86, 88, 93.

[54] Stephen Nissenbaum, *The Battle for Christmas,* 153.

[55] An example was Cornelius Mathews, *Chanticleer: A Thanksgiving Story of the Peabody Family* (Boston, 1850).

[56] Although there are special holiday M and M's for Easter, Christmas and Valentine's Day, there are none for Thanksgiving. Jack Santino, *New Old-Fashioned Ways: Holidays and Popular Culture* (Knoxville, 1996), 33. For Thanksgiving advertisements, see *Saturday Evening Post* v. 204, No. 22 (November 28, 1931), 42–43; William Leach, *Land of Desire: Merchants, Power, and the Rise of a New American Culture* (New York, 1993), 334, 335; Susan Strasser, *Satisfaction Guaranteed: The Making of the American Mass Market* (New York, 1989), 120; Ernest A. Dench, "Thanksgiving Candy Displays Given More Attention," *Confectioner's Journal* v. XLIV, No. 586 (November, 1923), 96–97.

[57] William Leach argues that the Macy's Thanksgiving Day parade was the commercial inheritor of the Fantastic and ragamuffin parades since the two events occurred on Thanksgiving. He seems to have been unaware of football parades. Moreover, as Leach notes, the department store parade was copied from circus parades. Department stores had been staging small-scale parades since around 1900. By World War I they were holding parades to welcome home the troops.

Child welfare agencies, not Macy's, organized alternative activities to begging. Store executives were not interested in eliminating begging. Macy's parade does not appear to have led to the decline of child begging. Child begging was dying out gradually before the parade began, but continued on a small scale for about fifteen years after the parade was initiated. William R. Leach, *Land of Desire,* 331–336.

[58] William R. Leach, *Land of Desire,* 331–336.

[59] William R. Leach, *Land of Desire,* 336.

[60] S. W. Pope summarizes all the various claims made on behalf of football in S. W. Pope, *Patriotic Games,* 85–100; E. Anthony Rotundo, *American Manhood: Transformations in Masculinity from the Revolution to the Modern Era* (New York, 1993), 241.

[61] Barre Toelken, *The Dynamics of Folklore* (Boston, 1979), 132–135.

[62] Michael Messner, *Power at Play: Sports and the Problem of Masculinity* (Boston, 1992), 168–170.

[63] Tad Tuleja, "Trick or Treat: Pre-Texts and Contests," in Jack Santino, ed., *Halloween and Other Festivals of Death and Life* (Knoxville, 1994), 85.

Name: _____ Date: _____

UNDERSTANDING THE TEXT

1. What does Pleck mean by the "domestic occasion"? How did it evolve from the "communal celebration" that preceded it?

2. According to Pleck, why were "domestic occasions" designed to seem "old-fashioned"?

3. According to Pleck, how did football games come to be played on Thanksgiving? For many families, what were the consequences?

ADDITIONAL READINGS

Bordo, Susan. *The Male Body: A New Look at Men in Public and Private*. New York: Farrar, Straus and Giroux, 1999.

———. *Unbearable Weight: Feminism, Western Culture, and the Body*. Berkeley: U of California P, 1993.

Brownmiller, Susan. *Femininity*. 1984. New York: Fawcett-Ballantine, 1985.

Brumberg, Joan Jacobs. *The Body Project: An Intimate History of American Girls*. New York: Random House, 1997.

Byron, Christopher M. *Martha Inc.: The Incredible Story of Martha Stewart Living Omnimedia*. New York: John Wiley, 2002.

Coward, Rosalind. *Female Desires: How They Are Sought, Bought and Packaged*. 1984. New York: Grove Weidenfeld, 1985.

Douglas, Ann. *The Feminization of American Culture*. New York: Knopf, 1977.

Douglas, Susan. *Where the Girls Are: Growing Up Female with the Mass Media*. New York: Times Books, 1994.

Ehrenreich, Barbara. *The Hearts of Men: American Dreams and the Flight from Commitment*. New York: Anchor-Doubleday, 1983.

Faludi, Susan. *Backlash: The Undeclared War Against American Women*. New York: Crown, 1991.

———. *Stiffed: The Betrayal of the American Man*. New York: William Morrow, 1999.

Garvey, Ellen Gruber. *The Adman in the Parlor: Magazines and the Gendering of Consumer Culture, 1880s to 1910s*. New York: Oxford UP, 1996.

Hollander, Anne. *Sex and Suits: The Evolution of Modern Dress*. New York: Knopf, 1994.

Kitch, Carolyn. *The Girl of the Magazine Cover: The Origins of Visual Stereotypes in American Mass Media*. Chapel Hill: U of North Carolina P, 2001.

Luciano, Lynne. *Looking Good: Male Body Image in Modern America*. New York: Hill and Wang, 2001.

Macdonald, Myra. *Representing Women: Myths of Femininity in the Popular Media*. London: Arnold, 1995.

Nissenbaum, Stephen. *The Battle for Christmas*. New York: Knopf, 1996.

Shapiro, Laura. *Perfection Salad*. New York: Farrar, Straus and Giroux, 1986.

Shields, Vickie Rutledge and Dawn Heinecken. *Measuring Up: How Advertising Affects Self-Image*. Philadelphia: U of Pennsylvania P, 2002.

Strasser, Susan. *Never Done: A History of American Housework*. 1982. New York: Owl-Henry Holt, 2000.

Wolf, Naomi. *The Beauty Myth: How Images of Beauty Are Used Against Women*. New York: William Morrow, 1991.

CHAPTER IV

Dumb and Dumber: Anti-Intellectualism in American Life

Democracy and Anti-Intellectualism in America

Richard Hofstadter

INTELLECTUALISM AND DEMOCRACY

American education today is in the midst of a great crisis, the general outlines of which I believe we can all recognize. About the first part of this crisis, its financial aspect, I shall have nothing to say. A second part of it comes from outside education, in the shape of tremendous pressures to conform, for we live in a society in which the most dynamic force is provided by a small group of politicians who seek to base careers upon the policing of opinion. About the problems of freedom and conformity, I will speak briefly. The third part of this crisis, which concerns me most, is internal; it is less dramatic and perceptible than the others and it has been going on for a longer time. It stems from an inner failure of nerve, for it is nothing less than the growing loss of confidence among educators in the importance and value of the life of the mind, a capitulation within the educational world—indeed, in many quarters an eager capitulation—to the non-intellectual or anti-intellectual criteria that many forces in our society wish to impose upon education and which we might well consider it the bounden duty of educators to resist. It is about this that I wish primarily to speak; and I hope to suggest some relations between this species of educational failure and our popular democracy.

Since I am speaking about education and intellectualism, I want to make it entirely clear that I do not make the mistake of identifying higher education in general with intellectualism. Quite the contrary; I propose to emphasize the extent to which anti-intellectualism is

From *The Michigan Alumnus Quarterly Review,* Vol. LIX, Nu. 21, August 8, 1953 by Richard Hofstadter. Copyright © 1953 by Alumni Association of the University of Michigan. Reprinted by permission.

rampant within the educational community. But it is also probably true that in America the greater part of the leadership of those who can be called intellectuals lives and works in academic communities. And if higher education can be said to be under fire today, it can be said with greater certainty that the distinctively intellectual part of the educational community is the part that stands to lose most.

The crisis in higher education is also a crisis in the history of the intelligentsia. Today, everywhere in America, intellectuals are on the defensive. They have been identified with the now-defeated inheritance of the New Deal and the Fair Deal. That this identification should have been made is ironical, because the New Deal itself, for all its Brain Trusters, had its own streak of anti-intellectualism. But it has also been unfair: the intellectuals are never given credit for the successes of the New Deal, but they have had to take the blame for everything that has been charged up to the Democratic administrations of the past twenty years—with so-called creeping socialism, with the war, with the alleged failure at Yalta, even with treason. In the late presidential campaign a political leader who embodied the kind of traits that the intellectual would most like to see in our national leadership found the support of the intellectuals of slight value in overcoming the disadvantages of his party and his hour. During that campaign the nation also found the epithet for the intellectuals that it has so long wanted—"egg-heads."

Do not imagine, however, that the intellectual is going into permanent eclipse. He always has his day posthumously, for the very men who are most forward in proclaiming their dislike of living intellectuals are the most abject followers of the dead ones. They may not like contemporary intellectuals but they are often quite hypnotized by the intellectual leavings of Adam Smith or Herbert Spencer, or Edmund Burke, or Thomas Aquinas, or similar gods of the past. They have restored an old slogan of the frontiersman with a new meaning and a new object: "The only good intellectual is a dead intellectual."

But what is an intellectual, really? This is a problem of definition that I found, when I came to it, far more elusive than I had anticipated. A great deal of what might be called the journeyman's work of our culture—the work of engineers, physicians, newspapermen, and indeed of most professors—does not strike me as distinctively intellectual, although it is certainly work based in an important sense on ideas. The distinction that we must recognize, then, is one originally made by Max Weber between living *for* ideas and living *off* ideas. The intellectual lives for ideas; the journeyman lives off them. The engineer or the physician—I don't mean here to be invidious—needs to have a pretty considerable capital stock in frozen ideas to do his work; but they serve for him a purely instrumental purpose: he lives off them, not for them. Of course he may also be, in his private role and his personal ways of thought, an intellectual, but it is not necessary for him to be one in order to work at his profession. There is in fact no profession which demands that one be an intellectual. There do seem to be vocations, however, which almost demand that one be an anti-intellectual, in which those who live off ideas seem to have an implacable hatred for those who live for them. The marginal intellectual workers and the unfrocked intellectuals who work in journalism, advertising, and mass communication are the bitterest and most powerful among those who work at such vocations.

It will help, too, to make the further distinction between living for ideas and living for *an idea.* History is full of cases of great men with good minds, a capacity to deal with abstractions, and a desire to make systems of them—all qualities we associate with the intellectual. But when, as it has in many of them, this concern with ideas, no matter how dedicated and sincere, reduces in the end to the ingenious use of them for a central preconception, however grand, then I think we have very little intellectualism and a great deal of something else. A good historical illustration is that of Lenin, who, as his more theoretical works show, had in him a powerful element of intellectuality; but this intellectuality was rendered thin by his all-absorbing concern with certain very limiting political values. His book on philosophy, *Materialism and Empirio-Criticism,* a shrill work and an extremely depressing one to read, makes it altogether clear that the politician in him swallowed up the intellectual. I choose the illustration of Lenin because it helps me to make another point that seems unfortunately necessary because of the present tendency to identify intellectuals with subversives. That point is that the idea of a party line and political messianism is inherently inconsistent with intellectualism, and those few intellectuals who have in some way survived that tension are few, pitiable, and on the whole sterile.

The journeyman of ideas, and the janizary who makes a somewhat complicated but highly instrumental use of ideas, provide us with two illustrations of people who work with ideas but are not precisely intellectuals, as I understand the term. What, then, are the differences between the men who work with ideas but are *not* intellectuals and the men who work with ideas and *are* intellectuals?

Two things, that seem in fact to be mutually at odds, mark off the intellectual from the journeyman of ideas; one is playfulness, the other is piety.

Certainly the intellectual, if he is nothing else, is one who relishes *the play of the mind* for its own sake, for whom it is one of the major ends of life. The intellectual has a full quotient of what Veblen called "idle curiosity." His mind, instead of falling to rest when it has provided him with his girl and his automobile and his dinner, becomes even more active. Indeed if we had to define him in physiological terms, we might define him as the creature whose mind is *most* likely to be active after dinner.

I speak of playfulness too because of the peculiar nature of the relationship, in the intellectual's mind, between ideas and practicality. To the journeyman of ideas the be-all and end-all of ideas lies in their practical efficacy. Now the intellectual, by contrast, is not necessarily impractical; I can think of some intellectuals like Thomas Jefferson and Robert Owen and John Maynard Keynes who have been eminently practical, and I consider the notion that the intellectual is inherently impractical to be one of the most contemptible of the delusions with which the anti-intellectual quiets his envy—the intellectual is not impractical but primarily concerned with a quality of ideas that does not depend upon their practicality. He neither reveres nor disdains practical consequences; for him they are either marginal or irrelevant.

And when he does talk about the practicality or the "relevance" of ideas, the kind of practicality that he is concerned with is itself somewhat different from the practicality of building a bridge, curing a disease, or making a profit—it is practical relevance to spiritual values themselves.

The best illustration of the intellectual's view of the purely practical that has recently come to my attention is the reaction of Clerk Maxwell, the great nineteenth-century mathematician and theoretical physicist, to the invention of the telephone. Maxwell was asked to give a lecture on the workings of this wonderful new instrument, which he began by saying how difficult it was to believe, when the word first came from America, that such a thing had actually been devised. But then, he said, "when at last this little instrument appeared, consisting, as it does, of parts, every one of which is familiar to us, and capable of being put together by an amateur, the disappointment arising from its humble appearance was only partially relieved on finding that it was really able to talk." Perhaps, then, this regrettable appearance of simplicity might be redeemed by the presence somewhere of "recondite physical principles, the study of which might worthily occupy an hour's time of an academic audience." But no; Maxwell had not met a single person who could not understand the physical processes involved, and even the science reporters for the daily press had almost got it right! The thing was a disappointing bore; it was not recondite, it was not profound, it was not complex, it was not *intellectually* new.

To be sure, what this illustration suggests is not merely that the telephone disappointed Maxwell as a pure scientist and an intellectual, but that the strain of intellectuality in him was not as broadly developed as it might have been. The telephone might well excite not merely the commercial imagination but the historical imagination. But my point is, after all, not that Maxwell was a universal intellectual, but that he was displaying the attitude of the intellectual in his particular sphere of interest.

The second element in intellectualism is its religious strain, the note of piety. What I mean by this is simply that for the intellectual the whole world of moral values becomes attached to ideas and to the life dedicated to ideas. The life given over to the search for truth takes on for him a primary moral significance. Intellectualism, although hardly confined to doubters, is often the sole piety of the skeptic. A few years ago a distinguished sociologist asked me to read a brief manuscript which he had written primarily for students planning to go on to advanced work in his field, the purpose of which was to illustrate various ways in which the life of the mind might be cultivated. The essay had about it a little too much of the how-to-do books, and my friend abandoned it. But the nub of the matter from the standpoint of our present problem was that I found myself to be reading a piece of devotional literature, comparable perhaps to Cotton Mather's *Essays to do Good* or Richard Steele's *The Tradesman's Calling*. My friend was trying to communicate his sense of dedication to the life of ideas, which he conceived much in the fashion of the old Protestant writers as a *calling*. To work is to pray. Yes, and for this kind of man, to think—really to think—is to pray. What he knows best, when he is at his best, is the pursuit of truth; but *easy* truths bore him.

What he is certain of becomes unsatisfactory always; the meaning of his intellectual life lies in the quest for new uncertainties.

In a bygone day when men lived even more by dogma than they do now, there were two kinds of men whose special office it was to seek for and utter the truth; and they symbolize these two sides of the intellectual's nature. One was the angelic doctor, the learned schoolman, the conserver of old orthodoxies but also the maker of the new, and the prodder at the outer limits of received truths. The other was the jester, the professional fool, who had license to say on occasion for the purposes of amusement and release those things that bordered on lèse majesté and could not be uttered by others who were accounted serious men.

The fool and the schoolman are very far apart. No doubt you will ask whether there is not a contradiction between these two qualities of the intellectual, piety and playfulness. Certainly there is great tension between them; human beings are tissues of contradictions, and the life even of the intellectual is not logic, to borrow from Holmes, but experience. If you will think of the intellectuals you know, some will occur to you in whom the note of playfulness seems stronger, others who are predominantly pious. But I believe that in all intellectuals who have any stability as intellectuals—and that includes the angelic doctors of the middle ages—each of these characteristics is at some point qualified by the other. Perhaps the tensile strength of the intellectual can be gauged by his ability to maintain a fair equipoise between these aspects of himself. At one end of the scale, an excess of playfulness leads to triviality, to dilettantism, to cynicism, to the failure of all sustained creative effort. At the other, an excess of piety leads to fanaticism, to messianism, to ways of life that may be morally magnificent or morally mean, but in either case are not quite the ways of intellectualism. It is of the essence of the intellectual that he strikes a balance.

The widespread distrust of intellectuals in America reflects a tendency to depreciate their playfulness and distrust their piety. Ours is a society in which every form of play seems to be accepted by the majority except the play of the mind. It does not need to be explained to most people in America why sports, sex, liquor, gambling, motoring, and gourmandizing are all more or less legitimate forms of amusement for those who happen to find them amusing. The only forms of *mental* play that are similarly accepted and understood are those that do not involve the particular kinds of critical intelligence that are called into play by intellectualism; I refer, of course, to such highly cerebral amusements as bridge, chess, and the various forms of the crossword puzzle. I suppose that those who are inclined to find economic explanations will point out that the play of the mind, being the only kind that has not been susceptible to commercialization, has not been able to rally the support of a vested interest. I believe, however, that a large part of our common neglect of the humanities is attributable to the absence of a traditional and accepted leisure class which looks upon this kind of personal cultivation as a natural goal of life. The idea of leisured intellectual exercise, not put to the service of some external end, has been offensive to mass democracy. One of the best signs of this is the rhetoric adopted by college presidents and others who appeal to the public for support for education. Always these appeals tell how much education does for citizenship, science, technology, morals, or religion. Rarely do they point to the glories or pleasures of the human mind as an end in itself.

Just as the truly religious man is always a misfit in a secular society, so it is the piety of the intellectual that makes the greatest difficulties for him. Playfulness may be disdained or misunderstood, but it is not usually thought to be dangerous. Piety is another matter, for it is almost certain in the end to challenge something. It is the piety of the intellectual that puts iron into his nonconformism, if he happens to be a nonconformist. It is his piety that will make him, if anything does, a serious moral force in society. In our day the pressures operating against boldness in thought, as well as the sheer bureaucratization of intellectual life, bear hardest against the elements of piety in the intellectual. The temptation is very strong for some intellectuals to suppress the note of piety in themselves, to turn increasingly to the playful and generally more esoteric aspects of their work, to give up the office of spiritual leadership. Such self-suppression is psychologically and morally dangerous, and cannot be indulged in without paying a serious price. It does not become the intellectual, it is much too false to an important part of him, to give in altogether to playfulness and play the fool to the powerful. The jester had his prerogatives, to be sure, but we should also remember that he was usually a slave.

I have attempted thus far to define and elucidate intellectualism. Let me now explain what I mean by democracy when I say that in an important sense higher education and democracy have often been at odds. I do not mean by democracy simply the indispensable formal essentials of our society—constitutionalism, government by discussion, guarantees for the civil liberties of political minorities. These I neither challenge nor criticize; and I am sure that free higher education cannot in our time stand without them. But I do mean to criticize something that relates to the spirit of our politics, something that for lack of a better term I will call populistic democracy. Populistic democracy is neither progressive nor conservative, although it is in a perverse way equalitarian. Populistic democracy is the meeting ground, in fact, of the extreme left and the extreme right. It is government by or through the mass man, disguised behind the mask of an easy sentimentalization of the folk. It is the idea that anything done in the name of the people is *ipso facto* legitimate, even if the same act done in the name of a vested interest would be considered outrageous. It is the idea that a dozen postcards to a congressman from the wildest cranks should be given the same weight as a dozen reasoned letters from sober citizens. Transferred to the field of education, which is our concern, it is the idea that a university ought to cater to the needs of anybody who comes out of or pretends to represent the folk, whether or not he has any real need for or interest in the use of ideas. Put in terms of the state university, it is the idea that any graduate of the public high school should be accepted as a freshman no matter how dismal his prospects are as a student. Put in broader terms, it is the idea that any of the wants, real or fancied, of a mass society, should be absolute imperatives to its system of higher education.

We Americans are noted for our faith in both democracy and education. It has been our assumption that democracy and education, both being good, must be closely related and mutually reinforcing. We should have, it is argued, as much education and as much democracy as possible. It is also assumed that education serves democracy, and one of the most common shibboleths in our educational literature is the slogan "education for democracy." It is characteristically American that very few of us trouble to inquire whether democracy serves education. Whether it does indeed do so as fully and unambiguously as we might consider desirable is the question I insist we must face.

That there is any necessary relation between a vital system of higher education and a democratic society, one may readily deny on the basis of historical evidence. Two of the greatest periods in university history, that of the thirteenth and fourteenth centuries and that of the German universities in the nineteenth century, occurred in societies that were not notably democratic. In our own experience, I do not believe it incorrect to say that the great age of American university development from 1870 to 1910 was for the most part an age of political and economic oligarchy; and also that our finest universities and small colleges, by and large, have been those started and endowed by rich men and patronized chiefly by the upper classes.

All this does not mean, of course, that there is any necessary antagonism between democracy and higher education. Presumably there is no inherent or universally necessary opposition between a political democracy and a vital, respected, intellectually rich and alert university system. But I do wish to point out that there has been a historically persistent tension between our popular democracy and intellectualism that has been very sadly felt in the sphere of university and college life. The problem of how democracy and education can best serve and complement each other—as we would all, no doubt, like them to do—has not been nearly as constructively attacked as it might be for the simple reason that it has not often enough been candidly faced.

Long ago Tocqueville saw that the democratic culture that had emerged in the United States had brought with it pressures that were seriously hostile to the free use of the mind. He found that the democratic and equalitarian impulse had weakened the ability of the individual to resist the pressure of the opinion of the mass:

> The fact that the political laws of the Americans are such that the majority rules the community with sovereign sway, materially increases the power which that majority naturally exercises over the mind. For nothing is more customary in man than to recognise superior wisdom in the person of his oppressor. . . . The intellectual dominion of the greater number would probably be less absolute among a democratic people governed by a king than in the sphere of a pure democracy, but it will always be extremely absolute; and by whatever political laws men are governed in the ages of equality, it may be foreseen that faith in public opinion may become a species of religion there, and the majority its ministering prophet.
>
> Thus intellectual authority will be different, but it will not be diminished; and far from thinking that it will disappear, I augur that it may readily acquire too much preponderance and confine the action of private judgment within narrower limits than are suited either to the greatness

or the happiness of the human race. In the principle of equality I very clearly discern two tendencies; the one leading the mind of every man to untried thoughts, the other inclined to prohibit him from thinking at all. And I perceive how, under the dominion of certain laws, democracy would extinguish that liberty of mind to which a democratic social condition is favourable; so that, after having broken all the bondage once imposed on it by ranks or by men, the human mind would be closely fettered to the general will of the greatest number.

Tocqueville found that in his time the most absolute monarchs in Europe were unable to prevent certain heretical notions from circulating through their dominions and even in their courts:

> Such is not the case in America; as long as the majority is still undecided, discussion is carried on; but as soon as its decision is irrevocably pronounced, a submissive silence is observed, and the friends, as well as the opponents of the measure unite in assenting to its propriety. The reason of this is perfectly clear: no monarch is so absolute as to combine all the powers of society in his own hands, and to conquer all opposition with the energy of a majority which is invested with the right of making and of executing the laws. . . .
>
> I know no country in which there is so little true independence of mind and freedom of discussion as in America. In any constitutional state in Europe every sort of religious and political theory may be advocated and propagated abroad; for there is no country in Europe so subdued by any single authority as not to contain citizens who are ready to protect the man who raises his voice in the cause of truth from the consequences of his hardihood. If he is unfortunate enough to live under an absolute government, the people is upon his side; if he inhabits a free country, he may find a shelter behind the authority of the throne, if he require one. The aristocratic part of society supports him in some countries and the democracy in others. But in a nation where democratic institutions exist, organized like those of the United States, there is but one sole authority, one single element of strength and of success, with nothing beyond it.

While I do believe that Tocqueville was exaggerating the case of the United States in 1835, he pointed to the heart of the problem of majority tyranny over the soul. It is a problem that has grown still more acute in our own age, an age of mass communications and the mass man; for now the tyranny of the majority can be spread uniformly over the surface of a great nation otherwise well suited by size and diversity to a multiplicity of opinions, and it can be to some degree forged and manipulated from a few centers. If there were any horrors in that spontaneous, grass-roots variety of popular tyranny, as Tocqueville saw it, they must be greatly compounded by the artificial and centralized means of manipulation that the communications technology of our time has made possible.

But has there been substantial historical evidence in the development of American higher education for the validity of Tocqueville's fear of mass tyranny? I believe there is certainly enough evidence to warrant a reconsideration of our views of the relation between democracy and university culture. I propose to argue that while populistic democracy has been on the side of many educational improvements and reforms, it has often been aligned as sharply with forces tending to constrain freedom in higher education and to lower its devotion to intellectual goals.

DEMOCRACY AND HIGHER EDUCATION

There may have been some popular upsurges in our history that have been auspicious for intellectualism in general, and for higher education in particular; but the popular movements that have been notable for their failure to understand the place of learning in our culture, or even on occasion for their hostility to it, are quite numerous. One of the first, the Great Awakening of the mid-eighteenth century, was notable for its hostility to a free and liberal-minded theological education such as was emerging in the older colleges; and while the Awakening must be in the end credited for enlarging the number of colleges, the goal sought at first in these enterprises was not an enhancement of the sphere of free learning but simply the creation of schools that would teach the right brand of theology. Jeffersonian democracy was not, on the whole, what I call populistic—at least not in its leadership. Its most constructive work in education, the founding of a liberal university in Virginia, was the work of aristocratic leadership. Jacksonian democracy, whatever its benefits in other areas, was identified with a widespread deterioration in the standards of professional education, masquerading under the ideology that easier access to these privileged areas of life must be made available to the people.

The founding of early state universities was badly hampered by popular hostility to advanced education that was held to be of use chiefly to the aristocrats, who, in fact, usually provided the basic impetus to the cultivation of the higher learning, whether in state-founded or private institutions. The movement that destroyed the old classical curriculum and made American universities, especially our state universities, the nurseries of all kinds of subintellectual practical skills of less than university grade was in its impetus very largely a popular movement; and while many of the consequences of that movement must be set to its credit as compensations, the undercurrent of vocationalism and anti-intellectualism was undeniable. Our history books tell us—to come toward our own time—that during the Populist-Bryan period the university professors who failed to accept the gold-standard economics of the well-to-do classes were often victims of outrageous interference; they do not usually trouble to tell us that when the Populists captured Kansas they raised hob with the University of Kansas in much the same way that they complained of so bitterly when the shoe was on the other foot. One of the most genuinely popular, and I believe democratic, political leaders in our history was William Jennings Bryan; and the sort of respect he showed for science and academic freedom is familiar to you all. His concept of the rights of the dissenting teacher reduces to his famous comment: "A man cannot demand a salary for saying what his employers do not want said."

My aim in stressing these facts is not to cast discredit upon popular democracy, whose merit in our whole scheme of things must be weighed by taking into account all its achievements as well as its deficiencies; I am simply trying to suggest that many of us have in the past made a mystique of the masses and have tended too much to attribute all the villainy in our world to the machinations of vested interests. I find it rather suggestive that the sole ruling group in our history that could be called a vested intellectual interest of any considerable power—I refer, of course, to the early Puritan clergy—has suffered the fate of being scandalously libelled by our "liberal" historians who have written in the tradition of V. L. Parrington.

Why this persistent tension between popular democracy and free higher learning? Obviously it is to some degree an aspect of social striving: a college education is a privilege that has not been open to all. While it can open up otherwise unavailable opportunities to the children of the less favored classes, it can also confirm the privileges of the upper classes by adding to those social, political, and economic advantages which are theirs by birth and family, the advantages of a superior education. Much of the early opposition to state universities was based precisely upon this argument. Why tax the poor, it was repeatedly asked, to educate the sons of the rich? No doubt there is such an element of resentment on the part of the lower classes for the privileges and attainments of the upper classes. But this, to my mind, will not get us very far in explaining why the United States in particular has been a happy hunting ground for anti-intellectualism. Class divisions exist in all western societies. Moreover, of all western nations, the United States has given by far the greatest proportion of its total population an opportunity to have a college education. In our more than 1700 colleges, for instance, we offer higher education, or a reasonable facsimile thereof, to about ten times as large a portion of our population as is done in the British Isles. Moreover, while we have always had our class stratification, class lines have been less sharp in the United States, and mobility between classes somewhat easier, than in European countries. By the showing of these facts, the United States should, in accordance with the class envy theory, have much less resentment of higher education as a source of privilege than any other country on the globe.

The evidence is all to the contrary, and this is enough to give us pause. It remains to be explained why, in a culture that seems to value education very highly, that has provided an enormous apparatus for the collegiate education of its youth, the genuine intellectual content of higher education is so little esteemed, why the teacher in general and the college professor in particular has so much less social status than he does almost anywhere else. I believe that the problem of status is, indeed, quite crucial, but that the situation cannot be explained in terms of broad assertions about the envy of manual for intellectual labor, the poor for the well-to-do, or the middle classes for the leisure classes. We must look to some of the unique factors of American historical development for our answers.

From the beginning the American people were confronted with rich resources, an immense task of continental settlement, and a shortage of labor. Their culture thus came to set a premium on practical achievement, the manipulation of material reality, and quick decision. It did not encourage reflection or a respect for the ultimate and irreducible disagreements of life. On the contrary, it suggested that it was to everyone's interest to arrive at a quick consensus, general enough to get the work done, that any disagreement on details was, in the light of the rich potentialities of organized work, unimportant. The American still sets a very high premium on such a consensus; he implicitly approaches broad intellectual and philosophical problems with that model of prompt decision in mind. "What can we agree on?" he wants to know. The wonderful persistence of irreducible differences of opinion, of the plurality of human dreams and perspectives, the exchange or contemplation of differences as an exercise in mutual understanding—all these are likely to be dark mysteries to him. He makes an ideology of normality; he asks not "What am I?" but "What is it customary and proper to be around here?" He *thinks* he is an individualist because he does truly and genuinely resent any rude coercive efforts to make him conform, but he cannot realize that he spends half his time trying to figure out how he can conform "spontaneously." One of the most appalling things in American life is the failure of those who prate most about individualism to develop any understanding of individuality. The loudest hosannas to individualism are sung by grim, regimented choruses.

The effects of our chronic shortage of labor have also struck quite directly at the teaching profession from grammar schools to graduate schools. Our historic abundance of land and other resources has continually beckoned to the inadequate resources of our labor power. The consequences of this for other areas of life than education have often been noted. Our agriculture, for instance, was dedicated from the outset to extensive and wasteful cultivation and rapid mechanization rather than to intensive and careful cultivation and farming as a settled way of life. Too little has been said about a similar trend in our educational history. I think we have cultivated man wastefully and mechanically too. The teaching of our young, for instance, has been all too regularly left over to those whose imaginations and energies were not absorbed—or not yet absorbed—in the more exciting and lucrative life of physical and economic conquest, or to those who for one reason or another were altogether incapable of entering upon it. Ichabod Crane was, I suppose, the archetype of the American schoolmaster—the timid misfit, the amiable failure, the man who was scared out of town; and when Brom Bones chased him that terrible night through Sleepy Hollow and frightened him almost to death with a pumpkin, he was passing upon him the characteristic comment of the American philistine upon the American teacher. If the teacher was not Ichabod Crane, then it was the lonely spinster, driven by desperation to take up teaching when all else failed. If not the spinster, it was the young man who was merely marking time, supporting himself before launching upon a more permanent career in business or some really serious profession. "The men teachers," wrote an observer of early Massachusetts schools—mind you, even Massachusetts schools—

> may be divided into three classes: (1) Those who think teaching is easier and possibly a little more remunerative than common labor. (2) Those who are acquiring, or have acquired, a good education, and who take up teaching as a temporary employment, either to earn money for pressing necessities or to give themselves time to choose deliberately a regular profession. (3) Those who, conscious of weakness, despair of distinction or even the means of subsistence by other means. . . . They are often very young, they are constantly changing their employment,

and consequently can have but little experience; and what is worse than all, they have never had any direct preparation for their profession. . . . No standard of attainments is fixed . . . so that any one *keeps school,* which is a very different thing from *teaching school,* who wishes to do it, and can persuade by herself or her friends, a small district to employ her. And this is not a very difficult matter, especially when the remuneration for the employment is so very trifling. . . . If a young man be moral enough to keep out of State prison, he will find no difficulty in getting approbation for a schoolmaster.

An exaggeration? Possibly. But in 1930–31, even after much had been done to improve standards of teacher training in the United States, the National Survey of the Education of Teachers showed that American teacher education, although only slightly inferior to that of England, was drastically inferior to that of France, Germany, and the Scandinavian countries. The teacher of a high school in the continental countries was found to be a much superior person, attracted by the relatively high social position, higher salaries, and advanced professional morale. And while I have been speaking here of the teaching profession below the university grade, most of what I have said will apply almost as well to American colleges down at least to the last three decades of the nineteenth century.

Let us look for a moment at those old colleges and the situation of their faculties. One of the first things that any observer of American higher education is struck by is the fact that the American professoriat is the only profession in the United States that is governed by laymen. Outside the continent of North America university faculties are nowhere governed, as they are here, by lay boards of trustees. Of course it is not easy to say whether the American professor lacks status because he is not self-governing or whether he has failed to get self-government in part because he lacks status. Genetically, however, it is not too difficult to explain how the curse of absentee government came to afflict American education. American colleges were called into existence before the community had the full means to support them amply, and indeed before there was a body of learned men professionally given to teaching. The great independent, self-governing universities of the middle ages, which established the pattern for early modern university government, came into existence only where there were well-established bodies of students and masters; they took their political form from the guild model of corporate self-control and the church's model of independence from the power of the state. The American colleges were founded in a Protestant milieu, which, no longer accepting the principles of hierarchy and corporate independence, had introduced lay government of churches. From this to lay government of colleges was a natural step, made the more natural by the fact that the greater part of the teaching personnel in early American colleges, for over a century and a half, consisted of young tutors, recent graduates, who were merely waiting and studying preparatory to entering the ministry. These men usually had no permanent interest in teaching as a profession, no permanent stake in its welfare. And they were considered by the philanthropic non-teachers who founded the colleges to be too young and too transient to be entrusted with the task of governing the colleges and managing their resources. Hence governmental powers were kept in the hands of trustees. The only working member of the college who held the full stature of a master of university learning was the president who, in the absence of the trustees, took over a larger and larger share of the task of determining college policy. Hence to this day the only person in the American community who enjoys a measure of prestige and respect comparable to that enjoyed by the university professor in most countries of Europe is our college or university president. Needless to say, with the development of the modern university, a great deal of the power to govern academic affairs has informally passed into the hands of faculties. But in almost all cases, such powers are delegated and may be legally retaken on any issue at any time by trustees. While few American university professors would argue for full self-government at this date, the legal inability of the American academic community to govern itself in matters bearing on academic freedom and tenure is a major disability in its struggle against the external forces of anti-intellectualism.

It may also be said in passing that the historic lack of prestige within the American academic community has tended to feed on itself. I am sure that no man anywhere whose primary desire is for a large share of the material goods of life enters the teaching profession with the idea that it will supply them with any abundance. He enters it because of other inducements: because he wants to pursue knowledge, because he values leisure (he will be lucky if he gets it), because he likes the idea of living in an academic community, or because of the prestige of the office. But American academic life, having so little prestige to offer, has failed to recruit a very large percentage of its professorial personnel from the upper classes, as does the professoriat in England or on the continent. The American college professor is characteristically drawn from the lower middle classes. I hope you will not imagine that I am being snobbish when I argue that this has been a signal disadvantage both to the freedom and the intellectualism of the academic community. Logan Wilson, in his study of *The Academic Man* in the United States, has pointed out that the recruit from the lower middle classes often comes from a background of cultural poverty in which, of necessity, the view taken of most things has to be profoundly affected by their material efficacy. I should also add that a man who comes from a well-established family with secure connections, and has perhaps in addition some personal resources to draw on, can confront the problems of free expression with far greater boldness than the man who feels that he must cling to his academic job at all costs. I have been impressed, in studying the development of a certain measure of liberalism in the American colleges of the eighteenth century, by the important role played by men who came to academic life from secure positions of social prestige, either in great commercial families or the ministry. One of the boldest men in early academic life was Professor John Winthrop, the great Harvard astronomer, and no little part of his boldness rested upon the security derived from the fact that he was, after all, a Winthrop in Massachusetts.

The low prestige of the professor in America was matched by the low prestige of the college itself. At the end of the eighteenth century and the beginning of the nineteenth, as the

American population broke through the Allegheny mountains and began to spread across the continent, a process of educational fragmentation began which still profoundly afflicts our educational system. Every sect of Protestants wanted to have a little college to service every part of a great country. Localities thought that a community college would be good for local development. Parents welcomed the opportunity to educate their sons near at home in small schools whose annual tuition was often not much larger than the cost of transportation to a distant and perhaps more formidable seat of learning. They were advised, too, that the country college was socially democratic and that it protected their offspring from the corrupting atmosphere of great cities. This passion for breaking up the educational system into small units destroyed much of the potential strength and prestige of the old college. Where English colleges had clustered at a few university centers, American colleges were strewn across three thousand miles of continent. Innumerable colleges failed because they were so flimsily launched. Many that survived were much too tiny to maintain decent teaching staffs and adequate educational standards. It became a commonplace among serious educators before the Civil War that the American college was not, in the terms of international educational standards, a college at all, but a closer equivalent to the German gymnasium, the French lycée, the English public school.

After a time the old college became the butt of a great deal of criticism. It was, of course, devoted chiefly to the inherited classical curriculum, featuring Latin, Greek, and mathematics. This kind of schooling was increasingly held to be unadapted to the needs of American business, technology, and agriculture. It was held, and quite correctly, to be too limited and rigid to be adequate to the growing fund of human knowledge. Between the educational reformers, who were dissatisfied with the low level of work that the existing colleges were unable to transcend, and the practical reformers, who wanted to make American higher education work for the community in a clearer and more easily definable way, a curiously mixed transformation was finally effected in the last half of the nineteenth century. Universities, both state and private, were at last reared on adequate foundations; graduate and professional schools were created; schools of agriculture and engineering were founded; the curriculum was broadened; and the elective system was introduced.

Within only a few decades a curriculum system that had been too tight and too rigid was made too loose and too sprawling. All kinds of practical skills that had neither professional nor intellectual stature—no matter how necessary they might be to the community—were taught, or presumed to be taught, at universities. The president of a great state university was proud to say: "The state universities hold that there is no intellectual service too undignified for them to perform." Vast numbers of students without notable intellectual interests or skills flocked to the colleges and universities, availed themselves freely of the multitude of elective courses with little or no intellectual content, and passed out into the world with padded degrees. Much of the information thus inculcated may be thought to have no place in any system of formal education. A still larger part belongs to purely technical and mechanical education of the sort that can be properly taught in formal education but is not elsewhere considered proper to a university—the sort of thing that on the continent of Europe is to be found among the offerings of the German *technische Hochschule* and its many coun-terparts in other countries.

Now all this has taken place at serious cost to intellectualism. It is possible, of course, to argue that the professor of some field of pure learning is not interfered with in the pursuit of his work simply because his colleague in the school of agriculture is busy teaching farmers how to raise healthy pigs. Theoretically, no; but those who are familiar with the problems of university administration and finance know that these things have a way of pulling against or tripping over each other; and that when all kinds of skills of various levels are jumbled together and taught in one institution, the hierarchy of values that places intellectual accom-plishment at the top, as one would expect to do in a university, is somehow broken and destroyed. Thus the universities, that we might have expected to stand as solid barriers against the undercurrents of American anti-intellectualism, have actually intensified the push of the stream. How they could have resisted it, I do not honestly know. For one thing, our system of higher education is, unlike all the other systems in the world, a system of mass education, that today enrolls about 3,000,000 people. In a way, that is a preposterous figure, and I suppose it is altogether unreasonable to expect that students in such numbers will all get anything that could be called a common liberal education. All kinds of things pass for a college education in this country and will no doubt continue to do so for a long time to come. The difficulty is that we now have an educational system which rarely pro-duces educators who will themselves dare to defend an education wholeheartedly directed to the goal of increasing intellectual power. The famous report of the President's Commission on Higher Education published in 1948—a report prepared by a representative group of American educators and laymen interested in education—had this to say on the subject:

> We shall be denying educational opportunity to many young people as long as we maintain the present orientation of higher education toward verbal skills and intellectual interest. Many young people have abilities of a different kind, and they cannot receive "education commensu-rate with their native capacities" in colleges and universities that recognize only one kind of educable intelligence.
>
> Traditionally the colleges have sifted out as their special clientele persons possessing verbal aptitudes and a capacity for grasping abstractions. But many other aptitudes—such as social sensitivity and versatility, artistic ability, motor skill and dexterity, and mechanical aptitude and ingenuity—also should be cultivated in a society depending, as ours does, on the minute divi-sion of labor and at the same time upon the orchestration of an enormous variety of talents.

I can think of no more shameful capitulation than this to the canons of anti-intellectual-ism: a group of educators urging that our de-intellectualized colleges become still more de-intellectualized by giving up their alleged preoccupation with "verbal aptitudes" and "a capacity for grasping abstractions"—that is, the power to think and to express thought—for a motley batch of skills which, however valuable, one does not have to go to college to learn; for "social sensitivity" that no doubt includes ballroom dancing and parlor games; for "motor skill and dexterity" that must clearly mean athletics if it does not mean the ability to wash dishes without dropping them; and for "mechanical aptitude and ingenuity" that may very well mean the ability to drive and repair an automobile. Worthy skills every single one of them, and no doubt a necessary part of our life; but why they have to be acquired in something that calls itself a college or university the Commission, whose business was supposed to be with *higher* education, did not take the trouble to explain. No doubt its members did not feel themselves to be on the defensive, for they were expressing the dominant point of view in American society.

At the top of our educational system this attitude threatens to weaken whatever intellectualism we have. At lower levels, in our grammar and high schools, it threatens to wipe out literacy altogether in the name of "progressive education" or education for "life adjustment." If you think I exaggerate, listen to the principal of a junior high school in Urbana, Illinois, speaking to a meeting of the National Association of Secondary-School Principals:

> Through the years we've built a sort of halo around reading, writing, and arithmetic. We've said they were for everybody . . . rich and poor, brilliant and not-so-mentally endowed, ones who liked them and those who failed to go for them. Teacher has said that these were something "everyone should learn." The principal has remarked, "All educated people know how to write, spell, and read." When some child declared a dislike for a sacred subject, he was warned that, if he failed to master it, he would grow up to be a so-and-so.
>
> The Three R's for All Children and All Children for the Three R's! That was it.
>
> We've made some progress in getting rid of that slogan. But every now and then some mother with a Phi Beta Kappa award or some employer who has hired a girl who can't spell stirs up a fuss about the schools . . . and ground is lost. . . .
>
> When we come to the realization that not every child has to read, figure, write, and spell . . . that many of them either cannot or will not master these chores . . . then we shall be on the road to improving the junior high curriculum.
>
> Between this day and that a lot of selling must take place. But it's coming. We shall some day accept the thought that it is just as illogical to assume that every boy must be able to read as it is that each one must be able to perform on a violin, that it is no more reasonable to require that each girl shall spell well than it is that each one shall bake a good cherry pie. . . .
>
> When adults finally realize that fact, everyone will be happier . . . and schools will be nicer places in which to live. . . .

Of course this speaker, unlike the President's Commission, does not seem to be entirely in harmony with the prevailing sentiments of the country—at least, not yet; for it is clear that he thinks himself to be a visionary whose notions are considerably in advance of the times but whose high ideals for the future of illiteracy will some fine day be realized. I must ask you, however, to try to envisage the minds of a generation of young Americans who receive their lower education under men of this stamp and their higher education under a regime fully conforming to the President's Commission's disdain for verbal aptitudes and abstractions.

What is it, I think we may properly ask, that brings our nation's educators to such depressing disavowals of the fundamentally intellectual purposes of education? Much the same thing, I believe, that has them cringing before the onslaughts of politicians who are beyond the pale of moral decency—and that is the lack of a self-confident dedication to the life of the mind. What the root of that failure of self-confidence is, no one really knows; but I venture to suggest that it has a great deal to do with our false piety for populistic democracy, our sense of guilt at daring to suggest that there is anything wrong with the mob, even when a large part of it has obviously been whipped up by demagogues to a state of frantic suspicion of everything it does not care to understand. I think it would help us all morally, even if it would do nothing else, to face the fact that the very idea of intellectualism implies an elite of some kind—not, to be sure, a ruthless elite with special privileges or powers, but simply a group of people who have interests not shared by everyone in the community and whose very special interest is in freedom. Not everyone really wants to belong to that elite. But the primary fact is that this elite must maintain a certain spiritual autonomy in defining its own standards. I am not optimistic enough to believe that in any calculable future the rest of society can be brought to recognize that intellectuals have their own rights and interests, not special rights or privileged interests, but of the same sort that any other group has. What the intellectual community can do is what any group of sensible people will do whose values are under attack—and that is not to try to find some plausible reason for abandoning those values because they are not shared by the majority; and not to try to convince themselves that they really agree with the majority after all—but to show cohesion and firmness under fire, until the point has been reached when it is no longer profitable to encroach upon them.

This world will never be governed by intellectuals—it may rest assured. But *we* must be assured, too, that intellectuals will not be altogether governed by this world, that they maintain their piety, their long-standing allegiance to the world of spiritual values to which they should belong. Otherwise there will be no intellectuals, at least not above ground. And societies in which the intellectuals have been driven underground, as we have had occasion to see in our own time, are societies in which even the anti-intellectuals are unhappy.

Name: _____ Date: _____

UNDERSTANDING THE TEXT

1. According to Hofstadter, what is an intellectual?

2. What role does Hofstadter feel that democracy has played in education and anti-intellectualism in America?

3. Is Hofstadter hopeful about the fate of intellectualism in this country? Why or why not?

The Renaissance of Anti-Intellectualism

Todd Gitlin

The presidential campaign ended, effectively, in a tie, but it did speak clearly about the value accorded intellectuals and intellectuality in American culture. What it declared is, to say the least, inauspicious.

However the next four years play out in the White House, George W. Bush deserves a certain credit for resurrecting— though probably not intentionally—the subject of anti-intellectualism. Like Dan Quayle before him, but even more conspicuously (Bush's gaffes provided horror-comic relief during a campaign marked by its narrowed themes and horse-race obsessions), the governor of Texas proved an inadvertent shill for the comedy routines that have become an increasingly visible showcase for the spectacle of national politics.

Gov. Malaprop accomplished that dubious objective by various means: semantic spatter, most memorably "subliminable" for "subliminal," but also "subscribe" for "ascribe," "retort" for "resort," "hostile" for "hostage," and so on; inversions and juxtapositions of singular verbs and plural nouns, as in "Our priorities is our faith" and "Families is where our nation finds hope, where wings take dream"; and an ineptitude so guileless ("Social Security is not a federal program") as to embarrass the literal-minded who affect intellectual seriousness, for after a certain point it seems rude to call attention to the obvious, or "elitist" to notice something that viewers haven't noticed.

Early in the campaign, Bush had famously dubbed the inhabitants of Greece "Grecians" and flubbed a talk-show host's quiz about names of foreign leaders. There was so much ignorance on display as to raise the suspicion, on one hand, that Bush was dyslexic or, on the other, that this lazy-minded graduate of Andover, Yale, and Harvard Business School was a chip off his father's pork rinds, appealing self-consciously to his audience's resentment of brains. Thanks to videotape and a media maw hungry for simple charges and sound bites, Duh-bya seemed to have stridden right out of central casting, a veritable personification of the politician as clown.

Yet none of the easy charges against Bush touched upon his more substantial incapacities: his lack of curiosity about the world (he has scarcely traveled outside the United States and Mexico City) and the ample evidence that he does not reason. During the debates, he was unresponsive to questions the answers to which he had not memorized. In public appearances, he spoke in sloganistic lists, not arcs. It would seem that, precisely because his thinking was disordered, the governor lost track of his points, so that items came out nonsensical, as in: "Drug therapies are replacing a lot of medicines as we used to know it."

There has been much talk since the election to the effect that "two nations" were evenly matched in the contest: roughly speaking, the rural, inland, heavily male, and white Bushland versus the urban, coastal, heavily female, black, and immigrant Goreland. To be sure, suspicion of intellectuals and intellectuality was visible in both camps, but most plainly so in Bush's. So it came to pass that half of the voting population was appalled that the other half judged this man of little discernible achievement, little knowledge of the world or curiosity about it, to be an acceptable president of the United States. His defenders were in the position of claiming that it didn't matter whether the governor was smart or not, he could hire a smart staff, thereby certifying that intelligence was something for underlings.

In the minds of many of Bush's supporters, the absence of thoughtfulness, the narrowness of scope, the presence of diminished capacity were all reduced to a question of "management style." Gore, meanwhile, suffered bad reviews for his dismissive and overbearing style of intellectual combat. In the eyes of half the population, the vice president fell prey to a suspicion that he was not only preachy but also a sharpie. In the media's campaign story line, the standard charge against Gore, shared by the Bush campaign and the comedians, was that, like the traditional confidence man, Gore—too smart for his own good—lied, while Bush was the amiable common man.

Thirty-seven years have passed since the appearance of the last substantial book to take seriously, in the words of its title, *Anti-Intellectualism in American Life*. Richard Hofstadter's tour de force, appearing in 1963, is actually a product of the 1950's. Like many intellectuals, Hofstadter was disturbed by the general disdain for "eggheads," haunted by Joseph McCarthy's thuggish assault on Dean Acheson and his Anglophilic ways, and dismayed by Eisenhower's taste for Western novels and his tangled syntax (which was not yet understood to be, at least sometimes, not simply incompetent but deliberately evasive). Had not Eisenhower himself in 1954 (no doubt in words written for him by another hand) cited a definition of an intellectual as "a man who takes more words than are necessary to tell more than he knows"? (How much more congenial was Stevenson, who once cracked: "Eggheads of the world, unite! You have nothing to lose but your yolks!")

Probing for historical roots of a mood that was sweeping (if somewhat exaggerated by intellectuals), Hofstadter found that "our anti-intellectualism is, in fact, older than our national identity." He cited, among others, the Puritan John Cotton, who wrote in 1642, "The more learned and witty you bee, the more fit to act for Satan will you bee"; and Baynard

R. Hall, who wrote in 1843 of frontier Indiana: "We always preferred an ignorant bad man to a talented one, and hence attempts were usually made to ruin the moral character of a smart candidate; since unhappily smartness and wickedness were supposed to be generally coupled, and incompetence and goodness."

Yet, according to the historian Lawrence W. Levine, the illiterate Rocky Mountain scout Jim Bridger could recite long passages from Shakespeare, which he learned by hiring someone to read the plays to him. "There is hardly a pioneer's hut that does not contain a few odd volumes of Shakespeare," Alexis de Tocqueville found on his trip through America in 1831–32. Here lay a supremely American paradox: The same Americans who valued the literacy of commoners were suspicious of experts and tricksters.

In his unsurpassed survey, Hofstadter described three pillars of anti-intellectualism—evangelical religion, practical-minded business, and the populist political style. Religion was suspicious of modern relativism, business of regulatory expertise, populism of claims that specialized knowledge had its privileges. Those pillars stand. But, as Hofstadter recognized, something was changing in American life, and that was the uneasy apotheosis of technical intellect.

The rise of big science during World War II, and its normalization during the cold war, along with the Sputnik panic of 1957, made "brains" more reputable among respectable citizens who had their own ideas about the force of common sense but had to acknowledge that expertise delivered material goods Then as now, the "brains" that became admirable were brains kept in their place. To the extent that brains were admirable, it was because they were instrumental—they prevented polio, invented computers, launched satellites.

By the 1990s, the geek was an acceptable good guy, the nerd an entrepreneurial hero. That sense of the supreme position of useful intellect is preserved in the current phrase, "It's not rocket science"—implying that real rocket science is the grandest field of intellectual dreams.

Hofstadter did most of his research before Kennedy came to the White House, and he understood that Kennedy's brief ascendancy did not change the fundamentals. Kennedy was not especially serious about the life of the mind, but he was elegant, witty, and, by all accounts, enjoyed the occasional presence of intellectuals. John Kenneth Galbraith and Arthur Schlesinger Jr. were adornments. Never mind that Kennedy's reading tilted heavily toward Ian Fleming, who in the James Bond books supplied the president with a man of action's idea of the debonair, the sort of fellow whose European accent can be mistaken for mental accomplishment.

Even into the Johnson administration, the While House ceremonially invited intellectuals and high artists to visit, culminating in the public-relations disaster of a White House festival of the arts, in 1965, that was boycotted by some writers and artists while others circulated an antiwar petition at the event.

The force of Hofstadter's insight into persistent anti-intellectualism despite the rising legitimacy of technical experts would be clear five years after he published his book. George

Wallace ran well in several Democratic Party primaries, and eventually, too, as a third-party candidate, while campaigning against "pointy-headed bureaucrats"—precisely the classic identification of intellect with arbitrary power that Hofstadter had identified as the populist hallmark.

There was a left-wing version of this presupposition, too. A populist strain in the 60s student movement, identifying with the oppressed sharecroppers of the Mississippi Delta and the dispossessed miners of Appalachia, bent the principle "Let the people decide" into a suspicion of all those who were ostensibly knowledgeable. Under pressure of the Vietnam War, the steel-rimmed technocrat Robert S. McNamara came to personify the steel-trap mind untethered by insight, and countercultural currents came to disdain reason as a mask for imperial arrogance.

In his first gubernatorial campaign in 1966, Ronald Reagan deployed a classic anti-intellectual theme—portraying students as riotous decadents. Real education was essentially a matter of training, and breaches of discipline resulted in nihilism and softness on communism. The Nixon-Agnew team proceeded to mobilize resentment against "nattering nabobs of negativism," successfully mobilizing a "silent majority" against a verbose minority. That was to flower into a major neoconservative theme thereafter.

As candidate and president, the smooth-spoken if intellectually challenged Reagan succeeded in availing himself of an indulgent press and an adoring constituency that, at the least, did not mind his incapacity. He did not suffer from his evident contempt for professorial types, his half-educated ignorance of history and reliance on crackpot sources, his embrace of the notion that trees cause pollution. That he was opposed by sophisticated types only inflated his aura.

By the 1990s, "elitism" had become an all-purpose epithet, used by neoconservatives against the "new class" (consisting of all political intellectuals with the exception of themselves), but also by hard multiculturalists against "the neo-Enlightenment project," by relativists in general against objectivists in general. Populist resentment flourished even as (and, perhaps in part, because) populist egalitarianism of an economic stripe was dwindling.

The counterculture had introduced suspicion of professionalized rationality—swelling the reputation of "alternative" medicine and elevating herbs and homeopathic, chiropractic, and osteopathic treatments to alternatives to plodding old Western therapies. Hofstadter had made much of the distinction between critical intellectuals (suspected, sometimes justifiably, of being ideologues) and expert intellectuals ("on tap, not on top," in the terms of the early atomic scientists), but thanks to the postmodern mood of the intervening decades, many experts had come to be tarred with the same brush as ideologues. College students were heard to complain that certain professors were excessive in their vocabularies. Even in the classroom, "boring" became an epithet of choice.

A central force boosting anti-intellectualism since Hofstadter published his book has been the bulking up of popular culture and, in particular, the rise of a new form of faux cerebration: punditry. Everyday life, supersaturated with images and jingles, makes intellectual life look hopelessly sluggish, burdensome, difficult. In a video-game world, the play of intellect—the search for validity, the willingness to entertain many hypotheses, the respect for difficulty, the resistance to hasty conclusions—has the look of retardation.

Again, there is a continuity to the earlier nation. Long before Hollywood or MTV, Tocqueville observed that Americans were drawn to novelty, turnover, and sensation. How much more so in a world of cascading, all-pervasive images, where two-thirds of children grow up with 24/7 access to television in their bedrooms, where video and computer games flourish, where mobile phones guarantee access when and where one chooses, where the right to be instantly entertained and in-touch seems to preoccupy more of the citizenry than the right to vote and to have their votes properly counted.

There is a seeming paradox that Hofstadter did not anticipate, but would have appreciated. In the torrent of popular culture, there emerges more talk about public affairs than ever before—virtually nonstop talk about political concerns, debate on burning questions available at all hours of the day and night. But the talk that fills the channels amounts mainly to signals, gestures, and stances—not reasoning.

Television reporting and punditry are the tributes that entertainment pays to the democratic ideal of discourse. The political talk does not, in the main, evaluate or research: It "covers." When CNN's Washington bureau chief can say casually, "The Texas governor hammered home some of his major themes, including Social Security," this is shorthand, but not only shorthand—it is a surrogate for reasoning. Positions are signaled—candidates "position themselves"—rather than defended; no defending is demanded of them. A topic is a "theme" is a "position" is an "issue" is news.

All the more so does punditry diffuse a debased version of intellectual life, cornering intellect in the name of chat, operating by a sort of Gresham's law of discourse. Punditry is concerned with reviewing performances, rating "presidentiality," itemizing themes, relaying and interpreting spin, not thoughtfully assessing politicians' claims, evaluating their evidence, judging their reasoning. To assess the quality of what politicians say would require intellectual work for which the pundits do not demonstrate competency. Pundits are hired, rather, for the facility and pungency of their presentations and the ferocity and acceptability of their opinions.

The most bookish of pundits, George Will, was hired for the Anglophilic elegance of his sneers, not for logical mastery or historical depth. The punditocracy, as Eric Alterman calls it, does not assess either reason or reasons. Its job is simply to declare which issues are discussable, which positions presentable. It makes up for its intellectual deficits by supplying precooked opinion. The point is not to clarify: It is never to be at a loss for words. Surely the English infusion into American journalism—the premium on corrosive wit, the fusion of intellectual name-dropping with tabloid meanness—belongs to this trend: the show of intellect without the demanding work.

When Hofstadter wrote, the dominant intellectuals were either experts or ideologues. The most influential pundit was Walter Lippmann. But the crucial public development since Hofstadter's time is the rise of the pseudo-intellectual, thanks to the premium on smirking and glibness, which, in much of the popular mind, passes for intellect. The pundit is a smart person in both senses—intelligent and a smarty-pants— and his knowingness about how the game is played is a substitute for knowledge about what would improve society. Punditry is to intellectual life as fast food is to fine cuisine.

After Gore, self-cast as wonk-expert and therefore prey to precisely the anti-intellectualism that Hofstadter identified, challenged Bush to state his position on the Dingell-Norwood patients-rights' bill during the third debate, and Bush avoided the question, the pseudo-brains of ABC's *This Week,* Cokie Roberts and Sam Donaldson, made much mirth by mocking the names. They did not think it their obligation to clarify what Gore was talking about. Deadly, that would have been. Chock full of attitude, deploying the cheap gags and knowingness that mark them as qualified for their jobs, those maestros of the Beltway paraded their superiority to knowledge while (as Michael Kinsley pointed out) refraining from showing that they knew more than the public.

Surely television is a boon to anti-intellectualism, with its encouragement of emotional chords and comfort, but the degradations of public life that afflict us are not primarily visual achievements. It is language and sound, most of all, that warp the public discourse. That is true not only in the presentation of politics but of science, education, and many another subject. The sound-bite discourse cultivated by television pumps up the imperative "Cut to the chase," reinforcing the fetish of "the bottom line."

It is not that the sound-bite culture was imposed upon what was previously unrelievedly brilliant politics. From "Tippecanoe and Tyler too" to "I like Ike," American history is soaked in sound-bite prefigurations. Warren G. Harding may not have been much better than George W. Bush. But the more striking transformation in American commentary takes us in 50 years from Walter Lippmann, a man of tremendous historical and philosophical sophistication, to Tim Russert, an intelligent man who specializes in "Gotcha!" questions and gives Rush Limbaugh respectful interviews, defending that choice on the ground that, after all, Limbaugh "speaks to 20-million people." Thus does knowingness make its peace with populism.

In the Bushes, *père et fils,* we see another turn in the history of the American aversion to intellect. Hofstadter rightly noted the 19th-century aristocratic disdain for practical intellectuals, the business types and experts whose rising power displaced their own. The Roosevelt cousins, different in many respects, both honored the life of the mind: Theodore as writer, Franklin as a collector of advisers. Old money respected brains.

But the Bushes are men of social credentials who went to the right schools and passed through them without any detectable mark. They represent aristocracy with a populist gloss, borrowing what they can from the evangelical revival, siding with business and its distaste for time-wasting mind work, holding intellectual talent in contempt from both above and below. Pleasant enough for the pundits, they have been able to count on a surplus of populist ressentiment. That Bush *fils,* country-club Republican, could gain stature (and keep a straight face) in his presidential campaign for proposing an "education presidency" and denouncing an "education recession" tells us something about the closing of the American mind that Allan Bloom did not dream of.

Name: _____ Date: _____

UNDERSTANDING THE TEXT

1. How does Gitlin characterize Bush and Gore's performance during the 2000 campaign for president?

2. What former presidents does Gitlin discuss, and how does he assess their performance in regard to intellectualism?

3. What is "punditry"? According to Gitlin, how does it contribute to the rise of anti-intellectualism in American political discourse?

On the Uses of a Liberal Education: As Lite Entertainment for Bored College Students

Mark Edmundson

Today is evaluation day in my Freud class, and everything has changed. The class meets twice a week, late in the afternoon, and the clientele, about fifty undergraduates, tends to drag in and slump, looking disconsolate and a little lost, waiting for a jump start. To get the discussion moving, they usually require a joke, an anecdote, an off-the-wall question—When you were a kid, were your Halloween getups ego costumes, id costumes, or superego costumes? That sort of thing. But today, as soon as I flourish the forms, a buzz rises in the room. Today they write their assessments of the course, their assessments of *me,* and they are without a doubt wide-awake. "What is your evaluation of the instructor?" asks question number eight, entreating them to circle a number between five (excellent) and one (poor, poor). Whatever interpretive subtlety they've acquired during the term is now out the window. Edmundson: one to five, stand and shoot.

And they do. As I retreat through the door—I never stay around for this phase of the ritual—I look over my shoulder and see them toiling away like the devil's auditors. They're pitched into high writing gear, even the ones who struggle to squeeze out their journal entries word by word, stoked on a procedure they have by now supremely mastered. They're playing the informed consumer, letting the provider know where he's come through and where he's not quite up to snuff.

But why am I so distressed, bolting like a refugee out of my own classroom, where I usually hold easy sway? Chances are the evaluations will be much like what they've been in the past—they'll be just fine. It's likely that I'll be commended for being "interesting" (and I am commended, many times over), that I'll be cited for my relaxed and tolerant ways (that happens, too), that my sense of humor and capacity to connect the arcana of the subject matter with current culture will come in for some praise (yup). I've been hassled this term, finishing a manuscript, and so haven't given their journals the attention I should have, and for that I'm called—quite civilly, though—to account. Overall, I get off pretty well.

Yet I have to admit that I do not much like the image of myself that emerges from these forms, the image of knowledgeable, humorous detachment and bland tolerance. I do not like the forms themselves, with their number ratings, reminiscent of the sheets circulated after the TV pilot has just played to its sample audience in Burbank. Most of all I dislike the attitude of calm consumer expertise that pervades the responses. I'm disturbed by the serene belief that my function—and, more important, Freud's, or Shakespeare's, or Blake's—is to divert, entertain, and interest. Observes one respondent, not at all unrepresentative: "Edmundson has done a fantastic job of presenting this difficult, important & controversial material in an enjoyable and approachable way."

Thanks but no thanks. I don't teach to amuse, to divert, or even, for that matter, to be merely interesting. When someone says she "enjoyed" the course—and that word crops up again and again in my evaluations—somewhere at the edge of my immediate complacency I feel encroaching self-dislike. That is not at all what I had in mind. The off-the-wall questions and the sidebar jokes are meant as lead-ins to stronger stuff—in the case of the Freud course, to a complexly tragic view of life. But the affability and the one-liners often seem to be all that land with the students; their journals and evaluations leave me little doubt.

I want some of them to say that they've been changed by the course. I want them to measure themselves against what they've read. It's said that some time ago a Columbia University instructor used to issue a harsh two-part question. One: What book did you most dislike in the course? Two: What intellectual or characterological flaws in you does that dislike point to? The hand that framed that question was surely heavy. But at least it compels one to see intellectual work as a confrontation between two people, student and author, where the stakes matter. Those Columbia students were being asked to relate the quality of an *encounter,* not rate the action as though it had unfolded on the big screen.

Why are my students describing the Oedipus complex and the death drive as being interesting and enjoyable to contemplate? And why am I coming across as an urbane, mildly ironic, endlessly affable guide to this intellectual territory, operating without intensity, generous, funny, and loose?

Because that's what works. On evaluation day, I reap the rewards of my partial compliance with the culture of my students and, too, with the culture of the university as it now operates. It's a culture that's gotten little exploration. Current critics tend to think that liberal-arts education is in crisis because universities have been invaded by professors with peculiar ideas: deconstruction, Lacanianism, feminism, queer theory. They believe that genius and tradition are out and that P.C., multiculturalism, and identity politics are in because of an invasion by tribes of tenured radicals, the late millennial equivalents of the Visigoth hordes that cracked Rome's walls.

But mulling over my evaluations and then trying to take a hard, extended look at campus life both here at the University of Virginia and around the country eventually led me to some different conclusions. To me, liberal-arts education is as ineffective as it is now not chiefly because there are a lot of strange theories in the air. (Used well, those theories *can* be illuminating.) Rather, it's that university culture, like American culture writ large, is, to put it crudely, ever more devoted to consumption and entertainment, to the using and using up of goods and images. For someone growing up in America now, there are few available alternatives to the cool consumer worldview. My students didn't ask for that view, much less create it, but they bring a consumer weltanschauung to school, where it exerts a powerful, and largely unacknowledged, influence. If we want to understand current universities, with their multiple woes, we might try leaving the realms of expert debate and fine ideas and turning to the classrooms and campuses, where a new kind of weather is gathering.

From time to time I bump into a colleague in the corridor and we have what I've come to think of as a Joon Lee fest. Joon Lee is one of the best students I've taught. He's endlessly curious, has read a small library's worth, seen every movie, and knows all about showbiz and entertainment. For a class of mine he wrote an essay using Nietzsche's Apollo and Dionysus to analyze the pop group The Supremes. A trite, cultural-studies bonbon? Not at all. He said striking things about conceptions of race in America and about how they shape our ideas of beauty. When I talk with one of his other teachers, we run on about the general splendors of his work and presence. But what inevitably follows a JL fest is a mournful reprise about the divide that separates him and a few other remarkable students from their contemporaries. It's not that some aren't nearly as bright—in terms of intellectual ability, my students are all that I could ask for. Instead, it's that Joon Lee has decided to follow his interests and let them make him into a singular and rather eccentric man; in his charming way, he doesn't mind being at odds with most anyone.

It's his capacity for enthusiasm that sets Joon apart from what I've come to think of as the reigning generational style. Whether the students are sorority/fraternity types, grunge aficionados, piercer/tattooers, black or white, rich or middle class (alas, I teach almost no students from truly poor backgrounds), they are, nearly across the board, very, very self-contained. On good days they display a light, appealing glow; on bad days, shuffling disgruntlement. But there's little fire, little passion to be found.

This point came home to me a few weeks ago when I was wandering across the university grounds. There, beneath a classically cast portico, were two students, male and female, having a rip-roaring argument. They were incensed, bellowing at each other, headstrong, confident, and wild. It struck me how rarely I see this kind of full-out feeling in students anymore. Strong emotional display is forbidden. When conflicts arise, it's generally understood that one of the parties will say something sarcastically propitiating ("whatever" often does it) and slouch away.

How did my students reach this peculiar state in which all passion seems to be spent? I think that many of them have imbibed their sense of self from consumer culture in general and from the tube in particular. They're the progeny of 100 cable channels and omni-present Blockbuster outlets. TV, Marshall McLuhan famously said, is a cool medium. Those who play best on it are low-key and nonassertive; they blend in. Enthusiasm, à la Joon Lee, quickly looks absurd. The form of character that's most appealing on TV is calmly self-interested though never greedy, attuned to the conventions, and ironic. Judicious timing is preferred to sudden self-assertion. The TV medium is inhospitable to inspiration, improvisation, failures, slipups. All must run perfectly.

Naturally, a cool youth culture is a marketing bonanza for producers of the right products, who do all they can to enlarge that culture and keep it grinding. The Internet, TV, and magazines now teem with what I call persona ads, ads for Nikes and Reeboks and Jeeps and Blazers that don't so much endorse the capacities of the product per se as show you what sort of person you will be once you've acquired it. The Jeep ad that features hip, outdoorsy kids whipping a Frisbee from mountaintop to mountaintop isn't so much about what Jeeps can do as it is about the kind of people who own them. Buy a Jeep and be one with them. The ad is of little consequence in itself, but expand its message exponentially and you have the central thrust of current consumer culture—buy in order to be.

Most of my students seem desperate to blend in, to look right, not to make a spectacle of themselves. (Do I have to tell you that those two students having the argument under the portico turned out to be acting in a role-playing game?) The specter of the uncool creates a subtle tyranny. It's apparently an easy standard to subscribe to, this Letterman-like, Tarantino-like cool, but once committed to it, you discover that matters are rather different. You're inhibited, except on ordained occasions, from showing emotion, stifled from trying to achieve anything original. You're made to feel that even the slightest departure from the reigning code will get you genially ostracized. This is a culture tensely committed to a laid-back norm.

Am I coming off like something of a crank here? Maybe. Oscar Wilde, who is almost never wrong, suggested that it is perilous to promiscuously contradict people who are much younger than yourself. Point taken. But one of the lessons that consumer hype tries to insinuate is that we must never rebel against the new, never even question it. If it's new—a new need, a new product, a new show, a new style, a new generation—it must be good. So maybe, even at the risk of winning the withered, brown laurels of crankdom, it pays to resist newness-worship and cast a colder eye.

Praise for my students? I have some of that too. What my students are, at their best, is decent. They are potent believers in equality. They help out at the soup kitchen and volunteer to tutor poor kids to get a stripe on their résumés, sure. But they also want other people to have a fair shot. And in their commitment to fairness they are discerning; there you see them at their intellectual best. If I were on trial and innocent, I'd want them on the jury.

What they will not generally do, though, is indict the current system. They won't talk about how the exigencies of capitalism lead to a reserve army of the unemployed and nearly inevitable misery. That would be getting too loud, too brash. For the pervading view is the cool consumer perspective, where passion and strong admiration are forbidden. "To stand in awe of nothing, Numicus, is perhaps the one and only thing that can make a man happy and keep him so," says Horace in the *Epistles,* and I fear that his lines ought to hang as a motto over the university in this era of high consumer capitalism.

It's easy to mount one's high horse and blame the students for this state of affairs. But they didn't create the present culture of consumption. (It was largely my own generation, that of the Sixties, that let the counterculture search for pleasure devolve into a quest for commodities.) And they weren't the ones responsible, when they were six and seven and eight years old, for unplugging the TV set from time to time or for hauling off and kicking a hole through it. It's my generation of parents who sheltered these students, kept them away from the hard knocks of everyday life, making them cautious and overfragile, who demanded that their teachers, from grade school on, flatter them endlessly so that the kids are shocked if their college profs don't reflexively suck up to them.

Of course, the current generational style isn't simply derived from culture and environment. It's also about dollars. Students worry that taking too many chances with their educations will sabotage their future prospects. They're aware of the fact that a drop that looks more and more like one wall of the Grand Canyon separates the top economic tenth from the rest of the population. There's a sentiment currently abroad that if you step aside for a moment, to write, to travel, to fall too hard in love, you might lose position permanently. We may be on a conveyor belt, but it's worse down there on the filth-strewn floor. So don't sound off, don't blow your chance.

But wait. I teach at the famously conservative University of Virginia. Can I extend my view from Charlottesville to encompass the whole country, a whole generation of college students? I can only say that I hear comparable stories about classroom life from colleagues everywhere in America. When I visit other schools to lecture, I see a similar scene unfolding. There are, of course, terrific students everywhere. And they're all the better for the way they've had to strive against the existing conformity. At some of the small liberal-arts colleges, the tradition of strong engagement persists. But overall, the students strike me as being sweet and sad, hovering in a nearly suspended animation.

Too often now the pedagogical challenge is to make a lot from a little. Teaching Wordsworth's "Tintern Abbey," you ask for comments. No one responds. So you call on Stephen. Stephen: "The sound, this poem really flows." You: "Stephen seems interested in the music of the poem. We might extend his comment to ask if the poem's music coheres with its argument. Are they consistent? Or is there an emotional pain submerged here that's contrary to the poem's appealing melody?" All right, it's not usually that bad. But close. One friend describes it as rebound teaching: they proffer a weightless comment, you hit it back for all you're worth, then it comes dribbling out again. Occasionally a professor will try to explain away this intellectual timidity by describing the students as perpetrators of postmodern irony, a highly sophisticated mode. Everything's a slick counterfeit, a simulacrum, so by no means should any phenomenon be taken seriously. But the students don't have the urbane, Oscar Wilde-type demeanor that should go with this view. Oscar was cheerful, funny, confident, strange. (Wilde, mortally ill, living in a Paris flophouse: "My wallpaper and I are fighting a duel to the death. One or the other of us has to go.") This generation's style is considerate, easy to please, and a touch depressed.

Granted, you might say, the kids come to school immersed in a consumer mentality— they're good Americans, after all—but then the university and the professors do everything in their power to fight that dreary mind-set in the interest of higher ideals, right? So it should be. But let us look at what is actually coming to pass.

Over the past few years, the physical layout of my university has been changing. To put it a little indecorously, the place is looking more and more like a retirement spread for the young. Our funds go to construction, into new dorms, into renovating the student union. We have a new aquatics center and ever-improving gyms, stocked with StairMasters and Nautilus machines. Engraved on the wall in the gleaming aquatics building is a line by our founder, Thomas Jefferson, declaring that everyone ought to get about two hours' exercise a day. Clearly even the author of the Declaration of Independence endorses the turning of his university into a sports-and-fitness emporium.

But such improvements shouldn't be surprising. Universities need to attract the best (that is, the smartest *and* the richest) students in order to survive in an ever more competitive market. Schools want kids whose parents can pay the full freight, not the ones who need scholarships or want to bargain down the tuition costs. If the marketing surveys say that the kids require sports centers, then, trustees willing, they shall have them. In fact, as I began looking around, I came to see that more and more of what's going on in the university is customer driven. The consumer pressures that beset me on evaluation day are only a part of an overall trend.

From the start, the contemporary university's relationship with students has a solicitous, nearly servile tone. As soon as someone enters his junior year in high school, and especially if he's living in a prosperous zip code, the informational material—the advertising—comes flooding in. Pictures, testimonials, videocassettes, and CD ROMs (some bidden, some not) arrive at the door from colleges across the country, all trying to capture the student and his tuition cash. The freshman-to-be sees photos of well-appointed dorm rooms; of elaborate phys-ed facilities; of fine dining rooms; of expertly kept sports fields; of orchestras and drama troupes; of students working alone (no overbearing grown-ups in range), peering with high seriousness into computers and microscopes; or of students arrayed outdoors in attractive conversational garlands.

Occasionally—but only occasionally, for we usually photograph rather badly; in appearance we tend at best to be styleless—there's a professor teaching a class. (The college catalogues I received, by my request only, in the late Sixties were austere affairs full of professors' credentials and course descriptions; it was clear on whose terms the enterprise was going to unfold.) A college financial officer recently put matters to me in concise, if slightly melodramatic, terms: "Colleges don't have admissions offices anymore, they have marketing departments." Is it surprising that someone who has been approached with photos and tapes, bells and whistles, might come in thinking that the Freud and Shakespeare she had signed up to study were also going to be agreeable treats?

How did we reach this point? In part the answer is a matter of demographics and (surprise) of money. Aided by the G.I. bill, the college-going population in America dramatically increased after the Second World War. Then came the baby boomers, and to accommodate them, schools continued to grow. Universities expand easily enough, but with tenure locking faculty in for lifetime jobs, and with the general reluctance of administrators to eliminate their own slots, it's not easy for a university to contract. So after the baby boomers had passed through—like a fat meal digested by a boa constrictor—the colleges turned to energetic promotional strategies to fill the empty chairs. And suddenly college became a buyer's market. What students and their parents wanted had to be taken more and more into account. That usually meant creating more comfortable, less challenging environments, places where almost no one failed, everything was enjoyable, and everyone was nice.

Just as universities must compete with one another for students, so must the individual departments. At a time of rank economic anxiety, the English and history majors have to contend for students against the more success-insuring branches, such as the sciences and the commerce school. In 1968, more than 21 percent of all the bachelor's degrees conferred in America were in the humanities; by 1993, that number had fallen to about 13 percent. The humanities now must struggle to attract students, many of whose parents devoutly wish they would study something else.

One of the ways we've tried to stay attractive is by loosening up. We grade much more softly than our colleagues in science. In English, we don't give many Ds, or Cs for that matter. (The rigors of Chem 101 create almost as many English majors per year as do the splendors of Shakespeare.) A professor at Stanford recently explained grade inflation in the humanities by observing that the undergraduates were getting smarter every year; the higher grades simply recorded how much better they were than their predecessors. Sure.

Along with softening the grades, many humanities departments have relaxed major requirements. There are some good reasons for introducing more choice into curricula and requiring fewer standard courses. But the move, like many others in the university now, jibes with a tendency to serve—and not challenge— the students. Students can also float in and out of classes during the first two weeks of each term without making any commitment. The common name for this time span—shopping period— speaks volumes about the consumer mentality that's now in play. Usually, too, the kids can drop courses up until the last month with only an innocuous "W" on their transcripts. Does a course look too challenging? No problem. Take it pass-fail. A happy consumer is, by definition, one with multiple options, one who can always have what he wants. And since a course is something the students and their parents have bought and paid for, why can't they do with it pretty much as they please?

A sure result of the university's widening elective leeway is to give students more power over their teachers. Those who don't like you can simply avoid you. If the clientele dislikes you en masse, you can be left without students, period. My first term teaching I walked into my introduction to poetry course and found it inhabited by one student, the gloriously named Bambi Lynn Dean. Bambi and I chatted amiably awhile, but for all that she and the pleasure of her name could offer, I was fast on the way to meltdown. It was all a mistake, luckily, a problem with the scheduling book. Everyone was waiting for me next door. But in a dozen years of teaching I haven't forgotten that feeling of being ignominiously marooned. For it happens to others, and not always because of scheduling glitches. I've seen older colleagues go through hot embarrassment at not having enough students sign up for their courses: they graded too hard, demanded too much, had beliefs too far out of keeping with the existing disposition. It takes only a few such instances to draw other members of the professoriat further into line.

And if what's called tenure reform—which generally just means the abolition of tenure—is broadly enacted, professors will be yet more vulnerable to the whims of their customer-students. Teach what pulls the kids in, or walk. What about entire departments that don't deliver? If the kids say no to Latin and Greek, is it time to dissolve classics? Such questions are being entertained more and more seriously by university administrators.

How does one prosper with the present clientele? Many of the most successful professors now are the ones who have "decentered" their classrooms. There's a new emphasis on group projects and on computer-generated exchanges among the students. What they seem to want most is to talk to one another. A classroom now is frequently an "environment," a place highly conducive to the exchange of existing ideas, the students' ideas. Listening to one another, students sometimes change their opinions. But what they generally can't do is acquire a new vocabulary, a new perspective, that will cast issues in a fresh light.

The Socratic method—the animated, sometimes impolite give-and-take between student and teacher—seems too jagged for current sensibilities. Students frequently come to my office to tell me how intimidated they feel in class; the thought of being embarrassed in front of the group fills them with dread. I remember a student telling me how humiliating it was to be corrected by the teacher, by me. So I asked the logical question: "Should I let a major factual error go by so as to save discomfort?" The student—a good student, smart and earnest—said that was a tough question. He'd need to think about it.

Disturbing? Sure. But I wonder, are we really getting students ready for Socratic exchange with professors when we push them off into vast lecture rooms, two and three hundred to a class, sometimes face them with only grad students until their third year, and signal in our myriad professorial ways that we often have much better things to do than sit in our offices and talk with them? How bad will the student-faculty ratios have to become, how teeming the lecture courses, before we hear students righteously complaining, as they did thirty years ago, about the impersonality of their schools, about their decline into knowledge factories? "This is a firm," said Mario Savio at Berkeley during the Free Speech protests of the Sixties, "and if the Board of Regents are the board of directors, . . . then . . . the faculty are a bunch of employees and we're the raw material. But we're a bunch of raw material that don't mean . . . to be made into any product."

Teachers who really do confront students, who provide significant challenges to what they believe, *can* be very successful, granted. But sometimes such professors generate more than a little trouble for themselves. A controversial teacher can send students hurrying to the deans and the counselors, claiming to have been offended. ("Offensive" is the preferred term of repugnance today, just as "enjoyable" is the summit of praise.) Colleges have brought in hordes of counselors and deans to make sure that everything is smooth, serene, unflustered, that everyone has a good time. To the counselor, to the dean, and to the university legal squad, that which is normal, healthy, and prudent is best.

An air of caution and deference is everywhere. When my students come to talk with me in my office, they often exhibit a Franciscan humility. "Do you have a moment?" "I know you're busy. I won't take up much of your time." Their presences tend to be very light; they almost never change the temperature of the room. The dress is nondescript: clothes are in earth tones; shoes are practical—cross-trainers, hiking boots, work shoes, Dr. Martens, with now and then a stylish pair of raised-sole boots on one of the young women. Many, male and female both, peep from beneath the bills of monogrammed baseball caps. Quite a few wear sports, or even corporate, logos, sometimes on one piece of clothing but occasionally (and disconcertingly) on more. The walk is slow; speech is careful, sweet, a bit weary, and without strong inflection. (After the first lively week of the term, most seem far in debt to sleep.) They are almost unfailingly polite. They don't want to offend me; I could hurt them, savage their grades.

Naturally, there are exceptions, kids I chat animatedly with, who offer a joke, or go on about this or that new CD (almost never a book, no). But most of the traffic is genially sleepwalking. I have to admit that I'm a touch wary, too. I tend to hold back. An unguarded remark, a joke that's taken to be off-color, or simply an uncomprehended comment can lead to difficulties. I keep it literal. They scare me a little, these kind and melancholy students, who themselves seem rather frightened of their own lives.

Before they arrive, we ply the students with luscious ads, guaranteeing them a cross between summer camp and lotusland. When they get here, flattery and nonstop entertainment are available, if that's what they want. And when they leave? How do we send our students out into the world? More and more, our administrators call the booking agents and line up one or another celebrity to usher the graduates into the millennium. This past spring, Kermit the Frog won himself an honorary degree at Southampton College on Long Island; Bruce Willis and Yogi Berra took credentials away at Montclair State; Arnold Schwarzenegger scored at the University of Wisconsin-Superior. At Wellesley, Oprah Winfrey gave the commencement address. (*Wellesley*—one of the most rigorous academic colleges in the nation.) At the University of Vermont, Whoopi Goldberg laid down the word. But why should a worthy administrator contract the likes of Susan Sontag, Christopher Hitchens, or Robert Hughes—someone who might actually say something, something disturbing, something "offensive"—when he can get what the parents and kids apparently want and what the newspapers will softly commend—more lite entertainment, more TV?

Is it a surprise, then, that this generation of students—steeped in consumer culture before going off to school, treated as potent customers by the university well before their date of arrival, then pandered to from day one until the morning of the final kiss off from Kermit or one of his kin—are inclined to see the books they read as a string of entertainments to be placidly enjoyed or languidly cast down? Given the way universities are now administered (which is more and more to say, given the way that they are currently marketed), is it a shock that the kids don't come to school hot to learn, unable to bear their own ignorance? For some measure of self-dislike, or self-discontent—which is much different than simple depression—seems to me to be a prerequisite for getting an education that matters. My students, alas, usually lack the confidence to acknowledge what would be their most precious asset for learning: their ignorance.

Not long ago, I asked my Freud class a question that, however hoary, never fails to solicit intriguing responses: Who are your heroes? Whom do you admire? After one remarkable answer, featuring T. S. Eliot as hero, a series of generic replies rolled in, one gray wave after the next: my father, my best friend, a doctor who lives in our town, my high school history teacher. Virtually all the heroes were people my students had known personally, people who had done something local, specific, and practical, and had done it for them. They were good people, unselfish people, these heroes, but most of all they were people who had delivered the goods.

My students' answers didn't exhibit any philosophical resistance to the idea of greatness. It's not that they had been primed by their professors with complex arguments to combat genius. For the truth is that these students don't need debunking theories. Long before college, skepticism became their habitual mode. They are the progeny of Bart Simpson and David Letterman, and the hyper-cool ethos of the box. It's inane to say that theorizing professors have created them, as many conservative critics like to do. Rather, they have substantially created a university environment in which facile skepticism can thrive without being substantially contested.

Skeptical approaches have *potential* value. If you have no all-encompassing religious faith, no faith in historical destiny, the future of the West, or anything comparably grand, you need to acquire your vision of the world somewhere. If it's from literature, then the various visions literature offers have to be inquired into skeptically. Surely it matters that women are denigrated in Milton and in Pope, that some novelistic voices assume an overbearing godlike authority, that the poor are, in this or that writer, inevitably cast as clowns. You can't buy all of literature wholesale if it's going to help draw your patterns of belief.

But demystifying theories are now overused, applied mechanically. It's all logocentrism, patriarchy, ideology. And in this the student environment—laid-back, skeptical, knowing—is, I believe, central. Full-out debunking is what plays with this clientele. Some have been doing it nearly as long as, if more crudely than, their deconstructionist teachers. In the context of the contemporary university, and cool consumer culture, a useful intellectual skepticism has become exaggerated into a fundamentalist caricature of itself. The teachers have buckled to their students' views.

At its best, multiculturalism can be attractive as well-deployed theory. What could be more valuable than encountering the best work of far-flung cultures and becoming a citizen of the world? But in the current consumer environment, where flattery plays so well, the urge to encounter the other can devolve into the urge to find others who embody and celebrate the right ethnic origins. So we put aside the African novelist Chinua Achebe's abrasive, troubling *Things Fall Apart* and gravitate toward hymns on Africa, cradle of all civilizations.

What about the phenomenon called political correctness? Raising the standard of civility and tolerance in the university has been—who can deny it?—a very good thing. Yet this admirable impulse has expanded to the point where one is enjoined to speak well—and only well—of women, blacks, gays, the disabled, in fact of virtually everyone. And we can owe this expansion in many ways to the student culture. Students now do not wish to be criticized, not in any form. (The culture of consumption never criticizes them, at least not *overtly.*) In the current university, the movement for urbane tolerance has devolved into an imperative against critical reaction, turning much of the intellectual life into a dreary Sargasso Sea. At a certain point, professors stopped being usefully sensitive and became more like careful retailers who have it as a cardinal point of doctrine never to piss the customers off.

To some professors, the solution lies in the movement called cultural studies. What students need, they believe, is to form a critical perspective on pop culture. It's a fine idea, no doubt. Students should be able to run a critical commentary against the stream of consumer stimulations in which they're immersed. But cultural-studies programs rarely work, because no matter what you propose by way of analysis, things tend to bolt downhill toward an uncritical discussion of students' tastes, into what they like and don't like. If you want to do a Frankfurt School-style analysis of *Braveheart,* you can be pretty sure that by mid-class Adorno and Horkheimer will be consigned to the junk heap of history and you'll be collectively weighing the charms of Mel Gibson. One sometimes wonders if cultural studies hasn't prospered because, under the guise of serious intellectual analysis, it gives the customers what they most want—easy pleasure, more TV. Cultural studies becomes nothing better than what its detractors claim it is—Madonna studies—when students kick loose from the critical perspective and groove to the product, and that, in my experience teaching film and pop culture, happens plenty.

On the issue of genius, as on multiculturalism and political correctness, we professors of the humanities have, I think, also failed to press back against our students' consumer tastes. Here we tend to nurse a pair of—to put it charitably—disparate views. In one mode, we're inclined to a programmatic debunking criticism. We call the concept of genius into question. But in our professional lives per se, we aren't usually disposed against the idea of distinguished achievement. We argue animatedly about the caliber of potential colleagues. We support a star system, in which some professors are far better paid, teach less, and under better conditions than the rest. In our own profession, we are creating a system that is the mirror image of the one we're dismantling in the curriculum. Ask a professor what she thinks of the work of Stephen Greenblatt, a leading critic of Shakespeare, and you'll hear it for an hour. Ask her what her views are on Shakespeare's genius and she's likely to begin questioning the term along with the whole "discourse of evaluation." This dual sensibility may be intellectually incoherent. But in its awareness of what plays with students, it's conducive to good classroom evaluations and, in its awareness of where and how the professional bread is buttered, to self-advancement as well.

My overall point is this: It's not that a left-wing professorial coup has taken over the university. It's that at American universities, left-liberal politics have collided with the ethos of consumerism. The consumer ethos is winning.

Then how do those who at least occasionally promote genius and high literary ideals look to current students? How do we appear, those of us who take teaching to be something of a performance art and who imagine that if you give yourself over completely to your subject you'll be rewarded with insight beyond what you individually command?

I'm reminded of an old piece of newsreel footage I saw once. The speaker (perhaps it was Lenin, maybe Trotsky) was haranguing a large crowd. He was expostulating, arm waving, carrying on. Whether it was flawed technology or the man himself, I'm not sure, but the orator looked like an intricate mechanical device that had sprung into fast-forward. To my students, who mistrust enthusiasm in every form, that's me when I start riffing about Freud or Blake. But more and more, as my evaluations showed, I've been replacing enthusiasm and intellectual animation with stand-up routines, keeping it all at arm's length, praising under the cover of irony.

It's too bad that the idea of genius has been denigrated so far, because it actually offers a live alternative to the demoralizing culture of hip in which most of my students are mired. By embracing the works and lives of extraordinary people, you can adapt new ideals to revise those that came courtesy of your parents, your neighborhood, your clan—or the tube. The aim of a good liberal-arts education was once, to adapt an observation by the scholar Walter Jackson Bate, to see that "we need not be the passive victims of what we deterministically call 'circumstances' (social, cultural, or reductively psychological-personal), but that by linking ourselves through what Keats calls an 'immortal free-masonry' with the great we can become freer—freer to be ourselves, to be what we most want and value."

But genius isn't just a personal standard; genius can also have political effect. To me, one of the best things about democratic thinking is the conviction that genius can spring up anywhere. Walt Whitman is born into the working class and thirty-six years later we have a poetic image of America that gives a passionate dimension to the legalistic brilliance of the Constitution. A democracy needs to constantly develop, and to do so it requires the most powerful visionary minds to interpret the present and to propose possible shapes for the future. By continuing to notice and praise genius, we create a culture in which the kind of poetic gamble that Whitman made—a gamble in which failure would have entailed rank humiliation, depression, maybe suicide—still takes place. By rebelling against established ways of seeing and saying things, genius helps us to apprehend how malleable the present is and how promising and fraught with danger is the future. If we teachers do not endorse genius and self-overcoming, can we be surprised when our students find their ideal images in TV's latest persona ads?

A world uninterested in genius is a despondent place, whose sad denizens drift from coffee bar to Prozac dispensary, unfired by ideals, by the glowing image of the self that one might become. As Northrop Frye says in a beautiful and now dramatically unfashionable sentence, "The artist who uses the same energy and genius that Homer and Isaiah had will find that he not only lives in the same palace of art as Homer and Isaiah, but lives in it at the same time." We ought not to deny the existence of such a place simply because we, or those we care for, find the demands it makes intimidating, the rent too high.

What happens if we keep trudging along this bleak course? What happens if our most intelligent students never learn to strive to overcome what they are? What if genius, and the imitation of genius, become silly, outmoded ideas? What you're likely to get are more and more one-dimensional men and women. These will be people who live for easy pleasures, for comfort and prosperity, who think of money first, then second, and third, who hug the status quo; people who believe in God as a sort of insurance policy (cover your bets); people who are never surprised. They will be people so pleased with themselves (when they're not in despair at the general pointlessness of their lives) that they cannot imagine humanity could do better. They'll think it their highest duty to clone themselves as frequently as possible. They'll claim to be happy, and they'll live a long time.

It is probably time now to offer a spate of inspiring solutions. Here ought to come a list of reforms, with due notations about a core curriculum and various requirements. What the traditionalists who offer such solutions miss is that no matter what our current students are given to read, many of them will simply translate it into melodrama, with flat characters and predictable morals. (The unabated capitalist culture that conservative critics so often endorse has put students in a position to do little else.) One can't simply wave a curricular wand and reverse acculturation.

Perhaps it would be a good idea to try firing the counselors and sending half the deans back into their classrooms, dismantling the football team and making the stadium into a playground for local kids, emptying the fraternities, and boarding up the student-activities office. Such measures would convey the message that American colleges are not northern outposts of Club Med. A willingness on the part of the faculty to defy student conviction and affront them occasionally—to be usefully offensive— also might not be a bad thing. We professors talk a lot about subversion, which generally means subverting the views of people who never hear us talk or read our work. But to subvert the views of our students, our customers, that would be something else again.

Ultimately, though, it is up to individuals—and individual students in particular—to make their own way against the current sludgy tide. There's still the library, still the museum, there's still the occasional teacher who lives to find things greater than herself to admire. There are still fellow students who have not been cowed. Universities are inefficient, cluttered, archaic places, with many unguarded corners where one can open a book or gaze out onto the larger world and construe it freely. Those who do as much, trusting themselves against the weight of current opinion, will have contributed something to bringing this sad dispensation to an end. As for myself, I'm canning my low-key one-liners; when the kids' TV-based tastes come to the fore, I'll aim and shoot. And when it's time to praise genius, I'll try to do it in the right style, full-out, with faith that finer artistic spirits (maybe not Homer and Isaiah quite, but close, close), still alive somewhere in the ether, will help me out when my invention flags, the students doze, or the dean mutters into the phone. I'm getting back to a more exuberant style; I'll be expostulating and arm waving straight into the millennium, yes I will.

Name: _____ Date: _____

UNDERSTANDING THE TEXT

1. How does Edmundson characterize today's typical college students—physically, intellectually, emotionally?

2. How does Edmundson characterize the university, the faculty, and the quality of education they offer?

3. How does Edmundson propose to conduct himself in the future?

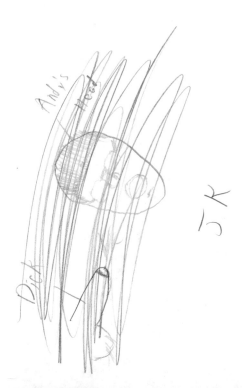

Stealth TV

Russ Baker

At Clifton High School, a mostly white, working-class institution in suburban New Jersey, it's time for second period—and for Channel One, a public-affairs TV broadcast available exclusively for school viewing. Mounted high in a corner of every classroom—as omnipresent an icon as the American flag—is a large-screen television set, provided by Channel One. The face on the screen is that of school principal William Cannici. Speaking into a microphone, he tries a few jokes, then announces student vocational-award winners. In Mrs. Rossi's Spanish class, restless students begin talking among themselves. Suddenly, the teacher shushes her charges: It's show time.

The hip-hop music starts. Heads bounce to the beat. Cut to two young, fashionably dressed anchorwomen, one white and one black. First up in the news is a tough sell to almost any viewership: the census. Point: Without an accurate count, schools can't get their rightful aid. The census form flashes on the screen. "Hey, I got that!" remarks a student. Channel One's reporter interviews a census spokesperson, a sexually ambiguous-looking woman with her hair pulled back in a ponytail. "What the heck is that?" a student in the back of the room asks with a chortle.

Time for a commercial break. Teens snowboard and dirt-bike their way through the Mountain Dew life (170 calories, 46 grams of sugar per can): "Do the Dew!" Then a Twinkies spot (150 calories, 14 grams of sugar per two-pack).

Back to the news. As a story airs about the pope's groundbreaking mea culpa over the Catholic Church's transgressions toward the Jews, much of the class is deep in chitchat; the teacher tries, without success, to silence the talk. Other students appear to be doing their homework. Two young women are checking their makeup, and four are resting their heads on their desks. Not one person has a comment about the story, described by *The New York Times* as "the most sweeping papal apology ever."

Another commercial break. As the first frames roll, a student shrieks, "Pokémon!" Declares another: "I need to get that." Next ad: Join the Marines. One viewer chimes along with the script: "The Few. The Proud. . . ."

For 10 years now, the folks behind Channel One have been able to offer advertisers a dream demographic: a captive audience composed of nearly half of all American teenagers. (And they truly are captive, as Carlotta and D.J. Maurer, two students at Perrysburg Junior High School in Ohio, can attest. Their refusal to watch Channel One in school bought them a day in the Wood County Juvenile Detention Center.) On the condition that all teachers will air and all students will watch its daily satellite-broadcast programs, Channel One lends television sets and other equipment to schools. The company, which claims to reach a teen market 50 times larger than MTV's, profits by selling two of every 12 program minutes for commercials coupled with call-in contests and cool banter.

As noxious as these school-sanctioned ads are, Channel One's success is part of a larger trend toward in-school marketing: Textbook manufacturers insert proprietary brand names into math equations, corporations provide book covers emblazoned with their logos, soda companies entice school officials into signing deals for on-campus product exclusivity, and companies donate computers that have the ability, in some cases, to track the online behavior of individual students. A whole new industry of consultants has sprung up to help corporate clients position their products in schools.

Even in today's thoroughly commercialized environment, there is something especially insidious about school-endorsed product pushing. For one thing, schools are supposed to offer a haven from the worst the world has to offer. We authorize metal detectors and locker sweeps to prevent deadly violence on campus. But there are other dangers to impressionable minds. Channel One's hyperkinetic blend of "current-affairs broadcasting" and carefully targeted commercials blurs the line between fact and fiction, between reporting that at least tries to be objective and the self-serving rhetoric of the advertising business. Unquestionably, young people lack the media "literacy" skills necessary to understand fully what they are dealing with: A recent study cited in *Education Week* shows that ninth-graders who watched ads in which professional athletes endorsed products thought the athletes had themselves paid for the ads.

CHANNEL WHAT?

Few American adults have ever heard of Channel One—a remarkable fact, considering that one in four middle and high schools now broadcasts it and an estimated 40 percent of all high school students are compelled to watch its programming every single school day. Perhaps parents do not know about Channel One because their kids (some eight million of them, in 12,000 schools) do not tell them about it. As for the key American institutions— governmental, educational—that might be expected to raise an alarm, they have mostly been looking the other way.

Last fall the first-ever government study of commercialization in the schools was published. The General Accounting Office (GAO) report, requested by two Democrats—Representative George Miller of California and Senator Christopher Dodd of Connecticut—notes that in-school marketing is dramatically on the rise and that deals between schools and companies are being made on a district-by-district basis. Local educators are not equipped to negotiate with crafty marketers bearing freebies, much less to address the larger educational issues. While the GAO study was being circulated, the Federal Trade Commission released a report specifically condemning the marketing of violent content to underage children.

In some ways, the "new" political interest in protecting our children from the onslaught of the marketers harks back to 1989, when Channel One was launched by entrepreneur Chris Whittle (later, in 1994, he sold the company to K-III Communications, now called Primedia). Initially, the service faced heavy criticism from liberal groups and from educational power-houses such as the national Parent-Teacher Association, the American Federation of Teachers (AFT), the National Education Association (NEA), and various principals' associations; even the American Academy of Pediatrics frowned upon for-profit classroom television. But the well-financed company won over school system after school system, and effective opposition dried up.

Of late, none of the major teachers' or school administrators' organizations has seemed willing to mount a serious challenge to Channel One. Two years ago, NEA officials told Channel One critics that while the association remains opposed to the service, removing it from America's classrooms was not a priority. The AFT offered a similar line. And the National Association of School Principals rebuffed Channel One opponents several times when they requested a meeting. As a result, the battle against Channel One is being waged by several tiny public-interest groups and through scattered, small-scale parent uprisings. The educational establishment apparently believes that the issue lacks urgency.

Governmental bodies tend to accept the claim that the free equipment and the "news value" of Channel One more than make up for any downside; besides, the argument goes, local governments can address the matter if they so choose. Even the GAO report declares that it is impossible to differentiate the effects of bombardment by Channel One from those of the commercial messages directed at young people outside school hours. Although the GAO researchers were undoubtedly well-meaning, such a claim is a cop-out: Many in-school marketers specially design ads, promotions, contests, and the like to track the impact of their sales pitches.

Can anyone doubt that the ads on Channel One are grossly out of place in an academic environment? Mark Crispin Miller, a professor of media and culture at New York University who studied Channel One's content in 1997, concluded that its commercial messages reinforced bad body image, emphasized the importance of buying things, and glamorized boorish and loutish behavior. To ensure "stickiness," the ad campaigns often feature interactive components. One that I saw urged students to watch a film called *Never Been Kissed,* then to call in and answer questions about the movie's content in order to qualify for a chance to win a $500 shopping spree and a watch.

Rather than defend the indefensible, Channel One insists that the ads are not what matters. At the company's Madison Avenue headquarters, sleek, gunmetal-silver placards fit for the starship *Enterprise* proclaim "Education" and "Our Missions: To Inform and Empower Young People." These displays imply that the ads are a necessary evil that makes possible a bounty of fresh educational content and free equipment. Indeed, in a meeting with me last year, Channel One officials sought repeatedly to focus attention on the educational merits of their product. The company has been able to orchestrate favorable publicity ranging from a laudatory *New York Times* op-ed by a Catholic priest who is also a principal in a Channel One school to supportive statements from the ordinarily populist Senator Paul Wellstone of Minnesota.

Company executives claim that the broadcasts hold students' interest because they deliver important information in an appealing manner. (The students appear to identify with the youthful newscasters as stars; indeed, one of them, Lisa Ling, has moved on to anchoring a commercial-network morning show.) The solution to disaffection among youths, say executives, is to deliver a product that shows them how world affairs are relevant to them and their families. "We go to Kosovo and talk to kids who are their age," said Susan Tick, an outside PR representative for Channel One. "You don't connect with them otherwise."

Even by these standards, the compilation tape Channel One gave me was not impressive: It included a segment summarizing the Bill Clinton impeachment situation, delivered at a rapid-fire pace that seemed harder for an average teen to follow than a conventional news broadcast. The commentary is often self-promotional, with Channel One correspondents and anchors gushing about how they've gotten to travel to exotic places, and with interviewed students identified as attendees of "a Channel One school."

If we are to accept Channel One's request that it be judged on its news content, we have to face the fact that there just isn't much there. Of the 10 minutes of "news," only two to three minutes is breaking news, according to William Hoynes, a Vassar College sociologist who studies the intersection of media and education. The remainder is a hodgepodge of contests, self-promotion, light features and profiles, music intros, and pop quizzes. And Hoynes concludes that even those paltry hard-news minutes frame the issues in rigid terms that do not promote original thought or critical thinking.

Not surprisingly, Channel One doesn't offer any statistics to prove that its programs benefit students. "We have attitudinal studies showing that teachers believe it to be productive," said Jeffrey Ballabon, a Channel One executive vice president. "They know kids don't read newspapers. They also don't watch the evening news." Perhaps the citation of "attitudinal" evidence is necessitated by the findings of one study the company did commission: A 1994 University of Michigan analysis found that students performed just 5 percent better in high schools that aired the programs and 8 percent better in participating middle schools—and then only in an "exemplary" (read: highly atypical) environment in which the teacher actively sought to incorporate the broadcast content into the class and made sure the students were paying attention. There was no measurable increase in discussion of news outside the school or in efforts to seek out additional information from outside news sources.

Nevertheless, most administrators and teachers seem to love their Channel One. With good reason: The company provides TV sets and a broadcast system that the schools use for their own purposes, including the principal's morning addresses. "Our district is not a real wealthy district," explains Lawrence Westerfield, principal of Mt. Healthy South Middle School in Cincinnati, Ohio, which airs Channel One. If you want the technology, says Westerfield, "you have to count on advertisers to pay."

Yet there is evidence that the schools aren't getting a very good deal. A 1998 study co-authored by Alex Molnar, an education professor at the University of Wisconsin-Milwaukee, concluded that broadcasting Channel One takes up six or seven days of instruction over the school year and costs American taxpayers $1.8 billion annually. Molnar, who heads the Center for Education Research, Analysis, and Innovation, compared the average cost of 12 daily minutes of a secondary school's time, or about $158,000 a year, with the total value of Channel One's equipment ($17,000) and the annual rental value of the equipment ($4,000). Even the value of the time spent watching the two minutes of commercials ($26,000) exceeded the value of the equipment. And those Channel One minutes add up. A child who views the shows from sixth grade to graduation will lose seven weeks of school time.

AD NAUSEAM

Despite Channel One's self-proclaimed educational mission, the company offers a different story to advertisers. As Channel One's then-president bragged to a youth marketing conference in 1994, "The biggest selling point to advertisers [is that] . . . we are forcing kids to watch two minutes of commercials. . . . The advertiser gets a group of kids who cannot go to the bathroom, who cannot change the station, who cannot listen to their mother yell in the background, who cannot be playing Nintendo, who cannot have their headsets on." Channel One continually conducts surveys about the spending patterns of teens; and its Web site, heavily touted on the shows themselves, provides an ideal means of obtaining direct feedback from the students.

Channel One also makes much of its public-service announcements, including those warning students to resist peer pressure to take drugs. Meanwhile, it airs ads stressing ways to be cool and brags to advertisers that controlled viewing in the classroom is the ideal way to play on teens' insecurity and desire to fit in.

Channel One makes a lot of money—$346 million in 1999 ad revenues—for its financially troubled parent company, Primedia, which reported a net loss of $120 million that year. With an estimated $200,000 price per 30-second ad (a rate comparable to the major networks'), Channel One is a crucial element in the company's future strategy. In its 1999 stockholder report, Primedia declared: "Our products serve highly specialized niches and capitalize on the growing trend toward targeted rather than mass information distribution. Many of the company's products, such as . . . CHANNEL ONE NEWS, . . . afford advertisers with an opportunity to directly reach niche market audiences. CHANNEL ONE NEWS *has no direct competition in the schools* [my emphasis] but does compete for advertising dollars with other media aimed at teenagers."

With so vast a market at stake, Channel One has not been reluctant to spend in order to protect its franchise. When Republican Senator Richard Shelby of Alabama, an ally of the ragtag band of Channel One opponents, initiated Senate hearings in 1999, Channel One dumped almost $1 million into a lobbying effort led by former Christian Coalition Director Ralph Reed and the powerful law firm of Preston, Gates, and Ellis—and effectively kept a lid on further action or hearings. Last spring a Shelby-sponsored sense-of-the-Senate resolution opposing commercialization of the schools was blocked by Republican Senator Sam Brownback of Kansas and heavy lobbying by Reed and former New York Senator Alfonse D'Amato. The company has other means of winning support: Channel One's Ballabon insisted on faxing me a mound of positive letters; several from students mentioned free trips to Channel One's Los Angeles production studios.

Lined up against Channel One's PR juggernaut is a spirited and diverse coalition that includes Professor Molnar's group; Ralph Nader's D.C.-based Commercial Alert; the Center for Commercial-Free Public Education, located in Oakland, California; and Obligation, Inc., a group from Birmingham, Alabama, headed by Republican businessman Jim Metrock. When Metrock found out that his children were watching Channel One, he did his own study; he's been a committed opponent ever since. He has helped recruit a number of socially conservative groups—like Phyllis Schlafly's Eagle Forum and James Dobson's Focus on the Family—some of which are more concerned with what they perceive as risqué content than with commercialism per se. In addition, Channel One's critics convinced the 15.8-million-member Southern Baptist Convention to pass a resolution in 1999 opposing the enterprise.

That's about it on a national scale. Channel One likes to keep the battleground local, where school officials often lack the training and policy sophistication to ask tough questions about content control and educational philosophy. Thus far, only one state, New York, has banned Channel One from the public schools.

Still, a few small districts have voted to bar Channel One, and Metrock says that some teachers in schools contractually obligated to show the programs are nevertheless switching them off. The company has apparently responded by warning errant schools that it will yank its equipment. And Channel One has now retained Nielsen Media Research to measure student viewing in 1,500 schools.

Sooner or later, it seems, educational advocates are going to have to make Channel One and its ilk a priority. If we are really on the brink of a top-to-bottom reconstitution of American education, then surely the intrusion of corporate products must be addressed. And enthusiasm for these new methods of "improving" the educational experience bears scrutiny if the letters of support from teachers and principals that Channel One's Ballabon forwarded to me are any evidence. Many contained the sorts of appalling errors—in spelling, grammar, syntax, and exposition—that these educators are supposed to be helping students avoid.

Were the topic ever to reach the national agenda, many vexing questions about education itself would be raised. For example, Channel One advocates contend that the broadcasts make it easier to teach young people about the news because the young hosts know how to speak kids' language. This, of course, suggests that adult educators (and parents, for that matter) are incapable of discussing the ways of the world in a compelling manner—a sentiment not everyone shares. And anyway, in an America awash in exhortations to buy and consume, shouldn't institutions of learning and discussion be free from the constant pressures toward superficiality and conformity?

Meanwhile, Primedia has announced a merger with the Internet company About.com, which has intricate business partnerships with pornography purveyors. Conservatives are upset by that, as they are with Senator Brownback, who is a leader in denouncing violence in the media yet enthusiastically backs Channel One, with its advertising for violent movies.

This year opponents are likely to concentrate on challenging the federal government's role as a major Channel One benefactor through its paid advertising for the armed services and the Office of National Drug Control Policy. But if there's strong, broad, untapped sentiment against the juggernaut, it probably needs to coalesce fairly soon: Channel One officials told me the company looks forward to rolling out the programs in thousands of additional schools.

Name: _____ Date: _____

UNDERSTANDING THE TEXT

1. According to Baker, what kind of material typically airs on Channel One? In how many states does Channel One provide programming?

2. What arguments do Channel One supporters offer in its favor?

3. What do its critics say against it?

Athletes, Outcasts and Partyers

Dianne Williams Hayes

Films about African Americans in higher education are a relatively new phenomenon but they, like other films about Blacks, still frequently resort to stereotypes.

In Spike Lee's *School Daze,* John Singleton's *Higher Learning,* and other less-known movies such as *Blue Chips* and *The Program,* African-American students tend to be shown as athletes, outcasts or partyers with little interest or engagement in the academic life of colleges and universities.

"There has been a very narrow portrayal," said Henry Hampton, producer of the award-winning *Eyes on the Prize* civil rights documentary. "For the last five to seven years, more Black films are in production, but the stereotypes persist and characters are one-dimensional. The problem is that we need to get more thoughtful portrayals," Hampton said.

"I am particularly concerned about the lack of portrayals of people who succeed academically. At the same time, we allow them without protest. Young people have got to have academic excellence as an attainable goal that is represented in film. There's a missed opportunity to show variety."

Reality for many minority students in higher education is that they often have to overcome the notion that they are getting a "free ride" or are in some way less qualified than other students. One of the reasons to be concerned about one-sided portrayals of the college experience for minorities is that the images may extend beyond the dark movie theaters into the minds of professors and fellow students.

Spike Lee's film *School Daze* was one of the first films produced by an African-American director that addressed life on a predominantly Black campus during the 1980s. While some report that many of the portrayals were accurate, it fell short of exploring the academic dimension of college life. Its premise was to take a hard and honest look at the social side of college life dealing with fraternities and sororities, classism and prejudice among African Americans.

Monty Ross, who co-produced the movie with Spike Lee, described it as an exercise in dealing with many of the issues that carry over into the classroom. "Overall, the weekend of homecoming was used to deal with issues affecting the school and inner activities of the student body as it relates to skin color, hair and African-American support of the school, as well as hazing," Ross said. "It explored the issues of sororities and fraternities, but the classroom was part of it."

Subtle Issues Overwhelmed

More recently, John Singleton attempted to address issues of race relations and campus polarization on a majority campus in his film *Higher Learning*. However, the day-to-day subtle issues that are a fact of life on many American campuses were overshadowed by stereotypical images outside the norm. Its main white character was recruited by neo-Nazis because of bad experiences with an insensitive Black roommate, and its main Black character spent his time demanding his athletic scholarship money and dodging bullets and violence on campus.

Singleton did offer some new elements, such as an older perpetual student played by rapper Ice Cube. Ice Cube began by benignly guiding newcomers, but his advice quickly became one of advocating violence as a solution to problems. The Black characters who weren't athletes were from the "hood." And none of the main Black characters were presented in a way to endear the audience. Before the athlete was hunted down by his former roommate-turned-neo-Nazi, we saw him expect special favors from the only Black faculty member we see, demand scholarship money, and show up late for track practice because he feels superior to everyone else on the team.

Frequently, African-American students on campus are portrayed as athletes with serious deficiencies in reading and basic skills and the classroom is merely a backdrop to the football field, basketball court or track. Movies such as *Blue Chips, The Program* and the highly-acclaimed documentary *Hoop Dreams* all deal with the experience of talented athletes whose primary goal is to transcend their struggling economic backgrounds with sports. College is simply a vehicle to their dreams.

While the movies address an overwhelming sentiment among many young students that sports can lead to riches and fame as coaches help them through college, there is little balance or representation of the majority of students who do not enter college on athletic scholarships. Nor do they tend to represent the middle- and upper-class students who go to class every day, graduate in four years and have aspirations of becoming doctors, lawyers and engineers.

"Blacks are portrayed as being generally deficient," said Dr. Jesse A. Rhines, assistant professor of African-American studies with a concentration in film at Rutgers University, Newark campus. "There is . . . a preference for sports and entertainment over education in these films."

Hoop Dreams is credited with being more ambitious in its complex depiction of the dream that many poor, urban youth carry of becoming the next Shaquille O'Neal. In the film, two boys are followed as they grow, from the playground to the Catholic high school that produced Isiah Thomas. Their lives are shown in detail as one is forced back to his neighborhood school while the other continues the struggle to lift his family out of poverty. College is only a way to continue to play basketball and be noticed by scouts. In this true story, few teachers or coaches talk to him about other career choices besides shooting a basketball.

"The current crop of jock films are primarily the fish out of water stories," said Butch Robinson, cowriter and producer of the film *Drop Squad,* which was released in 1994. The film, which Spike Lee executive produced, is about an African-American advertising executive who teaches his firm how to push unwanted products on his community in order to rise to the top. "The presentation of Blacks in higher education is extremely stereotypical in breadth, with no complexity to the characters." Robinson said.

"I think whites in general like their Negroes docile and concerned about things other than politics, education and their rights. The idea even with *Hoop Dreams* and the majority of films that receive the green light [is that they] provide a certain comfort for the majority viewers who do not see African Americans expressing the same desires as them. It makes more sense to perpetuate the idea of life in the ghetto and triumph if a jump shot is hit. The wonderful back story in *Hoop Dreams* was that it didn't work," said Robinson.

Robinson adds that stereotypes persist when it comes to higher education. African-American characters in these films are always characters where their "Blackness" is the prevalent issue in their role, he said. A 1970s comedy, *Soul Man,* depicted Black actress Rae Dawn Chung at Harvard University but, unlike her counterparts, she was a single mother working in the university's cafeteria to make ends meet.

THE MEN OF MOREHOUSE

Short films, which are not always seen by mass audiences, are credited with doing a better job at telling a broader range of stories that are rarely seen. For example, *The Men of Morehouse,* made by California Newsreel, examines the making of the Morehouse College student, and aired last year on public television.

California Newsreel, based in San Francisco, has released several movies that address aspects of Black life including documentaries such as *Frosh,* which looks at the first-year college experience through the eyes of an array of students, some African American. Another film, *Skin Deep,* features roundtable discussions between students of different ethnic backgrounds on the subject of race. A new film, *W.E.B. DuBois: A Biography in Four Voices,* features perspectives on the educator's life from author Toni Cade Bambara and others. Many of these documentaries are being used to fill the void through PBS and find their way into the classroom.

But with all of the criticism about the shortcomings of films that address the African-American experience, particularly on the college campus, many filmmakers and those in the industry point the finger back at viewing audiences who continue to support stereotypical films. For African Americans, Robinson describes it as simply a matter of limited opportunities for Black filmmakers.

"I have yet to see a film by a Black filmmaker that was not ambitious," Robinson said. "The prevailing thought is that they may not get another shot at it. But we are asked to solve all of the problems. The (Black) audience is starving to see themselves, see their story. We don't have the luxury to tell all the stories. If you go to see a Black film, nine times out of 10 it will be a ghetto film. We are allowed to make films about survival."

In the African-American community, the mission of telling the story of the community has frequently fallen in the hands of someone else. It wasn't until the beginning of this decade that doors have begun to open to more African-American directors, who have begun to control images (under the direction of funding studios).

Sensitivity about images in the African-American community is based on a long legacy of negative portrayals of Blacks in film. Some of the earliest films depicting African Americans produced by the American Mutoscope company included such fares as *Trilby,* an excerpted moment from the popular play *Trilby,* and *Little Billee,* vignettes of African Americans in "characteristic poses." *A Hard Wash,* shows a Black woman scrubbing her child. Spectators were to consider the scene humorous since no matter how hard the mother scrubbed, she would never get him "truly clean." *Watermelon Feast* and *Dancing Darkies* were filled with stereotypes and conformed to degrading, white-imposed stereotypes. That trend continued through *Birth of a Nation,* which played on white fears of newly-freed slaves and portrayed the Ku Klux Klan in a heroic role.

Even in the hands of African Americans, films sometimes perpetuate stereotypical images. In *House Party II* the main characters, Kid and Play, spend most of their time on the college campus partying, with little representation of the average student who can't sing or dance their way through the rigors of college life.

"It is a really complicated issue," said Cornelius Moore, co-director of California Newsreel. "The reality is that there have been few movies about education. We are only talking about a handful of movies during the past few years. The debate is much more charged, because there aren't that many Black films and we want to be portrayed in the right way, whatever that is. For us, it is more than just entertainment."

Name: _____ Date: _____

UNDERSTANDING THE TEXT

1. Hayes and those she interviews are quite critical of the mainstream films they discuss. Why? And why do they believe this is such a critical issue?

2. According to Hayes and those she interviews, what are the sources of these films' failings? (Identify two.)

3. According to Hayes, what kinds of films seem to represent the situation more accurately?

Lisa and American Anti-Intellectualism

Aeon J. Skoble

American society has generally had a love-hate relationship with the notion of the intellectual. On the one hand, there is a sense of respect for the professor or the scientist, but at the same time there is great resentment of the "ivory tower" or the "bookish"; a defensiveness about intelligent or learned people. The republican ideals of the Founders presuppose an enlightened citizenry, yet today, the introduction of even remotely sophisticated analysis of political topics is decried as "elitism." Everyone respects a historian, yet a historian's opinion may be disregarded on the grounds that it is "no more valid" than that of the "working man." Populist commentators and politicians frequently exploit this resentment of expertise while relying on it as it suits them, for example when a candidate attacks his opponent for being an "Ivy League elitist" while in fact being a product of (or relying on advisers from) a similar educational background.

Similarly, a hospital may consult a bioethicist, or it may reject the counsel of bioethicists, on the grounds that they are too abstract and unconnected to the realities of medicine. Indeed, it seems as though most people like being able to support their positions by citing experts, but then invoke populist sentiment when the experts don't support their view. For instance, I may lend support to my argument by citing an expert who agrees with me, but if an expert disagrees, I may respond "what does he know?" or "I'm entitled to my opinion too." Oddly, we see anti-intellectualism even among intellectuals. For example, at many universities today, both among the student body and the faculty, the role of the classics, and humanities generally, has been greatly diminished. The trend has clearly been to develop pre-professional programs and emphasize "relevance"; whereas traditional humanities classes are regarded as a luxury or an enhancement, but not truly necessary features of a college education. At best they are seen as vehicles for developing "transferable skills" such as composition or critical thinking.

There seem to be periodic pendulum swings: in the 1950s and early 1960s, there was tremendous respect for scientists, as the nation found itself competing against the Soviets in such areas as space exploration. Today, it seems the pendulum has reversed swing, as the current *Zeitgeist* holds all opinions to be equally valid. But at the same time, people still seem interested in what alleged experts have to say. A cursory review of TV talk shows or newspaper letters-to-the-editor reveals this ambivalence. The talk show will book an expert because, presumably, people will be interested in that person's analysis or opinion. But the panelists or audience members who disagree with the expert will argue that their opinions, their perspectives, are just as worthwhile. A newspaper will run an opinion column by a specialist, whose analysis on a situation may be better informed than the average person's, but the letters from people who disagree will often be based on the underlying (if unstated) premise that "No one really knows anything" or "It's all a matter of opinion, and mine counts too." This last rationale is particularly insidious: in fact, if it were true that everything were merely a matter of opinion, then it actually would follow that mine is as relevant as the expert's; indeed there would be no such thing as expertise.

So, it is fair to say that American society is conflicted about intellectuals. Respect for them seems virtually to go hand in hand with resentment. This is a puzzling social problem, and also one of great importance, for we seem to be on the verge of a new "dark ages," where not only the notion of expertise, but all standards of rationality are being challenged. This clearly has significant social consequences. As a vehicle for exploring this issue, it may be surprising to choose a TV show which, at first glance, seems devoted to the idea that dumber is better; but actually, of the many things that *The Simpsons* skillfully illustrates about society, the American ambivalence about expertise and rationality is clearly one of them.[1]

On *The Simpsons,* Homer is a classic example of an anti-intellectual dolt, as are most of his acquaintances, and his son. But his daughter, Lisa, is not only pro-intellectual, she is smart beyond her years. She is extremely intelligent and sophisticated, and is often seen out-thinking those around her. Naturally, for this she is mocked by the other children at school and generally ignored by the adults. On the other hand, her favorite TV show is the same one as her brother's: a mindlessly violent cartoon. Her treatment on the show, I argue, captures the love-hate relationship American society has with intellectuals.[2] Before turning to the ways in which it does this, let's have a closer look at the problem.

FALLACIOUS AUTHORITY AND REAL EXPERTISE

It is a staple of introductory logic courses that it is a fallacy to "appeal to authority," yet people typically make more out of this than is appropriate. Strictly in terms of logic, it's always a mistake to argue that a proposition is true because so-and-so says it is, but appeals to authority are more commonly used to show that we have good reason to believe the proposition, as opposed to being proof of its truth. Like all fallacies involving relevance, the problem with most appeals to authority is that they are invoking the authority in an irrelevant way. For example, in matters which really are subjective, such as which pizza or soft drink I should buy, invoking anyone else is irrelevant, since I may not have the same tastes.[3] In other cases, the error is in assuming that because a person is an authority about one thing, that person's expertise should carry the day in all areas. We see this in celebrity endorsements for products unrelated to that person's field. For example, Troy McClure endorsing Duff Beer would not constitute a valid appeal to authority, since being an actor doesn't make one an expert on beer. (And experience is not the same as expertise: Barney is not an expert on beer either.) In other cases, the appeal is fallacious on the grounds that some matters cannot be settled by appeal to experts, not because they are subjective, but because they are unknowable, for instance the future of scientific progress. The classic example here is Einstein's claim in 1932 that "there is not the slightest indication that [nuclear] energy will ever be obtainable."[4]

But after building up all this skepticism about appeals to authority, it's worth remembering that some people actually do know more about some things than other people, and in many cases, the fact that an authority on a subject tells us something really is a good reason to believe it. For example, since I have no first-hand knowledge of the Battle of Marathon, I am going to have to rely on what other people tell me, and a classical historian is precisely the sort of person I should go to, whereas a physician probably is not.[5]

Often what people resent is the application of wisdom, especially to moral or social ideals. People may argue that yes, there is such a thing as being an expert on the Greco-Persian Wars, but that doesn't mean that person can inform our discussion about world politics today.[6] You may be an expert on Aristotle's moral theory, but that doesn't mean you can tell me how I should live. This sort of resistance to expertise stems partly from the nature of a democratic regime, and the problem is not new, but was identified by philosophers as early as Plato. Since, in a democracy, all voices get heard, this can lead people to conclude that all voices have equal value. Democracies tend to justify themselves by contrast to the aristocracies or oligarchies they replace or resist. In those elitist societies, some presume to know more, or actually to be better people; whereas we democrats know better: all are equal. But of course, political equality doesn't imply that no one can possess knowledge that others lack, and indeed few people think this about most skills, for example plumbing or auto repair. No one, though (they say), can know more than anyone else about how to live, how to be just. Hence a kind of relativism develops: from the rejection of ruling elites, who in fact may not have had any better idea than anyone else about justice, to a rejection of the notion of objective standards of right and wrong entirely. What is right is what I feel is right, what is right-for-me. Today, there is a trend even in the academy to dispute notions of objectivity and expertise. There are said to be no true histories, only different interpretations of history.[7] There are no correct interpretations of literary works, only different interpretations.[8] Even physical science is said to be value-laden and non-objective.[9]

So we have all these factors contributing to a climate in which the notion of expertise is eroded, yet at the same time we see countervailing trends. If there's no such thing as expertise, and all opinions are equally valid, why are the talk shows and bestseller lists populated by experts on love and angels? Why watch those shows or read books in the first place? Why send the kids to school? Clearly, people do still put some stock in the notion of expertise, and in many cases, yearn for its guidance. People actually seem to have some tendencies towards wanting to be told what to do. Some critics of religion ascribe its influence to this psychological need, but we need look no further than the political realm to see evidence of it. People look to political figures for their "leadership": we're having a problem with unemployment—doesn't anyone know how to do something about that? This person would make a better president than that one because he knows how to reduce crime, end poverty, make our children better, and so on. But the ambivalence shows itself very clearly in these contexts. If candidate Smith bases his appeal on his expertise and ability to "get the job done," candidate Jones will likely charge Smith with being an elite, a "pointy-head." We also see the paradoxical situation wherein celebrities' pronouncements on political matters taken seriously, as if being a talented musician or actor gave greater weight to one's political views, while at the same time the notion of being an expert on government is derided. With whose views are most Americans more familiar, Alec Baldwin and Charlton Heston, or John Rawls and Robert Nozick?

In addition to political expertise, people also yearn for, and seem least ambivalent about, technological expertise. Most people are quick to acknowledge their own incompetence at plumbing, auto repair, and surgery, and happily turn those tasks over to the experts. In the case of the surgeon, we do see another manifestation of the ambivalence I have in mind, namely when people defend alternative medicine or spiritual healing—what do doctors know? This is a trickle-down from the currently-fashionable trend in academia which maintains that all science is value-laden and non-objective. But we don't have any advocates of "alternative plumbing" or "spiritual auto repair," so these people's expertise is more generally accepted; and do-it-yourselfers are not a counter-example, since that's more a matter of regarding oneself as that sort of craftsman, rather than denying that anyone else is. Also, since plumbers and mechanics less frequently position themselves as experts in fields beyond their own, as surgeons might position themselves as ethicists, they are less susceptible to being regarded skeptically.[10]

Do We Admire or Laugh at Lisa?

American anti-intellectualism, then, is pervasive but not all-encompassing. As it does with many other aspects of modern society, *The Simpsons* often uses this theme as fodder for its satire. In the Simpson family, only Lisa could really be described as an intellectual. But her portrayal as such is not unequivocally flattering. In contrast to her relentlessly ignorant father, she is often shown having the right answer to a problem or a more perceptive analysis of a situation, for example when she exposes political corruption[11] or when she gives up her dream of owning a pony so that Homer won't have to work three jobs.[12]

When Lisa discovers the truth behind the myth of Jebediah Springfield, many people are unconvinced, but Homer says, "you're always right about this sort of thing."[13] In "Homer's Triple Bypass," Lisa actually talks Dr. Nick through a heart operation and saves her father's life. But other times, her intellectualism is itself used as the butt of the joke, as if she were "too" smart, or merely preachy. For instance, her principled vegetarianism is revealed as dogmatic and inconsistent,[14] and she uses Bart in a science experiment without his knowledge,[15] evoking examples of the worst sort of arrogance, such as the infamous Tuskegee study.[16] She agitates to join the football team, but it turns out she is more interested in making a point than in playing.[17] So although her wisdom is sometimes presented as valuable, other times it is presented as a case of being sanctimonious or condescending.

One common populist criticism of the intellectual is that "you're no better than the rest of us." The point of this attack seems to be that if I can show that the alleged sage is "really" a regular person, then maybe I don't have to be as impressed with his opinion. Thus the expression "Hey, he puts his pants on one leg at a time just like the rest of us." The implication of this non-sequitur is clearly "he is just a regular person like you and me, so why should we be awed by his alleged expertise?" In Lisa's case, we are shown that she has many of the same foibles as many kids: she joins her non-intellectual brother in revelry as they watch the mindlessly violent *Itchy and Scratchy* cartoon, she worships the teen idol Corey, she plays with Springfield's analogue to the Barbie Doll, Malibu Stacy. So we are given ample opportunity to see Lisa as "no better" in many respects, thus giving us another window for not taking her smarts seriously. Of course, it is true that she is a young girl, and one might argue that this is merely typical young girl behavior, but since in so many other cases she is presented not simply as a prodigy but as preternaturally wise, the fondness for *Itchy and Scratchy* and Corey seem to be highlighted, taking on greater significance. Lisa is portrayed as the avatar of logic and wisdom, but then she also worships Corey, so she's "no better." In "Lisa the Skeptic," Lisa is the sole voice of reason when the town becomes convinced that "the skeleton of an angel" has been found (it's a hoax), but when it seems to speak, Lisa is as afraid as everyone else.

Lisa's relationship with the Malibu Stacy doll actually takes center stage in one episode,[18] and even this highlights an ambivalence in society about rationalism. It gradually occurs to Lisa that the Malibu Stacy doll does not offer a positive role model for young girls, and she presses for (and actually contributes to) the development of a different doll which encourages girls to achieve and learn. But the makers of Malibu Stacy counter with a new version of their doll, which triumphs on the toy market. The fact that the "less intellectual" doll is vastly preferred over Lisa's doll, even though all of Lisa's objections are reasonable, demonstrates the ways in which reasonable ideas can be made to take a back seat to "having fun" and "going with the flow." This debate is often played out in the real world, of course: Barbie is the subject of perennial criticism along the lines of Lisa's critique of Malibu Stacy, yet remains immensely popular, and in general, we often see intellectual critiques of toys dismissed as "out of touch" or elitist.[19]

PHILOSOPHER KINGS? D'OH!

A more specific instance of the way *The Simpsons* reflects American ambivalence towards the intellectual is found in the episode "They Saved Lisa's Brain."[20] In this episode, Lisa joins the local chapter of Mensa, which already includes Professor Frink, Dr. Hibbert, and the Comic Book Guy. Together they end up in charge of Springfield. Lisa rhapsodizes about the rule of the intellectuals, a true rationalist utopia, but too many of their programs alienate the regular citizens of the town (including, of course, Homer, who leads the charge of the idiot brigade). It would be easy enough to see this sequence of events as a satire on the way the average person is too stupid to recognize the rule of the wise, but more than that is being satirized here. Also under attack is the very notion of rule of the wise—the Mensans have some legitimately good ideas (more rational traffic patterns), but also some ridiculous ones (censorship, mating rituals inspired by *Star Trek*), and they squabble amongst themselves. The Mensans offer something of value, especially in contrast to the corrupt regime of Mayor Quimby or the reign of idiocy that Homer represents, and Lisa's intentions are good, but it is impossible to see this episode as unequivocally pro-intellectual, since one theme is clearly that utopian schemes by elites are unstable, inevitably unpopular, and sometimes foolish. As Paul Cantor argues, "the utopia episode embodies the strange mixture of intellectualism and anti-intellectualism characteristic of *The Simpsons*. In Lisa's challenge to Springfield, the show calls attention to the cultural limitations of small-town America, but it also reminds us that intellectual disdain for the common man can be carried too far and that theory can all too easily lose touch with common sense."[21]

It is actually true, however, that utopian schemes by elites tend to be ill-conceived, or are power-grabbing schemes masquerading as the common good. But is the only alternative Homer's mob or Quimby's oligarchy? The framers of the United States Constitution hoped to combine democratic principles (a Congress) with some of the benefits of an undemocratic elite rule (a Senate, a Supreme Court, a Bill of Rights). This has had mixed results, but in contrast to other alternatives seems to have fared well. Is all of our society's ambivalence about intellectuals due to this constitutional tension? Surely not. That is part of it, but, more likely than not, this ambivalence is a manifestation of deeper psychological conflicts. We want to have authoritative guidance, but we also want autonomy. We don't like feeling stupid, yet when we are honest we realize we need to learn some things. We respect the accomplishments of others, but sometimes feel threatened and resentful. We have a respect for authorities when it suits us, and embrace relativism in other cases. The "we" here is, of course, a generalization: some people manifest this conflict less than others (or in a few cases not at all), but it seems an apt description of a general social outlook. Unsurprisingly, *The Simpsons,* our most profoundly satirical TV show, both illustrates and instantiates it.

The ambivalence in American society towards the intellectual, if it is indeed a deep-rooted psychological phenomenon, is not likely to go away any time soon. But no one is better off for encouraging or promoting anti-intellectualism. Those who wish to save the republic from the tyranny of Professor Frink and The Comic Book Guy need to find ways to argue against it that do not entail a wholesale attack on the ideal of intellectual development. Those who champion the common man ought not do so in ways that belittle the achievements of the learned. That approach is tantamount to defending Homer's right to live as a stupid person by criticizing Lisa for being smart.[22] That's not a sound idea for the development of the nation or of any individual.[23]

ENDNOTES

[1] Is it anti-intellectual for a Ph.D. in philosophy to write an essay about a TV show? As we argued in the Introduction, not necessarily: it depends on whether or not the show can illuminate some philosophical problem, or serve as an accessible example when explaining a point. If we wanted to adopt an anti-intellectual approach, we could argue that all one needs to know about life can be learned from watching TV, but that's clearly not what we are saying; indeed, we're trying to use people's interest in the show as a way to get them to read more philosophy.

[2] Intellectuals and experts are not the same thing, of course: many intellectuals are not experts in anything. But I suspect that the antipathy towards both is similarly rooted, and that the distinction is lost on those who would be inclined to reject or scorn both.

[3] This is not to address the arguments concerning whether or not there can be objective criteria for judging food, but simply to distinguish between the way in which Smith's preference for chocolate over vanilla is really different from Jones's preference for murder over counseling.

[4] Quoted in Christopher Cerf and Victor Navasky, *The Experts Speak* (New York: Pantheon Books, 1984), p. 215.

[5] Of course, there are the odd cases where the physician in question is, say, as a hobby, also an expert on the Battle of Marathon, but I am speaking here of the physician qua physician.

[6] In case you're wondering, see Peter Green's *The Greco-Persian Wars* (Berkeley: University of California Press, 1996).

[7] See for example, Mary Lefkowitz's book *Not Out of Africa* (New York: Basic Books, 1996), in which she recounts her experiences as a classicist trying to maintain standards of rational inquiry in the heated area of race-based archeology.

[8] For a rare objective account of artistic interpretation, see William Irwin's *Intentionalist Interpretation: A Philosophical Explanation and Defense* (Westport, CT: Greenwood Press, 1999). Ironically, at the same time the notion of truth and expertise is being challenged within the academy—there are no such things as experts on morality—the talk shows and bestseller lists are populated with experts on such things as relationships, horoscopes, and angels. But these experts are heeded, I think, only to the extent that they confirm a person's predispositions, and rejected on grounds I have outlined when they do not. To be sure, the rejection of knowledge claims in the realm of values is different from the rejection of knowledge claims in physical matters, but what is interesting is that we do see both, and at the same time we also see bogus claims of expertise on a host of inappropriate matters.

[9] See, for example, Alan Sokal and Jean Bricmont, *Fashionable Nonsense: Postmodern Intellectuals' Abuse of Science* (New York: Picador, 1998). The springboard for this book was Sokal's now-famous hoax, in which he submitted a bogus essay based on this theme, which was readily accepted by scientifically challenged journal editors as a fine work. That essay was "Transgressing

the Boundaries: Toward a Transformative Hermeneutics of Quantum Gravity," originally published in *Social Text* 46–47, (1996), pp. 217–252.

[10] This also highlights ways in which popular attitudes towards "authorities" and "intellectuals" are not exactly the same. People are less resistant to an authority or expert when the area seems not to be an intellectual one, as for example we all recognize the plumber's expertise; but of course being an expert in anything requires a degree of intellectualism, so the distinction is a fallacious one, and is more a reflection of people's attitudes than a statement about the intellectual level of expert craftsmen. Expert craftsmen obviously do possess wisdom, but are often seen as less threatening to those who don't possess the wisdom. This might be due to the fact that when we speak of "intellectuals" or "smart people," we are describing a general characteristic which sets the person apart, whereas when we speak of an "expert," we are only describing an attribute which we may regard as isolated, and thus feel less threatened. Lisa is an intellectual (valuing the pursuit of wisdom) and very smart, while not specifically an "expert" on anything.

[11] "Mr. Lisa Goes to Washington."

[12] "Lisa's Pony."

[13] "Lisa the Iconoclast."

[14] "Lisa the Vegetarian."

[15] "Duffless."

[16] This was a case in which the doctors experimented without consent, and with little regard for the well-being of the "participants," who were infected with syphilis.

[17] "Bart Star."

[18] "Lisa vs. Malibu Stacy."

[19] GI Joe, for example, is criticized for promoting militarism and violence, as do all "gun" toys, yet parents overwhelmingly reject the calls of some intellectuals that kids should be guided towards different play.

[20] For futher discussion of this episode, see Chapter 11 of this volume.

[21] Ibid., p. 178.

[22] Some argue that, indeed, Homer does not have the right to live as a stupid person. There may be something to this, but it's neither here nor there with respect to the narrower argument I am making here.

[23] I am grateful to Mark Conard and William Irwin for helping me clarify several of my points and reminding me of several useful examples.

Name: _____   Date: _____

UNDERSTANDING THE TEXT

1. According to Skoble, how do Americans typically view expertise? Why?

2. Skoble entitles one section of his article, "Do We Admire or Laugh at Lisa?" What is his answer?

3. According to Skoble, how does the episode "They Saved Lisa's Brain" represent intellectualism?

Yes, America Has a Class System. See *Frasier.*

Anita Gates

D r. Frasier Crane's apartment says a lot about him. The tan suede sofa is a copy of one Coco Chanel had in her Paris atelier. The view is the Seattle skyline. There are Lichtensteins on the wall, a baby grand in the alcove and a finely ground Kenya blend in the coffeemaker.

All Frasier (Kelsey Grammer) really wants is to be Cary Grant, but he can never quite pull it off. Even when he, his ex-wife and his brother find themselves in bathrobes (but let's call them dressing gowns) in a great Art Deco hotel room discussing irony, superegos, eggs Florentine and—oh, by the way—a tiny sexual infidelity, as he did in a recent episode, Frasier can't help summing it all up with "Well, isn't this peachy?"

And if Frasier's own failings weren't enough to sabotage his efforts at urban sophistication, there's his father, Martin Crane (John Mahoney), retired cop, beer drinker, television watcher, plain speaker,whose sense of style is symbolized by the dreadful striped easy chair with duct-tape accents that he has plunked down in the middle of his son's elegant minimalism.

The dangers of class mobility in America have never been more eloquently addressed. And class is a subject long overdue for discussion, now that three or four people have admitted that they would have liked Paula Jones better if she'd gone to all the right schools.

There may be a hundred reasons why *Frasier* has been a hit sitcom since NBC introduced it in 1993 or why it has won the best-comedy Emmy Award every year it has been on the air, but for many viewers the heart of the series is the Cranes' intrafamily culture clash, the kind that's bound to occur when blue-collar Americans send their children to Harvard.

American television has never dealt much with the class system, possibly because of the lingering belief that we don't have one. Most series have picked a socioeconomic level and stuck with it: struggling working class from *The Life of Riley* to *Roseanne,* solidly, comfortably middle class from *Father Knows Best* to *Home Improvement,* or filthy rich on *Dallas* and *Dynasty.*

One of the few conspicuously rich households on the 1998 schedule belongs to Maxwell Sheffield on *The Nanny*, a sitcom about a Broadway producer with a British accent who hires and learns to love a loud young woman with a Queens accent and very short skirts. The class gap on *The Nanny* is exaggerated for broad laughs, just as a larger gap was on *The Beverly Hillbillies* 30 years ago. Even *Fresh Prince of Bel Air,* Will Smith's sitcom about an inner-city teen-ager relocated to his wealthy relatives' home in a posh part of Los Angeles, tended to rely on stereotypes about the stuffy rich.

The closest thing to a serious portrayal of class mobility must have been *The Millionaire,* the 1950s series about a billionaire who liked to amuse himself by giving $1 million (tax free, that was the great part) to some deserving stranger. The half-hour was devoted to the story of how the lucky man or woman handled that new-found wealth—usually badly.

But on innumerable shows, especially rags-to-riches mini-series, that sort of transition is a snap. Maybe that's because television has usually treated class differences as if they were strictly about net worth. Lucy and Ricky Ricardo often had more money than Fred and Ethel Mertz, because Ricky was a successful band leader (and eventually a movie actor), but they never seemed to have different tastes in fashion, food or art. At least not to the degree found among the Cranes.

Viewers quickly learned who they were dealing with during the first season of *Frasier* when, over latte at Cafe Nervosa, Frasier's dapper brother, Niles, described a trick he had played on someone at his wine club: switching labels between a Chateau Petrus and a Fourcas-Dupré. "What scamps you are!" said Frasier. "His face must have turned redder than a Pichon-Longueville." The difference between the brothers is that Frasier knows they're being pretentious; Niles honestly doesn't.

David Hyde Pierce, who plays Niles, has said that his character was originally explained to him as "what Frasier would be if he had never gone to Boston and never been exposed to the people at Cheers."

Frasier's character was created in 1984 for *Cheers,* then NBC's highest-rated sitcom, as a love interest for Diane Chambers (Shelley Long). A psychiatrist with elbow patches and pear-shaped vowels, he was an educated and sophisticated contrast to the jovially working-class gang that hung out at the show's namesake Boston bar. Diane left Frasier at the altar, but he kept his seat at the bar, looking down his nose at the others' failings for eight more seasons. Luckily for Frasier, Martin never flew into town to reveal his son's humble origins. *Cheers,* in the tradition of a class-free America, acknowledged taste and economic differences, but in script after script it insisted that the postal worker and the professor might really socialize.

Back in Seattle, Frasier has given that sort of thing up, possibly because he gets enough blue-collar atmosphere at home.

Maybe, the Crane boys sometimes wonder, there was a switched-at-birth mistake at the hospital. "Frasier, is he our real father?" Niles once asked. Frasier answered tolerantly: "Now don't start that again. We've been having this discussion since we were children."

At times the brothers think they might be able to sophisticate Martin by exposing him to the finer things. Frasier recalls that even their own tastes were not always beyond reproach. "Remember," he tells Niles, "when you used to think the 1812 Overture was a great piece of classical music?" Niles smiles wistfully. "Was I ever that young?" he says.

But that strategy doesn't work and neither does Frasier's attempt to buy his father an Armani suit. Martin insists on stopping at a discount store, where he finds a wrinkle-resistant sharkskin ensemble instead. Offered any restaurant in town for his birthday celebration, Dad wants to go to Hoppy's Old Heidelberg. Which may be better than the steak place he once dragged his sons to where patrons choose their meal from "the steak trolley" and anyone wearing a necktie has it cut off—even if it's Hugo Boss.

Although Frasier earns his living in broadcasting (giving psychiatric advice on a radio call-in show), he makes fun of his father's unfortunate television habit. When he buys Martin a telescope, he says "Just think of it as having 100 more channels to watch."

But Martin won't let his sons undermine his confidence in his common-man tastes and often gives as good as he gets. He refers to Frasier's breakfast of a bran muffin and a touch of yogurt as "girlie food" and corrects Niles when he describes the cuisine at a certain restaurant as "to die for." "Niles, your country and your family are to die for," Martin reminds him. "Food is to eat." Martin isn't oblivious to changing standards around him; he just thinks they're insane. "A dollar fifty for coffee?" he says in one show. "What kind of world are we living in?"

One of Martin's finest moments comes when Frasier, planning an old-fashioned live radio play, explains to Niles, "People of Dad's generation would sit around at night listening to the radio, absolutely mesmerized." Before Niles has a chance to say that yes, he's well aware of that, Martin gives his older son a look and says, "We were a simple people."

One reason *Frasier* works is that both classes are made up of good people with values, which happen to be expressed in different ways. The show gives both coastal yuppies and Middle America a good name.

Kelsey Grammer once described his character, at a Museum of Television and Radio seminar, as "flawed and silly and pompous and full of himself" but "genuinely kind" and "totally vulnerable."

And then there's Niles. Niles, who is so out of touch with the mainstream that he explains creative visualization by suggesting that a radio listener might have "a dog-eared copy of *Middlemarch*" nearby. That he tries to order a Stoli gibson with three pearl onions at a theme restaurant. (Niles who, by the way, mentions his $400 Bruno Maglis months before O. J. Simpson mentions his.) Niles of the cute smirk and boyish blond good looks (Leonardo DiCaprio in 15 years, if he takes care of himself) and tart tongue. Lilith, Frasier's formidable ex-wife, is in town. "Ah," says Niles, "that explains why blood was pouring from all my faucets this morning."

But also Niles who, despite his elegance, can't dance ("Start with your left foot," suggests his instructor. "Which one?" Niles asks, all too honestly). And who has a painful case of unspoken, unrequited love for Daphne Moon (Jane Leeves), his father's young English (working-class) live-in physical therapist.

Which could begin a list of things the *Frasier* writers are doing right: unrequited love as an opportunity for bawdy double-entendre (Daphne to Niles: "I'm beginning to think I should spend an hour or two on the couch with you"), the lovable dog whom the lead character hates, Niles's never-seen monster of an estranged wife and occasional excursions into farce.

The writers throw in literary and theatrical references— without explanation, God bless them—to the likes of Dorothy Parker ("What fresh hell is this?"), *A Chorus Line* ("I'm a dancer. A dancer dances.") and *Hamlet,* sort of ("We're a hit. A palpable hit.").

While most sitcoms change scenes with a shot of the exterior of a building and some perky music, *Frasier* does it with subtitles like "A Coupla White Guys Sittin' 'Round Talkin'" and "Could Guy's Last Name Be Feydeau?"

The show is just plain smart. But America might not forgive the Crane brothers their sophistication, their culinary pretensions and their decorating budgets if they didn't have Martin around to remind them where they came from.

Name: _____ Date: _____

UNDERSTANDING THE TEXT

1. According to Gates, what is the chief difference between Frasier and Niles?

2. *Frasier* has been a top-rated show since it first aired in 1993. How does Gates account for its continued popularity?

3. "The show is just plain smart," Gates concludes. What, specifically, does she think is "smart" about it?

ADDITIONAL READINGS

Birkerts, Sven: *The Gutenberg Elegies: The Fate of Reading in an Electronic Age.* 1994. New York: Fawcett-Ballantine, 1995.

Bloom, Alan. *The Closing of the American Mind.* New York: Simon and Schuster, 1987.

Denby, David. *Great Books: My Adventures with Homer, Rousseau, Woolf, and Other Indestructible Writers of the Western World.* New York: Simon and Schuster, 1996.

Hirsch, E. D. *Cultural Literacy: What Every American Needs to Know.* Boston: Houghton, Mifflin, 1987.

Hofstadter, Richard. *Anti-Intellectualism in American Life.* New York: Random House, 1963.

Jacoby, Russell. *The Last Intellectuals: American Culture in the Age of Academe.* New York: Basic Books, 1987.

Marc, David. *Bonfire of the Humanities: Television, Subliteracy, and Long-Term Memory Loss.* The Television Series. Syracuse: Syracuse UP, 1995.

Miller, Mark Crispin. *The Bush Dyslexicon: Observations on a National Disorder.* New York: Norton, 2001.

Newman, John Henry. *The Idea of a University.* 1852. Notre Dame: U of Notre Dame P, 1982.

Shor, Ira. *Culture Wars: School and Society in the Conservative Restoration, 1969–1984.* Critical Social Thought. Boston: Routledge & Kegan Paul, 1986.

Washburn, Katharine and John Thornton. *Dumbing Down: Essays on the Strip-Mining of American Culture.* New York: Norton, 1996.

CHAPTER V

That's Entertainment: Politics and the News

The Age of Show Business

Neil Postman

A dedicated graduate student I know returned to his small apartment the night before a major examination only to discover that his solitary lamp was broken beyond repair. After a whiff of panic, he was able to restore both his equanimity and his chances for a satisfactory grade by turning on the television set, turning off the sound, and with his back to the set, using its light to read important passages on which he was to be tested. This is one use of television—as a source of illuminating the printed page.

But the television screen is more than a light source. It is also a smooth, nearly flat surface on which the printed word may be displayed. We have all stayed at hotels in which the TV set has had a special channel for describing the day's events in letters rolled endlessly across the screen. This is another use of television—as an electronic bulletin board.

Many television sets are also large and sturdy enough to bear the weight of a small library. The top of an old-fashioned RCA console can handle as many as thirty books, and I know one woman who has securely placed her entire collection of Dickens, Flaubert, and Turgenev on the top of a 21-inch Westinghouse. Here is still another use of television—as bookcase.

I bring forward these quixotic uses of television to ridicule the hope harbored by some that television can be used to support the literate tradition. Such a hope represents exactly what Marshall McLuhan used to call "rear-view mirror" thinking: the assumption that a new medium is merely an extension or amplification of an older one; that an automobile, for example, is only a fast horse, or an electric light a powerful candle. To make such a mistake in the matter at hand is to misconstrue entirely how television redefines the meaning of public discourse. Television does not extend or amplify literate culture. It attacks it. If television is a continuation of anything, it is of a tradition begun by the telegraph and photograph in the mid-nineteenth century, not by the printing press in the fifteenth.

What is television? What kinds of conversations does it permit? What are the intellectual tendencies it encourages? What sort of culture does it produce?

These are the questions to be addressed in the rest of this [essay], and to approach them with a minimum of confusion, I must begin by making a distinction between a technology and a medium. We might say that a technology is to a medium as the brain is to the mind. Like the brain, a technology is a physical apparatus. Like the mind, a medium is a use to which a physical apparatus is put. A technology becomes a medium as it employs a particular symbolic code, as it finds its place in a particular social setting, as it insinuates itself into economic and political contexts. A technology, in other words, is merely a machine. A medium is the social and intellectual environment a machine creates.

Of course, like the brain itself, every technology has an inherent bias. It has within its physical form a predisposition toward being used in certain ways and not others. Only those who know nothing of the history of technology believe that a technology is entirely neutral. There is an old joke that mocks that naive belief. Thomas Edison, it goes, would have revealed his discovery of the electric light much sooner than he did except for the fact that every time he turned it on, he held it to his mouth and said, "Hello? Hello?"

Not very likely. Each technology has an agenda of its own. It is, as I have suggested, a metaphor waiting to unfold. The printing press, for example, had a clear bias toward being used as a linguistic medium. It is *conceivable* to use it exclusively for the reproduction of pictures. And, one imagines, the Roman Catholic Church would not have objected to its being so used in the sixteenth century. Had that been the case, the Protestant Reformation might not have occurred, for as Luther contended, with the word of God on every family's kitchen table, Christians do not require the Papacy to interpret it for them. But in fact there never was much chance that the press would be used solely, or even very much, for the duplication of icons. From its beginning in the fifteenth century, the press was perceived as an extraordinary opportunity for the display and mass distribution of written language. Everything about its technical possibilities led in that direction. One might even say it was invented for that purpose.

The technology of television has a bias, as well. It is conceivable to use television as a lamp, a surface for texts, a bookcase, even as radio. But it has not been so used and will not be so used, at least in America. Thus, in answering the question, What is television?, we must understand as a first point that we are not talking about television as a technology but television as a medium. There are many places in the world where television, though the same technology as it is in America, is an entirely different medium from that which we know. I refer to places where the majority of people do not have television sets, and those who do have only one; where only one station is available; where television does not operate around the clock; where most programs have as their purpose the direct furtherance of government ideology and policy; where commercials are unknown, and "talking heads" are the principal image; where television is mostly used as if it were radio. For these reasons and more television will not have the same meaning or power as it does in America, which is to say, it is possible for a technology to be so used that its potentialities are prevented from developing and its social consequences kept to a minimum.

But in America, this has not been the case. Television has found in liberal democracy and a relatively free market economy a nurturing climate in which its full potentialities as a technology of images could be exploited. One result of this has been that American television programs are in demand all over the world. The total estimate of U.S. television program exports is approximately 100,000 to 200,000 hours, equally divided among Latin America, Asia and Europe.[1] Over the years, programs like *Gunsmoke, Bonanza, Mission: Impossible, Star Trek, Kojak,* and more recently, *Dallas* and *Dynasty* have been as popular in England, Japan, Israel and Norway as in Omaha, Nebraska. I have heard (but not verified) that some years ago the Lapps postponed for several days their annual and, one supposes, essential migratory journey so that they could find out who shot J.R. All of this has occurred simultaneously with the decline of America's moral and political prestige, worldwide. American television programs are in demand not because America is loved but because American television is loved.

We need not be detained too long in figuring out why. In watching American television, one is reminded of George Bernard Shaw's remark on his first seeing the glittering neon signs of Broadway and 42nd Street at night. It must be beautiful, he said, if you cannot read. American television is, indeed, a beautiful spectacle, a visual delight, pouring forth thousands of images on any given day. The average length of a shot on network television is only 3.5 seconds, so that the eye never rests, always has something new to see. Moreover, television offers viewers a variety of subject matter, requires minimal skills to comprehend it, and is largely aimed at emotional gratification. Even commercials, which some regard as an annoyance, are exquisitely crafted, always pleasing to the eye and accompanied by exciting music. There is no question but that the best photography in the world is presently seen on television commercials. American television, in other words, is devoted entirely to supplying its audience with entertainment.

Of course, to say that television is entertaining is merely banal. Such a fact is hardly threatening to a culture, not even worth writing a book about. It may even be a reason for rejoicing. Life, as we like to say, is not a highway strewn with flowers. The sight of a few blossoms here and there may make our journey a trifle more endurable. The Lapps undoubtedly thought so. We may surmise that the ninety million Americans who watch television every night also think so. But what I am claiming here is not that television is entertaining but that it has made entertainment itself the natural format for the representation of all experience. Our television set keeps us in constant communion with the world, but it does so with a face whose smiling countenance is unalterable. The problem is not that television presents us with entertaining subject matter but that all subject matter is presented as entertaining, which is another issue altogether.

To say it still another way: Entertainment is the supra-ideology of all discourse on television. No matter what is depicted or from what point of view, the overarching presumption is that it is there for our amusement and pleasure. That is why even on news shows which provide us daily with fragments of tragedy and barbarism, we are urged by the newscasters to "join them tomorrow." What for? One would think that several minutes of murder and mayhem would suffice as material for a month of sleepless nights. We accept the newscasters' invitation because we know that the "news" is not to be taken seriously, that it is all in fun, so to say. Everything about a news show tells us this—the good looks and amiability of the cast, their pleasant banter, the exciting music that opens and closes the show, the vivid film footage, the attractive commercials—all these and more suggest that what we have just seen is no cause for weeping. A news show, to put it plainly, is a format for entertainment, not for education, reflection or catharsis. And we must not judge too harshly those who have framed it in this way. They are not assembling the news to be read, or broadcasting it to be heard. They are televising the news to be seen. They must follow where their medium leads. There is no conspiracy here, no lack of intelligence, only a straightforward recognition that "good television" has little to do with what is "good" about exposition or other forms of verbal communication but everything to do with what the pictorial images look like.

I should like to illustrate this point by offering the case of the eighty-minute discussion provided by the ABC network on November 20, 1983, following its controversial movie *The Day After*. Though the memory of this telecast has receded for most, I choose this case because, clearly, here was television taking its most "serious" and "responsible" stance. Everything that made up this broadcast recommended it as a critical test of television's capacity to depart from an entertainment mode and rise to the level of public instruction. In the first place, the subject was the possibility of a nuclear holocaust. Second, the film itself had been attacked by several influential bodies politic, including the Reverend Jerry Falwell's Moral Majority. Thus, it was important that the network display television's value and serious intentions as a medium of information and coherent discourse. Third, on the program itself no musical theme was used as background—a significant point since almost all television programs are embedded in music, which helps to tell the audience what emotions are to be called forth. This is a standard theatrical device, and its absence on television is always ominous. Fourth, there were no commercials during the discussion, thus elevating the tone of the event to the state of reverence usually reserved for the funerals of assassinated Presidents. And finally, the participants included Henry Kissinger, Robert McNamara, and Elie Wiesel, each of whom is a symbol of sorts of serious discourse. Although Kissinger, somewhat later, made an appearance on the hit show *Dynasty,* he was then and still is a paradigm of intellectual sobriety; and Wiesel, practically a walking metaphor of social conscience. Indeed, the other members of the cast—Carl Sagan, William Buckley and General Brent Scowcroft—are, each in his way, men of intellectual bearing who are not expected to participate in trivial public matters.

The program began with Ted Koppel, master of ceremonies, so to speak, indicating that what followed was not intended to be a debate but a *discussion.* And so those who are interested in philosophies of discourse had an excellent opportunity to observe what serious television means by the word "discussion." Here is what it means: Each of six men was given approximately five minutes to say something about the subject. There was, however, no agreement on exactly what the subject was, and no one felt obliged to respond to anything anyone else said. In fact, it would have been difficult to do so, since the participants were called upon seriatim, as if they were finalists in a beauty contest, each being given his share of minutes in front of the camera. Thus, if Mr. Wiesel, who was called upon last, had a response to Mr. Buckley, who was called upon first, there would have been four commentaries in between, occupying about twenty minutes, so that the audience (if not Mr. Wiesel himself) would have had difficulty remembering the argument which prompted his response. In fact, the participants—most of whom were no strangers to television—largely avoided addressing each other's points. They used their initial minutes and then their subsequent ones to intimate their position or give an impression. Dr. Kissinger, for example, seemed intent on making viewers feel sorry that he was no longer their Secretary of State by reminding everyone of books he had once written, proposals he had once made, and negotiations he had once conducted. Mr. McNamara informed the audience that he had eaten lunch in Germany that very afternoon, and went on to say that he had at least fifteen proposals to reduce nuclear arms. One would have thought that the discussion would turn on this issue, but the others seemed about as interested in it as they were in what he had for lunch in Germany. (Later, he took the initiative to mention three of his proposals but they were not discussed.) Elie Wiesel, in a series of quasi-parables and paradoxes, stressed the tragic nature of the human condition, but because he did not have the time to provide a context for his remarks, he seemed quixotic and confused, conveying an impression of an itinerant rabbi who has wandered into a coven of Gentiles.

In other words, this was no discussion as we normally use the word. Even when the "discussion" period began, there were no arguments or counterarguments, no scrutiny of assumptions, no explanations, no elaborations, no definitions. Carl Sagan made, in my opinion, the most coherent statement—a four-minute rationale for a nuclear freeze—but it contained at least two questionable assumptions and was not carefully examined. Apparently, no one wanted to take time from his own few minutes to call attention to someone else's. Mr. Koppel, for his part, felt obliged to keep the "show" moving, and though he occasionally pursued what he discerned as a line of thought, he was more concerned to give each man his fair allotment of time.

But it is not time constraints alone that produce such fragmented and discontinuous language. When a television show is in process, it is very nearly impermissible to say, "Let me think about that" or "I don't know" or "What do you mean when you say . . . ?" or "From what sources does your information come?" This type of discourse not only slows down the tempo of the show but creates the impression of uncertainty or lack of finish. It tends to reveal people in the *act of thinking,* which is as disconcerting and boring on television as it is on a Las Vegas stage. Thinking does not play well on television, a fact that television directors discovered long ago. There is not much to *see* in it. It is, in a phrase, not a performing art. But television demands a performing art, and so what the ABC network gave us was a picture of men of sophisticated verbal skills and political understanding being brought to heel by a medium that requires them to fashion performances, rather than ideas. Which accounts for why the eighty minutes were very entertaining, in the way of a Samuel Beckett play: The intimations of gravity hung heavy, the meaning passeth all understanding. The performances, of course, were highly professional. Sagan abjured the turtle-neck sweater in which he starred when he did *Cosmos.* He even had his hair cut for the event. His part was that of the logical scientist speaking in behalf of the planet. It is to be doubted that Paul Newman could have done better in the role, although Leonard Nimoy might have. Scowcroft was suitably military in his bearing—terse and distant, the unbreakable defender of national security. Kissinger, as always, was superb in the part of the knowing world statesman, weary of the sheer responsibility of keeping disaster at bay. Koppel played to perfection the part of a moderator, pretending, as it were, that he was sorting out ideas while, in fact, he was merely directing the performances. At the end, one could only applaud those performances, which is what a good television program always aims to achieve; that is to say, applause, not reflection.

I do not say categorically that it is impossible to use television as a carrier of coherent language or thought in process. William Buckley's own program, *Firing Line,* occasionally shows people in the act of thinking but who also happen to have television cameras pointed at them. There are other programs, such as *Meet the Press* or *The Open Mind,* which clearly strive to maintain a sense of intellectual decorum and typographic tradition, but they are scheduled so that they do not compete with programs of great visual interest, since otherwise, they will not be watched. After all, it is not unheard of that a format will occasionally go against the bias of its medium. For example, the most popular radio program of the early 1940's featured a ventriloquist, and in those days, I heard more than once the feet of a tap dancer on the *Major Bowes' Amateur Hour.* (Indeed, if I am not mistaken, he even once featured a pantomimist.) But ventriloquism, dancing and mime do not play well on radio, just as sustained, complex talk does not play well on television. It can be made to play tolerably well if only one camera is used and the visual image is kept constant—as when the President gives a speech. But this is not television at its best, and it is not television that most people will choose to watch. The single most important fact about television is that people *watch* it, which is why it is called "tele*vision.*" And what they watch, and like to watch, are moving pictures—millions of them, of short duration and dynamic variety. It is in the nature of the medium that it must suppress the content of ideas in order to accommodate the requirements of visual interest; that is to say, to accommodate the values of show business.

Film, records and radio (now that it is an adjunct of the music industry) are, of course, equally devoted to entertaining the culture, and their effects in altering the style of American discourse are not insignificant. But television is different because it encompasses all forms of discourse. No one goes to a movie to find out about government policy or the latest scientific advances. No one buys a record to find out the baseball scores or the weather or the latest murder. No one turns on radio anymore for soap operas or a presidential address (if a television set is at hand). But everyone goes to television for all these things and more, which is why television resonates so powerfully throughout the culture. Television is our culture's principal mode of knowing about itself. Therefore—and this is the critical point—

how television stages the world becomes the model for how the world is properly to be staged. It is not merely that on the television screen entertainment is the metaphor for all discourse. It is that off the screen the same metaphor prevails. As typography once dictated the style of conducting politics, religion, business, education, law and other important social matters, television now takes command. In courtrooms, classrooms, operating rooms, board rooms, churches and even airplanes, Americans no longer talk to each other, they entertain each other. They do not exchange ideas; they exchange images. They do not argue with propositions; they argue with good looks, celebrities and commercials. For the message of television as metaphor is not only that all the world is a stage but that the stage is located in Las Vegas, Nevada.

In Chicago, for example, the Reverend Greg Sakowicz, a Roman Catholic priest, mixes his religious teaching with rock 'n' roll music. According to the Associated Press, the Reverend Sakowicz is both an associate pastor at the Church of the Holy Spirit in Schaumburg (a suburb of Chicago) and a disc jockey at WKQX. On his show, *The Journey Inward,* Father Sakowicz chats in soft tones about such topics as family relationships or commitment, and interposes his sermons with "the sound of *Billboard's* Top 10." He says that his preaching is not done "in a churchy way," and adds, "You don't have to be boring in order to be holy."

Meanwhile in New York City at St. Patrick's Cathedral, Father John J. O'Connor put on a New York Yankee baseball cap as he mugged his way through his installation as Archbishop of the New York Archdiocese. He got off some excellent gags, at least one of which was specifically directed at Mayor Edward Koch, who was a member of his audience; that is to say, he was a congregant. At his next public performance, the new archbishop donned a New York Mets baseball cap. These events were, of course, televised, and were vastly entertaining, largely because Archbishop (now Cardinal) O'Connor has gone Father Sakowicz one better: Whereas the latter believes that you don't have to be boring to be holy, the former apparently believes you don't have to be holy at all.

In Phoenix, Arizona, Dr. Edward Dietrich performed triple bypass surgery on Bernard Schuler. The operation was successful, which was nice for Mr. Schuler. It was also on television, which was nice for America. The operation was carried by at least fifty television stations in the United States, and also by the British Broadcasting Corporation. A two-man panel of narrators (a play-by-play and color man, so to speak) kept viewers informed about what they were seeing. It was not clear as to why this event was televised, but it resulted in transforming both Dr. Dietrich and Mr. Schuler's chest into celebrities. Perhaps because he has seen too many doctor shows on television, Mr. Schuler was uncommonly confident about the outcome of his surgery. "There is no way in hell they are going to lose me on live TV," he said.[2]

As reported with great enthusiasm by both WCBS-TV and WNBC-TV in 1984, the Philadelphia public schools have embarked on an experiment in which children will have their curriculum sung to them. Wearing Walkman equipment, students were shown listening to rock music whose lyrics were about the eight parts of speech. Mr. Jocko Henderson, who thought of this idea, is planning to delight students further by subjecting mathematics and history, as well as English, to the rigors of a rock music format. In fact, this is not Mr. Henderson's idea at all. It was pioneered by the Children's Television Workshop, whose television show *Sesame Street* is an expensive illustration of the idea that education is indistinguishable from entertainment. Nonetheless, Mr. Henderson has a point in his favor. Whereas *Sesame Street* merely attempts to make learning to read a form of light entertainment, the Philadelphia experiment aims to make the classroom itself into a rock concert.

In New Bedford, Massachusetts, a rape trial was televised, to the delight of audiences who could barely tell the difference between the trial and their favorite mid-day soap opera. In Florida, trials of varying degrees of seriousness, including murder, are regularly televised and are considered to be more entertaining than most fictional courtroom dramas. All of this is done in the interests of "public education." For the same high purpose, plans are afoot, it is rumored, to televise confessionals. To be called *Secrets of the Confessional Box,* the program will, of course, carry the warning that some of its material may be offensive to children and therefore parental guidance is suggested.

On a United Airlines flight from Chicago to Vancouver, a stewardess announces that its passengers will play a game. The passenger with the most credit cards will win a bottle of champagne. A man from Boston with twelve credit cards wins. A second game requires the passengers to guess the collective age of the cabin crew. A man from Chicago guesses 128, and wins another bottle of wine. During the second game, the air turns choppy and the Fasten Seat Belt sign goes on. Very few people notice, least of all the cabin crew, who keep up a steady flow of gags on the intercom. When the plane reaches its destination, everyone seems to agree that it's fun to fly from Chicago to Vancouver.

On February 7, 1985, *The New York Times* reported that Professor Charles Pine of Rutgers University (Newark campus) was named Professor of the Year by the Council for the Support and Advancement of Education. In explaining why he has such a great impact on his students, Professor Pine said: "I have some gimmicks I use all the time. If you reach the end of the blackboard, I keep writing on the wall. It always gets a laugh. The way I show what a glass molecule does is to run over to one wall and bounce off it, and run over to the other wall." His students are, perhaps, too young to recall that James Cagney used this "molecule move" to great effect in *Yankee Doodle Dandy.* If I am not mistaken, Donald O'Connor duplicated it in *Singin' in the Rain.* So far as I know, it has been used only once before in a classroom: Hegel tried it several times in demonstrating how the dialectical method works.

The Pennsylvania Amish try to live in isolation from mainstream American culture. Among other things, their religion opposes the veneration of graven images, which means that the Amish are forbidden to see movies or to be photographed. But apparently their religion has not got around to disallowing seeing movies *when* they are being photographed. In the summer of 1984, for example, a Paramount Pictures crew descended upon Lancaster County to film the movie *Witness,* which is about a detective, played by Harrison Ford, who falls in love with an Amish woman. Although the Amish were warned by their church not to interfere with the film makers, it turned out that some Amish welders ran to see the action as soon as their work was done. Other devouts lay in the grass some distance away, and looked down on the set with binoculars. "We read about the movie in the paper," said an Amish woman. "The kids even cut out Harrison Ford's picture." She added: "But it doesn't really matter that much to them. Somebody told us he was in *Star Wars* but that doesn't mean anything to us."[3] The last time a similar conclusion was drawn was when the executive director of the American Association of Blacksmiths remarked that he had read about the automobile but that he was convinced it would have no consequences for the future of his organization.

In the Winter, 1984, issue of the *Official Video Journal* there appears a full-page advertisement for "The Genesis Project." The project aims to convert the Bible into a series of movies. The end-product, to be called *The New Media Bible,* will consist of 225 hours of film and will cost a quarter of a billion dollars. Producer John Heyman, whose credits include *Saturday Night Fever* and *Grease,* is one of the film makers most committed to the project. "Simply stated," he is quoted as saying, "I got hooked on the Bible." The famous Israeli actor Topol, best known for his role as Tevye in *Fiddler on the Roof,* will play the role of Abraham. The advertisement does not say who will star as God but, given the producer's background, there is some concern that it might be John Travolta.

At the commencement exercises at Yale University in 1983, several honorary degrees were awarded, including one to Mother Teresa. As she and other humanitarians and scholars each in turn, received their awards, the audience applauded appropriately but with a slight hint of reserve and impatience, for it wished to give its heart to the final recipient who waited shyly in the wings. As the details of her achievements were being recounted, many people left their seats and surged toward the stage to be closer to the great woman. And when the name Meryl Streep was announced, the audience unleashed a sonic boom of affection to wake the New Haven dead. One man who was present when Bob Hope received his honorary doctorate at another institution said that Dr. Streep's applause surpassed Dr. Hope's. Knowing how to please a crowd as well as anyone, the intellectual leaders at Yale invited Dick Cavett, the talk-show host, to deliver the commencement address the following year. It is rumored that this year, Don Rickles will receive a Doctorate of Humane Letters and Lola Falana will give the commencement address.

Prior to the 1984 presidential elections, the two candidates confronted each other on television in what were called "debates." These events were not in the least like the Lincoln-Douglas debates or anything else that goes by the name. Each candidate was given five minutes to address such questions as, What is (or would be) your policy in Central America? His opposite number was then given one minute for a rebuttal. In such circumstances, complexity, documentation and logic can play no role, and, indeed, on several occasions syntax itself was abandoned entirely. It is no matter. The men were less concerned with giving arguments than with "giving off" impressions, which is what television does best. Post-debate commentary largely avoided any evaluation of the candidates' ideas, since there were none to evaluate. Instead, the debates were conceived as boxing matches, the relevant question being, Who KO'd whom? The answer was determined by the "style" of the men—how they looked, fixed their gaze, smiled, and delivered one-liners. In the second debate, President

Reagan got off a swell one-liner when asked a question about his age. The following day, several newspapers indicated that Ron had KO'd Fritz with his joke. Thus, the leader of the free world is chosen by the people in the Age of Television.

What all of this means is that our culture has moved toward a new way of conducting its business, especially its important business. The nature of its discourse is changing as the demarcation line between what is show business and what is not becomes harder to see with each passing day. Our priests and presidents, our surgeons and lawyers, our educators and newscasters need worry less about satisfying the demands of their discipline than the demands of good showmanship. Had Irving Berlin changed one word in the title of his celebrated song, he would have been as prophetic, albeit more terse, as Aldous Huxley. He need only have written, There's No Business But Show Business.

ENDNOTES

[1] On July 20, 1984, *The New York Times* reported that the Chinese National Television network had contracted with CBS to broadcast sixty-four hours of CBS programming in China. Contracts with NBC and ABC are sure to follow. One hopes that the Chinese understand that such transactions are of great political consequence. The Gang of Four is as nothing compared with the Gang of Three.

[2] This story was carried by several newspapers, including the *Wisconsin State Journal,* February 24, 1983, Section 4, p. 2.

[3] As quoted in *The New York Times,* June 7, 1984, Section A, p. 20.

Name: _____ Date: _____

UNDERSTANDING THE TEXT

1. "A news show," Postman asserts, "is a format for entertainment, not for education, reflection or catharsis." Why does he think so? (Identify four reasons.)

2. Why is Postman critical of the "discussion" that followed ABC's airing of *The Day After* in 1983? (Identify two reasons.)

3. The "critical point," Postman says, is that "how television stages the world becomes the model for how the world is properly to be staged." What, exactly, does he mean by this, and why is it a problem?

Jesse Ventura™ and the Brave New World of Politainer Politics

Ann Conley and David Schultz

"We shocked the world."

So stated former pro wrestler, action film movie actor, and AM radio talk show host Jesse Ventura in November, 1998, as the election results revealed that he had been elected governor of Minnesota (Schultz, "Kenny Meets" xi).

The example of celebrity-turned-politician Jesse Ventura is but one clear indication of how the media, politics, and popular culture are becoming increasingly intertwined in our lives, and in the lives of politicians. Here, an individual named James Janos rose to fame as a popular, cult-like, outlandish personality in the televised world of wrestling with the assumed persona Jesse Ventura. From there, he appeared in several films popular with teenagers and college students; then he moved on to be a controversial host of several AM radio talk shows in Minnesota. As a host, he was known for his brash, hard-talking, "take no prisoners" views that often criticized the political establishment. Jesse carried that persona over into his surprise run for governor, using it as a way to distinguish himself from the political establishment and to demonstrate that, if elected, he would be a different kind of governor.

And elected he was. Using his media image in televised debates, and even in commercials that featured "Jesse Ventura action figures," Jesse Ventura did shock the world. Since his election he has become an international celebrity, merging his role as governor with that of professional wrestler into a unique figure in American politics.

Since taking office, Ventura has continued to capitalize on his fame, selling his action figures and other merchandise bearing his name and returning to the wrestling ring to referee a 1999 World Wrestling Federation "Summer Slam" event. The media popular culture icon's personality and his role as governor have become indistinguishable.

What Jesse Ventura has taught us all, besides the level of his marketing genius, is the incredible potential to reach the public (read: voters) through entertainment venues. Jesse's power and value as a politician come not just from his use of a particular venue. Because Jesse is a politician who is also an entertainer, he has become what other politicians, thus far, will never be—a politainer.

This article explains what it means to be a politainer, why the time is right for the politainer in our society, and what the implications of politainment are.

EMERGENCE OF THE POLITAINER

Jesse Ventura emerged from a long line of predecessors who are celebrities (actors, newscasters, and athletes) turned politicians: Ronald Reagan, Sonny Bono, Clint Eastwood, Jack Kemp, Bill Bradley, and Fred Grandy (*Love Boat's* "Gopher"), to name just a few. While following in the footsteps of such notable politicians who have traded in their celebrity for political power, Jesse is forging his own distinct political path—one that others are sure to follow. He takes the trend of entertainer turned politician one step further because he is more than just a celebrity turned politician; he is simultaneously an entertainer and a politician; he is, in other words, a politainer.

Jesse's path has been marked by many firsts for an American politician: action figures modeled after his television persona; a not for-profit company ("Ventura for Minnesota, Inc.") that sells official, licensed Jesse Ventura paraphernalia, along with a trademarked name; a tell-all autobiography published in his first few months as Governor of Minnesota; a second book published (and aggressively promoted and publicized) just over a year later; an appearance on the soap opera *The Young and the Restless;* an appearance as the referee in a World Wrestling Federation match; and a weekly Minnesota radio show. His meteoric rise into the statewide, and now the national, political scene has been incredibly instructive for those who follow and study politics.

It is from Jesse's colorful activities that we can deduce the characteristics of a politainer. A politainer is simultaneously an entertainer and a politician; his persona is a fiction; his persona is a commodity; and he uses multi-media venues (many of which are entertainment outlets) and sophisticated mass-marketing techniques to distribute "message," and/or to market himself as a politician and as an entertainer.

SIMULTANEOUSLY AN ENTERTAINER AND A POLITICIAN

A politainer has a dual career: he uses his entertainment career to benefit his political career, and he uses his political career to benefit his entertainment career. Jesse Ventura's autobiography, *I Ain't Got Time to Bleed,* his appearances on the late night shows (Jay Leno and David Letterman), a controversial interview in *Playboy,* and the sale of Jesse Ventura action figures might not have occurred had he never run for governor. Likewise, it would have been impossible for Jesse to become governor without the celebrity status that accompanied his role as

Jesse Ventura, the wrestler. He capitalized on his entertainer status, ran for governor as a publicity stunt, and, much to his and everyone's surprise, was elected.

ENTERTAINMENT PERSONA IS A FICTION, YET WE ELECT THE PERSONA RATHER THAN THE PERSON

Minnesota's current governor was born James Janos, not Jesse Ventura; yet Minnesotans elected with Jesse Ventura™, a man a trademarked name fashioned after a coastal California city and a persona fashioned as an over-the-top wrestler. Ventura the wrestler/governor beats up "special interest man"; he sells officially-licensed bumper stickers that say "My governor can beat up your governor"; and he refereed a World Wrestling Federation wrestling match. For Jesse Ventura the wrestler/governor, politics has become the crucible in which he continues to forge his persona as the tough-talking renegade wrestler. Where James Janos ends and Jesse Ventura begins, or where the entertainer or governor begins and ends, is not clear, but there is no doubt that the Jesse Ventura persona is a fiction—a fiction that he sold to the public and upon which he has built his political base. The public has always made a distinction between the public and private sides of politicians' personalities and lives. For a politainer, the public/private tension is far less relevant than the tension between fiction and nonfiction.

Indeed, the public allows a politainer to get away with behavior that falls within expected parameters of that particular politainer's entertainment persona. Since Jesse has always been over-the-top, people allow and even expect him to be consistent with that persona, even if his behavior is very different from what we might expect from an ordinary politician. He can be blunt, use coarse and vulgar language, and refer to his critics as "gutless cowards," and the public views each instance as simply another example of the Governor telling it like it is. Ventura is examined not through the lens normally used to evaluate elected officials, but instead through the magnifying glass normally used on movie stars and celebrities. Such a standard is less critical and introspective, and tolerant of the latest foibles so long as they entertain and amuse us. And just like in an all-star wrestling match, the public suspends its beliefs in order to participate in the myth and fiction of Jesse "The Body" Ventura, the wrestler in the governor's office. He is the Postmodern version of the Horatio Alger story: anyone can grow up and become famous, and the television viewer vicariously participates in the story. In its desire to be entertained, the public is willing to leave its critical faculties at the door and accept behavior from the politainer that it would not accept from another elected official.

ENTERTAINMENT PERSONA IS A COMMODITY

The last two to three decades of the twentieth century are distinguishable from any others in their increasingly widespread and rampant consumerism. It is in this context that our culture (with the help of marketers and our mass media) has broken new ground in its ability to commodify almost anything. While the political world has never been immune to the influence of the marketplace, one can argue that the politainer becomes a commodity like Coke or Snicker's bars. Jesse's use of a trademarked name, his enforcement of his rights, his precluding others from capitalizing on his fame, and all the accompanying paraphernalia reinforce this fact (Caple). In fact, in an August, 1999 news conference, he refused to rule out any future product endorsements (Ragsdale A1).

USE OF MULTI-MEDIA VENUES AND MARKETING TECHNIQUES TO DISTRIBUTE "MESSAGE" AND/OR TO MARKET HIMSELF AS A POLITICIAN AND AS AN ENTERTAINER

Politicians throughout U.S. history have made use of the media in their campaigns and during their terms of office. Political campaigns have continually adapted to the media and marketing practices of their times. In his book, *Adcult USA,* James Twitchell cites the "defining event of political maneuvering" in advertising as the 1952 election campaign of Dwight Eisenhower. A man named Rossier Reeves masterminded a highly successful campaign called "Eisenhower Answers America," in which Eisenhower answered on television a series of questions generated by Reeves but asked on camera by average citizens. Decades later, "Reagan did exactly what Rossier Reeves was attempting to do for Eisenhower. He traded intellectual content for emotional appeal" (Twitchell 121–22).

John F. Kennedy, too, innovatively used television. Common wisdom has it that it was Kennedy's appearance on the first televised presidential debate with Nixon that helped him win the election. Kennedy's superb television presence contrasted so greatly with Richard Nixon's lack of presence that some say it cost Nixon the election. Bill Clinton, too, pushed his use of the media farther than any previous president when he went on MTV, and when he played the saxophone on Arsenio Hall's TV show. He and his wife Hillary have periodically used morning and prime time interview shows (e.g., the *Barbara Walters Specials* and *The Today Show*) to get particular messages Out.

Finally, during the 2000 presidential race, Jay Leno and David Letterman hosted candidates John McCain, George W. Bush, and Al Gore. David Letterman even employed a long-running stunt, Campaign 2000, in a successful effort to hype ratings by enticing New York candidate Hillary Clinton to appear on his show. For Letterman the purpose was clear: better ratings. But for the candidates, the free exposure was invaluable, and the result was a faint effort at emulating Ventura's success in bridging the politics and entertainment gap. In fact, Ms. Clinton, who used "Hillary!" as her slogan (reminiscent of other first-name-only celebrities such as Madonna and Cher), seemed poised to make a bid for public office using her first name much like a brand name for a product. "Buy Hillary! New and improved!" Overall, the trend toward celebrity news (Hess 28) dovetails with the emergence of celebrity politicians.

Clearly there is historical precedent for politicians' use of the media. What is different about a politainer's use of the media is the degree to which it is done. What the politainer represents is the complete saturation of politics by media and marketing.

POLITAINER POSTMODERN ROOTS

The politainer is a creature of Postmodern culture. Postmodern society is characterized by:

1. the increasing heterogeneity or diversity of the public;
2. relativism (a core challenge to our cohesion as a culture in the Postmodern world is the relativism of values in the absence of shared foundational assumptions);
3. the blurring of the line between public and private life (improvements in technology, advancements in information processing, and flexible job structures allow us to do work anywhere and anytime, which leads to the blending of our work and private lives);
4. a multiplicity of roles (a denizen of the Postmodern world can be overwhelmed by the number of competing roles that she fulfills at any given moment; even more difficult is the task of trying to prioritize these multiple roles [Cooper 364]); and
5. consumerism and the commodification of knowledge.

In the United States, we are chronically inundated with what James Twitchell calls "commercial speech" (16), the language of advertising. Behind that language is the powerful, and frequently unchallenged, assumption that money will buy happiness, and that by consuming enough of the right products, we will eventually achieve personal satisfaction. Additionally, Jean-Francois Lyotard's criticism of Modernity implies that we must now recognize the new information society of the computer and the changing role of knowledge and knowing in the Postmodern world (36). Knowledge is not a ground, but a commodity for exchange and power. It is transmutable and its commodification reveals its nonpermanent nature. Lyotard thus proposes that this change in knowledge undermines Modernity and its belief in a fixed epistemological center. Knowledge is a commodity no different from any other, and it can be exchanged or changed on the market for any other thing. Knowledge has been reified, implying that it can be manipulated to suit the needs of the market or the electorate.

Postmodernism challenges the traditional foundational basis of knowledge characteristic of Modernity, seeing in its place a more subject-oriented theory of truth that contests the clear boundaries demarcated by a rational-scientific conception of the world. According to Richard Rorty, a sense of commonness or agreement on what truth and knowledge are lies at the heart of the epistemological foundationalism of Modernity. Rorty believes that this foundationalism is either false or illusionary, since we do not really have access to some Archimedean epistemological point—because such a point does not exist (316). Kantian epistemological categories are not universal, but historical, and they are the product of individual cultures and psychologies. Knowledge is not universal but particular, more like perspectives or ideologies than anything else.

Rorty's point is that the confrontational (or subject/object) model of knowledge is an inadequate model of cognition. Rorty also denies that epistemology is an adequate ground for politics. In rejecting the notion that a fixed reality exists out there (or, for Kant, in the objective categories of the mind), Rorty rejects the belief in a fixed terra firma upon which one can build a permanent base of knowledge. This rejection leads to a denial of an epistemological center for politics. There is no one political truth or authority for political propositions, but many. One cannot assert that any natural laws validate universal truths of politics or prove that a political doctrine is the only correct one. Instead, there are many ways to view political questions, and all of us have the right to adjudicate them.

Rorty thus dismisses as failed the confrontation theory of knowledge. With that rejection, the epistemological ground of Modernity is gone and the entire project of Modernity is moribund. Rorty argues that we should instead view knowledge as conversational (163, 389–93) and dispense with the belief in a cognitive center. We should look to knowing as being plural and diverse (316). What we know, or what knowledge is (if we can even continue to use that term), is determined in some conventional conversational mode of unity being produced out of the many localized understandings or meanings found in the diversity of social practices (178, 361). There is no social or political center of truth. Claims to truth, or verifications of truth propositions, reside not in appeals of correspondence to some object, or in appeal to some political authority. Truth resides in how we can justify or persuade others to accept our beliefs (141).

Similarly, Paul Feyerabend also attacks the totalizing force of science as a paradigm for politics in Modernity (106–07). Modern science, as the paradigm for modern politics, has thus supported an elitist notion of politics that claims there are experts in scientific and political matters. This means that there are correct political truths and technical experts, who, when employing the correct tools, can find these truths and scientifically run the state and the polity.

Scientific rationality and politics discourages the role of opinion in politics in the same way Plato discouraged doxa. Only a few really know, and are entitled to participate. Modern scientific politics, then, is antidemocratic and non-participatory, and enjoys its privileged status through its protection by the state. For Feyerabend, science has become the new state religion.

In medieval times, Christianity was the legitimizing force of monarchial power. Now, it is science justifying the modern state. While Christianity supported kings, kings supported Christianity. Similarly, science supports, and is supported by, the modern state. Feyerabend thus divorces science from politics. This presents Postmodern culture with a choice—either a foundationless politics or a politics searching for a new ground—that is filled by linking politics to entertainment.

Postmodern life is marked by shifting and uncertain identities, assumptions, and values. At the same time, Postmodern culture is saturated by the influence of commerce and consumerism. Despite our great diversity in the United States, we are tied together by our shared identity as marketplace consumers. It is the relative strength of our shared marketplace values and the relative weakness of other potentially competing value systems that makes Postmodern society particularly vulnerable to the influence of consumerism. Our shared materialism fills a cultural need for commonality. The common experience of shopping at Wal-Mart, eating at McDonald's, or watching television serves more to tie people together than anything else. The equality of Postmodern life is the shared experience of being consumers.

Postmodernism is the backdrop against which a number of interrelated trends play out: the deepening of the relationship between entertainment and advertising, the convergence of entertainment and the news media, and the convergence of politics and entertainment—all of which create the crucible in which a politainer is created.

Entertainment is obviously a common thread running throughout the trends mentioned above. A key ingredient of Postmodern culture is that people have a fundamental need to be entertained—to engage in the suspension of beliefs, the escapism, the imaginative process, the archetypal struggles (e.g., good vs. evil), and the emotional stimulation that are part of being entertained. It is from this need that the "entertainment imperative" arises in the advertising, news, and political arenas (McAllister 43).

The relationship between entertainment and advertising has been provocatively analyzed by James Twitchell, who coined the term "Adcult" as a way of capturing the degree that advertising has become the central institution in American society. In his thumbnail sketch of the advertising industry, he makes the link between advertising and entertainment: "The business of advertising is essentially the business of trafficking in audiences. After an audience has been gathered, its attention is rented to an agent who inserts a message from a sponsor. The audience pays attention because it is traded something in return, namely, entertainment" (5).

Twitchell highlights six characteristics of Adcult that demonstrate its cultural influence and importance. According to Twitchell, Adcult is:

- Ubiquitous. Advertising is everywhere.
- Anonymous. It is extremely difficult to determine authorship in advertising.
- Symbiotic. "Adcult shares the energy of other social organisms. The something with which it lives is on the surface entertainment and below the surface deep concerns of the specific culture." Advertisement merges with other cultural trends, like music. By viewing MTV videos, for example, one sees "how the colonizing power of commercial speech can quickly consume discrete forms and make them one."
- Syncretic. "Adcult layers itself on top of other cultures." It builds on what has come before, like the Burger King commercial that has two diapered babies chatting as in *Look Who's Talking*. Twitchell likens this self-referential aspect of Adcult to religious ceremonies.
- Profane. Advertising must excite and shock to get the consumers' attention.
- Magical. Twitchell contends that he is "hardly the first to recognize that advertising is the gospel of redemption in the fallen world of capitalism, that advertising has become the vulgate of the secular belief in the redemption of commerce. In a most profound sense advertising and religion are part of the same meaning-making process: they occur at the margin of human concern about the world around us, and each attempts to breach the gap between us and objects by providing a systemic understanding. Whereas the Great Chain of Being organized the world of our ancestors, the marketplace of objects does it for us. They both promise redemption: one through faith, the other through purchase. But how are order and salvation affected? By magical thinking, pure and simple" (16–30).

The concept of magic needs more exploration because, while it is the most surprising of the characteristics described above, it is also the most profound. We are so immersed in advertising that it is easy to miss the degree to which it promises us magical transformations, both big and small, from our current state of being. Through advertising we might come to believe that we can stop the aging process with the right skin cream or hair coloring; or we might become convinced that by purchasing the right make-up or beer, we could be more attractive to the opposite sex.

On one level, this kind of magical transformation is entertaining. On another, this type of advertisement goes far beyond entertainment, speaking to some of our deepest hopes (e.g., defeating loneliness) and fears (e.g., rejection or death). Twitchell contends that it is the conversation that advertising carries on with these deeper issues in our lives that puts it on a par with religion.

Twitchell goes on to draw parallels between the ancient gods (Zeus, Hera, Jupiter, etc.) and the commercial "gods" of today: The Jolly Green Giant, the Michelin Man, and Aunt Jemima, among others. The difference between modern and ancient gods is that modern gods "now reside in manufactured products and that, although earlier gods were invoked by fasting, prayer, rituals, and penance, the promise of purchase calls forth their modern ilk" (30). Through magic, disposable goods become "long-lasting charms." Through magic, a pitcher of Kool-Aid smiles and Dow Cleanser develops scrubbing bubbles that talk (30). Later, this article will return to the religious significance of advertising and will address how this point is relevant to the role of the politainer.

Matthew McAllister speaks more specifically about the tactics of what he calls "new advertising," which include cross-promotion, sponsorship, and place-based advertising. These three tactics have a particular salience when it comes to understanding the milieu from which a politainer emerges.

The first tactic, cross-promotion, is an increasingly-used practice in which companies pool their economic and symbolic resources to create joint advertising. McAllister believes that "cross-promotion increases the symbolic power of one product by using it as a referent system for another product" (250). This practice is further enhanced when database marketing is used to help the marketer precisely deduce what referent systems a consumer does or doesn't like.

Jesse Ventura's press conference regarding his foray back into the wrestling ring as a referee for a World Wrestling Federation (WWF) match could be viewed as cross-promotion—Jesse and the WWF received mutual benefit from Ventura's appearance. Jesse's symbolic power enhanced the WWF's and the WWF's symbolic power enhanced Jesse's (in the eyes of some, at least). Similarly, the sale of Jesse dolls by Ventura's political campaign reinforced the similar sale of the dolls by his nonprofit corporation Ventura for Minnesota, Inc.

A second tactic is sponsorship, a practice that McAllister defined as "an act of corporate giving to some activity—sometimes for-profit, sometimes not—in an attempt to capitalize on the philanthropic ethos of patronage as well as the promotional functions of advertising" (178). This tactic is not new, but it is provocative when viewed in the context of politics. In the next section of this article, we will discuss the ethical implications of a politainer with corporate sponsorship.

A third tactic is place-based advertising, which is a form of advertising that places advertising at the location or destination in which a particular audience is found. Advertising along the walls of an ice arena during a hockey game is one example. As McAllister states, "[p]lace-based advertising is not simply an ad-supported medium in a social place; it is also the use of the place (the school, the doctor's office) as a way to increase the credibility of the advertising message" (250).

All of these—cross-promotion, sponsorship, and place-based advertising—are practices that could be used by a politainer, and all create specific ethical concerns for politainers and the public. These will be discussed in the next section of this essay.

The world of advertising has had an enormous impact on the institutions surrounding it. The news media/journalism is one of the institutions that have fallen under the spell of the advertising industry's twin values of entertainment and profit. The result is infotainment, the merging of entertainment and journalism. Bill Kovach and Tom Rosenstiel lament the demise of journalistic integrity at the altar of profit and entertainment. They believe that we are living in an era of "post-O. J. media" in which "the cultures of entertainment, infotainment, argument, analysis, tabloid, and mainstream press not only work side by side but intermingle and merge" (4).

Put another way, ours is a "Mixed Media Culture" in which the "classic function of journalism to sort out a true and reliable account of the day's events is being undermined" (5). Kovach and Rosenstiel conclude that news programming is driven by, among many other things, the twenty-four hour news cycle, a fascination with a polarized story, and a desire to find "the 'big story' that will temporarily reassemble the now-fragmented [read: Postmodern] mass audience" (5). Ironically, the Mixed Media Culture weakens the press's ability to "serve as a cohesive cultural force, and weakens the public's tether to a true account of the news" (4–5). Under corporate control, news has simply become another form of entertainment (Schultz, "Cultural" 19–21).

News producers unfortunately are unable to afford, or keep up with, the information demands of round-the-clock news coverage. According to Kovach and Rosenstiel, channels do not adequately invest in reporting infrastructure. Short-staffed and in need of programming that will capture audiences' attention, news producers have been pushed into the "journalism of assertion" (8). The journalism of assertion has the feel of a talk show; it is populated with pundits who do not gather the news as much as they comment and speculate on it; and it entertains by engaging in polarized argumentation (1–9). News producers are falling sway to the same "entertainment imperative" that mobilizes the advertising industry.

Infotainment emerges from a milieu defined by consumerism and mass marketing. Taking its cue from the advertising industry, the news industry is becoming the infotainment industry, migrating ever closer toward the world of the entertaining, the unsubstantiated, the titillating, and the fictional. Aping a television commercial that opened with the line "I'm not a doctor, but I play one on television," infotainment takes as its slogan, "I'm not a real politician, but I play one on television."

Thus we have Jesse Ventura, who embodies all of the above in a parallel arc in politics. What we observe in Jesse is the convergence of entertainment and politics to meet the demands of a populace that is cynical about most politicians, that wants to be entertained, and that is willing to suspend their beliefs to do so.

The Implications of Politainment

As politics merges with entertainment, entertainment becomes a doorway through which politics (and, by extension, governance) immerses itself in the vocabulary and behavior of mass marketing. What are the ethical implications of this trend for politicians and for democracy?

In light of the trends toward Adcult and infotainment, there are several emerging ethical concerns for the politainer, for his audience (the public), and for the institution of democracy.

For the politainer, the previous discussion about Adcult begs the question of whether a politainer is more vulnerable to individual corruption and conflicts of interest. Dennis Thompson defines individual corruption as private gain from public office (29). This is an ongoing concern for any politician, but a politainer has even more opportunity for conflicts of interest because she has a dual career in both the political and the entertainment fields. How can the public (or the politainer) determine which hat she is wearing? When is she acting in the interest of her entertainment career, and when is she acting on behalf of her political career? When might either or both careers conflict with her duty to act in the best interest of the people she was elected to represent? When it comes to having a multiplicity of roles, the politainer is surely a Postmodern phenomenon!

Furthermore, the politainer's entertainment career, with its immersion in Adcult and mass media, makes the politainer particularly susceptible to conflicts of interest. As described earlier, the advertising industry employs the tactics of cross-promotion, sponsorship, and place-based advertising. If we apply these advertising tactics to a politainer like Jesse Ventura™—who is, for all practical purposes, a marketable commodity—then it is logical to assume that he influences and is influenced by the advertising process. Indeed, the politainer in this situation is vulnerable to undue influence in the advertising process.

If, for example, Jesse Ventura were the recipient of corporate sponsorship from a nuclear power company for an entertainment event in which he was participating or that he was hosting, would Jesse be more inclined to sign a piece of legislation that would permit it to expand its storage of nuclear waste? Jesse Ventura says that he is not beholden to special interests—but what kind of influence would a lucrative sponsorship deal have on his decision-making? This same line of thinking would hold true for other advertising deals like endorsements and cross-promotion. Jesse Ventura™ cannot separate his interests, those of his sponsor, and those of the public, because he and his governorship are simply products of the corporate infotainment culture, lacking distinct identities. Louis XIV once remarked, "L'dtat c'est moi," demonstrating an incapacity to distinguish himself from France. Perhaps Jesse Ventura™, who exclaimed in a *Playboy* interview that it was "good to be the king"

(Sweeney, "Governor"), should have as his slogan either "L'marchandise c'est moi" or "L'idole c'est moi."

In the case of Jesse Ventura, as with all politainers, a dynamic that complicates this issue is his apparently deep philosophical grounding in what Terry Cooper identifies as the "spirit of western individualism" (114). Cooper contends that Americans place a high value on respecting an individual's right to protect his self-interest.

Small (554), in his survey of the problem of conflict of interest in American government, has produced findings that support the conclusion that this tendency has been on the increase in modern society. He writes, "Increasingly, then, in the late Twentieth Century it becomes more and more difficult to separate the simplistic, completely personal interest from the public interest. Because these interests are overlapping and no longer separable, older norms of right and wrong, desirable or undesirable are inadequate" (554). He concludes that it is "part of the human condition" to seek money and power from public sources for the sake of private gain (Cooper 116).

This trend does not bode well for those who believe elected office is a form of public service. Jesse Ventura™ justifies his pursuit of private gain by claiming that he is doing it in his off hours, and that if one bans outside gain, then only rich professional politicians can run for office. In short, the politainer sets a standard of conduct clearly lower than we set for traditional politicians and government officials, and the public—rather, we consumers—seem to accept this behavior much in the same way that we accept other celebrities pursuing commercial ventures. In fact, since first being elected governor, Ventura has been subject to numerous criticisms of his behavior as violating generally-applicable codes of ethics (Sweeney, "Top Ethics").

Some suggest that using government or the public sphere for private purposes can be viewed as one way in which our "commons" are being exploited. "Conflict of interest, therefore, is an insidiously difficult problem [. . .]. Citizens in public administrative positions have special access to the governmental commons that most ordinary citizens do not. This access presents unusual opportunities and, therefore, temptations to exploit governmental resources for personal gain" (Cooper 117). The emergence of the politainer, as embodied by Jesse Ventura, is a signal that this individualistic ideology is indeed winning out over a concern for the common good. Jesse's own mantra of "personal responsibility" echoes this very trend.

Another ethical question that arises in this context of mass marketing and politics relates to whether a politainer devalues the public office he holds by selling himself as a commodity. In his critique of new advertising, Matthew McAllister points out that advertising practices "devalue original institutions" (250). For example, when a school participates in place-based advertising, it is "no longer a place where advertising does not influence," and therefore it is a little less special. When Jesse Ventura™, the Governor of Minnesota, becomes a de facto advertisement for the World Wrestling Federation through cross-promotion, he not only loses some of his authority as Minnesota's highest official in state office, but he also breaks down a wall that has traditionally kept commercialism out of the role of a serving public official. Perhaps this is not a terribly compelling argument in an era where a large segment of the population already has little regard for public office and believes that all politicians are corrupt. It is, however, noteworthy that Ventura the politainer has made an unprecedented move by allowing the office of governor to be commercialized.

Unfortunately, there are no clear answers to concerns about conflicts of interest and undue influence. There is not a great deal of political will to legislate restrictions on the actions of politainers. The public seems indifferent so long as the politainer entertains, and other legislators, either fearful of public wrath or hopeful that they too can profit from the bounty, steer away from acting. Indeed, public vigilance may be the most important remedy for potential conflicts of interest on the part of the politainer.

Ironically, even though a politainer is more susceptible to conflicts of interest, she is less likely to be scrutinized for it by the public. As the first section of this article pointed out, the public has different expectations for a politainer's behavior than it does for the behavior of an ordinary politician. We allow greater flexibility in how a politainer behaves, which might mean that we are more accepting of her conflicts of interest. Additionally, the relationship between the politainer and the public is one of audience to entertainer. This means that the audience's (the public's) critical faculties have been suspended—that, again, creates a situation in which the politainer is subject to less oversight by the public. As with a movie star or other celebrity, foibles and personal failings are part of the entertainment and attraction. Finally, Ventura often claims he is "just kidding" when he makes remarks which would damage other politicians, and the public seems to accept this as an apology.

Politainment raises ethical concerns for the public as well. These concerns could be viewed as questions of access. The politainer presents both opportunities and challenges to public participation in the democratic process.

What is clear from Jesse Ventura's campaign is the degree to which he mobilized previously unmobilized voters. Because of significant media access, and through the use of sophisticated marketing strategies, politainers like Jesse Ventura now have unprecedented access to multiple markets—i.e., markets that vary by race, ethnicity, socioeconomic status, and gender. That is good news for the "23 million American adults [who] are functionally illiterate and therefore are almost entirely beyond the reach of print media" (Graber 203). Mass media marketing through entertainment venues present incredible possibilities for reaching out to alienated or disenfranchised groups.

One might argue that, because of whom he mobilized, Jesse Ventura's victory is something of a Jacksonian "common man" revolution. One essayist in *Harper's Magazine* described the following scene at the Ventura victory party on election night:

> The betting windows are closed but the Ascot Lounge to the right of the escalators is open, and Ventura's supporters wait three deep for a chance to take full advantage. I try to move past them for a closer look but get cut off by a train of manly men who are using their 16-ounce Leinenkugel's as wedges against the crowd. All four of them are wearing army jackets, camouflage pants, and hunting boots. The only thing missing, so I hope, are the guns.
>
> I drop into their slipstream and ride it into the party, a fat, sweaty weisswurst of baseball hats, Twins sweatshirts, and high-school letter jackets in a makeshift staging area surrounded

by television crews, whose lights fence in the dense crowd like a cattle pen. Thick of neck and stout of heart, Ventura's supporters are bleaching under the hot lights, but none of them seem to care. Next to me on the fringe, a ratty Vikings parka encases a man in his thirties. A thin layer of foam coats his mustache, and his brow is knit in drunken concentration as he tries to decide between the whiskey in his left hand and the beer in his right.

All white and all worked up, the crowd near the stage builds up a stadium chant of "Packers suck! Packers suck!" which inexplicably segues into "Bikers suck! Bikers suck!" I look around and see one such biker walking out of the Ascot Lounge carrying a big beer and a paper plate with a pyramid of cocktail franks. Flipping his long black hair, he angrily surveys the pit. For a moment I think he's going to throw down his snack and put up his fists, but he only smiles and struts into the room, holding his beer high above his head like a torch (Cass 65).

To what degree might we have heard the elite utter parallel sentiments about Andrew Jackson's supporters in the 1800s? However, despite the classist overtones in this passage, it is clear that Jesse Ventura's candidacy excited and mobilized an unusual group of voters. If it is true that Jesse is reaching disenfranchised voters, are we not one step closer to achieving a goal of full citizen participation in government? Perhaps yes, but is this an informed citizenry coming together to articulate the public good, or is it merely another form of Nielsen rating or consumer choice of a brand name product? Or is it simply swapping votes for entertainment? Are elections simply People's Choice Awards? And do we have real political debate and discourse, or a brave new form of Huxleyian hypnopaedia that lulls us into McWorld (Barber 1–3)?

In addition, human communication researchers have discovered that "individuals who consume a lot of media, particularly television, are more knowledgeable about politics and other social issues" (Emmers-Sommer and Allen 490). If this is true, then a politainer's use of multiple media venues might provide a greater opportunity for a broader number of people to engage in our democratic process.

Along with opportunities come challenges. A politainer's increased level of access to the public certainly has a bright side. It also has a dark side. Increased access to and engagement of the public through advertising and entertainment venues creates the potential to manipulate who gets access to political information. It also has the potential to fictionalize the political process. Politainment is Orwellian in a doublethink or Newspeak sense: Politicians merge two arenas not previously combined—politics and entertainment—where fiction is reality, and where the message does not ask citizens to render careful political judgments, but instead asks for blind acceptance of the product being sold.

Indeed, a positive interpretation of the access argument assumes a free market of consumer choice in media venues. Ideally, demand determines what venues are available, and as our population becomes more diverse, so does the variety of media available to meet the population's needs. But perhaps the opposite is true. Perhaps the consumer does not choose the media, but, rather, the media choose the consumer.

Matthew McAllister contends that advertising-based media seek out the demographic groups that have the money to buy the advertised products. He paraphrases the thinking of

C. E. Baker: "[A]udiences who are not 'demogenic' are ignored or seriously underrepresented by advertising-supported media. Those who are poor, elderly or live in rural areas have less media options designed to appeal to them than those who are rich, young and urban [. . .]. Advertising is much more likely to subsidize, with advertising revenue, media aimed at the upper-class than media aimed at the poor" (46).

In addition, McAllister says that media create and alter program content in order to gain audiences and to make these audiences more receptive to certain ads. Conversely, programming that makes audiences less receptive to certain advertising is less desirable to advertisers and therefore more difficult to maintain. Obviously, "advertising has an ideological effect upon media content. Advertising's economic presence significantly influences the view of the world that the media present, a view embedded in and influenced by social power and social relations" (47).

Clearly, this dynamic has implications for access to information. In the past, one might have argued that even though advertisers have a great deal of control over certain media venues, at least the news media could still be relied upon to protect some level of democratic public discourse. Bill Kovach and Tom Rosenstiel contend that "the news culture still shapes the lines of the political playing field and the context in which citizens define meaning for political events" (3). What the infotainment trend shows us, however, is the degree to which the news media have joined advertisers in turning public discourse into commercial speech. Advertising-based media, including the news media, are manufacturing and limiting the political debate.

Following the same logic, one might speculate that the politainer, with his vulnerability to advertisers and entertainment media, might engage in the same process of limiting public debate in order to please advertisers. The politainer is symbolic of how commercial speech has now permeated the political arena. All political speech is now commercial, and vice versa, challenging yet another barrier within First Amendment free speech jurisprudence that seeks to distinguish the two.

There is yet another problem with the optimistic view that the methods of a politainer might improve the political process. The same researchers who proposed that media can be educative also showed that there is a problem with "impressionable" individuals whose "learning and beliefs are influenced by fictional media" (Emmers-Sommer and Allen 491). For example, viewers of Oliver Stone's *JFK* are more likely to accept as truth his and James Garrison's view of the Kennedy assassination than that of the Warren Commission (Kelly and Elliot 191). These researchers might have made a case study of the thirty-seven percent of the Minnesota electorate who voted for the fictional candidate, Jesse Ventura™. They are prime examples of the impressionable individuals who feel that they "know" Jesse Ventura through his character in the wrestling ring.

If we concur with the assertions made about the deep and pervasive influence of Adcult, then it is likely that to some degree, we are all impressionable. We are all, to varying degrees, well-conditioned congregants in the church of the marketplace in America; so much so that we are willing to believe in the magic that advertising offers us. With the convergence of politics and entertainment, and the concomitant influence of advertising on politics, one can foresee a future in which our notion of an educated electorate deliberating about candidates and public policy has been swept away. In its place is a populace that favors fictionalized candidates who not only entertain, but promise magic—such as simultaneously cutting taxes, raising military spending, and balancing the budget, all without smoke and mirrors!

One result of the merger of politics and entertainment is that the impression people now have of public officials is framed more by jokes and less by their stances on the issues. Thus, in the 2000 presidential race, George Bush was seen as an intellectual light-weight and a frat boy and Al Gore depicted as wooden. And because candidates were treated more like movie stars, politics is now thought of as entertainment, campaigning is like acting, and politicians are like actors. All this clearly leads to a loss of substance in politics and a degeneration into politainment.

In an essay reviewing five pieces of anti-utopian literature from the early twentieth century, Christopher Dornan comments on the prescience of the authors in their assessment of where our society would be at the end of this century. In our market-induced predilection for the world of fantasy and fiction, we are moving closer to this anti-utopian vision than we ever anticipated: "So as the 20th century draws to a close, its signature futurist motif is one of escaping reality into a media-maintained imaginary dimension where all fantasies are possible, all desires can be fulfilled. As the Microsoft ad put it, 'Where do you want to go today?' The very question presumes that the answer is elsewhere: somewhere more interesting than here and now" (Dornan 129).

Perhaps we are destined for a dual reality in which our hoped-for future is "Adtopia," the world of magic and wish fulfillment, and the reality an antiutopia in which commercial speech passes for public discourse and advertisers control public discourse and thereby control political decisions (Twitchell 39). Dornan asks the question, "Who could have imagined that the media would come to usurp political authority, buffeting a political process and decision-making in the chaotic turbulence of perception" (129)?

CONCLUSION

Jesse Ventura™ did shock the world with his election, but the real shock is perhaps more Orwellian in what it bodes for politics. Perhaps Jesse Ventura™ is just the first of a new wave of politainers who will come to dominate politics in the twenty-first century. He is the culmination of many forces. As *The Wall Street Journal* proclaimed, "America is reaching the climax of a generation-long trend: the melding of entertainment and politics into a hybrid, all-purpose celebrity culture"—where, according to Frank Mankiewicz, a political consultant, "We're talking about seeing politics as an extension of popular culture" (Seib). Candidates for public office need not be real candidates or politicians; instead, it is enough, as with Warren Beatty, to have played one in a movie (*Bulworth*). Or, reality can mirror fiction, which mirrors reality, as in the movie *Wag the Dog,* which told the tale of a United States president starting a war to distract the public away from a sex scandal in which he was entwined. In 1998, as impeachment was bearing down on President Clinton because of allegations that he lied about an affair he had with White House intern Monica Lewinsky, he announced that he would begin bombing Iraq. Almost immediately, the public and the press stated this was simply "wagging the dog," using this phrase to describe what they assumed to be the real motives Clinton had in this military action.

Is the future of politics in the twenty-first century really so bleak? Perhaps not. But we can be sure that there will be many more politainers to come. Future candidates for office may not come from state houses and the halls of Congress, but from television shows such as *The West Wing,* movie houses, and sports arenas. The power of Adcult and the shaping influence of infotainment almost require it. Politics, like the news, will become yet another entertainment medium through which products are sold—including the politicians/politainers themselves. We are sure to see more Bob Doles selling Viagra, Mario Cuomos selling Doritos, and Jesse Venturas™ selling World Wrestling Federations, with little regard for whether the politician is currently in office. And, as for the public, as long as we are entertained—we simply will not mind.

WORKS CITED

Barber, Benjamin R. *Jihad Vs. McWorld: How Globalism and Tribalism Are Reshaping the World.* New York: Ballantine, 1996.

Beatty, Warren, dir. and writer. *Bulworth.* Perf. Warren Beatty, Hallie Berry. Twentieth Century Fox, 1998.

Caple, Jim. "Ventura Won't Let Others Cash in on his Cachet." *St. Paul Pioneer Press* 24 Dec. 1998: A1.

Cass, Dennis. "An Action Figure for All Seasons." *Harper's Magazine* Feb. 1999: 65.

Cooper, Terry L. *The Responsible Administrator.* San Francisco: Jossey-Bass, 1998.

Dornan, Christopher. "Peering Forward: The Conduct of the News Media is Part of a Fretful Arc of Apprehension That Spans the Twentieth Century." *Media Studies Journal* 13:2 (1999): 120–29.

Emmers-Sommer, Tara, and M. Allen. "Surveying the Effect of Media Effects." *Human Communication Research* 25:4 (1999): 478–98.

Feyerabend, Paul. *Farewell to Reason.* London: Verso, 1987.

Graber, Doris A. *Mass Media and American Politics.* Washington, DC: Congressional Quarterly, Inc., 1993.

Hess, Stephen. "Federalism & News: Media to Government: Drop Dead." *Brookings Review,* Winter 2000: 28–31.

Kelly, Jim, and Bill Eliott. "Synthetic History and Subjective Reality: The Impact of Oliver Stone's Movie *JFK.*" *It's Show Time! Media, Politics, and Popular Culture.* Ed. David Schultz. New York: Peter Lang, 2000. 171–96.

Kovach, Bill, and Tom Rosenstiel. *Warp Speed: America in the Age of Mixed Media.* New York: The Century Foundation Press, 1999.

Lyotard, Jean-François. *The Postmodern Condition: A Report on Knowledge.* Minneapolis: U of Minnesota P, 1984.

McAllister, Matthew. *The Commercialization of American Culture.* Thousand Oaks, CA: Sage Publications, 1996.

Ragsdale, Jim. "Ventura Lambastes His Critics on Radio." *St. Paul Pioneer Press* 21 Aug. 1999: Al.

Rorty, Richard. *Philosophy and the Mirror of Nature.* Princeton: Princeton UP, 1980.

Schultz, David. "The Cultural Contradictions of the American Media." *It's Show Time! Media, Politics, and Popular Culture.* Ed. David Schultz. New York: Peter Lang, 2000. 13–28.

———. "Kenny Meets George Washington or 'Come on Down, Your 15 Minutes of Fame Are Now!'" *It's Show Time! Media, Politics, and Popular Culture.* Ed. David Schultz. New York: Peter Lang, 2000. xi–xiv.

Seib, Gerald F. "Live From Hollywood, It's American Politics with Warren Beatty." *The Wall Street Journal* 14 Sept. 1999: A1.

Small, J. "Political Ethics: A View of the Leadership." *American Behavioral Scientist* 19 (1976): 543–66.

Sweeney, Patrick. "Governor Bares All (Opinions) in *Playboy.*" *St. Paul Pioneer Press* 30 Sept. 1999: Al .

———. "Top Ethics Official's Memo Says Ventura Ventures Violated State Statutes." *St. Paul Pioneer Press* 10 Sept. 1999: Al.

Thompson, Dennis F. *Ethics in Congress: From Individual to Institutional Corruption.* Washington, DC: The Brookings Institution, 1995.

Twitchell, James B. *ADCULT USA.* New York: Columbia UP, 1996.

Wag the Dog. Dir. Barry Levinson. Perf. Dustin Hoffman, Robert DeNiro, Anne Heche, Denis Leary. New Line, 1997.

Name: _____ Date: _____

UNDERSTANDING THE TEXT

1. According to Conley and Schultz, what is the difference between a celebrity turned politician, like Ronald Reagan, and a "politainer" like Jesse Ventura?

2. According to Conley and Schultz, what social forces have converged to bring us the politainer?

3. What ethical concerns do Conley and Schultz consider at issue when a politainer holds public office? (Identify and discuss two.)

The Yuckster: Bob Dole, After Politics

John J. Miller

When the people behind *Bartlett's Familiar Quotations* consider whether to put any of Bob Dole's utterances in their next edition—he has none in the current one—they'll have plenty of choices. There's the bitter line from the 1988 GOP primaries, spoken to then-Vice President George Bush: "Stop lying about my record." There's one of the great blunders of recent political history, from the 1976 debate with Walter Mondale: "I figured it up the other day: If we added up the killed and wounded in Democrat wars in this century, it would be about 1.6 million Americans—enough to fill the city of Detroit." A later, self-deprecating quip on this unfortunate statement may itself deserve status as a minor classic: "They told me to go for the jugular, so I did: mine."

Now there's a very late entry: "Easy, boy."

On March 25, during ABC's broadcast of the Oscars, Pepsi unveiled an ad in which belly-baring 19-year-old pop star Britney Spears vamps about shaking her hips, flaunting her cleavage, and singing her tune. Flash to Bob Dole, sitting in an armchair and watching the same commercial. He appears transfixed at the sight of Spears and her come-hither looks. His dog barks. Dole doesn't budge, except to nod and speak two words: "Easy, boy."

It's the sort of double entendre more suited to a cheap sitcom than to a former presidential candidate, and it's hard to imagine, say, Michael Dukakis pulling it off. Dole can, simply because he's universally known not just as a former politician, but as a septuagenarian pitchman for an erection drug.

What a long way we've come since Dole ran for the White House. Back in 1995, he traveled to Hollywood and delivered a bold speech attacking the entertainment industry for its "mindless violence and loveless sex." It was a fight Dole didn't especially need to pick, and it voiced the belief of millions of Americans that contemporary movies and music pander far too much to people's worst urges. Dole's rhetoric soared, in what remains one of the finest speeches of his career: "The mainstreaming of deviancy must come to an end, but it will only stop when the leaders of the entertainment industry recognize and shoulder their responsibility." "The mainstreaming of deviancy"—that's a nice phrase, and a useful one. So it's too bad that Bob Dole, by portraying a dirty old man in a Pepsi commercial, now embodies a trend he once condemned with such eloquence.

Conservatives never were entirely comfortable with Dole as the Republican nominee— Newt Gingrich once described him as "the tax collector for the welfare state"—but the stoic Kansan nevertheless earned respect on the right for his rugged Midwestern dignity. He was a plainspoken war hero, a gruff member of the Greatest Generation who seemed attractively out of place in the age of Slick Willie. During one of the debates in 1996, Dole even criticized Clinton's manners: "I'm addressing [Clinton] all evening as 'Mr. President,'" he said. "He didn't extend that courtesy to President Bush." Here was a man who probably would have refused to answer the most memorably indecent question of the 1992 presidential campaign: boxers or briefs? Conservatives also admired his loyalty: Dole was capable of resilient partisanship when necessary, and remained faithful to the first President Bush even after they fought through that rough primary in 1988.

Despite this appeal, Dole was not a good presidential candidate. It would have taken a truly exceptional campaign to beat Bill Clinton in 1996, but Dole's effort was worse than lackluster. The one thing most people remember is not that he proposed a tax cut or that he promised to restore character to the Oval Office, but that time he tumbled off the stage in Chico, California

It's hard to believe, then, that Dole has been even worse as an ex-presidential candidate— but it's true. Dole started out playing the good loser, and his shtick worked. He went on David Letterman's show within days of his defeat. "Bob, what have you been doing lately?" asked Letterman. "Apparently not enough," Dole deadpanned. He also showed up on *Saturday Night Live* for a skit with Norm MacDonald, the man who had been impersonating him. They commiserated about their dim futures. Dole said that at least he had a job answering phones at the Red Cross. "My wife pulled some strings," he explained, referring to the fact that Elizabeth Dole was president of the organization. Then he satirized his own penchant for talking about himself in the third person by demonstrating his telephone skills: "Hello, Red Cross. How might Bob Dole direct your call?"

These appearances were funny. They also communicated the fundamentally conservative message that politics isn't everything. As Dole wrote in his recent book, *Great Political Wit* (an amusing collection of one-liners and anecdotes), "I wanted to show that there is indeed life after politics. And that losing an election does not mean losing your sense of humor."

But some of his behavior following the election was a bit unsettling. Dole immediately reneged on what seemed a simple promise, made during his surprise speech announcing he would retire from the Senate: "I will seek the presidency with nothing to fall back on but the judgment of the people, and nowhere to go but the White House or home." By "home," most listeners assumed he meant Kansas, which he had represented in Congress for decades. But it turned out that home really meant the Watergate complex, where he owned a one-bedroom apartment; Kansas was no more Bob Dole's home than Tennessee was Al Gore's.

Next came a slew of commercials. Other losing candidates—Dan Quayle, Geraldine Ferraro, Mario Cuomo—had made commercials, but for Dole it amounted to a new career. First was an ad for Air France, featuring Dole's picture under the caption, "Not doing anything?" Then there was one for Visa, which set Dole in what seemed to be a "homecoming" parade in Russell, Kansas. (It was actually shot in a couple of Texas towns.) Dole winds up in a local store, tries to make a purchase, and is asked for ID. "I just can't win!" he cracks. Dole also appeared in ads for Dunkin' Donuts and Target. He gave much of his personal proceeds to charity, yet there was still something unseemly about it all. Losing with a smile is one thing; repeatedly poking fun at your loss—in a campaign to which thousands of people anonymously devoted themselves because they seriously believed in a man and his ideas—is another. Nowadays Dole is more likely to be seen on Comedy Central's *Daily Show* than on *Meet the Press*. He's not an elder statesman so much as an aging comic.

He is best known, of course, as a poster boy for Viagra. Impotence is surely a difficult condition, and one of the primary hurdles facing men who might benefit from the drug is the awkwardness of asking for a prescription. The whole object of Viagra's ongoing ad campaign is to destigmatize the product. As Dole himself said in his commercial, "You know, it's a little embarrassing to talk about E.D. [erectile dysfunction], but it's so important to millions of men and their partners that I decided to talk about it publicly." It's a little embarrassing to listen to Bob Dole talk about it publicly. Frankly, I'd rather know whether he wears boxers or briefs. And what's this business about men and their "partners"? Would it be too judgmental and exclusionary simply to say "wives"? Some things apparently could benefit from restigmatizing.

Bob Dole once knew the value of a good stigma. "Those who cultivate moral confusion for profit should understand this," he warned in his Hollywood speech, before turning positively Churchillian. "We will name their names and shame them as they deserve to be shamed. We will contest them for the heart and soul of every child, in every neighborhood. If we refuse to condemn evil, it is not tolerance but surrender. And we will never surrender."

At least not until we can appear in a Pepsi commercial with Britney Spears.

Name: _____ Date: _____

UNDERSTANDING THE TEXT

1. Miller praises several passages from Bob Dole's 1995 campaign speech. What was the subject of that speech?

2. Why do you think Miller quotes those passages in his essay?

3. Since he lost the 1996 presidential election, what has Bob Dole become best known for? What is Miller's response to this?

Power of Ads to Shape News

Kathleen Hall Jamieson

In October 1980 Citizens' Party candidate Barry Commoner, who would garner a quarter of a million votes in the general election, bought air time for a radio commercial that opened with the word "Bullshit!" As the ad itself admitted, it had used that word to secure news coverage for a campaign that had been ignored by the press. ABC complied (October 15, 1980). CBS and NBC ignored the ad. By getting access to ABC network news time, Commoner's ad producer Bill Zimmerman parlayed a $5000 radio buy into free television attention previously denied that campaign. But the coverage ABC gave the ad was hardly a producer's dream. Throughout, Susan King, the network reporter, uses every available moment to convey her personal distaste and that of the network for the ad.

> *King:* "Political commercials you hear on the radio are broadcast from network studios like this one at ABC in New York. Later this month ABC will be forced to carry the Citizens' Party presidential ad which ran across the country yesterday at CBS and NBC radio and which begins with the unprecedented use of vulgarity."
> *Ad:* "Bullshit. What? Reagan and Anderson—it's all bullshit."
> *King:* "Shocked? Many listeners were when they heard the ad and complained to their local radio station, but when it comes to political advertising, the candidate controls. By law the studio, or in this case the network, is bound to air the politician's message if he is involved in the ad, no matter what the message says."

An expert then agrees that the law requires airing bona fide candidate ads if the candidate's picture appears or his voice is heard. [The "expert" should have added that this requirement goes into effect only when the station has aired an ad for any candidate for that office.]

King: "Section 315 of the Federal Communications Act dealing with political commercials says, 'The licensee shall have no power of censorship over the material broadcast.'"

Commoner: "I think the American public is mature enough to be able to withstand certain messages and register their reaction to that at the polls."

A spokesperson for Commoner decries a situation that dictates that "the only way we can attract attention is to remind people that this campaign is a hollow sham." King closes by noting that the few stations that refused the ad were being sued by the Citizens' Party. The piece ends with King saying, "No matter how uncomfortable the listener is, the candidate has the last word."

News reporting can provide a frame through which viewers understand ads. Conventional campaign wisdom holds that news sets the context for ads. If the news accounts are inconsistent with the ad, the power of the ad is diminished. When the two are consistent, the power of both is magnified. But news can only reframe ads if reporters question the legitimacy of their claims, point out the false inferences that they invite, and so on. Without such reframing by reporters, campaign ads have the potential to shape the visual and verbal language of news, and in recent campaigns they have been increasingly successful.

Eleven years after the Commoner ad aired, network norms for coverage had changed. On September 4, 1991, CBS, NBC, ABC, and CNN news stories all carried an excerpt from a Conservative Victory Committee ad urging Senate confirmation of Supreme Court nominee Clarence Thomas and attacking the integrity of his likely opponents including one who was not even on the Senate Judiciary Committee.

As a result, viewers saw and heard content they would not otherwise have been exposed to on these news programs. "Who will judge the judge?" asked a segment of the ad. "How many of these liberal Democrats could themselves pass ethical scrutiny?" [Pictures of Alan Cranston, Joseph Biden, and Edward Kennedy are shown.] As the charges unfold, they are repeated in print on the screen. "Ted Kennedy, suspended from Harvard for cheating, left the scene of the accident at Chappaquiddick where Mary Jo Kopechne died" [a headline from the *Washington Star* appears] "and this year Palm Beach [on screen, a photo of the front page of the *New York Post* showing a picture of Kennedy in casual wear and the headline "Teddy's Sexy Romp."] "Joseph Biden, found guilty of plagiarism during his presidential campaign. Alan Cranston, implicated in the Keating Five S&L scandal. Whose values should be on the Supreme Court? Clarence Thomas's or Ted Kennedy's" [The headline "Teddy's Sexy Romp" with the attached photo is juxtaposed with a photo of Thomas].

With the exception of CNN's *Crossfire,* the news broadcasts did not focus on the accuracy or fairness of the attacks but rather on the potential impact of the campaign on the Thomas hearings. A small Conservative group with a membership of 80,000 had managed to garner over a million dollars' worth of network time with an ad that cost $20,000 to produce and just under $40,000 to air on Fox and CNN in the Washington, D.C., area.

In the process of relaying the controversial segments of the ad to their viewers, the networks legitimized the unsupported inference that Kennedy had either engaged in questionable sexual behavior or, worse, was an accomplice in the alleged rape of a young woman by his nephew at the Kennedy Palm Beach home. The headline in the *New York Post* referred to a later discredited report that Kennedy, wearing only an undershirt, had chased a young woman around the Palm Beach residence. As corrected, the report revealed that the Senator had simply appeared in a living room in which a young woman was talking with Kennedy's son. The senator was at the time wearing a nightshirt that went down to his knees.

As the controversy about the ad raged, the *New York Times* ran a still from the ad on its front page. Where in 1980 two of the three networks ignored the Commoner ad, in 1991 all four networks centered coverage on the Conservative ad. Where the frame created by ABC for the Commoner ad distanced the network from it and treated it negatively, coverage of the anti-Biden, -Cranston, -Kennedy ad focused on its strategy and likely outcome.

But what the ABC coverage of 1980 and the 1991 coverage of the Thomas ad have in common is also important. Neither ABC in 1980 nor any of the networks in 1991 examined the legitimacy of the ads' claims. The Commoner ad alleged that there were no substantive differences among the major party candidates; the Conservative Victory Fund ad posited that the morality of those who would determine the qualifications of a Supreme Court nominee was a legitimate subject of inquiry. Until a subsequent charge of sexual harassment surfaced, no questions about Thomas's morality had been publicly raised by anyone.

News can provide a frame through which viewers are invited to see an ad. But 1988 was the year in which ads began routinely to contextualize news. As many have argued, in 1988 the Republicans defined the campaign terrain for Dukakis, for the press, and for voters. Ads played an important role in the Republicans' ability to set this agenda. To the extent that the spots succeeded and their images were used as visual illustration of the power of the Bush appeals, ads were contextualizing news.

Ads also contextualized news in a second sense. After a viewer has seen the same ad many times, exposure to a small segment of it can evoke the whole ad. My work with focus groups across a twenty-year period suggests that unless the verbal message is highly salient (e.g., the mention of your profession in the ad), reinforced by print on the screen, or repeatedly uttered in the ad, it is not until the third exposure to a typical production ad that the typical viewer is able to recall a substantial amount of the ad's spoken content.

But weeks after exposure to a single ad image, viewers can accurately recall whether or not they have seen it before. The discussion of whether pictures dominate words or words pictures is confused by its assumptions that one invariably dominates the other, that music plays no role in cueing recall, and that the impact of each remains the same with repeated exposure.[1]

Ads have an additional recall advantage over news. Most ads are "bedded" in a sound track that invites emotions consistent with the ad's message. So, for example, the musical backtrack for an ad about the candidate's accomplishments is upbeat and often patriotic. When a segment of the ad airs in news, its soundtrack is usually preserved. Lee Greenwood's "I'm Proud to Be an American" hitchhiked into network news in 1984 when the Reagan ads incorporating it were clipped into broadcast news stories. Although network news opens and closes with theme music, the news segments themselves aren't musically scored.

Moreover, the announcer's voice on the ad is usually more resonant than the reporter's. These factors increase the power of the embedded ad segment and dampen the corrective words spoken by the reporter.

Repeated exposure increases the likelihood that the words and pictures will be remembered. When a segment from a remembered ad is then shown on news, two things happen. First, if the segment is able to function synecdochically for the whole ad, the viewer will recall a larger part of the ad than that shown. Second, the audio that is likely to be remembered is not the reporter's words about the ad but rather some form of the audio from the ad itself.

ADS CAN SHAPE THE VISUAL AND VERBAL LANGUAGE OF NEWS

Critics from Coleridge to Kenneth Burke have recognized the power of naming. For Coleridge, a word doesn't "convey merely what a certain thing is, but the very passion and all the circumstances which were conceived as *constituting* the perception of the thing by the person who used the word."[2] One might paraphrase Burke to say that language does our thinking for us.[3] Along these lines, if the language of a candidate's ads infuses the vocabulary of reporters, the candidate has obtained a significant advantage.

In the 1988 general election the Republicans' ads, reinforced by news coverage of speeches and debates, created a pro-Bush vocabulary for reporters. Others had done so, although with less impact, before. In 1976 the Ford campaign succeeded in getting reporters to adopt the language of its most powerful attack ads. Repeatedly, Carter was faced by press queries about being or being perceived to be "wishy-washy on the issues."

In 1980 Carter achieved the same effect when the press accepted the question raised in Democratic ads and speeches, "Is Reagan too reckless to be president?" "Aides acknowledge that Reagan is having trouble shaking the perception that he might be militarily reckless," noted Barry Serafin (ABC, October 20, 1980). "Critics say his proposals border on recklessness," noted John McWethy (ABC, October 28, 1980). So, for example, after the Carter-Reagan debate, Barry Serafin (ABC, October 31, 1980) commented that Reagan's "advisers think that in his debate with Mr. Carter, he went a long way toward assuring a big audience that he would not be reckless." In their only debate, Reagan was able to dispatch the reckless image more by manner than matter. "There you go again" just aren't the words Hollywood usually scripts for Dr. Strangelove.

But where in these earlier campaigns, one side or the other occasionally enticed the press into embracing one of its words or phrases, in 1988 the Bush campaign managed to insinuate an entire vocabulary about the campaign into press coverage. Reporting on the Dukakis record on crime is illustrative. Here the Republicans secured the complicity of the press in renaming convicted murderer William Horton, in redefining the relationship between Horton's Maryland victims, in adopting such words as "torture" and "terrorize" to describe his actions while on furlough, in defining the furlough program's purpose as dispensing "weekend passes," and in talking of the policy as a "revolving door." Each of these acts of naming biased the discussion against Dukakis. Each was inaccurate. To the extent that the Republicans were able to put this language in place, however, they demonstrated the power of ads, reinforced by candidate speeches and campaign hype, to contextualize news.

Although his given name is William, he calls himself William, court records cite him as William, a July 1988 *Reader's Digest* article identifies him as William J. Horton, Jr.,[4] and press reports before the Republican ad and speech blitz name him "William," the Bush campaign and its supporting PACs identified the furloughed convict as "Willie" Horton. Even the crusading anti-Dukakis newspaper that won a Pulitzer Prize for its exposé on the furlough program consistently identifies Horton as William Horton or William Horton, Jr. When the Maryland man stabbed by the furloughed convict contacted the Lawrence *Eagle-Tribune* reporter, he too referred to Horton as William Horton.[5] In his account of the attack in the PAC ad, however, that man, Clifford Barnes, instead identifies the convict as "Willie" Horton.

One might trace the familiar "Willie" to the naming practices of slavemasters, to our patterns of talk about gangsters, or to the sort of benign paternalism that afflicts adults around small children. But whatever its origin, when discussing murder, kidnapping, and rape "Willie" summons more sinister images of criminality than does William. After all, it wasn't J. Eddie Hoover who hunted down Albert (or was it Alfred?) Capone. And during his trial, the person to that point known as Willie Smith was identified by family and attorney as either William or Will. After his acquittal on charges of rape, the family reverted to the name by which he had been known before.

The PAC ad titled "Weekend Prison Passes" as well as the PAC ads featuring Horton's victims all refer to him as "*Willie* Horton." When his mug shot appears on the screen of "Weekend Prison Passes," print under it reads "Willie Horton." Reporters reduced Dukakis on crime to the Republican sculpted image of "Willie Horton." In news reports, "*Willie*" Horton's name was mentioned more often by reporters than by George Bush or any of his representatives. Use of dramatic, coherent narrative increases the likelihood of recall.[6] Once the Horton narrative was embedded in public consciousness, mention of his name should have been sufficient to evoke the entire story.

By the campaign's end, even the Democratic candidates had accepted the Republican identification of Horton. (Bentsen in Rather interview, CBS, October 26, 1988; Dukakis interview with Rather, October 27, 1988; Dukakis in interview with Jennings, November 9, 1988). The most prominent exception occurred before Horton became a stock feature in the Bush stump speech and the subject of PAC ads. On July 8, 1988, in the *Washington Post* Richard Cohen wrote about "*William* Horton's Furlough."

The schizophrenic labeling by the *New York Times* seemed to invite a Woody Allen to shout that the czar and the tsar were the same person. An editorial on June 30, 1988, labels Horton "Willie Horton" as do articles on October 3 and 21. Yet pieces by Robin Toner on July 5 and Martin Tolchin on October 12 refer to him as "William R. Horton." In Tolchin's article, it is Clifford Barnes who refers to Horton as "Willie Horton."[7] The difference between the two sets of articles appears to be that "Willie Horton" is written about by anonymous reporters tasked with inside reporting and given filler space. By contrast, "issue" pieces carrying bylines write of "William Horton." The contrast raises the unconfirmed possibility that the more contact a reporter had with Bush campaign insiders, the more likely the use of "Willie." The hypothesis falters on the editorial presumably written by someone safely anchored to a desk in New York.

In an October 10, 1988, *New York Times* piece, Horton is initially tagged "Willie" and then accorded "Mr. Horton," the *Times'* usual mode of address. "Clifford Barnes is making a radio commercial—to the delight of George Bush and the concern of Michael Dukakis," says the report. "More than a year ago, Mr. Barnes and his wife [*note:* she wasn't his wife at the time; they were engaged and living together], Angela, were *viciously* attacked in their suburban Maryland home by *Willie* Horton, who had fled Massachusetts while out of prison under that state's furlough program. Mr. Horton broke into their home, *slashed* Mr. Barnes with a knife, and raped Angela Barnes. *Mr. Horton* is now serving two life sentences plus 85 years in prison for the attack. Vice President Bush repeatedly cites the attack and Mr. Dukakis's support for the furlough program to charge that his rival is soft on crime. Mr. Barnes will recount his grim experience in a radio ad for a pro-George Bush group in California, the Committee for the Presidency." About the *Times'* naming of Horton, one *New York Times* reporter observed, "Once when an editor changed his name to William, I argued that no one would know who I was talking about [if he weren't called 'Willie']."

The Republicans also controlled the language that characterized the furlough program itself. The Bush furlough ad describes Dukakis's policy as giving "*weekend furloughs to first-degree murderers.*" The PAC ad titled "Weekend Passes" shows pictures of Bush, Dukakis, and Horton as it claims that Dukakis "allowed first-degree murderers to have *weekend passes* from prison. . . . Horton received ten *weekend passes* [a statement reprinted on the screen]. . . ." The ad is tagged "*Weekend prison passes:* Dukakis on crime" (emphasis added).

The press adopted the phrases "weekend furloughs" and "weekend passes" from the Republican speeches and ads that in turn located them in the Lawrence *Eagle-Tribune*. The phrases are inaccurate. Furloughs in Massachusetts ranged from one to seventy-four hours in 1987 and from one to 170 hours in 1986[8] and furloughs could be granted for any day or days of the week. In 1987, the median number of hours of leave per furlough was 19, five less than a full day and 29 less than a weekend. Horton's approved 48-hour furlough began on Friday, June 6, 1986, which means he should have returned to prison while most of us were still enjoying what we usually define as a weekend.

Bush reinforced the notion that these were weekend events by averring that he says to criminals "Make my day!" while Dukakis says "Have a nice weekend." "Weekend" suggests that the furloughs occur frequently when in fact in 1988 as in 1986 a prisoner is permitted no furloughs for the first half of his or her sentence and in 1988 may be furloughed only in the final three years before eligibility for parole or release.[9] In April 1988, Dukakis signed a bill ending furloughs for those who once were first-degree murderers not eligible for parole.

Weekend is a time for recreation. This association suggests that the assault and rapes were leisure activities for the prisoners. Bush implied as much when he asked those in his audience to question Dukakis why he had let "murderers out on vacation" (June speech to Illinois Republican Convention in Springfield).

The Bush furlough ad is titled "Revolving Door" and speaks of Dukakis's "revolving door prison policy." Although the visual in the ad itself shows not a revolving door but a turnstile, reporters also adopted the Republican announcer's characterization of the program as a "revolving door" policy. So, for example, Dan Rather asked the Democratic vice presidential nominee "[C]an't a person, or can a person, be deeply concerned about *revolving-door justice* and laxity toward criminals, even when the criminal happens to be someone who is black and still not be a racist?" (CBS, October 26, 1988).

In describing the ad, reporters adopted the Bush language as well. In an article examining inaccuracies in the ads of both campaigns, the *Washington Post's* Lloyd Grove describes "[A]nother Bush campaign commercial featuring hard-eyed men in prison garb streaming through a *revolving door*" (*Washington Post,* October 31, 1988, p. A8).

So clear was the identification that reporters quote viewers using it. In Texas Bill Cockerill described the ad to a *New York Times* reporter as "the revolving door commercial, implying that they come out as fast as they go in" (*New York Times,* October 22, 1988).[10] Despite the use of the words "turnstile or gate" in all questions to our Texas focus groups, 36 percent of respondents referred to the "furlough ad" as the "revolving door ad."

Here is an instance of the complexity of the visual-verbal relationship. The repeated use of the phrase "revolving door" couples with repeated viewing of the image of the circling actors as convicts to situate the visual-verbal link in memory. "Revolving door" too suggests a frequency and casualness in the administration of the furlough program that did not characterize the Massachusetts system.

From PAC ads made by Horton's victims, reporters adopted the words "slashed," "brutally," "terrorized," and "tortured." "For twelve hours I was beaten, slashed, and terrorized," says Clifford Barnes, "and my wife Angie was brutally raped." "Horton went on to rape and torture others," says the sister of the man killed by Horton. Bush helped set the language in place. On June 24, he stated, "In no other state would a cold-blooded murderer like *Willie* Horton have been set free to *terrorize* innocent people" (emphasis added).

"Slashed," "terrorized," and "tortured" are not the words usually used by reporters to characterize crime. Nor was it the language first used by the national press to describe Horton's actions. Before the furloughs became a campaign issue, on December 2, 1987, CBS aired a segment that "took a hard look today at a standard procedure for many of the nation's prisons. Forty-five states," says Rather, "offer furlough programs which release inmates from prison for limited times to see how they handle freedom." The language of the correspondent is the factual, calm, descriptive language characteristic of crime reporting in network news. "William Horton did strike again in this Maryland house where Cliff and Angela Barnes lived. He held them hostage for 12 hours. Horton raped her twice, tied her husband up in the basement and stabbed him 22 times." But by June 26 (Adams) and July 20 (Stahl), CBS reporters were calling Horton "Willie" and adopting the tabloid-like language of torture and terror.

Once the Republican language was in place, it became the optic through which the print media saw and invited us to see Horton's actions as well. The *Washington Post* favored the word "terrorized" (October 22, 1988; October 25, 1988; June 23, 1988, "terror"), as did columnist Tom Wicker (*New York Times,* June 24, 1988). *Newsweek* preferred to label "*Willie* Horton" "the Massachusetts murderer who *tortured* a Maryland couple" (October 31, 1988, p. 16). The *New York Times,* which on July 5 described "William Horton" as "a convicted murderer" who "broke into the couple's home, bound and stabbed Mr. Barnes and raped his wife" by mid-October had "*Willie* Horton" "viciously" attacking and also adopted Barnes's word "*slashed* with a knife" (*New York Times,* October 10, 1988, "Convict's Victim Makes an Ad" [emphasis added]).

Academics also embraced the Republican language. "The furlough program was emphasized," writes journalism professor David Myers, "because *Willie* Horton, a black man who had been convicted of first-degree murder, had escaped to Maryland on a *weekend pass,* where he *brutalized* a white man and raped his fiancée."[11]

As interesting is the fact that when offered two different constructions of the relationship of the couple assaulted by Horton, press reports adopt the more incendiary of the two until late in the campaign. At the time of the Horton attack, Clifford Barnes and his fiancée were living together. The first PAC ad to air on the topic says accurately that Horton "kidnapped a young couple, stabbing the man and repeatedly [twice] raping his *girlfriend.*"[12] That ad began airing September 9. On October 20 a second PAC ad is aired in California. This spot features Clifford Barnes, who is now married to the woman who was his fiancée at the time of the attack by Horton. "My wife Angie was brutally raped," says Barnes.

The sources that identify "Angie" as Barnes's "wife" at the time of the attack include CBS (December 1987), Cohen in the *Washington Post,* Holman of *MacNeil/Lehrer,* and Toner in the *New York Times.* Although in an October 23 ABC report, Joe Bergantino identifies Barnes as her "boyfriend," two days later ABC's Britt Hume identifies Barnes as her husband (October 25, 1988). On NBC (October 28, 1988), this identification was reinforced in what I define as a "newsad," a segment of news that might as well have been paid candidate advertising:

> *Ken Bode:* "George Bush was here [California] again today. Again talking about crime."
>
> *Bush:* "I believe in safe neighborhoods, and I say I believe it is time for America to take back our streets."
>
> *Bode:* "Like everywhere else the Democrats have been on the defensive about crime. Willie Horton's victims made a campaign commercial."
>
> *Cliff Barnes in ad clip:* "For twelve hours I was beaten, slashed, and terrorized, and my wife Angie was brutally raped."
>
> *Bode:* "But mostly, Bush's tough talk on crime works, because it fits with what Californians see on their news each day."
>
> *Man:* "When you have gang murders in the headlines, day after day, I think the voters understand that there is only one candidate in this race who is truly tough on crime. Only one candidate for President who really supports the death penalty."

My final claim is that the Republican use of Horton shaped the visual portrayal of crime in network news in ways that reinforced the mistaken assumption that violent crime is disproportionately committed by blacks, disproportionately committed by black perpetrators against white victims, and disproportionately the activity of black males against white females. In other words, Republican use of Horton shaped the visuals in 1988 network crime coverage in a way that underscored the Bush message.

James Devitt and I have systematically examined the way in which alleged criminals are portrayed in network news from 1985 to 1989. In 911 scenes of alleged criminals in 530 network news stories, blacks are proportionately more likely than whites to be shown restrained and in actual mug shots—the two visuals shown in the Horton PAC ads. Robert Entman has found the same pattern in local news.[13]

I suspect that this disproportionate exposure to black males in mug shots increases the telegraphic power of the use of the Horton mug shot in the PAC ads. This tendency is then magnified at a statistically significant level in coverage of crime as a 1988 campaign issue ($p = .0011$). This finding raises the question: What subtle chain of inferences or visceral responses might be invited by Senator Jesse Helms's showing of a closeup still photo of his opponent Harvey Gantt?

Our data also provide a baseline telling us how often blacks are likely to appear as "alleged criminals" in news and what visual forms this representation will take. By comparing the appearance of blacks as alleged criminals in crime stories from 1985 to 1989 with appearance in stories about the issue of crime in the 1988 general election, we can determine whether the crime stories of 1988 differed significantly from earlier norms. They do. The increase in the proportion of blacks identified or shown as criminals in 1988 general election stories about crime is statistically significant ($p = .0139$). Moreover, the number of female victims per news story doubled in 1988 stories about crime.

Just as the Bush campaign verbally primed reporters' discussion of crime, so too the issue of Horton subtly primed producers and editors to include more blacks in their covering shots showing presumed criminals. The most egregious example of this occurred October 31, 1988 on ABC. The reporter was Ken Kashiwahara. All of the presumed criminals but one are black or Hispanic. All of those who say that they are afraid are white. Most are women.

To portray a black male who "killed" one white male, stabbed a second, and raped a white woman as a typical criminal is inaccurate. Blacks run a greater risk of forcible rape, robbery, and aggravated assault than whites. Low-income individuals are the most likely victims of violent crime. Men are more likely than women to be the victims of violence, blacks more often than whites.[14] FBI statistics confirm that, unlike robbery, rape and murder in the United States are primarily intraracial not interracial phenomena. In 1988, for example, 11.3 percent of reported rapes involved a black rapist and a white victim.[15]

I do not intend to minimize Thomas and Mary Edsall's claims that a higher percent of the crime committed by blacks is interracial and that in the categories of assault and robbery more than half of the robberies committed by blacks have white victims.[16] Rather, my point is that raising the fear of whites that they are likely to be murdered or raped by blacks is unjustified. It is racist to identify William Horton's actions as somehow typical, as George Bush did when he said that the Horton case had "come to symbolize, and represent . . . the misguided outlook of my opponent."

Moreover, disproportionate portrayal of blacks as criminals plays on racial fears. When discussion of crime in network news occurs in segments in which blacks are visually cast in disproportion as criminals, the news stories themselves are priming both a pro-Bush and a racist response.

In 1988 the power of the Republican campaign to export the visual and verbal language of its ads to news was indicative of a change in the relationship between news and political advertising. Where news once contextualized ads, visually evocative and easily edited oppositional ads backed by reinforcing candidate speeches and pseudo-events now have the capacity to shape the language and pictures of news.

ENDNOTES

[1] This conclusion is consistent with that of scholarship about recall of advertising and of television. Cf. D. S. Hayes and S. Pingree, "Television's Influence on Social Reality," in D. Pearl and J. Lazar, *Television and Behavior* (Washington, D.C.: U.S. Government Printing Office, 1982), 224–47; D. S. Hayes and D. W. Birnbaum, "Preschoolers' Retention of Televised Events: Is a Picture Worth a Thousand Words?" *Developmental Psychology* 16 (1980), 410–16; D. S. Hayes, B. E. Chemelaki, and D. W. Birnbaum, "Young Children's Incidental Retention of Televised Events," *Developmental Psychology* 17 (1981), 230–32; K. Pezdek and E. F. Hartman, "Children's Television Viewing: Attention and Comprehension of Auditory Versus Visual Information," *Child Development* 54 (1983), 1015–23.

The evidence does not suggest that the visual interferes with comprehension of the audio, however. Cf. D. R. Rolandelli, "Children and Television: The Visual Superiority Effect Reconsidered," *Journal of Broadcasting and Electronic Media* 33 (1989), 69–81; C. Hoffner, J. Cantor, and E. Thorson, "Children's Responses to Conflicting Auditory and Visual Features of a Televised Narrative," *Human Communication Research* 16:2, (1989), 256–78. There is evidence that the visual imagery of television changes the processing of audio. Cf. J. Beagles-Roos and I. Gat, "Specific Impact of Radio and Television on Children's Story Comprehension," *Journal of Educational Psychology* 75 (1983), 128–35.

Some have argued that Iyengar and Kinder's research calls the impact of vivid communication into question. Their summary of the existing scholarly literature states that "When vividness is defined as the contrast between personalized, case history information and abstract statistical information, the vividness hypothesis is supported every time" (p. 35). The structure of their chapter seems to suggest that they then take issue with this consensus. Yet they conclude that "Our results do not argue against vividness effects in general; they indicate only that dramatic vignettes of personal suffering do not enhance agenda setting" (p. 46). See S. Iyengar and D. Kinder, *News that Matters* (Chicago: University of Chicago Press, 1987).

Additional information on verbal/visual processing can be found in Laura M. Buchholz and Robert E. Smith, "The Role of Consumer Involvement in Determining Cognitive Response to Broadcast Advertising," *Journal of Advertising* 20:1 (1991), 4–17, and Julie Edell and Kevin Lane Keller, "The

Information Processing of Coordinated Media Campaigns," *Journal of Marketing Research* 26 (May 1989), 149–63.

[2] Samuel Taylor Coleridge, *Shakespeare Criticism,* Middleton Raysor, ed. (London: Dutton, 1907).

[3] Cf. *The Philosophy of Literary Form,* 3rd ed. (Berkeley: University of California Press, 1973), 3 ff.

[4] Robert James Bidinotto, "Getting Away With Murder," *Reader's Digest* 133 (July 1988), 57–63.

[5] Susan Forrest, "How 12 Hours Shattered Two Lives," *Lawrence Eagle-Tribune,* August 16, 1987.

[6] See N. S. Johnson and J. M. Mandler, "A Tale of Two Structures: Underlying and Surface Forms in Stories," *Poetics* 9 (1980), 51–86.

[7] "Furloughs From Common Sense," *New York Times,* June 30, 1988, A22; Robin Toner, "Prison Furloughs in Massachusetts Threaten Dukakis Record on Crime," *New York Times,* July 5, 1988, B5.

[8] "1987 Annual Statistical Report of the Furlough Program," Massachusetts Department of Correction, December 1988, 6.

[9] 103CMR-157. February 2, 1990, 3.

[10] Cf. Gerald Boyd, "Bush's Attack on Crime Appeals to the Emotions," *New York Times,* October 11, 1988, 12: "In addition, Mr. Bush's campaign has aired television commercials that portray the prison system in Massachusetts, where Mr. Dukakis is the Governor, as a revolving door that releases inmates on weekend passes." Gerald Boyd "Despite Vow to be 'Gentler,' Bush Stays on Attack," *New York Times,* October 29, 1988, 8: "Mr. Fuller said that although Mr. Bush hoped to end the campaign on a 'positive note,' there were no plans to remove television commercials like the one that accuses Mr. Dukakis of operating the Massachusetts prison program as a 'revolving door.'"

[11] *The Media in the 1984 and 1988 Presidential Campaigns,* Guido H. Stempel III and John W. Windhauser, eds. (New York: Greenwood Press, 1991), 169. Note the tacit assumption that because the man is white, his fiancée must be white as well.

[12] "Weekend Prison Passes," produced by Larry McCarthy for Americans for Bush.

[13] Entman, 30.

[14] *Sourcebook,* 1988, 298. Table 3.17.

[15] *U.S. Dept. of Justice "Criminal Victimization in the United States, 1988."* December 1990. NCJ-122024. Table 43.

[16] Edsall and Edsall, *Chain Reaction,* 236.

Name: _____ Date: _____

UNDERSTANDING THE TEXT

1. According to Jamieson, when television news programs "analyze" a political ad on the air, what do they typically focus upon, and what do they ignore?

2. According to Jamieson, in what ways do ads "shape news"? (Identify and discuss two.)

3. What, according to Jamieson, were some of the inaccuracies of the Willie Horton ad? (Identify and discuss two.)

Trout or Hamburger: Politics and Telemythology

Michael Schudson

Has television taken over the practice of American politics? Have cynically manipulated images and sound bites mesmerized the American public? Have politicians bypassed the citizen's rational decision-making process with a shortcut to some image center in the brain that values appearance over substance, flash over philosophy? In American politics today, do the eyes have it?

Anyone listening to political commentary in any recent election would surely answer yes. The airwaves teem with political commercials. The newspapers overflow with commentary about the broadcast spots. And then new TV spots incorporate the print commentary about the old spots. At times, candidates and voters seem to be on the sidelines, passively observing the media consultants and ad agencies on the playing field.

As soon as the election is over, however, talk about the brilliance or mendacity of 30-second demagoguery fades. On the day before the election, every politician is a candidate, and takes a candidate's obsessive interest in every little bit of good or harm that might come from advertising. On the day after there are only winning candidates, glad to be in office, and losers, seeking some kind of solace in a bad time. The losers seem to change quickly from activists to philosophers, from political strategists to political scientists. Thus in 1990 Dianne Feinstein's campaign manager, Duane Garrett, was suddenly reminding people that for twenty-five years (with the exception of 1974, the Watergate year) California voted Republican for president and governor—so what else could one expect in 1990? In his post-election assessment, the story was not that Feinstein lost but that she came as close as she did.

Did Feinstein's TV spots make a difference? Did Paul Wellstone's in Minnesota? Or Jesse Helms's in North Carolina? The question is still important, but it is notoriously elusive.

Despite all the attention that the press has lavished on political commercials, it is no simple task to evaluate their potency, as opposed to observing their ubiquity and decrying their negativity. Even newspaper "truth box" commentaries, which began in 1990 to monitor the accuracy of political ads on television, have been criticized for focusing on the commercials' explicit claims rather than their visual imagery—for reading television as if it were radio and failing to understand the overwhelming power of the image.

But is the image overpowering? Does the image conquer all in political television? Even that apparently safe assumption can be questioned.

Take, for instance, the story told by the media critic Michael Arlen in *Thirty Seconds* about the making of an AT&T "Reach Out and Touch Someone" commercial.[1] In one version of the commercial, a group of men have gone off to a rural retreat for a weekend of fishing. The weekend is a disaster; it is pouring rain the whole time. We see the men huddled in their cabin in the woods, cooking hamburgers, while one of them talks to friends back home, singing the praises of their manly adventure. The man on the phone is staring into a frying pan full of hamburgers while he says into the receiver, "Boy, you should see the great trout we've got cooking here." When test audiences were asked what the men were cooking for dinner, they replied overwhelmingly—trout. One of the advertising executives in charge of the project comments:

> I have to tell you we were very discouraged. Some of our guys were even talking of junking the commercial, which was a good one, with a nice humorous flow to it. Well, we ended up making it, but what we had to do was, when we came to that segment, we put the camera almost inside the frying pan, and in the frying pan we put huge, crude chunks of hamburger that were almost red. I mean, just about all you could see was raw meat. This time, when we took it to the audience, it tested OK. That is, most of the test audience—though, in fact, still not everybody—finally said "hamburger."

The trout/hamburger story has not made its way into the common culture of media consulting, political journalism, or academic criticism. The ability of verbal cues to trump the visual is forgotten, while the contrary lesson, that a picture overrides ten thousand words, is regularly retold.

A current favorite is the story of the Lesley Stahl four-and-a-half-minute piece that CBS ran during the 1984 presidential campaign. Its subject was how the White House staged events for Ronald Reagan and manipulated the press, especially television. Stahl later said that a White House official called her soon after the piece aired and said he'd loved it. "How could you?" she responded. He said, "Haven't you figured it out yet? The public doesn't pay any attention to what you say. They just look at the pictures." Stahl, on reflection—but not, I think, on very much reflection—came to believe that the White House was probably right: all she had done was to assemble, free of charge, a Republican campaign film, a wonderful montage of Reagan appearing in upbeat scenes.

In the world of media criticism and political consulting, the Stahl story is presented as powerful evidence of the triumph of pictures over words and emotion over rationality in American politics. It is a major piece of evidence for *New York Times* reporter Hedrick Smith's conclusion that the eye is more powerful than the ear in American politics; it opens journalist Martin Schram's account of television in the 1984 election; it is cited to similar account by *Washington Post* columnist David Broder and communications scholar Kathleen Jamieson.[2] But the story's punch depends on our believing that the White House official knew what he was talking about. Did he?

In this case, no one really knows. But in another case we have information that indicates that the Reagan White House did *not* understand the power of pictures on television. In 1982 the country was in the midst of a recession and the Reagan administration was faring badly in the polls. The networks were making efforts to dramatize the country's economic plight not only by reporting the national unemployment figures, but also by focusing on a particular person or family hurt by hard times. The White House was outraged and criticized the networks for presenting the sad tale of the man in South Succotash and missing the general economic trends that, according to the White House, were more positive. Obviously, the White House assumed that the emotionally compelling, visually powerful vignette had much more impact on the American public than dry statistics. But when Donald Kinder and Shanto Iyengar conducted a series of careful experiments on television viewing, they found that the captivating vignette on economic affairs did no more than the bare statistics to lead viewers to believe that economic affairs were a major problem facing the nation. In fact, the evidence in Kinder and Iyengar's *News That Matters* ran modestly in the other direction— viewers were more impressed by statistics than by down-home stories about the gravity of the economic crisis.[3] This result runs counter to common sense. Isn't it true that a picture is worth more than all those words? Are the social scientists in this case (and not for the first time) just plain wrong?

I don't think so. There is a way to understand their results that is consistent with other well-established research. People do not automatically extrapolate from individual experience, even their own, to the nation as a whole. When American citizens go to the polls, for instance, they distinguish between their own personal economic situation and their sense of how the nation as a whole is doing—and typically they vote according to their sense of how the nation as a whole is doing. They do not cast reflex-like "pocketbook" votes.[4] When people see a television story on the plight of an individual family, they do not automatically generalize to the state of the nation. Indeed, the form of the vignette encourages them to discount the story as unrepresentative. If, say, the vignette pictures a black family, a significant number of whites may routinely discount the story as a special case, not a representative one, because they do not identify with blacks. If the news pictures a farm family, an urban family may not identify with them. In a sense, these viewers are not "visually literate"; they do not follow the visual logic by which one instance of poverty or unemployment is meant to represent the general phenomenon. Viewers find more general significance, then, in

Department of Labor statistics than in artfully composed and emotionally compelling photographic essays on the economy.

The Lesley Stahl episode has become part of our telemythology, a set of widely circulated stories about the dangerous powers of television. With respect to politics, three key episodes contribute to the general mythology:

- Kennedy defeated Nixon in 1960 because he presented a more attractive image in the first television debate.
- Television's graphic portrayal of the war in Vietnam sickened and horrified American viewers, who were led by harsh photographic reality to oppose the war.
- The unprecedented popularity of President Reagan has no rational explanation but can be accounted for only by the power of an actor skilled at manipulating a visual medium.

But look again at each of the episodes. Kennedy just barely defeated Nixon in November 1960, and perhaps did not actually defeat him at all—we will never know just how many ballot boxes were stuffed in Cook County on election day. Many observers of the election, including Kennedy himself, attributed his success to his fine showing in the television debates. The most discussed part of the debates concerns the failure of Nixon's makeup artists to prepare him properly for the hot lights of the television studio. Where Kennedy seemed cool, Nixon appeared to be sweating; where Kennedy was self-assured, Nixon seemed to strain. Kennedy's appearance on national television galvanized his campaign; crowds instantly seemed larger and more enthusiastic in his campaign appearances. For Nixon, who added to Kennedy's stature simply by accepting the challenge to debate in the first place, the first debate was deeply unsettling.

Social scientists cite the finding that citizens who listened to the Kennedy-Nixon debate on the radio judged Nixon the winner; those who watched television found Kennedy the winner. As with the Stahl story, this is presented as conclusive evidence of the distorting lens of television. On radio, it is assumed, one listens to pure argument; on television, one is distracted by the appearance of things, the superficial look of people rather than the cogency of their arguments.

The basis for all this is a study undertaken by a Philadelphia market research firm that found that radio listeners judged Nixon the winner by 43 percent to 20 percent, while a majority (53 percent) of television viewers judged the debate a draw or refused to name a winner. Of those willing to name a winner, 28 percent chose Kennedy and 19 percent Nixon.[5]

Even if we accept this study as valid (and it was never reported in a form to make serious analysis possible), there are two problems with the way it has been used. The first problem concerns the presumption that radio is a distortion-free medium. Is the human voice itself not a medium? Is radio not a medium, too? Are words conveyed through radio a pure rendering of logical relations? Or does the voice—specifically, the radio-transmitted voice—give special weight to sonority and to the verbal tics and tricks of an experienced and skilled debater that have no necessary relation to the validity of the arguments themselves? Might radio have exaggerated Kennedy's Boston accent as part of his nature and therefore put people off? The human voice, from the cry of a baby onward, can stir passions. It can as easily be an enemy of reason as its epitome. A medium like radio that separates the human voice from the body is not necessarily a guardian of rationality.

Second, is television imagery so obviously superficial? Was it not important, and truthful, to see that Kennedy, despite his relative youth, was able to handle the most public moment of his life with assurance? Was it not important, and truthful, to see Nixon, despite his vast experience, looking awkward and insecure? Isn't it possible to argue that the insecurity he showed betrayed his manner and motive in public life?

Let me turn briefly to Vietnam. Here we have been told repeatedly about the power that television had to turn the American public against the war. The general argument has been that the horror of war, graphically shown to the viewing public, sickened Americans. Anything that the narration might have said about the legitimacy of the military effort, the pictures stunningly undermined. What is the evidence for this belief? There is, it turns out, almost no evidence at all. The public did, over time, become more and more disenchanted with the war in Vietnam—but at just about the same rate and to just about the same degree as the public became disaffected with the untelevised Korean war. Moreover, contrary to some popular reconstructions of television coverage, the TV coverage of the Vietnam war provided very little combat footage in the years during which opposition to the war mounted. It is possible, of course, that isolated instances of combat coverage had great impact; but, as Peter Braestrup points out in his book *Battle Lines,* the television archives provide no basis for the view that a day-in, day-out television portrait of bloodshed was ever presented to the American public.[6]

The general understanding behind the "TV-turned-us-against-the-war" argument is that TV photography comes to us unmediated—it forces itself upon the viewer, who then recoils from war. In fact, Daniel Hallin argues in *The Uncensored War* that "television's visual images are extremely ambiguous." We don't know very much about how audiences construct the meaning of TV images, but "it seems a reasonable hypothesis that most of the time the audience sees what it is told it is seeing."[7] Trout, in short, not ground beef.

The final piece of telemythology I want to examine is the view that Ronald Reagan's mastery of television led to his mastery of the American public. This is another curious story. Reagan's extraordinary popularity was heralded by the news media months before he took office. The sense in Washington of his popularity was so powerful that on March 18, 1981, not yet two months into Reagan's first term, James Reston reported that Congress was very reluctant to vote against the budget of so popular a chief executive. Reston's column appeared prominently on the *New York Times* op-ed page on the same day that, in a three-inch story at the bottom of page 22, a report on the latest Gallup poll coolly stated that Reagan's public approval ratings were the lowest in polling history for a newly elected president.

As it turned out, Reagan's average approval rating for his first year in office was, according to the Gallup survey, 57 percent compared with Carter's 62 percent, Nixon's 62 percent,

Kennedy's 76 percent. His second-year average was 43 percent compared with Carter's 46 percent, Nixon's 56 percent, Kennedy's 72 percent.[8] Polls that tried to separate Reagan's personal appeal from the appeal of his policies found the President to be notably more popular than his program; however, this has been the case with every president, and the margin of difference was smaller for Reagan than for other presidents.[9] Later in his first term and in much of his second term, Reagan had unusually high public approval ratings. Still, the public impression and the media consensus about his general popularity were firmly established before there was any national polling evidence to corroborate it. How did this happen?

There are a number of explanations. The most important, I think, is that the Washington establishment *liked* Reagan. That establishment, Republican and Democrat, politician and journalist, had had enough of Jimmy Carter's puritanical style of socializing and humorless style of leadership. "For the first time in years, Washington has a President that it really likes," *Washington Post* political analyst Haynes Johnson concluded by the fall of 1981.[10] Reagan was very likable, yes. He brought with him the allure and glamour of Hollywood. More than this, he turned out to be a first-rate politician in the most old-fashioned sense: he could count votes, he knew whom to invite to breakfast or dinner and when, and he employed expert staff to deal with the Congress. When his aides asked him to make a phone call here or a public appearance there, he obliged. And if this direct courtship from the White House were not enough, Reagan succeeded in mobilizing a small but highly vocal right-wing constituency that, with just a whisper from the White House staff, would deluge congressional offices with telegrams and letters.

That is probably the heart of it, but I think there is something more—the strong belief of Washington elites that the general public can be mesmerized by television images. Many journalists shared a kind of "gee whiz" awe at the media skills of the White House, according to Laurence Barrett, senior White House correspondent for *Time*. Their sense of White House media omnipotence was particularly strong because of the contrast between Reagan's smooth administrative machinery and the ineffective Carter White House.[11] Consider the view of Barrett's colleague at *Time,* Thomas Griffith, who wrote that the "people in Peoria" are more receptive to Reagan's message than people who follow public affairs closely. The Reagan administration, he felt, aimed its message at the television audience, not the close readers of print. Reagan's was a "TV presidency."[12]

What is a TV presidency? Reagan's was scarcely the first to be declared one. There was Kennedy's, of course. Even Nixon gets a vote: "Nixon is a television creation, a sort of gesturing phantom, uncomfortable in the old-fashioned world of printer's type, where assertions can be checked and verified." That unlikely judgment comes from novelist and critic Mary McCarthy.[13] Carter was regularly declared a master of symbolism and images in his first year in office. In 1976, Carter flew into office hailed as a genius at media manipulation. His own media adviser, perhaps not surprisingly, called him "the biggest television star of all time. He is the first television president." The comic strip *Doonesbury* added a new cabinet officer, the secretary of symbolism, early in the Carter administration. The *New York*

Times television critic reported in 1977 that Carter is "a master of controlled images." David Halberstam wrote in 1976 that Carter "more than any other candidate this year has sensed and adapted to modern communications and national mood . . . Watching him again and again on television I was impressed by his sense of pacing, his sense of control, very low-key, soft, a low decibel count, all this in sharp contrast to the other candidates."[14] Note, however, that as is so often the case with discussions of Reagan, Halberstam attributes Carter's television power to sound, not look. A case could be made that Reagan's presence on television has to do most of all with his voice. People thought of Carter in his first years as a master of images—the President walking, rather than riding, in his inaugural procession; the informal, down-home Jimmy wearing a cardigan sweater. Reagan riding his horse on the ranch never gained the same kind of power. I suspect that we will one day recall Reagan as one of the least visual but most auditory of our presidents. What is memorable is the Reagan with the slight choke in his voice when he told a melodramatic story about a G.I. or read a letter from a little girl, his quick intelligence with a joke or a quip, the comfort, calm, and sincerity in his voice. It was not even his look. It was not his words, as such, but his way with them. Reagan knew, if his critics did not, that it was his voice, his long-lived radio asset, that made his television appearance so effective.

The power of television is perhaps more firmly an article of faith in Washington than anywhere else in the country. There is an odd sense inside the beltway that the rest of the nation is not so much concerned with freeway traffic, paying bills at the end of the month, waiting for the plumber, getting the kids off to school, and finding a nursing home for Grandma as it is with watching Washington, especially in an election year. Otherwise it seems inexplicable that George Will, for instance, should have judged Robert Dole's relatively high poll ratings among Democrats early in the 1988 Republican primary season as "an effect of the televised Senate—he's had a chance to be seen in what is manifestly his home turf, where he is very comfortable."[15] Who is watching the televised Senate? C-SPAN is just not much competition for *Wheel of Fortune, General Hospital, Roseanne,* or, I'm afraid, even *Sesame Street.* How could anyone be so hopelessly out of touch? But so as not to pick on a Republican unfairly, I call to mind Walter Mondale's mournful plaint after his landslide loss to Reagan that television never warmed up to him nor did he warm up to television.[16] Did Hoover lose to Roosevelt because he didn't warm up to radio? Could a Depression have had something to do with it? And might Mondale have lost because 1984 was a time of peace, apparent prosperity, and a likable incumbent Republican?

The phenomenon of people believing that only *others* are influenced by the mass media is what W. Phillips Davison calls the "third-person effect" in communication.[17] The assumption that gullible others, but not one's own canny self, are slaves to the media is so widespread that the actions based on it may be one of the mass media's most powerful creations. The power of the media resides in the perception of experts and decision makers that the general public is influenced by the mass media, not in the direct influence of the mass media on the general public. That is to say, the media's political appeal lies less in its ability to bend minds than in its ability to convince elites that the popular mind can be bent.

If experts overestimate the direct power of the visual, they underrate their own power to reinterpret the visual. In 1976, Gerald Ford said in his debate with Carter that "there is no Soviet domination of Eastern Europe." Although recent events suggest that his misstatement was truer than he knew, that gaffe was reputed to be a major break for Carter and the beginning of the Ford campaign's unraveling. Again, it appears, television demonstrated its enormous power in American politics.

But few television viewers noticed or cared about Ford's remark. A poll conducted by a market research organization employed by the President Ford Committee found that people judged Ford to have done a better job than Carter by 44 percent to 35 percent in the two hours immediately after the debate on the evening of October 6. By noon on October 7, Carter was judged the winner by 44 percent to 31 percent, and by that evening he was judged the winner by 61 percent to 19 percent. On the evening of October 6, not a single person interviewed mentioned the Eastern Europe statement as one of the "main things" the candidate had done "well" or "not well" during the debate. But the next morning 12 percent of the respondents mentioned it, and the next evening 20 percent mentioned it. By that time it was the most frequently mentioned criticism of Ford's performance.[18]

What happened in the interim, of course, is that the news media intervened. Journalists, print and broadcast, told viewers what they had seen and heard. Viewers did not take their hint from the cathode ray tube but from the lessons the journalists taught them after the fact. Trout or hamburger? People did not know until they were told.

In 1984, in Mondale's first debate with Reagan, there was widespread agreement that Mondale was impressive and Reagan surprisingly ill at ease and defensive. Polls conducted during the debate, however, showed that people felt, by a slight margin, that Reagan was winning. An hour after the debate, Mondale had a 1 percent edge in a poll on who won. A day later his advantage was 37 percent, and two days later 49 percent. Again, the evidence compellingly shows that even when people "see for themselves," they take as cues for their own thinking suggestions from experts that come after the fact.[19]

In this respect, Reagan's administration did understand television very well. Reagan's aides did not expect television by itself to implant in Americans a love of Reagan or his policies, and they did not treat a television appearance as simply a matter of finding an appropriate stage set and working on the president's makeup. They did all they could to assure the success of a television appearance by preparing the audience for it in rather old-fashioned ways. Before a presidential TV address, the administration's public liaison office arranged for Reagan to meet personally with groups of allies, several hundred at a time, and brief them on what he would say on television so that they could alert their comrades at home. According to political analyst Stephen Wayne, these briefings helped unleash the flood of responses the White House and Congress received on the budget and tax proposals during Reagan's first year in office.[20] This is not to say that the television appearance was without effect on the public—although recent analysis by political scientists indicates that the influence of staged television appearances was very slight in the Reagan years.[21] It is to suggest that even here Reagan was more successful at manipulating congressional opinion than public opinion—but the manipulation came through encouraging the Congress to believe that the public at large was aroused by television. Since this so readily coincided with a view that Washington elites already held as gospel, it was a relatively easy trick to manage.

If the belief in television power is a large part of what makes television powerful, it may be not television but our beliefs about it that help undo a vital politics. The fascination of critics with television as devil, in any event, takes political discourse off track. We— American citizens, cultural critics, social scientists—seek some kind of reckoning with television, the culture it presents and the culture it represents. But despite the growing abundance of media critics, I don't think we have found the language for that reckoning yet. The object of our attention keeps shifting, for one thing; we've gone from an era of the sponsor to an era of the network to the present (still undefined) era of the proliferation of cable and the declining network-share of the television audience. The kinds of television experience also seem too varied to be easily encapsulated—from the live coverage of the Kennedy funeral, the Olympics, a presidential debate, or a natural disaster to the evening news, daytime soap operas, old movies, or reruns of old sitcoms. The judgment we make of one of these genres is not likely to stick when applied to the next.

Beyond the difficulties in keeping the object of our attention steadily in view, there is the complicated problem of the mixed motives of our own curiosity. There are professional career-making ambitions, an inevitable product of the proliferation of the study of communication in the universities; there is the *ressentiment* of intellectuals who feel unfairly overlooked in an era of celebrity; there is the anger, seeking an object, that arises in the general population from a sense of impotence in dealing with the wider world that both print and television news bring to our homes daily. There is also a sense, one I certainly share, that television executives live in time-and-space capsules closely linked to research reports on market trends but very far from deeper currents of experience in the contemporary world. And since they do not yet know this, may never know this, may not want to know this, they may never tell us the stories about ourselves from which we could genuinely learn.

ENDNOTES

[1] Michael Arlen, *Thirty Seconds* (New York: Penguin, 1980).

[2] Hedrick Smith, *The Power Game* (New York: Ballantine Books, 1988) p. 409; David Broder, *Behind the Front Page* (New York: Simon & Schuster 1987), p. 182; Martin Schram, *The Great American Video Game: Presidential Politics in the Television Age* (New York: William Morrow, 1987), pp. 23–27; and Kathleen Hall Jamieson, *Eloquence in an Electronic Age* (New York: Oxford University Press, 1988), pp. 60–61.

[3] Shanto Iyengar and Donald Kinder, *News That Matters* (Chicago: University of Chicago Press, 1984), pp. 36–42.

[4] See D. Roderick Kiewiet, *Macroeconomics and Micro-politics: The Electoral Effects of Economic Issues* (Chicago: University of Chicago Press, 1983).

[5] *Broadcasting* 59 (November 7, 1960): 27–29. When I originally published this chapter, I was unaware of a very good paper criticizing the conventional wisdom on the Kennedy-Nixon debate by David L. Vancil and Sue D. Pendell, "The Myth of Viewer-Listener Disagreement in the First Kennedy-Nixon Debate," *Central States Speech Journal* 38 (1987): 16–27. Vancil and Pendell nicely demonstrate both how pervasive the myth about the Kennedy-Nixon debate is and how meager is the evidence to substantiate it.

[6] Peter Braestrup, *Battle Lines* (New York: Priority Press, 1985), pp. 68–69.

[7] Daniel C. Hallin, *"The Uncensored War": The Media and Vietnam* (New York: Oxford University Press, 1986), p. 131.

[8] Calculated from Gallup polls reported in "Reagan and His Predecessors," *Public Opinion* (September/October 1987): 40.

[9] *The Gallup Poll* 1982 (Wilmington, Del.: Scholarly Resources, 1983), pp. 107, 243.

[10] *Washington Post,* November 22, 1981.

[11] Laurence I. Barrett, *Gambling with History: Ronald Reagan in the White House* (Harmondsworth, England: Penguin Books, 1984), p. 443.

[12] *Time,* August 16, 1982.

[13] Mary McCarthy, *The Mask of State: Watergate Portraits* (New York: Harcourt Brace Jovanovich, 1974), p. 5.

[14] Barry Jogoda, quoted in William Lunch, *The Nationalization of American Politics* (Berkeley: University of California Press, 1987), p. 79; John J. O'Connor, *New York Times,* April 14, 1977, quoted in Joshua Meyrowitz, *No Sense of Place* (New York: Oxford University Press, 1985), p. 273; David Halberstam cited in Meyrowitz, *No Sense of Place,* p. 297.

[15] *San Diego Union,* January 31, 1988, p. C-8.

[16] *Los Angeles Times,* November 8, 1984, p. 1.

[17] W. Phillips Davison, "The Third-Person Effect in Communication," *Public Opinion Quarterly* 47 (1983): 1–15.

[18] Frederick T. Steeper, "Public Response to Gerald Ford's Statements on Eastern Europe in the Second Debate," in George F. Bishop, Robert G. Meadow, and Marilyn Jackson-Beeck, *The Presidential Debates: Media, Electoral, and Policy Perspectives* (New York: Praeger, 1978), pp. 81–101.

[19] Michael Robinson, "Where's the Beef? Media and Media Elites in 1984," in *The American Elections of 1984,* ed. Austin Ranney (Durham, N.C.: Duke University Press, 1985), pp. 198–199.

[20] Stephen J. Wayne, "Congressional Liaison in the Reagan White House: A Preliminary Assessment of the First Year," in *President and Congress: Assessing Reagan's First Year,* ed. Norman J. Ornstein (Washington, D.C.: American Enterprise Institute, 1982), p. 55.

[21] Charles W. Ostrom, Jr., and Dennis M. Simon, "The Man in the Teflon Suit: The Environmental Connection, Political Drama, and Popular Support in the Reagan Presidency," *Public Opinion Quarterly* 53 (1989): 353–387.

Name: _____ Date: _____

UNDERSTANDING THE TEXT

1. What assumption about the relative power of images vs. words does Schudson challenge in his essay?

2. What three historical events does Schudson examine to support his challenge? Choose one, and summarize his argument about it.

3. To what does the "Trout or Hamburger" of Schudson's title refer? What is the lesson he extracts from this reference, and how does this relate to his understanding of the influence of television upon viewers?

The Incredible Shrinking Sound Bite

Kiku Adatto

Standing before a campaign rally in Pennsylvania, the 1968 Democratic vice presidential candidate, Edmund Muskie, tried to speak, but a group of anti-war protesters drowned him out. Muskie offered the hecklers a deal. He would give the platform to one of their representatives if he could then speak without interruption. Rick Brody, the students' choice, rose to the microphone where, to cheers from the crowd, he denounced the candidates that the 1968 presidential campaign had to offer. "Wallace is no answer. Nixon's no answer. And Humphrey's no answer. Sit out this election!" When Brody finished, Muskie made his case for the Democratic ticket. That night Muskie's confrontation with the demonstrators played prominently on the network news. NBC showed fifty-seven seconds of Brody's speech, and more than a minute of Muskie's.

Twenty years later, things had changed. Throughout the entire 1988 campaign, no network allowed either presidential candidate to speak uninterrupted on the evening news for as long as Rick Brody spoke. By 1988 television's tolerance for the languid pace of political discourse, never great, had all but vanished. An analysis of all weekday evening network newscasts (over 280) from Labor Day to Election Day in 1968 and 1988 reveals that the average "sound bite" fell from 42.3 seconds in 1968 to only 9.8 seconds in 1988. Meanwhile the time the networks devoted to visuals of the candidates, unaccompanied by their words, increased by more than 300 percent.

Since the Kennedy-Nixon debates of 1960, television has played a pivotal role in presidential politics. The Nixon campaign of 1968 was the first to be managed and orchestrated to play on the evening news. With the decline of political parties and the direct appeal to voters in the primaries, presidential campaigns became more adept at conveying their messages through visual images, not only in political commercials but also in elaborately staged media events. By the time of Ronald Reagan, the actor turned president, Michael Deaver had perfected the techniques of the video presidency.

For television news, the politicians' mastery of television imagery posed a temptation and a challenge. The temptation was to show the pictures. What network producer could resist the footage of Reagan at Normandy Beach, or of Bush in Boston Harbor? The challenge was to avoid being entangled in the artifice and imagery that the campaigns dispensed. In 1988 the networks tried to have it both ways—to meet the challenge even as they succumbed to the temptation. They showed the images that the campaigns produced—their commercials as well as their media events. But they also sought to retain their objectivity by exposing the artifice of the images, by calling constant attention to their self-conscious design.

The language of political reporting was filled with accounts of staging and backdrops, camera angles and scripts, sound bites and spin control, photo opportunities and media gurus. So attentive was television news to the way the campaigns constructed images for television that political reporters began to sound like theater critics, reporting more on the stagecraft than the substance of politics.

When Bush kicked off his campaign with a Labor Day appearance at Disneyland, the networks covered the event as a performance for television. "In the war of the Labor Day visuals," CBS's Bob Schieffer reported, "George Bush pulled out the heavy artillery. A Disneyland backdrop and lots of pictures with the Disney gang." When Bruce Morton covered Dukakis riding in a tank, the story was the image. "In the trade of politics, it's called a visual," said Morton. "The idea is pictures are symbols that tell the voter important things about the candidate. If your candidate is seen in the polls as weak on defense, put him in a tank."

And when Bush showed up at a military base to observe the destruction of a missile under an arms control treaty, ABC's Brit Hume began his report by telling his viewers that they were watching a media event. "Now, here was a photo opportunity, the vice president watching a Pershing missile burn off its fuel." He went on to describe how the event was staged for television. Standing in front of an open field, Hume reported, "The Army had even gone so far as to bulldoze acres of trees to make sure the vice president and the news media had a clear view."

So familiar is the turn to theater criticism that it is difficult to recall the transformation it represents. Even as they conveyed the first presidential campaign "made for television," TV reporters in 1968 continued to reflect the print journalist tradition from which they had descended. In the marriage of theater and politics, politics remained the focus of reporting. The media events of the day—mostly rallies and press conferences—were covered as political events, not as exercises in impression management.

By 1988 television displaced politics as the focus of coverage. Like a gestalt shift, the images that once formed the background to political events—the setting and the stagecraft—now occupied the foreground. (Only 6 percent of reports in 1968 were devoted to theater criticism, compared with 52 percent in 1988.) And yet, for all their image-conscious coverage in 1988, reporters did not escape their entanglement. They showed the potent visuals even as they attempted to avoid the manipulation by "deconstructing" the imagery and revealing its artifice.

To be sure, theater criticism was not the only kind of political reporting on network newscasts in 1988. Some notable "fact correction" pieces offered admirable exceptions. For example, after each presidential debate, ABC's Jim Wooten compared the candidates' claims with the facts. Not content with the canned images of the politicians, Wooten used television images to document discrepancies between the candidates' rhetoric and their records.

Most coverage simply exposed the contrivances of image-making. But alerting the viewer to the construction of television images proved no substitute for fact correction. A superficial "balance" replaced objectivity as the measure of fairness, a balance consisting of equal time for media events, equal time for commercials. But this created a false symmetry, leaving both the press and the public hostage to the play of perceptions the campaigns dispensed.

Even the most critical versions of image-conscious coverage could fail to puncture the pictures they showed. When Bush visited a flag factory in hopes of making patriotism a campaign issue, ABC's Hume reported that Bush was wrapping himself in the flag. "This campaign strives to match its pictures with its points. Today and for much of the past week, the pictures have been of George Bush with the American flag. If the point wasn't to make an issue of patriotism, then the question arises, what was it?" Yet only three days later, in an ABC report on independent voters in New Jersey, the media event that Hume reported with derision was transformed into an innocent visual of Bush. The criticism forgotten, the image played on.

Another striking contrast between the coverage of the 1968 and 1988 campaigns is the increased coverage of political commercials. Although political ads played a prominent role in the 1968 campaign, the networks rarely showed excerpts on the news. During the entire 1968 general election campaign, the evening news programs broadcast only two excerpts from candidates' commercials. By 1988 the number had jumped to 125. In 1968 the only time a negative ad was mentioned on the evening news was when CBS's Walter Cronkite and NBC's Chet Huntley reported that a Nixon campaign ad—showing a smiling Hubert Humphrey superimposed on scenes of war and riot—was withdrawn after the Democrats cried foul. Neither network showed the ad itself.

The networks might argue that in 1988 political ads loomed larger in the campaign, and so required more coverage. But as with their focus on media events, reporters ran the risk of becoming conduits of the television images the campaigns dispensed. Even with a critical narrative, showing commercials on the news gives free time to paid media. And most of the time the narrative was not critical. The networks rarely bothered to correct the distortions or misstatements that the ads contained. Of the 125 excerpts shown on the evening news in 1988, the reporter addressed the veracity of the commercials' claims less than 8 percent of the time. The networks became, in effect, electronic billboards for the candidates, showing political commercials not only as breaking news but as stand-ins for the candidates, and file footage aired interchangeably with news footage of the candidates.

The few cases where reporters corrected the facts illustrate how the networks might have covered political commercials. ABC's Richard Threlkeld ran excerpts from a Bush ad attacking Dukakis's defense stand by freezing the frame and correcting each mistaken or distorted claim. He also pointed out the exaggeration in a Dukakis ad attacking Bush's record on Social Security. CBS's Leslie Stahl corrected a deceptive statistic in Bush's revolving-door furlough ad, noting: "Part of the ad is false. . . . Two hundred sixty-eight murderers did not escape. . . . [T]he truth is only four first-degree murderers escaped while on parole."

Stahl concluded her report by observing, "Dukakis left the Bush attack ads unanswered for six weeks. Today campaign aides are engaged in a round of finger-pointing at who is to blame." But the networks also let the Bush furlough commercial run without challenge or correction. Before and even after her report, CBS ran excerpts of the ad without correction. In all, network newscasts ran excerpts from the revolving-door furlough ad ten times throughout the campaign, only once correcting the deceptive statistic.

It might be argued that it is up to the candidate to reply to his opponent's charges, not the press. But the networks' frequent use of political ads on the evening news created a strong disincentive for a candidate to challenge his opponent's ads. As Dukakis found, to attack a television ad as unfair or untrue is to invite the networks to run it again. In the final weeks before the election, the Dukakis campaign accused the Republicans of lying about his record on defense, and of using racist tactics in ads featuring Willie Horton, a black convict who raped and killed while on furlough from a Massachusetts prison. (See "The Making of Willie Horton" by Martin Schram.) In reporting Dukakis's complaint, all three networks ran excerpts of the ads in question, including the highly charged pictures of Horton and the revolving door of convicts. Dukakis's response thus gave Bush's potent visuals another free run on the evening news.

The networks might reply that the ads are news and thus need to be shown, as long as they generate controversy in the campaign. But this rationale leaves them open to manipulation. Oddly enough, the networks were alive to this danger when confronted with the question of whether to air the videos the campaigns produced for their conventions. "I am not into tone poems," Lane Venardos, the executive producer in charge of convention coverage at CBS, told *The New York Times*. "We are not in the business of being propaganda arms of the political parties." But they seemed blind to the same danger during the campaign itself.

So successful was the Bush campaign at getting free time for its ads on the evening news that, after the campaign, commercial advertisers adopted a similar strategy. In 1989 a pharmaceutical company used unauthorized footage of Presidents Bush and Gorbachev to advertise a cold medication. "In the new year," the slogan ran, "may the only cold war in the world be the one being fought by us." Although two of the three networks refused to carry the commercial, dozens of network and local television news programs showed excerpts of the ad, generating millions of dollars of free airtime.

"I realized I started a trend," said Bush media consultant Roger Ailes in *The New York Times*. "Now guys are out there trying to produce commercials for the evening news." When Humphrey and Nixon hired Madison Avenue experts to help in their campaigns, some worried that, in the television age, presidents would be sold like products. Little did they imagine that, twenty years later, products would be sold like presidents.

Along with the attention to commercials and stagecraft in 1988 came an unprecedented focus on the stage managers themselves, the "media gurus," "handlers," and "spin-control artists." Only three reports featured media advisers in 1968, compared with twenty-six in 1988. And the numbers tell only part of the story.

The stance reporters have taken toward media advisers has changed dramatically over the past twenty years. In *The Selling of the President* (1969), Joe McGinniss exposed the growing role of media advisers with a sense of disillusion and outrage. By 1988 television reporters covered image-makers with deference, even admiration. In place of independent fact correction, reporters sought out media advisers as authorities in their own right to analyze the effectiveness and even defend the truthfulness of campaign commercials. They became "media gurus" not only for the candidates but for the networks as well.

For example, in an exchange with CBS anchor Dan Rather on Bush's debate performance, Stahl lavished admiration on the techniques of Bush's media advisers:

> STAHL: "They told him not to look into the camera. [She gestures toward the camera as she speaks.] You know when you look directly into a camera you are cold, apparently they have determined."
>
> RATHER [laughing]:"Bad news for anchormen I'd say."
>
> STAHL: "We have a lot to learn from this. Michael Dukakis kept talking right into the camera. [Stahl talks directly into her own camera to demonstrate.] And according to the Bush people that makes you look programmed, Dan [Stahl laughs]. And they're very adept at these television symbols and television imagery. And according to our poll it worked."
>
> RATHER: "Do you believe it?"
>
> STAHL: "Yes, I think I do, actually."

So hypersensitive were the networks to television image-making in 1988 that minor mishaps—gaffes, slips of the tongue, even faulty microphones—became big news. Politicians were hardly without mishaps in 1968, but these did not count as news. Only once in 1968 did a network even take note of a minor incident unrelated to the content of the campaign. In 1988 some twenty-nine reports highlighted trivial slips.

The emphasis on "failed images" reflected a kind of guerrilla warfare between the networks and the campaigns. The more the campaigns sought to control the images that appeared on the nightly news, the more the reporters tried to beat them at their own game, magnifying a minor mishap into a central feature of the media event.

Early in the 1988 campaign, for example, George Bush delivered a speech to a sympathetic audience of the American Legion, attacking his opponent's defense policies. In a slip, he declared that September 7, rather than December 7, was the anniversary of Pearl Harbor. Murmurs and chuckles from the audience alerted him to his error, and he quickly corrected himself.

The audience was forgiving, but the networks were not. All three network anchors highlighted the slip on the evening news. Dan Rather introduced CBS's report on Bush by declaring solemnly, "Bush's talk to audiences in Louisville was overshadowed by a strange happening." On NBC Tom Brokaw reported, "He departed from his prepared script and left his listeners mystified." Peter Jennings introduced ABC's report by mentioning Bush's attack on Dukakis, adding, "What's more likely to be remembered about today's speech is a slip of the tongue."

Some of the slips the networks highlighted in 1988 were not even verbal gaffes or mis-statements, but simply failures on the part of candidates to cater to the cameras. In a report on the travails of the Dukakis campaign, Sam Donaldson seized on Dukakis's failure to play to ABC's television camera as evidence of his campaign's ineffectiveness. Showing Dukakis playing a trumpet with a local marching band, Donaldson chided, "He played the trumpet with his back to the camera." As Dukakis played "Happy Days Are Here Again," Donaldson's voice was heard from off-camera calling, "We're over here, governor."

One way of understanding the turn to image-conscious coverage in 1988 is to see how television news came to partake of the postwar modernist sensibility, particularly the pop art movement of the 1960s. Characteristic of this outlook is a self-conscious attention to art as performance, a focus on the process of image-making rather than on the ideas the images represent.

During the 1960s, when photography and television became potent forces for documenta-tion and entertainment, they also became powerful influences on the work of artists. Photographers began to photograph the television set as part of the social landscape. Newspapers, photographs, and commercial products became part of the collage work of painters such as Robert Rauschenberg. Artists began to explore self-consciously their role in the image-making process.

For example, Lee Friedlander published a book of photography, *Self Portrait,* in which the artist's shadow or reflection was included in every frame. As critic Rod Slemmons notes, "By indicating the photographer is also a performer whose hand is impossible to hide, Friedlander set a precedent for disrupting the normal rules of photography." These "post-modernist" movements in art and photography foreshadowed the form television news would take by the late 1980s.

Andy Warhol once remarked, "The artificial fascinates me." In 1988 network reporters and producers, beguiled by the artifice of the modern presidential campaign, might well have said the same. Reporters alternated between reporting campaign images as if they were facts and exposing their contrived nature. Like Warhol, whose personality was always a presence in his work, reporters became part of the campaign theater they covered—as pro-ducers, as performers, and as critics. Like Warhol's reproductions of Campbell's soup cans, the networks' use of candidates' commercials directed our attention away from the content and toward the packaging.

The assumption that the creation of appearances is the essence of political reality per-vaded not only the reporting but the candidates' self-understanding and conduct with the press. When Dan Quayle sought to escape his image as a highly managed candidate, he resolved publicly to become his own handler, his own "spin doctor." "The so-called handlers story, part of it's true," he confessed to network reporters. "But there will be no more handlers stories, because I'm the handler and I'll do the spinning." Surrounded by a group of reporters on his campaign plane, Quayle announced. "I'm Doctor Spin, and I want you all to report that."

It may seem a strange way for a politician to talk, but not so strange in a media-conscious environment in which authenticity means being master of your own artificiality. Dukakis too sought to reverse his political fortunes by seeking to be master of his own image. This attempt was best captured in a commercial shown on network news in which Dukakis stood beside a television set and snapped off a Bush commercial attacking his stand on defense. "I'm fed up with it," Dukakis declared. "Never seen anything like it in twenty-five years of public life. George Bush's negative television ads, distorting my record, full of lies, and he knows it." The commercial itself shows an image of an image—a Bush television commercial showing (and ridiculing) the media event where Dukakis rode in a tank. In his commercial, Dukakis complains that Bush's commercial showing the tank ride misstates Dukakis's position on defense.

As it appeared in excerpts on the evening news, Dukakis's commercial displayed a quintessentially modernist image of artifice upon artifice upon artifice: television news covering a Dukakis commercial containing a Bush commercial containing a Dukakis media event. In a political world governed by images of images, it seemed almost natural that the authority of the candidate be depicted by his ability to turn off the television set.

In the 1950s Edward R. Murrow noted that broadcast news was "an incompatible combination of show business, advertising, and news." Still, in its first decades television news continued to reflect a sharp distinction between the news and entertainment divisions of the networks. But by the 1980s network news operations came to be seen as profit centers for the large corporations that owned them, run by people drawn less from journalism than from advertising and entertainment backgrounds. Commercialization led to further emphasis on entertainment values, which heightened the need for dramatic visuals, fast pacing, quick cutting, and short sound bites. Given new technological means to achieve these effects—portable video cameras, satellite hookups, and sophisticated video-editing equipment—the networks were not only disposed but equipped to capture the staged media events of the campaigns.

The search for dramatic visuals and the premium placed on showmanship in the 1980s led to a new complicity between the White House image-makers and the networks. As Susan Zirinsky, a top CBS producer, acknowledged in Martin Schram's *The Great American Video Game,* "In a funny way, the [Reagan White House] advance men and I have the same thing at heart—we want the piece to look as good as [it] possibly can." In 1968 such complicity in stagecraft was scorned. Sanford Socolow, senior producer of the *CBS Evening News with Walter Cronkite,* recently observed, "If someone caught you doing that in 1968 you would have been fired."

In a moment of reflection in 1988, CBS's political correspondents expressed their frustration with image-driven campaigns "It may seem frivolous, even silly at times," said Schieffer.

"But setting up pictures that drive home a message has become the No. 1 priority of the modern-day campaign. The problem, of course, is while it is often entertaining, it is seldom enlightening."

Rather shared his colleague's discomfort. But what troubled him about modern campaigns is equally troubling about television's campaign coverage. "With all this emphasis on the image," he asked, "what happens to the issues? What happens to the substance?"

Name: _____ Date: _____

UNDERSTANDING THE TEXT

1. According to Adatto, how did the focus of presidential campaign coverage change from 1968 to 1988?

2. Why is Adatto critical of the television news programs in 1988 excerpting 125 candidate ads during their broadcasts? (Identify two reasons.)

3. Adatto reports that even in the early days of television news, Edward R. Murrow, a prominent journalist, observed that it was "an incompatible combination of show business, advertising, and news." According to Adatto, what has become of this "combination" since? What evidence does she cite to support her view?

Politics and the English Language

George Orwell

Most people who bother with the matter at all would admit that the English language is in a bad way, but it is generally assumed that we cannot by conscious action do anything about it. Our civilization is decadent and our language—so the argument runs—must inevitably share in the general collapse. It follows that any struggle against the abuse of language is a sentimental archaism, like preferring candles to electric light or hansom cabs to aeroplanes. Underneath this lies the half-conscious belief that language is a natural growth and not an instrument which we shape for our own purposes.

Now, it is clear that the decline of a language must ultimately have political and economic causes: it is not due simply to the bad influence of this or that individual writer. But an effect can become a cause, reinforcing the original cause and producing the same effect in an intensified form, and so on indefinitely. A man may take a drink because he feels himself to be a failure, and then fail all the more completely because he drinks. It is rather the same thing that is happening to the English language. It becomes ugly and inaccurate because our thoughts are foolish, but the slovenliness of our language makes it easier for us to have foolish thoughts. The point is that the process is reversible. Modern English, especially written English, is full of bad habits which spread by imitation and which can be avoided if one is willing to take the necessary trouble. If one gets rid of these habits one can think more clearly, and to think clearly is a necessary first step towards political regeneration: so that the fight against bad English is not frivolous and is not the exclusive concern of professional writers. I will come back to this presently, and I hope that by that time the meaning of what I have said here will have become clearer. Meanwhile, here are five specimens of the English language as it is now habitually written.

These five passages have not been picked out because they are especially bad—I could have quoted far worse if I had chosen—but because they illustrate various of the mental vices from which we now suffer. They are a little below the average, but are fairly representative samples. I number them so that I can refer back to them when necessary:

(1) I am not indeed sure whether it is not true to say that the Milton who once seemed not unlike a seventeenth-century Shelley had not become out of an experience ever more bitter in each year, more alien *[sic]* to the founder of that Jesuit sect which nothing could induce him to tolerate.

> —Professor Harold Laski, Essay in *Freedom of Expression*

(2) Above all, we cannot play ducks and drakes with a native battery of idioms which prescribes such egregious collocations of vocables as the Basic *put up with* for *tolerate* or *put at a loss* for *bewilder.*

> —Professor Lancelot Hogben, *Interglossa*

(3) On the one side we have the free personality: by definition it is not neurotic, for it has neither conflict nor dream. Its desires, such as they are, are transparent, for they are just what institutional approval keeps in the forefront of consciousness; another institutional pattern would alter their number and intensity; there is little in them that is natural, irreducible, or culturally dangerous. But *on the other side,* the social bond itself is nothing but the mutual reflection of these self-secure integrities. Recall the definition of love. Is not this the very picture of a small academic? Where is there a place in this hall of mirrors for either personality or fraternity?

> —Essay on psychology in *Politics* (New York)

(4) All the "best people" from the gentlemen's clubs, and all the frantic fascist captains, united in common hatred of Socialism and bestial horror of the rising tide of the mass revolutionary movement, have turned to acts of provocation, to foul incendiarism, to medieval legends of poisoned wells, to legalize their own destruction of proletarian organizations, and rouse the agitated petty-bourgeoisie to chauvinistic fervour on behalf of the fight against the revolutionary way out of the crisis.

> —Communist pamphlet

(5) If a new spirit *is* to be infused into this old country, there is one thorny and contentious reform which must be tackled, and that is the humanization and galvanization of the B.B.C. Timidity here will bespeak cancer and atrophy of the soul. The heart of Britain may be sound and of strong beat, for instance, but the British lion's roar at present is like that of Bottom in Shakespeare's *Midsummer Night's Dream*—as gentle as any sucking dove. A virile new Britain cannot continue indefinitely to be traduced in the eyes or rather ears, of the world by the effete languors of Langham Place, brazenly masquerading as "standard English." When the Voice of Britain is heard at nine o'clock, better far and infinitely less ludicrous to hear aitches honestly dropped than the present priggish, inflated, inhibited, school-ma'amish arch braying of blameless bashful mewing maidens!

> —Letter in *Tribune*

Each of these passages has faults of its own, but, quite apart from avoidable ugliness, two qualities are common to all of them. The first is staleness of imagery; the other is lack of precision. The writer either has a meaning and cannot express it, or he inadvertently says something else, or he is almost indifferent as to whether his words mean anything or not. This mixture of vagueness and sheer incompetence is the most marked characteristic of modern English prose, and especially of any kind of political writing. As soon as certain topics are raised, the concrete melts into the abstract and no one seems able to think of turns of speech that are not hackneyed: prose consists less and less of *words* chosen for the sake of their meaning, and more and more of *phrases* tacked together like the sections of a pre-fabricated hen-house. I list below, with notes and examples, various of the tricks by means of which the work of prose-construction is habitually dodged:

DYING METAPHORS

A newly invented metaphor assists thought by evoking a visual image, while on the other hand a metaphor which is technically "dead" (e.g. *iron resolution*) has in effect reverted to being an ordinary word and can generally be used without loss of vividness. But in between these two classes there is a huge dump of worn-out metaphors which have lost all evocative power and are merely used because they save people the trouble of inventing phrases for themselves. Examples are: *Ring the changes on, take up the cudgels for, toe the line, ride roughshod over, stand shoulder to shoulder with, play into the hands of, no axe to grind, grist to the mill, fishing in troubled waters, on the order of the day, Achilles' heel, swan song, hotbed.* Many of these are used without knowledge of their meaning (what is a "rift," for instance?), and incompatible metaphors are frequently mixed, a sure sign that the writer is not interested in what he is saying. Some metaphors now current have been twisted out of their original meaning without those who use them even being aware of the fact. For example, *toe the line* is sometimes written *tow the line.* Another example is *the hammer and the anvil,* now always used with the implication that the anvil gets the worst of it. In real life it is always the anvil that breaks the hammer, never the other way about: a writer who stopped to think what he was saying would be aware of this, and would avoid perverting the original phrase.

OPERATORS OR VERBAL FALSE LIMBS

These save the trouble of picking out appropriate verbs and nouns, and at the same time pad each sentence with extra syllables which give it an appearance of symmetry. Characteristic phrases are: *render inoperative, militate against, make contact with, be subjected to, give rise to, give grounds for, have the effect of, play a leading part (role) in, make itself felt, take effect, exhibit a tendency to, serve the purpose of, etc., etc.* The keynote is the elimination of simple verbs. Instead of being a single word, such as *break, stop, spoil, mend, kill,* a verb becomes a *phrase,* made up of a noun or adjective tacked on to some general-purposes verb such as *prove, serve, form, play, render.* In addition, the passive voice is wherever possible used in preference to the active, and noun constructions are used instead of gerunds (*by examination of* instead of *by examining*). The range of verbs is further cut down by means of the *-ize* and *de-* formations, and the banal statements are given an appearance of profundity by means of the *not un-*formation. Simple conjunctions and prepositions are replaced by such phrases as *with respect to, having regard to, the fact that, by dint of, in view of, in the interests of, on the hypothesis that;* and the ends of sentences are saved from anticlimax by such resounding commonplaces as *greatly to be desired, cannot be left out of account, a development to be expected in the near future, deserving of serious considera-tion, brought to a satisfactory conclusion,* and so on and so forth.

PRETENTIOUS DICTION

Words like *phenomenon, element, individual* (as noun), *objective, categorical, effective, virtual, basic, primary, promote, constitute, exhibit, exploit, utilize, eliminate, liquidate,* are used to dress up simple statements and give an air of scientific impartiality to biased judg-ments. Adjectives like *epoch-making, epic, historic, unforgettable, triumphant, age-old, inevitable, inexorable, veritable,* are used to dignify the sordid processes of international pol-itics, while writing that aims at glorifying war usually takes on an archaic colour, its charac-teristic words being: *realm, throne, chariot, mailed fist, trident, sword, shield, buckler, banner, jackboot, clarion.* Foreign words and expressions such as *cul de sac, ancien regime, deus ex machina, mutatis mutandis, status quo, gleichshaltung, weltanschauung,* are used to give an air of culture and elegance. Except for the useful abbreviations *i.e., e.g.,* and *etc.,* there is no real need for any of the hundreds of foreign phrases now current in English. Bad writers, and especially scientific, political and sociological writers, are nearly always haunted by the notion that Latin or Greek words are grander than Saxon ones, and unnecessary words like *expedite, ameliorate, predict, extraneous, deracinated, clandestine, subaqueous* and hun-dreds of others constantly gain ground from their Anglo-Saxon opposite numbers.[1] The jar-gon peculiar to Marxist writing (*hyena, hangman, cannibal, petty bourgeois, these gentry, lacquey, flunkey, mad dog, White Guard,* etc.) consists largely of words and phrases trans-lated from Russian, German or French; but the normal way of coining a new word is to use a Latin or Greek root with the appropriate affix and, where necessary, the -ize formation. It is often easier to make up words of this kind (*deregionalize, impermissible, extramarital, non-fragmentatary* and so forth) than to think up the English words that will cover one's meaning. The result, in general, is an increase in slovenliness and vagueness.

MEANINGLESS WORDS

In certain kinds of writing, particularly in art criticism and literary criticism, it is normal to come across long passages which are almost completely lacking in meaning.[2] Words like *romantic, plastic, values, human, dead, sentimental, natural, vitality,* as used in art criti-cism, are strictly meaningless in the sense that they not only do not point to any discoverable object, but are hardly ever expected to do so by the reader. When one critic writes, "The outstanding feature of Mr. X's work is its living quality," while another writes, "The immediately striking thing about Mr. X's work is its peculiar deadness," the reader accepts this as a simple difference of opinion. If words like *black* and *white* were involved, instead of the jargon words *dead* and *living,* he would see at once that language was being used in an improper way. Many political words are similarly abused. The word *Fascism* has now no meaning except in so far as it signifies "something not desirable." The words *democracy, socialism, freedom, patriotic, realistic, justice,* have each of them several different meanings which cannot be reconciled with one another. In the case of a word like *democracy,* not only is there no agreed definition, but the attempt to make one is resisted from all sides. It is almost universally felt that when we call a country democratic we are praising it: consequently the defenders of every kind of regime claim that it is a democracy, and fear that they might have to stop using the word if it were tied down to any one meaning. Words of this kind are often used in a consciously dishonest way. That is, the person who uses them has his own private definition, but allows his hearer to think he means something quite different. Statements like *Marshal Pétain was a true patriot, The Soviet Press is the freest in the world, The Catholic Church is opposed to persecution,* are almost always made with intent to deceive. Other words used in variable meanings, in most cases more or less dishonestly, are: *class, totalitarian, science, progressive, reactionary, bourgeois, equality.*

Now that I have made this catalogue of swindles and perversions, let me give another example of the kind of writing that they lead to. This time it must of its nature be an imaginary one. I am going to translate a passage of good English into modern English of the worst sort. Here is a well-known verse from *Ecclesiastes:*

> I returned and saw under the sun, that the race is not to the swift, nor the battle to the strong, neither yet bread to the wise, nor yet riches to men of understanding, nor yet favour to men of skill; but time and chance happeneth to them all.

Here it is in modern English:

> Objective consideration of contemporary phenomena compels the conclusion that success or failure in competitive activities exhibits no tendency to be commensurate with innate capacity, but that a considerable element of the unpredictable must invariably be taken into account.

This is a parody, but not a very gross one. Exhibit (3), above, for instance, contains several patches of the same kind of English. It will be seen that I have not made a full translation. The beginning and ending of the sentence follow the original meaning fairly closely, but in the middle the concrete illustrations—race, battle, bread—dissolve into the vague phrase "success or failure in competitive activities." This had to be so, because no modern writer of the kind I am discussing—no one capable of using phrases like "objective consideration of contemporary phenomena"—would ever tabulate his thoughts in that precise and detailed way. The whole tendency of modern prose is away from concreteness. Now analyse these two sentences a little more closely. The first contains forty-nine words but only sixty syllables, and all its words are those of everyday life. The second contains thirty-eight words of ninety syllables: eighteen of its words are from Latin roots, and one from Greek. The first sentence contains six vivid images, and only one phrase ("time and chance") that could be called vague. The second contains not a single fresh, arresting phrase, and in spite of its ninety syllables it gives only a shortened version of the meaning contained in the first. Yet without a doubt it is the second kind of sentence that is gaining ground in modern English. I do not want to exaggerate. This kind of writing is not yet universal, and outcrops of simplicity will occur here and there in the worst-written page. Still, if you or I were told to write a few lines on the uncertainty of human fortunes, we should probably come much nearer to my imaginary sentence than to the one from *Ecclesiastes.*

As I have tried to show, modern writing at its worst does not consist in picking out words for the sake of their meaning and inventing images in order to make the meaning clearer. It consists in gumming together long strips of words which have already been set in order by someone else, and making the results presentable by sheer humbug. The attraction of this way of writing is that it is easy. It is easier—even quicker, once you have the habit—to say *In my opinion it is a not unjustifiable assumption that* than to say *I think.* If you use ready-made phrases, you not only don't have to hunt about for words; you also don't have to bother with the rhythms of your sentences, since these phrases are generally so arranged as to be more or less euphonious. When you are composing in a hurry—when you are dictating to a stenographer, for instance, or making a public speech—it is natural to fall into a pretentious, Latinized style. Tags like *a consideration which we should do well to bear in mind* or *a conclusion to which all of us would readily assent* will save many a sentence from coming down with a bump. By using stale metaphors, similes and idioms, you save much mental effort, at the cost of leaving your meaning vague, not only for your reader but for yourself. This is the significance of mixed metaphors. The sole aim of a metaphor is to call up a visual image. When these images clash—as in *The Fascist octopus has sung its swan song, the jackboot is thrown into the melting pot*—it can be taken as certain that the writer is not seeing a mental image of the objects he is naming; in other words he is not really thinking. Look again at the examples I gave at the beginning of this essay. Professor Laski (1) uses five negatives in fifty-three words. One of these is superfluous, making nonsense of the whole passage, and in addition there is the slip *alien* for akin, making further nonsense, and several avoidable pieces of clumsiness which increase the general vagueness. Professor Hogben (2) plays ducks and drakes with a battery which is able to write prescriptions, and, while disapproving of the everyday phrase *put up with,* is unwilling to look *egregious* up in the dictionary and see what it means. (3), if one takes an uncharitable attitude towards it, is simply meaningless: probably one could work out its intended meaning by reading the whole of the article in which it occurs. In (4), the writer knows more or less what he wants to say, but an accumulation of stale phrases chokes him like tea leaves blocking a sink. In (5), words and meaning have almost parted company. People who write in this manner usually have a general emotional meaning—they dislike one thing and want to express solidarity with another—

but they are not interested in the detail of what they are saying. A scrupulous writer, in every sentence that he writes, will ask himself at least four questions, thus: What am I trying to say? What words will express it? What image or idiom will make it clearer? Is this image fresh enough to have an effect? And he will probably ask himself two more: Could I put it more shortly? Have I said anything that is avoidably ugly? But you are not obliged to go to all this trouble. You can shirk it by simply throwing your mind open and letting the ready-made phrases come crowding in. They will construct your sentences for you—even think your thoughts for you, to a certain extent—and at need they will perform the important service of partially concealing your meaning even from yourself. It is at this point that the special connection between politics and the debasement of language becomes clear.

In our time it is broadly true that political writing is bad writing. Where it is not true, it will generally be found that the writer is some kind of rebel, expressing his private opinions and not a "party line." Orthodoxy, of whatever colour, seems to demand a lifeless, imitative style. The political dialects to be found in pamphlets, leading articles, manifestos, White Papers and the speeches of under-secretaries do, of course, vary from party to party, but they are all alike in that one almost never finds in them a fresh, vivid, homemade turn of speech. When one watches some tired hack on the platform mechanically repeating the familiar phrases—*bestial atrocities, iron heel, bloodstained tyranny, free peoples of the world, stand shoulder to shoulder*—one often has a curious feeling that one is not watching a live human being but some kind of dummy: a feeling which suddenly becomes stronger at moments when the light catches the speaker's spectacles and turns them into blank discs which seem to have no eyes behind them. And this is not altogether fanciful. A speaker who uses that kind of phraseology has gone some distance towards turning himself into a machine. The appropriate noises are coming out of his larynx, but his brain is not involved as it would be if he were choosing his words for himself. If the speech he is making is one that he is accustomed to make over and over again, he may be almost unconscious of what he is saying, as one is when one utters the responses in church. And this reduced state of consciousness, if not indispensable, is at any rate favourable to political conformity.

In our time, political speech and writing are largely the defence of the indefensible. Things like the continuance of British rule in India, the Russian purges and deportations, the dropping of the atom bombs on Japan, can indeed be defended, but only by arguments which are too brutal for most people to face, and which do not square with the professed aims of political parties. Thus political language has to consist largely of euphemism, question-begging and sheer cloudy vagueness. Defenceless villages are bombarded from the air, the inhabitants driven out into the countryside, the cattle machine-gunned, the huts set on fire with incendiary bullets: this is called *pacification*. Millions of peasants are robbed of their farms and sent trudging along the roads with no more than they can carry: this is called *transfer of population* or *rectification of frontiers*. People are imprisoned for years without trial, or shot in the back of the neck or sent to die of scurvy in Arctic lumber camps: this is called *elimination of unreliable elements*. Such phraseology is needed if one wants to name things without calling up mental pictures of them. Consider for instance some comfortable English professor defending Russian totalitarianism. He cannot say outright, "I believe in killing off your opponents when you can get good results by doing so." Probably, therefore, he will say something like this:

> While freely conceding that the Soviet regime exhibits certain features which the humanitarian may be inclined to deplore, we must, I think, agree that a certain curtailment of the right to political opposition is an unavoidable concomitant of transitional periods, and that the rigours which the Russian people have been called upon to undergo have been amply justified in the sphere of concrete achievement.

The inflated style is itself a kind of euphemism. A mass of Latin words fall upon the facts like soft snow, blurring the outlines and covering up all the details. The great enemy of clear language is insincerity. When there is a gap between one's real and one's declared aims, one turns as it were instinctively to long words and exhausted idioms, like a cuttlefish squirting out ink. In our age there is no such thing as "keeping out of politics." All issues are political issues, and politics itself is a mass of lies, evasions, folly, hatred and schizophrenia. When the general atmosphere is bad, language must suffer. I should expect to find— this is a guess which I have not sufficient knowledge to verify—that the German, Russian and Italian languages have all deteriorated in the last ten or fifteen years, as a result of dictatorship.

But if thought corrupts language, language can also corrupt thought. A bad usage can spread by tradition and imitation, even among people who should and do know better. The debased language that I have been discussing is in some ways very convenient. Phrases like *a not unjustifiable assumption, leaves much to be desired, would serve no good purpose, a consideration which we should do well to bear in mind,* are a continuous temptation, a packet of aspirins always at one's elbow. Look back through this essay, and for certain you will find that I have again and again committed the very faults I am protesting against. By this morning's post I have received a pamphlet dealing with conditions in Germany. The author tells me that he "felt impelled" to write it. I open it at random, and here is almost the first sentence that I see: "[The Allies] have an opportunity not only of achieving a radical transformation of Germany's social and political structure in such a way as to avoid a nationalistic reaction in Germany itself, but at the same time of laying the foundations of a cooperative and unified Europe." You see, he "feels impelled" to write—feels, presumably, that he has something new to say—and yet his words, like cavalry horses answering the bugle, group themselves automatically into the familiar dreary pattern. This invasion of one's mind by ready-made phrases (*lay the foundations, achieve a radical transformation*) can only be prevented if one is constantly on guard against them, and every such phrase anaesthetizes a portion of one's brain.

I said earlier that the decadence of our language is probably curable. Those who deny this would argue, if they produced an argument at all, that language merely reflects existing social conditions, and that we cannot influence its development by any direct tinkering with words and constructions. So far as the general tone or spirit of a language goes, this may be true, but it is not true in detail. Silly words and expressions have often disappeared, not through any evolutionary process but owing to the conscious action of a minority. Two recent examples were *explore every avenue* and *leave no stone unturned,* which were killed by the jeers of a few journalists. There is a long list of flyblown metaphors which could similarly be got rid of if enough people would interest themselves in the job; and it should also be possible to laugh the *not un-* formation out of existence,[3] to reduce the amount of Latin and Greek in the average sentence, to drive out foreign phrases and strayed scientific words, and, in general, to make pretentiousness unfashionable. But all these are minor points. The defense of the English language implies more than this, and perhaps it is best to start by saying what it does *not* imply.

To begin with it has nothing to do with archaism, with the salvaging of obsolete words and turns of speech, or with the setting up of a "standard English" which must never be departed from. On the contrary, it is especially concerned with the scrapping of every word or idiom which has outworn its usefulness. It has nothing to do with correct grammar and syntax, which are of no importance so long as one makes one's meaning clear, or with the avoidance of Americanisms, or with having what is called a "good prose style." On the other hand it is not concerned with fake simplicity and the attempt to make written English colloquial. Nor does it even imply in every case preferring the Saxon word to the Latin one, though it does imply using the fewest and shortest words that will cover one's meaning. What is above all needed is to let the meaning choose the word, and not the other way about. In prose, the worst thing one can do with words is to surrender to them. When you think of a concrete object, you think wordlessly, and then, if you want to describe the thing you have been visualizing you probably hunt about till you find the exact words that seem to fit. When you think of something abstract you are more inclined to use words from the start, and unless you make a conscious effort to prevent it, the existing dialect will come rushing in and do the job for you, at the expense of blurring or even changing your meaning. Probably it is better to put off using words as long as possible and get one's meaning as clear as one can through pictures or sensations. Afterwards one can choose—not simply *accept*—the phrases that will best cover the meaning, and then switch round and decide what impression one's words are likely to make on another person. This last effort of the mind cuts out all stale or mixed images, all prefabricated phrases, needless repetitions, and humbug and vagueness generally. But one can often be in doubt about the effect of a word or a phrase, and one needs rules that one can rely on when instinct fails. I think the following rules will cover most cases:

1. Never use a metaphor, simile or other figure of speech which you are used to seeing in print.
2. Never use a long word where a short one will do.
3. If it is possible to cut a word out, always cut it out.
4. Never use the passive where you can use the active.
5. Never use a foreign phrase, a scientific word or a jargon word if you can think of an everyday English equivalent.
6. Break any of these rules sooner than say anything outright barbarous.

These rules sound elementary, and so they are, but they demand a deep change of attitude in anyone who has grown used to writing in the style now fashionable. One could keep all of them and still write bad English, but one could not write the kind of stuff that I quoted in those five specimens at the beginning of this article.

I have not here been considering the literary use of language, but merely language as an instrument for expressing and not for concealing or preventing thought. Stuart Chase and others have come near to claiming that all abstract words are meaningless, and have used this as a pretext for advocating a kind of political quietism. Since you don't know what Fascism is, how can you struggle against Fascism? One need not swallow such absurdities as this, but one ought to recognize that the present political chaos is connected with the decay of language, and that one can probably bring about some improvement by starting at the verbal end. If you simplify your English, you are freed from the worst follies of orthodoxy. You cannot speak any of the necessary dialects, and when you make a stupid remark its stupidity will be obvious, even to yourself. Political language—and with variations this is true of all political parties, from Conservatives to Anarchists—is designed to make lies sound truthful and murder respectable, and to give an appearance of solidity to pure wind. One cannot change this all in a moment, but one can at least change one's own habits, and from time to time one can even, if one jeers loudly enough, send some worn-out and useless phrase—some *jackboot, Achilles' heel, hotbed, melting pot, acid test, veritable inferno* or other lump of verbal refuse—into the dustbin where it belongs.

Endnotes

[1] An interesting illustration of this is the way in which the English flower names which were in use till very recently are being ousted by Greek ones, *snapdragon* becoming *antirrkinum, forget-me-not* becoming *myosotis,* etc. It is hard to see any practical reason for this change of fashion: it is probably due to an instinctive turning-away from the more homely word and a vague feeling that the Greek word is scientific.

[2] Example: "Comfort's catholicity of perception and image, strangely Whitmanesque in range, almost the exact opposite in aesthetic compulsion, continues to evoke that trembling atmospheric accumulative hinting at a cruel, an inexorably serene timelessness. . . . Wrey Gardiner scores by aiming at simple bull's-eyes with precision. Only they are not so simple, and through this contented sadness runs more than the surface bitter-sweet of resignation." (*Poetry Quarterly.*)

[3] One can cure oneself of the *not un-* formation by memorizing this sentence: *A not unblack dog was chasing a not unsmall rabbit across a not ungreen field.*

Name: _____ Date: _____

UNDERSTANDING THE TEXT

1. In Orwell's view, what is the nature of the relation between language and thought?

2. What typifies writing that Orwell considers "easy"?

3. What social improvement does Orwell think would follow if writers improved their use of the English language? Why?

ADDITIONAL READINGS

Adatto, Kiku. *Picture Perfect: The Art and Artifice of Public Image Making.* New York: Basic Books, 1993.

Alterman, Eric. *Sound and Fury: The Washington Punditocracy and the Collapse of American Politics.* New York: HarperCollins, 1992.

Bagdikian, Ben. *The Media Monopoly.* 1983. Boston: Beacon Press, 2000.

Fallows, James. *Breaking the News: How the Media Undermine American Democracy.* New York: Pantheon 1996.

Hertsgaard, Mark. *On Bended Knee: The Press and the Reagan Presidency.* 1988. New York: Schocken, 1989.

Jamieson, Kathleen Hall. *Dirty Politics: Deception, Distraction, and Democracy.* New York: Oxford UP, 1992.

———. *Packaging the Presidency: A History and Criticism of Presidential Campaign Advertising.* 1984. New York: Oxford UP, 1996.

Kalb, Marvin. *One Scandalous Story: Clinton, Lewinski, & 13 Days That Tarnished American Journalism.* New York: Free Press, 2001.

Lapham, Lewis. *Lights, Camera, Democracy!: Selected Essays.* New York: AtRandom.com, 2001.

McChesney, Robert W. *Rich Media, Poor Democracy: Communication Politics in Dubious Times.* New York: New Press, 2000.

Postman, Neil. *Amusing Ourselves to Death: Public Discourse in the Age of Show Business.* New York: Viking, 1985.

Scheuer, Jeffrey. *The Sound Bite Society: How Television Helps the Right and Hurts the Left.* New York: Routledge, 2001.

Schroeder, Alan. *Presidential Debates: Forty Years of High-Risk TV.* New York: Columbia UP, 2000.

Schudson, Michael. *The Power of News.* Cambridge: Harvard UP, 1995.

CHAPTER VI

Is Nothing What It Seems?: Mediation and Its Problems

Allegory of the Cave

Plato

FROM BOOK VII

Next, said I, compare our nature in respect of education and its lack to such an experience as this. Picture men dwelling in a sort of subterranean cavern with a long entrance open to the light on its entire width. Conceive them as having their legs and necks fettered from childhood, so that they remain in the same spot, able to look forward only, and prevented by the fetters from turning their heads. Picture further the light from a fire burning higher up and at a distance behind them, and between the fire and the prisoners and above them a road along which a low wall has been built, as the exhibitors of puppet shows have partitions before the men themselves, above which they show the puppets.

All that I see, he said.

See also, then, men carrying past the wall implements of all kinds that rise above the wall, and human images and shapes of animals as well, wrought in stone and wood and every material, some of these bearers presumably speaking and others silent.

A strange image you speak of, he said, and strange prisoners.

Like to us, I said. For, to begin with, tell me do you think that these men would have seen anything of themselves or of one another except the shadows cast from the fire on the wall of the cave that fronted them?

How could they, he said, if they were compelled to hold their heads unmoved through life?

And again, would not the same be true of the objects carried past them?
Surely.

If then they were able to talk to one another, do you not think that they would suppose that in naming the things that they saw they were naming the passing objects?

Necessarily.

And if their prison had an echo from the wall opposite them, when one of the passers-by uttered a sound, do you think that they would suppose anything else than the passing shadow to be the speaker?

By Zeus, I do not, said he.

Then in every way such prisoners would deem reality to be nothing else than the shadows of the artificial objects.

Quite inevitably, he said.

Consider, then, what would be the manner of the release and healing from these bonds and this folly if in the course of nature something of this sort should happen to them. When one was freed from his fetters and compelled to stand up suddenly and turn his head around and walk and to lift up his eyes to the light, and in doing all this felt pain and, because of the dazzle and glitter of the light, was unable to discern the objects whose shadows he formerly saw, what do you suppose would be his answer if someone told him that what he had seen before was all a cheat and an illusion, but that now, being nearer to reality and turned toward more real things, he saw more truly? And if also one should point out to him each of the passing objects and constrain him by questions to say what it is, do you not think that he would be at a loss and that he would regard what he formerly saw as more real than the things now pointed out to him?

Far more real, he said.

And if he were compelled to look at the light itself, would not that pain his eyes, and would he not turn away and flee to those things which he is able to discern and regard them as in very deed more clear and exact than the objects pointed out?

It is so, he said.

And if, said I, someone should drag him thence by force up the ascent which is rough and steep, and not let him go before he had drawn him out into the light of the sun, do you not think that he would find it painful to be so haled along, and would chafe at it, and when he came out into the light, that his eyes would be filled with its beams so that he would not be able to see even one of the things that we call real?

Why, no, not immediately, he said.

Then there would be need of habituation, I take it, to enable him to see the things higher up. And at first he would most easily discern the shadows and, after that, the likenesses or reflections in water of men and other things, and later, the things themselves, and from these he would go on to contemplate the appearances in the heavens and heaven itself, more easily by night, looking at the light of the stars and the moon, than by day the sun and the sun's light.

Of course.

And so, finally, I suppose, he would be able to look upon the sun itself and see its true nature, not by reflections in water or phantasms of it in an alien setting, but in and by itself in its own place.

Necessarily, he said.

And at this point he would infer and conclude that this it is that provides the seasons and the courses of the year and presides over all things in the visible region, and is in some sort the cause of all these things that they had seen.

Obviously, he said, that would be the next step.

Well then, if he recalled to mind his first habitation and what passed for wisdom there, and his fellow bondsmen, do you not think that he would count himself happy in the change and pity them?

He would indeed.

And if there had been honors and commendations among them which they bestowed on one another and prizes for the man who is quickest to make out the shadows as they pass and best able to remember their customary precedences, sequences, and coexistences, and so most successful in guessing at what was to come, do you think he would be very keen about such rewards, and that he would envy and emulate those who were honored by these prisoners and lorded it among them, or that he would feel with Homer and greatly prefer while living on earth to be serf of another, a landless man, and endure anything rather than opine with them and live that life?

Yes, he said, I think that he would choose to endure anything rather than such a life.

And consider this also, said I. If such a one should go down again and take his old place would he not get his eyes full of darkness, thus suddenly coming out of the sunlight?

He would indeed.

Now if he should be required to contend with these perpetual prisoners in 'evaluating' these shadows while his vision was still dim and before his eyes were accustomed to the dark—and this time required for habituation would not be very short—would he not provoke laughter, and would it not be said of him that he had returned from his journey aloft with his eyes ruined and that it was not worth while even to attempt the ascent? And if it were possible to lay hands on and to kill the man who tried to release them and lead them up, would they not kill him?

They certainly would, he said.

This image then, dear Glaucon, we must apply as a whole to all that has been said, likening the region revealed through sight to the habitation of the prison, and the light of the fire in it to the power of the sun. And if you assume that the ascent and the contemplation of the things above is the soul's ascension to the intelligible region, you will not miss my surmise, since that is what you desire to hear. But God knows whether it is true. But, at any rate, my dream as it appears to me is that in the region of the known the last thing to be seen and hardly seen is the idea of good, and that when seen it must needs point us to the conclusion that this is indeed the cause for all things of all that is right and beautiful, giving birth in the visible world to light, and the author of light and itself in the intelligible world being the authentic source of truth and reason, and that anyone who is to act wisely in private or public must have caught sight of this.

I concur, he said, so far as I am able.

Come then, I said, and join me in this further thought, and do not be surprised that those who have attained to this height are not willing to occupy themselves with the affairs of men, but their souls ever feel the upward urge and the yearning for that sojourn above. For this, I take it, is likely if in this point too the likeness of our image holds.

Yes, it is likely.

And again, do you think it at all strange, said I, if a man returning from divine contemplations to the petty miseries of men cuts a sorry figure and appears most ridiculous, if, while still blinking through the gloom, and before he has become sufficiently accustomed to the environing darkness, he is compelled in courtrooms or elsewhere to contend about the shadows of justice or the images that cast the shadows and to wrangle in debate about the notions of these things in the minds of those who have never seen justice itself?

It would be by no means strange, he said.

But a sensible man, I said, would remember that there are two distinct disturbances of the eyes arising from two causes, according as the shift is from light to darkness or from darkness to light, and, believing that the same thing happens to the soul too, whenever he saw a soul perturbed and unable to discern something, he would not laugh unthinkingly, but would observe whether coming from a brighter life its vision was obscured by the unfamiliar darkness, or whether the passage from the deeper dark of ignorance into a more luminous world and the greater brightness had dazzled its vision. And so he would deem the one happy in its experience and way of life and pity the other, and if it pleased him to laugh at it, his laughter would be less laughable than that at the expense of the soul that had come down from the light above.

That is a very fair statement, he said.

Then, if this is true, our view of these matters must be this, that education is not in reality what some people proclaim it to be in their professions. What they aver is that they can put true knowledge into a soul that does not possess it, as if they were inserting vision into blind eyes.

They do indeed, he said.

But our present argument indicates, said I, that the true analogy for this indwelling power in the soul and the instrument whereby each of us apprehends is that of an eye that could not be converted to the light from the darkness except by turning the whole body. Even so this organ of knowledge must be turned around from the world of becoming together with the entire soul, like the scene-shifting periactus in the theater, until the soul is able to endure the contemplation of essence and the brightest region of being. And this, we say, is the good, do we not?

Yes.

Of this very thing, then, I said, there might be an art, an art of the speediest and most effective shifting or conversion of the soul, not an art of producing vision in it, but on the assumption that it possesses vision but does not rightly direct it and does not look where it should, an art of bringing this about.

Yes, that seems likely, he said.

Then the other so-called virtues of the soul do seem akin to those of the body. For it is true that where they do not pre-exist, they are afterward created by habit and practice. But the excellence of thought, it seems, is certainly of a more divine quality, a thing that never loses its potency, but, according to the direction of its conversion, becomes useful and beneficent, or, again, useless and harmful. Have you never observed in those who are popularly spoken of as bad, but smart men how keen is the vision of the little soul, how quick it is to discern the things that interest it, a proof that it is not a poor vision which it has, but one forcibly enlisted in the service of evil, so that the sharper its sight the more mischief it accomplishes?

I certainly have, he said.

Observe then, said I, that this part of such a soul, if it had been hammered from childhood, and had thus been struck free of the leaden weights, so to speak, of our birth and becoming, which attaching themselves to it by food and similar pleasures and gluttonies turn downward the vision of the soul—if, I say, freed from these, it had suffered a conversion toward the things that are real and true, that same faculty of the same men would have been most keen in its vision of the higher things, just as it is for the things toward which it is now turned.

It is likely, he said.

Well, then, said I, is not this also likely and a necessary consequence of what has been said, that neither could men who are uneducated and inexperienced in truth ever adequately preside over a state, nor could those who had been permitted to linger on to the end in the pursuit of culture—the one because they have no single aim and purpose in life to which all their actions, public and private, must be directed, and the others, because they will not voluntarily engage in action, believing that while still living they have been transported to the Islands of the Blessed?

True, he said.

It is the duty of us, the founders, then, said I, to compel the best natures to attain the knowledge which we pronounced the greatest, and to win to the vision of the good, to scale that ascent, and when they have reached the heights and taken an adequate view, we must not allow what is now permitted.

What is that?

That they should linger there, I said, and refuse to go down again among those bondsmen and share their labors and honors, whether they are of less or of greater worth.

Do you mean to say that we must do them this wrong, and compel them to live an inferior life when the better is in their power?

You have again forgotten, my friend, said I, that the law is not concerned with the special happiness of any class in the state, but is trying to produce this condition in the city as a whole, harmonizing and adapting the citizens to one another by persuasion and compulsion, and requiring them to impart to one another any benefit which they are severally able to bestow upon the community, and that it itself creates such men in the state, not that it may allow each to take what course pleases him, but with a view to using them for the binding together of the commonwealth.

True, he said, I did forget it.

Observe, then, Glaucon, said I, that we shall not be wronging, either, the philosophers who arise among us, but that we can justify our action when we constrain them to take charge of the other citizens and be their guardians. For we will say to them that it is natural that men of similar quality who spring up in other cities should not share in the labors there. For they grow up spontaneously from no volition of the government in the several states, and it is justice that the self-grown, indebted to none for its breeding, should not be zealous either to pay to anyone the price of its nurture. But you we have engendered for yourselves and the rest of the city to be, as it were, king bees and leaders in the hive. You have received a better and more complete education than the others, and you are more capable of sharing both ways of life. Down you must go then, each in his turn, to the habitation of the others and accustom yourselves to the observation of the obscure things there. For once habituated you will discern them infinitely better than the dwellers there, and you will know what each of the 'idols' is and whereof it is a semblance, because you have seen the reality of the beautiful, the just and the good. So our city will be governed by us and you with waking minds, and not, as most cities now which are inhabited and ruled darkly as in a dream by men who fight one another for shadows and wrangle for office as if that were a great good, when the truth is that the city in which those who are to rule are least eager to hold office must needs be best administered and most free from dissension, and the state that gets the contrary type of ruler will be the opposite of this.

By all means, he said.

Will our alumni, then, disobey us when we tell them this, and will they refuse to share in the labors of state each in his turn while permitted to dwell most of the time with one another in that purer world?

Impossible, he said, for we shall be imposing just commands on men who are just. Yet they will assuredly approach office as an unavoidable necessity, and in the opposite temper from that of the present rulers in our cities.

For the fact is, dear friend, said I, if you can discover a better way of life than office holding for your future rulers, a well-governed city becomes a possibility. For only in such a state will those rule who are really rich, not in gold, but in the wealth that makes happiness—a good and wise life. But if, being beggars and starvelings from lack of goods of their own, they turn to affairs of state thinking that it is thence that they should grasp their own good, then it is impossible. For when office and rule become the prizes of contention, such a civil and internecine strife destroys the office seekers themselves and the city as well.

Name: _____ Date: _____

UNDERSTANDING THE TEXT

1. What are the circumstances of the prisoners in Socrates' story? What do they consider to be real? Who do the prisoners symbolize?

2. What does Socrates imagine to be the initial response of a prisoner who is released from the cave and exposed to the light? What would be the prisoner's response after he became accustomed to the light?

3. What role does Socrates envision for those who have seen the light? Why?

Molding Our Lives in the Image of Movies

Neal Gabler

Nearly 160 years ago, Alexis De Tocqueville observed that Americans lacked an appreciation for what he called the "pleasures of mind." Instead, he wrote, they "prefer books which may be easily procured, quickly read, and which require no learned researches to be understood. They ask for beauties self-proffered and easily enjoyed. . . .They require strong and rapid emotions, startling passages, truths or errors brilliant enough to rouse them up and to plunge them at once, as if by violence, into the midst of the subject."

Those words remain, in fact, a pretty good description of the impulses that drive American popular culture, what one might call a constant quest for ever greater sensationalism. But the characteristics Tocqueville ascribed to our books, poetry and theater are now no longer confined to amusements; they have leached into almost every aspect of American life. Any putative Tocqueville looking at America today would see a whole Republic of Entertainment in which strong and rapid emotions, startling passages and rousing truths pervade journalism, politics, education, religion, art and even crime. Indeed, ours seems to be a world molded in the image of the movies and intended for our viewing pleasure.

To most of us, this has been obvious for some time in the country's public life. However serious their subtext may be, news events like the O. J. Simpson trials and Lewinskygate are vastly entertaining spectacles that are promoted, packaged and presented very much like the latest Hollywood blockbusters, only these stories happen to be written in the medium of life.

What has been less evident than the transformation of public events into entertainment, however, is something arguably much more important: the extent to which entertainment has gradually infested our own personal lives, converting them into "movies" too. It is not just that audiences may find daily life as entertaining as fictionalized stories, as *The Truman Show* and the director Ron Howard's forthcoming *EdTV* have it. It is that over the years our movie-going and television watching has been impregnating the American consciousness with the conventions and esthetics of entertainment, until we have become performers ourselves, performing our own lives out of the shards of movies. One might even think of American life, including quotidian American life, as a vast production in which virtually every object is a prop, every space is a set, every person is an actor and every experience is a scene in a continuing narrative.

It has been a long process that has brought us to this point—a process that may have been set in motion by the country's very active sense of democracy. In Europe, where the class hierarchy was rigid and class distinctions obvious, any sort of personal theatricality, aside from that of self-conscious, rebellious Bohemians, was limited to the upperclasses, which could afford flamboyant display. But in America, where class boundaries were more porous and distinctions less apparent, citizens quickly learned that how one looked and behaved largely determined how one was perceived, prompting Walt Whitman to lament the "terrible doubt of appearances."

This emphasis on class by style infused 19th century American life with a kind of subtle theatricality as the middle class and later the working class imitated the affectations of the gentry in hopes of being regarded as gentry themselves. By the early 20th century, though, these old models of gentility had yielded to new models in the mass media, especially the movies, and the change ushered in a marked difference in aspiration. What had begun in the 19th century as a way of appropriating class became in the 20th a way of making one's life more closely approximate the glamorous visions one read about in novels and picture magazines or saw on the screen.

Today, with the burgeoning of mass culture, this everyday performance art may be America's most ubiquitous art. Though obviously not everyone is willing to concede that he or she is becoming a performer, there are telltale signs everywhere that ordinary life is cinematic. Take fashion. There was a time when fashion was, as Tom Wolfe once put it, the "code language of status," a way to express where one stood in the social order. Nowadays, when nearly everyone has access to designer clothes, even if it is only a pair of jeans, fashion is less expressive than imaginative. What one wears doesn't necessarily convey who one is: it projects who one wants to be—which makes clothing into costume.

It is certainly no coincidence that America's most popular and influential designer, Ralph Lauren, has demonstrated the greatest appreciation for the costume functions of fashion. What Mr. Lauren, born Ralph Lifshitz, understood from his own love of the movies as a boy growing up in the Bronx was that people would pay to transform their lives into their cinematic fantasies: safari outfits to make one a colonialist from *Out of Africa;* denim jackets and jeans to make one a cowboy from a Hollywood western; finely tailored English suits to make one an aristocrat from any number of crisp drawing room melodramas.

At the same time, he realized that these transformations were more than a matter of costuming. With his home furnishings and accessories as well as his ad campaigns, Mr. Lauren sells an image of life, a kind of collage of movie fantasies that, in his own words, "represent living, not fashion" and that, more specifically, provide the "whole atmosphere of the good life" that movies had always purveyed. One writer called him the first image manager, which is exactly what he is. He *gave* the middle class what the upper classes and celebrities had always had: a conscious esthetic.

What Ralph Lauren is to the materials of image, Martha Stewart is to their deployment. Like Mr. Lauren's, Ms. Stewart's origins were humble, but like Mr. Lauren, she has an instinct for transporting her followers from their daily grind. Identifying with the bedraggled, unfulfilled, unappreciated middle-class housewife, Ms. Stewart, as a life style consultant, offers a vision of domestic perfection that owes more to movies and television sitcoms than to reality. "We have come to realize that the creation of a fine family, a lovely life style and a comfortable home is kind of a national art form in itself," she told her readers of her syndicated column with a nod to the theatricality of it. So devout an esthete is Ms. Stewart that she has even issued instructions on how to shovel the snow from your sidewalk: "Always leave an inch of snow so it looks nice and white. Esthetics are very important in snow removal."

While designers like Mr. Lauren and life style counselors like Ms. Stewart are in the business of image management, more and more architects are in the business of creating the sets on which the life movie could unfold. Stores like Niketown and malls like the Mall of America outside Minneapolis or Horton Plaza in San Diego, theme restaurants like the Hard Rock Cafe, Planet Hollywood or Jekyll and Hyde, and hotels, museums, churches and schools were now furnishing stages for the performance of shopping, eating, sleeping, watching, worshiping or learning. As Andy Warhol once said of New York restaurants, "They caught on that what people really care about is changing their atmosphere for a couple of hours"—that is, escaping into their own life movies.

Nor was the set restricted to individual spaces. Whole areas had become back lots, to use the Hollywood term for the studios' old tracts where outdoor scenes were shot—areas like West 57th Street and the South Street Seaport in New York or Peachtree Center in Atlanta or Navy Pier in Chicago. The intellectual historian Thomas Bender, looking at the way America's inner cities were being colonized and commercialized by chain stores, theme restaurants and other tourist attractions, summoned a new urban vision in which the city was an "entertainment zone—a place to visit, a place to shop; it is no more than a live-in theme park," which he believed was designed to hide a grittier, dirtier, more problematic city from us.

Even so, if many of us now live on stages, dress in costumes and follow esthetic guidance, these things are only symptomatic of a larger reconceptualization of life itself. Nearly 50 years ago, the sociologist David Riesman identified the emergence of a new type of social character in America that he called "other-directed," by which he meant, essentially, that one's goals were directed toward satisfying the expectations of others—an audience. By definition, other-directed Americans were conscious of performance and of the effects of affect, a self-consciousness that led another sociologist, Erving Goffman, to conclude that in the 20th century "life itself is a dramatically enacted thing."

In Goffman's analysis, every American was engaged in a series of plays and a series of roles, an "exchange of dramatically inflated actions, counteractions, and terminating replies"—in short, an enactment of the scenes of daily life. What Goffman didn't seem to foresee when he was writing in the late 1950's was how much more complex the performance would become, how many more scenes and roles there would be to play on a daily basis and how much farther the front stage would extend into the backstage until the show never seemed to end.

In effect, the demands of daily performance at work, at school, at social engagements, even at home, would become so onerous that one could no longer be compared to a classical actor digging into his kit bag to find a character the way a Laurence Olivier had. Rather, Americans were on stage so often that they were forced to become Method actors mastering the art of playing themselves by, as Elizabeth Taylor once described the technique, "making their fiction reality." Daily life had become a show. "A whole day of life is like a whole day of television," Andy Warhol observed, anticipating *The Truman Show*. "TV never goes off the air once it starts for the day, and I don't either. At the end of the day the whole day will be a movie."

But if one lived a movie, as Warhol said, it wasn't just the day that qualified as a performance; it was the entire life. It was *life* now that had a beginning, a middle and an end like conventional movies. It was *life* now that was increasingly being plotted to let the "actor" live out his or her fantasies, albeit within the restraints of physical appearance, financial resources, talent, cooperation and a myriad of other impediments. One now chose a genre to which one aspired and then eased into the role. If you wanted to be a young professional or a Bohemian artist or a man of leisure or an outdoorsman, you conformed your life to the conventions of each. You dressed the way they dressed, acted the way they acted, associated with the kinds of people with whom they associated.

Though in practice this was all somewhat amorphous, what really seemed to illustrate how rapidly personal life was advancing toward theater was the advent of a new profession: self-styled "life coaches," reportedly 1,300 of them, as of last year, who advise clients on how to reorient their lives to reach what one coach calls fulfillment but what someone else might call a happy ending. What the coaches do, along with routine ego boosting, is replot the client's life. They tell him how he should organize his time, how he should deal with business matters, whether or not he should host a party or take a trip. "It's like painting a canvas for a 'life assignment,'" said one coach.

Few people are as overtly self-conscious about their life movies as these clients, but a good many Americans are still embarked on a campaign to live out their life vision as it has been shaped by mass culture. "At one point in cultural history we asked whether movies furnished an adequate likeness of real life," the psychologist Kenneth Gergen once observed. "The good movies were the more realistic. Now we ask of reality that it accommodate itself to film. The good person, like the good party, should be more 'movieistic.'" Or to put it another way, where we had once measured the movies by life, we are learning to measure life itself by how well it satisfies the narrative expectations created by the movies.

In doing so, we have been changing not only the contours of our lives but the very justification for our existence. Traditionally, realizing one's dreams was only one part of the life experience. It was understood that a full life necessarily entailed both our failures and our triumphs, our agonies and our ecstasies. This was why Aldous Huxley's brave new world seemed so terrifying even though its inhabitants were in a perpetual state of bliss. In Huxley's view, they had sacrificed their humanness to their happiness.

Clearly we have not yet arrived at the point where we can shape our lives to our specifications as writers shape movies, but we are probably closer to living in *Pleasantville*, to cite the title of the new film about a 1950s television universe of unruffled joy, than any previous generation. In the movie, the town of Pleasantville is disturbed by the arrival of "real" humans who bring with them a pungent taste of "real" life. In our own Pleasantville, though, the issue is not how much more exciting reality is than our movie and television glosses; it is how little reality seems to count when life itself is a gloss. After all, when life is a movie, who needs reality?

Huxley notwithstanding, that may just turn out to be the central question of the next millennium.

Name: _____   Date: _____

UNDERSTANDING THE TEXT

1. In Gabler's view, what insights did Alexis de Tocqueville provide into the American character?

2. According to Gabler, in what ways has entertainment "infested" our lives? Why is he concerned about this?

3. Gabler suggests that America's "very active sense of democracy" might account for why elements of performance have come to so thoroughly pervade our lives. Why does he think so?

The Reality Effect

Joel Black

FROM CINEMA VERITÉ TO REALITY TV

> The networks not only remain enthusiastic about the reality genre,
> but the next iterations are all about one-upping the others.
>
> —Ben Silverman, the William Morris Agency

The media's growing influence in the digital age would seem to support the claims of critics such as Jean Baudrillard and Paul Virilio about the "crisis in the reality principle," and has led a number of commentators to lament the gradual disappearance and ultimate loss of "reality" itself.[1] For some, the problem goes back six thousand years to the earliest media technology, writing, which heralded the separation of signs and things that caused reality to become increasingly symbolic and virtual.[2] Others, such as James Carey, call attention to the fact that reality is increasingly being coopted, "preempted," "defined," and "restricted" by ever more powerful global media conglomerates that debase news and history into mindless diversions.[3] Such critiques of the media and information technology are valid as far as they go, but they overlook several key matters. By calling attention to the media's distortions of reality, they give the impression that there is some independent state of affairs "out there" that can be objectively verified. Yet as philosophers from Vico onward have insisted, human reality is always a construct and has been so since the earliest poets came up with supernatural explanations for natural phenomena. If anything, the recording revolution of the nineteenth and twentieth centuries has worked to stabilize meaning and limit interpretation rather than promote rampant invention and distortion. (Of course, this could all change with the digital revolution now under way, in which fabricated images are capable of simulating indexical records.)

Then there are claims such as Neal Gabler's that entertainment now plays such an overwhelming role in people's lives that reality hardly "seems to count . . . After all, when life is a movie, who needs reality?"[4] On the contrary, reality is never more in demand than it is in our global mass-mediated film culture, where it has become, in Carey's words, "a scarce resource." And while reality has never been more in demand, it has also never been more at issue. Reality in liberal, democratic, mass-mediated societies no longer is self-evident, but is constantly contested and up for grabs. It isn't merely that movies compete with reality; rather, movies compete with other movies (and studios with other studios) in rendering an authentic—that is, graphic—view of reality. Thus in 1998, for example, the movies *Deep Impact* and *Armageddon* both took up the hot new post–Cold War scare of an asteroid hitting the earth, while *Saving Private Ryan* and *The Thin Red Line* presented directors Steven Spielberg's and Terrence Malick's strikingly different accounts of American soldiers' experiences of World War II, and *Antz* and *A Bug's Life* offered the DreamWorks and Disney/Pixar studios' competing computer-animated visions of the anthropomorphized world of insects.

Besides the rival views of reality presented by different movies is the competition in our "mixed media culture" between movies and other media, such as TV, video, and the Internet.[5] An entire subgenre of movies has emerged, from *Network* to *Quiz Show,* critiquing the impact of television on daily life. While the protagonist of the 1998 movie *The Truman Show* is the unwitting star of a real-life TV serial and the two 1990s teenagers in *Pleasantville* become the unwilling captives of a 1950s black-and-white television drama, Ed of *EdTV* is only too eager (at least at first) to allow himself to become the star of a real-life soap opera. In each case, the medium of television is presented in all its contrived artificiality—especially in its pretense as reality TV to give viewers a direct glimpse of life. Yet movies critical of television do precisely what they fault television for doing: they present themselves as a transparent lens through which we watch the absurd interaction unfold between the artificial medium of TV and "real life." Film's own status as an artificial (and artificing) medium goes unexamined in these intramedial movies that critique TV as a mediating agency standing between viewers and (one particular view of) reality. Watching these movies about TV, we are led to forget that we are watching a movie, and more precisely a movie fiction. When the protagonists Truman and Ed renounce their fake TV world for real life, no acknowledgment is made that "real life" in these movies is nothing but another media fiction—that of *The Truman Show* and *EdTV* themselves.

Even as these end-of-the-century films critique television as an artificial medium, a case can be made that movies themselves have historically been a fantasy medium and that it is in fact TV that has led the way in presenting the real in all its gritty, graphic immediacy.[6] Whereas cinema verité uses the pretense of documentary to dramatize events or fabricate a story in order to present a thesis or to convey some deeper truth, reality TV documents "actual" events that are intrinsically dramatic, sensational, and voyeuristic (car chases and crashes, man-made and natural disasters, feuding spouses, even surgical operations).[7] The fact that the phrase "reality TV" has largely displaced "cinema verité" is itself revealing: in contrast to the immediacy of television, movies only offer a staged (after)image of reality,

reality as an effect. Yet as media researcher Sandra J. Ball-Rokeach asks of infotainment TV, "in what sense is it reality programming? . . . These shows desensitize the audience to the fear and the emotions [of actual chases and shoot-outs]. The fictional police dramas are sometimes more 'real' because they give you that context. You get a much more subtle understanding of character instead of just the action."[8] Arguing along similar lines, Lincoln Kaplan points out that fictional police and courtroom dramas on television "are more effective in framing important legal choices than most of what [the real-life cable channel] Court TV broadcasts. In an era when 'reality' TV blurs the line between nonfiction and fiction by recreating events, what people see on [fictional television dramas] gets closer to the truth—especially since the events they stage are often taken from the news."[9] Once again, what is graphic and documentary is not necessarily real or true. The so-called "caught-on-video" footage of reality TV is marked by its own artificial

> vérité aesthetic (shaky camerawork, static and technical glitches, time codes, and other aesthetic techniques that suggest that the footage was not studio-produced) . . . [Reality TV's] claim of realism is not achieved by stripping the imagery of all mediation to somehow reveal an unadulterated "reality"—an impossible feat. In fact, it tends to require *more* mediation to assert that these images are real.[10]

Narrative filmmakers might think twice before emulating the dubious realism of reality TV. Still, the fact that a number of filmmakers are striving for television's nonfictional edginess suggests that "reality" still counts for a great deal in the movies, and that film has a deeper commitment to, and connection with, the "real world" than formalist critics suspect.

Nowhere is television's vaunted realism more dubious than in the new genre of "reality shows" flourishing at the turn of the century. Many of these popular American products are not even original, but recycled European imports. The number one U.S. TV program *Who Wants to Be a Millionaire* was a British quiz show that ABC first acquired as a summer series. After its success (and the fiasco of Fox's prime-time, publicity-driven special *Who Wants to Marry a Multi-Millionaire*), three networks vied for the rights to the Dutch program *Big Brother* (another losing proposition, it turned out), in which a group of young people is confined to a house loaded with cameras and microphones that record their every move. The CBS summer-of-2000 blockbuster *Survivor,* in which sixteen contestants were stranded on (and gradually eliminated from) a jungle island near Borneo, was originally a Swedish hit. In that version, one cast member committed suicide after receiving a negative vote. If *Los Angeles Times* television columnist Brian Lowry is right, more deaths can be expected as these ratings-driven shows continue "to push the envelope farther and farther in order to make them interesting"[11]—and, we might add, in order to pursue an elusive reality which must appear ever more violent and graphic.

Not only did reality shows have the potential to be immensely popular with audiences, but they were far cheaper to produce, and therefore far more profitable, than sitcoms and crime dramas. As a partner at one talent agency remarked, "Game shows and reality shows will occupy real estate previously rented to fictional entertainment programs."[12] As of this writing, plans are already in place for a televised worldwide scavenger hunt; an American version of the European show *Jailbreak,* in which a group of contestants compete to be the first to break out of a high-technology prison; and a show in which a group of people live in an environment approximating conditions on Mars. There's even a new all-out space race for the new century: NBC's deal with Russia to broadcast a contest in which the winner is sent into space aboard a Russian rocket was followed up by negotiations between the other major networks and NASA for a show in which twenty contestants train with the space agency for the chance to spend a week aboard the new International Space Station.[13]

While the hegemony of the Hollywood movie industry is threatened by far cheaper independent films and video games, the reign of costly fictional programming on TV has been put in jeopardy by the groundswell of inexpensive "reality shows." Clearly the term is an egregious misnomer. The fact that such shows are unscripted hardly makes them real. The ubiquitous presence of television cameras and film crews, and above all the actors' awareness that they are being filmed, undercuts the pretense of reality that informs the film *The Truman Show* or, for that matter, a TV program such as *Candid Camera*—"shows" in which the subject is genuinely ignorant that he or she is on film and is being seen by millions of knowing viewers. But while shows such as MTV's *The Real World* continued to cling to the pretense of presenting people as they are, the new breed of hyperreality shows has dropped this conceit once and for all. The over-the-top, soap-opera stories contrived by the World Wrestling Federation's Vince McMahon have given up any "pretense that wrestling was real." Far from making the sport seem more legitimate and lifelike, McMahon introduced "a second layer of unreality" by alternating the rounds with a lurid, behind-the-scenes glimpse into his own dysfunctional family. In John Leland's words, "here was something to believe in: the candidly, honestly fake."[14] But McMahon seriously misgauged matters when, instead of the honestly fake, he attempted to bring a new level of realism to the hallowed institution of professional football. The XFL, or Extreme Football League, was expressly created in 2000 for a new generation of viewers who appeared to be steadily losing interest in the increasingly artificial spectacle of NFL games. By placing cameras and microphones everywhere—on the field and off the field, in the players' helmets, and in the locker rooms—the XFL promised a glimpse into the behind-the-scenes reality of the game. Such realism couldn't compete with the over-hyped spectacle of the NFL, and the XFL folded after only one season.

If viewers of the common run of reality shows willfully suspend their disbelief to the point that they can believe the "candidly, honestly fake," what's to stop them from doubting the documented truth? Indeed, while a surprising number of people are disposed to believe photographic "evidence" of UFOs and other fantastic phenomena, others reject filmed evidence of the moon landing or the liberation of the death camps at the end of World War II. Straightforward, undoctored amateur recordings of sensational events, such as the Zapruder film of JFK's assassination or the Holliday video of the Rodney King beating, not only fail to show "what really happened," but actually provoke more controversy than if they hadn't been made and hadn't become part of the public record.[15] Such seemingly accurate but ultimately ambiguous and inconclusive recordings have contributed to the skeptical attitude that many feel toward the documentary media today. Others, meanwhile, are disposed to accept whatever they are shown in the movies, regardless of its veracity or even its authenticity, as long as the special effects are sufficiently spectacular and graphic.

More than ever, film audiences are in need, if not of a new hermeneutics of suspicion, then of a code of cinematic literacy that will allow them to maintain a healthy skepticism in the face of ever more spectacular special effects. An innovative media criticism is called for that can expose the ways that film distorts the world in the process—and under the pretense—of documenting it. Of particular interest in this regard are a line of narrative films from the second half of the century—from Hitchcock's 1958 *Vertigo* to Antonioni's 1966 *Blow-Up* and Neil Jordan's 1992 *The Crying Game*—that thematize the pitfalls of credulity and stress the need to doubt visible evidence in the primarily visual medium of film. "You can't believe everything you see" ran the advertising tag for Brian De Palma's 1984 film *Body Double,* while the ads for his 1998 *Snake Eyes* warned, "Believe everything, except your eyes."[16] It's as if filmmakers increasingly find themselves in the role of sorcerer's apprentices, wielding a medium whose seductive power has become so great, thanks to ever more realistic special effects, that they actually need to remind their supposedly media-savvy audiences to suspend not their disbelief but their belief. Yet it may be too much to expect such warnings to be taken seriously by most viewers growing up in the society of the spectacle of contemporary film culture. From their earliest years they have learned that the visible is the only reality that matters and that the truth is out there—namely, on the airwaves, on whatever channel the most vivid and awesome spectacle can be found.

ENDNOTES

[1] John Johnston, "Machinic Vision," *Critical Inquiry* 26 (1999): 31.

[2] Albert Borgmann, *Holding on to Reality: The Nature of Information at the Turn of the Millennium* (Chicago: University of Chicago Press, 1999).

[3] Quoted by Eric Alterman, "A Euro without a Europe," *The Nation,* Oct. 11, 1999, 10.

[4] Neal Gabler, "Molding Our Lives in the Image of Movies," *New York Times,* Oct. 25, 1998.

[5] See Bill Kovach and Tom Rosenstiel, *Warp Speed: America in the Age of Mixed Media* (New York: The Century Foundation Press, 1999).

[6] Thus Sterngold observes that "real life, as portrayed on television, has grown so graphic that the people who write teleplays and screenplays have been forced into greater luridness just to keep up" ("For Artistic Freedom, It's Not the Worst of Times"). Don DeLillo has contrasted "choreographed movie violence" with the surveillance videos of bank robberies and shoot-outs that are shown and reshown on television news programs, commenting that while such television images are "produced in a mass-market kind of fashion," they're "also real, it's real life. It's as though this were our last experience of nature: seeing a guy with a gun totally separate from choreographed movie violence. It's all that we've got left of nature, in a strange way. But it's all happening on our TV set" (quoted in David Remnick, "Exile on Main Street," *The New Yorker,* Sept. 15, 1997, 48).

[7] Examples of medical reality shows are the Discovery Health Channel's *Operation,* the Health Network's *O.R.: Behind the Mask,* and the Learning Channel's *Trauma: Life in the E.R.* See Craig Tomashoff, "When the Reality Is Inside the Body," *New York Times,* June 11, 2000.

[8] Quoted in James Sterngold, "Bruce Nash: Seeking to Go Beyond the 'Shockumentary,'" *New York Times,* Jan. 25, 1999.

[9] Lincoln Caplan, "The Failure (and Promise) of Legal Journalism," in J. Abramson, ed., *Postmortem: The O.J. Simpson Case: Justice Confronts Race, Domestic Violence, Lawyers, Money, and the Media* (New York: Basic Books, 1996), 199–207.

[10] Tarleton Gillespie, "Narrative Control and Visual Polysemy: Fox Surveillance Specials and the Limits of Legitimation," *The Velvet Light Trap* 45 (Spring 2000): 40.

[11] Interview with Mandalit Delbarco on NPR's "Morning Edition" (Feb. 9, 2001).

[12] Peter Benedek, quoted in Bernard Weinraub, "Sudden Explosion of Game Shows Threatens the Old TV Staples," *New York Times,* Feb. 9, 2000.

[13] Bill Carter, "Space: Network TV's Commercial Frontier," *New York Times,* Sept. 21, 2000.

[14] John Leland, "Why America's Hooked on Wrestling," *Newsweek,* Feb. 7, 2000, 48.

[15] The unreliability of video evidence in the courtroom became especially apparent in the 1999 antitrust case against Microsoft; a videotape demonstration that the corporation had prepared in its defense backfired when troubling inconsistencies on the tape prompted the judge to reject it as evidence.

[16] In a marketing ploy devised by producers of the film *The X-Files,* ads for the video version advised viewers who had already seen the movie in theaters that "if you've seen it once, you haven't seen it all; now you can look closer, dig deeper." While this promotion ostensibly referred to the fact that the video—like many DVD releases—included additional scenes that weren't shown in theaters, it also hinted that *The X-Files* was a kind of hermetic text with hidden clues that required endless study, and that the video was a medium more conducive to in-depth research than the movie's theatrical presentation.

UNREAL ESTATE: FAKE TOWNS, REAL PEOPLE

Nowadays when a person lives somewhere, in a neighborhood, the place is not certified from him. More than likely he will live there sadly and the emptiness which is inside him will expand until it evacuates the entire neighborhood. But if he sees a movie which shows his very neighborhood, it becomes possible for him to live, for a time at least, as a person who is Somewhere and not Anywhere.

—Walker Percy, *The Moviegoer*

Besides *Wag the Dog,* two other noteworthy movies about the media appeared in 1998. In Gary Ross's *Pleasantville,* two contemporary siblings are transported back into a 1950s-era TV show, experiencing and exposing the blandness of that artificial world. And Peter Weir's *The Truman Show* presents the ultimate paranoid scenario: Jim Carrey's character, Truman Burbank, is a man whose entire life is a staged, ongoing soap opera, filmed by five thousand tiny hidden cameras and watched by millions on TV. Reality triumphs over artifice at the end of both movies: the TV characters in the *Pleasantville* series wake up to the unpredictability of real life, and Truman discovers the elaborate deception in which he has been both dupe and star, whereupon he abandons his closed sound-stage world in order to live an authentic life beyond the cameras' myriad probing eyes.

The Truman Show and *Pleasantville* are movies whose stories play on the unprecedented power of the visual media of television and, by extension, film at the end of the twentieth century. They especially call attention to Americans' obsessive fascination with "the surreal ordinariness" of life as embodied in the character of Truman or in the town of Pleasantville, and they self-reflexively examine the willingness of viewers "to find the most nondescript . . . experiences" of a character such as Truman "more poignant and meaningful than one's own."[1] But why do viewers find the ordinary so fascinating? Perhaps because it's become so rare in a society of the spectacle where more and more of life is mediated by the mass media. Or perhaps because in such a society the "ordinary" is anything but natural, but is itself the most surreal and extraordinary effect of all.

It's worth noting in this regard that both *The Truman Show* and *Pleasantville* are situated in towns that look like sets staged for movies or television. Oddly, the fake town of Seahaven portrayed in *The Truman Show* was *not* a set, but the actual planned community of Seaside on Florida's panhandle. The film's producers had simply reversed the customary practice of building an artificial set that looks real; instead they used a real town that looked like a set to evoke "a setting that becomes a character in its own right."[2] Viewers unaware of the fact that Seahaven is not just a set but the real town of Seaside miss the irony in the film's premise that enormous effort, incalculable expense, and ingenious special effects have been used to provide Truman with the illusion of reality—that he is living a normal life in an ordinary town—when the film was in fact shot in an actual (although thoroughly movie-mediated) town. If, as J. G. Ballard said, "the fiction is already there" for the writer whose only "task is to invent the reality," the setting for Peter Weir's film already existed as the town of Seaside. Rather than create a fake town as an "effect," Weir merely had to give this ready-made town a slightly altered name.

It's not often that the real thing suits Hollywood's artificial purposes. When an existing historical monument figures prominently in a movie, it's usually necessary to construct a fake alternative. Thus when a film about the Alamo was being made in Texas, moviemakers considered the real landmark "small and unprepossessing." As a result, they arranged for "a bigger and better Alamo" to be built in a nearby town, and today it is as much a tourist attraction as the genuine Alamo.[3] (One is reminded of the exact copy of Goethe's Garden House built a hundred yards from the original in Weimar to celebrate the writer's 250th birthday.)

Similarly, in seeking set locations, Hollywood production designers routinely settle on small, historic American towns to create a feeling of authenticity—for example the Rhode Island towns of Wickford in *Meet Joe Black* (1998) and Jamestown in *Me, Myself, and Irene* (2000). Yet although these traditional towns would seem to be utterly unlike the artificial fantasy worlds of Hollywood or the synthetic sprawl of Los Angeles, they increasingly seem quaint and unreal, as if they were constructed as movie sets. In fact, a growing number of residential communities have so assiduously simulated the pristine towns portrayed in the movies that they themselves take on the appearance of movie sets. And so the producers of *The Truman Show*—a movie satirizing the media's idealized depictions of post-World War II American life—were able to use a real-life town as a set precisely because it looked so artificial. The logical next step was for the movie companies themselves to construct new "real" communities that replicate the appearance of the few remaining towns of yesteryear, and then to use these new-old, fake-real hybrid towns as movie sets.[4]

The fact that real and fake towns can no longer be distinguished in the movies is another sign that the traditional distinction between narrative films and documentaries has been thoroughly blurred. After Michael Moore's *Roger & Me* documented the ravaged economy of Flint, Michigan, in the aftermath of General Motors plant closings and layoffs, it was only a matter of time before a virtual documentary such as Russ Hexter's 1997 movie *Dadetown* would portray the economic woes of a fake town.

> The film unrolled like an as-it-happened documentary of a small town where the factory economy was dying and giving way to the software business. Not until the credits rolled was it revealed that the town, the citizens and the upheaval were entirely fictional.
> Any critic who raced out at the close of the final scene reviewed a documentary they only thought they saw.[5]

While *Roger & Me* depicts the decline of an actual industrial city, a finde-siècle documentary such as James Marsh's *Wisconsin Death Trip* insidiously suggests that the apparent prosperity of the rural farming community of Black River Falls is deceptive, and that the pleasant rituals of small-town life—parades, beauty contests, high-school football games—mask occasional eruptions of criminal violence that are painfully reminiscent of the town's harrowing gothic past.

These documentaries about decaying cities and troubled towns are giving way to a new phenomenon: real towns whose survival depends on their becoming an artificial film set, a theme park, or even an advertisement. Take the small Cascade Mountain town of Cashmere, Washington, which recently faced economic ruin when its principal business, a candy company that had been based there since 1918, threatened to move to a nearby "Bavarian theme town." The company, Liberty Orchards, would agree to stay in Cashmere only if a list of demands were met that would effectively turn the town into an advertisement for its business—changing road signs and renaming streets to refer to Liberty Orchards' products, and even letting the company buy the town hall.

"It is not surprising," writes architecture critic Ada Louise Huxtable, "that much of the most popular and profitable development of the [theme park] genre is spearheaded and bankrolled by the masters of illusion; the movie and entertainment businesses have become the major innovators and investors in theme parks and related enterprises."[6] But it should also come as no surprise to learn that the media company most adept in constructing amusement parks and entertainment complexes as well as movie sets simulating small-town life in America would enter the real estate business and build actual residential communities. This is what the Walt Disney Company did when it created the town of Celebration in Florida on land acquired in the 1960s for Walt Disney World. Disney himself had wanted to create "a real town with real citizens" in central Florida to be called Epcot, the Experimental Prototype Community of Tomorrow.[7] But the Epcot that eventually opened in the early '80s as part of Disney World was a futuristic theme park that hardly conformed to the original project. Disney's dream had to wait until the company came under the management of Michael Eisner, who agreed to develop a five-thousand-acre tract of land that wasn't needed for the park's expansion into a town that he hoped "would be a model for development in the next millennium."[8] But far from being a futuristic town, Celebration—which was designed by the same architects who planned Seaside, that other artificial-looking Florida site where *The Truman Show* was filmed—is an example of "New Urbanism," a style modeled on Savannah, Georgia, and other pre-1940s southern towns. The exterior appearance of the homes are carefully regulated, from the landscaping to the pastel shades of paint to the white and off-white color of the window curtains.[9] It's fitting that the town's central feature is its movie house, designed by Cesar Pelli in the style of 1930s theaters.

For critics such as Neal Gabler, Celebration's nostalgic creation of a movie-mediated past is a sign of its unreality. Celebration is *The Truman Show* come true—a town in which all the inhabitants "were cast members on the set of their own life movies."[10] But the New Urbanist invocation of an earlier period in American culture can also be seen as a move toward a new reality. In contrast to Disney's futuristic Epcot, Celebration may be, as Kurt Andersen suggests, "the real EPCOT—the quasi-democratic, postmodern fulfillment of Walt's totalitarian, late-modern vision." To those critics who would sneer at Celebration's "picturesque fakery," Andersen responds,

> Isn't the obligatory American lawn a form of fakery? Isn't air-conditioning a fake? Aren't the crazy architectural mongrels built every day in every city in America—all the tarty Mediterranean-Colonial-Norman-Palladian raised ranches—thoroughly (and wretchedly) fake? . . . Celebration's "fakery"—its small scale, its density, its hidden garages, its pre-mall commercial core—is in the service of a coherent vision, as opposed to the accumulation of developers' cost-efficient short cuts and aesthetic bad habits that produce the random, sprawling, ghastly "real" suburbs of the late twentieth century.[11]

For end-of-the-century advocates of New Urbanism, planned fakery has become preferable to a ruthlessly unregulated reality. And Celebration's particular brand of fakery is also preferable to all the other forms of artificiality that characterize modern American life, not so much because it is more picturesque or more up-front about its pretense, but because its coherent vision of small-town life (which is really a cinematic vision à la Capra and Disney) comes closest to creating the ultimate reality effect—the illusion of "a real town with real citizens." According to this logic, the only place in late-twentieth-century America to find real people who can be spontaneously and genuinely themselves is in fake towns, communities deliberately designed to recapture the supposed simplicity of a bygone era before the advent of the very technology that transformed reality into—or revealed it as—an effect.

Ants Wars

While families were moving into Celebration's movie-set community in an attempt to re-experience real life at the close of the twentieth century, another building project of a different kind was under way on the other side of the country that was intended to challenge Disney's media hegemony. (Under Eisner's leadership, the Disney corporation had acquired the film company Miramax, allied itself with the software company Pixar, and was once again producing cutting-edge feature animation as in the days of its founder.) On a 1,087-acre stretch of marshland on the California coast, the first new Hollywood studio in sixty years was being planned by DreamWorks SKG. The complex was to be a state-of-the-art technological marvel, constructed on the very site where former film mogul Howard Hughes had built his "Spruce Goose" seaplane. Headed by director Steven Spielberg, former Disney movie chief Jeffrey Katzenberg, and record mogul David Geffen, the company was valued at $2.7 billion before it even produced its first product.[12] A project of this size had to be more than just a complex of sound stages; DreamWorks was to be the anchor tenant of the projected Playa Vista development, which, with thirteen thousand new condos and commercial space including a new marina, and at least $75 million in city and state tax incentives, was intended to be a self-sufficient residential community with an estimated worth of $6 billion to $8 billion.

From the start, however, the ambitious project was headed for trouble. Environmentalists charged that Playa Vista threatened the Ballona wetlands, the last undeveloped tract in Los Angeles County. Ultimately, financing difficulties led DreamWorks to pull out of the project in 1999. There are limits, it seems, to the joint business ventures envisioned by dream movies and "real" estate.[13]

Nevertheless, DreamWorks was—and still is—clearly positioning itself to give Disney, one of the world's largest media companies, a run for its money. Specifically, it has sought to challenge Disney in the domain where it reigns supreme—animation—and especially in the new generation of computer-generated animation that Disney had inaugurated with its partner Pixar (the software company that Apple Computer cofounder Steve Jobs bought from George Lucas in 1986). Since the huge success of the first computer-animated feature, *Toy Story,* Pixar's staff focused exclusively on making movies, entering into a five-picture partnership with Disney and building its own base of operations on sixteen and a half acres in Emeryville, California.

Competition between DreamWorks and Disney/Pixar came to a head in the fall of 1998 with each studio's release of a blockbuster computer-generated animation feature dealing with the unlikely subject of ants. Although DreamWorks started work on *Antz* in 1995, a full year after Pixar began developing *A Bug's Life,* the film was rushed into production so that it could be released more than a month ahead of its competitor. Pixar protested that its idea for an ant movie had been stolen by Katzenberg when he quit his post as chairman of Disney Studios to join DreamWorks in August 1994—two days before the idea was pitched to Disney by Pixar director John Lasseter. (Katzenberg has denied knowing about the project.) But while DreamWorks scooped Disney in the ants animation war, *A Bug's Life* held its own and was widely hailed as a superior achievement. Besides, the technical innovations of *Antz* did not go without criticism. Film critic Anthony Lane complained about the movie's "decorative uniformity," its shiny surfaces that show no trace of

> the random ways on which physical surfaces are rubbed and scarred. This was no problem with "Toy Story," where the natural sheen of the animation coincided happily with the fact that the heroes were molded from plastic; it is more of a letdown in "Antz," which is, by definition, set in a universe of trash and crap.[14]

The movie's key scene in a garbage dump dubbed "Insectopia" fails to come off "because the garbage cannot help but suffer from the same spooky, enhanced cleanness in which computer design has wrapped the entire movie." The contradiction Lane finds between computerized cleanliness and a sort of sanitized filth that appeals to humans and vermin alike would seem to be an inevitable result of the new technology which is incapable of simulating oldness and waste.

And why two ant films anyway? The life of insects, typically the subject of nature documentaries, became the ideal subject for filmmakers eager to demonstrate the new capabilities of the most artificial of cinematic forms—animation—to reproduce the natural world. What better subject, as Edward Rothstein observes, to display "texture, character, individuality, nuance and other un-antlike characteristics" created by the new technology? "Computer animation was once the sign of artificiality; now it is humanized, naturalized, and we are meant to see it at work bringing a human touch to the inhuman realm of the ant. Nature is transformed by artifice into seeming more natural."[15] Computer animation, the latest breakthrough in cinematic special effects, was used to produce the illusion not of the supernatural but of nature at its most ordinary, familiar, and homely. The greatest technical feat in *Toy Story 2* wasn't the lifelike animation of the toy characters but the digitized portrayal of the dachshund Buster; the four million hairs on his body are visual effects made possible by fur software developed during the movie's production. It's as if nature presents the computer-animation wizards not only with the greatest challenge, but also with an unprecedented opportunity to re-create it into something altogether new, artificial, and supremely graphic—to make reality over once and for all as an effect.

Back to the Future: Movies, the Ride

At the end of the twentieth century, Neal Gabler's claim that life has become "the biggest, most entertaining, most realistic movie of all, one that played twenty-four hours a day, 365 days a year, and featured a cast of billions" itself became the subject of movies.[16] In *The Truman Show* one man's life is nothing more than a cinematic illusion; the following year *The Matrix* revealed *all* life to be an illusion. The latter film is based on the Kabbalistic premise that the world as we know it is no longer real but a "computer-generated dream" that only a few select individuals can penetrate to the reality beyond. The irony here, of course, is that the movie *The Matrix* is itself a computer-generated dream that envelops its viewers, sealing them off in its own substitute reality. It doesn't take much imagination to see *The Matrix* as an allegory of the pervasive power of movies—especially movies loaded with special effects—to create an alternate, substitute, but ultimately false reality. A key problem with such movies is that they are utterly incapable of critically looking at or reflecting upon new developments in digital media and virtual-reality technology because for the most part they are themselves a product of that technology. A better title for the movie might have been *The Möbius Strip* since the mediated reality it depicts loops back into its own production. The use of all the advanced special effects— especially the well-hyped "Flo-Mo" sequences—give the movie the look not of real life, but of a spectacular sci-fi comic book.

The explicit thematization of virtual reality machines in movies such as *The Matrix* calls attention to the fact—already anticipated by early-twentieth-century writers such as Pirandello and Schwartz—that the ultimate machine of this kind, the ideal dream machine, is the cinematic apparatus itself and its more recent televisual derivatives. Most of today's commercial films do not encourage such reflection, however, but rather employ a powerfully synchronized combination of digital audio and visual effects to plunge the viewer into an all-encompassing, somnambulent state that all but screens out the real world. Caught up in the overwhelming imagery of Tony Scott's 1998 thriller *Enemy of the State, Newsweek's* Jack Kroll describes the

> scary fun of the movie . . . embodied in a brilliantly filmed and edited chase sequence in which [Will] Smith tries to escape the ubiquitous cyber-eyes that see every inch of his flight. In such passages Scott . . . creates a new cinematic landscape out of hurtling satellite images and flashing computer screens, turning the whole earth into a claustrophobic space that affords no escape.[17]

Scott's creation of a "new cinematic landscape" is an instance of the Kuleshov effect taken to the extreme: now not merely does the swift sequencing of scenes shot at different locations serve to create an artificial space for the viewer, who remains outside the action, but the film surrounds the viewer with a total surveillance space in which there is no escape from remote cameras, bugging devices, and concealed monitoring systems. The wording of Kroll's description leaves it unclear whether it is the actor Smith or the viewer who is unable to escape the "claustrophobic space" of the "cinematic landscape" into which "the whole earth" has been transformed—the world made film. Whether viewers want it or not, they are along for the ride.

Many of Hollywood's blockbuster films are really no longer movies, but are better described (and evaluated) as rides or games. Some movies, such as *Raiders of the Lost Ark* or *Back to the Future,* become actual rides in theme parks such as Walt Disney World and Universal City, where visitors are no longer passive spectators but have the sense of being interactive participants in cinematic events. Yet there is also a sense in which some of the most entertaining special-effects movies are more than mere rides, providing graphic, documentary evidence or even proof of a reality that has never been, and can never be, recorded on film. One thinks of the prehistoric dinosaurs reconstructed in Steven Spielberg's *Jurassic Park*: although this movie itself became a ride, and is itself *about* a ride in a futuristic theme park, it also presents a vivid picture of a "lost world" that no human being has ever witnessed, let alone documented. In contrast to Disney's talking-dinosaur movie a few years later, Spielberg endeavored to use special effects to reconstruct the most realistic visual simulation possible of these prehistoric creatures. Like all those cinematic reconstructions of JFK's assassination that tried to fill in the gaps left by the spotty film record, Spielberg was making up for the absolute absence of cameras, recording technology, or eyewitnesses during the Jurassic period. Beyond providing a graphic "record" of that lost world, he may have been giving it a kind of reality. For as the real is increasingly identified with recorded audiovisual "evidence" that dates back only to the twentieth—or the first filmed—century, there is a chance that history may appear to future generations as *beginning* with the twentieth century, or at least with what was graphically recorded at that time. (This was, after all, the logic behind the Kansas Board of Education's 1999 decision to drop evolution and the big bang theory from the state's science curriculum since such unobserved and unrecorded events are open to doubt.) The corollary of the literalist belief that the whole world is on film is the view that there's every reason to doubt the reality of whatever *isn't* on film. Given such a view, events in earlier times will have to be photographically reconstructed through dramatization and special effects if they are to appear real. A popular commercial filmmaker such as Spielberg may find himself as a documentarian not only preserving history (as in his project to record the recollections of Holocaust survivors), but also creating history as he and others face the daunting task of having to fill in the yawning gap of all of unrecorded history with realistic, graphic reconstructions.

The longest running back-to-the-future ride is George Lucas's *Star Wars* series. In a curious temporal twist, *Episode 1: The Phantom Menace*—the 1999 sequel to the trilogy of movies that appeared in the 1970s—purported to be a *prequel* that depicted events a generation before those shown in the earlier films. The first three movies dealt with the aftermath of a great debacle that reduced the former Galactic Empire (derived from Isaac Asimov's *Foundation* stories) to a primitive condition of nomadic warriors working with salvaged weaponry; the new film introduced viewers to the period preceding the debacle, when the Empire was at the height of its technological glory.[18]

In fact, this was all an ingenious strategy on Lucas's part to showcase the special-effects wizardry of his company Industrial Light and Magic, effects that were necessary to bring the pre-debacle Empire to the screen in the first place. Twenty years earlier, when the original *Star Wars* movies appeared dealing with the Empire's aftermath, a movie about the Empire could not be made because the special effects needed to represent—and, indeed, create—it did not yet exist. And so Lucas found it necessary to put the series on hold. The depiction of a lost world of marvelous but dangerous technology had to be postponed until end-of-the-century computer technology could catch up with his own imaginative scenarios. (The contradiction between the antitechnological thrust of Lucas's films and his love of special-effects technology has not gone unnoticed.)[19] As late as 1990, Lucas still didn't consider computers sufficiently cost-effective to create the effects he wanted. But with the release of his friend Spielberg's *Jurassic Park* he realized that "we can create a photo-realistic, digital character that can look as real as any actor. . . . I was just so desperate to have an alien character that I can turn into a real character who interacts with other humans." Here was a case in which a certain spectacle—in this case, the world of the Empire—could not be "recorded" on film until the special effects needed to represent that spectacle became available.

But the epic saga doesn't end here. The images of the Galactic Empire with their vast scale that Lucas's FX-driven movies made so popular have gone on to generate our very conception of the actual cosmos. It's now common to hear the three-dimensional universe described cinematically, as a thin membrane in which we are trapped like "characters playing out their lives within the confines of a movie screen. Unknown to these shallow, two-dimensional players, a larger universe spreads into numerous extra dimensions, like theaters in a multiplex."[20] Or, as Dick Teresi puts it more dramatically, "With its fiery explosions, wormholes, white dwarfs, red giants and black holes, the big bang universe satisfies our Lucasfilm sensibilities. . . . It is the biggest-budget universe ever, with mind-boggling numbers to dazzle us. . . . Who wants to live in a smallish, low-budget universe?"[21]

ENDNOTES

[1] Janet Maslin, "'The Truman Show': So, What's Wrong with This Picture?" *New York Times,* June 5, 1998.

[2] Ibid.

[3] Ada Louise Huxtable, *The Unreal America: Architecture and Illusion* (New York: New Press, 1997). See also the scene in Walker Percy's *Lancelot* where a film company shooting a movie near New Orleans needs "to use the hurricane machine even though a real hurricane is coming, not just because the real hurricane is not yet here, but because even if it were it wouldn't be as suitable for film purposes as an artificial hurricane" (1977; New York: Picador, 1999), 191.

[4] A similar retrolook was adopted by automakers for the new millennium—e.g., Volkswagen's new Beetle and Chrysler's PT Cruiser.

[5] "Photos that Lie—and Tell the Truth," *New York Times,* Mar. 16, 1997.

[6] Timothy Egan, "Candymaker Wants to Use Town as Advertisement," *New York Times,* Oct. 6, 1997.

[7] Kurt Andersen, "Pleasantville," *The New Yorker,* Sept. 6, 1999, 74.

[8] Douglas Frantz, "Living in a Disney Town, with Big Brother at Bay," *New York Times,* Oct. 4, 1998.

[9] Ibid.

[10] Neal Gabler, *Life the Movie: How Entertainment Conquered Reality* (New York: Knopf, 1998), 213 n.

[11] Andersen, "Pleasantville," 79.

[12] Allan Sloan, "Pennies from Heaven," *Newsweek,* Apr. 3, 1995, 44–45. DreamWorks should not be confused with Dreamtime Holdings, Inc., the multimedia company based in Moffett Field, California. The company has been involved in many media projects with NASA and is currently trying to broker a new reality show with one of the major networks in which the winner of a group of contestants training at the Johnson Space Center in Houston would spend a week aboard the International Space Station.

[13] Thus, in order to expedite the creation of Disney World, the Walt Disney Company had founded an independent governmental jurisdiction called the Reedy Creek Improvement District; two decades later, when the company developed Celebration, it removed its name from the title, turned matters of land use over to Osceola County, and turned the business of buying and selling the town's houses over to out-of-state companies.

[14] Anthony Lane, "No Picnic," *The New Yorker,* Oct. 19, 1998, 94.

[15] Edward Rothstein, "Heed the Arthropods; They May Have the Answers," *New York Times,* Nov. 23, 1998.

[16] Gabler, *Life the Movie,* 58.

[17] Jack Kroll, "Cyberspies," *Newsweek,* Nov. 23, 1998, 83.

[18] See Oliver Morton, "In Pursuit of Infinity," *The New Yorker,* May 17, 1999, 84–89. Morton argues, however, that the antitechnological thrust of Lucas's *Star Wars* films "is the antithesis of what Asimov believed. Asimov had an Enlightenment love of reason above all things; and he wanted a better future, not a stirring past" (88).

[19] See Morton: "'Star Wars' treats technology as essentially malign, inhuman, and untrustworthy (except when producing special effects)" (ibid., 88).

[20] K. C. Cole, "Unseen Dimensions Hold Theory Aloft," *Los Angeles Times,* Nov. 18, 1999, B2.

[21] Dick Teresi, "The First Squillion Years," *New York Times Book Review,* Aug. 8, 1999, 6.

Name: _____ Date: _____

UNDERSTANDING THE TEXT

1. Why is Black critical of *The Truman Show, Pleasantville,* and *EdTV*—films that are critical of television?

2. What town provided the set for *The Truman Show?* How does Black characterize this town, and why does he find it significant that *The Truman Show* was filmed there?

3. While Disney's Celebration has many critics, such as Neal Gabler, it has its supporters, too. On what basis does Kurt Andersen defend Disney's "ideal" town?

The Capital of Loneliness

Jane Rosenzweig

The advent of television has long been associated with the beginning of the end of the "good old days." Historians, sociologists, filmmakers, and yes, even TV shows (think *Brooklyn Bridge* and *The Wonder Years*) have explored this relationship. In his 1990 film *Avalon,* Barry Levinson heartbreakingly rendered the effects of TV on three generations of an immigrant family in Baltimore, Maryland, as frequent family gatherings were replaced by solitary TV dinners and aching loneliness. I was 20 years old when *Avalon* came out. The irony of watching it on video, alone in my parents' basement, didn't escape me. The experience left me feeling more palpably than ever before that I had missed out by not being part of the pre-TV, sing-around-the-piano generation.

I thought of *Avalon* again while I was reading *Bowling Alone: The Collapse and Revival of American Community,* Robert Putnam's recent book analyzing the role of television in society. Putnam argues that there is a strong correlation between the rise in television watching and the decline in civic engagement over the past 30 years. We are, at the dawn of the twenty-first century, a society lean on what Putnam calls "social capital," the complex network of human interactions and community connections that lead to "mutual support, cooperation, trust, institutional effectiveness"—in short, the stuff that makes society work. Putnam emphasizes that while TV is certainly not the only factor in social disengagement, those who consider TV their main form of entertainment are less involved in everything else—from community projects to socializing with friends to giving blood. And, he argues convincingly, watching TV isn't just what we do instead; it actually helps to make us isolated, uninvolved, and even cynical.

Without equating TV with reality (it's not), I think it's fair to say that television programs of the past two decades have reflected a society in a social-capital crisis, even if they've simultaneously helped to cause that crisis. Workplace dramas—from *LA Law* to *Hill Street Blues* to the world according to David E. Kelley (*The Practice* and *Boston Public*) depict characters that exist almost entirely at work and seem disconnected from any community larger than the office.

Putnam suggests—and he may be right—that our exposure to so many social problems on TV deflates any hope that we could actually make an impact. Perhaps this is the message to take from the popularity of sitcoms like *Friends* and *Seinfeld,* which—while appearing to suggest community in the form of friends hanging out in one another's apartments and in local restaurants—really portray a social-capital wasteland in which the world beyond a small group of sidekicks in a big, anonymous city barely exists. Can the benefits of talking about *Friends* around the water cooler undo the costs of time spent sitting home watching it?

Through the years of *Seinfeld* and Kelley, there have been a few shows that seem aware of the need for social capital—shows I'd call "family values" TV. Most prominent among these is CBS's popular *Touched by an Angel.* But even this series, with its emphasis on the intervention of angels, reinforces the idea that we are isolated and misguided and need outside help.

Over the past two seasons, though, a new trend has emerged: television characters don't necessarily see a solution to the disjunction of society in terms of their jobs (workplace dramas) or religion or two-parent families (family-values TV) but, rather, in social-capital terms. Just as *The Waltons* and *Little House on the Prairie* presented a pre-TV good-old-days in which society brimmed with social capital, programs like NBC's *Providence* and *Ed* and CBS's *Judging Amy* and *That's Life* present characters at least in search of a contemporary version of connectedness. These shows don't promise overnight solutions to society's ills, but their characters do seem to fulfill the prerequisites of social capital by returning to and participating in their communities.

The social-capital trend began in January 1999 with the premiere of *Providence.* The show features Dr. Syd Hansen (Melina Kanakaredes), a strikingly attractive, thirty-something plastic surgeon in Los Angeles who, after the death of her mother, moves back to her hometown of Providence, re-establishes ties with her family and friends, and takes a job working at a clinic for low-income patients. Considering the program's weak dialogue and silly supporting characters, it's a surprise that this show has been so popular. Can it have anything to do with the premise mirroring our own longings? From the anonymity of the big city (where, Putnam says, significantly fewer people are actively engaged in community activities), Syd returns home to a smaller city where she is part of a complex web of social relationships, both formal and informal. Her father (played by Mike Farrell) is a pre-baby boomer veterinarian—a member of the generation that was, according to Putnam, the last truly civic-minded one—with strong personal ties to his clients. Through her work at the clinic, Syd is suddenly a community activist, chasing down at-risk patients and calling in favors to get them treated. What sets *Providence* apart from family-values TV is that it doesn't promote a particular type of connectedness—only the importance of being connected. Syd's younger sister is a single mother who also lives at home, and the adult children regularly sit down to dinner—and breakfast—with their father.

While the multigenerational television family of the *All in the Family* era lived together for economic reasons, the likes of Syd—and her CBS counterpart Amy Gray (played by

Amy Brenneman) in *Judging Amy*—have actually given up inflated incomes in exchange for something less tangible: emotional support and a sense of belonging. *Judging Amy* premiered in the fall of 1999 with the heroine, divorced Manhattan corporate lawyer Amy Gray, moving herself and her daughter back into her widowed mother's home in Hartford, Connecticut, and accepting an appointment as a family-court judge. While the scripts and the characters are much smarter than *Providence's,* the shows' similarities in content are striking. Amy's mother (Tyne Daly) is a social worker and, like Syd's father, a community-minded representative of the pre-baby boomer generation. In more than one episode, Amy talks of wanting her own daughter to have a "normal life," a vision she equates with her own childhood, which included a dog and a close family. At work she makes decisions for other children who have been deprived of this kind of life.

These shows tell us that people who are ensconced in smaller cities and tied to a community are happier, do more good for others, and find themselves participating in civic causes in ways that TV viewers, apparently, are not. Certainly this is the case with *That's Life,* which takes place in a blue-collar New Jersey town and follows the plight of thirtysomething Lydia, who breaks her engagement to be married in order to fulfill her dream of going to college. As the show has developed, Lydia's civic life has moved more and more to the forefront. *That's Life* really went Putnam in early February, when Lydia began working in a community center to meet a college requirement. When she handed over her hard-earned $500 in rent to keep the center open, she had no choice but to move back into her parents' home. Soon her father was involved, and comments overheard by an acquaintance allowed the family to save the center. And because this is television, civic involvement led to romance.

Similarly, love is integral to a thriving community on *Ed.* After thirty-something Ed is fired from a job as a corporate lawyer and finds his wife in bed with a mailman she picked up at Starbucks (not even their own mailman, which might at least have been a sign of some kind of social capital at work), he moves back to his hometown of Stuckeyville, Ohio. On a whim, he buys the local bowling alley, which, according to an employee, is "as dead as my Aunt Frances." When Ed arrives in Stuckeyville, residents of the town are not just bowling alone; they're not bowling at all. And so, for every customer who bowls three games, Ed promises to provide free legal advice. Granted, Putnam might be skeptical about Ed's choice of solution—the whole litigious thing has replaced the kind of social-capital interaction that Putnam discusses—but he also notes that it's hard to know what solutions best suit current times. Might *Ed*—or any of these shows, for that matter—be onto something? (Full disclosure: I went to my senior prom with one of the creators of *Ed.* Shouldn't there be some social capital in it for me?)

What does it mean that as a society we are comforted and entertained by the idea of adult children, even those with successful careers, moving home and pursuing community connectedness? It doesn't take a sociologist to imagine that the disconnected post-baby boomers who write and watch these shows might yearn to be somewhere where everyone knows their name—not just for a drink after work, but for life. If these shows echo, in their own way, Putnam's call for social capital, is there anything we can learn from how they do it? At best, it seems, they reinforce the appeal of community ties while suggesting that we should reshape what we actually have rather than return to the good old days. Of course, we probably have the best shot of living as these characters do if we stop watching them: One of the great ironies of TV is that its heroes are rarely seen watching it, except when they're depressed. It will be another great irony if these social-capital shows contribute to our social-capital deficit.

Name: _____ Date: _____

UNDERSTANDING THE TEXT

1. According to Rosenzweig, what does Robert Putnam suggest about the effects of television viewing?

2. Which television shows does Rosenzweig praise? Why?

3. What does Rosenzweig find ironic about the way most television shows represent the act of viewing television?

The Numbing of the American Mind: Culture as Anesthetic

Thomas de Zengotita

... the massive influx of impressions is so great; surprising, barbaric, and violent things press so overpoweringly—"balled up into hideous clumps"—in the youthful soul; that it can save itself only by taking recourse in premeditated stupidity.

—Friedrich Nietzsche

It was to have been the end of irony, remember? Superficial celebrity culture was over; a new age of seriousness was upon us. Of course, the way media celebrities focused on their own mood as the consequence of September 11 was in itself an irony so marvelous you knew immediately how wrong they were. And sure enough, the spotlight never wavered. It went on shining as it always had, on those it was meant for—on them. A guarantee of continuing superficiality right there, quite apart from unintended irony.

So we shared Dan Rather's pain, marveled at intrepid Ashleigh Banfield, scrutinizing those ferocious tribal fighters through her designer specs, and Tom Brokaw, arbiter of greatness among generations, took us on a tour of the real West Wing. But these iconic moments swam into focus only momentarily, soon to be swept away in a deluge of references, references so numerous, so relentlessly repeated, that they came at last to constitute a solid field, a new backdrop for all our public performances. How often did you hear, how often did you say, "Since the events of 9/11"? A new idiom had been deposited in the language, approaching the same plane of habituality as "by the way" or "on the other hand." And in the process we got past it after all. Six months or so was all it took. The holidays came and went, and—if you were not personally stricken by the terror of September—chances are you got over it. You moved on.

How is that possible?

Nietzsche was not thinking I.Q. or ignorance when he used the word "stupidity." He meant stupidity as in clogged, anesthetized. Numb. He thought people at the end of the *nineteenth* century were suffocating in a vast goo of meaningless stimulation. Ever notice how, when your hand is numb, everything feels thin? Even a solid block of wood lacks depth and texture. You can't feel the wood; your limb just encounters the interrupting surface. Well, numb is to the soul as thin is to a mediated world. Our guiding metaphor. And it isn't just youthful souls either.

Here's the basic situation. On the one hand: the Web, satellite cable TV, PalmPilot, DVD, Ethernet—Virtual Environments everywhere. On the other hand: cloning, genetic engineering, artificial intelligence, robotics—Virtual Beings everywhere. Someday, when people (or whatever they are) look back on our time, all this will appear as a single development, called something like "The Information Revolution," and the lesson of that revolution will have been this: what counts is the code. Silicon- or carbon-based. Artifact or animate. The difference between them is disappearing. This is not science fiction. This is really happening. Right now, in an Atlanta hospital, there is a quadriplegic with his brain directly wired to a computer. He can move the cursor with his thoughts.

The moving cursor doesn't really need explaining—it comes down to digital bytes and neurochemical spikes. What needs explaining is our equanimity in the face of staggering developments. How can we go about our business when things like this are happening? How can we just read the article, shake our heads, turn the page? If creatures from outer space sent a diplomatic mission to the U.N., how long would it be before we were taking that in stride? Before Comedy Central send-ups were more entertaining than the actual creatures? About six months?

Soap-opera politics. The therapy industry. Online communities. Digital effects. Workshops for every workplace. Viagra, Prozac, Ritalin. Reality TV. Complete makeovers. Someday, it will be obvious that all the content on our information platforms converges on this theme: there is no important difference between fabrication and reality, between a chemical a pill introduces and one your body produces, between role-playing in marital therapy and playing your role as a spouse, between selling and making, campaigning and governing, expressing and existing. And that is why we moved on after September 11, after an event that seemed so enormous, so horrific, so stark, that even the great blob of virtuality that is our public culture would be unable to absorb it. But it could. It has. Here's how.

FABRICATION

Some people refuse to believe that reality has become indistinguishable from fabrication. But beliefs are crude reflections of the psychological processes that actually determine how we function. Fat people believe they are on the stocky side. Abject drunks believe they are poetical free spirits. Malicious prudes believe they are selfless do-gooders. And a lot of people still believe that, with some obvious exceptions involving hoaxes and errors, we know what's real and what's not. We can tell the difference between the *Kursk* and the *Titanic* (meaning the movie, of course), for example.

And maybe we can—when specifically focused on the issue. It might take a while, of course, because there *are* so many gradations when you stop to think about it. For example:

- Real real: You fall down the stairs. Stuff in your life that's so familiar you've forgotten the statement it makes.
- Observed real: You drive by a car wreck. Stuff in your life in which the image-statement is as salient as the function.
- Between real real and observed real: Stuff that oscillates between the first two categories. Like you're wearing something you usually take for granted but then you meet someone attractive.
- Edited real real: Shtick you have down so pat you don't know it's shtick anymore, but you definitely only use it in certain situations. Documentaries and videos in which people are unaware of the camera, though that's not easy to detect, actually. Candid photographs.
- Edited observed real: Other people's down-pat shtick. Shtick you are still working on. Documentaries in which people are accommodating the camera, which is actually a lot of the time, probably.
- Staged real: Formal events like weddings. Retail-clerk patter.
- Edited staged real: Pictures of the above. Homemade porn.
- Staged observed real unique: Al kisses Tipper. *Survivor.*
- Staged observed real repeated: Al kisses Tipper again and again. Anchor-desk and talk-show intros and segues. Weather Channel behavior.

(In the interests of time, we can skip the subtler middle range of distinctions and go to the other end of the spectrum:)

- Staged realistic: *The English Patient* and *NYPD Blue.*
- Staged hyperreal: Oliver Stone movies and *Malcolm in the Middle.*
- Overtly unreal realistic: S.U.V.'s climbing buildings. Digitized special effects in general, except when they are more or less undetectable.
- Covertly unreal realistic: Hair in shampoo ads. More or less undetectable digital effects, of which there are more every day.
- Between overtly and covertly unreal realistic: John Wayne in a beer ad (you have to know he's dead to know he isn't "really" in the ad).
- Real unreal: Robo-pets.
- Unreal real: Strawberries that won't freeze because they have fish genes in them.

See? No problem. The differences are perfectly clear.

But the issue isn't *can* we do it; it's *do* we do it— and the answer is, of course not. Our minds are the product of total immersion in a daily experience saturated with fabrications to a degree unprecedented in human history. People have never had to cope with so much stuff, so many choices. In kind and number.

FLOOD

And sheer quantity really matters, because here we collide with a real limit, one of the few that remain—namely, how much a person can register at a given instant. No innovation in techno-access or sensationalism can overcome this bottleneck. It determines the fundamental dynamic, the battle to secure attention, in every domain of our lives.

Compare, say, the cereal and juice sections of a supermarket today with those of years ago. For you youngsters out there, take it from Dad: it used to be Wheaties, Corn Flakes, Cheerios (oats), Rice Krispies—and that was about it. One for each grain, see? Same for fruit juice. But now? Pineapple/Banana/Grape or Strawberry/Orange/Kiwi anyone? And that's just a sample from Tropicana—check out Nantucket Nectars. Makes of cars? Types of sunglasses? Sneaker species? Pasta possibilities? On and on. It's all about options, as they say.

Umbrella brands toss off diverse and evolving lines of market-researched products for niches of self-inventing customers with continual access to every representational fabrication ever produced in the whole of human history. That's "the environment." You like Vedic ankle tattoos? 1930s cockney caps? Safari jackets? Inca ponchos? Victorian lace-up high-heel booties? Whatever.

No wonder that word caught on.

The moreness of everything ascends inevitably to a threshold in psychic life. A change of state takes place. The discrete display melts into a pudding, and the mind is forced to certain adaptations if it is to cohere at all.

When you find out about the moving cursor, or hear statistics about AIDS in Africa, or see your 947th picture of a weeping fireman, you can't help but become fundamentally indifferent because you are exposed to things like this all the time, just as you are to the rest of your options. Over breakfast. In the waiting room. Driving to work. At the checkout counter. *All the time.* I know you know this already. I'm just reminding you.

Which is not to say you aren't moved. On the contrary, you are moved, often deeply, very frequently—never more so, perhaps, than when you saw the footage of the towers coming down on 9/11. But you are so used to being moved by footage, by stories, by representations of all kinds—that's the point. It's not your fault that you are so used to being moved, you just are.

So it's not surprising that you have learned to move on so readily to the next, sometimes moving, moment. It's sink or surf. Spiritual numbness guarantees that your relations with the moving will pass. And the stuffed screen accommodates you with moving surfaces that assume you are numb enough to accommodate them. And so on, back and forth. The dialectic of postmodern life.

One might say, "Well, people didn't respond deeply to every development in the world 200 years ago either." And that's true, but it isn't an objection, it's a confirmation. Until the new media came along, people didn't even *know* about such developments, or not as quickly, and above all not as dramatically or frequently. Also, there weren't as many developments, period. This is crucial, another aspect of sheer moreness that gets overlooked. *Less was happening.*

The contrast is stark with, say, the Middle Ages. By the industrial era, a lot more was happening, and numbness became an issue then. Think of Baudelaire, adrift in the crowd, celebrating the artist for resisting numbness, for maintaining vulnerability—thus setting the standard for the genius of modernism. But a qualitative threshold has since been breached. Cities no longer belong to the soulful *flâneur* but to the wired-up voyeur in his soundproofed Lexus. Behind his tinted windows, with his cell phone and CD player, he gets more input, with less static, from more and different channels, than Baudelaire ever dreamed of. But it's all insulational—as if the deities at Dreamworks were invisibly at work around us, touching up the canvas of reality with existential airbrushes. Everything has that edgeless quality, like the lobby of a high-end Marriott/Ramada/Sheraton. Whole neighborhoods feel like that now. And you can be sure that whatever they do at "the site" will feel like that, too. Even if they specifically set out to avoid having it feel like that—it will still feel like that. They can't control themselves. They can't stop.

Take the new Times Square, everybody's icon for this process. All the usual observations apply—and each contributes its iota to muffling what it meant to expose. But the point here is the way everything in that place is *aimed.* Everything is firing message modules, straight for your gonads, your taste buds, your vanities, your fears. These modules seek to penetrate, but in a passing way. A second of your attention is all they ask. Nothing is firing that rends or cuts. It's a massage, really, if you just go with it. And why not? Some of the most talented people on the planet have devoted their lives to creating this psychic sauna, just for you.

And it's not just the screens and billboards, the literal signs; it's absolutely everything you encounter. Except for the eyes of the people, shuffling along, and the poignant imperfections of their bodies; they are so manifestly unequal to the solicitations lavished upon them. No wonder they stuff themselves with junk—or, trying to live up to it all, enslave themselves to regimes of improvement.

Yes, there were ersatz environments and glitzy ads back in the fifties, but this is a new order of quality and saturation. Saying that it's just more of what we had before is like saying a hurricane is just more breeze. For here, too, there is a psychological threshold. Today, your brain is, as a matter of brute fact, full of stuff that was *designed* to affect you. As opposed to the scattered furniture of nature and history that people once registered just because it happened to be there. September 11 had to accommodate the fact that our inner lives are now largely constituted by effects.

To get relief, you have to stumble into the Greyhound bus station in Albany, or some old side-street barbershop that time forgot, into someplace not yet subjected to the renovating ministrations of the International Red Brick and Iron Filigree Restoration Corporation. And "stumble" is the key concept here. Accidental places are the only real places left.

That's why a couple of weeks out in Nature doesn't make it anymore. Even if you eschew the resonant clutter of The Tour and The Gear, you will virtualize everything you encounter anyway, all by yourself. You won't see wolves, you'll see "wolves." You'll be murmuring to yourself, at some level, "Wow, look, a real wolf, not in a cage, not on TV, I can't believe it."

That's right, you can't. Natural things have become their own icons.

And you will get restless really fast if that "wolf" doesn't do anything. The kids will start squirming in, like, five minutes; you'll probably need to pretend you're not getting bored for a while longer. But if that little smudge of canine out there in the distance continues to just loll around in the tall grass, and you don't have a really powerful tripod-supported telelens gizmo to play with, you will get bored. You will begin to appreciate how much technology and editing goes into making those nature shows. The truth is that if some no-account chipmunk just happens to come around your campsite every morning for crumbs from your picnic table, it will have meant more to you than any "wolf."

Precious accidents.

Back to the new Times Square—do you parse out the real from the fabricated in that mélange? Not *can* you, but *do* you. The Fox screen is showing Elián in his Cuban school uniform on the side of a building—real or not? Some glorious babe in her underwear is sprawled across 35 percent of your visual field. She's looking you right in the eye. You feel that old feeling—real or not? A fabulous man, sculpted to perfection by more time in the health club than most parents have for their kids, is gliding by on Day-Glo Rollerblades eight inches high. He's wearing Tex-tex gear so tight it looks like it's under his skin, and the logos festooning his figure emit meaning-beeps from every angle—real or not? What about the pumped-up biceps? If he uses steroids? But, once again, the issue isn't what you *can* do when I call your attention to it. The real issue is *do* you do it as a matter of routine processing? Or do you rely instead on a general immunity that only numbness can provide, an immunity that puts the whole flood in brackets and transforms it all into a play of surfaces—over which you hover and glide like a little god, dipping in here and there for the moving experience of your choice, with the ultimate reaches of your soul on permanent remote?

FINITUDE

What about that feeling that it's all been done? Not in the techie department, of course; there, the possibility of novelty seems to be unlimited. But in those areas occupied by what platform proprietors call "content providers." What a phrase! Could anything register devastation of the spirit more completely than that little generic? Could meaning suffer more complete evacuation? Not since we landed on the moon and found nothing has our cultural unconscious encountered so traumatic a void.

Maybe the postmodern taste for recycling and pastiche is more than a phase? Maybe it's necessity. Maybe more or less everything that can be done in the plastic arts, say, has been done? How many different ways can a finite set of shapes and colors be arranged in a finite space? We aren't talking infinitely divisible Platonic geometry here. Maybe there just isn't any really new way to put *x* shapes and *y* colors into *z* permutations. Maybe some day it will be obvious that the characteristic gestures of twentieth-century art were flailing against this fact. Cézanne's planes, Magritte's pipe, Pollock's swirls, Warhol's soup can, Christo's draperies, Serrano's piss, the "installations"—so many desperate efforts to elude the end of originality?

Likewise with music? How many distinguishable sounds can be put in how many patterns? There has to be some limit. After you've integrated techno and Brazilian-Afro and Tibetan monko and Hump-backed Whalo, at some point, surely, there's going to be nothing left but play it again, Sam. Maybe that's why it's the age of the mix. And characters and plots, in stories and shows? What's the raw material? Sex, outlaws, illness, death, master villains, guilt, the fall of giants, fate, just deserts, the dark side, redemption by the little things, a few other themes—we all know the repertoire. Maybe it's just impossible to think of anything that couldn't be described, after the fashion of all contemporary pitches, as "It's *To the Lighthouse* meets *Married with Children*" or "It's Hannibal Lecter meets Peter Pan."

The prospect of finitude helps to account for the turn to sensation, as if intensity of presentation could make up for repetition. Of course, sensation is also a response to sheer clutter on the screen, a way to grab the most possible attention in the least amount of time. But that clutter also accounts for why everything's already been done, and so it cycles on relentlessly—fill the pages, fill the time slots, fill the channels, the websites, the roadsides, the building facades, the fronts and backs of shirts and caps, everything, everything must be saying something, every minute. But what? What's left to say? It doesn't matter. Cut to the response.

Zap. Whimper. Flinch. Cringe. Melt. Assert! Exult! Weep. Subside. Ahhh . . .

Eventually we can just wire our glands directly to a console of sensation buttons, platform to platform, and be done with this tiresome content altogether. Call it P2P communication. Talk about interactive. Thus will the human soul be compensated for the despair of finitude.

FAST

Remember that T-shirt from the eighties that said "High on Stress"? It was sort of true and sort of a way to bluff it out and sort of a protest—it had that "any number of meanings" quality we now prefer to depth. That's because the any-number-of-meanings quality keeps you in motion, but depth asks you to stop. Depth is to your life what dead air is to a talk show.

Being numb isn't antithetical to being totally stressed, 24-7—and asking for more. Overscheduled busyness might seem like the opposite of numbness, but it is just the active aspect of living in a flood of fabricated surfaces. Consider the guiding metaphor again. The (absence of) sensation that is physical numbness is constituted by a multitude of thrills and tingles at a frequency beyond which you feel nothing. The numbness of busyness works on the same principle, but it relies upon its agents to abide by an agreement they must keep secret, even from themselves. The agreement is this: we will so conduct ourselves that everything becomes an emergency.

Under that agreement, stress is how reality feels. People addicted to busyness, people who don't just use their cell phones in public but display in every nuance of cell-phone deportment their sense of throbbing connectedness to Something Important—these people would suffocate like fish on a dock if they were cut off from the Flow of Events they have conspired with their fellows to create. To these plugged-in players, the rest of us look like zombies, coasting on fumes. For them, the feeling of being busy *is* the feeling of being alive.

Partly, it's a function of speed, like in those stress dramas that television provides to keep us virtually busy, even in our downtime. The bloody body wheeled into the ER, every per-sonjack on the team yelling numbers from monitors, screaming for meds and equipment, especially for those heart-shocker pads—that's the paradigm scene. All the others derive from it: hostage-negotiator scenes, staffers pulling all-nighters in the West Wing, detectives sweeping out of the precinct, donning jackets, adjusting holsters, snapping wisecracks. Sheer speed and Lives on the Line. That's the recipe for feeling real.

The irony is that *after* we have worked really hard on something urgent for a long time, we do escape numbness for a while—stepping out of the building, noticing the breeze, the cracks in the sidewalk, the stillness of things in the shop window. During those accidental and transitional moments, we actually get the feeling of the real we were so frantically pur-suing when we were busy. But we soon get restless. We can't take the input reduction. Our psychic metabolism craves more.

Actually, stress dramas are about the lives of the media people who make them. They purport to be about hospitals or law firms, but they are actually about what it is like to make TV shows, about high-stakes teamwork in the land of celebrity, where, by definition, every-thing matters more than it does anywhere else, a land that welcomes diversity and foibles as long as The Job Gets Done, a land where everything personal, unconditional, intimate—everything unbounded by the task—takes place on the side. That's why, in these shows through which the celebrated teach the rest of us how to be like them, the moments of heart-felt encounter that make it all worthwhile are stolen in the corridors of power, while the ver-dict is awaited. If we get that real-folks-rushing-to-get-out-of-the-house-in-the-morning scene, it's just to underscore the priority of the Flow of Events that protects the busy from being left alone in the stillness with what makes it all worthwhile. Lest direction be lost, motion must be maintained.

MOVING ON

So life in a flood of surfaces means a life of perpetual motion, and TV provides the model in other modes as well. Take the transitions from story to story in newscasts, that finishing-with-a-topic moment. "Whether these supplies, still piling up after weeks of intense effort by these humanitarian workers, will actually reach the victims (pause) remains to be seen." A hint of a sigh, a slight shake of the head, eyes down-turning; the note of seasoned resigna-tion. Profound respect is conveyed for the abandoned topic even as a note of anticipation rises to greet the (also interesting, but less burdensome) next topic—and the new camera angle at the anchor desk makes it clear that stern and external necessity, rather than any human agency, governs the shift from two minutes on mass starvation to the next episode of The Fall of the House of Enron.

Judy Woodruff is especially good at this, her particular little head nod, or shake, as the case may be, and the way her lips tighten up a tad. "If it were up to me as a human being I would *never* leave this coverage of thousands of dying innocents, but, as a newscaster, of course, I have to." And her speaking voice says, "All right, Jim, we have to go to a break now, but we will be following this story as it develops—and thanks again." "Thank you, Judy," says Jim, echoing her gesture, and we understand that he, too, as a human being, would never allow us to move on from so ghastly and demanding a reality, but it isn't up to him as a human being either. It isn't up to anybody, actually. That's the one real reality. Moving on.

It would be irrelevant to object by asking, "Well, how else are we supposed to do it?" There isn't any other way to do it. That's the point. This isn't a consultant's memo. This is a serious diagnosis of a serious condition. Would we rather not know about it because it happens to be incurable? This goes much deeper than subject matter, or political bias, the usual fodder. It determines the way we frame everything. Like all that is most profound in human custom, this agreement is almost physical, an attunement, more music than semantics. It instills and expresses, moment by moment, the *attitude* we bring to living in this world of surfaces.

So, for example, you don't have to wait for the anchorperson to change the topic. You can change it yourself, and you don't have to sigh or tighten your lips as you make the transition. But you do. Monitor yourself next time you zap away from some disturbing something on *Lehrer* to catch the action on the *Law & Order* reruns. You mime those little gestures as you punch the buttons. These are the constituting habit structures of our culture.

And we've touched already on what awaits you when you join the gang on *Law & Order.* The stress drama re-creating, more elaborately, the basic gesture of the news show, the one you just performed when you slid away from those refugee visuals. Everything's in motion, elliptical, glancing, fungible. You see the sides of faces, the slope of shoulders, the beginnings of expressions but not the ends, the ends of expressions but not the beginnings. No matter the horror, no matter the injustice, no matter how passionate McCoy may feel, no matter how angry Bratt gets at Briscoe (actors or characters?), no matter how obnoxious the defense attorney or impatient the judge (especially in chambers), they all keep moving. And the camera keeps moving, too, gliding, peeking, glimpsing. Frightened witnesses, incoming lawyers, outgoing suspects, they're all moving—as is the traffic, the doors, hands, phones, everything. Meaningful personal encounters are bound to be interrupted, and the performers, like would-be fighters in a bar relying on friends to keep them apart, anticipate the interruption. Ferociously or tenderly, they emote in transitional interlude, awaiting inevitable rescue by events, and, gratefully regretting the passing of the moment of communion, they watch the D.A. step into the elevator and deliver the homily as the door slides shut across his grizzled visage, a homily that is never merely upbeat or despairing, never final or conclusive in any way. Because the one thing people in a TV series know is that tomorrow is another show, and they will be ready to roll. For they are pros, and pros know how to deal. It's not that they're indifferent or cynical. They care. Sometimes they win, sometimes they lose—but, either way, they move on. That's the lesson, the ultimate homily of all shows. The way we live now.

So, if we were spared a gaping wound in the flesh and blood of personal life, we inevitably moved on after September 11. We were carried off by endlessly proliferating representations of the event, and by an ever expanding horizon of associated stories and characters, and all of them, in their turn, represented endlessly, and the whole sweep of it driven by the rhythms of The Show—anthrax, postal workers, the Bronx lady, the Saddam connection, Osama tapes, Al Jazeera's commentary on Osama tapes, Christiane Amanpour's commentary on Al Jazeera's commentary on Osama tapes, a magazine story about Christiane Amanpour . . .

And that's just one thread in this tapestry of virtuality. The whole is so densely woven and finely stranded that no mind could possibly comprehend it, escape it, govern it. It's the dreamwork of culture. It just proceeds and we with it, each of us exposed to thousands, probably millions of 9/11-related representations—everything from the layout of the daily paper to rippling-flag logos to NYPD caps on tourists to ads for *Collateral Damage*. Conditioned thus relentlessly to move from representation to representation, we got past the thing itself as well; or rather, the thing itself was transformed into a sea of signs and upon it we were borne away from every shore, moving on, moving on.

What else could we do?

Name: _____ Date: _____

UNDERSTANDING THE TEXT

1. de Zengotita writes: Someday, it will be obvious that all the content on our information platforms converge on this theme: there is no important difference between fabrication and reality. . . .” What evidence does he offer to support this notion that no such “important difference” exists? (Identify two instances.)

   Fat people believe they are on the stocky side.

   Abject drunks believe they are poetical free spirits.

2. de Zengotita claims that “[a]ccidental places are the only real places left.” What does he mean by this, and why does he think it is true?

   nil.

3. "Flood," "Finitude," "Fast," "Moving On": de Zengotita uses each of these headings to describe a condition of contemporary life that shapes our consciousness. To what, specifically, does each refer? Together, how does he think these conditions affect our response to the events of 9/11?

Flood - flood of information about everything.

Finitude — the intensity of presentation could make up for repetition.

Fast — to move fast, you have a busy life.

Moving On — life will move on.

People are used to being moved by footage. It is not our fault (we're) use to being moved, we cant help it. We were flooded w/ information on the attacks and we all eventually moved on.

CASE STUDY

Representing the West

Fighting for the West

Eric Foner and Jon Wiener

"The West as America: Reinterpreting Images of the Frontier, 1820–1920," an exhibit at the Smithsonian Institution's National Museum of American Art, has become the latest target in the assault on "politically correct" thought by longtime conservatives, onetime radicals and academics enamored of campus life before the advent of large numbers of women and minority students. Critics accusing this show of being "P.C." have once again wrapped themselves in the mantle of intellectual liberalism, while accusing their opponents of political indoctrination and thought control (see Alexander Cockburn, "Beat the Devil," May 27 and June 24). But at the Smithsonian, as on most college campuses, abuses inspired by political correctness remain a minor problem. Their significance is dwarfed by the myriad real crises in university and cultural life—among them dwindling public funds, rising corporate influence, the fragmentation of scholarship and widespread illiteracy. "Political correctness" ranks with the swine flu epidemic and comet Kohoutek as molehills transformed into mountains by a gullible media. The Smithsonian controversy suggests that it is the right, not the left, that today poses the real threat to intellectual freedom.

Senator Ted Stevens, the Alaska Republican, made the Smithsonian show a national issue in a Senate Appropriations Committee hearing in May, when he accused the museum of advancing a leftist political agenda and threatened to cut the institution's budget in retaliation. "You're in for a battle," he told Smithsonian officials. Washington Republican Senator Slade Gorton echoed the charge. (Stevens later acknowledged that he had not, in fact, seen the show. What prompted his crusade was a well-publicized remark by former Librarian of Congress Daniel Boorstin in the museum's comment book that the exhibit was "perverse, historically inaccurate, [and] destructive.")

The press quickly entered the fray. *The Washington Post*'s Ken Ringle called the show "the most cynical exhibit . . . ever presented under the aegis of your tax dollars and mine." *The New York Times*'s senior art critic, Michael Kimmelman, blasted the show's "simplistic" and "forced" analyses. The wildest attack came from political columnist Charles

Reprinted with permission from the July 29, 1991 issue of *The Nation*.

Krauthammer: The exhibit, he wrote, had "a crude half-baked Marxist meanness"; it could have appeared "thirty years ago in Moscow."

Those who actually visit "The West as America" may well be disappointed to discover that the exhibit is decidedly unscandalous. It begins with a seemingly unexceptional premise: that nineteenth-century paintings do not simply record Western "reality." Instead, as a wall label states, they are "products of convention" rooted in the dominant ideologies of their time. Of course, placing the work of artists in historical context is hardly a new idea. What the critics object to is the nature of the historical interpretation presented in tandem with these particular works of art.

In most assaults on "political correctness," the bogyman is "multiculturalism"—the movement to expand subjects like history and literature to include the experiences of previously neglected groups. Critics of "The West as America," however, are after larger game—nothing less than an entire interpretation of the American past. What they want is the kind of relentlessly celebratory account of American development so common in the 1950s. To Krauthammer, the show expresses "contempt for every achievement of Western expansion"; the *Post*'s Ringle complained that the show "trashes . . . most of our national history."

Scholars may be excused for finding this somewhat tendentious. As Patricia Nelson Limerick of the University of Colorado at Boulder, a leading historian of the West, puts it, "This show is about as revolutionary as if you had a Southern history exhibit, hung romantic paintings of plantations, and then said slavery was a rough business—not a very wild proposition, and the same kind of proposition this show offers about the West."

Limerick, of course, knows full well that a heroic vision of the West retains a powerful hold on the American imagination. She and others founded the "New Western History," which has transformed our understanding of the region over the past decade or so (see Sarah J. Stage, "Tales of the New West," October 22, 1990). These scholars have hammered the final nail into the coffin of Frederick Jackson Turner's "frontier thesis," which saw westward expansion as a mystical social process in which European culture was stripped away by settlers' encounter with nature. On the frontier emerged the quintessential American, cut free from the European past and devoted to individualism, democracy and equality.

In the New Western History, the West is not a process but a place—a place inhabited by people, not just nature, and fought over by a multi-ethnic cast of characters including Easterners, Mexicans, Native Americans and blacks. The conquest of the West is a story of success and failure, heroism and betrayal, capitalist triumph and labor exploitation. Colorado miners and Mexican peons are as much a part of the story as pioneers on the Oregon Trail. In other words, the West's development was a complex history, not a simple heroic progress.

Howard Lamar, the Yale historian whose work inspired much of this new history, writes in the exhibition catalogue that the West has always been "a place to project wishes and dreams," and that in so doing, Americans "reveal themselves and their own ideologies." American history contained many Wests, all more or less "invented," all different from the prosaic and intermittently violent reality of white settlement and Native American dispossession. At the Constitutional Convention, Madison argued that the West could save America from Old World class conflict. Half a century later Horace Greeley saw it as a safety valve for oppressed Eastern workers. The doctrine of Manifest Destiny held that the West would fulfill America's divinely ordained role as savior of the world. Economic writers often viewed the West as a passage to India, a route by which America could dominate trade with the Far East. Today, it seems, the New World Order requires a West free of exploitation, racism and other inconvenient realities of American life.

That the West has always existed in the imagination as much as in reality is the theme of the Smithsonian show. *The Washington Post* declared it "curious" that "the art and the arguments of the show's organizers tend to operate at cross-purposes." But that is precisely the show's message. The nineteenth- and early twentieth-century paintings on display celebrated the conquest of the West. The accompanying wall labels challenge viewers not to take the paintings at face value, but to reinterpret them in terms of what historians have come to understand about Western expansion.

The show emphasizes that artists painted the West to conform to the expectations of Easterners, especially wealthy patrons of the arts and railroad companies interested in promoting Western settlement and tourism. Easterners wanted to see a West more honest and clean, more stirring and uplifting, than their own troubled region, suffering in the late nineteenth century from periodic depressions and violent class conflict. The paintings promised settlers a peaceful journey to fertile lands, and the artists paid special attention to "the triumphs of engineering"—railroads, bridges, etc. The wall texts take note of what the paintings left out: abandoned homesteads and mining towns that went bust; social conflict and environmental damage.

Often, artists portrayed the West as if it were entirely uninhabited. When they did depict Native Americans, much of their work tended to be stereotypical. The exhibition section "Inventing the Indian" has turned out to be one of the most controversial. These paintings, the much-maligned wall text declares, "tell more about the feelings and ideas of artists and patrons than about the 'Indians' whose lives they represent." Early in the nineteenth century, Native Americans were portrayed as noble savages; later, as they were being driven off their land, they were portrayed as violent aggressors (even though they were usually the victims of aggression). Later still, the "doomed Indian" (representing the fantasy that the whole problem might be eliminated by Indians simply dying out) and the acculturated Indian became prominent themes.

The final room, on early-twentieth-century painters, also aroused considerable ire. One guide who has taken groups around the museum reported that while many visitors accept the idea that paintings of Indians are not entirely "accurate," they nevertheless become irate when presented with the idea that the West may not have "really" been the way Frederic Remington painted it.

Nor do they appreciate being confronted by Remington's racism. "Jews— inguns—chinamen—Italians—Huns—" he wrote, were "the rubbish of the earth I hate." In the same letter to a friend, he boasted, "I've got some Winchesters and when the massacreing begins . . . I can get my share of 'em and whats more I will." It does not seem entirely far-fetched to speculate, as the wall text does, that Remington's painting *Fight for the Water Hole,* in which some tough-looking Texans defend themselves from Comanche attack, may have been colored by these prejudices. And when the work is placed in the context in which it was painted—America in 1903, thirty years after the event it portrayed—it can be viewed as an allegory in which a native-born white elite is surrounded by menacing and uncivilized immigrants. But Krauthammer ridiculed those interpretations, describing the painting as simply "a classic cowboys vs. Indians gunfight," and *The Washington Post's* Ringle approvingly quoted an assertion that it portrays nothing more or less than "the truth . . . basic reportage."

Critics also objected to the museum's interpretation of *The Captive,* by Irving Crouse, which portrays a helpless young white woman in a flowing white dress, her hands and feet tied, lying unconscious at the feet of an Indian warrior, who quietly stares at her. The wall text suggests that the painting expresses white culture's "fears of miscegenation," which aroused a storm of protest from, among others, *The New York Times* and *Newsweek,* both of which ran reproductions of the painting. The warrior's arrows, on the ground, point at the helpless woman, suggesting a sinister version of Cupid; the catalogue interpreted the arrows as phallic symbols, an idea critics dismissed with contempt.

The painting's sexual imagery is ambiguous, but the critics seem most offended not by the museum's Freudianism (hardly a new idea, even in Stevens's Alaska) but by any effort to interpret a work of art. Krauthammer's argument that Remington painted only "a classic cowboys vs. Indians gunfight" falls into this category. This view reveals the deep strain of anti-intellectualism and provincialism that lies just beneath the surface of the assault on "political correctness."

Some of the show's wall texts are, indeed, didactic—a common failing in museum prose—but the critics are upset by its substance, not just its style. Rather than criticism, however, the exhibition curators deserve praise for the extensive archival work that has enabled them to place these mostly mediocre and forgotten paintings in a historical context. The show includes Henry Farny's 1902 portrait of Ogallala Fire in full warrior regalia. However, as Alex Nemerov's catalogue essay reports, Ogallala Fire was at that time not a warrior on the plains but a janitor in the Cincinnati Art Club. "The hand that erstwhile wielded the tomahawk and scalping knife now handles the broom and dustpan," Farny wrote.

What the catalogue calls "the hopeless separation of Western artists from the era they sought to document" was evident in other cases. A revealing photo of Charles Schreyvogel at work shows him at his easel, in front of a cowboy who crouches as he aims his revolver. They are on the roof of an apartment building in Hoboken, New Jersey, in 1903. Schreyvogel actually went to Colorado to sketch Pike's Peak in 1911; he wrote home to his wife, "I started [sketching] with Pike's Peak in the back ground and it looked fine. I was there at 7:30 a.m. Then the smelters started in and the black smoke just covered the whole valley so that I couldn't see a thing and had to stop." Of course, in his paintings the Western landscape always appears luminous and pristine—a West of the imagination rather than reality.

Although Senators Stevens and Gorton, and many Eastern critics, are outraged by the New Western History, in the West itself the regional political establishment has a different view. Increasingly, it welcomes the new history for its emphasis on the region's diversity of peoples and experiences. The Western Governors' Association invited Limerick and other practitioners of the new history to speak at their conference last summer, and has published a collection of essays on new ways of looking at the region's past, *Beyond the Mythic West*. (The first essay was written by former Secretary of the Interior Stewart Udall.) "Inside the beltway is a special place," Limerick argues, "a place where Western senators dress up as quaint prospectors. But if that exhibit had come to Denver it would get nowhere near the amount of whining it did in D.C."

"The West as America," however, will not travel to Denver. Previously scheduled appearances at the art museums there and in St. Louis have now been canceled. Both museums plead a shortage of funds rather than fear of political controversy, but surely if the exhibit had received the praise it deserved rather than a politically inspired assault, money would have been found to bring the show west.

Despite fears that "The West as America" reflects yet another takeover of a cultural institution by 1960s radicals, Senator Stevens can rest assured that the Smithsonian is no hotbed of political correctness. Most of the exhibitions in its complex of museums are thoroughly conventional. The National Air and Space Museum is nothing more than a celebration of American greatness; it must warm Professor Boorstin's heart. In the Ceremonial Court of the National Museum of American History, the visitor can view ball gowns of the last seven first ladies—with no embarrassing mention of the scandal over Nancy Reagan's requisitioning of hundreds of thousands of dollars' worth of "gifts" from the world's top designers. Nearby is a display of presidential memorabilia: Wilson's golf clubs, Cleveland's trout flies, Harding's riding crop; no Freudian interpretation, no historical context, no mention of Wilson's Red Scare, Cleveland's economic depression or Harding's sexual escapades; just a reliquary.

Indeed, critics of "The West as America" will be delighted to find in the National Museum of American History the show "Westward to Promontory," presenting photos of the building of the transcontinental railroad. Here, the labels are wholly celebratory of "the great enterprise of the nineteenth century." The theme is the triumph of capitalism and the reknitting of the post–Civil War Union, with barely a mention of exploited Chinese laborers or dispossessed Indians, and none at all of the struggle over Reconstruction taking place at the same time.

The Smithsonian, according to one staff member who preferred to remain anonymous, is "the most reactionary place I've ever been. It's anything but liberal." Nonetheless, Stevens's threats have had a chilling effect on an already conservative institution. Curators have changed some of the wall texts for "The West as America" to soften the impact. The changes have not been extensive—five rewritten labels and five new ones out of a total of fifty-five, according to exhibition curator William Truettner. Many of the changes were made in the section

"Inventing the Indian." One label no longer states that Indians were considered "racially and culturally inferior." Apparently in response to the complaint that the show has nothing good to say about the paintings, another now credits them with "valuable ethnographic detail."

Truettner insists that the changes were planned before Stevens launched his assault—although they were not executed until the political controversy began. He admits that curators in the future will have to be more "careful" about labels that may offend powerful interests. His observation is reinforced by reports from other Smithsonian employees, speaking off the record, that labels for future shows are being edited to avoid provoking right-wing senators or the White House.

Another example of the chill emanating from Stevens's office can be found at the Hirshhorn Museum, which took the unusual step of posting a warning that visitors "may find disturbing" some of the work in the Awards in the Visual Arts exhibit that opened there in June. The Hirshhorn is part of the Smithsonian, and its curators worried especially about a piece by Adrian Piper depicting a lynching. A museum spokesperson said the warning was posted because of the "climate," which *The Washington Post* took to be a reference to Stevens's threat.

The attack on "The West as America" comes after *The New Republic, Newsweek, Time, New York* magazine and others have blasted away at the campus left, portraying it as "thought police" out to destroy intellectual freedom. Dinesh D'Souza's *Illiberal Education* has reached the best-seller list, arguing as Roger Kimball did in a similar book that "tenured radicals" now control the universities and suppress freedom of speech with tactics that "border on the totalitarian." President Bush himself recently joined the chorus. These laments, however, ring a bit hollow when one reflects that none of these self-proclaimed opponents of censorship have uttered a word of protest against a senator's threat to cut the Smithsonian budget because he dislikes an exhibition's interpretation of American history.

The Smithsonian, it seems certain, will ride out this storm, but the controversy over "The West as America" is a harbinger of more trouble to come. The museum world, like academia, has lately been changing in ways many conservatives find deeply threatening. Long devoted simply to collecting and displaying memorabilia of prominent men and emblems of American greatness, museums are now seeking to present a more complex, diversified and critical portrait of the American past.

The Chicago Historical Society, for example, recently dismantled its Lincoln Gallery, complete with his top hat, ice skate and pieces of wood from his log cabin, and replaced it with an exhibit emphasizing the centrality of slavery and racism in nineteenth-century American history. Richmond's Valentine Museum currently displays a pioneering exhibition on "Jim Crow: Racism and Reaction in the New South." The Museum of the Confederacy in Richmond recently opened a major show on slavery, a far cry from its usual preoccupation with Robert E. Lee, Stonewall Jackson and the Lost Cause. (For reviews of similarly innovative exhibits, see Edward Chappell, "Museums," July 17, 1989, and December 18, 1989.)

"The West as America" is part of this development and represents a significant achievement for the Museum of American Art. We need more shows like this—exhibits that bring forgotten paintings back to life as documents of social and cultural history. Since most of these mediocre genre paintings and banal landscapes long ago lost their status as art, today they are viewed by few people outside the Buffalo Bill Historical Center or the Cowboy Hall of Fame. This exhibition has given us a new way to see them: as images that convey white Americans' obsessive preoccupation with their country's virtue. The Smithsonian, unfortunately, now plans to close this show July 28; it's too bad it can't remain open longer.

All these new exhibits offend some viewers, who go to museums for "old-fashioned" history. But they are appreciated by many others. At "The West as America," the visitors' comment book is filled with perceptive remarks; not everyone wants an exhibit about the West where never is heard a discouraging word. "Where's the paintings the Indians did of the whites?" asks one visitor, a legitimate question. Some comments are sharply critical, but more are rather favorable. "This exhibit," one visitor wrote, "helps me think about the art, the artists, the patrons, the audience, the subjects. Thanks." Is it possible that ordinary people actually appreciate being challenged by new ideas? Senator Stevens, please take note.

Name: _____ Date: _____

Understanding the Text

1. According to Foner and Wiener, what in the Smithsonian exhibit did critics object to? What do Foner and Wiener think of these objections?

2. According to Foner and Wiener, what are the tenets of the "New Western History"?

3. According to historian Howard Lamar, why are our conceptions of the West so important? What do Foner and Wiener claim to be the major "theme" of the exhibit?

Disney's "Politically Correct" Pocahontas

Jacquelyn Kilpatrick

W hen I walked into the theater to see *Pocahontas,* I had my choice of venue. It was playing on three of six screens, and the line waiting to get in never seemed to diminish. Later, I looked at the film section of the local paper and found that somewhere in the vicinity the movie was starting every fifteen minutes. Now that was a depressing thought.

In an interview with *The New York Times,* Eric Goldberg, the film's codirector (with Mike Gabriel), said, "We've gone from being accused of being too white bread to being accused of racism in *Aladdin* to being accused of being too politically correct in *Pocahontas.* That's progress to me." As much as I wanted to like Disney's production, I must disagree with Goldberg. Instead of progress in depicting Native Americans, this film takes a step backwards—a very dangerous step because it is so carefully glossed as "authentic" and "respectful."

The visual is emotionally more compelling than the written word, to say nothing of being more accessible, and since few people will read about Pocahontas, this film will exist as "fact" in the minds of generations of American children. They will believe in the Romeo and Juliet in the wilds of North America that Disney has presented, which, as Robert Eaglestaff, principal of the American Indian Heritage School in Seattle, has said, is much like "trying to teach about the Holocaust and putting in a nice story about Anne Frank falling in love with a German officer."

It might seem a moot point at best to debate the authenticity or reality of an animated film in which a tree speaks words of wisdom and the protagonist guides her canoe over a deadly looking waterfall without mussing her hair. If this were a story about a fictional character in a fictional situation, I would agree. I like Mickey Mouse, too. But Pocahontas was a real woman who lived during the pivotal time of first contact with the outside force that would ultimately decimate her people. Although we know of her only from the English reports, and some of the details are a bit hazy, there are some facts that are well supported. For one thing, she was not a voluptuous young woman when she met John Smith but a ten- to twelve-year-old girl, and John Smith was a thirty-something mercenary who more resembled a brick than a blond Adonis.

Smith's report of Pocahontas's brave act in saving his life was nowhere to be found in his initial description of his capture by Powhatan in 1608, surfacing only eight years later in a letter to the queen. There are a couple of possibilities to explain why that might have been. He could have been embarrassed, given the macho community of Jamestown boys, to admit a child had saved his life, or he might have stolen the story, possibly from the account published around the same time about Juan Ortiz and the Utica woman who saved him about eighty years before Smith met Pocahontas.

Assuming she did save his life, it could have been her idea, or it could have been her father's. If Powhatan had his own reasons for wanting Smith to live, he might have instructed her to do as she did to save face. Smith's report said she wanted her father to keep him alive but in captivity so he could make bells and beads for her, which, according to John Gould Fletcher (*John Smith—Also Pocahontas,* 1928), would have provided a cover story to eliminate the censure of the tribe for Powhatan's benevolent act and which would have been in keeping with their traditions.

Assuming Smith stole the story, he could have done so because he turned into a chronicler of his adventures in the New World after it became clear he was not going to be able to return to America to have more of them. He tried repeatedly to return, but even the first settlers in New England were happy to accept his advice but refused his company.

What we do know of Pocahontas is that she met John Smith in 1608, was probably responsible for some trading between the settlers and her people, was kidnapped and raped by the English but later married a tobacco planter named John Rolfe, had a son in 1615 and sailed to England in 1616. She was introduced to Ben Johnson and made such an impression that he wrote her into one of his comedies, *The Staple of News;* she attended a court masque that he wrote and evidently impressed the king and queen as well. She attempted to return home but became ill on the voyage and had to turn back to England, where she died, probably of smallpox, at the age of twenty-two. We have no idea how she or her people felt about any of this, except that some of the contemporary reports said she died "of a broken heart."

That's a pretty interesting story, but not the sort of thing animated Disney films are known for. For one thing, it's much too violent and sad. According to James Pentecost, the film's producer, the changes that were made were due to the fact that Pocahontas's real story was simply too long. He said, "We decided to dramatize what we felt was the *essence* of Pocahontas." Now the logic may be a little tough to follow here, but evidently what that means is that they changed her age, her body, and gave her a motive for her actions that boils down to going gaga over the first white man she sees.

Ignoring for a moment the very non-PC, nonfeminist content of that change, there lies within it a very old stereotype of Native American women. In hundreds of films made during the last century, Indian women have been seen sacrificing themselves and their tribal communities for their white lovers. I'm sure the irony is unintentional in *Pocahontas* as she paddles her canoe along, having just refused to marry the stereotypically stoic and noble Kocoum, singing about the change that is waiting "just around the river bend." The change that waits is another man and another culture in the form of John Smith.

The Disney folks have made much of the fact that Pocahontas is the driving force of this movie, which is, I suppose, to mean it makes some sort of feminist statement. She does sing to John about living naturally in tune with the Earth—also skirting dangerously close to another stereotype, that of the "natural ecologist"—but does she have to do it in an off-the-shoulder miniskirt? And I would love to see a report on the physics of her body. Would she, like Barbie, fall over if really given those dimensions? Glen Keane, the film's supervising animator, researched the paintings of the real Pocahontas but wasn't very impressed, so he made a few "adjustments." Besides her beautiful "more Asian" eyes, he gave her a body with a wasp waist, sexy hips and legs, and breasts that are *truly* impressive. He says, "Some people might see her as sexy, but she's not Jessica Rabbit. I think she looks rather athletic." Uh huh. Mel Gibson (the voice of John Smith) put it more succinctly when he said, "She's a babe." Or, what the heck, maybe she's just drawn that way.

To give the Disney folk their due, they apparently made some effort to be nonoffensive, hiring Native Americans to work on the film and to act as consultants. Unfortunately, there seems to have been some miscommunication of concept. The Disney people were making an animated film about a fictional character. They knew she was fictional because they created her. The Native Americans on the team had other interests. Russell Means, the voice of Powhatan, likes the film, even though they were willing to take his advice about a detail such as the father referring to Pocahontas as Daughter instead of her name, but were unwilling to change important aspects of the image of the Indians as warlike, as established by the return from war at the beginning of the film. He says, "There are scenes where the English settlers admit to historical deceit . . . their animated settlers say they are here to rob, rape, pillage the land and kill Indians. This is the truth that Disney is entrusting with children while the rest of Hollywood won't trust that truth with adults."

As a mixedblood woman, I too am concerned with the truth of the colonization of America, but establishing another stereotype isn't the way to go about it. Even given that Disney's animated characters are by nature larger than life, the English in the film are extremely one-dimensional in their bumbling greed. As Terry Russio, a screenwriter for Disney, said, "You can judge the sentiments of the country by who you can confidently make fun of. Nowadays the ultimate villain, I suppose, would be a fat, white male terrorist who ran a Fortune 500 company on the side." That fairly well describes the governor in *Pocahontas,* a description which renders the history of first contact literally cartoonish.

Disney also hired Shirley (Little Dove) Custalow-McGowan, a Powhatan who travels through Virginia teaching the history and culture of her people, to work as consultant for the film. When she saw the early rushes, she said, "My heart sorrowed within me . . . Ten-year-old Pocahontas has become twenty-year-old Pocahontas. The movie was no longer historically accurate."

According to the film's producer, James Pentecost, all this talk about historical accuracy is somewhat irrelevant. He believes that "Nobody should go to an animated film hoping to get an accurate depiction of history." Okay, I'll buy that, as long as you're talking about *The Lion King,* but Pocahontas was real, and most people have heard her name even if they know nothing about her reality. Most of the adults who view this film, however, will not have the background to judge whether it is accurate or not, and since the hype has been toward the 'political correctness' of the film, I would think they'd be more apt to trust it than not. And those are the adults. What about the children? As Linda Woolverton, screenwriter for *Beauty and the Beast* and *The Lion King* said, "When you take on a Disney animated feature, you know you're going to be affecting entire generations of human minds." In this case, the effect is one more misconception advertised in the guise of authenticity and respect for Native American values.

As Custalow-McGowan said, "History is history. You're not honoring a nation of people when you change their history."

Name: _____ Date: _____

Understanding the Text

1. Why does Kilpatrick think that Disney's publicity for *Pocahontas* makes the film especially "dangerous"?

2. What "very old stereotype of Native American women" does Kilpatrick especially object to?

3. How does the film represent Pocahontas physically, and what is Kilpatrick's response to this representation?

Prelude to World War II: Racial Unity and the Hollywood Indian

Angela Aleiss

W orld War II laid the foundation for a re-evaluation of the American Indian's screen image. Even before "tolerance," "brotherhood," and "unity" became catchwords in a society engaged within another world conflict, the movie industry had responded to the growing fascism in Europe with more ambiguity in its Indian portrayals. Like Black Americans who would find a place in the racially integrated units of Hollywood's war films (years before actual military desegregation), movie Indians would form a political alliance with their white counterparts.[1] Previous images of menacing warriors who blocked Westward expansion gradually began to fade into one in which Indians stood as allies—rather than as enemies—alongside America's frontier heroes.

Several scholars have noted the transformation of the Indian's screen image throughout the second world war. John A. Price observed that "the decline of Indian stereotyping seems to have begun during World War II when the Germans, Italians, and Japanese replaced the Indian as the major villains," although he argues that both *Geronimo* (1939) and *They Died with Their Boots On* (1941) contain unsympathetic portrayals of their Indian leaders (170).[2] Ted Siminoski concluded in his dissertation, "Sioux Versus Hollywood," that the Sioux's image reversed from a villain to a hero during the war. He explains, however, that the most dramatic shift occurred immediately after World War II when racially liberal attitudes began to influence minority portrayals (60–61). Donald Kaufmann points out that unscrupulous whites often misled otherwise friendly Indians in World War II Westerns, but these Native portrayals were merely "caught up in a fad for sympathetic treatment" along with other minorities (499).[3]

While these scholars agree that World War II reshaped the Indian's screen images, several points require further clarification:

1. As studios grew more circumspect about antagonistic Indian/white relations in light of growing European fascism, Americans and their Canadian/British allies would evolve into models of racial diplomacy. Selective Service was enforced by 1940, and scenes of the U.S. Cavalry killing Indians en masse could easily equate American militarism with Gestapo leadership.

2. The pro-interventionist politics of Hollywood studios helped to create a mindset that would reshape the Indian's image at least two years before America's entry into the war. The prevailing anti-fascist mood in the movie industry (best exemplified by the Hollywood Anti-Nazi League, with its roster of studio moguls and liberal screenwriters) peaked in 1936, and studio executives freely trumpeted their anti-Nazi ideology in many pre-forties films.[4] National unity was a powerful weapon against fascism, and Blacks, Indians, and Mexicans soon joined their white counterparts in the movies' effort to "racially integrate" the home front.

3. These "friendly" Indian portrayals were more enduring than a fad. The wartime image of Indians-as-allies would eventually give way to a postwar assimilationist theme: many Westerns further developed the Indian/white brotherhood concept, with *Broken Arrow* (1950) often cited as the most significant example.

Three popular Westerns mark a visible change from the "hostile warrior" stereotype and thus represent the first stage of a trend toward interracial harmony. *Susannah of the Mounties* (1939), *North West Mounted Police* (1940), and *They Died with Their Boots On* (1941) were each produced by major Hollywood studios whose large budgets and aggressive promotion would introduce the films' more complex Indian/white relations to a wider audience.[5] All three films include star performers—Shirley Temple, Gary Cooper, and Errol Flynn—and their established box-office reputations would bolster the pictures' popularity and thus secure these newfound racial themes within the Western genre.[6] Individually, each film exemplifies thematic characteristics that would serve as prototypes for later Indian-theme Westerns; taken together, they reveal an industry struggling to redefine its Indian/white relations in a rapidly changing world. *Susannah* demonstrates, through the perspective of two children, a symbolic interracial brotherhood: its co-mingling of blood between an Indian and a white would not occur again until *Broken Arrow*. *North West Mounted Police* casts Indians as American and Canadian allies against the French—its theme of an interracial allegiance a reverse of *Rose Marie's* (1936) enemy Indians who steal money and hide an American fugitive from the Royal Canadian Mounted Police. In *They Died with Their Boots On,* the legendary "Indian fighter" of America—George Armstrong Custer—becomes the friend, admirer, and guardian of the Sioux. His role as the Indians' protector—its departure from history notwithstanding—would be a model for other frontier epics like *Buffalo Bill* (1944), in which the hero publicly condemns white exploitation of Indian people.

The Westerns' concept of racial brotherhood was a sharp departure from the previous portrayals of hostile Indian/white relations. During the mid-30s, the 19th-century belief in a Manifest Destiny—the idea of United States' expansion across the North American continent—emerged as a common theme in Hollywood Westerns. The renaissance of the "Western hero" in the mid-30s, writes Andrew Bergman, brought law and government to a strong position in American culture.

> The revival of the cowboys spoke automatically to the benevolence of the federal law, which in turn was vanquishing bad men and releasing the old competitive energies in America. Hollywood constructed a government which it identified with justice and order, and which delivered the nation from external threats to its safety and industry. (169)

The cowboy became the benevolent hero, while the Indian emerged as civilization's alien—and eventually enemy—to progress. Such portrayals often cast Indians in an unambiguously hostile light: King Vidor's *Texas Rangers* (1936), for example, showed that while "savages" rule the plains, Texas is hardly a safe place. Only when the Rangers "put them on the reservation for good" can Texas look forward to real progress. So prevalent was the Indian-as-obstacle theme that a non-Western like Gregory La Cava's *Stage Door* (1937) included Katharine Hepburn's remark: "And if my grandfather hadn't crossed the country in a Conestoga wagon, there would *still* be Indians living in Wichita!"

The French and Indian War was Manifest Destiny displaced into colonial America in George Seitz's *The Last of the Mohicans* (1936), another remake based upon the enduring James Fenimore Cooper novel. The 1920 silent version (directed by Maurice Tourner and Clarence Brown) had blended romantic imagery with a foreboding atmosphere: its enemy Hurons were shadowy figures gliding across moonlit rocks or perched high atop jagged cliffs, and their silhouettes were often framed within cavernous entrances that receded into picturesque backgrounds. Seitz's version instead delivered an unabashed portrayal of bloodthirsty, scalp-hungry (Huron) savages who literally scream into the camera and defy the French and British armistice when they attack Fort William Henry. Magua was "as evil a Huron as ever you pictured him and his misdeeds . . . are even more ghastly than those the original text cited," declared the *New York Times,* noting that the British massacre was especially brutal (September 3, 1936). The more savage the Indians, *Mohicans* seemed to imply, the easier to justify their removal.

America's ability to rid the West of its marauding natives was glorified in Paramount's *Geronimo* (1939). Director Paul Sloan introduces *Geronimo* as "the story of a great enemy," then cautions that the Indian leader (portrayed by "Chief Thundercloud") remains unconquered. President Ulysses S. Grant admits that "our whole handling of the Indian problem has been wrong, unjust," and reiterates Abraham Lincoln's ideology that "the frontiers of the nation must be made safe." The studio's promotional campaign exploited the Apache leader's resistance: Geronimo was "The red terror of the American screen!" and "That most feared Apache that ever ravaged the West," who, obviously, had to be subdued or eliminated in order to open the doors to white settlement.

John Ford's *Stagecoach* (1939) flatly—and unambiguously—declared that white civilization had no room for American Indians. The film's opening titles warn of the Indians' "savage struggle" to oust white settlers and of the name Geronimo that struck terror into the hearts of innocent travelers. *Stagecoach's* references to Indians are consistently ominous: characters remark how Apaches burn every ranch in sight, and one even learns that these Indians strike like rattlesnakes. In a particularly disturbing scene, the charred remains of a house lie smoldering with a woman's body hunched over a burnt chair, her head partly scalped. The final attack upon the stage with the cavalry's fortuitous appearance (similar to *Union Pacific's* 1939 military rescue) suggests that America will be safe only when its hostile natives vanish forever.

The increasing conflict in Europe, however, began to influence Hollywood politics and consequently to reshape minority images even before America's entry into the war. Previous Westerns could boast of conquest, but a national campaign to purge the land of its Indian inhabitants smacked of fascist genocide. At the very least, the Manifest Destiny theme painted a racially intolerant picture of America's frontier heroes. King Vidor's *Northwest Passage* (1940), the story of Rogers' Rangers and their 1759 expedition to destroy the French/Abenaki stronghold in their war against England, shows early signs of ambiguity toward its Indian characters.[7] Rogers (Spencer Tracy) refers to the Indians as "red hellions" who hack and murder whites, steal women, roast officers, and brain babies: "If it were over quick," he explains, "they were lucky." During the village ambush, however, he instructs his men to kill only "every fighting Indian," and when one maniacal Ranger tries to attack two Indian women and a child, another orders him to leave women and young children alone. The deranged man murders a warrior out of sheer delight, infuriating his comrade: "Haven't you had enough?" Rogers tells his men to release the Indian prisoners because "they're not going to do us any good," and he enlists a Mohawk as his scout. Meanwhile, the disturbed Ranger (who has pilfered an Indian head) later plunges to his death—the film's retribution (and the Hay's Office compensation) toward an unfit soldier.[8]

At Twentieth Century-Fox, Darryl Zanuck's pro-interventionist perspective conveyed a theme of racial unity in his World War II Westerns. (As Vice President of Production, Zanuck closely supervised each film script and insisted upon numerous modifications.) Zanuck's sympathy for the French and the British against Nazi Germany developed years before America's entry into the war (he had contributed heavily to William Allen White's Committee to Defend America by Aiding the Allies); his zeal for military preparedness surfaced in *A Yank in the R.A.F.,* a 1941 film that drew much criticism from the media's isolationist factions (Mosley 195, 197).[9] Among his Westerns, a similar theme prevailed: *Hudson's Bay* (1941) favored a British/Canadian alliance against its French counterparts, but Pierre Radisson champions the Indian cause and requests that New France make provisions with the Cree before settling upon Native territory. Zanuck advised during story conferences that a Canadian/Indian alliance dominate the film: thus, Radisson's code of fair dealings with the Indians should be written into Canada's Charter, and the chiefs and white men should show allegiance to the British flag ("Rough Draft" 12). Similarly, the friendly (and comical) Oneida in *Drums Along the Mohawk* (1939) assists the American colonists in the Revolution and reminds whites that he is (in Henry Fonda's words) "as good a Christian as you and me are."

Zanuck's 1939 film, *Susannah of the Mounties,* was an earlier World War II Western whose political tone was noticeably one of racial tolerance. Directed by William A. Seiter and starring Shirley Temple, *Susannah* promotes a pacifist theme that leads to interracial harmony. Susannah is the only survivor of a wagon train massacre; despite the fact that the Indians have killed her grandfather, she befriends a Canadian Blackfoot boy and brings peace between both races. The chief agrees to help locate the Indians who raided the wagon and offers his son "Little Chief' (portrayed by Martin Goodrider, a Blackfeet Indian) as a token of promise to the whites.[10] The Canadian Mounties (who look after Susannah) accept the chief's gesture gratefully, adding, "It will do no harm for your son to learn the ways of the white man." Sue and Little Chief, after a few cultural clashes (he orders her to walk behind him like a squaw) develop a mutual friendship: they later join their fingers in a "blood brother" ceremony—a symbolic gesture that broke the barriers of Manifest Destiny separating Indian and white societies and pointed toward racial unity.

The underlying message is that Canada, England, and the Blackfoot are all united in the national welfare. Canadian expansion occurs through a peaceful resolution—rather than a hostile clash—between both races. When the Indians kidnap Sue's Mountie friend (Randolf Scott) she implores the chief (Maurice Moscovich) for his release: the real culprit is the tribe's warrior (Victor Jory) who has been selling stolen horses to the whites. The Mountie assures the chief that only the Redcoats can speak for England and honor their word; thus, Canada intends to respect Blackfoot territory in the building of the railroad. Zanuck's political sympathies toward the allies helped to shape the film's Indian portrayals: "Don't give impression that the Queen mother will send soldiers to annihilate the Indians—as this may get us in trouble with England" ("Conference . . . 11/12/38" 4–5). The conclusion shows the Mountie, Sue, and two Indians sitting underneath the British flag and sharing the peace pipe—the film's gesture of solidarity during the present European conflict.

Newspapers approvingly took note of *Susannah*'s theme. The *New York Evening Journal* noted that Temple "showed the red man and white man how to live together like brothers." The *Star Telegram* argued that the Indians were the movie's real heroes: Little Chief had taught "hostile Susannah how to ride, how to do Indian war dances . . . and at last the meaning of blood brotherhood." Other reviews, however, balked at the film's newfound interracial harmony: "The Indian raids and fights are rather unimpressive," *Variety* alerted exhibitors. Perhaps, the trade journal surmised, audiences might still prefer bloody Indian/white clashes to peace parleys (16).

The Canadian wilderness provided another setting for an American/British alliance with its Indian neighbors in Cecil B. DeMille's *North West Mounted Police* (1940). DeMille began making feature films in 1914 with his production of *The Squaw Man,* based upon Edwin Milton Royle's play about a marriage between an Indian woman and an English man that tragically ends in her suicide. (The miscegenation theme was popular enough, for he remade the same picture twice, in 1918 and 1931). Conversely, in 1917, DeMille directed *The Woman God Forgot,* the story of Montezuma's daughter and her love for and subsequent marriage to a white officer of Cortez's army. Such variety was the spice of DeMille's

Indian portrayals, and the producer/director could easily cast them as villains (*The Virginian,* 1914) or as aides (*Girl of the Golden West,* 1915), depending on what the film's story (or even current politics) demanded.

DeMille's later sound Westerns—*The Plainsman* (1936) and *Union Pacific* (1939)—championed the theme of Manifest Destiny with Indians as obstacles to frontier settlement. In *The Plainsman,* production personnel instructed that the audience immediately recognize Indians as "really a menace—burning settlements and massacring whites" (Pine Memo) and the film's promotional campaign boasted of "Heroes of the Dusty Past Slashing an Empire from Savage Hands" ("Advertising Approach").[11] Suggestions for interviews and speeches on *Union Pacific* emphasized the film's timely message of "preserving the unity of this nation," which embraced Irish laborers and Chinese coolies, but not the recalcitrant Indians ("Line on the Golden Spike" 3). "The railroad builders are continually harassed by Indians, who stole supplies, burned houses and killed workmen," the picture's titles warned.

A year later, however, Paramount's *North West Mounted Police* would reevaluate the white relationship to America's natives. The 1885 Métis uprising in Saskatchewan of the French and Indian mixed bloods and their Cree support against the Canadian government (the "Riel Rebellion") was the basis for DeMille's first Technicolor film. DeMille portrayed the French as enemies to Canadian progress and extolled the growth of the British empire; like Zanuck, he "never had any doubt, from the outbreak of World War II, where America must and eventually would take her stand" (Hayne 370).

The film's story of the friendship and mutual respect between Canada and the United States now included its Indian allies (DeMille, "In Chicago" 2–3). The Cree Indians, led by Chief Big Bear (Walter Hampden), initially defy British allegiance and become caught in a power struggle between the Métis and the Canadian government; the Mounties, however, succeed in retaining the chief's loyalty to the British. The American interest is represented by a Texas Ranger (Gary Cooper), who pursues a criminal across the Canadian border where the Mounted Police claim he is also wanted for murder. Americans and Mounties unite to capture the man (Louis Riel, leader of the Métis uprising) and succeed in preventing "a war that might have torn Canada to fragments (DeMille, "In Chicago" 2–3).

DeMille's respect for historical accuracy extended as far as his Anglo-American sympathies would allow. Numerous notations on Indian sign language and dialect accompanied careful research on Cree costumes and equipment; citations included a glossary of Blackfeet words gathered by Henry Schoolcraft and descriptions of Cree camps by Edward Curtis.[12] "History should be honestly and diligently respected," DeMille said in a 1939 interview, but he noted that dramatic license sometimes took precedent over historical truth. "For the sake of dramatic construction, I am justified in making some contradictions or compressions of historical details, so long as I stick to the main facts," he added (Crowther).

DeMille did take liberties in the portrayal of Big Bear by combining his character with Crowfoot, leader of the Blackfoot, who prevented his people from joining the Riel Rebellion (DeMille, Letter 1). (Big Bear actually joined the Métis and was later imprisoned for his part in the rebellion.) In *North West Mounted Police,* Big Bear's composite character supports the

British and emerges as a timely metaphor for wartime propaganda: Indians would clearly remain on the side of Canadian and American—rather than French—political interests. When a New York newspaper questioned Big Bear's ability to speak fluent English, DeMille replied with three pages of quoted passages from Crowfoot's eloquent oratory. (The director had explained that both leaders were impressive speakers.) His detailed response carefully positioned Indian chiefs among the ranks of other legendary American heroes: "The Indians of the American continent have produced some great men, and I fear we are all a little apt to confuse these fine philosophers and statesmen with the Indians of the comic strip, whose accepted rhetorical attainment is "ugh!" (DeMille, Letter 3).

The film's villains, then, are the French and Indian Métis. Their leader's daughter is Louvette (Paulette Goddard), whose unsavory habits are intended as a reflection of her mixed-blooded ancestry. Louvette eats on the dirt floor with her hands, prowls barefoot around the campsite, and entices a naive Mountie away from his post when she learns of an attack. Originally named "Lupette" (a parody on the word lupine), Louvette "has the instincts of a wolf, lives by robbing traps, and gets into every possible difficulty" (Rosson Letter).[13] Louvette's connivery is akin to treason: when she seduces the Mountie, she fails to warn Canadian forces of an ambush. This act of treachery immediately casts her as Canada's political enemy, a fitting statement for any pro-British sentiment during the war

The pro-ally sympathies of DeMille and other studio moguls were gradually becoming the rule—rather than the exception—in Hollywood. "The film industry will not shirk from its chance to aid immeasurably in the strengthening of national morale," a *Variety* editorial announced in 1940 (5). Hollywood supported military readiness by providing studio facilities for Army training films and reshaping the movies' content in response to a world fascist threat. Westerns followed with a step toward racial unity: a year before Pearl Harbor, one veteran producer observed that scheming businessmen and crooked bankers began to replace Indians as the frontier's villains (*New York Times*). By 1942, the trend had become noticeable: when MGM resorted to the cowboy-vs.-Indian formula in *Apache Trail,* the results were hackneyed. "The uprising of the Apaches against the whites is something that's long since seen its best picture days," *Variety* complained (MacRae 20).

At Warner Brothers' studio, the concept of racial brotherhood began to influence its Indian/white portrayals at least two years before America's entry into the war. Like his contemporaries at Twentieth Century Fox and Paramount, Jack Warner (Vice President of Production) supported the allies long before the fateful events at Pearl Harbor. In 1940, he sent money to London for the purchase of two fighter planes and produced *London Can Take It,* a documentary that raised thousands of dollars toward British aid. His feature films of the late 30s conveyed the studio's anti-Nazi sentiments; *Confessions of a Nazi Spy* (1939) and *Underground* (1940) both elicited sharp criticisms from pro-German sympathizers (namely, the German-American Bund) as well as the nation's isolationist groups.[14]

As a member of the Hollywood Anti-Nazi League, Warner joined his colleagues in promoting national unity as democracy's toughest enemy against fascism. The studio's Westerns would echo this same political theme with their symbolic interracial alliance. *Dodge City*

(1939) celebrated the building of the West and the settlement of a Kansas town; when a citizen drives a golden spike through the town's railroad terminal, an Indian holds it steady. The community is plagued by villainous cowboys (who were initially reprimanded for killing buffalo on Indian territory); the new threat to law and order is civilization's corruption and greed. Warner's *Santa Fe Trail* (1940) was another variation on the Western theme without the usual cowboy-and-Indian skirmishes and wagon train attacks. The frontier's new villain is the abolitionist leader John Brown (Raymond Massey), whose armed resistance further divides a politically torn Kansas just prior to the Civil War. Brown smuggles rifles in Bible boxes and attacks the people of Harpers Ferry. His "reasons may be good," observes one cavalry officer, "but what he's doing is wrong." Led by George Armstrong Custer and Jeb Stuart, the cavalry finally seizes Brown and orders the rebel hung, a fitting victory against an enemy of the Union and foe of the human race, as one officer puts it.

Santa Fe's pro-Southern sympathy notwithstanding, its friendly Indian character is a barometer of America's changing sentiments during World War II. As Custer eagerly awaits romance, he seeks the advice of an Indian fortune teller. The old woman pokes at the campfire and solemnly predicts that Americans soon will be enemies in battle: a fight has started in the east, a man is lighting a torch, she warns, "but none of us can stop him." The men laugh at her prophecy, but the allusion to a fascist enemy and the urgency for national unity were more than a coincidence. The film skillfully uses Indian mysticism to serve America's political interests.

A year later, Warners' leaning toward Indian/white solidarity grew even more pronounced in *They Died with Their Boots On,* a biography of George Armstrong Custer. "Most Westerns had depicted the Indian as a painted, vicious savage," director Raoul Walsh explained of his 1941 film, in which the real villains are the unscrupulous railroad companies. "In *They Died With Their Boots On,* I tried to show him as an individual who only turned vindictive when his rights as defined by treaty were violated by white men" (qtd. in Walsh 325).

Noting its timely release, Warners seized the opportunity to exemplify American militarism. "In preparing this scenario," screenwriter Aeneas MacKenzie explained in 1941, "all possible consideration was given to the construction of a story which would have the best effect upon public morale in these present days of a national crisis" (Memo).[15] Hence, the studio built an image of an efficient—albeit pompous and bureaucratic—American military. "I need not mention," MacKenzie continued, "that this picture will be released at a moment when thousands of youths are being trained for commissions, and when hundreds of new and traditionless units are being formed" (MacKenzie). Warners' research department noted that during President Grant's era, army officers were appointed as Acting Superintendents for the Indian Service, making "an impressive show of efficiency by enforcing programs for Indian welfare with prompt military action" (Lissauer Memo).[16] In *They Died with Their Boots On,* the United States Army would protect the Indians' best interest.

White paternalism replaced Manifest Destiny as hostile interracial relations became politically unwise for a nation on the throes of fighting genocide in Europe. Warners thus whitewashed Custer's career to create a more racially "sympathetic" hero: the Lieutenant Colonel's massacre of the Cheyenne village in the Battle of Washita was completely ignored, and the events at the Little Bighorn were rearranged so that the loss would not "result from Custer's greed for glory" (Churchill).[17] Further, the hero's feats result from luck rather than foresight: Custer is promoted to (brevet) General by an administrative error, and he claims a victory medal during the Civil War by flouting orders and saving an entire regiment from extermination.

"The Indians need not be presented as lay figures whose sole function in life is to 'mas[s]acre' and be wiped out," advised studio executive Melvin Levy, "but as real people having desires, hopes, loves and hates." Levy thus attempted to convince associate producer Robert Fellows to create a relationship of respect and friendship between Custer and Crazy Horse, as it was "a basis of actuality" (Levy, Memo). Fellows solicited the opinion of his close friend (and history buff) Lee Ryan, who recommended a scene in which Sitting Bull speaks to the chiefs, and Chief Joseph [White Bull] of the Minneconjou Sioux outlines battle strategy. It was "a bit gushy," Ryan explained, to have Custer as the last survivor in a battle not borne out by a conversation with Sioux braves (Memo).[18]

The movie's Custer hero (Errol Flynn) thus emerges as the guardian of Indian welfare: he defends the Sioux's treaty rights and even admires the tactical abilities of the Oglala leader, Crazy Horse (Anthony Quinn).[19] Custer temporarily imprisons Crazy Horse for attacking his wagon train, but he reminds the regiment to treat the Indian leader well. When Crazy Horse escapes, Custer actually praises him as "the only cavalryman I've seen around this fort so far." The narrative titles warn of "a ruthlessly advancing civilization that spelled doom to the red race," and a montage of Indian/cavalry battles follows. Crazy Horse demands a peace powwow with Custer: framed equally in low-angle shots, the two face each other mounted on horseback. The Indian leader says that his people will give up everything but the Black Hills, and Custer promises to defend the sacred land against whites. "I listen to my brother," the officer assures him in another wartime gesture toward interracial cooperation.

The Western Railroad Land & Trading Company, however, has other ideas. The railroad's only route is through the Black Hills, and its corrupt owners (including Custer's former West Point classmate) devise a plan to wipe out the Sioux and snatch their territory. Newspapers announce a "Second California gold Rush" in the Black Hills, and Custer warns officials that the Indians will unite in retaliation. "If I were an Indian, I'd fight beside Crazy Horse to the last drop of my blood!" the officer thunders during his court-martial.

Crazy Horse, meanwhile, invites Sitting Bull to a war council, and Indians from several nations convene to plan an attack. The night before, Custer requests that an English soldier escape with a message because he does not want to endanger a foreigner's life. The Briton refuses to leave, and in the spirit of Anglo-American wartime solidarity and racial tolerance, he adds that the Indians are the only real Americans. "You're probably right about that," Custer agrees. The officer ultimately "sacrifices" his regiment at the Battle of Little Bighorn to protect General Alfred Terry and his men; his dying declaration stipulates that the Indians be protected in their right to the existence of their own country—a request that General Philip Sheridan pledges to enforce.[20]

The November 20, 1941, premiere of *They Died with Their Boots On* was just 17 days prior to America's entrance into World War II. The movie's theme of an interracial alliance was not far from wartime rhetoric: as Indians fought in the battlefields, they stood alongside white Americans and gradually melted into society. The Office of Indian Affairs announced that, despite years of discrimination, Native Americans "responded earnestly and enthusiastically" to the challenge of war (Collier, June 1942: 238), and tribes even dropped claims against the United States for "patriotic reasons" (June 1944: 252). The Iroquois Confederacy had issued a declaration of war upon the Axis Powers in 1942 (June 1942: 240), and 18,000 Indians had joined the armed services by 1943 (June 1943: 237). Indians stood beside whites and captured military honors: 75 received the Purple Heart and 16 the Distinguished Flying Cross, while a Second Lieutenant Childers (a Creek) picked up the Congressional Medal of Honor (June 1944: 235–36). Perhaps the most memorable event occurred on Mt. Suribachi in Iwo Jima, where the Pima Indian Ira H. Hayes was one of six men who helped raise the American flag. "The impact of the wartime experience on the Indians was immeasurable," wrote historian Francis Paul Prucha, "for the war suddenly threw thousands of reservation Indians into the midst of white society and greatly accelerated the movement toward assimilation" (1009).

By World War II, the hostile, conniving Indian characters of *The Plainsman* and *Stagecoach* could stand in friendship alongside America's heroes in *Susannah of the Mounties, North West Mounted Police,* and *They Died with Their Boots On.* For a nation preparing to enter yet another world conflict, these Indian/white portrayals offered a powerful message about America's emerging solidarity with its Natives. Three years prior to the formation of the Office of War Information [OWI]—a federal agency that advised the film industry on its promotion of war-related themes—Hollywood had taken a major step toward an Indian/white interracial alliance. "Any form of racial discrimination or religious intolerance, special privileges of any citizen are manifestations of Fascism, and should be exposed as such," the Office lectured Hollywood studios ("Government").[21] The OWI routinely recommended script modifications, advising producers to treat "dark-skinned peoples" as allies to American heroes. "Our sincerity," the agency explained, "is judged by the attitude and treatment we accord those dark-skinned peoples within our own borders" (Rev. of "Road to God's Country" 1).

The OWI's presence war short-lived (Congress slashed its budget in 1943), but the concept of racial brotherhood would continue to permeate Hollywood Westerns. Twentieth Century-Fox's *Buffalo Bill,* released in 1944, signaled the return to frontier epics (following their temporary decline during the war) that would take a close look at racial relations. The film's depiction of William Frederick Cody (Joel McCrea) resembles Warner's Custer: the hero is the Indian's friend and protector, and the villains are the railroad owners. But Cody's relationship with the Indians is more personalized: when his Indian-schoolteacher friend dies in battle, Cody carries her limp body across the field. "They are *all* friends of mind," he confesses to a soldier.

Buffalo Bill was released amidst a growing liberal outlook within the film industry. As American postwar society readjusted to changing social values, political "messages" began cropping up in stories condemning anti-Semitism—*Crossfire* (1947) and *Gentleman's*

Agreement (1947)—and those advocating black racial tolerance—*Intruder in the Dust* (1949) and *No Way Out* (1950). Westerns also began examining interracial relations in a more serious light, showing conspicuous tolerance and sympathy toward their Indian characters. *Black Gold* (1947) appeared to promote the racial issue on several fronts: Indian, white, and Chinese. "Use tolerance, Americanism to win heavy publicity," the studio advised. "The picture carries a message that will have a wholesome effect upon the community" ("Use Tolerance"). Similarly, in *The Last Round-Up* (1947), a group of young boys engage in a game of cowboys-and-Indians, and predictably, one of them feigns a scalping. One lad objects because "Indians don't scalp people anymore"—a reminder that traditional beliefs of Indians as bloodthirsty savages should be passé in a more tolerant postwar society.

The movies' themes of a postwar brotherhood pointed to racial assimilation within American society. Although still reluctant to embrace fully this liberal policy (Hollywood would readily promote it by the 1950s), cultural pluralism was growing politically suspect among the industry's conservative ranks. One outspoken adherent to the right-wing faction was the redoubtable Cecil B. DeMille, and his story of Pontiac's rebellion in *Unconquered* (1947) was a fitting analogy to the industry's present communist purge.[22] "America today resists red ideas as it once resisted Red Indians in the pioneer days of *Unconquered*," boasted Paramount's ad campaign ("Suggestions"). Beneath its anti-communist rhetoric, *Unconquered* hinted that a person's "Indianness" was politically risky during a Cold War era.

Equating Indians with communists, however, was the exception and not the rule in postwar Westerns; many instead emerged as allegories of the Cold War mentality in which national unity and conformity stood side by side. Westerns could easily "erase" cultural/racial differences between Indians and whites by assimilating the former into mainstream American society. By 1950, *Broken Arrow* showed that racial tolerance could exist if Indians would agree to compromise. (A peaceful co-existence is achieved only when the Apaches relinquish their warfare and accept the Army's terms.) Several of *Broken Arrow*'s successors—*Battle at Apache Pass* (1950); *Taza, Son of Cochise* (1954); *Apache* (1954); *Chief Crazy Horse* (1955); and *Walk the Proud Land* (1956) advocate Indian/white co-existence as a long-term solution to racial problems.[23] In *White Feather* (1955), a liberal successor to *Broken Arrow,* an interracial marriage between a Cheyenne woman and a white man absorbs Indian culture and produces a mix-blooded offspring who enters the Military Academy at West Point. The transition from a segregated vision of Indian/white relations into one in which assimilation dominated the Westerns' themes had finally been achieved—at least by the movies' standards. Whether the industry openly acknowledged these political implications or not, the Hollywood Indian—once the enemy of the great frontier—was gradually being transformed into a white American.

ENDNOTES

[1] Hollywood "racially integrated" military units in many popular war films, including: *Star-Spangled Rhythm* (1942), *Bataan* (1943), *Crash Dive* (1943), *Sahara* (1943), *This Is the Army* (1943).

In these films, Black Americans were often performing a service to their country in violation of more traditional "segregated" customs. For a further discussion of this theme, see Thomas Cripps, *Slow Fade to Black: The Negro in American Film, 1900–1942* (New York: Oxford UP, 1977) 249–389. Clayton R. Koppes and Gregory D. Black offer another point of view in "Blacks, Loyalty, and Motion-Picture Propaganda in World War II," *Journal of American History* 73.2 (Sept. 1986).

[2] While I concur with Price's opinion of *Geronimo* as perpetuating another hostile Indian stereotype, *They Died with Their Boots On* portrays the Sioux as allies to Custer, and the railroad owners as the movie's villains. See my discussion in this article.

[3] Michael Hilger disagrees with the aforementioned opinions: he believes instead that the Western heroes' struggle to "conquer and punish the hated Indians parallels the effort of American soldiers to defeat the hated Germans and Japanese" during and after World War II. See *The American Indian in Film* (Metuchen, NJ: Scarecrow, 1986) 54. Hilger's book—an annotated list of Westerns with Indian characters—is a reference guide with no sustained argument.

[4] Many prominent Hollywood executives, writers, and directors were Jewish whose families and relatives in Europe were targets of anti-Semitism long before U.S. entry into the war. Beginning in 1936, the Hollywood Anti-Nazi League openly condemned German fascism and the Japanese invasion of China; so vocal was their opposition that isolationist groups criticized the industry's pro-interventionist (and pro-leftist) politics. For a further discussion of the motion picture community's prewar sentiments, see Neal Gabler, *An Empire of Their Own: How the Jews Invented Hollywood* (New York: Doubleday, 1988) 311–47.

[5] "Major" studios were the five production companies in Hollywood that owned affiliated distributor and exhibitor chains. They were: Paramount, Metro-Goldwyn-Mayer, Radio-Keith-Orpheum, Twentieth Century-Fox, and Warner Brothers. Major studio films often had greater financing and were more widely marketed than their "minor" counterparts (United Artists, Columbia, and Universal).

[6] Hollywood studios often contracted performers, and their popularity became a key factor in the films' promotion. In 1940, Twentieth Century-Fox studio boasted Shirley Temple as its second popular star; Paramount placed Gary Cooper fourth, and Warner put Errol Flynn third. See *Variety,* 3 Jan. 1940: 29.

[7] The Indian massacre in *Northwest Passage* has prompted many recent scholars to attack the movie as "the single, most ferocious prewar film" ever known. See Raymond Durgnat and Scott Simmon, *King Vidor: American* (Berkeley: U of California P, 1988) 190.

[8] The Hays Office Production Code of 1930–34 insisted upon a moral compensation within motion pictures. Loosely interpreted, this meant that a wrongful death was to be compensated by the death (or arrest) of the perpetrator. Examples abound, but the most contrived is William Wyler's *The Letter* (1940), which added a policeman's arrest of the murderess' murderess in the remote Malaysian jungle. This was a significant departure from the conclusion that W. Somerset Maugham wrote in his original play.

[9] Zanuck espoused the same anti-fascist ideology in several war pictures (all written by him under the pseudonym Melville Crossman); namely, *Secret Agent of Japan* (1942), *To the Shores of Tripoli* (1942), *Tonight We Raid Calais* (1943), and *They Came to Blow Up America* (1943). Zanuck was raised in Nebraska, and his parents were from a Methodist/Episcopal background.

[10] Contrary to critical opinion, Hollywood employed Indians in major roles even prior to World War II. Not only did Chief Thundercloud appear as the Apache leader in *Geronimo* (although his grimacing character was far from flattering), but films included other Indian performers as well: Redwing

(who appeared in DeMille's 1914 *The Squaw Man*) Chief Thunder Bird (who appeared as Sitting Bull in *Annie Oakley,* 1935), Chief John Big Tree (Ford's Indian lead in *Drums Along the Mohawk,* 1939), to name only a few.

[11] All subsequent material from the Brigham Young University Collection will be noted as CBD.

[12] F. Calvin researched and compiled notes for *North West Mounted Police* from the following sources: *Harper's Magazine* (Dec. 1891); *The War Trail of Big Bear* by William Cameron; *History of the Northwest Rebellion of 1885* by C. P. Mulvaney; *The Silent Force* by M. Longstreth; *Information Respecting the History, Condition, and Prospects of the Indian Tribes of the United States* by Henry Schoolcraft; and *North American Indians* by Edward S. Curtis (typed Aug.–Oct. 1939, Box 377 Folder 4, CBD).

[13] The letter indicated that DeMille personally had chosen the name Louvette.

[14] In his autobiography, *My First Hundred Years in Hollywood* (New York: Random House, 1964), Jack L. Warner describes—albeit cautiously—his own political sentiments prior to and during World War II. For a detailed discussion of the later 30s films, see Charles Higham, *Warner Brothers* (New York: Scribner, 1975) 139–43. The German-American Bund actually sued Warner for $500,000 in alleged damages from *Confessions of a Nazi Spy.* (The lawsuit was later dropped.)

[15] All production correspondence from *They Died with Their Boots On* was obtained from the Warners' archives at University of Southern California.

[16] Such gestures failed to impress the War Department, which criticized the script's depiction of officers and enlisted men as corrupt or drunk. Executive producer Hal B. Wallis believed that although the military would not assist in production, Warner should incorporate the Army's suggestions so as not to "build up antagonism against possible future cooperation." Colonel E. R. Householder, Letter to William Guthrie (at Warner Brothers), [n.d.], Motion Picture Association of America, and Hal Wallis, Memo to Robert Fellows, 10 June 1941, File 2303.

[17] The studio's liberal interpretation of history prompted MacKenzie to comment that Warner had "an eye more to generosity than to fact."

[18] Although some scholars have incorrectly interpreted Chief Joseph's name (in a studio memo) to mean the Nez Perce leader, a previous citation (File 1018) had referred to *The Battle of the Little Big Horn,* by Chief Joseph White Bull (as told to Stanley Vestal), which describes the latter's role in the battle. Lee Ryan was the captain of Warner's Security Department; how much influence he had on the movie's actual content is questionable. It is worth noting, however, that the film did show Crazy Horse requesting Sitting Bull to join a war council with other Indian leaders.

[19] There has been much disagreement over Anthony Quinn's heritage. According to Quinn's autobiography, *The Original Sin* (A Self-Portrait) (Boston, MA: Little, Brown and Company, 1972) 11, the actor was born in Chihuahua, Mexico in 1915; his father was part Irish and his mother was Mexican with Indian blood.

[20] The movie's depiction of Custer's heroic sacrifice prompted studio head Jack Warner to remark—perhaps, with a twinge of sarcasm: "If Custer died like that, we should applaud him!" Walsh, *Each Man in His Time,* 327.

[21] While it is not within the scope of this article to examine the function of the OWI, it is worth noting that the agency did scrutinize Westerns for domestic and foreign release. Koppes and Black, in "Blacks, Loyalty, and Motion-Picture Propaganda in World War II," *op. cit.* state that every studio (except Paramount) submitted all scripts to the OWI for review, and that by mid-1943, the agency's recommendations were almost always followed (393).

[22] The movie's release in September 1947 was just one month prior to the testimony of Hollywood's 19 "unfriendly" witnesses before the House Un-American Activities Committee in Washington, in which 10 were eventually cited for contempt and sent to prison.

[23] For a further discussion of this trend, see Angela Aleiss, "Hollywood Addresses Postwar Assimilation: Indian/White Attitudes in *Broken Arrow*," *American Indian Culture and Research Journal* 11.1 (1987): 67–79. John H. Lenihan's *Showdown: Confronting Modern America in the Western Film* (Chicago: U of Illinois P, 1980), devotes an entire chapter to the emerging theme of racial liberalism in Hollywood Westerns (55–89) passim. For better or worse, these fifties Westerns— with their message of tolerance and racial inclusion—echoed the concurrent Federal Termination policy of assimilating Indians into mainstream American society.

WORKS CITED

"Advertising Approach to *Plainsman*." C. J. Dunphy staff memo to Zukor, Le Baron, DeMille, Gilliam [n. d.], Box 353, Folder 1, Cecil B. DeMille Collections, Archives and Manuscripts, Harold B. Lee Library, Brigham Young U.

Bergman, Andrew. *We're In the Money: Depression America and Its Films*. New York: New York UP, 1971.

Churchill, Douglas. "A Cowboy's Feud with Hollywood." *New York Times* 19 Oct. 1941.

Collier, John. *Annual Report of the Commissioner of Indian Affairs*. Washington, DC: GPO, June 1942.

———. June 1943.

———. June 1944.

"Conference with Zanuck on Temporary Script of 11/12/38." *Susannah of the Mounties*. Dir. William A. Seiter. With Shirley Temple. 23 Nov. 1938: 4–5, Box FX-PRS-122, Collection 010. Twentieth Century-Fox Film Corp. Produced Scripts, U of California at Los Angeles.

Crowther, Bosley. "DeMille Checks the Facts." *New York Times* 5 July 1939.

DeMille, Cecil B. "In Chicago Tonight." 27 Oct. 1940, Box 387, Folder 6: 2–3, CBD.

———. Letter to Mr. Archer Winsten. (Critic, *New York City Post* [sic]). 28 Nov. 1940: 1, Box 388, Folder 17, CBD.

Geronimo. Dir. Paul Sloan. Paramount, 1939. Paramount Press Sheets from 1 Aug. 1939 to 31 July 1940, Academy of Motion Picture Arts & Sciences, Margaret Herrick Library, Beverly Hills, CA.

"Government Information Manual for the Motion Picture Industry." Summer 1942, Record Group 208, National Archives & Record Administration, Office of War Information, Bureau of Motion Pictures (Hollywood Office), General Records of the Chief, Suitland, Maryland.

Hayne, Donald. Ed. *The Autobiography of Cecil B. DeMille*. New Jersey: Prentice, 1959.

Kaufmann, Donald L. "The Indian as a Media Hand-Me-Down." *The Colorado Quarterly* 23 (Spring 1974): 489–504.

Levy, Melvin. Memo to Robert Fellows, 30 Apr. 1941, File 2303, Warner Brothers Archives, USC.

"Line on the Golden Spike Itself." *Union Pacific* Apr. 1939: 3. Box 374, Folder 7, CBD. Notes for Speeches and Interviews.

Lissauer, Herman [Head, Warner's Research Department]. Memo to Aeneas MacKenzie, 17 June 1941, File 1018, Warner Brothers Archives, USC.

MacKenzie, Aeneas. Memo to Hal Wallis, 13 May 1941, File 2303, Warner Brothers Archives, USC.

MacRae, Henry. "The Perennial Western." Editorial. *Variety* 8 Jan. 1941: 20.

Mosley, Leonard. *Zanuck: The Rise and Fall of Hollywood's Last Tycoon.* Boston: Little, 1984.

"Movies Will Produce Army Training Films: Industry Organizes to Aid Citizen Soldiers." *New York Times* 1 Nov. 1940.

Pine, Bill [Associate Producer]. Memo to DeMille, 18 Feb. 1936. Box 342, Folder 12, CBD.

Price, John A. "The Stereotyping of North American Indians in Motion Pictures." *Ethnohistory* 20.2 (Spring 1973): 153–71.

Prucha, Francis Paul. *The Great Father: The United States Government and the American Indians II.* Lincoln: U of Nebraska P, 1984.

Rev. of *Apache Trail. Variety* 24 June 1942: 8.

Rev. of *Last of the Mohicans. New York Times* 3 Sept. 1936.

Rev. of "Road to God's Country," by Lillian R. Bergquist. 13 Apr. 1943, Record Group 208, OWI.

Rev. of *Susannah of the Mounties. New York Evening Journal* 24 June 1939.

Rev. of *Susannah of the Mounties. New York Star Telegram* 24 June 1939.

Rev. of *Susannah of the Mounties. Variety* 21 June 1939: 16.

Rosson, Gladys. Letter to Baron Valentin Mandelstamm, 29 Jan. 1940, Box 384, Folder 7, CBD.

"Rough Draft of New Line Suggested by Mr. Zanuck." First Draft Continuity of 10/12/37. *Hudson's Bay* 12. Box FX-PRS-809, Collection 010. Dir. Irving Pichel. 20th Century-Fox Film Corp. Produced Scripts, U of California at Los Angeles.

Ryan, Lee. Memo to Robert Fellows, [n.d.], File 2303, Warner Brothers Archives, USC.

Siminoski, Ted. "Sioux Versus Hollywood: The Image of Sioux Indians in American Film." Diss. U of Southern California, 1979.

"Suggestions for Promotion of *Unconquered.*" n.d. Box 430, Folder 7, 6, 10, CBD.

"Use Tolerance, Americanism to Win Heavy Publicity." *Black Gold* Pressbook, New York Public Library at Lincoln Center, Library and Museum of the Performing Arts.

Variety. Editorial. 29 May 1940: 5.

Walsh, Raoul. *Each Man in His Time: The Life Story of a Director.* New York: Farrar, 1974.

Name: _____ Date: _____

UNDERSTANDING THE TEXT

1. According to Aleiss, what events in Europe prompted Hollywood to change its depiction of Native Americans? What, in particular, did these events make the U.S. government's policy toward Native Americans in the past look like?

2. According to Aleiss, what did Native Americans represent in most Hollywood films before these events? What did they represent during and immediately after?

3. According to Aleiss, how, during the early years of the Cold War, did Cecil B. DeMille in *Unconquered* (1947) choose to depict Native Americans?

What Rough Beast—New Westerns?

John G. Cawelti

In *Gunfighter Nation* (1992), the third volume of his monumental study of the myth of the frontier in American culture, Richard Slotkin suggests that the disillusionment resulting from our disastrous involvement in the Vietnam War and our growing uncertainty about the American economy and its future have deeply eroded the ideology of American uniqueness that the traditional western mythicized. Slotkin thinks that the notable decline of the western in the 1970s means that "the western has therefore been relegated to the margins of the 'genre map'" (633) and will never again occupy the central place it once held in the expressive patterns of American culture. Though, according to Slotkin, the western film "reached the peak of its popularity and cultural pre-eminence from 1969 to 1972" (627), its decline has been precipitous since then, and "the failed attempts to revive the western after Vietnam indicate the character and strength of the social and cultural forces that fractured the myth/ideology of the liberal consensus" (628). Just as almost exactly a century ago Frederick Jackson Turner inspired a redefinition of the meaning of American history by his commentary on the end of the frontier, today "it may be time for a post-mortem assessment of the significance of the Frontier *Myth* in American history" (627).

Slotkin goes on to suggest that "the rejection of the western had gone beyond antipathy for a particular ideology to a rejection of the very idea that the Frontier could provide the basis of a national public myth" (632). We have arrived at a "'liminal' moment in our cultural history" when we are "in the process of giving up a myth/ideology that no longer helps us see our way through the modern world" (654). In particular, we need new mythical patterns that express "the fact that our history . . . was shaped from the beginning by the meeting, conversation and mutual adaptation of different cultures." In short, the old epic of the American frontier as locus for white America's conquest of a savage wilderness is in the

ANQ, Vol. 9, No. 3, Summer 1996. Reprinted with permission of the Helen Dwight Reid Educational Foundation. Published by Heldref Publications, 1319 Eighteenth St., NW, Washington, DC 20036-1802. Copyright © 1996.

process of giving way to a new mythical dialectic of multiculturalism that cannot be contained within the patterns of the western.

Slotkin's argument is very persuasive, both in relation to the significance of the frontier myth in American history and in light of the precipitous decline in the creation and popularity of western films and TV programs during the later seventies and throughout most of the eighties. Yet, strangely enough, in the middle of the 1990s, we seem to be in the midst of a remarkable revival of the western. "Today westerns are back, guns blazing" a lead essay in the November 15, 1993, issue of *Time* announced with great éclat (Richard Zoglin, "Return from Boot Hill," 90–95). *Time* traces this upsurge in the production of westerns to the 1989 television mini-series based on Larry McMurtry's *Lonesome Dove,* the popular TV series *Dr. Quinn, Medicine Woman,* and the combined critical and popular acclaim that greeted two recent films, Kevin Costner's *Dances with Wolves* and Clint Eastwood's *Unforgiven.* The popular success of these works paved the way for such productions as three versions of *Geronimo* (PBS, TNT, and Walter Hill), two variations on the Wyatt Earp saga, a new *Maverick,* a plethora of new TV documentary series (Wests "Untold," "Real," and "Native American"), a *Return to Lonesome Dove,* and such gender westerns as *The Ballad of Billie Joe.* Still another Larry McMurtry mini-series based on his *Buffalo Girls* premiered in the spring of 1995.

This flurry of new westerns clearly indicates that the genre is far from dead, but there is some question as to just what this new activity signifies. Is the genre experiencing a revival, that is to say, the continuation of an established tradition after a period of interruption, or can we better characterize what is going on as a rebirth, a much more significant artistic and cultural event that involves not just a revitalization, but a significant transformation of cultural traditions? Although it is clearly premature to attempt a definitive answer to this question, some attempt to see these new western films in the context of other contemporary developments in our understanding of the American West may offer at least some preliminary guesses.

Dances with Wolves seemed to be at once a radical departure and a significant reaffirmation of the major traditions of the western. Most obviously, by making a group of Native Americans the sympathetic protagonists and by showing the U.S. Cavalry as an aggressive and brutal invader, the film reversed the western's mythical polarity between savage Indians and civilizing pioneers. However, as many critics have pointed out, this was not as much of a departure from tradition as it might seem. From the earliest European encounters with non-European cultures, there has always been a certain ambivalence about Native Americans, which manifested itself in divided portrayals of native peoples as diabolical savages on the one hand and noble innocents on the other. As Slotkin points out, this doubleness toward the Native American was always a significant part of the myth of the West, from James Fenimore Cooper's magnificent Mohicans to what Slotkin calls the "cult of the Indian" in the western film. Was there any significant difference in the way the Native American was portrayed in *Dances with Wolves* than in earlier "cult of the the Indian westerns" such as *Broken Arrow, Soldier Blue,* or *Little Big Man?*

Certainly the film could be criticized for simply revising the old stereotype of the white man's ambiguous encounter with the noble savage. One Native American critic observed that *Dances with Wolves* should really be called *Lawrence of South Dakota*. The movie is clearly connected to earlier westerns and to the long tradition of frontier narrative going back to the seventeenth century by its adaptation of the theme of "captivity," which has always been one of the most potent of western themes. But there are significant departures. The leading female character, Stands-with-a-Fist, is actually a white woman captured as a girl and raised by the Indians. She has even married a warrior, who has recently died, and she sincerely mourns him. Though in traditional terms she has suffered a "fate worse than death," she seems to have thrived on it and has become so completely integrated into the tribe that she has almost forgotten her original language. She becomes the teacher and guide for Lt. Dunbar's willing "captivity" by the tribe. Dunbar himself has "lit out for the territory" after being symbolically killed and reborn in the violent madness of the Civil War. He seeks something better than the "civilized" military culture of madness and destruction. Eventually he relinquishes his former identity and becomes a member of the tribe. When the madness of civilization follows after him, he is forced to leave the tribe. However, he vows to continue his opposition to the destructiveness of white civilization.

There are many similarities between *Dances with Wolves* and *Little Big Man* (1970), which appeared just before the western began its precipitous decline in the early 1970s. Both were strongly influenced by the tragedy of the Vietnam War and portray the invasion of the American West very critically. Both center around a protagonist who becomes integrated into a tribe that is experiencing the destruction of its traditional culture, that of the migratory buffalo hunters of the Great Plains. Finally, both treat Native American cultures— the Sioux in *Dances with Wolves* and the Cheyenne in *Little Big Man*—with some attempt at historical accuracy and complexity as well as great sympathy.

Though *Dances with Wolves* may be overly romantic in its view of Native American cultures, it is still a remarkably effective film and a unique attempt to represent the Native American perspective in a popular cultural form. It does have similarities with *Little Big Man,* but there are some important new elements. Jack Crabb of *Little Big Man* is captured as a child and brought up by the Cheyenne. He has already been acculturated as a Cheyenne when he is taken back by the whites, recaptured again by the Indians, and so on. This is an excellent premise for satirizing cultural differences and inverting conventional perceptions, which *Little Big Man* effectively does. But throughout his story, Jack Crabb remains essentially external to both the cultures he is involved in. To the end, he is, like Huckleberry Finn, always on the outside. Dunbar is not a more complex character, but his role is different. He enables us to participate vicariously in the realization of, and finally the initiation into, a different culture.

This aspect of the narrative is further supported by three other aspects of the film. First, there was the decision to use Native American actors for several of the most important roles. In the traditional western, of course, it was most common to use white actors for the major Indian roles.[1] One of the striking exceptions to this practice, Chief Dan George's delightful portrayal of Old Lodge Skins in *Little Big Man,* was really more caricature than character. On the other hand, Graham Greene's portrayal of Kicking Bird in *Wolves* was a fully rounded and persuasive portrayal of a strong and dignified human being who represented a different set of cultural norms. This effect was reinforced by the use of the Sioux language, which helped give us the sense of encountering the world of another culture. Finally, the film's choice of location was extremely important. Instead of being filmed in the conventional western landscape of desert, mountain, and frontier town, *Wolves* was filmed in South Dakota on the Great Plains, which was, in fact, the real locale of the Sioux culture. This landscape differs enough from the traditional western setting that our sense of the mythical frontier world is subtly displaced, and we do not immediately recognize the familiar mythic West.

Two other recent "Cavalry and Indian" films attempt to acknowledge more fully a Native American perspective. Significantly, both these films center around the most feared and hated of Indian war leaders, the Apache Geronimo. Can anyone forget the famous opening scene of Ford's *Stagecoach,* where the soldiers at an isolated cavalry post suddenly realize that the telegraph wire has been cut, and one of them pronounces in awed tones the dread word "Geronimo!"? In TNT's version, the story is narrated by the aged Geronimo, who has been made into a celebrity by his former enemies, though never really freed from the imprisonment he entered after his surrender. From this standpoint at the end of his life, Geronimo tells a younger Apache warrior, now a West Point Cadet, about his long resistance to the white incursion. The film also contains a few scenes of Apache religious ceremonies and other cultural episodes beyond the stereotypical image of Apaches as fearsome raiders and torturers. Walter Hill's *Geronimo* is an even more complex and powerful film that suggests that the destruction of the Apache culture was not only a historical tragedy but a betrayal as well.

These new representations of the Native American situation in the history of the West are not without unintentional ironies or occasional reversions to the sentimentalizing stereotypes of the noble savage tradition. Still, the films I have been discussing illustrate a new concern for historical complexity and for the acknowledging of different cultural perspectives. In this way, they relate to other important developments in our treatment of the western past.

One of these is particularly evident in the new western history, which rejects the traditional approach to that history as centered around the European settlement of the western frontier. Instead, contemporary historians emphasize the clash of cultures and its lasting implications for the present. Significantly, one of the most widely read of the new histories is Limerick's *The Legacy of Conquest* (1987), which not only rejected the Turnerian emphasis on the uniqueness of America's frontier experience, but insisted on the American West as "an important meeting ground, the point where Indian America, Latin America, Anglo-America, Afro-America, and Asia intersected. . . . The workings of conquest tied these diverse groups into the same story" (27).

Another important contemporary development is the great flowering of Native American fiction and poetry in English. More than anything else, the fascinating novels and poems of writers like N. Scott Momaday, Leslie Silko, James Welch, Gerald Vizenor, and Louise Erdrich have offered a new kind of insight into the cultures and the perspectives on America of a variety of Indian groups. One of the most striking of these works, Leslie Silko's contemporary epic fantasy, *Almanac of the Dead* (1991), startlingly displaces our traditional sense of the West as the victory of American civilization over savagery by representing the present as a time in which the temporary European incursion into the Americas is beginning to show signs of drawing to an end. These Native American fictions should provide a rich literary source for the western films of the future.

A second aspect of recent western films reflects important changes in our understanding of the significance of the West but involves Native Americans only tangentially. This appears in Clint Eastwood's film *Unforgiven* and the television series based on Larry McMurtry's best-selling novel, *Lonesome Dove.* One striking quality shared by both these works is a highly complex and many-sided relationship to the traditional mythology of the West. Both works begin by placing themselves in well-established generic traditions: *Unforgiven* is clearly in the line of gunfighter westerns, most notably perhaps that of *Shane* and its ilk, whereas *Lonesome Dove* relates to cattle-drive westerns such as Howard Hawks's *Red River.* In addition, both films make continual allusions to earlier western films, and this allusive texture is so complex that one is sometimes reminded of modernist novels and poems by writers such as Joyce, Faulkner, Eliot, and Pound, in whose works layers of the mythical past are also continually invoked through allusions. But allusions to western mythology are counterpointed in these films by a constant sense that the characters and action are in continual danger of falling out of the mythical world. In *Unforgiven,* for example, the gunfighter is almost unable to carry out his mission when he nearly dies from a bad case of the flu. In *Lonesome Dove,* accidents, chance encounters, and sudden revelations are continually undercutting and reducing to absurdity the significance of the protagonists' mythical quest. As if to remind us of the falsity of the gunfighter myth, *Unforgiven* provides us with a dime-novel hero accompanied by his writer. English Bob is, in good postmodernist fashion, ambivalently referred to throughout his episode as the "Duke (Duck) of Death" and is literally deconstructed by the sadistic sheriff Little Bill, who reduces him to a pathetic victim. On the other hand, in the film's violent climax, Will Munny actually improves on dime-novel shootouts by escalating the body count when he kills the bar-and-brothel owner, the sheriff, and three deputies.

These works neither affirm nor reject the myth, and that is the way they differ significantly from most previous westerns, which either repeated some version of the myth or claimed to reveal at last the "true" history that lay behind the myth, a "reality" that, more often than not, turned out to be another mythical invention. *Lonesome Dove* and *Unforgiven* manage, it seems to me, to do something still more complex: they show both the power of myth and its dangers, revealing not just the ambiguity of the myths, but the way in which myth and history are engaged in a problematic dialectic. The chaos, randomness, and futility of history call forth the great excitements and simplicities of myth, but once evoked or entered, the mythic world develops an impetus of its own that, imposed on history, can generate a new and more terrifying apocalypse.

In *Lonesome Dove* and *Unforgiven,* the mythic world is associated with the violence and heroism of the protagonists' youths, just as the mythic era of the wild West is associated with an earlier period of America's history. In *Lonesome Dove* Gus and Call have a nostalgic feeling for their earlier lives as Texas Rangers, and they seek to recreate this time of adventure by leaving behind the dull and predictable world of *Lonesome Dove.* William Munny of *Unforgiven* looks back on his violent youth with fear and regret, but he too feels trapped in the present on a wretched hardscrabble farm, trying to raise pigs. The lure of money and adventure draws him once again into a vortex of drunkenness and violence, which leaves a trail of corpses and his best friend dead. It is perhaps the ultimate irony that he is rumored after that to have become a successful merchant in San Francisco.

The ambivalence of these westerns toward the traditional mythic world of the frontier is also related to a more complex treatment of gender issues, for one characteristic of the western was its stereotyping of women by simplification (as in the limitation of women's roles to schoolmarms and dancehall girls) or subordination (by arranging for any important women characters to be converted to the patriarchal code of values). *Lonesome Dove* and *Unforgiven* unfurl a variety of new gender possibilities, from the virtual marriage of Gus McCrae and Woodrow Call to the employer-employee relationship between the victimized prostitutes of *Unforgiven* and the retired gunfighter William Munny. The complexities of gender were even more fascinatingly deployed in another recent western, *The Ballad of Billie Joe,* in which the central character is forced to masquerade as a man to make a decent life for herself in the West. But perhaps in part because this film went even further in its exploratory probing of the absurdity of traditional gender stereotypes as a foundation of the myth of the West, it did not achieve the wide popularity of *Lonesome Dove* and *Unforgiven.*

These changes in the treatment of the West are also reflected in much new fiction and in the revisionist approach to western history. Such cultural phenomena as the extraordinary vitality of Native American and Hispanic writing suggest that the new western is not just part of a momentary revival, but may be one sign of an important cultural renaissance of the sort that another major American region—the South—underwent in the course of the 1920s and 1930s, when a new generation of writers struggled to free themselves from the cultural devastation of another great myth of American history, that of the Lost Cause. In that case, the result was some of the greatest novels and stories ever written about the American dream and its tragic failure. Perhaps today, it is the final decay of the myth of the frontier that makes possible the creativity of the new western literature, film, and history.

Among the themes that express the particular concerns of the new western literature and film are the sense of the loss of a world that seemed to be more fulfilling and more human than the present and the story of the initiation of potentially heroic young men into a world where there is no longer any room for the kind of meaningful action that was once possible.[2] The new western, like many novels of the Southern renaissance, is filled with a deep sense of belatedness and nostalgia for a more unified traditional culture. Larry McMurtry pioneered this genre of western literature with his two early novels of Thalia, Texas, *Horseman, Pass By* (1961) and *The Last Picture Show* (1966). In both these novels, the protagonists not only confront the usual strains of growing up and accepting the knowledge and limitations of adulthood, but also must deal with a very difficult sense of diminishing expectations and of the loss of a bygone time of greater significance and meaning associated with the heyday of the cattle industry and the great cattle drives of the nineteenth century. In *Horseman, Pass By,* the young narrator feels a deep sense of loss: "'Things used to be better around here,' I said. 'I feel like I want something back'" (123). And loss does come to characterize young Lonnie's world, when his beloved grandfather's diseased cattle must be destroyed and the grandfather himself is killed after he is terribly hurt in an accident. *The Last Picture Show* ends with the closing of Thalia's one movie theater and with it, the dream of the old West, which inspired so many of the pictures shown there. Peter Bogdanovich, who directed the excellent movie based on McMurtry's novel, appropriately ended the film with the great scene from Howard Hawks's western *Red River* (1947) in which John Wayne sets off on the first great cattle drive from Texas. In contrast to this heroic moment, the young people of Thalia are left only with the vacuous emptiness of a depressed oil boomtown.

This sense of the end of the heroic West haunts such major works of the new western fiction as Norman Maclean's *A River Runs through It* (1976), in which an old man is haunted by memories of his long-dead father and brother and of the fishing that they shared, and still broods about his inability to save his brother from the violence that destroyed him. In other stories, Maclean evokes a lost world of skill with tools and heroic physical labor and shows how powerful an experience it was to be initiated into such a world. His nonfiction study *Young Men and Fire* (1992) beautifully represents the heroism and tragedy of traditional western work in his reconstruction of the last hours of a fire-fighting crew destroyed by a great fire in Montana in 1949 in the words of an old man who is facing his own encounter with death. Like the mythical western, these works portray a West that is largely gone, but unlike the once-dominant tales of wild cowtowns and cattle drives, outlaws and marshals, gunfighters and schoolmarms that populated the nation's imagined West, they celebrate the heroism not of gunfighters, but of loggers, miners, forest service workers, and firefighters— those ordinary people who built the West and then saw it transformed into something else.

Thus far, the greatest treatment of the western theme of initiation and belatedness may be found in the transplanted Southerner Cormac McCarthy's novel *All The Pretty Horses* (1992). McCarthy transforms the mythical fantasy world of wild western gunfighters, outlaws, and savage Indians into the last remnant of an age-old world of traditional work in which men are part of the unity of life and find great fulfillment in their actions, because these actions are integral with horses and the rest of nature. Horses, which have been man's primary instrument in the use of nature and the creation of culture for centuries, are, as the novel's title would suggest, the symbol of a traditional unity between man and the world that is being increasingly destroyed by modern technology and industrialism. As McCarthy portrays it, west Texas, once one of the last bastions of traditional pastoralism in America,[3] is already a wasteland of oil derricks and on the verge of the postwar oil boom that will utterly destroy the traditional cattle culture (111).

Like Larry McMurtry's earlier work, *All The Pretty Horses* begins in a depressed west Texas, in the immediate aftermath of World War II. Its protagonist, John Grady Cole, is sixteen years old and very much alone in the world. His father is separated from his mother and is slowly dying from a condition incurred in a prison camp in the war. Cole's grandfather is a rancher, and Cole, loving horses and ranching, would like nothing better than to continue the ranch, but the old man dies, and Cole's mother plans to sell the family ranch and leave the area. To continue the work he loves, Cole crosses the border into Mexico with a young friend, and the two find work on a large hacienda where the traditional work with horses and cattle is still carried on.

However, this momentary recovery of paradise is disrupted when Cole falls desperately in love with the daughter of the great hacienda's proprietor. When she returns his love and the two embark on a passionate affair, her powerful family has Cole wrongfully arrested. After being nearly killed in a Mexican prison, Cole is freed after his lover promises never to see him again. The last section of the novel deals with Cole's revenge on the corrupt Mexican policeman who has betrayed him and stolen his horses. Finally, hardened and matured by his ordeal and deeply saddened by the loss of his love and his encounters with death, Cole returns to Texas.

The Texas he finds is on the verge of the postwar oil boom that will destroy the traditional cattle culture, the same process McMurtry portrayed in his series of Thalia novels and which furnished the background for television's popular western soap opera *Dallas*. Although the traditional culture still exists in the late 1940s on the great haciendas of Mexico, it too is clearly on borrowed time. It is significant that the wealthy hacendado of McCarthy's novel keeps his ranch more as a hobby than a way of life and uses an airplane to fly back and forth between the hacienda and his other life in Mexico City.

John Grady Cole is not only a master of horses but something of a visionary as well, and the story is punctuated by his dreams of horses, which picture an eternal paradise where wild horses symbolize the possibility of man's redemption:

> That night as he lay in his cot he could hear music from the house and as he was drifting to sleep his thoughts were of horses and of the open country and of horses. Horses still wild on the mesa who'd never seen a man afoot and who knew nothing of him or his life yet in whose souls he would come to reside forever. (117–18)

One of the most striking moments in the novel comes in a conversation between Cole, his young friend Rawlins, and an old man who symbolizes the traditional wisdom of the world of natural work. It is this old man who expresses most clearly the full spiritual significance of horses in this traditional vision of the world:

> Finally he said that among men there was no such communion as among horses and the notion that man can be understood at all was probably an illusion. Rawlins asked him in his bad spanish if there was a heaven for horses but he shook his head and said that a horse had no need of heaven. Finally John Grady asked him if it were not true that should all horses vanish from the face of the earth the soul of the horse would not also perish for there would be nothing out of which to replenish it but the old man only said that it was pointless to speak of there being no horses in the world for God would not permit such a thing. (111)

The major thing John Grady Cole must learn in the process of his initiation into mature life is the hardest to accept: that such a world no longer exists for him. The Mexican hacienda is, for him, a Paradise Lost. Even in Mexico, the modern world of politics and revolution, technology and cities, is eroding and destroying the traditions of the countryside, and in the Texas to which he must return, the only vestiges of the traditional world of man and nature are in the few remaining Indian encampments in the midst of the oil fields:

> In tour days' riding he crossed the Pecos at Iraan Texas and rode up out of the river breaks where the pumpjacks in the Yates Field ranged against the skyline rose and dipped like mechanical birds. Like great primitive birds welded up out of iron by hearsay in a land perhaps where such birds once had been. At that time there were still indians camped on the western plains and late in the day he passed in his riding a scattered group of their wickiups propped upon that scoured and trembling waste. They were perhaps a quarter mile to the north, just huts made from poles and brush with a few goathides draped across them. The indians stood watching him. He could see that none of them spoke among themselves or commented on his riding there nor did they raise a hand in greeting or call out to him. They had no curiosity about him at all. As if they knew all that they needed to know. They stood and watched him pass and watched him vanish upon that landscape solely because he was passing. Solely because he could vanish. (301)

In this profoundly elegiac conclusion McCarthy evokes that mythical western scene of the hero riding off into the sunset, but for John Grady Cole there is no more mythical world to cross over into, there is only "the darkening land, the world to come" (302). In the end, McCarthy's vision of the West is as apocalyptic in its way as Leslie Silko's, though he sees only a darkening wasteland, whereas Silko imagines the ultimate restoration of the land through an ecological catastrophe of modern technological civilization and a return of tribal cultures.

The new western literature, like that of the Southern renaissance before it, is centrally concerned with the failure of white American civilization and with the burden of guilt left by the exploitation of nature and the tragic heritage of racism. The contemporary literary exploration of the history and culture of these regions, once so important as sources of romantic myths of otherness in American culture, has produced compelling reevaluations of the basic myths of American exceptionalism and superiority and powerful critiques of the multiple failures of the American dream.

It's striking, though perhaps not surprising, that these deeply critical literary movements have emerged almost simultaneously with a new surge of political conservatism and fundamentalism in America, also centered in the South and the West and seeking to manipulate the same symbolic and ideological traditions for their own very different purposes. As many commentators have noted, Ronald Reagan tried to reenact the western myth of the shootout between the heroic marshall and the lawless outlaw on the national and international scenes. The new breed of Southern Republicans who have recently become so important in American politics have found that a traditional Southern rhetoric of less government, family values, localism, and even a coded white supremacy disguised as opposition to affirmative action has proved highly effective on the national scene. These reactions are almost always antithetical to those of serious contemporary Southern and Western writers, but though differently focused, they are responses to the same uncertainties that have beset America in the last quarter of the twentieth century: a profound loss of confidence in America's uniqueness, moral superiority, and global omnipotence. In the context of this ongoing spiritual crisis, the South and the West, which once helped define America mythically and symbolically through their otherness, are now being pursued by both intellectual critics and conservative fundamentalists as symbols of the real truth of America.

ENDNOTES

[1] One of the most successful of these portrayals was that of the Apache chief Cochise by Jeff Chandler in *Broken Arrow,* a portrayal that Chandler repeated in *The Battle at Apache Pass* and *Taza, Son of Cochise.*

[2] The concern for the loss of a traditional way of life is also reflected in the recent reactions of some westerners against the Federal Government's control of public lands and environmental regulations. These are reported in a recent cover story in *Time* magazine, "Don't Tread On Me: An Inside Look at the West's Growing Rebellion" (October 23, 1995, pp. 52–71). Ironically, if these movements succeed, they will probably accelerate the very transformations they seem to deplore. Similarly, the period of the Southern literary renaissance, the 1920s and 1930s, was also marked by a reactionary resurgence of social movements like the Ku Klux Klan and Protestant fundamentalism, which sought desperately to hold on to the traditional social, racial, and economic patterns of the "Solid South."

[3] West Texas was also the ostensible setting of John Ford's great movie *The Searchers* (1956), a powerful treatment of the clash between pioneers and Indians and of the mythical version of the Indian captivity and the initiation of a young man. Actually, the movie was largely filmed in Ford's favorite locale of Monument Valley. *The Searchers* is considered by many to be the finest of all Western films.

WORKS CITED

Berger, Thomas. *Little Big Man.* New York: Dial, 1964.

Limerick, Patricia. *The Legacy of Conquest: The Unbroken Past of the American West.* New York: Norton, 1987.

Maclean, Norman. *A River Runs Through It and Other Stories.* Chicago: U of Chicago P, 1976.

———. *Young Men and Fire.* Chicago: U of Chicago P, 1992.

McCarthy, Cormac. *All the Pretty Horses.* New York: Knopf, 1992.

McMurtry, Larry. *Horseman, Pass By.* New York: Harper, 1961.

———. *Lonesome Dove.* New York: Simon and Schuster, 1985.

Name: _____ Date: _____

UNDERSTANDING THE TEXT

1. Early in his essay, Cawelti wonders whether the "flurry of new westerns" produced in the mid-1990s is the product of a "revival" or a "rebirth" of the genre? What is the difference, in Cawelti's view, and, ultimately, which term does he think is more appropriate? Why do you think so?

2. What, overall, is Cawelti's assessment of *Dances with Wolves?*

3. In his conclusion, Cawelti ties the motifs of "new western literature" to national political trends. What, ultimately, does he say about the relation between the two?

ADDITIONAL READINGS

Black, Joel. *The Reality Effect: Film Culture and the Graphic Imperative.* New York: Routledge, 2002.

Boorstin, Daniel J. *The Image: A Guide to Pseudo-Events in America.* 1961. New York: Atheneum, 1987.

Braudy, Leo. *The Frenzy of Renown: Fame and Its History.* New York: Oxford UP, 1986.

Coontz, Stephanie. *The Way We Never Were: American Families and the Nostalgia Trap.* New York: Basic Books, 1992.

Czitrom, Daniel J. *Media and the American Mind: From Morse to McLuhan.* Chapel Hill: U of North Carolina P, 1982.

DeLillo, Don. *White Noise.* New York: Viking 1985.

Ewen, Stuart. *All Consuming Images: The Politics of Style in Contemporary Culture.* New York: Basic Books, 1988.

Frantz, Douglas and Catherine Collins. *Celebration, U.S.A.: Living in Disney's Brave New Town.* New York: Henry Holt, 1999.

Gabler, Neal. *Life the Movie: How Entertainment Conquered Reality.* New York: Knopf, 1998.

Gitlin, Todd. *Media Unlimited: How the Torrent of Images and Sounds Overwhelms Our Lives.* New York: Metropolitan Books, 2001.

Lazere, Donald, ed. *American Media and Mass Culture: Left Perspectives.* Berkeley: U of California P, 1987.

McKibben, Bill. *The Age of Missing Information.* New York: Random House, 1992.

Miller, Mark Crispin, ed. *Seeing Through Movies.* Pantheon Guide to Popular Culture Series. New York: Pantheon, 1990.

Ross, Andrew. *The Celebration Chronicles: Life, Liberty, and the Pursuit of Property Value in Disney's New Town.* New York: Ballantine, 1999.

Tye, Larry. *The Father of Spin: Edward L. Bernays & The Birth of Public Relations.* New York: Crown, 1998.

Case Study: Representing the West

Berkhofer, Robert. *The White Man's Indian: The History of an Idea from Columbus to the Present.* New York: Knopf, 1978.

Cawelti, John G. *The Six-Gun Mystique Sequel.* Bowling Green, OH: Bowling Green State U Popular P, 1999.

Limerick, Patricia Nelson. *The Legacy of Conquest: The Unbroken Past of the American West.* New York: Norton, 1987.

Slotkin, Richard. *The Fatal Environment: The Myth of the Frontier in the Age of Industrialization, 1800–1890.* New York: Atheneum, 1985.

——. *Gunfighter Nation: The Myth of the Frontier in Twentieth-Century America.* New York: Atheneum, 1992.

——. *Regeneration Through Violence: The Mythology of the American Frontier, 1600–1860.* Middletown, CT: Wesleyan UP, 1973.

Smith, Henry Nash. *Virgin Land: The American West as Symbol and Myth.* Cambridge: Harvard UP, 1950.

Tompkins, Jane. *West of Everything: The Inner Life of Westerns.* New York: Oxford UP, 1992.

Turner, Frederick Jackson. *The Significance of the Frontier in American History.* New York: Holt, 1947.

Ward, Geoffrey C. *The West: An Illustrated History.* Boston: Little Brown, 1996.

Wills, Garry. *John Wayne's America: The Politics of Celebrity.* New York: Simon and Schuster, 1997.